CLIFFORD SIFTON

Very best wishes—

David Hall

CLIFFORD SIFTON

Volume Two

A LONELY EMINENCE

1901-1929

D. J. HALL

UNIVERSITY OF BRITISH COLUMBIA PRESS
VANCOUVER
1985

CLIFFORD SIFTON

Volume 2, A Lonely Eminence, 1901-1929

This book has been published with the help of a grant from the Canadian Federation for the Humanities, using funds provided by the Social Sciences and Humanities Research Council of Canada.

Canadian Cataloguing In Publication Date

Hall, D.J. (David John), 1943-
  Clifford Sifton

Includes bibliographical references and indexes.
Contents: v. 1. The young Napoleon, 1861-1900 —
v. 2. A lonely eminence, 1901-1929.
ISBN 0-7748-0135-2 (v. 1.) — ISBN 0-7748-0209-X
(v. 2)

1. Sifton, Clifford, Sir, 1861-1929.
2. Politicians - Canada - Biography. 3. Canada -
Politics and government - 1896-1911.* 4. Manitoba
- Politics and government - 1870-1900.* I. Title.
FC551.S53H3 1981   971.05'6'0924   C81-091153-1
F1033.S53H3 1981

INTERNATIONAL STANDARD BOOK NUMBER 0-7748-0209-X

Printed in Canada

Contents

Illustrations

Preface

This is the concluding volume of a life of Sir Clifford Sifton, 1861-1929. The first covered his Ontario boyhood, his provincial political career in Manitoba, and the first part of his years in Ottawa as minister of the interior under Sir Wilfrid Laurier, concluding with his contribution to the Liberals' triumphant re-election in 1900. Brought into the cabinet as spokesman for the West, his extraordinary energy, incisive analytical skills, attention to organizational details, and refusal to be bound to a narrowly regional perspective quickly gave him prominence. He was recognized as one of the ablest, and certainly the most combative and controversial, of Laurier's English-speaking colleagues. His leadership of the Liberal party machinery, his hard-hitting political tactics, and his unapologetic use of patronage made him a prime target for the Conservative opposition. It was difficult to gainsay his great success in promoting immigration and western settlement, but the scandal-filled administration of the Yukon and the evidence of a growing and conspicuous personal fortune made him seem vulnerable.

These themes all continue after 1900, but new ones also emerge: the development of Sifton's concern for a rational all-Canadian transportation policy; his differing views from Laurier on the role of government and the nature of Canada, resulting in his gradual estrangement from the prime minister; his evolution toward a central Canadian perspective on public policy; his growing dissatisfaction with the unreformed political system combined with an inability to break entirely from the constraints of past practice. Despite a gift for creating enemies on all sides of the political spectrum and consequent growing isolation, he maintained a remarkable prominence and influence in Canadian affairs almost until his death. He always was a nationalist who was proud of his country and assumed throughout his career that he had an important contribution to make in shaping its destiny.

As was the case with the first volume, this is essentially a political biography. A bit more light can be shed on Sir Clifford's business activities, but business and personal papers remain disappointingly scanty. Still, the vitality and significance of his public career seems ample justification for a new study of his life.

Many of those, both individual and institutional, whose aid was acknowledged in volume 1 contributed also to the completion of the project in this volume. Professors R. Craig Brown and John A. Eagle kindly gave considerable time to reading and commenting upon a large manuscript. Their suggestions helped to make this a better work. I also would like to acknowledge the unusually constructive suggestions from the anonymous readers for the University of British Columbia Press and the Canadian Federation for the Humanities, many of whose suggestions I was happy to adopt.

I was fortunate to have the capable aid of three research assistants who looked into aspects of Sifton's later career for me: Judy Hill, David Lupul, and Bruce Hughson. They will scarcely know how much I appreciated their efforts when I began to write this book.

There are three other people to whom I owe a special thanks. Mrs. Eli Brooks cheerfully and speedily typed and retyped the manuscript. Dr. Jane C. Fredeman, Managing Editor of the University of British Columbia Press, evinced enthusiasm for the project and demonstrated a sympathetic, knowledgeable, and critical skill in editing. Above all, my wife Ann has been a constant encouragement, a skilled proofreader, a patient listener; and, with Jimmy, has put up with my long absences for research and writing. She will be especially thankful to see the biography completed.

1

Cleaning Up the Klondike
(1900-1901)

"My verdict is,—criminal administration by the Min. of the Interior."[1] Lord Minto was scandalized. A journey in August 1900 to Dawson City had permitted the governor general a rare view behind the scenes of Canadian political life. He was disgusted and fascinated, in approximately equal proportions, by what he saw. With an undiscriminating naïveté he rushed to share his findings with Queen Victoria, Colonial Secretary Joseph Chamberlain, and other relatives and friends in Britain. They commiserated with one another over the sad descent of dominion politics into the cesspool of corruption. Such a state of affairs, moralized Chamberlain, was "a feature of all young democracies." Minto surmised that the problem resulted from the lack of a "leisured class with a stake in the country" who might exercise an uplifting influence on the political process. "In any case," concluded Chamberlain, "Canada will work out its own salvation and we have no right and no wish to interfere."[2]

But Minto had no intention of refraining from interference. He had concluded that Clifford Sifton, minister of the interior, was a blackguard and a villain, and he would exercise whatever influence he possessed to have Sifton removed from Prime Minister Laurier's cabinet. The relationship between the two men had begun on a sour note when Sifton's newspaper, the *Manitoba Free Press*, had suggested that Minto was no more than a "second or third rate man" who would probably take himself and his position too seriously. A few months later Minto had supported some Indians who had exercised their right of appeal to the Crown concerning an aspect of Indian policy. Sifton had bluntly informed the governor general that the power of the Crown to influence government policy was negligible.[3] Minto's aggressive imperialism during the early stages of the South African war had further irritated Sifton; while the governor general, for his part, had concluded that Sifton's Yukon administration "would not bear very close scrutiny."[4]

There can be no doubt that Minto intended his Yukon tour of 1900 to be more than a royal progression. It would be an excellent opportunity to bring the searchlight of public scrutiny to bear on the dark corners of the Yukon administration at an acutely embarrassing juncture for the minister of the interior, who was embroiled in preparations for the 1900 election campaign. Prior to his arrival in Dawson, Minto sent a telegram declaring "that I would listen to nothing of a political (i.e. a party) nature," and he even tried to persuade himself that he had succeeded. In fact, however, he had listened avidly to representations by prominent Conservatives, responding favourably and publicly to them, while dismissing Liberal counter arguments as merely the words of creatures of the government.[5]

Among the grievances were complaints about the 10 per cent royalty on gross output of gold from claims; the reservation of alternate groups of claims for the dominion government; the neglect of interior improvements, such as roads; the neglect of representations to Ottawa; abuse of the liquor permit system; and lack of an elective assembly and representation in Parliament. Generally, Minto believed that the administration permitted substantial corruption and was lax in enforcement of morality laws. The one bright spot seemed to be the success of the North-West Mounted Police in maintaining law and order and gaining popular respect. By contrast, Commissioner William Ogilvie was found to be "weak, and vacillating, and does not even possess any social weight."[6] Ultimate responsibility lay with Clifford Sifton, whom Minto believed to have manipulated the system for his own personal and partisan profit.

Some assessment of these charges must be undertaken if Sifton's record in the Yukon administration is to be evaluated. It was unfortunate that Minto so determinedly refused to listen to Sifton's side of the issue; he would have had to modify at least some of his conclusions. In fact, after a fashion, Sifton had been trying to clean up and straighten out the Klondike administration in face of an extraordinary range of conflicting representations. Since the fall of 1898 he had been directing a constant stream of orders to Commissioner Ogilvie, trying to rectify the damage done by some incompetent and a few corrupt officials. "*At any cost*," ordered Sifton, "put the Gold Commissioner's office in perfect order." If it was necessary to change the entire staff in order to restore public confidence, then it would have to be done. The same should be done with the Post Office.[7] Because of the distance and difficulties of communication, the government had been forced to allow officials considerable discretion. To avoid further embarrassment, Finance Minister W.S. Fielding told Sifton, it would be necessary "to guard against the repetition of the irregularities which appear to have occurred, and to mould the financial system there as nearly as possible to the system that prevails in the Dominion generally."[8]

Unfortunately, so laudable an objective would not be easily accomplished. Officials used to exercising discretionary power did not willingly relinquish it, nor did they much respect Ottawa authorities who issued orders and made policy without any first-hand knowledge of Yukon problems. On several occasions Sifton planned visits to the gold districts, but he never actually found it convenient to go. That fact certainly did not diminish his confidence in his own ability to comprehend and rule on various problems. He once told Ogilvie, "I may say that I have not found very much difficulty in understanding appeals that have come before me; in fact, I think I have understood them better than the people who originally decided them."[9] The commissioner had made it clear that he disapproved of many of Sifton's directives and did not consider himself bound by them. Repeatedly Sifton had to tell Ogilvie that "the administration of the Yukon district is essentially a departmental administration," and because ultimate responsibility lay with the minister, Sifton expected his orders to be carried out.[10]

This was especially true with respect to civil service appointments. Ogilvie had assumed he could appoint whomever he wished and selected several known Conservatives. Sifton bluntly told him that "under our system of Government we cannot appoint our opponents to office, and while you are an Administrator under a party Government you will have to be guided by this rule." When the Yukon Advisory Council demurred at accepting Sifton's old political crony from Brandon, J.D. McGregor, as chief licence inspector, he angrily reminded Ogilvie that the members of the council "all owe their positions to me," and "I did not appoint them for the purpose of advising me as to the character and responsibility of a man that I have known over fifteen years."[11] The evidence would suggest that Ogilvie's stance derived, not from objection in principle to patronage, or even from a knowledge that his appointees were especially qualified, but rather from personal preference for some people on the spot.

This willingness to let his personal prejudices intrude in administrative decision-making was perhaps most pronounced with respect to French-Canadian civil servants. Of an estimated six thousand "French Canadians" in the Yukon, about half were from Canada, and the remainder were mostly American citizens. They constituted nevertheless a substantial element in the Yukon, and they did not hesitate to complain to Ottawa when they thought their interests were suffering. French-Canadian civil servants believed they were discriminated against, particularly in terms of pay; and French-speaking miners were annoyed when they were unable to communicate in government offices.[12] Laurier and Public Works Minister Israel Tarte made it clear that French Canadians must have their share of available patronage and be treated equitably. That Sifton shared Ogilvie's antipathy to French Canadians is certain; but he also understood practical politics much better than the Yukon commissioner. "There is an extremely strong feeling that I have overlooked the French people in the appointment of officers," he wrote, "and the share of patronage that I have given them is the least that I could possibly give them. You will have to do the best you can with them." When Ogilvie still complained, Sifton pointed out that half the members of Parliament on the government side were French. "I do not care whether the cry of French domination is raised in the Yukon or not. A reasonable number of officials in the district will have to be appointed from the Province of Quebec. Up to the present time I do not think they have received their share of the patronage."[13] Antagonism to the French Canadians remained, however, and Sifton continued to receive letters from the Yukon declaring that "there should be no more of that class here."[14]

The dominance of the patronage system perhaps impeded efficient reform of the Yukon administration, though there was no particular reason why the gold district should have been less subject to the requirements of the system than any other part of Canada. A greater effort was being made to select qualified officers and to exercise a more direct supervision when they were sent in. By the fall of 1899 a former critic of the administration was able to tell Laurier, "The complaint is no longer against the officials, who fortunately are of a good class, but against the laws and regulations governing the country.[15]

This struck close to the heart of the grievances voiced to Lord Minto in 1900. Seven times the mining regulations had been changed since 1896, redefining the size and nature of claims and leading to constant confusion. But the basic principles of the policy had remained unchanged in over two years and remained an even more serious basis for complaint. A 10 per cent royalty was still levied on gross output; and alternate groups of ten claims, as well as "fractions,"[16] were still reserved for the government. To all pleas for change Sifton returned a stubborn refusal. He had come to believe that issuing a commission to Ogilvie in 1898 to investigate miners' grievances had been a mistake. He was convinced that time would prove his mining policy correct, and in the meantime he would not be stampeded. Canada, he contended, had a right to a proportion of the profits from her own gold-regions; and in any case it was necessary to defray the expense of government.

From the commissioner down to the individual miners, the people of the Yukon claimed that the royalty was unrealistically high, inequitable, and widely avoided. [17] Most believed that false declarations were so widespread that no royalty was collected on more than half the gold actually produced. The reasons were simple. Few claims were very rich. Most required intensive investment in material and labour, leaving a very narrow profit margin, if indeed there was any. Judge C.A. Dugas, who, like other officials, had been personally interested in a number of gold claims, contended that "in the present state of affairs, there is not [*sic*], in the whole Territory, 10 claims out of 100 which are sufficiently remunerative for investment, and that only about 50 per cent of them can pay a fair remuneration to those who work *them themselves* with their own hands, after having staked and recorded them." Dugas agreed with those who gloomily attributed the exodus of miners to the baneful effects of excessive taxation and regulation." [18]

Realistically, however, as Dugas himself pointed out, much of the gold was being extracted from hundreds of marginal claims, not the few that were highly profitable. Any miner who could demonstrate that his labour and material costs were so high that the royalty would create a net loss could have the royalty remitted by the Commissioner. Obviously that exempted a significant portion, and Sifton's policy was not quite so harsh as it was often made to appear. Furthermore, to improve the rate of collection he empowered the NWMP, highly respected in the Territory, to collect the royalty and other dues and fees directly on the creeks. The officers were paid a commission of 2.5 per cent on royalties collected and 5 per cent on items such as timber dues. [19]

Meanwhile there was the problem of government-reserved claims and fractions. Sifton had told Ogilvie that this land was to be "sold in such a way as to get the largest amount of money out of it," to help defray the administrative burden. The land was to be disposed of only by public auction after being advertised in London, New York, and across Canada, as well as in the Yukon. [20] No doubt Sifton fully intended to implement such a procedure when he initiated the reservation policy. Events gradually changed his attitude. First there was a long period of total suspension of sales while surveys were completed and government holdings were delineated and evaluated. Great pressure was brought to bear upon Sifton to allow friends of the government access to the most valuable of these lands, pressure which he was determined to resist. [21] Angry miners and speculators in Dawson naturally put the worst interpretations upon the delays. They were doubly infuriated when what they believed to be some of the most valuable lands were withheld from public sale altogether. Actual sales of lands produced a steady but very modest income for the government, about $63,000 to $65,000 each year from 1899 to 1902. [22]

By 1900, however, Sifton had decided upon a different policy. He had become convinced that the future development of the Yukon depended, not upon the individual placer miner, but upon large-scale mechanized development through so-called hydraulic concessions.[23] It was scarcely coincidental that the new policy became effective prior to the 1900 federal election, when those fortunate enough to obtain concessions could demonstrate their gratitude to the government in a concrete way. Little wonder that the people of Dawson were irate and frustrated at their own impotence in the determination of policy. The reforms that they had urged on Ottawa to strengthen the placer mining system were being ignored, a new and alien system was being substituted for it, and there was little attempt made to conceal the blatant patronage associated with it. It was understandable, if regrettable, that the people of Dawson would attribute the basest of personal motives for Sifton's policy; it also was simply irresponsible of the governor general to give credence to such rumours without some concrete evidence.

By early 1900 Sifton's colleagues were beginning to bow to public pressure, urging him to moderate his policy. The publicity surrounding Minto's Yukon trip would make it exceedingly difficult for the minister of the interior to continue to resist. In July the government passed an order-in-council which extended free miners' privileges in renewing their claim certificates. The new policy was announced in Ottawa just as Minto was reaching Dawson in August. Undoubtedly, it was calculated to moderate the attacks upon the government, but it failed to do so. At the end of August Sifton decided to abandon the policy of government-reserved claims. The changes were attributed by the populace solely to Minto's visit. Moreover, the change of heart appeared hollow because so many of the valuable government reserves had already been disposed of, so that there was little boost for the placer-mining community.[24]

Minto also was credulous with respect to complaints concerning Sifton's responsibility for the internal communications of the Yukon, particularly roads, trails and bridges. Undeniably they were in deplorable condition and a leading source of local grievance. Minto did not bother to check the information he was given in Dawson; consequently his conclusions were wrong.[25] The condition of the roads was more a function of difficulty in dealing with permafrost than a result of government inaction. Moreover, Sifton had been as anxious as anyone to get adequate roads. His belief was that the commissioner-in-council ought to have the authority to act in such local matters on behalf of the entire government, and most of his colleagues co-operated in letting him shape government policy in the Yukon. There was, however, one important exception — Joseph Israel Tarte, minister of public works. Tarte firmly believed that his department must retain control over all public works, and unfortunately the Yukon was not high on his list of priorities.[26] His officials were engaged in completing the telegraph to the Yukon in 1899, and needed government buildings and roads simply had to wait. Public Works was also improving navigation on Yukon rivers, and constructing huts and buildings to facilitate the carriage of mail in the winter. The government, then, was spending hundreds of thousands of dollars annually in improving communications and responding to grievances of the past.[27] But as the problems of poor mail service and isolation were solved, new grievances, such as those concerning internal roads, took their place.

The issue came to a head only a few weeks prior to Minto's arrival in the Yukon. Ogilvie had been promised that J.B. Charleson, a public works official, would arrive with sixty thousand dollars to spend on roads, and the commissioner made this information public to quell the agitation. "You can imagine my surprise, therefore, and mortification," Ogilvie bitterly told Sifton,

> when Mr. Charleson arrived to find, according to his allegation, he knew nothing of any such sum of money to be expended on roads; remained one day, and went out again almost as soon as his presence was known. I was beset on the street and everywhere by a crowd who grew angry when I had to tell them that I could do nothing for the present. This looked to them very much like a breach of faith on my part....and while it may be very easy to suffer these things 4000 miles away they are not pleasant to live in.[28]

Still burning from this humiliation, Ogilvie poured his heart out to the willing ear of the governor general in August 1900. It was but a small consolation when Sifton replied, "Next year I hope to place the estimates for the construction of trails, roads, and bridges entirely under the control of the Local Council where it ought to be."[29]

By contrast, among the areas of administration that would not be suitable for local control was the North-West Mounted Police. "The respectable people," commented Sifton when the subject was broached, just "lift up their hands in horror" at the very idea. "They say it would be simply mob rule, and I think they are right."[30] Although the NWMP normally fell under the jurisdiction of the prime minister, Laurier had given Sifton substantial control over the force in the North-West Territories and the Yukon. The minister of the interior rarely interfered in the normal duties of the force, but he did not hesitate to supervise postings of individual officers and matters subject to the rules of patronage, such as supply contracts.[31] The very success of the NWMP over the previous quarter century had depended in part upon the willingness of the force to accommodate the political realities of the day and upon the willingness of the government to recognize the independence of the force in upholding the law.

The officer in charge of the Police in the Yukon, Superintendent Sam Steele, never understood the delicate balance inherent in this relationship. In most respects Steele was an excellent officer. He had a strong sense of moral rectitude, was deeply conscious of the majesty of the law which he represented, and saw himself as a leading figure in the great saga of introducing law and order to the far reaches of the Canadian frontier. He had become an extraordinarily popular figure in the Yukon and very proud of his success. "We have some of the greatest criminals on the continent here," he wrote from Dawson, "and yet the vigilance exercised has made the place as orderly as Montreal, in fact, as far as public resorts go, the city is much rougher than this town."

> Crimes are all brought to justice promptly. The town is so orderly that any lady can walk with more safety from insult (in the middle of the night) than in any place I know of. It shews plainly the system of police that is necessary for towns and cities. A high order of discipline is required and the power to enforce it. [32]

Almost everyone agreed with Steele's assessment, regardless of political affiliation.

Unfortunately, Steele seemed to believe that his popularity and position would enable him to resist the exigencies of the patronage system, a challenge which Sifton could not permit. It was Steele who pressured the Yukon council, of which he was a member, to refuse to accept J.G. McGregor as liquor licence commissioner. McGregor apparently had been tried and acquitted on charges of horse-stealing, but Steele believed him guilty anyway and considered that his appointment to a responsible office would be "an insult to the police." [33] Eventually Sifton won his point, although, as he noted with irritation, "I find a good deal of difficulty in convincing people in the Yukon District that orders have to be obeyed, but I think I will succeed before I get through." [34] However, Steele broke the rules again, awarding a supply contract for the Police to another—and higher—bidder than one recommended by Sifton. On 24 August, 1899 Sifton ordered that Steele be transferred from the Yukon to Fort Macleod. [35]

Perhaps no single action of Sifton's administration in the Yukon caused so much popular hostility toward him and the Laurier government. "The condemnation of it is general," Henry J. Woodside of *The Yukon Sun* told Sifton, "and most of the people here ascribe the most sinister motives."

> You are taking away the man, who more than any official here, is endeavoring to make conditions more tolerable to the people of the Yukon, just as he is striving to modify the evil effects of unwise

legislation and poor regulations. In this without in the least iota trying to become popular, he has really become the most popular man in the Yukon.[36]

Despite the short-term obloquy directed against Sifton, the removal of Steele probably was beneficial. The force had been effective and respected before he assumed command and would continue to be so after his departure. His replacement, the much more intelligent and sensitive Aylesworth Bowen Perry, would prove to be one of Sifton's most successful appointments.[37] Perry, in turn, would be succeeded by Zachary Taylor Wood in 1900. Both Perry and Wood would have to adjust the Police to a town and territory fast losing their rough and informal frontier ways. The population was beginning to shrink and stabilize, and the "rough characters" who had so concerned Steele either disappeared or settled into colourless respectability.

A sign of the times was the mounting interest in more rigorous restriction of alcohol, gambling, and prostitution. The convenor of the Vigilance Committee of the Toronto WCTU solemnly warned Sifton of the "feelings of deep indignation" that would be roused in the breasts of "nearly five thousand Presbyterian women, and...three thousand, five hundred women of the Toronto WCTU" if action were not taken to dry up the Yukon, and in particular to eliminate an alleged "floating grog-shop" on the Yukon River.[38] Such complaints were not new, but they were now being joined by growing numbers of similar appeals from Dawson itself.[39]

Underlying much of the complaint about Sifton's policies was the conviction that he had been using his control of liquor permits to enrich the Liberal party and its friends. There was indeed some substance to the charges, although the true story was more complex than it appeared to his critics. Even Solomon could not have devised a policy to pacify both wets and drys. Sifton's sympathies lay with the latter; yet compromise had been necessary from the early days of the gold rush. In the first place, total prohibition would have been unenforceable. In the second place, revenues from alcoholic beverages were second only to the royalty on gold in defraying the cost of local government. Revenue from liquor licences and permits constituted the bulk of the budget of the Yukon Council: some $215,317.48 out of total revenues of $319,632.41 in 1899-1900 for example.[40]

In 1898 Sifton shifted the responsibility for issuing liquor permits to the Yukon Council, partly because it was in theory a local matter and partly to evade the contumely being heaped on his head by irate prohibitionists. Although the North-West Territories government had issued permits for more than sixty-five thousand gallons, he told a Toronto correspondent, "no permits have been issued by or under the authority of the Federal Government since the discussion of the question first arose and it was brought to my attention." In February 1899 he sent in J.D. McGregor as liquor licence commissioner, with the idea that only McGregor would have authority to issue permits for importation—and McGregor, of course, was under Sifton's personal control. At the same time he directed the NWMP to stamp out smuggling and illicit stills.[41]

Much to Sifton's surprise and fury, Ogilvie and the council simply ignored his direct orders. One observer told him that the permit business was in a "mess" owing to "the wholesale way in which Mr. Ogilvie has been issuing permits to anybody & everybody who has chosen to apply."[42] In April 1899 Sifton directed that all existing permits were to be cancelled, that only permits solely for personal use were to be permitted, that only the Interior Department could issue permits for amounts over fifty gallons, and that Ogilvie could issue permits for smaller amounts. Five months later, however, Sifton still found it necessary to upbraid the Yukon commissioner for ignoring direct orders. No liquor whatever was thereafter to enter the Yukon, except on the order of the department.[43]

Not until early in 1900 did Sifton succeed in imposing his plan. McGregor was officially in charge of permits; in fact, none were to be issued except upon Sifton's personal order.[44] By this time the government had suffered substantial embarrassment on the liquor question. Ogilvie had granted permits totalling some 246,138 gallons before he was stopped. The government did prevent approximately 175,000 gallons from being imported, at the cost of some threatened lawsuits and the loss of some prestige.[45]

The drought was temporary. Yukoners could not long be denied their liquor, the local government had to be funded and the Liberal party required financial aid during the 1900 election. Between 27 July and 12 October the government issued permits for 74,800 gallons of beer, wine, and liquor. Of these, more than 42,000 gallons were permitted in the three weeks preceding Lord Minto's arrival in Dawson.[46] Ogilvie was already miffed at the way Sifton had overridden his authority and cancelled so many permits. He was simply livid about Sifton's new issue of permits, and on this subject also poured out his heart to the governor general. Permits, complained Ogilvie, were "given solely to political supporters & friends" of the government and were best obtained in the lobby of the House of Commons. "Permits are saleable," noted Minto, "& the liquor traffic in Dawson is at present in the hands of a very few (two Jews I believe), these people absolutely control the liquor market & in selling to the saloons can make their own price."[47] Following the election the issuance of permits was again suspended, and in February and March 1901 power to issue them was again reposed in the Yukon commissioner—by which time Ogilvie was on his way out of power.[48]

Sifton had been heavy-handed in his use of patronage, but he had done nothing illegal or criminal. Even the vigilant Conservative opposition could find little with which to berate him in connection with the liquor question. The Tories resented the size of the patronage pie available to the Grits in the Yukon, but they were not as yet prepared to assault the roots of the patronage system. If there was reason to question Sifton's actions, it was more with respect to his personal inconsistency. His policy appeared to be vacillating, though Ogilvie must shoulder a substantial portion of the blame. Prohibitionists too considered Sifton inconsistent, professing sympathy with the objectives of temperance organizations, while permitting a substantial flow of alcohol. A free system was politically impossible, and prohibition was practically unenforceable, replied Sifton, so a policy of controlled supply was the only alternative.[49]

Alcohol was an especially complicated issue in a frontier environment where it was closely associated with gambling and prostitution, which in turn involved a greater proportion of the population than in the rest of Canada. By 1899 an informal understanding had been reached that gambling houses and prostitutes would be fined on a monthly or yearly basis, allowing them to carry on their trade and enabling the NWMP to uphold the law without driving the sinners underground. The fines in turn were an important part of the Yukon Council's revenues, reaching $70,650, or about 22 per cent of the total revenues in 1899-1900.[50]

> It is a vexed question here [A.B. Perry told Sifton]. I have talked to many people on the subject, and many are of the opinion that gambling is a necessity in a mining country. A few others take a different view but they are in a minority. I find that business men are more or less directly interested in it. Gambling causes miners to spend their money. The gamblers who win it spend it on restaurants, and prostitutes who in turn largely patronize stores and purchase very freely at extravagant prices. Some leading business men in the place are owners or part owners of the leading saloons. If therefore any attempt is made to stamp out what is undoubtedly a very serious evil a strong opposition will be created in the town itself.[51]

Perry added that he thought that the worst gamblers could be run out of town, preferably at the opening of navigation. Sifton appears not to have been unduly concerned, however, and no action was taken in the spring of 1900. Complaints about the situation increased nevertheless, and with a general election in the offing, Sifton could not appear to be inactive. He therefore told Ogilvie and the NWMP that more stringent action was necessary and that gambling and the dance-halls frequented by prostitutes should "be summarily suppressed." Once again the new policy was announced to coincide with Minto's Yukon visit and it reinforced the hostility of the businessmen of Dawson as they delivered their petitions to Minto.[52]

Sifton probably knew that late summer was the wrong time to enforce the law and that no serious change could be brought about until after the election.[53] In February 1901 he directed that his order of the previous summer be carried out, a step which Ogilvie and Major Z.T. Wood of the Police reluctantly announced. The outcry of dismay and anger was instantaneous. "Property will depreciate 75 per cent," read one telegram. "Five hundred men will be thrown out of employment...and will have to be supported on charity....This mining Town cannot be run on Sunday school lines." Many businesses ran at a loss during the winter and counted on the spring clean-up to recoup their losses.[54] At midnight on Saturday 16 March the gambling dens and dance-halls were closed. But the government capitulated to the unanimous outcry from the Dawson business community, and the following Monday granted a stay of execution until 1 June by which time it was hoped that the so-called "undesirable element" would have departed with a minimum of disruption.[55]

If respectability was descending upon Dawson, the increased stability of the population convinced the government that some elective institutions should be granted. Early in 1900 the most prominent Liberals in the Yukon were sounded out about the probable result of allowing the election of two representatives to the Yukon Council. The replies were unanimous: so deep was the hostility to the government that there was no hope of electing Liberal supporters.[56] Agitation on the subject persisted in Dawson through out the spring and summer, however, and finally in mid-July the Laurier government bit the bullet and announced that election of two representatives to the council would take place.[57] The decision probably was taken in anticipation of Minto's visit, as with so many of the changes of that summer, to undermine the agitation. As predicted, the polling in the fall resulted in an embarrassingly decisive victory for two anti-government candidates.[58] It remained to be seen, however, if the success in obtaining a measure of local representation would release some of the accumulated steam in the Yukon pressure cooker or whether it would be encouragement to even stronger agitation.

What substance, then, underlay Lord Minto's conclusion that Clifford Sifton had been guilty of "criminal administration" in the Yukon? Very little, it would appear. Sifton did use the patronage system freely and openly, but there was nothing new in that. His failure to go to Dawson suggests that the Yukon was not near the top of his list of priorities. He was stubborn; many questioned his judgment; some thought him incompetent. He was loyal to a fault in supporting the officials he sent to the Yukon. He had no qualms about the need to maintain a paternal supervision of the gold rush society to keep it peaceful, law-abiding, and British. Equally he would be prepared to shape its future, to oversee a transition from a placer-mining, individualistic society to capital-intensive development under big business. In the tradition of frontier mining towns, the people of Dawson wanted a government that was responsive to their demands and that would encourage a continued placer-mining society. They sometimes forgot that there was a price to be paid for the order guaranteed by the Police, whom they so admired. They failed to realize that Sifton had to govern with broader considerations in mind than the immediate concerns of the people of Dawson. His record was imperfect, but it was far from the total disaster implied in Minto's remarks.

Perhaps Minto was influenced as much by his personal distaste for the minister of the interior as by the alleged evidence. On their way back from Dawson, in the midst of the 1900 election campaign, the Mintos ostentatiously stayed in Brandon with Senator Kirchhoffer, whom Sifton angrily described as "the most violent opponent I have" in the constituency.[59] Upon reaching Ottawa Minto told his brother that Laurier "must get rid of some of his present colleagues...the Govnt. of the Yukon has been too infamously corrupt, and I shall absolutely refuse to accept the present Minister who is answerable for it, again—and I feel sure Sir Wilfrid will agree with me."[60] The governor general's resolution collapsed however in face of Laurier's determination to defend his colleague. "My visit has done a great deal of good," observed Minto complacently.[61] But, he added sourly, "how [my ministers] can whitewash their colleague of the Interior with their eyes open I don't know—However he has won an important election for them, which goes a long way—."[62]

The 7th of November 1900 presented not only electoral victory for Sifton and the Laurier government, but the conclusion of more than a year of constant preparation and campaigning. What with the Manitoba election of 1899, defusing agrarian protest, travel to Europe in search of a cure for his deafness, and running much of the Liberal campaign in addition to his regular administrative duties, Sifton had left the Yukon simmering on the back burner for too long. Early in 1901 he moved decisively to improve the situation. As noted above, he attempted to end the lax enforcement of morality laws in Dawson; he decided to reduce the royalty to 5 per cent of gross output; and he decided to replace Ogilvie.

He had had high hopes for the commissioner, and whether out of loyalty, or out of deference because Ogilvie was older and his wife's uncle, he had been exceptionally patient. Certainly anyone else who so disregarded Sifton's orders would have been promptly dismissed. He explained administrative procedures repeatedly and in detail, attempting to compensate for Ogilvie's lack of experience. When it was reported that Ogilvie consorted too much with the ordinary people of Dawson, Sifton instructed him to establish separate quarters "and have a little more of the Government dignity." The higher officials should not eat with subordinate officials and must "keep aloof from the crowd."[63] More than social snobbery was involved in these sentiments. Sifton well understood that a successful administrator had to appear to be in authority, that style was as necessary as substance.

Unhappily, Ogilvie lacked both; he never grew into the job. He remained vacillating, indecisive, inconsistent, complaining. A separate quarters could not provide him with the social presence that should have accompanied his high office. Early in 1901 Sifton finally bowed to the inevitable. An office like that of commissioner, he told Ogilvie awkwardly, was not like a civil service position, but was analogous to "the Governorship of a Province." He had served three years, and "I am writing you in this way so that you may be able to intimate from your end your intention to retire and thus prevent either your enemies or mine from being able to put upon your retirement anything of an unpleasant construction."[64]

Even the offer of another civil service appointment did not shield the blow to Ogilvie's pride contained in Sifton's somewhat curt and insensitive letter. He announced his retirement, for reasons of health, and promptly shut himself up in his house for two weeks, seeing no one. Sifton later tried to soothe the pain, explaining that the change was calculated to coincide with the spring break-up and that the circumstances of his successor, J.H. Ross, had forced Sifton to make a rapid decision.[65]

In the absence of evidence to the contrary, one must remain sceptical of Sifton's explanations. Ogilvie had to be replaced in any event, Ross was available, and—scarcely coincidentally—the appointment made it possible for Sifton's brother Arthur to succeed Ross as commissioner of public works and territorial treasurer in the government of the North-West Territories. Ross also happened to be an excellent choice. He was an experienced and capable administrator, a committed Liberal, and had Sifton's full confidence. He was immediately popular in the Yukon. "Ross is an entire success," wrote one enthusiastic correspondent. "He possesses all the qualities required by his office. Most of all he is shrewd."[66] In conjunction with other changes and knowing that Ross had the ear of the government, Yukoners began to hope that a new era of renewed fortunes lay ahead.

2

Settling Old Scores:
Politics in Western Canada
(1901-1902)

The dominion general election of 1900 had confirmed Liberal predominance in western Canada. A sustained effort would be essential to retain the initiative in western politics, particularly given the social and economic dislocation caused by rapid immigration and settlement and the increasingly strident demands of the organized farmers. Manitoba, however, had sounded a dissonant note in the otherwise harmonious western approval of the Liberal record. The fractious politics of that province had produced neither a Liberal nor a Conservative victory in 1900. Clifford Sifton would have to wrestle for the advantage with his wily—and worthy—Conservative opponents in Winnipeg, Premier Rodmond P. Roblin and his skilled organizer, Robert Rogers. Meanwhile, political changes put off for too long must soon be implemented: the Manitoba Liberals required new leadership and revitalized organization; the *Manitoba Free Press* had been found wanting during the elections of 1899 and 1900; and the remaining centre of disaffected Liberalism in Manitoba, R.L. Richardson, must be purged to allow the wounds of division to heal. Sifton hoped that a few months of respite from partisan conflict would permit him ample time to effect his reforms.

Roblin, not Sifton, made the first move, as daring as it was unexpected. He did what Thomas Greenway had never succeeded in doing in twelve years: he devised effective competition for the Canadian Pacific Railway, in an agreement with the Northern Pacific and Canadian Northern. It was fully as popular as Greenway's triumphant slaying of the monster of monopoly in 1888 and fully as discomfitting to the premier's hapless political opponents. New divisions appeared among Manitoba Liberals. They found little leadership from Sifton, who flip-flopped woefully on the issue and seemed at times to be dancing to Roblin's tune.

Provision of effective competition for the CPR had been the goal of every premier of Manitoba since John Norquay. The Greenway Liberals thought they had succeeded in 1888-89 when they brought in the Northern Pacific and Manitoba, along with slightly lower freight rates. The failure of the NP&M to become profitable during the next decade, however, led the parent Northern Pacific company to seek one of two solutions: expansion to Duluth or sale of the NP&M. The Greenway Liberals could not see their way clear to support expansion unless it was accompanied by significant freight rate reductions, including a ten-cent per hundredweight rate for grain between Winnipeg and the Lakehead. The Northern Pacific was unable to meet the government demands. The same dilemma faced the Conservative administration of Hugh John Macdonald and Rodmond Roblin. As an alternative, the Northern Pacific was anxious to sell its NP&M subsidiary, but it was forbidden by law to sell to the one obvious purchaser, the CPR. The latter, for its part, desired to re-establish its absolute dominance in the West; it was just because of such a contingency that the Greenway government had stipulated that the NP&M lines must never come under CPR control.

The NP&M nevertheless had been a popular line in Manitoba. By contrast, its eventual successor, the Canadian Northern, was not. The promoters of the CN, William Mackenzie and Donald Mann, were widely, if erroneously, perceived to be front men for the CPR. As one observer put it, "many think MM & co are just a sort of Donkey Engine for the C.P.R."[1] By 1900 they had acquired or constructed lines northwest from Gladstone, southeast from Winnipeg, and the Ontario and Rainy River charter which would give the eventual access to Port Arthur, but which was still far from complete. Acquisition of the NP&M lines would link together their Manitoba lines and make the CN the only potentially viable western competition for the CPR. Their Ontario and Rainy River bonds were not selling well in London, however, and what they most needed was the backing of the Manitoba government.

When Premier Roblin assumed office in the fall of 1900, he quickly jettisoned the plank of government ownership in his predecessor's platform. President T.G. Shaughnessy of the CPR tried desperately to gain control of the NP&M lines, but politically Roblin could scarcely coun-tenance such a solution. That left the premier with one alternative: he had to deal with Mackenzie and Mann.[2] And Roblin could not settle for a grain rate higher than the ten-cent rate promised by Greenway. This left him comparatively little room to negotiate. On 15 January, 1901 the Manitoba government leased the NP&M lines for 999 years, with an option to purchase for $7,000,000. Rental of the lines would start at $210,000 per year, rising to $300,000 after thirty years. Nearly a month later an agreement was signed with the CN, which agreed to take over the NP&M lease, to reduce passenger rates, and to accept government control of freight rates within Manitoba and between Manitoba and Port Arthur. In return the provincial government undertook to guarantee the principal and interest at 4 per cent on bonds at $20,000 per mile for 290 miles in Ontario, and at $8,000 per mile on the shorter Minnesota section.[3] Roblin knew the deal would be popular, particularly the ten-cent rate and the effective competition for the CPR. He promptly set about booming the CN, while somewhat exaggerating the unwillingness of the NP to negotiate favourable terms.[4] The result was a massive boost in popular support for Mackenzie and Mann.

Sifton was placed in an awkward position. He had long supported Mackenzie and Mann, and late in 1900 he had given public support to their goal of transcontinental expansion. At the same time he had for some years mistrusted the NP and believed that they were more likely to conspire with the CPR. He could not very well criticize the method of support for the CN, because he himself had pioneered it on a smaller scale in 1895-96. As events unfolded, therefore, it appeared that there might be more that he could support in the Conservatives' plans than in anything that Greenway had devised since 1896. He reacted cautiously. After Manitoba had leased the NP&M lines in January, he told Arnott J. Magurn, editor of the *Free Press*, that any bargain with the CPR should be fought "to a finish." In the more likely event that a deal was struck with the CN, "it will be necessary for the paper to steer a very careful course." Any reduction in rates should be heartily approved, but the financial burden assumed by the province must be carefully examined. At all costs, the paper must avoid a blanket condemnation of the scheme, because that would be taken as proof that the *Free Press* and Sifton were still closely identified with CPR interests.[5]

When the CN agreement became public, the *Free Press* continued in its non-partisan coolness to the contract. This outraged many Liberals. They believed that the arrangement was "simply appalling" and that if it passed the provincial Liberal party would be obliterated.[6] Some assumed that Sifton was in cahoots with Mackenzie and Mann. In fact, however, he opposed the contract for the same reasons the local Liberals did, and once the *Free Press*'s independence from the CPR had been established, he allowed it to enter aggressive opposition. "I am satisfied," he told Magurn, "that the contract if it passed would simply ruin the Province of Manitoba."[7] The contract essentially was a gamble upon the future prosperity of the province. If the economy continued to expand rapidly, the people of Manitoba might never have to pay a cent. But if bad times recurred, some estimated that the province could have to pay anywhere from $200,000 to $500,000 per annum, equivalent to nearly the total provincial revenues a few years previously.

Even if it did pass the local legislature, the legislation would have to be confirmed by the dominion Parliament because both railways were under dominion charter and because the agreement affected interprovincial trade. Such legislation would be "extremely unlikely" to pass in Ottawa, Sifton assured Magurn:

> The argument that it is a local matter would not apply. The province no doubt has a perfect right to bankrupt itself if it can do so by the exercise of its own legislative power, but if it wishes to have the assistance of the Dominion the Dominion Parliament may very readily and properly refuse. My own private impression is that an Act to confirm this agreement would not have a ghost of a chance of getting through.[8]

Buoyed by these assurances and by the vigorous leadership of the *Free Press,* local Liberals fought valiantly against the legislation, which nevertheless passed by mid-March. Sifton tried and failed to persuade the lieutenant governor to reserve the legislation.[9]

Roblin was cockily confident that the overwhelming popularity of his legislation would force Sifton's hand. "Sifton daren't refuse us legislation at Ottawa," he reportedly boasted, "and, of course, such legislation will really make the Dominion a party to the deal, so that if things should go wrong, it will have to come to the aid of the Province."[10] The Manitoba premier was right. The ink was hardly dry on the royal assent when Sifton began to reverse his stand. "I do not think the Free Press should keep up the fight with the same vigour which has been exercised so far," he told Magurn. Reports began to descend upon him that not only was the arrangement popular in rural Manitoba but that it was supported by such leading Liberal businessmen as J.H. Ashdown and G.F. Galt.[11] By late March Sifton decided that the politically wise thing to do would be to confirm the Manitoba legislation. Refusal, he told his father, would simply permit Roblin to call an election, accusing the Dominion of coercion and siding with the CPR:

> In that event he would have a very strong case when he is backed by the opinions of a considerable number of prominent business men that the road will pay its fixed charges. Our opinion, after going into the matter

fully, is that it is a matter for the province to settle, and if the people have been foolish enough to elect legislators who make improvident bargains, they will have to stand it. It will probably put an end to railway agitation for some years to come at any rate.[12]

Enabling legislation was introduced into Parliament in April, second reading occurring uneventfully on the 15th. The government nevertheless had not finally made up its mind on the issue, and there were evidently divisions in the cabinet, with the minister of railways, A.G. Blair, known to be opposed. At the end of the month Sifton heard that his father was very ill, and he at once set out for Winnipeg. En route he wrote the prime minister, suggesting that he "quietly see that the Manitoba railway bills are pushed along. I have gone over the whole matter carefully in my mind and am satisfied that it is in every way the best policy that they should pass. I think you should speak to Blair & [Sir Louis] Davies *particularly the former.*"[13] At once Laurier complied, and a series of contentious debates occurred at the committee stage. The government brought in an amendment to make it clear that the power to control interprovincial freight rates was vested in the Dominion.[14]

Sifton returned in time to support the bill on the last day of debate.[15] He claimed that while he still opposed the agreement in principle, it was a matter purely of local concern. He observed that it also fulfilled policies espoused in different forms by Premiers Greenway, Macdonald, and Roblin to provide Manitoba with a second railway outlet to the Great Lakes and effective competition for the CPR. The Dominion was not ratifying the agreement, but merely enabling the province to proceed. He drew a comparison with the Manitoba school question. The Judicial Committee of the Privy Council had determined the right of the federal government to override the Manitoba legislation. "There was no question as to the legislative power, but, the question was as to whether it was wise to interfere—that was the question. And I cannot but feel that in connection with a matter of this kind, where the province takes hold of a question and acts within its own jurisdiction, it will prove to be an unwise course for this parliament to interfere." Let the Manitobans decide for themselves: "I would be inclined to think that the most effective way of making them all think this was a good contract, would be for the parliament of Canada to refuse to pass it." The legislation promptly passed by an overwhelming majority from both parties.[16]

The contract proved extremely successful, belying all the dismal forebodings of the Liberals. It redounded to the credit of Premier Roblin, firmly establishing his leadership in the province. Sifton was briefly concerned that Mackenzie and Mann were busy replacing existing Northern Pacific employees, many of whom were Liberals, with appointees of Roblin. Such a situation, Sifton declared, would be "an impossible one and could not be tolerated." Mann hastened to reassure him that such was not CN policy, and "you may rest assured that our Company will not use their power to the disadvantage of any of your political friends." Not wholly satisfied, Sifton ordered Immigration Commissioner J. Obed Smith to keep him informed about all new men employed by the railway. [17]

Not only was the contract a successful gamble on Roblin's part, but it was effective tactically on the political scene. The Liberals looked foolish and inept, particularly when Greenway's dismal record of recent years was contrasted with that of Roblin. The local Liberals were divided, and they resented Sifton's seeming vacillation and half-hearted opposition. His actions left doubt in many minds about his independence from Mackenzie and Mann and his continued loyalty to the local Liberal cause.The available evidence does not support these suspicions, but once roused they were not easily allayed.

As the Canadian Northern affair unfolded, Sifton had maintained a steady stream of detailed directions to Magurn at the *Free Press*. The correspondence typified a problem of long standing. Magurn had commenced a three-year contract on 1 August, 1898, but he had failed to grow into the position. His intentions were good. Yet he had alienated the Manitoba Liberals, whose confidence he required. He quarrelled incessantly with the business managers, first the conservative J.B. Somerset and then the imaginative E.H. Macklin. He was ineffective as an office manager, inclined to grandiose ideas to promote the paper, and his writing, though competent, carried little weight. As one of Sifton's confidants in Winnipeg wrote, with a touch of malice, "Magurn is a man here without friends, if he left there would be no band playing, torch light processions or suppers. He is quite without influence." [18]

Sifton had already reached the same conclusion. He had long defended Magurn against Winnipeg Liberals, but his experience with the paper during the 1899 provincial election and the 1900 dominion election had convinced him that it was time for a change. Late in 1900 a rumour that a change was contemplated reached the ears of J.S. Brierley, managing director of the Montreal *Herald*, who promptly recommended a good friend of his, J.W. Dafoe. "Doubtless you know him well. He is at present editor of the weekly Star; is an ardent Liberal; well posted in political matters; of keen and sound judgment, and has a comprehensive knowledge of the North West." Sifton's reply was immediate and enthusiastic. He had tried to secure Dafoe "a couple of years ago"—probably before Magurn was hired—but he had not then been available. "I shall be very happy to have a talk with him in absolute confidence." [19]

Indeed the minister of the interior was well acquainted with Dafoe. Almost exactly five years younger than Sifton, John Wesley Dafoe was born near Arnprior, Canada West, in March 1866. He was scarcely seventeen when he began a life-long career in journalism, starting in Montreal with the *Family Herald and Weekly Star*. In 1885 he became editor of the *Ottawa Evening Journal*; and a few months later the city editor of the *Manitoba Free Press*, with which he was associated from 1886 until 1892. It was in 1888 that Dafoe first heard Sifton speak, was struck with the dynamism of the young MLA for Brandon North, and sought to make his acquaintance. In 1892 Dafoe joined the editorial staff of the Liberal Montreal *Herald* and then in 1895 returned to edit the *Family Herald and Weekly Star*—the weekly edition of the Tory *Montreal Star*. He was a committed Liberal who had learned while with the *Herald* to revel in fiercely partisan combat, but he was bound to a non-partisan stance with the *Family Herald and Weekly Star*. Dafoe's abilities were forcefully brought home to Sifton, for the circulation of the *Weekly Star* doubled from 50,000 to 100,000 during Dafoe's tenure, much of the increase occurring in the rural West at the expense of Sifton's *Free Press* weekly.[20] Taking Dafoe from the *Star* thus would be a double coup. An able and committed Liberal editor would be returned to the party fold. It would also remove the chief inspiration from the greatest competitor of the *Free Press*.

Yes, Sifton definitely wanted Dafoe. And Dafoe was equally anxious to secure the *Free Press* editorship. When Sifton offered him the position early in January 1901, Dafoe later recalled, "it only took me the millionth part of a second to accept."[21]

There was, however, the problem of Magurn, whose contract ran until 1 August. Magurn appears still to have been labouring under the delusion that Sifton did not own the paper, but merely had been given control over editorial policy by its owners. Lately the *Free Press* editor had been pestering Sifton to use his influence with the owners to secure him an increase in salary or at least compensation for out-of-pocket expenses incurred in entertaining on behalf of the paper. Directly after his meeting with Dafoe, Sifton used this situation in a not very subtle attempt to secure Magurn's resignation. "I have for some time been trying to get your letter on the subject of Finances before my friends of the Free Press board," he told Magurn, "and have at last succeeded, but with very unsatisfactory results." The proprietors had incurred such heavy expenses lately that "they absolutely refuse even to take your claim into consideration." The minister of the interior claimed that he had exhausted his influence. Magurn evidently had earlier declared that if his case was not decided favourably, he might resign. Sifton, "as a matter of friendship," reminded him of this, noted that no increase in salary was likely in the foreseeable future, and concluded, "I have thought that under all the circumstances I ought to say just how the matter stands according to the best of my judgment so that you will be enabled to form an opinion as to what you should do. With kind regards, and wishing you the Compliments of the Season."[22] Magurn was quite taken in by Sifton's deception, but he obstinately refused to take the hint and resign. He was angry both at the decision of "the board" and at Sifton's failure to exert his influence fully,[23] but he was determined to stay on and fight.

By late March Dafoe was becoming uneasy. The lease on his house would have to be renewed shortly if he was to stay in Montreal. Sifton hastened to reassure him: the *Free Press* position would be open soon, and "I do not think we can afford to let you work for the Tories any longer."[24] But no way could be found to force Magurn's early retirement without unpleasantness and disruption potentially damaging to the *Free Press*. In mid-June Sifton made his move. The figurehead president of the company, John Mather, wrote a cold letter to Magurn informing him that new editorial arrangements had been made, effective 1 August: "I trust that in leaving the service of the Company you will find no cause to complain of the manner in which we have fulfilled our obligations to you."[25] Dumbfounded, Magurn frantically wired and wrote Sifton, convinced that Mather had taken leave of his senses. Finally Sifton wired a response that was an entire fabrication: "President informed me some days ago of letter written you. Has taken matter into his own hands. I can do nothing to alter his arrangements."[26]

Magurn was prevented from exercising his editorial duties during July, lest he attempt to harm the paper. He rushed to Ottawa to interview Sifton; his Irish temper provided some fireworks, but eventually Sifton soothed him with the offer of a year's salary as severance pay.[27] Magurn even offered to introduce Dafoe, whom he claimed to admire, to his new charge, so the final parting was quite amicable. Though scarcely predictable, the termination of his contract seemed to destroy Magurn. He drifted in and out of several unsuccessful journalistic ventures, periodically appealing to friends in government for civil service positions. In 1914 Sifton was trying to secure a position for Mrs. Magurn, because her husband "apparently has done little to support his family for some time now." On 4 February 1923, he died, apparently impoverished and almost forgotten.[28]

Despite his shortcomings, Magurn had devoted himself to the *Free Press*, and it was a much stronger property when he left than it had been in 1898. Even Sifton was pleased with its progress, noting that "the daily circulation of the Free Press is 13,000 and the combined circulation of the Morning Telegram and Winnipeg Tribune is not 8,000." There was a strong foundation upon which J.W. Dafoe, one of the supreme figures in the history of Canadian journalism, could build. Sifton was confident about the future prospects of his paper. "I have no doubt," he told J. D. Cameron, "that with Dafoe in the editorial chair and Macklin at the other end the active progress which the paper has lately been making will be not only maintained but accelerated."[29]

Sifton, Dafoe later recalled, "was always deeply interested in the *Free Press*—in its plans, its methods, and its policies; but he never forgot his self-denying ordinance by which he left the last word upon policy to those in charge of the paper." From the beginning Sifton exhibited a much greater confidence in his new editor than he ever had in Magurn. It is true that Dafoe was by far the abler man. But it is equally true that Sifton temperamentally could not long have adhered to any "self-denying ordinance" had he and his editor not seen eye-to-eye on most major policy issues and had the two men not found their relationship to be consistently intellectually stimulating. At first, however, they agreed that the *Free Press* "must be the champion of the West's interests,"[30] and that—at least as long as Sifton was in politics—the interests of the West were intimately bound up with the fortunes of the Liberal party.

Magurn had been inclined to resent Sifton's blunt and frequently proffered advice as an infringement upon his editorial freedom and a commentary upon his professional competence. Certainly it was true, Sifton admitted to him, "that you have confidence in your own judgment and of course a managing editor must not only have such confidence but in the main act upon it. Nevertheless there is very great necessity for every editor[']s judgment to be tempered by the opinions of others."[31] This was a principle that Dafoe well understood, and he never failed to give Sifton the impression that his advice was taken seriously, whether it was acted upon or not. Sifton had, in fact, had occasion to consider seriously the proper relationship of an editor and his newspaper to a political party some months before Dafoe assumed his new post. The *Globe* of Toronto, the leading English-Canadian Liberal paper, had been the subject of abuse by Ontario Liberals for its allegedly ineffectual partisan leadership during the 1900 dominion election campaign. Undoubtedly a scapegoat was needed to account for the party's dismal showing in that province, so the Liberals complained of too much space being devoted to Tory speeches and very mild editorial attacks on the Opposition.[32] J.S. Willison, editor of the *Globe*, bitterly resented the complaints. He had been friendly with Sifton and used the occasion to ask his opinion. "The idea of a great newspaper suppressing the speeches of its political opponents," he wrote indignantly, "is to me so absurd and stupid that it is simply not worth discussion." Could Liberal politicians not appreciate the fact that he too was a professional and knew better than they how to run a newspaper? The *Globe*, he claimed, owed the Liberal party nothing; it had greatly aided the party and received little but abuse in return. "I have always been willing to take kindly advice from any quarter," he added. "But I am not willing to be the football of every querulous and disgruntled Liberal in the country."[33]

Sifton replied that there was no "balance of obligation between a great party newspaper and the party it supports." The *Globe* and the Liberals needed one another, for the party supported the paper as much as the paper supported the party. From the party standpoint, the *Globe*

> lacks aggressiveness, stands too much on the defensive, and in politics seems to regard everything that the party does as having to be defended instead of carrying the war into Africa. I share this opinion myself, but....I recognize that you are the trustee for a large property and that your duty is to conduct it in such a way as to make it most successful....
>
> I think that in election campaigns from a party standpoint you advertise the Opposition a great deal too much....In a campaign the object of a party is to get the public mind saturated with its own views and ideas. When we send out campaign literature we don't send the Tory stuff with ours. We would prefer that the people did not read the Opposition literature. Hence The Globe in an election campaign is not the best kind of literature to send. The theory that you want the elector to read both sides and trust to him that you are right, is not practical politics....
>
>
> My own opinion is that when approaching an election a great party paper can afford to alter its tactics, put more ginger into its fighting, rake the other side and devote its space to its own friends and when the campaign is over go back to its former style....
>
> I may add on this point that I think the entire trouble with the Liberal party of Ontario is lack of aggressiveness. Young men don't enthuse over a party that is not aggressive. Any success I ever had in the west was due to the fact that under all the attacks I *never* apologized, fought everybody. Tupper, Macdonald, Richardson, Tribune and everyone else—fired a Tory whenever I wanted to and never explained or apologized. I don't mean by this that I was personal or abusive. I mean that I never turned to the wave of feeling. They said I was too much for bonuses to railways and stood in with capitalists. I never spent a half minute trying to prove that it was not true. The policy of the Government has been bold and progressive and I kept right on hammering that in, while the fellows like Dr. Rutherford [MP for Macdonald, Manitoba, 1897-1900] who spent their whole time defending, were whipped both in the west and in Ontario.[34]

Sifton and Willison more or less had to agree to disagree. In John Dafoe, by contrast, Sifton had found an editor whose views paralleled his own, whose youthful zeal for partisan conflict still surged strong in his veins. Western Canadian Liberals had gained a vigorous associate, and prospects for a bumper harvest augured well for the beginning of the new era. It would be necessary to get to work right away on "the fall campaign for the weekly," Dafoe enthusiastically wrote, "if we are to capture some of the wealth that is going to be poured into the pockets of the farmers this fall."[35]

Clifford Sifton celebrated his fortieth birthday on 10 March 1901. It was not a watershed in his life, but he seems about this time to have begun to review his private affairs. He and Arma were happy in Ottawa, and their five sons, ranging in age from four to fifteen, were demanding more and more of his time. Political life, he had once said, was a "treadmill," and he was determined to be able to escape from it and relax with his family more regularly. In 1901 the Siftons vacationed near Brockville in the beautiful Thousand Islands district of the St. Lawrence. The following year Sifton purchased Whitney's Point, where he would erect a comfortable summer establishment known as Assiniboine Lodge, complete with a dock and a yacht for summer cruises.[36]

Indeed, the opulence of Sifton's life was beginning to cause widespread comment. His splendid Ottawa home, called "Armadale," was lavishly furnished. According to one report, it had a music room, "devoted to a weekly dance"; a drawing room with satin furnishings, polar bear rugs, and beautiful paintings; a billiard room with still more valuable paintings; and a library, "full of books from floor to ceiling." Sifton also maintained a notable stable of horses, and in 1903 became president of the Ottawa Racing Association.[37] In 1902 his old political enemy, Senator Kirchhoffer, was so busy regaling "the boys" back in Brandon with stories of Sifton's wealth that the minister's former law partner, A.E. Philp, wanted to launch a libel suit. Sifton naturally ignored the idea; but in Brandon, where many people well remembered the impecunious if hard-working young lawyer of nearly twenty years before, embroidered stories of his "magnificent institution," carriages, horses and footmen, his supposed interests in various companies and banks, invariably attracted a wide-eyed audience.[38] But Sifton believed that his wealth was his personal affair, that it had been obtained perfectly legally, that it was no sin to be wealthy, and that there was nothing for which to apologize.

In the opinion of many, however—including some Liberals—a little discretion would have been appropriate. It hardly seemed decent for a minister of the Crown whose wealth obviously was increasing rapidly to be so ostentatious. The situation was perhaps best summed up in a story attributed to Sir Richard Cartwright, Laurier's minister of trade and commerce. As they watched Sifton step into his carriage one day, Cartwright supposedly said to a young Liberal acquaintance:

> Young man, do you note this display of affluence on the part of a minister so new and so young? Do you note those spirited horses, that silver-mounted harness, and the magnificent chariot behind? Shall I tell you what Sir John Macdonald would have said to one of his ministers if he'd appeared thus? Sir John would have said, "My dear fellow, it is bad enough to do it, but for heaven's sake don't advertise it." [39]

Sifton also decided in 1901 to reorder his financial affairs. The *Manitoba Free Press* was by far his largest single investment, but he had interests in many other areas such as land and various securities, and he also wished to use his position and talents as a broker or investment agent for others. He wanted to incorporate an umbrella company under which all these activities could be conducted. Through his lawyer, C.A. Masten of Toronto, he began to explore the possibilities and discovered that only in New Jersey could a company be incorporated with the wide-ranging powers he desired. [40] Tempting as such an incorporation appeared, the company would still be subject to various Canadian and provincial laws so far as most of Sifton's interests were concerned and therefore would not serve the purpose. Ultimately, if reluctantly, Sifton decided that he would have to incorporate under the more restrictive Ontario laws.

The greatest problem was the distinction drawn between "loan corporations" and "trust companies," which were not allowed to infringe upon the jurisdiction of one another. Lending money or investing in real estate or other securities came under the former, which also required a much higher proportion of paid up stock. Masten told Sifton that the proposed company "would be both a loan company and a trust corporation within the meaning of these acts." In October 1901 they decided to file for incorporation of a joint stock company, trying to push the Ontario authorities for an even broader range of powers than was normally granted. After protracted negotiations, the Canadian Investment & Brokerage Company Ltd. was incorporated in the spring of 1902, with Masten as president. Sifton held forty-eight shares, Masten one, and A.P. Collier, Sifton's private secretary, one. The presidency was quickly transferred to Sifton, and Collier became secretary treasurer. [41] Early in 1905 it became the Canadian Assets & Brokerage Co., with considerably extended powers, "granted now without demur." "I have no doubt," Masten told Sifton, "that if at any time you find the Charter not necessary for your own purposes, that you can sell it for a good deal more than it has cost. I do not think that I could undertake with any one to get another such Charter."[42]

Sifton nevertheless was annoyed at the red tape which forced disclosure of what he regarded as purely private business. He had designated Masten's Toronto law office as the nominal head office of his firm and was greatly irritated when he discovered that by law the head office must display a proper sign. And the required annual returns seemed to him excessively detailed. "All that in any reason the Company should be required to state in its return," he snorted, "is the place of the Head Office, the names of the Officers of the Company, the amount of the stock, and the amount that is paid up."[43]

During the course of his investigations into creating his company, Sifton decided that an overhaul of the dominion government's Joint Stock Companies Act was overdue. The old act, he later claimed, "was in a most ridiculous condition and the administration of it was a relic of the dark ages." In 1902 the new bill was introduced in the Senate by R.W. Scott, the secretary of state, under whose jurisdiction the legislation fell. After extensive debate, it passed late in the session to the Commons, where Laurier tried to pass it off as a minor amendment to joint stock companies law. The Leader of the Opposition demurred; it was, he declared, an important departure from past practice and the time for proper debate was too short. Laurier backed off, agreeing not to press the legislation.[44] But Sifton was not satisfied, apparently persuaded Laurier to let him take charge of the bill, and pushed it through in short order. It generally followed English law, with the intention of facilitating the incorporation of joint stock companies by enabling the secretary of state to issue letters patent, rather than going through the lengthy legislative process which then existed. The avoidance of parliamentary examination of companies seeking incorporation indeed seems to have been Sifton's main object. His attitude was reflected in other provisions of the legislation. For example, if those controlling two-thirds of the shares were agreed upon a course of action, the remaining shareholders need not even be notified. For someone like Sifton, who tried to control every possible share in his companies, the new law would make life much easier. Another provision eliminated the need for detailed annual returns concerning the shareholders and activities of the company, except at the discretion of the secretary of state. Annual returns, in effect, became a mere formality.[45] Undoubtedly the legislation had its strong points from a businessman's perspective, but it removed from public scrutiny much connected with the business interests of Canada and consolidated greater power in the hands of those controlling the corporations.

Real estate remained a favoured field of investment for Sifton. He continued to own both town and rural lots scattered in Manitoba and the

Territories. He invested heavily in 1904 in lots in Port Arthur, speculating upon their increased value when the Grand Trunk Pacific terminal was built. In 1904 he appears to have established the Canadian Northern Land Company through which he could more easily carry on his land trans-actions.[46] At one stage he also invested in the Canada North West Land Company, a subsidiary of the CPR.[47] Occasionally he purchased trust company debentures, as in 1902 when he invested $100,000 in Canada Permanent and Huron and Erie.[48] Sifton frequently exhorted Canadians to invest in their own resources, such as spruce forests and the pulp and paper industry, before American and other foreign interests did. He followed his own advice, and there is evidence that probably he, and certainly his brother-in-law, T.A. Burrows, were busily acquiring timber lands during his term of office.[49] He also believed in the profitability of Canada's hydro-electric potential, and in 1901 was involved in a scheme of the Keewatin Power Company, of which John Mather was president, to sell power to the City of Winnipeg.[50] He was a primary moving force in setting up the United Empire Life Assurance Company in 1902. And he was cautiously interested in a scheme to establish a new bank in the West, if it were "conducted upon conservative principles." New banks were tricky affairs to get safely launched, he warned, and "it is easier to lose money than to make it."[51] Over all, Sifton was an astute if cautious investor, not given to high-risk gambling. He liked to have nearly absolute control of ventures in which he was involved, to play his cards close to his chest, and to have the prospect of a certain, steady return on investment. He was extremely well placed to take advantage of the economic boom that was launched with the new century.

One old political score remained to be settled: that with Robert Lorne Richardson, Independent MP for Lisgar, and proprietor of the *Winnipeg Daily Tribune*. Following the general election of November 1900, Sifton had ordered petitions filed against all Conservatives elected in the West, and against Richardson, in order to protect Liberal members whose elections might be protested. "One difficulty," he wrote smugly, "is that there are not quite enough Conservatives elected, but we cannot help that."[52] The Liberals were serious about two of the protests in Manitoba: that against Richardson in Lisgar and that against A.A.C. LaRivière in Pro-vencher. With respect to the latter petition, however, the Manitoba Liberals made a ridiculous political blunder, alleging "improper acts" between Archbishop Langevin of St. Boniface and Premier Roblin. This open accusation irrevocably alienated the Church from the Liberal cause and made success in a by-election exceedingly improbable, so the petition was not seriously pressed.[53]

The Lisgar case was altogether different. During the late election campaign Richardson had been happy to welcome the assistance of the Roblin-Rogers Manitoba Conservative machine in defeating the Liberal candidate. He would shortly discover that he had sold his soul to the devil and that there would be a price. The *Tribune*'s intemperate attacks on the Roblin government's railway policy early in 1901 were somewhat foolhardy under the circumstances, as were Richardson's parliamentary speeches. Not surprisingly, the Tories retaliated. They turned over to the Liberals a great deal of incriminating correspondence and aided in every way the collection of evidence. The bill of particulars was astonishingly complete, ranging from the amounts of liquor at various polls, to bribery of voters, to free tickets for Richardson's supporters on the NP&M lines. Sifton wanted to do more than unseat Richardson; he desired to have him disqualified from running again because of his personal knowledge of the corrupt acts. The latter charge, however, was so serious that for success the evidence had to be overwhelming; it was not sustained in the courts. There was ample evidence for the previous charge, however, and on 20 July 1901 the courts unseated Richardson. Sifton personally absorbed the bill for the prosecution.[54]

Richardson reacted predictably, defending his "exceptionally clean" election: "A candidate who was elected by force of overwhelming public opinion in spite of the most unscrupulous tactics, is unseated by a conspiracy between the dictators of the two political organizations, because he refused to connive with either of them in the betrayal of the public good to the exploiters who control them, and because his presence in parliament...is a hindrance in the way of their illicit designs." His denunciation of political machines would have been more convincing had he not availed himself of them in 1896 and 1900. In a futile gesture, he joined with A.W. Puttee and other Winnipeg independents to create a stillborn new independent party of purity and progress, called the Political Reform Union.[55]

Sifton wanted J.D. Cameron, his former colleague in the Greenway cabinet, to be the Liberal candidate in the forthcoming Lisgar by-election. Unfortunately, Cameron was losing another in his series of battles with the bottle, and would not do.[56] Then there was some hope of persuading Greenway himself to run in what would have been his home district, but after an initial expression of interest the ex-premier declined.[57] The dispirited leaders of Manitoba Liberalism plainly had lost their old zeal and fire. Sifton concluded that he would have to take matters directly into his own hands. A full-time organizer, J.M. Robinson, was put to work in Lisgar by early November. In December Sifton himself came to supervise the preparations. He arranged for Edward Farrer, the ubiquitous Tory-Grit-CPR journalist, to work the constituency as well and to serve as contact with the Manitoba government. Premier Roblin, through his organizer Robert Rogers, fully supported Sifton's efforts. The Tories agreed to run a weak candidate, J.M. Toombs, to split Richardson's vote. Naturally the Roblin government had a price for this co-operation. In January 1902 the Laurier government advanced to Manitoba the school lands money which had been denied to the Greenway government, an action the timing of which outraged many local Liberals. There may also have been co-operation on certain railway affairs. [58]

Finally the by-election was announced for 18 February 1902. Again Sifton came from Ottawa to speak every evening in the constituency during the last two weeks of the campaign. He also had his cohorts W.F. McCreary, J.D. Cameron, Isaac Campbell, Senators Finlay Young and Robert Watson, Greenway, and others campaigning just as hard. The constituency was blanketed with special literature and the *Free Press*. But who, it may be asked, was the Liberal candidate? Sifton personally selected D.A. Stewart, a local farmer with neither political ambition nor speaking ability. The candidate was furnished with a written speech, a very few minutes in length, which he dutifully read at every meeting and then retired to permit the more experienced gladiators to battle on his behalf. [59] Against such an awesome machine Richardson had little chance, and Stewart received a comfortable plurality of over a thousand votes. Immediately after the election the flow of the *Free Press* into the constituency was cut off. [60]

Sifton had by no means heard the end of R.L. Richardson, although the former MP never wholly recovered his political influence. Richardson protested the election with good evidence, but Sifton secured the best available legal counsel and outmanoeuvred him on the legal front as well. [61] "Stewart was a very poor witness," wrote H.M. Howell, Sifton's lawyer, after the trial; he had been put on the stand only because "it was absolutely necessary for him to show that he had no notice or knowledge of any expenses for transport of voters and [that] those who are charged with bribery were conducting the election entirely without his knowledge and that he had no connection with them in any way whatever." Poor Stewart seemingly had no idea of what was going on. "He proved this," added Howell, "but he did make a sorry appearance in the witness box. It seems to me you could get better timber next time." [62]

The by-election was a great triumph for machine politics and probably reinforced Sifton's cynical assessment of the voters and his belief in the effectiveness of thorough organization. He was convinced that the Liberals had lost Manitoba in 1899, and several provincial by-elections since, by failing to organize properly. Beyond ridding the political scene of Richardson, whom he had come to despise, his purpose was to provide an object lesson and to revive the party's spirit. At least there were now as many

Liberals as Tories representing Manitoba in Ottawa, and the Martin-Richardson faction of dissident Liberals was discredited, if not routed. Sifton's authority seemed unchallenged. But Howell's letters, nevertheless, remain a depressing commentary upon the sordid morality of the political process in early twentieth-century Canada.

Ironically, during the by-election there also were encouraging signs that there was still vitality in the grass roots, that forces were taking shape which would be beyond the control of mere political machines. The democratic process was, indeed, very much alive. It was, perhaps, evident in the fact that Stewart's victory was less than overwhelming despite the immense influence and many able speakers and organizers who laboured mightily on his behalf. Richardson, for all his shortcomings, had touched a responsive chord in his rural audiences on two issues: government ownership of railways and the great grain blockade of 1901. A third issue, resentment of high tariffs on the necessities of life, was only barely submerged in the tide of prosperity.[63]

The difficulties of the grain trade predominated. The growing western population and near-perfect weather conditions in 1901 combined to produce a record 63 million bushel crop of wheat—a sharp increase over 1900, and more than double the crop of 1898.[64] The CPR had insufficient rolling stock and was quite unequal to the occasion. By the time the shipping season closed on the Great Lakes, only one-third of the crop had been moved, while half remained in the farmers' hands for lack of storage facilities.[65] The Manitoba Grain Act of 1900, the supposed guardian of farmers' rights, proved ineffective under the pressures of the 1901 crop. Farmers anticipating healthy profits were unable to secure cars to ship their grain individually, often could not beg or buy space in existing elevators, and lacked even storage facilities on their own farms. The blockade of 1901, as this constipation of grain handling and transportation facilities was called, led directly to the first effective, permanent agrarian organization, the Territorial Grain Growers' Association, formed in November 1901. It forced the government to recognize the validity of many of the farmers' complaints. And the blockade pressed upon the government's attention the urgent need for a second transcontinental railway, proving that the West could generate the necessary business.

The failure of the system was obvious by October; early in November J.W. Dafoe told Sifton that the railways were not erecting platforms or supplying cars as called for in the Grain Act. Hostility was mounting, and Dafoe thought the *Free Press* should protest the CPR's inaction. Sifton's reply was brief: "Give it to them hot." Dafoe did, in a series of editorials praising the Grain Act and denouncing the railways.[66] The impending by-election in Lisgar made the situation particularly embarrassing for the government, and Richardson was able to make a great deal of political hay by rubbing in the fact that he had opposed the 1900 measure, predicting it would be ineffective. A wave of protests descended upon the government. Demanded one farmer, was the CPR "to be allowed to override the law at their own sweet will & leave the farmers to the tender mercies of the elevator men—if so it is a gross outrage."[67]

Unhappily anger and "hot" attacks on the CPR in the press did nothing to alleviate the situation. In fact, as Dafoe began to investigate more carefully, he came to the conclusion that the railway company was doing the best it could under impossible conditions. Too much criticism, moreover, would play directly into Richardson's hands. Dafoe attempted to hold to a middle course in his editorials, which "were written very carefully to create three impressions: to serve notice on the railway officials that the Free Press was quite prepared to criticize them[;] to satisfy the farmers that the F.P. is quite free from railway control: and at the same time to keep the agitation within reasonable bounds by pointing out that the situation had been created in large part by the fact that we are having almost too much of a good thing." Nevertheless, he advised Sifton, "if a clear case of discrimination could be located and a prosecution actually begun...the effect would be immense in a political sense."[68]

When Sifton visited the West in December 1901, he was left in no doubt that this was the question of the day. He returned to Ottawa determined to retain the political initiative in the West, and accordingly he joined the battle on several fronts. Under the CPR charter, when the company's earnings exceeded 10 per cent of capital expended in construction, the governor general in council had the right to reduce freight rates; a court case was launched to determine upon exactly what base the 10 per cent was to be calculated so that action might be taken.[69] Second, the CPR had applied for an increase of $20 million in its capital stock. The government was disposed to grant the increase only with extensive conditions. About three-quarters of the increase would have to "be spent for the direct benefit of the West," including about $8 million for rolling stock; and about $5 million for double tracking west of the Lakehead and increasing elevator facilities. "You might incidentally invite the attention of the public in Lisgar," Sifton told Dafoe, "to deciding whether they would rather have this $15,000,000.00 spent in improving their transportation facilities or in enjoying the sentimental satisfaction of voting for Richardson." The implied threat was hollow, for Sifton knew that the entire West, and not merely Lisgar, was demanding vigorous action. The attachment of such conditions to the CPR application and the amount to be spent in and for the West, he observed proudly, would be "altogether unprecedented in Canada."[70] Scarcely coincidentally, the public announcement of this deal was made on the same day that the Lisgar by-election was called. It was intended to provide ample evidence of energetic government response to western problems. And it gave Sifton some grounds for his favourite line of attack on proponents of government ownership: through regulation of private companies the government could achieve every bit as much public benefit as a public system could provide, without the alleged inefficiency of publicly owned enterprises and the expenditure of public capital.

A third line of attack was to meet charges that the West was under-represented in the dominion cabinet; Laurier, Sifton told a Lisgar audience, had promised increased representation.[71] Fourth, and probably most important, was the promise that the demands of the TGGA and other grain growers would be met and that real teeth would be put into the Manitoba Grain Act. Introduced in May, the amendments established a system for compulsory supplying of railway cars without discrimination; local railway agents were required to keep an order book and to supply cars in the order in which applications were made, whether to elevators flat warehouses, loading platforms, or otherwise. To avoid block bookings by elevators, it was stipulated that when insufficient cars were supplied to cover out-standing orders, they were to be distributed in rounds at the rate of one car per applicant in the order on the list. Limits on the construction of flat warehouses were lifted, and any person within forty miles of a given shipping point could apply to erect one, the railway being compelled to provide land and a siding.[72] The purpose of the amendments, Sifton told the House of Commons , was "to put the farmer in as independent a position as possible, so far as the wheat buyer is concerned," to enable the farmers to tell the grain buyers, "we are independent and we can deal with it ourselves."[73]

The problem could hardly be solved within a year. President Shaugh-nessy of the CPR told Sifton in November that his employees had been ordered to adhere to the provisions of the Grain Act and that the company had so far "handled 40% more grain than we did in the corresponding period a year ago."[74] The completion of the Canadian Northern line to Port Arthur also relieved some of the pressure. Still, there was in 1902 another, less severe, grain blockade that inevitably produced another rash of complaints. Sifton was now disinclined to denounce the railways, stressing that the wheat boom was a continent-wide phenomenon which neither government nor the railways could have foreseen. Factories producing rolling stock were unable to meet the demand, and it would perhaps take two or three years before the situation was fully corrected.[75] So obviously were the railways struggling to do their best that Dafoe was having trouble producing reasonable editorials that did not sound too friendly to the railways. Finally Sifton advised him that it was a waste of time to argue with those who blamed the railways: "The class feeling amongst the farmers is strong, and you will find I think in the course of time that even if you are successful in proving these fellows to be wrong, which no doubt is a comparatively easy matter, the average farmer will stick with him. A controversy with anyone of a class who incline to stick together is very unprofitable, and in the case of such controversy it matters little whether you are right or wrong the antagonism is created."[76]

Far better, if the class sentiment could not be overcome, to take advantage of it. A clear case of discrimination in the distribution of cars was found at Sintaluta, NWT, and the federal government supported the grain growers who wanted to take the CPR to court. The Supreme Court found in favour of the farmers, a decision interpreted in the West as a great agrarian victory. Yet it certainly did the government no harm, as Dafoe had suggested in 1901, to be publicly identified with the case.[77]

An even better opportunity presented itself to Sifton early in 1903. While he was on a visit to Winnipeg, representatives of the Manitoba grain dealers waited upon him to register their dissatisfaction with the new Grain Act. After a single season's operations, they had concluded that the Act "is detrimental to the best interests of the country in restricting and interfering in trade and commerce, and is manifestly unfair to those in the grain trade, who have capital invested in elevators." It was "class legislation" and so discriminatory with respect to distribution of cars that many elevator men were unlikely to remain in business. Perfectly sensing the mood of the West, Sifton replied that usually it was the farmers who were complaining and accusing him of conspiring with the grain dealers; now he heard the reverse accusation. Certainly the question was complex, and each side had its rights. "But," he stated firmly, "when the grain producer comes to parliament, and says: 'I have produced a commodity which is in universal demand, and I object to its going through the hands of middle-men who will take an undue toll on the product of my labor,' then I want to say plainly, that this is a complaint and an objection that parliament is bound to recognize. And I tell you, moreover, gentlemen, that no parliament will ever be elected in Canada that can afford to disregard this protest." The long-term solution lay with the transportation question: "It seems to me that the railways have utterly failed to apprehend and comprehend the task they were supposed to accomplish. Nine-tenths of the trouble we now labor under is due to that fact." These remarks, Sifton was told later, were worth several thousand votes to the Liberal party.[78]

The grain dealers next presented their case to Sir Richard Cartwright, under whose department the legislation fell. To an anxious correspondent, Sifton pledged, "I shall not under any circumstances agree to the Grain Act being so amended as to take away from the farmers any privileges which they have at the present time." The object of the grain men, Sifton warned Cartwright, was to seek amendments to the Grain Inspection Act "in order to manipulate and mix Manitoba wheat, committing at once a fraud on the producer and the purchaser and ruining the reputation of Manitoba wheat.'' They also would seek changes in the Grain Act: ''This Act, while it has been the subject of a good deal of criticism, has in reality met the views of the farmers and strengthened the Government with the farming population in the West more than anything we ever did.'' The Act should be left alone. Any amendments that infringed upon the farmers' rights ''would raise a storm from which every Liberal Member would have to hide.''[79]

A major redrafting of the legislation did take place in 1903, but the effect was to clarify and strengthen the hastily drawn provisions of 1902. Once more, in 1904, Sifton found it necessary to resist the pressures from the grain dealers for modifications, owing to the ''extremely sensitive'' political situation with an impending election.[80] The government had gradually been tightening legislation each year to establish permanent grades for grain and a better system of inspection. The various measures were consolidated in 1904 in the Grain Inspection Act, another important victory for the burgeoning farmers' movements of the West.[81]

The organized farmers had become a major political force in the West, a fact that Sifton recognized in 1903 when writing to Dafoe:

> I have acquired in the last three years the opinion that the farmers' vote in the west is going to be influenced along lines somewhat different to what we have been accustomed to the past. I think that with a reasonable amount of effort the Liberal party may be kept in line with the trend of thought amongst the farmers. What I mean is that such organizations as the Grain Growers' Association demanding emancipation from disabilities which are in themselves unjust and unfair ought to receive straightforward and emphatic support from the Liberal party....
>
> There are, no doubt, in the resolutions passed by some of the farmers' meetings fantastic and impracticable propositions, but this always happens in such cases. Nevertheless if the reasonable and practicable demands are met the others are generally lost sight of. In fact as a rule they are passed to placate cranks who are in the meetings.
>
> I think you should take strong grounds in favour of retaining and perfecting the privileges given to the farmers by the Grain Act, and resisting any kind of legislation which will ever again compel the farmers to ship through elevators against their will.[82]

Coming from the man who three or four years earlier had dismissed the farmers' demands as impossible, who had suggested that agrarian agitation had been roused by mere self-seeking demagogues, and that the demands could be defused by thorough organization and manipulation of farmers' meetings and the press, such views were astonishing. They reflect the transformation that had taken place in the relations between the farmers and the government. The federal Liberal party in western Canada could no longer be simply the party of capitalism and the nationalism of central Canada. It would have to take into account the real problems of the western wheat economy and a developing regional consciousness. The "simple-minded farmer," to use Sifton's term of 1900, had formed the TGGA and, early in 1903, the Manitoba Grain Growers' Association, and demonstrated a willingness to vote according to his perceived class interests. Now the problem was to keep the Liberal party "in line with the trend of thought amongst the farmers." To be sure, Sifton never became a radical populist, anxious to rouse and lead agrarian opinion. The majority of farmers, in his estimation, were not radical either, and if their reasonable and moderate demands were met in a friendly spirit, they would continue to support the Liberal cause. A reasonable solution, in his view, was to place the farmers in a position to deal as equals with the grain dealers; beyond this, he would not go.

Constantly lurking in the background of Ottawa-Winnipeg relations was the spectre of the Manitoba school question. Neither Prime Minister Laurier nor Premier Roblin wanted to risk another public debate on the racial or religious aspects of the issue. Both, however, were under some pressure: Laurier, to ensure that the Winnipeg Catholics were accorded an equitable settlement; and Roblin, to stake out the provincial claims to school lands, school lands funds and accumulated interest and to demonstrate that the Manitoba Conservatives would be no less aggressive in their pursuit of provincial rights than the Liberals had been under Thomas Greenway. There were some satisfying signs that Laurier's policy on the issue had been successful. By 1900 almost all the Roman Catholic schools outside Winnipeg had accepted the modified provincial system, under the concessions gained in 1899. And in 1899 the Vatican signalled acceptance of Laurier's policy in its appointment of Archbishop Falconio of Larissa as permanent papal delegate to Canada. Falconio was a moderating influence and sincerely sought a reasonable and realistic solution to outstanding difficulties.[83]

Laurier personally supervised negotiations over the Winnipeg schools, and the even more sensitive issue of the school lands funds. The Manitoba premier and his attorney general, Colin Campbell, had placed their case for control of the lands and funds before the Liberal government early in 1901. Although Roblin was believed to be sympathetic to the plight of the minority and not personally opposed even to the re-establishment of separate schools, he was constrained by overwhelming popular opinion. Laurier, who personally believed in provincial control of the school lands and school funds (as did Sifton), promised the Church authorities that control would not be turned over until concessions wholly satisfactory to the minority had been guaranteed. The result was a stand-off between the premier and the prime minister that would prevail for a decade.

Meanwhile, however, there was an issue that could be resolved. Interest on the fund had been accumulated for some years and could be turned over to the province without sacrificing federal control of the lands or the principal of the fund. This was the same money that Laurier and Sifton had promised Greenway three years earlier, but which the Senate had refused to grant. Laurier put off Roblin and Campbell during most of 1901, probably to ensure their co-operation in settling the difficulty in Winnipeg, and they seem to have bargained in good faith, even if the situation in the city was not wholly resolved. Laurier seemed anxious to give the money to the province and to obtain church approval for the gesture. Probably after some judicious arm-twisting by Falconio, the usually reluctant Langevin told Laurier in December that, in light of concessions and promises made, "I am of opinion that it is more advisable for the good of our country and for our own advantage, that the whole of the interest [*sic*] of the school money be paid to the Government of Manitoba."[84] The intention of the federal government to transfer some $224,000 to the province was announced accordingly in January 1902.

The timing was perfect for the Roblin government, helping them to avoid embarrassment in their education estimates for 1902. It was precisely the sort of gesture that Greenway had repeatedly and unsuccessfully sought from Laurier. Why, demanded the enraged local Liberals, had this step been taken without any consultation with Greenway on timing? The dominion Parliament was not even sitting; could the announcement not have waited a few months, allowing the provincial opposition to hammer the Roblin government for financial incompetence? "Our friends are fairly wild," Sifton's father wrote; "They say you have sold the province to save Lisgar."[85]

Naturally Sifton refused to apologize, and he took the high ground of considerations of public policy. The government, he told Dafoe while blithely brushing over inconvenient facts, had always been consistent in its attitude since 1898. The money had been paid to the Roblin government because there was "no ground upon which we could refuse to pay it." He added:

I have always myself taken the ground that the School Fund ought to be handed over completely to the Province to administer, and I do not propose to make myself responsible for any such picayune humbug as having one policy for a Grit local Government and another policy for a Tory local Government. If our fellows in the legislature know how to use it it will do them good instead of harm. If we had refused to pay the money the Roblin Government would have had a grievance and our fellows would have been put to apologizing for what we were doing. Now they can tell the other fellows that if it were not for our generosity they would be in the hole, and draw contrast between the method in which we are treating them and the action of Bowell and his followers in the Senate towards Greenway.[86]

Despite his remarks, as an old hand in politics Sifton must have known that the advantage lay with the Tories in Manitoba, not the Grits. It might be tempting to believe that Sifton and Laurier had higher considerations in mind than mere partisan advantage. But the local Liberals probably were not far off the mark when they guessed that the Lisgar by-election had more to do with the timing of the announcement than anything else. The Tory candidate was thinking of withdrawing, and Sifton was desperately anxious that he be kept in the field to divide Richardson's vote. It seemed a small price to placate the Roblin government. At any other time neither Sifton nor Laurier would have been above manipulating the announcement to give maximum advantage to the local Grits. And, given the minimal concessions gained by the minority under Roblin, Greenway must have wondered why his earlier request had been refused, yet now it was imperative to conciliate Roblin. All in all, it was not a good way to build mutual trust and teamwork between the provincial and federal Liberal organizations.

A new team spirit was what Sifton had been trying for months to infuse into the Manitoba Liberals. Thus it was ironic that he should have failed so completely to be conciliatory to the disappointed and bitter local Grits on the school fund issue. For several years Sifton had believed that the "indolent" leadership of the provincial Liberals was their greatest hindrance. In the elections when he had been successful, Thomas Greenway had had energetic assistants invigorating the party organization—Joseph Martin in 1888 and Sifton in 1892 and 1896. With Sifton's removal to Ottawa, the provincial government appeared to have little sense of direction, its organization lapsed into lassitude, and the government was defeated in 1899. Of course, there were other factors that contributed to the defeat, but in Sifton's mind the lack of energy and organization were most fundamental. Various expedients to ease Greenway out of the leadership — a senatorship after his defeat, a federal constituency during the 1900 dominion elections, the Lisgar nomination in 1901—all had failed. Whether driven by ambition, a sense of duty, or the importuning of his friends, Greenway stubbornly refused to budge.

Periodically he threatened resignation. At one stage, expecting Greenway to leave, Sifton proposed calling a convention for the summer of 1901, "where we will straighten things out and, according to my present view, probably appoint a Committee of Management." That certainly would have been an unsatisfactory solution, but once more Greenway's hesitations scotched Sifton's schemes. "I have been unable to get the old man's resignation," wrote Sifton's agent in the matter, Frank O. Fowler, in July, "although he still declares he is going to resign."[87] Even the local Liberals realized that if Roblin were to call a snap election they would be hopelessly unprepared. Several party members met in Winnipeg during Exhibition Week in August and decided to press for a provincial convention in the late fall. Sifton was invited to come, accepted, and began preparations to ensure its success.[88] The arrival of Dafoe as editor of the *Free Press* was an important part of his plan. In September an editorial appeared on the history of the Liberals in western Canada,[89] followed by many editorials and articles in praise of the Liberal cause. On 14 October the Winnipeg Liberal Association met in a unified, confident mood, no longer torn by dissident anti-Sifton forces, a dramatic change from two and three years earlier.[90]

If Greenway would not resign, concluded Sifton, the party must stand strongly behind him. He wrote an unusually diplomatic letter to the ex-premier, suggesting that "the party is in a much more satisfactory position than it has been since '96." There were few grievances and even fewer of "the kicking element" left. The organizer's office had been closed, and no money was being expended for that purpose; this produced a good effect, because "the men willing to work without money have emerged and there seems to be a healthy state of affairs throughout the party generally." In view of the "recklessness" of the Roblin government, the Liberals had a good chance if an election were called soon. If Greenway did not continue in the leadership, he added, "I am wholly and totally at a loss."[91] Sifton was attempting to put the best possible face on a bad situation, even to the extent of this hypocritical statement. The *Free Press* energetically joined in praising the ex-premier and refurbishing his image: no longer was he to be "the old man," as Liberals were wont to call him in private; he was now "Manitoba's G.O.M."[92]

As the delegates from across the province assembled in Winnipeg for the convention on 11 and 12 December, the *Free Press* published photographs and short biographies of each, duly inflating their egos and enhancing the spirit of the proceedings. Dafoe also gave special attention to sketches and biographies of the editors of the provincial Liberal weekly press, some nineteen papers outside Winnipeg at that time. Sifton addressed both the convention and the Young Liberals while in the city. The hopes for renewal climaxed with the enthusiastic endorsement of Greenway's leadership on 11 December . The whole affair, reported the *Free Press*, was an emphatic declaration of Liberal unity.[93]

Unfortunately, a dose of enthusiasm could only temporarily mask the real problems of the Manitoba Liberals. Within a few months their flagging zeal was made painfully obvious by contrast with the spirit of the Roblin-Rogers Conservative machine. Greenway was simply not an aggressive personality, and he was further hampered by ill health. Early in December 1902 Sifton told J.D. Cameron that "in view of the close proximity of the [provincial] elections I think it is absolutely suicidal for the local organization to remain quiescent. You ought to be at work now and you ought to have a candidate in every constituency in the province in the field. You remember that in 1896 we had our candidates nominated nine months before the election." As before, Sifton was willing to help, "but it is quite useless for me to go unless the local members are prepared to take hold and go to work. There ought to be 75 or 100 meetings at the very lowest calculation before the lst of January. Every local member ought to cover his own county with local meetings in addition to meetings in the larger places. The Government cannot be defeated without some work." Finally, he added, "There is no use in looking around and waiting for Greenway to move because he won't move a step—he will do absolutely nothing."[94]

Predictably, little was accomplished. The Liberals remained dispirited. Part of the problem, undoubtedly, was tired blood at the top. In prosperous times, too, it was a daunting prospect to battle a popular new administration with a powerful machine behind it. But Sifton and, indeed, the Laurier administration generally had contributed to the situation. They had done relatively little on a continuing basis to build up a sense of trust and co-operation with the local Liberals, as exhibited by their attitude on both Roblin's railway policy and the school funds issue. They too often appeared to be covering themselves, with only a very secondary concern for the local Grits. It would take more than a periodic injection of enthusiasm to overcome the lack of sympathy for, and unwillingness to consult with, the local leadership.

The months following the Dominion elections of 1900 had not permitted Sifton any respite from the political struggle. In addition to his heavy administrative responsibilities, there had been a constant succession of political difficulties in the West. The struggle for advantage with the Roblin government had been hard and not very successful. R.L. Richardson had been removed, but the spreading agrarian protest movement was creating new problems for the Liberals. As the tension and pressure mounted early in 1902, Sifton became irritable, his nerves were "badly upset," and probably he suffered again from severe headaches, high blood pressure, and insomnia. At Laurier's insistence he went to Virginia for a holiday. Cheerfully he wrote to his private secretary, A.P. Collier, "Weather is delightful & overcoats superfluous....I sleep about two thirds of the time & find it the easiest work I ever did."[95] He needed the rest; it was the last extended vacation he would have for many months.

3

From "Dismal Failure" to "Magnificent Success": Policies of Development (1901-1904)

In Clifford Sifton's view, the Department of the Interior was an agency of material growth and progress. Rare were those who dissented from the general goals of his policies, though many found grounds for disagreement with his methods and in some details. During the years after 1900 he succeeded in completing important administrative reforms, particularly with respect to the labyrinthine difficulties of the railway lands problem. He gave special attention to mining and forestry development. The astounding growth of immigration and western settlement not only appeared to justify Sifton's administration, but substantially contributed to the boundless optimism and self-confidence of Canadians as they entered the twentieth century. That immigration and settlement were basic to Canadian prosperity seemed a self-evident principle to the minister of the interior. Could not every Canadian comprehend that? "I am afraid you are too appreciative of my weak efforts," he told J.S. Willison in 1902, with a touch of false modesty. "I find some ground for wonder however in the lack of appreciation of what is going on in the West where we have turned dismal failure into magnificent success. The foundation of Canadian prosperity will be securely laid in another two years."[1]

The Department of Indian Affairs remained difficult to fit in to Sifton's general development strategy. He was neither a political nor a social reformer, as J.W. Dafoe once remarked,[2] a limitation which was underlined by his administration of Indian affairs. The goals of Indian policy seemed in Sifton's day both simple and unexceptionable: in the long run, assimilation; in the short run, "elevation" and "civilization" of the Indian to the point where he would be self-sustaining, productive, and no longer a drain on the national treasury. There was little appreciation, either on the part of the department or the minister, of how demoralizing a sedentary, agricultural life on the reserves was for Indians, many of whom vividly recalled the freedom of a nomadic hunting existence. Equally demoralizing was the constant, pervasive paternalism of the whites, the refusal to regard Indians as equals, the stamping of Indian ways and customs as inferior. Through formal education, agricultural instruction, and in other ways, the Indian was to be persuaded to transform himself and his culture. In 1901 Sifton assured the House of Commons that "great progress" had been made and continued:

> In the organized portion of the country there is no Indian population that may be considered dangerous so far as the peace of the country is concerned. The Indians are becoming rapidly a peaceful population and self-sustaining. The expenditure we are making is very large but it is made in the pursuance of a policy favoured by parliament for many years based upon a belief that it is better—aside from the justice of the question—to bring the Indians into a state of civilization or comparative civilization, so that they may not be a menace to the country, than to take any chances of their becoming a disturbing factor in the community. Generally the results have been satisfactory.[3]

The rapid expansion of the responsibilities of the Interior Department and other political interests preoccupied Sifton to the point that the Indian administration was of little more than parenthetical concern. Indeed even Deputy Minister James Smart could no longer cope with the responsibilities of two departments, and so in 1902 Sifton restored the separate post of deputy superintendent general of Indian Affairs. Promoted to this position was Frank Pedley, formerly superintendent of immigration in the Department of the Interior.[4] The administration simply continued for the most part in well-established grooves, with officials anxious to prove that economies were being effected, that the Indians were becoming more productive and self-sustaining, and less reliant on rations supplied by the department.[5]

Yet statistical compilations of progress ignored the real poverty and appalling health of many of Canada's Indians. Several of the western treaties had included provision for medical attendance as required, a service extended in practice to most of Canada's Indians in one form or another. The problem was that such medical services were regarded more as a patronage plum to reward partisan but often impecunious practitioners than as a moral obligation to the Indians. Poor diet, relative inactivity, psychological and sociological problems, along with limited resistance to white men's disease, induced extraordinarily high levels of disease and mortality among the Indians. Vaccination for smallpox had almost eliminated that historic scourge of the Indian populations, but now pulmonary diseases—particularly tuberculosis—were ravaging the western tribes. Early in 1901 Dr. G.A. Kennedy of Fort Macleod wrote Sifton at length about the shocking conditions and inadequate care for Indians in his district. "The death rate for the past year in both the Blood and Piegan reserves," he claimed, "has been over *ninety* per thousand." He added that "comparisons have been drawn in the past between the Canadian and the American treatment of the Indians, very much to the disparagement of the latter, but if one were to institute a comparison now between the South Piegan Reserve, immediately south of the line, and our own Blood Reserve here, the facts would hardly be flattering to Canadian self-complacency."[6]

It was a striking indictment of past policy, but Sifton apparently was unimpressed, merely directing one of his officials to acknowledge receipt of the letter. Two months later he made it clear to another correspondent that his objective was to keep medical expenditures down. Rather than pay doctors for each visit, the department began paying a fixed stipend.[7] Since most doctors did not live on reserves but in nearby towns this would have the effect of discouraging allegedly unnecessary visits. It was a continual struggle to keep medical costs down, he assured his fellow MPs: "When an Indian gets medicine one day, he imagines he cannot get along unless he gets more the next, and there are bound to be increases from time to time, but we are doing the best we can to keep down the expenditure." "You never can satisfy Indians that they are being properly attended to medically," he declared. "The more medical attendance that is provided the more they want."[8] At first Sifton's political opponents tended generally to agree with him, only demanding even more rigour in curbing costs. But the facts would not go away. By 1903 they generated a fairly substantial debate on the subject.[9] This pressure, combined with popular demand for more effective medical attendance for immigrants, led Sifton to relent slightly in 1904 when he appointed Dr. P.H. Bryce as the "medical inspector" of the Interior and Indian departments.[10] Bryce was an excellent choice who energetically conducted the first systematic survey of the health of Canada's Indians and attempted to press the government to accept higher standards of health care, particularly in the field of preventive medicine.[11]

The cost of Indian education was also regularly under attack. Since he first had assumed the office of superintendent general of Indian affairs,

Sifton had believed that the industrial school system was expensive and woefully inefficient, if not a waste of time. "I have no hesitation in saying," he told the Commons, "—we may as well be frank—that the Indian cannot go out from a school, making his own way and compete with the white man." Why? "He has not the physical, mental or moral get-up to enable him to compete. He cannot do it."[12] The industrial school system had been "artificial," keeping some Indian pupils in school into their twenties, whether out of fear of their inability to survive back on the reserves or to improve their skills. Sifton decreed that no child should be kept in school beyond the age of eighteen and promoted a "less elaborate" boarding school system,

> where a larger number of children can for a shorter time be educated more economically and generally more effectively. What we desire to do is not to give a highly specialized education to half a dozen out of a large band of Indians, but if possible to distribute over the whole band a moderate amount of education and intelligence, so that the general status of the band would be raised.[13]

Existing industrial schools were largely permitted to continue, but Sifton preferred to have students start in the day or boarding schools, so that a process of selection could determine those most likely to succeed in the more specialized trade schools. In general, too, he believed that it was better to reserve the trade schools for boys. As for the girls, "in their case the domestic work in which they can assist at the [boarding] schools in the later years of their pupilship is the best sort of industrial training that they can obtain."[14] Some people denied that any progress was being made in Indian education. Sifton flatly disagreed, but he added that perhaps the schools were not as efficient as white schools because "you cannot press the Indian children as you can the children of white people, you cannot require so much from them." He confessed also that it was difficult to find competent teachers. Although they were required to have third-class certificates, "when you pay $300 a year and send a young woman, or a young man, out to a lonesome place where there are no social advantages it is very difficult to get a competent teacher under those circumstances."[15] Most members were well aware of the fact that $300 was less than half what most teachers could expect in urban schools and less even than what was offered in most rural schools. Yet when Sifton was criticized, it was for spending too much, not for niggardliness.

In part it was this attitude of scrimping on public funds wherever possible that led to continuation of the church-dominated school system, despite mounting evidence of its inefficiency. The government shared the costs with various denominations, which allowed some control without full responsibility. The churches were anxious to take on the task, both as a means of denominational proselytizing and as a contribution to a national mission of "Canadianizing" both immigrants and Indians; but they laboured with a perpetual desperate shortage of funds and qualified personnel. Within the department some officials believed that the failures of the system could be laid directly at the doors of the churches. Inspector Martin Benson commented in 1903, "The Indians do not appreciate the instruction in religion and manners their children receive at these schools. What would impress them would be a practical education that would fit them to earn their own living and assist them to better their condition. That they do not receive such an education is generally admitted."[16] Nevertheless the government wanted to have it both ways. Most Canadians believed that the Indians ought to be instructed in the Christian religion and moral values of the white society if they were to be "civilized," and that was the province of the churches. But the church schools were inadequately funded to provide the practical education which also was recognized to be necessary. Neither Sifton nor Parliament would have countenanced any secularization of the system with a concomitant rise in costs to improve standards or efficiency.

The superintendent general was a believer in practical agricultural education both within and outside the school system. The department encouraged both Indians and farm instructors who demonstrated significant progress. Its goal, as one official put it, was "to hasten the day when ration houses shall cease to exist and the Indians be self-supporting."[17] Indians were taught the value of cereal agriculture for profit, and principles of cattle-breeding, and were discouraged from concentrating on horses and ponies. At least one farm instructor was being supported by the department in a programme to settle Indian couples who had graduated from the schools away from the main body of their tribes. There they would be urged to farm like whites, growing a surplus to their immediate needs, not sharing with the tribes, and keeping the profits for themselves. "As a matter of practice," stated Sifton, "one of the most serious difficulties in improving an Indian band is that just as soon as an Indian couple show an inclination to thrift and gather a little property around them, all their Indian relations think it is not necessary for them to work just in proportion as this couple is prosperous. Their relations take their supplies, and consequently they have no encouragement to accumulate property." Settled separately, graduates of Indian schools could have a "much higher type of civilized life than they could if they settled amongst the other Indians."[18] The scheme enjoyed some success, as Sifton noted with satisfaction in later years.[19]

It also may have been useful in bringing underutilized portions of reserves under cultivation. As the West became settled, Indian reserve land became more attractive to white speculators and settlers, and the department came under increasing pressure to obtain surrenders for those reserves or portions of reserves which the Indians could not use efficiently. Sometimes the department was sympathetic because it was persuaded that sale of land might benefit one or more Indian bands. The cash obtained could repay band debts, alleviate distress, provide capital for economic development or, if invested, the capital could provide long-term cash benefits. The surrender and sale of reserve lands, notes one authority, constituted "a particularly conspicuous reflection of the Indians' failure to meet the expectations of the department." Even so, "there was nothing like the United States' policy of speeding the assimilation of Indians into the wider society by granting allotments of reservation lands to individual Indians, a scheme which brought the rapid transfer of Indian lands into white hands."[20] Beginning in 1901, the number of surrenders was more marked than previously, and they increased sharply in the latter part of the decade.

It is fair to say, however, that relatively few surrenders took place during Sifton's tenure of office and that generally the department attempted to protect what it believed were the best interests of the Indians. Often it was not sale of the land, but leasing it for exploitation of resources that created difficulties. On the Dokis reservation in Ontario, for example, there stood a mature forest which, if harvested, was likely to produce nearly $300,000 for a band of eighty members; if not harvested, it would rot and lose its value. But an elderly chief was opposed to the proposal because he believed he had a moral or spiritual obligation to preserve the forest intact for his successors.[21] It was impossible to permit the exploitation of timber, mineral or grazing rights without the Indians' consent—though there were, of course, ways of inducing the Indians to respond favourably to departmental initiatives. Sifton told the House of Commons that the government would seek such consent only "when we think it will not interfere with the means of livelihood of the Indians."[22]

In southern Alberta the Blackfoot reserve proved very difficult for the department. Private capital had been interested during the 1890's in developing a coal seam on the reserve. The department preferred to see the Indians develop it on their own and advanced $1,000 to begin the work. Unfortunately, a much larger amount of capital was required for large-scale development, and the Indians viewed mining as a part-time or casual occupation. With major competition springing up elsewhere in the district, it was clear that failure was inevitable unless private capital could be induced to begin substantial mining. Throughout the negotiations, however, the department insisted upon protecting the Indians' rights to royalties and jobs. By contrast, the Indians flatly refused to co-operate in leasing part of their reserve as grazing land for ranchers.[23]

In yet a different case, Sifton wanted to prevent a surrender of land to protect an Indian band on the Coté Reserve in northeast Assiniboia. Mackenzie and Mann, promoters of the Canadian Northern railway, wanted a block of land in 1904 for a townsite and divisional point. Both the local Indian agent and the Indians were anxious to reach an agreement, probably because of the high cash value of the land. Sifton foresaw serious social problems with a town (Kamsack) on the reserve. Only reluctantly was he persuaded to consent to the arrangement, after ensuring that the Indians would make a substantial profit. Unhappily, the adverse effects that he predicted were realized in the future.[24]

Such examples of transactions involving Indian lands could readily be multiplied. In general they suggest that within the context of the times the department usually was fair and conscientious in its role as protector of the Indian interest. With hindsight many have come to deplore the alienation of any part of original reserve lands and to question the procedures used. Undeniably there were occasional abuses, although often the dubious procedures were used to bring about a result that officials genuinely believed was in the Indians' interest. But the context of the times assumed that the department knew what was best and that land and other transactions were to be considered with white, not Indian, values in mind.

One of the few prominent observers of the day who partially understood this shortcoming of Sifton and his department was Governor General Lord Minto. Having concluded a tour of the West in the fall of 1902, he undertook to present a number of Indian grievances to Sir Wilfrid Laurier. The department seemed too rigorous in repressing the Sun Dance, too willing to depose mildly troublesome chiefs, too determined to control the day-to-day lives of the Indians. "Speaking generally," he added, "while fully recognizing the great success of Canadian administration of Indian affairs, it has seemed to me that there is a want in many cases of human sympathy between the white administrator and the Indian, and that possibly... somewhat narrow religious sentiments have not conduced to a sympathetic understanding of the Indian races."[25]

Although not wholly accurate, Minto's observation does underline the outstanding characteristics of Sifton's policy: success defined in white terms with little empathy for the Indian point of view. The governor general himself professed to recognize that "as civilization advances. barbarism must go to the wall."[26] Certainly Sifton would have concurred, but he saw little to be gained in the interim by mollycoddling the customs and sensibilities of "barbarism." Directness and firmness would more rapidly persuade the Indians to accept the idea of a competitive society. In all probability they were saved from more draconian measures simply by the fact that they were not a major concern. The Indians were "wards of the state," a responsibility to be lived with, unlikely to contribute significantly to the progress of the country.

Also spared rigorous reform by virtue of not being central to Sifton's purposes was the Department of the Geological Survey. Indeed, the relative neglect may have been somewhat harmful to the survey, which spent several years in an administrative limbo.[27] It had always had an enviable professional and scientific record in the discovery and mapping of Canada's geological structure and mineral resources. Except for extraordinary parsimony, Sifton apparently preferred to keep his hands off the Survey so long as it was under the directorship of the redoubtable and acclaimed Dr. G.M. Dawson. Sifton and Dawson did not much like one another. The minister wanted to popularize and circulate more widely the findings of the Survey with respect to mining resources; and in general he wanted the Survey to become more "practical"—that is, to concentrate on providing all the knowledge necessary for the economic exploitation of Canada's mineral resources and to de-emphasize what he regarded as purely scientific but uneconomic work. He also frankly saw no reason why the Survey should be any more immune from the requirements of patronage than any other branch of the civil service. To Dawson these ideas were almost intolerable. He was a man of high, uncompromising standards who "refused to stoop to the geological illiterate" in his reports. "The central quality of Dawson's directorship," writes Professor Morris Zaslow, "was conservatism, the avoidance of new departures." He also bitterly resented the exigencies of political patronage, from which the Survey had been comparatively free in the past, for it impaired the efficiency of the work to employ people without scientific qualifications.[28]

Dawson died suddenly in the prime of his life on 2 March 1901. Apparently Sifton believed that it was an excellent opportunity to realize the changes he had vaguely formulated in the past. Dr. Robert Bell was appointed acting director. His scientific credentials were impeccable, his longevity of service equalled by few. Yet Bell was an insecure personality and a poor administrator whose leadership generated rather than softened personal rivalries and quarrels within the department. He was under pressure from Sifton to make signifcant changes. "My idea," Sifton told the Commons a few weeks after Dawson's death, "is that the time has now arrived when some practical method should be adopted in carrying out the idea of the founder of the Survey [Sir William Logan], namely, to make it the practical means of developing the country." Shorter, more frequent and less technical summaries of the work than appeared in the annual reports should receive wide circulation. That way, "many men who are practical miners and prospectors,'' but who did not understand the "Scientific terms and the technical manner of describing formations'' would benefit.[29]

Bell proved much more responsive than Dawson. The former director had never assumed that the work of the Survey required justification or explanation; his reports were virtually unrelieved technical and scientific accounts in extended essay form, all but indigestible to an average reader. Bell, by contrast, was anxious to make it clear that the work was highly beneficial to the Dominion. In 1904, for example, he began his report by stating, "The field work extended to all parts of the country....It will be seen that it was nearly all of a thoroughly practical character, intended to promote the discovery and development of the mineral wealth of the Dominion.'' Numerous examples of the practical effects of the Survey were cited, and there was even a separate section entitled "Practical Character of the Work of the Department.'' The reports had certainly become more useful and accessible in format.[30]

In part these changes may have reflected the fact that Sifton had created a competitor for the Survey within the Department of the Interior, a move that generated bitter rivalry in the civil service. The Survey already had a section of mines, but Sifton was dissatisfied with its work and decided to transform the post of superintendent of mines, hitherto under the Dominion Lands Branch of the Department of the Interior. The incumbent superintendent, William Pearce, had had limited duties with respect to collecting fees and royalties and enforcing mining regulations on federal mining concessions; in practice, he had spent much time labouring to solve the railway lands problem, and his reports focused on agricultural problems in the Territories. He was transferred to the chief inspectorship of surveys, and in June 1901 Dr. Eugene Haanel, Sifton's old mentor from Victoria College, was appointed superintendent of mines.[31] With limited funds and authority, Haanel concerned himself in the first two years with establishing an assay office in Vancouver, and reporting on mining operations in the Yukon. But Sifton moved more decisively in 1903, when he sought a larger parliamentary appropriation for what amounted to a new mines branch of the Department of the Interior.[32] Thus two competing bureaucratic complexes were created with overlapping jurisdiction, resulting in unnecessary hostility and some duplication of work. In 1904 Sifton attempted to clarify the situation when he announced that he intended to reorganize both the Geological Survey and the Mining Branch the following year. His resignation precluded this action, but Haanel was carving out a useful and important area of expertise nonetheless. He focused mostly on metallurgy, the extractive and refining processes and the economic potential of mineral resources in various regions.[33]

As it stood, Sifton's administration of the Geological Survey was unimpressive. An efficient and respected body lost some of its sense of direction and much of its morale during this period. Forcing it to be less elitist and more "practical" might have been arguably laudable goals had they been pursued with expeditiousness and consistency. The areas of metallurgy and promoting exploitation of mineral resources might well have been covered by the Survey had Sifton been less miserly. He tended to respond to crises with special appropriations, rather than planning a systematic expansion of the Survey on a scale commensurate with the growth of the Canadian economy and the mining industry. Probably he feared that the theoretical scientific mentality of the Survey would stifle rather than stimulate the objectives he had in mind. In any case, he, as well as Bell, set the survey irrevocably in a new direction, culminating in 1907 when it and the Mines Branch were at last brought together under a new Ministry of Mines.[34]

Sifton gave some attention to National Parks policy after 1900 for two principal reasons. First, the CPR was pressing for expansion and development of the Rocky Mountains (Banff) Park to attract tourists. Second, expansion of the parks could aid in efficient management of the eastern watershed of the Rockies, vital to ensure a reliable water supply in dry southern Alberta.[35]

Created in 1887, the Rocky Mountains Park was Canada's sole national park prior to the turn of the century. Sifton had done little to affect parks policy after he assumed office, save to appoint Howard Douglas, a Calgary Liberal, as park superintendent.[36] Douglas turned out to be an excellent choice, promoting the park and advocating expansion of its boundaries to facilitate conservation of the flora and fauna. He also believed in development of bridle paths and hiking trails to make the park more attractive to tourists.[37] Sifton remained oblivious to such suggestions until the CPR requested action and until investigation of the irrigation potential in southern Alberta made clear the necessity of careful management of the eastern watershed. Between 1901 and 1903 he moved decisively, expanding the Rocky Mountains Park from 260 square miles to 4,900 square miles and establishing Yoho Park (832 square miles) and Glacier Park (600 square miles).[38]

Conservation of resources in Sifton's day meant efficient management, not preservation. It was an era when Canada still had vast tracts of scarcely explored wilderness, and the need to conserve resources or preserve the wilderness was only beginning to touch the public consciousness.[39] The Rocky Mountains Park was developing an international reputation not only for its scenery, but also for its hot springs, climbing, hunting, and fishing. For the CPR the parks were justified by attracting business to a comparatively unproductive stretch of their main line. For the government too the parks were assessed in terms of economic benefit. The exploitation by the CPR of high-grade coal deposits only five miles from Banff townsite was viewed as an important economic development, definitely not a blight on the landscape or at odds with the purpose of the park. Superintendent Douglas reported that it added "another to the many and varied attractions of the neighbourhood." Lumbering also was carried on, though the government decided to issue no new leases and not to renew old ones when they had expired. As the *Manitoba Free Press* put it, when announcing the expansion of the Rocky Mountains Park boundaries, "The reserving of the land will not interfere with the development of mineral and other wealth in the park. The reserving of the land will simply give the government authority to say how much development shall be carried on and what steps are necessary for the preservation of the natural beauty of the parks."[40] So long as the number of tourists increased and expenditure was minimal, Sifton faced few complaints. Some 5,087 visitors had arrived in 1897; in 1905 the total was 17,605, and another 5,000 had to be turned away for lack of accommodation. In his report for 1905 Douglas cheerfully observed, "The revenue of the National Park is now far in excess of the amount necessary for the ordinary expenditure for salaries and maintenance." Banff was a thriving recreational centre, and Deputy Minister James Smart suggested in 1901 that "there could be no better investment for the enterprising capitalist than the erection of summer cottages" in the Park.[41] His views were not only reflective of Sifton's ideas, but were very much in line with policy since 1887.

The minister of the interior was much more interested in extending the principles of conservation to forests under federal jurisdiction, undertaking initiatives that would have a permanent impact. The necessity of government regulation of forests in the public interest had long been obvious in Europe, where forestry was a well-established profession. North Americans, by contrast, had faced from the early settlement period a seemingly endless ocean of forests stretching across the continent in unlimited abundance. Only after the Civil War did Americans slowly begin to comprehend the extent to which extravagant exploitation had diminished this great resource and the need for effective forest management. It was understandably "within the realm of forestry that conservation thought in America first developed."[42] The first national forestry association in the United States was formed in the mid-1870's; although it met in Montreal in 1882, there was no broad support in Canada for the movement at that time.[43] In the early 1880's the American government recognized the need for systematic forestry and in 1886 established a Division of Forestry within the Department of Agriculture. In the 1890's two vital laws were passed by the American Congress, the Forest Reserves Act of 1891, and the Forest Management Act of 1897. With the former act, comments one authority, "the government began changing its philosophy from one of disposing of all lands to private individuals and corporations as rapidly as possible to that of retaining forest areas for the welfare of society as a whole."[44]

Enthusiasm for forestry and conservation could not be confined to the United States, and a number of Canadians had followed developments in the Republic with intense interest. Yet several factors made the Canadian situation somewhat different. One was that a small population facing the vast forests of the Canadian Shield, the northern prairies, and the Cordillera could not believe that the issue was urgent. Another was that in most of the country forests were under provincial jurisdiction, and provincial governments in Quebec, Ontario, and British Columbia were competing for capital to exploit their resources.[45] They were hardly going to put themselves at a disadvantage by regulating the forest industry too closely. The federal government controlled northern prairie forests, those on the eastern slope of the Rockies, and a limited railway belt in British Columbia. Exploitation of these forests was comparatively light prior to 1896, and the Department of the Interior was naturally more concerned with settling the prairies than with regulating its peripheral forests.

Sifton's attitude differed markedly from that of his predecessors. He was a careful observer of American politics and certainly well aware of the scientific and economic reasoning behind forestry and the mounting popular enthusiasm for it. Moreover, he found within his department some pressure for action from officials like William Pearce and E.F. Stephenson, the inspector of crown timber agencies. Sifton entered upon his task with few philosophical qualms about governmental regulation. Within weeks of assuming office in 1896 he had moved briskly on several fronts. The nine dominion lands agents were also appointed crown timber agents for their respective land districts, thus requiring them to supervise forests which had not previously come under their jurisdiction. Homestead inspectors were also appointed forest rangers, both they and the dominion lands agents being carefully instructed in their new duties. Two mounted policemen were assigned to the international boundary area to control "depredations" committed by Americans on crown timber lands. Work was begun on fire guards in some timber reserves. Finally, within less than a year E.F. Stephenson presented to Sifton a report on forest issues, pointing out "the necessity of a comprehensive consideration of the whole question of timber supply and forest preservation in this country, in all its bearings." A commissioner should be appointed "to go thoroughly into the whole subject of forest management, to look into forest protection, the matter of forest reserves and their influence on climate and water supply, to look into planting trees on agriculturally unproductive land, to look into means of preventing prairie fires, and to collect information to enable the government to frame its future timber policy."[46]

In western Canada there was a continuing interest among both government officials and the press in government action to protect forest reserves. Even before Sifton finally acquired the *Manitoba Free Press*, it began a remarkable series of editorials advocating a forest bureau in the Department of the Interior to spearhead policies to preserve the nation's forests.[47] Within the department able men like William Pearce continued to promote a policy of forest protection.[48] Following his suggestions the decision was made not to allow cutting of timber on crown lands on the eastern slope of the Rockies and the foothills near the Bow River, "to preserve the timber as far as possible from being destroyed with the view of securing a permanent supply of water for irrigation purposes." Action also was taken to ensure full government control of timber reserves in Manitoba.[49]

On 15 August 1899, Elihu Stewart, a former dominion land surveyor, was appointed the first chief inspector of timber and forestry within the department. The new officer, Sifton told the House of Commons, "should give special attention to forest preservation and renewals" and help the Department determine effective regulations for that purpose. The information and resulting policies would be useful in dealing with timber on Indian reservations across the country. Furthermore, Sifton wanted his new officer to take a lead in determining what kinds of trees might be most suited to the settlement lands of the North-West, and to aid farmers in their planting and growth.[50]

Stewart was yet another of Sifton's many successful appointees. With remarkable energy he regularly travelled across the country, assessed problems, and made recommendations, always fervently promoting the ideas of the conservation movement. "The whole forestry problem of our North-west," he wrote in 1899, "may be included in two words: conservation, and propagation." Management of the forests, he contended, was "a legitimate function of government" because of "the communal interest in the forestry of a country being so large as compared with the individual interest" and because of "the length of time required for trees to attain maturity." Because it affected climate and watershed conditions, the cutting of forests could not be regarded as simply an opportunity for individual profit. The length of time necessary to grow forests demanded government control in the interest of the nation; individuals desirous of immediate profits would not share this long-term concern. Public management of forests, argued Stewart, was no threat to private enterprise; indeed in the long run expenditure on fire prevention and reproduction would be profitable for everyone. Not only was the activity "well within the limits of state authority," but "it is the duty of the government to expend such of the public funds as may be necessary for such service."[51]

Although Sifton was never able to be so free with public funds for forestry as Stewart suggested, presumably he endorsed the general sentiment. And he had given an enthusiastic promoter of the cause a national platform from which to propagate his ideas. It was on Stewart's initiative that the Canadian Forestry Association was founded in March 1900, and through publications and lectures the chief inspector did everything to sustain the organization and bring forest conservation to public attention.[52] He worked particularly hard to create local branches of the Association across the West, supplying speakers to local farmers' groups and information to individual farmers on conserving and cultivating trees, preventing fires, and so forth. Thus at the same time that conservation enthusiasm was mounting in the United States, it was being strongly encouraged in Canada. The programme was part of Sifton's broader scheme to ensure the success and prosperity of those settling in the West, enriching the entire country.

Sifton also recognized that if his plan was to be successful, it had to be placed on a more scientific footing. Training of foresters was still in its infancy in North America, so at one stage Sifton considered bringing in a German expert to teach his officials or to found forestry schools in Canada.[53] It was decided finally to ask C.A. Schenck, forester to the Biltmore estate in North Carolina where he headed a forestry school, and forest assessor to the Grand Duchy of Hesse-Darmstadt, to make a report on Canadian forests and the Forestry Branch. It was completed early in 1902, and Norman M. Ross, a Canadian who had studied with Schenck, became one of the leading permanent officials of the branch. The report itself praised Canadian policies which had created over four million acres of forest reserves, the leasing rather than sale of crown timber lands, and encouragement of tree-planting on the prairies.[54]

The latter activity was the most controversial of all the forestry policies adopted by Sifton. Indeed the issue of tree-planting divided the forestry movement itself, with figures such as the august B.E. Fernow, chief forester of the United States until 1898 and thereafter a professor of forestry at Cornell University, opposed to it as a waste of effort, diverting public attention from proper principles of forest management. Schenck, by contrast, not only supported it, but believed that without government assistance the programme could not be successful on the prairies. Dr. Saunders, the eminent Canadian government scientist, stated that it had been proven experimentally that fields protected by trees yielded up to twice as much grain as unprotected fields.[55] Sifton had been converted to the concept by 1901, when he began in a small way by distributing some 58,800 seedlings to forty-seven settlers; the programme was expanded rapidly, and by 1904, some 1,800,000 seedlings went to more than 1,000 settlers, as well as distribution of 2,000 pounds of maple and ash seed. The minister of the interior had begun what became a major programme of the Department of the Interior, which distributed over 116,000,000 trees to more than 100,000 settlers during the next three decades.[56]

The scheme may have done much to change the face of the West, but the Opposition naturally attributed dire motives to the minister. Was it not obvious that he was merely creating sinecures for his favourites and hirelings? It was inappropriate to have the government involved in aiding individual farmers; it should confine itself to "the general good." It was "a slander on the intelligence" of the average settler, claimed James Clancy, MP for Bothwell, to suggest that, with a little common sense, he could not plant a tree. The true difficulty, Clancy sneered, was that "the Minister of the Interior has brought a class of people to the country, who live by camp fires, and who might require assistance in tree planting, as well as assistance to keep body and soul together in many cases. But I venture the statement that three-fourths of the people in fact, every man in Manitoba and the Territories who is worth having there, knows how to plant a tree, because he is guided by common sense and has had experience in the older provinces."[57]

Tree-planting in the prairie West, replied Sifton, was altogether different from the East, and experiments were still in progress to determine the best varieties for given soil and climatic conditions. Very few farmers had the special knowledge required to select and raise trees successfully. The general purpose of the Forestry Branch, he added, was twofold: to preserve existing forest reserves, especially against fire; and to disseminate knowledge about trees in the West. Admittedly, the trees grown on the prairies had little commercial value except as firewood. But even that was significant because depletion of limited forest resources in the past had made settlers heavily dependent upon costly coal, and renewal of firewood resources was desirable. Even more important, the use of trees as windbreaks was viewed as vital. Trees helped to prevent erosion and to hold moisture in the soil. Sifton operated on the premise that small beginnings by the government would be multiplied as farmers saw the success of individual examples. "If one farmer in a township proceeds under our legislation and has a little plantation, very great benefits result as farmers for miles around try to emulate him." He even prophesied that if the demand became great enough, "the natural result would be that people would go into the nursery business on a large scale; and...the government would cease to supply the trees, and leave the work to private enterprise."[58]

There is no doubt that the scheme was popular in the West, where "woodlots sprang up to supply the settlers with fuel, the shelterbelts helped to preserve their fields, and the farmsteads served as their retreats." The trees served a psychological as well as a practical need for settlers to close off the view of the endless prairie landscape, allowing them to recreate within the walls of their tree-enclosed farmsteads, however tenuously, reminders of the landscape and culture from which they had come.[59] It is also worth noting that the Canadian programme of direct assistance to individual farmers which Sifton initiated was well in advance of anything in the United States or elsewhere in the world.[60]

The ever-growing waves of settlers flooding into western Canada after 1900 generated a new optimism and fueled a rapid economic expansion across the Dominion. The extraordinary increase in activity forced on the Department of the Interior in these years was reflected in three major areas: the sale and granting of western lands, resource exploitation, and surveying and mapping.

In the five years ending 30 June 1905, some 111,115 homestead entries were made; in the previous twenty-six years, the total had been 88,863.[61] That meant an average of three or four million acres a year being granted in homesteads in the years 1901 to 1905. Just as significant, however, was the enormous sale of railway and Hudson's Bay Company lands: of some 11.5 million acres sold between 1893 and 1905, just under ten million were sold in the period 1900 to 1905.[62] Added to these totals were some 230,000 acres granted "in redemption of half-breed scrip, a very large proportion of which it is reasonable to suppose had been taken up by actual settlers."[63] In a time of prosperity, and as a direct result of government policy, great tracts of land previously unsettled because of legal complications or want of settlers were at last yielding to the plough.

Resource exploitation kept up with settlement. In 1896 some 34.8 million board feet of lumber were cut from forests under dominion licence in Manitoba, the Territories, and the railway belt of British Columbia. By 1901 this total had increased to 78.8 million board feet, and in 1904 to 94.7 million board feet.[64] Grazing leases rose from 236 (258,000 acres) in 1896, to 889 (2,293,000 acres) in 1904.[65] Up to 1896 a total of 15,200 acres of coal lands had been sold, with sales in that year yielding but $168; by 1904, the total sold was 86,200 acres, with sales that year bringing in $68,500.[66] New regulations were effected in 1901 with the objective of encouraging dredging for minerals and petroleum exploration.[67] The promotion of irrigation in the West continued apace, so that the 65,000 acres subject to irrigation in 1896 had grown to 614,700 in 1901, while by 1904 the total area in process of reclamation by irrigation exceeded 4.1 million acres.[68]

The growth of immigration and settlement put tremendous pressures on the topographical survey branch of the Department of the Interior. "It is all that the department can accomplish to survey the land that is required for settlement," Sifton told the House of Commons in 1901. In that year officials struggled to survey 1.6 million acres in Manitoba, the Territories, and British Columbia, or some 10,000 farms of 160 acres each. But in 1903-4 the totals were 12.7 million acres, or 79,000 farms of 160 acres, by far the largest number since the record year of 1883. The seven or eight survey parties sent out in 1896 had grown to some eighty-two by 1903-4.[69]

One result of this western boom was that it forced the railways and the government to settle the outstanding land problem. Basically two issues were at stake. One was the need to have the railways select and patent lands earned by construction, so that the encumbrances to settlement on millions of acres of railway reserves could be removed. The second was whether the land, once patented, would be subject to taxation. Under the terms of the CPR contract, the company's lands would not be taxable for twenty years. At issue was whether the twenty years dated from the passage of the contract in 1881, from the completion of the main line in 1885 (that is, when the lands were "earned"), or from the date of issue of the land patents—a large portion of which were not issued until the period 1901-3. Both were burning issues in the West. The enormous land grants to the railways, especially the CPR, seemed bad enough, breaking up settlements with the reservation of alternate sections, and the rapid rise in land values enormously benefitted the hated monopoly. But that the company should not be paying its fair share of taxes for schools, roads, bridges, and other local improvements, while benefitting from them in terms of appreciating land values, seemed grossly unjust to western settlers. After unsuccessful attempts to resolve the issue between 1898 and 1900, the government and the CPR finally settled down to productive discussions between 1901 and 1903.

The railway company had been unco-operative in part because it claimed that the government had violated the letter and spirit of the contract of 1881 by granting valuable lands to other lines, making it difficult, if not impossible, for the company to find sufficient land "fairly fit for settlement" in alternate sections anywhere in the fertile belt of the West. It did, however, explore the potential of irrigation in the dry lands of southern Alberta, and a favourable report pointed to a way out of the deadlock. Available land in existing reserves came to 14.9 million acres of some 18.2 million to which the railway was entitled. Most of the remaining 3.3 million acres, it was found, could be made up if the government agreed to grant irrigable land en bloc (instead of in alternate sections) between Medicine Hat and Calgary. In July 1903 Sifton and Sir Thomas Shaughnessy finally agreed upon a basis of settlement whereby some 2.9 million acres would be granted for the irrigation project and the remainder in smaller grants elsewhere. The result was "to develop perhaps the largest irrigation scheme in North America, as well as a program of assisted settlement and colonization far more extensive than anything which other land grant railway companies had attempted."[70] The tremendous progress made in resolving the railway land problem is reflected in the fact that when Sifton assumed office in 1896, only 1.8 million acres of land had been patented, though some 24 million acres had been earned by all land grant railways. By the time he left office in 1905, another 22.5 million acres had been patented.[71]

At the same time the government was testing the taxation issue in the courts. This issue was particularly sensitive in the West. R.L. Richardson, for example, had cut a popular figure by insisting that the government ought to force the CPR to pay taxes on its land. In the 1901 session of Parliament he repeated this position, contending that Parliament was supreme and had the power to legislate whatever terms it chose, even to unilaterally altering the terms of the original contract. Sifton took the position that the government could not interpret the law nor enter into a breach of contract. The courts, he declared, would have to decide. During the 1900 election campaign he announced that the government would underwrite the costs of any municipal court action brought against the CPR seeking to collect taxes.[72] In 1902 the government launched three carefully planned court actions, two in Manitoba and one in the Territories. Decision was rendered early in 1903. In the two Manitoba cases the court ruled that the twenty-year exemption dated from the issuance of the letters patent—in other words, the decision favoured the Canadian Pacific. But in the territorial case the government lawyers almost accidentally discovered a loophole which, in the judgment of the court, meant that the CPR never had been exempt from school taxes on all its land and properties in the Territories, though the judgment did not cover taxation for other purposes.[73]

As soon as a settlement was reached and the railway lands finally selected, Sifton proposed using the arable land in odd-numbered sections now freed from railway reserves, and others remaining at the disposal of the government, for the purpose of funding the western portion of the trans-continental railway project also announced in 1903:

> With the release of large quantities of land-from the railway reser-vations [he told Land Commissioner J.G. Turriff] we shall be at once attacked from all quarters by persons desirous under one excuse and another of getting hold of this land. Moreover we shall very soon be forced to throw the odd-numbered sections open for homestead, which would be foolish policy. There is no reason why the country should not get a fair price for these lands, but unless a comprehensive policy is adopted it will not be done. I propose as a corollary to the proposition to build the Grand Trunk Pacific Railway to introduce an Act providing for the sale of odd numbered sections at the disposal of the Government

at prices to be fixed as above stated [by a board], the money to be funded for the purpose of providing means for paying for the railway. I have no doubt that inside of twenty or thirty years the land will produce enough money to pay for the whole railway, in fact there is practically no doubt that such will be the result, but the only way in which that can be accomplished is by fastening it down by an Act of Parliament so that no one else can divert the lands for any other purpose, or in any other way.

It will also be the best policy to pursue respecting settlement because as we know it leaves land for sale to persons who want more than a homestead, and that class of settlers is the class which we desire particularly to encourage.[74]

Exactly why Sifton and the government failed to pursue these ideas is unclear. Nevertheless, it suggests that he was fully as prepared as the Conservatives had been two decades earlier to fund major railway projects through the sale of land when that land became available. Certainly the government's role as a major speculator in prairie lands—as it was in the case of school lands—would have been greatly expanded. However much it might have aided in funding the railway, the proposal in all likelihood would have been a political hot potato, especially in the West. Perhaps Sifton believed that selling the odd-numbered sections would not impede the process of settlement as long as the even-numbered sections remained available for free homesteading. In 1902 he had estimated that "fully one-half of the settlers that are actually located on the land in the West are located on purchased land and have not taken up homestead at all."[75] Plainly a substantial proportion of settlers, constituting the "best class" in Sifton's view, had some means and did not require the advantage of a free homestead.

Nevertheless, it was one thing for railways to sell land grants and another for the government to do so on a large scale. Only two weeks before he addressed his memorandum to J.G. Turriff, Sifton had told the House of Commons that "it is against the policy of the department to sell, generally speaking. Until three or four years ago sales were made from time to time, but not of an important character. But even small sales are discontinued and are discouraged by the department." In a few exceptional cases, he admitted, he did permit small sales, for example, to those who had failed on their first homestead, or occasionally a section or two to ranchers (most of whose land was leased, not purchased). The standard departmental reply to those who wished to purchase land was that the railway and land companies had a good deal for sale and that government lands were reserved for homesteading.[76] Perhaps Sifton simply thought better of his scheme to sell the railway reserve lands, for in 1905 he defended the homestead system as the "successful settlement policy upon which the greatness and increase in the financial strength and resources of Canada depend."[77] These remarks notwithstanding, no action was taken to throw open the railway reserves to homesteading until 1908 when Sifton's successor, Frank Oliver, "officially abrogated" the railway land grant system.[78]

Sifton also revived an old method for settling land, the colonization company. The Tories had endowed several such companies in the 1880's, with little result, and since 1896 no further grants had been made.[79] Generally private capitalists had been unwilling to expend large sums of money to induce settlers to purchase land in their grants; they preferred to let the settlers come to them as surrounding areas were gradually settled and the land appreciated in value. There was, however, in the North-West Territories a large block of land that had been passed over by the railways as not "fairly fit for settlement," that was widely reputed not to be arable, and yet had been largely withheld from any form of settlement as a railway reserve pending final selection by the railways. When five American and two Canadian capitalists expressed interest in purchasing the tract, Sifton quickly changed his policy with respect to land companies and with extraordinary speed approved the project. Beginning some thirty miles north of Regina, the tract continued a further sixty-five miles north, comprising some 839,000 acres of railway reserve lands and 250,000 acres of government lands. The capitalists were allowed to purchase the railway lands at an average price of $1.53 per acre and government lands at $1 an acre, enabling them to secure a solid block of land, subject to fairly stringent settlement conditions. The Saskatchewan Valley Land Company, as the venture was known, was very successful. It spent large sums of money advertising and bringing in potential settlers to inspect the land and easily met the conditions imposed by the government. That it also turned a handsome profit, selling the land at prices between $5 and $10 an acre, seemed incidental to Sifton. Land previously passed over, regarded as semi-desert, was rapidly settled with long-term benefits to the country. Tory cries about the profits realized sounded hollow when it was shown that such eminent Conservatives as E.B. Osler and G.E. Foster were themselves making a tidy profit in land speculation and were perhaps more dubious in some of their methods. The Saskatchewan Valley Land Company was a striking success both as a business and as an immigration venture. Although controversial, it seemed to justify Sifton's flexible administration of lands policy.[80]

By no means, however, was Sifton prepared to support non-productive land companies. In 1901 he announced that individuals and companies holding land that was not settled would be notified that under the Dominion Lands Act they were required to place settlers on each homestead within two years of receiving patent for the land. The law, long ignored, was now to be enforced.If necessary, they would have to sell their land to any bona fide settler at cost or else forfeit it altogether.[81] Stringent enforcement of the law was probably the only way to stir the nearly moribund land companies into active encouragement of settlement.

There was one area of public lands administration, however, in which Sifton proved indecisive and the results of his policy—or lack of policy—were much less satisfactory. The ranching community of the southwestern plains had for many years been a bastion of Conservatism, well placed to solicit and receive favours from Tory officials. But even the Tories had concluded that the closed grazing lease policy favoured by the older and larger ranchers needed to be reviewed, and in 1892 the government announced that such leases would be terminated in four years, at which point the Liberals came to power with no new policy having been established. For a decade prior to the Liberal ascendancy, the ranchers had been under growing attack from smaller operators and would-be dryland homesteaders in the district and their political sympathizers who tended to be Liberals. Leading the assault was none other than Frank Oliver. The ranchers claimed—correctly, as events would prove—that much of the region was too arid for raising crops, at least without irrigation. But the homesteaders would hear none of it; the ranchers, they claimed, merely sought to secure their old and illegitimate privileges against the forces of progress and democracy.[82]

Sifton was caught in the crossfire.He neither liked nor trusted Frank Oliver, but there was no political advantage in supporting the ranchers. Oliver demanded the removal of William Pearce, who was believed to be the official who had engineered the pro-rancher policy of the department prior to 1896. After listening to Pearce's arguments, however, Sifton chose to leave him in office, seeming to understand that the grasslands were more economically productive when used for grazing cattle. Yet in the ensuing years, although the department did not encourage settlement in the region, thousands of drylanders drifted in, many from the United States. Nor for political reasons could the department discourage the movement. As was the case in the United States, writes David Breen, Canada was attached "to the myth that the nation's progress could be measured by the expansion of ploughed acres and the number of homesteads taken each year, with little or no thought to climate or soil type."[83] Furthermore, in the absence of regulations or any lease policy, the ranchers overgrazed several districts, rendering them nearly useless. As the situation became critical, and after several of Sifton's close political allies, such as A.E. Philp, J.D. McGregor, and J.H. Ross, entered ranching, the minister of the interior belatedly moved to reinstate a closed grazing lease system. A few ranchers were helped, but the tide of immigrants would not long be denied, particularly when it was announced in 1905 that Frank Oliver would succeed Sifton.

Then the prevailing uncertainty of the Sifton years would turn to gloom and despair for the ranching community.

Despite this blemish on his record, it is fair to say that Sifton continued and extended a Canadian approach of flexibility in land use in the West. "The system in Canada," writes J. B. Hedges, "was adapted and altered to fit particular situations in a way which was quite unheard of south of the border." The Canadians "were much more willing to experiment, and to adjust their policy to the special conditions prevailing in different areas."[84] Sifton's consistent objective was to get western land settled and productive. In part he did this by securing to himself and his deputies a vast amount of discretionary power. It enabled him to be flexible with respect to land suited to different purposes—homesteading, irrigation, or ranching. It permitted development of integrated policies to facilitate large projects, such as irrigation in southern Alberta. Moreover, while he believed that the government must take the initiative in promoting immigration and settlement, he was willing to recognize a role for private enterprise.

"The whole immigration work has...been placed upon a business basis and organized into systematic effectiveness, and is carried on with unremitting energy, altogether and wholly on business lines with results for the sole aim and object." So declared the *Manitoba Free Press* as Sifton renewed his labours in 1901.[85] The phrasing was infelicitous, but it drove to the heart of the philosophy of the minister of the interior. There appeared to be no gainsaying his success: the flow of immigrants which had more than trebled between 1896 and 1901, when 55,747 arrived, nearly trebled again by 1905, when 141,465 entered Canada. The 8,167 homestead entries of 1901 became an average of nearly 30,000 a year between 1903 and 1905.[86] Good times, energetic advertising and promotion, and the booming reputation of western Canada brought in the settlers. Efficient and thorough organization permitted them to arrive, locate land, and establish themselves with astonishingly few difficulties. Sifton's abilities to attract immigrants were now scarcely questioned. Yet the political debate over "quality" persisted as the numbers of immigrants swelled, and he was regularly compelled to defend his policies in face of nativist opposition.

Controversy was bound to arise, given the distribution of the immigrants. The government focused its attention on attracting intending farmers for the prairie West, yet the majority of immigrants reaching Canada's seaports had no intention of seeking a homestead. Of 102,723 arrivals at the ports in the year ending 30 June 1905, for example, only 37,672 gave Manitoba or the North-West Territories as their ultimate destination; almost 35,000 were going to Ontario, and more than 23,000 to Quebec. The totals were swelled by 43,000 Americans, most of whom sought to settle in the West.[87] Nevertheless, whether they came of their own free will or were encouraged by potential employers in search of skilled labour, or were sent across by the numerous charitable organizations that sought to locate the distressed and disadvantaged of British society overseas, it was clear that Canada had become attractive to immigrants for reasons other than the appeal of prairie farming. From the point of view of many westerners, it was distressingly apparent that Britishers were less inclined than most groups to settle in the West. On average, perhaps one-third of all immigrants in these years were of British origin, yet they filed only about one-sixth of the homestead applications. Fortunately, from the perspective of the dominant society, Canadian and American applications together constituted about half the total in each year, but the rapid growth in the West of ethnic groups from continental Europe continued to be a subject of great popular concern.[88]

Deputy Minister James A. Smart, whom Lord Minto accurately termed Sifton's "alter ego," continued to maintain a general supervision of immigration policy.[89] It was the most visible, and vulnerable, aspect of Sifton's administrative responsibilities, and Smart found it desirable to undertake a close personal examination of the organization in Britain, Europe, and the United States. The removal of Frank Pedley to Indian affairs resulted in the appointment as superintendent of immigration of W.D. Scott, formerly an immigration agent for the Manitoba government. W.F. McCreary, who had been very successful as immigration commissioner in Winnipeg, was elected to the House of Commons in 1900. He was succeeded by the former Liberal organizer in Manitoba, J. Obed Smith. Sifton did not alter the basic structure of his organization, though some changes were necessary here and there. For example, in 1903 it was discovered that "a large number" of sub-agents in the United States "were simply using their position as Government Agents in order to transact real estate deals." They did little actually to promote immigration, simply issuing certificates to intending immigrants to collect the commission—and there was evidently considerable falsification and abuse of the system. The sub-agents were normally working at best only part-time in promoting immigration and were much less effective than the permanent agents. As a result, more than 280 sub-agencies were closed out, and only the few who had proven to be effective were reappointed to the service.[90]

The work in the United States was, nevertheless, one of the department's greatest success stories. From an average of little over 10,000 immigrants a year between 1897 and 1900, the flow increased to 45,000 between 1903 and 1905. Moreover, the Americans generally were very welcome in the West. One observer commented in 1902 that "they are by general consent the best & most enterprising people coming in." Sifton shared these opinions. A small proportion of them were former Canadians, he admitted. However, "I am disposed to think that the greater proportion of them are American farmers whose ancestors have within the last two generations come from Northern Europe, mostly of Scandinavian origin. There are a few of what might be called Simon Pure Americans, but not very many. They are a strong vigorous people, capable, very alert, and progressive in their ideas."[91]

By contrast, there were many more difficulties associated with the work in Europe and Great Britain. The North Atlantic Trading Company, for example, constantly roused the suspicions of the opposition because of the secrecy surrounding its operations. The very nature of its activities in Europe was necessarily clandestine, and Sifton and his civil servants resisted repeated pressure to reveal the names of the companies involved and the details of the arrangements.[92] The minister of the interior remained very happy with the arrangement, because the company acted as a kind of initial screening agency with regard to the quality of immigrants. The company knew that they would not be paid for non-agriculturalists or paupers, to say nothing of diseased or otherwise unacceptable immigrants. "There has never been anything as effective as the old system under the North Atlantic Trading Company," Sifton recalled years later, "who selected the immigrants and gave us the pick of all those who were booking from continental ports, letting the riff-raff go to the United States and to South America."[93]

There were some changes in the contract after 1900 which should be noted. By 1902 France, Belgium, northern Italy, and Roumania had been dropped as sources of agricultural immigrants upon whom a bonus would be paid. Substituted were the Scandinavian countries, Luxembourg, and the term "Germans from Switzerland." Holland, Russia, and Austria-Hungary remained. However, a limitation was imposed on certain groups, in response to public opinion: "It is agreed in respect to settlers from Galicia, Buskowinia [sic], and Poland, excepting Germans, that the bonus allowed under this arrangement be paid on a total number not to exceed a combined number of 5,000 immigrants annually coming from these countries."[94] Such was the uneasy compromise between Sifton, who wished to encourage what he viewed as desirable "peasant races" who would make marginal farmland productive, and those who wanted a ban on all immigration from east central Europe.

A more delicate problem concerned the relationship of the immigration agents in Great Britain to the office of the high commissioner. Lord Strathcona believed that all Canadian agencies in Britain should naturally fall under his jurisdiction—a view common to high commissioners both before and after him. But Strathcona was elderly, having celebrated his eightieth birthday in 1900, his energy was failing, and promotion of immigration was not as high on his list of priorities as it naturally was on that of Sifton. The difficulty was compounded by the fact that the irascible and partisan Liberal inspector of agencies, W.T.R. Preston, could not tolerate Strathcona nor endure being his subordinate. In addition, Preston's relations with J.G. Colmer, an unrepentant Conservative who ran the high commissioner's office, were quite impossible.[95] An arrangement to give Preston full control of immigration concerns within the high commissioner's office failed because Colmer insisted on running everything. Sifton objected to Strathcona about "Mr. Colmer's evident determination to prevent the Department from controlling its own work." The high commissioner claimed that he was willing to allow Preston considerable administrative freedom, but strongly opposed payment of immigration officials through the inspector of agencies rather than Colmer. All such money, he claimed, should be paid out of one central bank account in London.[96] The interminable wrangling finally decided Sifton to make a clean break. The immigration offices were moved to new quarters in Charing Cross in 1903. He did ask Preston to continue to make a weekly report to the high commissioner, but even this attempt at smoothing relations between the two men failed.[97]

With the turn of the century the political controversy over numbers and quality of immigrants intensified. Labour unions incessantly clamoured for a halt to the encouragement of immigration or, failing that, the institution of a much more rigorously selective system to ensure that only actual farmers reached Canada. All who were headed directly or potentially for the urban labour market should, insisted the unions, be excluded. Fear of competition from "foreigners" preoccupied labour organizations, which also demanded that the Alien Labour Act must be strictly enforced. By the turn of the century the government had simply decided to look the other way while extensive systems were established to import migrant workers, as much to undermine unions and wage structures as to meet any shortage of labour. When the CPR imported Italian scab labour from the United States during a trackmen's strike in British Columbia in 1901, an angry correspondent told Sifton, "It is simply monstrous that this corporation should be permitted to set at defiance" the Alien Labour Act. The government's response was unsympathetic. In the spring of 1901 it had amended the act so that the aggrieved parties rather than the government would have to initiate court action, knowing full well that rarely could individuals or even unions afford such action.[98] It also transferred administration of the act from the Department of Justice to the newly created Department of Labour. But since enforcement of the act had generally been associated with immigration officials empowered from time to time to do so, it was not unnatural that many appeals concerning enforcement should be directed at Sifton. Deputy Minister Smart summarized the government's point of view well in a memorandum drawn up for Sifton to use in reply to a labour petition. He disagreed that "the result of bringing in farmers to settle on the lands in Manitoba and the North West Territories" was to intensify the competition for labour. Indeed, he pointed out, there had not been for some years sufficient labour for harvesting the huge western crops:

> It may be added that no assistance is given to any persons, labourers or otherwise, to move to Canada. The assistance that is granted out of the Immigration Vote is simply to the Agents who properly represent Canada to intending emigrants and present its claims. The suggestion that the Government does not control the ultimate destination of settlers is quite true, but the experience of the Department and the results which are shown by the Government records with respect to the grants of land prove pretty conclusively that the efforts of the Department to induce *only* agriculturalists to come to Canada have been successful. The movement of population, of course, from country to towns is one that no Government nor any set of men can prevent, and it is presumably the tendency of the age not only in Canada but in every country in the world. That is, however, no reason why the Government should not undertake to expend money in the development of its western lands by locating actual settlers who will be not only taxpayers but who will afford home markets for products which they can exchange for those which they may produce themselves, the result naturally being of most direct benefit to the manufacturers, merchants (& particularly laborers) and consequently all those engaged in trades and labour throughout the country. [99]

Smart and Sifton, of course, were simply wilfully ignoring the heart of labour's case and distorting the obvious evidence of their own statistics. Enforcement of the Alien Labour Act was not Sifton's responsibility, and he seemed to believe that because he was not directly promoting the migration of industrial workers, he could be absolved of blame for what was occurring. It is true that the Department of the Interior concentrated on procuring agricultural settlers and that it could not control where such people went after settling in Canada. Still it must be admitted that, as will be seen, sometimes officials disobeyed direct orders and encouraged non-agricultural emigration from Europe. It is also true that the government occasionally diverted poor settlers who wanted but could not afford western farms into Ontario where there was a shortage of agricultural labour; probably many of these people drifted eventually into the urban labour market rather than to western Canada. [100]

On balance, however, it is fair to say that the thrust of Sifton's immigration policy was to seek farmers for the West, a policy for which he made no apology. He openly admitted that his was a selective approach. He rejected the fears of the nativist in his cool, businesslike assessment of which races seemed most suited to Canada's requirements. Orientals, Blacks, Jews, southern Europeans, even the English city-dwellers would, in his judgment, create more problems than they would solve because they seemed unlikely to be successful prairie farmers. Typical of his attitude was his discouragement of a proposal in 1901 to settle some Roumanian Jewish farmers in the West: "Our desire is to promote the immigration of farmers and farm labourers. We have not been disposed to exclude foreigners of any nationality who seemed likely to become successful agriculturists.... Experience shows that the Jewish people do not become agriculturists. However strong the attempts that are made to induce them to remain upon the land and become cultivators of the soil, such efforts have, so far as Canada is concerned, proved an undoubted failure. The Jewish population of Canada today, like that of the United States, is to be found entirely in the cities and towns." The government was not concerned with increasing the size of urban centres, but rather with "the development of natural resources and the increase in production from these resources."[101] Similarly with respect to Italians, Sifton irritably told Smart in 1901, "I have explained at least a dozen times that I don't want anything done to facilitate Italian immigration....It seems to be difficult to get it through the heads of our officers." Elaborating on these instructions, Smart noted that while no offence should be given the Italians and no prohibition would be enacted against those who came to Canada on their own, "the Minister is of the opinion that it is not desirable to encourage any class of this nationality for the reason that it may have the effect of bringing out undesirable persons from Italy."[102]

In 1903 and 1904 the relationship between Sifton and organized labour threatened to become more strained. With a federal general election pending, both he and the government were anxious not to offend labour unduly. An unofficial Canadian Labour Bureau took offices in 1903 in the same building in Charing Cross in which the immigration offices were housed. Engaged in promoting the emigration of skilled and unskilled industrial workers, the bureau was happy to benefit by the implied association with the official government immigration services. The government was acutely embarrassed because the apparent connection between the two offices gave both Canadian labour leaders and the political opposition an opportunity to attack it for promoting the immigration of mechanics and labourers. Smart was sent to London early in 1904 under specific instructions to see that the bureau was removed from the building. Yet the operation must be done diplomatically, Sifton cautioned, to avoid any open quarrel with labour people.[103] The separation of the offices was doubly important, for Sifton believed that his officers, including Preston and possibly even Smart, "in the fulness of zeal for the work," were "inclined to take too favorable a view of the class of people who are sent out by societies and charitable institutions of one kind and another." Officials anxious to swell the total flow of immigrants were apt not to discourage non-agricultural emigration, and of course those sent by the Labour Bureau all helped. Nevertheless, Sifton indignantly declared, numerous people were arriving in Canada who were "perfectly helpless, that is to say, people who neither know how to take care of themselves nor want to do it." If there was the slightest doubt about the suitability of any class, "shut them off summarily. Shut off also all possibility of any connection between the immigration of mechanics being connected with our office." At all costs Sifton wanted to avoid being "drawn into a movement which will result in a lot of helpless people being lodged in the cities and towns."[104]

A case in point was a society which brought over twenty tailoresses from England. "These people are simply displacing Canadian girls who are working for their living," he wrote, "and they do not fill any requirements in this country." Could the societies not be persuaded to do something useful, such as "bringing out a good class of domestic servants"? In fact, the perpetual shortage of domestics in Canada made that class one of the few exceptions to Sifton's concentration on agricultural immigrants. Whatever happened, he directed, there was to be no assistance, direct or indirect, to anyone bringing over "men or women to displace industrial workers." "We are in a position now to take our choice," he added, "and we do not want anything but agricultural laborers and farmers or people who are coming for the purpose of engaging in agriculture, either as farmers or laborers."[105]

During Sifton's entire period in office this was practically the sole endeavour of the Immigration Branch, to ensure that within the stream of inmigrants who would come to Canada regardless of government policies there would be a steadily growing flow of intending farmers for the prairies. The most desirable, in his view, were those with sufficient capital and initiative to reach Canada on their own and with minimal assistance make a success of farming in the West. His efforts naturally focused on the states of the American Great Plains, on northern England and Scotland, and— through the North Atlantic Trading Company—on Scandinavia and central Europe.

Two major difficulties with immigrant groups confronted the Department of the Interior in these years. One was the ongoing controversy over the Doukhobors; the second concerned the difficult group of English settlers known as the Barr or Britannia colony. A persistent debate raged over the Doukhobors both in the public press and in Parliament. No group seemed so to symbolize the evils of Sifton's policies, in the eyes of his critics. The Doukhobors were allegedly unassimilable, unappreciative of Canadian law and liberty, poverty-stricken, government-supported, and they had been brought over at great cost to the taxpayer. And all for what? A people that refused to take up arms in defence of Canada; that demanded concessions in law to allow them to occupy the land in the way they chose, rather than in accordance with a system good enough for everyone else; a group which seemed obstinately and ostentatiously unco-operative, determined to resist the institutions and values of the dominant culture. What could they possibly contribute to the Canadian society or economy?[106]

Repeatedly Sifton explained that not only had they turned out to be excellent farmers but also that the cost to the taxpayer of bringing over the Doukhobors had been $7.47 per head, much less than expenditure for British immigrants. "These are the cheapest immigrants that ever came to Canada," he assured J.W. Dafoe, with a touch of exaggeration:

> As to special privileges; the feed, grain, stock and agricultural implements that were furnished were furnished by their friends and not by the Government, except in some trifling cases, and whatever has been advanced has been paid back. A reserve was made and a certain time allowed for the performance of homestead duties & payt of fees on condition of the people taking up their residence there and doing substantial improvements. There is not one of these inducements that would not be given in the case of any large body of desirable settlers from any other part of the world. The cry against the Doukhobors and Galicians is the most absolutely ignorant and absurd thing that I have ever known in political life. There is simply no question in regard to the advantage of these people, and I do not think there is anyone in the North West who is so stupid as not to know it—even the editor of the [Winnipeg] Telegram.
>
> The policy adopted of exciting racial prejudice is the most contemptible possible policy because it is one that does not depend upon reason. As you know you can excite the prejudice of one nationality against another by simply keeping up an agitation. You can excite the French against the English or the English against the French or the Germans against the English or vice versa. All you have to do is keep hammering away and appealing to their prejudices, and in the course of time you will work up an excitement, but a more ignorant and unpatriotic policy could not be imagined.[107]

"Cheap" the Doukhobors might have been, and excellent farmers they may have proved. Yet their religious fanaticism caused many problems even for a sympathetic government. Believing in a communal existence, they decided and held all things in common. For many months they refused to enter individually for homesteads because such an action was held to go against their beliefs. Patiently the department tried to explain that they could assign their homesteads to whomever they wanted after filing individually; improvements would be assessed proportionately for all Doukhobor holdings in a district, rather than individually; the entry fee was postponed; and they were allowed to dwell in villages rather than on their individual homesteads, and still meet the residence requirement. Finally in 1902 most of them filed their application, but some fanatical holdouts refused to comply, even after the arrival from Russia of spiritual leader Peter Verigin at the end of 1902.[108]

Public opinion was further roused in October and November of that year when a number of the more extremist Doukhobors embarked on a kind of religious protest march from the colony near Yorkton toward Winnipeg. It took place under bitterly cold conditions, the pilgrims living on handouts and charity as they went. Short of using force, the department officials had done everything possible to discourage the march, the object of which was obscure. According to one account, they hoped to "find the promised land where, under the beneficent sun, they would live upon fruit and meet their Messiah."[109] In any event, the demonstration was supervised by officials of the Interior Department, while officers of the NWMP observed at a distance to prevent violence or injury. "Our hope is that the electric current will expire and that after a little while the men will return to their villages," wrote Sifton. "I perfectly realize that any attempt to oppose them or exercise force would be extremely foolish. They are actually feeling neglected because no one is persecuting them, and the least attempt to interfere with them by force would be welcomed as an opportunity to die for their faith." The march petered out inside Manitoba, as Sifton anticipated. Then the Police and immigration officials under Frank Pedley loaded the marchers, despite some passive resistance, on a train and returned them to Yorkton. This was but the beginning of the difficulty, however, and even the arrival of Verigin did not end it. The radicals, who developed into the Sons of Freedom sect, steadfastly refused to file for their lands. Being vegetarians, they had given away or "liberated" their animals; and they believed that physical work was sinful. A nude march by some of them in 1903 simply confounded many Canadian observers, for many of whom these events were proof positive of Sifton's monstrous error in accepting these people.[110]

Despite the bad publicity, the department's handling of the outbreaks was exemplary. There was no violence; the marches were carefully supervised and fully reported. Both Sifton and Smart recognized that it was a mistake to identify the entire productive and successful Doukhobor population with the extreme tactics of a small minority. It is clear, too, that Sifton had a long-term goal in mind as he sought through Verigin to naturalize many of them and persuade them to vote Liberal at the next general election.[111] Whatever the reasons, what might have been a serious crisis and embarrassment to the government was skilfully defused.

By mid-1903 the Doukhobor question was paling in comparison with a new crisis over the controversial Barr colony. Many schemes for the establishment of block settlements for English settlers had been mooted over the years; few had seemed likely to succeed. The plan that the charismatic Reverend Isaac Barr proposed in 1902 promised to be an exception to the rule.[112] He had emerged as a focus for hundreds of Englishmen who had been considering a move to the Canadian prairies. The proposal entailed a wholly English colony, surrounded by Canadian and American farmers, immensely appealing to Englishmen troubled by rumours about the hordes of Europeans and other "foreigners" allegedly flooding the prairies. "People here," Smart told Sifton from London, "seem to have a great antipathy to mixing up with foreigners....You will notice that the English are just the same as any foreign element so far as wanting to get together."[113] Moving hundreds of people in one large party was a risky business at the best of times and with the most careful management. W.L. Griffith, Canadian emigration agent in Wales, warned that "there is an inevitable percentage of those who will be failures in all emigration movements, and the disadvantage of large parties lies in the fact that this element becomes formidable, whereas in the ordinary way their dispersal all over the country prevents this."[114] Not only was the concentration of potential failures "formidable," but they were English, which made their failure politically more dangerous.

Nevertheless, after some hesitation, Sifton accepted the enthusiastic recommendations of Smart and granted a suitable reservation of land near present-day Lloydminster. In principle both he and Smart wanted to treat the Barr colonists like any other immigrants, on an individual basis and with little or no government assistance. In fact, Sifton recognized that some concessions would have to be made, because "in as much as the people themselves organized it and took it up in consequence of our immigration propaganda we...could not refuse to give them reasonable facilities. I am doing everything that it is possible to do to give them a fair start, and have...authorized the employment of two farm instructors who will stay with them the whole summer and make themselves generally useful. We will do everything that the Government can do, but we cannot hold the plow for a settler, and that is, I am afraid, where some of the colonists will fail."[115]

Officially the government had committed itself to do nothing but reserve the land, leaving the rest to Barr. That was a serious error, for Barr, a well-intentioned visionary enamoured of grandiose schemes, was hopelessly out of his depth when it came to the logistics of moving and supplying hundreds of settlers. Unfortunately, Sifton was in England when the colonists reached Canada, and his officials realized too late the degree of Barr's ineptitude. In the long run the colony would work out very well, but in the short run the scrambling and apparent confusion of immigration officials and a flood of complaints from the settlers fed directly to an eager corps of newspaper reporters gave the Opposition a rare opportunity to attack the efficiency of Sifton's department. Yet the fact remained, as Sifton pointed out during a parliamentary debate in the summer, that the government had made much more extensive preparations for the movement than for any comparable group of settlers.[116] The rule of not assisting settlers had been bent a good deal more than usual, though rather hastily. The troubles of the colony, which the Opposition exaggerated, arose largely from Barr's mismanagement and from his incautious statements about the glorious prospects in Canada. In turn, this led to unrealistically high expectations on the part of many settlers, resulting in great discontent when they actually encountered the treeless plains. Undoubtedly the argument is strong that the government should have taken charge and supervised Barr's arrangements,[117] but it ought to be remembered that numerous groups of other nationalities, including the Doukhobors, had been settled with much less trouble. The experience could only serve to confirm Sifton's belief that the average Englishman was not cut out to be a successful settler in the Canadian West—and when he did succeed, the cost, time and trouble of enabling him to do so far exceeded that for other groups.

The experience also caused Sifton to terminate the policy of making reservations for block settlements. The policy had originated, he told one correspondent, "in the early days of the immigration movement when we were forced to do anything and everything to get people. What we were compelled to do in those days is no indication at all of what we ought to do now." On balance, such schemes would no longer add significantly to the flow of immigration to the West. The department had gone to a great deal of trouble and expense to advertise Canada and was now barely able to cope with the existing flow of settlers. The additional work and expense of reservations were not necessary. "It leads to a great deal of trouble and dissatisfaction," wrote Land Commissioner J.G. Turriff, "and proves conclusively that none of them can place settlers on the lands in as satisfactory a manner as the Agents of the Department."[118]

On the political front, Sifton had to be ever vigilant to defend his policies in face of constant attack. Typical, perhaps, was the demand of the Calgary Board of Trade that "measures be adopted to exclude the ignorant, improvident and vicious element of foreign populations." "The colonization of large numbers of unenlightened Europeans," the memorial went on, "whose customs, habits of thought and traditions are not compatible with our institutions, seriously threatens to degrade our social and political life and to introduce amongst us problems whose solution may be extremely difficult.''[119] Responses to such statements had to be undertaken immediately and regularly, a burden normally assumed by J.W. Dafoe and the *Free Press*. From them the Liberal press of the West would normally take its cue. Regular articles appeared describing all aspects of the immigration work: the numbers and types of settlers arriving on the trains, the work of placing them on the land, the progress of each settlement, the work of land offices, and so forth.

Early in his tenure as editor Dafoe set down the principle "that that immigration is desirable which can be assimilated."[120] Thus there was no disagreement with Sifton's critics as to the ultimately desirable end; no one seemed to support the virtues of ethnic diversity. The disagreement was over whether the various immigrant groups could be assimilated or at least whether it could be done without "degrading" Canada's social and political life. The *Free Press* set out to prove that there was no basis for these fears. Group settlement was said to be justified because it had attracted settlers who otherwise would not have come to build up the country, including many Britishers. Nevertheless, all would be assimilated eventually. Various articles on the Doukhobors, for example, claimed that they were progressive, anxious to learn English, and would be quickly assimilated. Similarly the *Free Press* defended the Galician colonies, particularly after a delegation demanded of the Roblin government a policy of unilingual English education aimed specifically at the Galicians. The newspaper also contended that fear of "foreigners" expressed by American nativists arose from concerns in American cities. Such fears were supposedly groundless in Canada, which was said to be securing only agriculturalists.[121]

An editorial even appeared in praise of the British race,[122] and British institutions were constantly referred to with glowing warmth. These institutions had wonderful absorptive powers. Did some fear the great influx of Americans into the prairies as likely to undermine British values and Canadian independence? There was nothing to worry about, counselled the *Free Press*:

> [They] are coming into a country where they will very soon realize that the will of the people rules. There is a greater freedom, a better administration of justice and greater respect for the law, guaranteeing the equal rights of all, in Canada than there is in the United States. The security of life and property is greater. The accessions to our population which we are now receiving from the United States are very largely of British origin. They are of our own stock. Their interests, once they make their homes on Canadian soil, become Canadian. So it

has always been; and that it will continue so is not to be doubted.[123]

Not infrequently the *Free Press*, as did Sifton himself, found it necessary to explain that no one received direct aid to migrate to Canada. A commission fee of $5 per adult was paid to immigration agents and shipping companies; occasionally when an organization sent over settlers, it was paid the same bonus. The paper denied, for example, that the government had paid any direct aid to the Welsh (Llewellyn) colony near Saltcoats. Only the usual $5 per head had gone to the committee arranging to bring in the settlers—a bonus which helped to defray but by no means covered expenses.

> The Government of Canada has never, since Canada was a Dominion, given any settlers or body of settlers a bonus to induce him or it to locate in Canada. The offer of free land, the protection of liberal laws, freedom from oppression and disability, and the prospects of a competence acquired through industry—these are among the inducements Canada offers to the individual settler. But for those who will send settlers to the Dominion—to steamship and immigration agents in other countries—Canada has for years established a system of bonuses.[124]

Occasionally aid in the form of repayable loans was made for settlers once they arrived. But Sifton remained distinctly opposed to outright financial aid or grants, "I have never known anybody that was materially assisted by the Government to amount to anything," he declared bluntly some years later. This was precisely the logic of James Smart when he recommended refraining from assisting the Barr colonists, lest they come "to expect a great deal from the Government."[125] Not only was direct assistance an undesirable extension of the powers of government, it was morally reprehensible because it would tend to weaken the virtuous character and self-reliance developed solely in the struggle to survive on the land.

It ought to be emphasized that the message of Sifton and of the *Free Press* was not defensive in character. Immigration was portrayed as a positive achievement. Canada's supervised selective policy was considered decidedly superior to that of the United States. They attempted to market the myth that only a high quality of agricultural immigrant was coming in, while the Republic was absorbing thousands of southern Europeans and "riff-raff" who merely contributed to urban congestion and social problems. The immigration into Canada, Sifton proudly told Robert Jaffray of Toronto, "is the one work which is propelling Canada forward and laying the foundation for future prosperity."[126]

Clifford Sifton was justifiably satisfied with what he had achieved. His characteristic caution was on occasion even discarded in favour of a spirit of boosterism. In Boston in 1902, for example, he optimistically predicted that Manitoba alone would have a population of two million within a few years. [127] Nevertheless, by that time Sifton had come to regard immigration and settlement no longer as a challenge, but as an achievement. The major obstacles had been overcome. Little land remained encumbered by red tape, and most was available for settlement. Confidence in Canada and the West had been restored. Immigrants were flooding in, attracted and placed on the land by an efficient, businesslike machinery. Sifton was not interested in merely running an efficient organization. He thrived on challenge. By 1902 or 1903 he exhibited perceptible slackening of energy and interest in departmental detail; his concerns spread to other wider problems of Canadian development: mineral and forest exploitation and, above all, the Canadian transportation problem. By 1904 he was concerning himself very little with plans for the future of his department, compared to previous years. Apart from all other circumstances, one might have guessed simply from changes in attitude to administration that Sifton had little desire to continue much longer in the position he occupied.

4

The Politics of Progress
(1901-1904)

The god of the young twentieth century was Progress, and his prophet was Laurier. "The twentieth century shall be the century of Canada," predicted the prime minister to a cheering crowd at Massey Hall in 1904. The gods indeed smiled warmly upon the Dominion in those years, and the Priestly Order of Material Growth and Prosperity—Laurier's cabinet— took full credit for the heavenly beneficence. Never since Confederation had optimism and confidence taken such hold. These sentiments had grown slowly since 1896, being cautiously nurtured and then exuberantly propagated by the government. Prosperity and development were evident on every hand. Cities were swelling with new industries, mineral and timber resources were being exploited, record wheat crops were straining transportation facilities to their limit, immigrants were streaming in to multiply the rate of growth, and the dominion government was happily reaping surpluses almost one-third as large as the annual budget.

Such growth needed to be harnessed and organized. Policies of development needed to be devised, a process which produced severe strains upon the cabinet. Deep cleavages resulted from disagreements over tariff and transportation policies in particular. Though they were not immediately fatal to the ministry, its internal strength was weakened. Haste and excessive optimism produced decisions dubious in their long-term effects upon the country. But Laurier and his cohorts captured the mood, hearts, and votes of the country, while the Opposition languished, colourless and divided.

Clifford Sifton was one of the principal disciples of Progress in Canada. Buoyed by rapid material development, he cast aside his former caution and projected a hard-nosed optimism. His prophecies of continuing prosperity never appeared rashly emotional; rather, he always gave the image of one who based his predictions on a sober calculation of realities. He understood that public opinion must be carefully cultivated if it was to identify Liberalism with the good times. Withal, he was restless and discontented. Within the cabinet there was constant friction, and even Laurier's leadership seemed at times unsteady. Western representation in the government was inadequate, given the expanding strength of the region. Differences on tariff policy resulted in a public dispute. Even more divisive was the problem of transportation policy, in which Sifton clearly wished to have an influential, if not decisive voice. Above all, the government, in his opinion, must both generate and shape national development policies. It must be a dynamic leader, creating both a favourable investment climate and a framework to ensure that private enterprise also would operate in the public interest. The philosophic gulf between Sifton and Laurier became steadily more obvious. The prime minister's principles, though flexible and governed by expediency, were firmly rooted in the laissez-faire liberalism of the mid-nineteenth century. Sifton, by contrast, was one of those Liberals who "saw no contradiction in defending the authority of the state in the collective interest."[1]

Beginning late in 1902, Sifton elected to take his case to the public. Possibly he wished to give the impression that the government had given comprehensive consideration to the kind of Canada that it wanted to develop, that it knew precisely where it was going. Possibly he was seeking a constituency of support for his own ambitions. At the very least he was trying to influence the railway policies then being considered. Whatever the case, he commenced a series of pronouncements setting out his matured views on the problems facing Canada, and their best solution. For the moment the political battles seemed almost subordinated as he ruminated in an unusually philosophical, non-partisan vein.

What might be taken as his keynote address was delivered on 17 November 1902 to the General Assembly of the Methodist Church in Toronto. The Methodists, and indeed most Canadians, needed to acquire a new vision of the West and what it meant to the Dominion, he asserted.

> Doubtless you have for a good many years looked upon it as a land of large promise but somewhat slow and poor performance, as a land of

illimitable possibility but limited realities, a land generally described, indeed, with a fine flow of rhetoric, but which had so far failed to realize the hopes which had been entertained of it. But a change has come, and all in a very short time. Stagnation has given way to abounding activity, production is now reckoned by tens of millions instead of by hundreds of thousands. Where we counted our incoming settlers by hundreds we now count them by thousands, and the whole situation has undergone an alteration that is little short of phenomenal.

Waxing eloquent, he continued, "But the tide of population is only beginning to rise. We see only what the American poet so well described in speaking of his own country, as 'the first low wash of waves where soon shall roll a human sea'." Within less than three years, predicted Sifton, the population of Manitoba and the Territories would triple, to 750,000. Very quickly the production of the western farmers would make them "one of the richest and most independent agricultural communities in the world." These people would "in a short time...constitute a most potent factor in the national life of Canada."

This would affect and benefit the entire country. What required to be done to facilitate and sustain this growth? "First there is the material side of the question; the necessary machinery of progress must be furnished. It will not do to attempt to follow the example of the slow growth of the older Provinces. Nowadays new districts must move rapidly or they do not move at all. Therefore railways must be constructed, roads and bridges built, public buildings and institutions provided, and these must be done in time to prevent the new population becoming discouraged and losing heart." The second requirement was education, so that "we shall be certain of a new generation which will furnish intelligent and progressive citizens." A third requirement, he told the Methodists, was religious work—the home missions in the West. These were essential "if in the new Canada we are to have a population animated by the same motives, actuated by the same ideas and governed by the same principles as obtain among the rest of our people." This process was not a proper function for government. Rather, it was "a fundamental principle of our public policy that while material and educational progress is to be fostered by the care and subsidized by the funds of the Government, the full enjoyment of freedom, toleration and complete religious liberty and equality can best be maintained by the absolute non-intervention of the State in the propagation of religious tenets." The church should look to the example of the state, where cash expended had resulted in "rapid development and progress," and "instead of a great lone land we...have a land teeming with a production which far outstrips the capacity of transportation agencies and commercial facilities." Money expended was an investment that would be handsomely returned both in religious and in national growth.[2]

Naturally it was material growth that most concerned Sifton. Speaking to the Boston Canadian Club on 21 November, he surveyed Canadian material progress.[3] The great requirement and the great achievement of Confederation, he argued, had been in the field of transportation, linking the country together and opening up its resources. "No known country of similar population has presented such tremendous difficulties of distance and material obstacles, but the triumph of human energy over nature has been complete."[4] Canada had more railway mileage per person than either the United States or Australia, and "easily the finest system of inland water transportation in the world." Shortly, he predicted, there would be at least two or three transcontinental lines, "not destroying each other, but each laboring with difficulty, as the Canadian Pacific is now laboring, to handle the increasing volume of business which is forced upon it."

The strain on transportation facilities, he informed his American audience, arose from the rapid exploitation of Canada's natural wealth and the growth in population. The dominion had scarcely begun to tap her hydroelectric potential; she had "inexhaustible" spruce resources for pulp and paper; and she benefitted from growing iron and steel industries and mineral development in British Columbia, as well as the great agricultural progress on the prairies. Now Canada was turning to "practical and technical education," preparing a new generation who would be even more adept at exploiting and developing Canadian resources.

Sifton carried this message, with appropriate variations, to St. Paul, Winnipeg, Brandon, and Regina early in 1903 and also published a version of his views in the *Canadian Magazine*.[5] While they touched on many topics, the one central, reiterated theme was the need for a comprehensive transportation policy: expansion of existing railways, control of freight rates, improvement of the waterway system, and Canadian-controlled internal and external shipping lines. Privately he was very unhappy with the inactivity of the cabinet on this subject, and he was eager to rouse public interest and support for a government initiative. When Charles Fitzpatrick told him that he had raised the subject with the prime minister, it occasioned a quick, impassioned response from the minister of the interior:[6]

> I have perhaps given more thought to this subject [transportation] than any other not directly connected with my own Department, and notwithstanding the fact that for six years we have been in power and spending a great deal of money I deplore the fact that the Government is yet without any expert professional advice of such a character as to enable any of its members to form an intelligent opinion upon this

subject. Nearly six years ago I expressed the opinion to Sir Wilfrid that almost the only two problems of government which we had to deal with of a serious character after the revision of the tariff was [*sic*] the immigration question, the question of securing a large addition to the agricultural population of the West, and the transportation question, the question of getting their products to market. I said then and I have not since altered my opinion, that to place a large producing population upon the Western prairies and to inaugurate a system whereby the products of their labours should be brought to the seaboard through exclusively Canadian channels and shipped from Canadian ports would of itself be enough glory for one Government, and would bring such prosperity to the Dominion of Canada as to wholly transform the financial difficulties of the country.

The immigration question was left to my charge, and without discussing the details, I may say that it may be regarded as practically solved. The population is increasing faster than we can take care of it.

Practically nothing has been done towards solving the transportation question, and the last conversation that I had with the late Minister of Public Works [Israel Tarte] upon the subject indicated that as a result of six years of effort he had then no real conception of the bearings of the problem....My judgment as to the course to be pursued now is that we should do now what we ought to have done six years ago. Three Members of the Government should be appointed to take the question under consideration.... They should be instructed to procure whatever expert advice and assistance they deem necessary, and the whole question from one end to the other should be thoroughly investigated....It involves an accurate knowledge of the hauling power of every eastern Canadian railroad; the nature of its grades; the size of the loads that it can haul; the cost price of hauling; the nature of the ocean tonnage facilities that can be furnished at each port; the causes which lead to the tonnage being abundant or otherwise; the methods that must be adopted to attract tonnage to keep the ocean rates sufficiently low to enable Canadian ports to compete with Boston, Portland, New York and Baltimore; and generally, a complete systematic and scientific knowledge of the whole situation must be acquired. I would then proceed to expend whatever amount of money was necessary to bring about the result that we have in view, and I would not be governed by precedents or by past theories in regard to policy. If it became necessary to extend the Government system of railways to Georgian Bay I would do so. If it became necessary to construct the French River Canal....I would do that. In fact whatever was necessary to accomplish the purpose I would do, because the purpose must be accomplished if

the commercial life of Canada is to be preserved, and we are to derive as
a country the benefits which are going on in the West at the present
time.

Such was the measure of Sifton's discontent. Canada's great future, which
he had been proclaiming publicly, was in danger of slipping from her grasp if
the government did not act quickly to devise a comprehensive policy to
keep the trade, both internal and external, firmly Canadian. The country
must be physically knit together. "Canada," Sifton told a Winnipeg
audience, "is a national entity. Canada is an organism, and you cannot
develop a single part of an organism satisfactorily. Each and all parts must
contribute to the vitality of the whole." The growth of the West, in this
context, would "send a flood of new blood from one end of this great
country to the other, through every artery of commerce."[7]

The optimism and confidence of these years produced a renewed nationalism which affected Canadian attitudes to both the United States and
Great Britain. Sifton was never an imperialist, and he did not identify
Canadian greatness with the Imperial connection. On the other hand, he
recognized that the British connection could be useful, even as it underwent significant changes. In Boston he claimed that the real significance of
the Colonial Conference of 1902 had been that it was "a conference of
statesmen representing the free self-governing colonies of the empire...
where, perhaps, for the first time it was thoroughly realized by the world
that the British self-governing colonies are in the fullest sense of the word
free communities." The tie binding the empire was "one of mutual
citizenship and good-will."[8] In St. Paul he said, "We are bound to Great
Britain by the fundamental law, and are as well attached to her by mutual
good feeling, and the sense of security induced by the assurance that she
will use her power to protect her colonies."[9]

The emphasis on the "ties that bind" was intended for an American
audience. When in Britain in the spring of 1903, Sifton stressed the theme of
independence and freedom. He told the Royal Colonial Institute that the
Colonial Conference of 1902 had "made manifest to the world...that the
British Empire was generically different from any of the great Empires of
history in the fact that, in addition to what might be termed its depen-
dencies, it reckoned within its borders practically a community of nations
....Freedom carries with it responsibilities, and powers, and rights, and the
fact that a Colony is a self-governing Colony gives to that Colony the right
to think and decide for itself." Periodic disagreements were bound to arise:

> There is in the Dominion a distinctly national sentiment of its own. We
> have a Canadian sentiment, but...it is also a British sentiment. It is the
> sentiment that we are engaged in overcoming a great many natural

. difficulties for the purpose of building up what we believe will be outside of England, perhaps, the greatest British community in the world.

For myself I have serious doubts about the effectiveness of any attempt to more closely unite the different members of the Empire by anything in the nature of a paper constitution....[I]t would be...more likely that a paper union would result in disunion and discontent than in greater union or in greater feeling on the part of the Colonies for the Mother Country....

Whatever may be the exact technical nature of the constitution which binds Canada to the Empire, this you will find—that as she grows, as she becomes stronger, and develops in wealth and strength and population, so will she become a stronger bulwark of British ideas and supremacy.[10]

During 1902 and 1903 the issues of imperial defence and an imperial preferential tariff came to the fore in British politics, and to a lesser extent in the Dominions. In colonial conferences since 1887 the British had tried to devise means to induce the Dominions to share in the burden of imperial defence. Canada had regularly resisted these pressures, most recently in 1902 when Laurier reiterated the Canadian position, but made vague pledges to form a distinctly Canadian navy. Sifton evidently concurred in the prime minister's views and told a British MP that in light of the opposition in Canada to any form of direct contribution to imperial defence, the British could only obtain relief by "inducing her to make expenditures that would be upon her own territory and under her own control." For example, the Dominion might be willing to take over the imperial garrison at Halifax. He added that "at the moment it would be a brave man who would bring down to the Canadian Parliament any proposition for expenditure of money in connection with the navy."[11]

Even more contentious was Joseph Chamberlain's campaign to pledge the Unionist Government in Britain to tariff reform and an enhanced imperial preference. To such a policy Sifton was firmly opposed. Chamberlain, he concluded while in England, had "completely wrecked the Unionist party," and all on the flimsiest foundation. The former colonial secretary apparently assumed that the colonies supported his scheme, which was certainly incorrect so far as Canada was concerned. Both sides in the controversy anxiously sought from the colonial politicians statements supporting their respective views. The Laurier government remained determinedly non-committal, having no wish to interfere in British politics. Privately, however, Sifton declared that Chamberlain's proposals "seem to me to be thoroughly impracticable and quite inconsistent with the logical development of our theory of self-government."[12]

Thus it is clear that even before the Alaska boundary award of 1903 Sifton had rejected any form of imperial federation or imperial centralization. He was indeed chary of any formal ties constricting Canada's freedom to chart her own course. Neither did he advocate complete independence; rather, he envisaged a shouldering of responsibilities commensurate with the Dominion's growing strength and evolution toward a co-equal status with Britain. Canada would remain within the British orbit by choice and by tradition.

If he was dubious about the advantages of closer trade relations with Great Britain, Sifton was equally cautious when the subject of reciprocity with the United States was raised. In St. Paul, the question was put to him by the National Reciprocity League. Publicly he was non-committal, stating that if an agreement were reached, it would have to benefit Canada as much as the United States. In the meantime those Americans who favoured the idea had a large task before them to educate their fellow countrymen to accept it. When that was accomplished, Canada might consider the question.[13] Privately, however, Sifton evinced little interest in the idea. Indeed, while the government was not likely to raise the protective tariff, he told Dafoe, "as far as I can see myself the whole country is becoming rabidly protectionist at a very rapid rate." The editor of the *Free Press* quickly replied that there was yet a good deal of low tariff sentiment in the West to be reckoned with.[14] Canada always had to reconcile these economic differences, and Sifton's approach was pragmatic. As with transportation policy, he would adjust the tariff as required to stimulate the Canadian economy and still protect legitimate industry. The general structure seemed admirably suited to dominion requirements, if the prevailing prosperity was any indication. While minor adjustments might be made from time to time, there was no justification for a major overhaul and redirection of the economy, such as would result from reciprocity.

These, then were Sifton's general views on Canada's situation and necessary policies of development. His solutions were national in focus. eschewing a merely regional perspective. Tying Canada more closely to either Britain or the United States could hinder Canada's long-term prosperity and independence. On the other hand, Canadian government policies must be both comprehensive and dynamic, national and international in scope, having a vision of how Canada should develop and how her prosperity might be retained.

Occasionally Sifton stopped briefly to reflect on the question, development and prosperity to what end? For its own sake? Why the insistence upon an independent and strong Canada? Philosophical utterances upon such questions were not part of his stock-in-trade. He made no pretence of being an original thinker; nevertheless his views, infrequently expressed, deserve note. To an American audience he deplored the limited knowledge of Canada in the United States, and informed them, "Our constitution is purer and freer than your own. In our government the will of the people is given more immediate effect. But I have no disposition to criticise your form of government." Canadians were satisfied with their government, "and believe it is effective and pure....But government is a mere device, the end of which is to afford administration of laws, and to maintain society. The essential thing about a people is virtue, and having that they will be able to carry out their ends and designs without any difficulty."[15] Such sentiments reflected no desire to change society; they were in the mainstream of late nineteenth-century liberalism. Government, in Sifton's view, might properly be a powerful agent in material development; it was not a vehicle for social reform.

Such change, if it were to come about, must arise from the people themselves, from a regeneration of the moral character of individuals. As a true liberal, he believed that within the people lay sufficient "virtue" to realize any necessary change and to produce a great civilization. "What do we expect this great west to accomplish for itself and for its people?" he asked in Winnipeg in 1904.

> We know now that there is no place known to civilization, where the poor man with willing and strong hands, and a mind disposed to success, may find a more certain reward for his labor; where he is more assured by reasonable diligence and frugality of social advancement and prosperity to himself and his family. And we know that the home-seekers of the world, at present, are aware of this fact, and are coming to cast their destinies amongst us. And therefore, sir, we look in the near future, to see upon these western plains, and in this western province and territories, a great population; great not only in numbers, but in other respects; not depressed by poverty; but a population characterized in its social conditions by a high degree of comfort and prosperity. We look forward to other things. We look forward to production of natural wealth of all kinds....We expect to see cities and towns springing up, in which the comforts and refinements of civilization will be within the reach of all. We expect to see a creditable system of education amongst our people, in which intellectual advancement and intellectual culture will go hand in hand with material progress. We expect another thing. We know that we have shown to the world that a western community is not necessarily a lawless community. But we hope to exhibit a great community, great in numbers and prosperity, built up within a single generation, in which respect for life and property is as profound, in which the administration of the law is as good as it is in the oldest and best organized communities of the world. We desire, in the end, that the accumulation of wealth and the

observance of social obligations shall not exhaust the energies of our people, but that our educational system may be crowned by institutions of learning, that our culture may not be forgotten, that the arts and sciences may not be neglected; so that Canadians may not fail in their duties to civilization. [16]

Such were Sifton's dreams of the future. The words constitute an epitome of his social thought. The ideas reflect the precepts and goals of the age of progress, within the context of the British heritage. Tremendous faith is placed in individualism and competition, in education, and in exploitation of natural resources and material progress. There is the conviction that inevitably out of all this activity a better life for everyone would result. There is also a confidence that the British way, respect for traditions and the law, for cultural values and for social obligations, was better than that of the United States. Development of Canada's material resources within the framework of the British heritage could produce a civilization that was great materially and culturally, fulfilling the deepest needs and aspirations of the human spirit.

Sifton's speeches were in part a response to the malaise that permeated the Laurier ministry early in the new century. The lassitude even touched the prime minister himself. So long as he won elections and remained in power, Laurier apparently did not care about policies of leadership or reform. "Reforms are for Oppositions," he curtly told J.S. Willison in 1897. "It is the business of Governments to stay in office." That certainly typified his attitude in 1901-2, when a lack of tight control and absence of a sense of purpose began to eat at cabinet solidarity and to widen divisions. "Politics seems to be dead at this moment," he wrote complacently in the summer of 1901. "The Government cannot seriously complain of this, and there is really nothing to do here [Ottawa] but the mere routine business of every day." [17] There was no hint of any desire to use the lull to reassess the position and direction of his government. Generally speaking there had been a sense of teamwork between 1896 and 1900, when many of the ministers—despite Laurier's disclaimer—had been implementing important reforms or fighting for the re-election of the ministry. Such dynamic ministers were bound to become restless and to require a firm rein and a sense of purpose from the leader of the government once their position again was secure and their reforms largely accomplished. However both his philosophy and ill health in 1902 and 1903 predisposed Laurier to indecision or inactivity. The result was that between 1902 and 1906 he lost five powerful ministers—Israel Tarte, A.G. Blair, William Mulock, Charles Fitzpatrick, and Sifton— who in most cases probably would have remained

Plate 1. "A second or third rate man," said Sifton of Governor General Lord Minto. For his part, Minto respected Sifton's abilities, but believed him guilty of "criminal administration."

Plate 2. The parliament buildings, Ottawa, draped for Queen Victoria's funeral in 1901, redolent of a brand of imperialism that was already being questioned by men like Sifton.

Plates 3 & 4. The ''dance hall girls of Dawson'' were associated in the public mind with gambling, alcohol and prostitution, all of which Sifton was expected to suppress. These women are identified as ''Snake Hips Lulu'' and ''Belgian Queen.''

Plate 5. ''Have a little more of the Government dignity,'' Sifton told Commissioner Ogilvy. In other words, dine and socialize with the upper classes, such as the N.W.M.P. officers, judges and government officials who frequented the Officers' Mess in Dawson.

Plates 6 & 7. The fears of the placer miners that they could not compete with large-scale, capital-intensive mechanical dredging operations are possibly more understandable with photographs such as these.

Plate 8. John W. Dafoe, one of the greatest Canadian journalists, edited the *Manitoba Free Press* from 1901 to 1944 and became one of Sifton's closest friends and confidants.

Plate 9. Sir John S. Willison was close to Sifton w̶ editor of the Toronto *Globe*; his switch to indepen̶ Conservatism with *The News* cooled, but did̶ end, their friendship.

Plate 10. Occupied in 1913, this building on Carlton Street became the permanent home of the *Free Press*.

with skilful handling. Their replacements generally were weak and ineffectual, suggesting that Laurier was willing to seek peace and avoid challenges to his leadership at any price.

So long as he remained in the government, however, Clifford Sifton was a loyal team player. He and Laurier could never have been close friends, but each respected the other's political abilities. There were frequent charges in these years that Sifton was the "master of the administration." He must have smiled wryly at such moments, for there never was any doubt that Laurier was in charge, and at no point does Sifton appear to have contemplated a challenge to him. Nevertheless, the minister of the interior not infrequently was as abrasive and difficult a colleague as he had been for Premier Greenway prior to 1896. More than once his hostility to Israel Tarte appeared directly in his correspondence with the minister of public works. [18] Even so sympathetic a colleague as Postmaster General Mulock complained to Sifton that "lately I have received various letters from you couched in language that I certainly would not use to you and I question if any good comes from your writing me in this strain." [19] The prime minister himself once found cause to reprove Sifton for a letter which "has a rasping tone, for which there is no cause." [20] There is little evidence that the minister of the interior felt personal animosity toward most of his colleagues, but on certain issues or under stress he was apt to vent his irritation. For example, as the sole western representative in the government he had to be constantly at pains to educate his colleagues on the need to be sympathetic to western views. To a friend in Virden, Manitoba, he complained of "the many and great difficulties that I have had to meet as the representative of western interests in the Cabinet." All western affairs, he told another correspondent, required his personal attention, as otherwise "owing to Eastern politics nothing would be done." [21] Often the cause of irritation was trivial: Mulock increasing the salary of a Virden postmaster whom Sifton had recommended be fired for partisan reasons; failure of Laurier to appoint a westerner to head at least one parliamentary committee; failure of Finance Minister Fielding to transfer government accounts in Brandon from a Tory bank to a Liberal bank. [22]

Indeed Sifton disliked the failure of any colleague to act in the party interest at all times. Almost insufferable in this respect was David Mills, minister of justice. He entertained high philosophical ideals about the impartiality of the law and of his civil servants and refused to manipulate the law or undertake thorough political reforms in his department in the manner which both Sifton and Solicitor General Fitzpatrick thought desirable. [23] They shared this opinion sufficiently to overcome their mutual coolness, and when Mills went on a tour to inspect western penitentiaries in 1899, Fitzpatrick suggested that Sifton try to be named acting minister of justice, "and we could work it [the Department] together. In this way you will I think realize what I have said so frequently about what is going on....I presume Mills would like to have [Senator R.W.] Scott or someone of that stamp, but this will not do. The opportunity is a good one to find out what is going on and we should take advantage of it."[24] The minister of justice particularly angered Sifton in 1901 when he ignored the latter's recommendations for Territorial KCs and instead consulted Senator Lougheed, a partisan Conservative.[25]

At the end of 1901 Mills indicated that he wished to be elevated to the Supreme Court bench. Who, then, should succeed him? Laurier discussed the possibility with Sifton, who was interested, especially if it would clear the way for another westerner in the cabinet. Justice was one of the most prestigious and potentially influential posts. Its incumbent was relatively free of patronage problems on any large scale and theoretically could interest himself in a wide range of policies. Whatever his reasons, however, Laurier decided against moving Sifton and elected to make the change while the minister of the interior was embroiled in battle with R.L. Richardson in Lisgar. "I have the assurance of the leader of the government," Sifton told the Lisgar Liberal nominating convention, "that such a change will be made in the representation of the West in the near future, that will more adequately represent the needs of this western country in the Dominion cabinet."[26] Little more than a week later, the same day that the cabinet changes were announced in the press, Laurier decided that he should write about them to Sifton. Mills, he declared weakly, had become "fidgety & nervous," and so Laurier had to act. The choice of a successor lay between Blair, Fitzpatrick, and Sifton. The former refused to be moved.

> From the conversation that I had with you I understood that it would be acceptable to you, but I saw insuperable difficulty in removing you from the Interior at this moment. Moreover I finally made up my mind to avail myself of the occasion to endeavor to ward off, as much as I can, the insidious movement which is now attempted against me in Q.[Quebec] So I raised F. [Fitzpatrick] to Justice, & called [H.G.] Carroll to be Solicitor General. I expect very good results from this combination & if any one can help me at this juncture, Carroll is the boy.
>
> My intention is to take [Senator William] Templeman without portfolio, so as to pave the way for the plans which you have in view.[27]

Needless to say, Sifton was embarrassed at the prime minister's decision and annoyed to read about it in the press a week before Laurier's explanations finally reached him. He was blunt in reply:

I presume it is unnecessary for me to say that the arrangements made are from my standpoint wholly unsatisfactory. You could hardly fail to be aware of this fact. I do not refer to any personal feeling because my suggestion that I might take the Justice Dept was only made to facilitate matters, & not because I had any particular desire for it.

I understand however that there was a clear agreement on your part that the vacant portfolio should be given to the West. When it was announced that it had been given to Quebec it was to put it mildly somewhat of a surprise.

I quite recognize however that in these matters you are the judge and must act on what seems to you to be the best course.[28]

There is little evidence that Sifton badly wanted Justice, despite the attractions of its prestige. He did want the vacancy made available to be filled, one way or another, by a westerner. All the evidence suggests that his personal ambitions lay in the direction of the railways and canals portfolio. Still, Laurier's decision was a slap in the face. Appointment of a weak senator to the cabinet without portfolio utterly failed to satisfy western ambitions.

The incident was a perfect example of Laurier's mastery of the fait accompli. Acting in Sifton's absence, he left the minister of the interior little choice but to accept the situation. For the Prime Minister, the decision was a comfortable one. Fitzpatrick and he were friends ("My dear Fitz," he would write) and shared a reasonably similar outlook on political affairs.[29] Certainly it was no way to win Sifton's affection. It also was the first time that Laurier had failed so completely to accede to Sifton's demands concerning an issue important to the West; in retrospect it appears to have been a turning-point in their relationship. There were several subsequent opportunities when the prime minister might have moved Sifton and strengthened western representation. Most memorable were the dismissal of Tarte in 1902 and the resignation of Blair in 1903, both better discussed in other contexts. Not until 1906 did Laurier strengthen western representation even slightly, when he appointed Templeman minister of inland revenue.

Occasionally difficult, Sifton at least knew the importance of getting along with his colleagues. With the governor general it was a different story. Minto and Sifton shared a cordial dislike for one another. Even while recognizing his great talents, the governor general despised what he believed was Sifton's unprincipled and corrupt public life. In fact, at Rideau Hall the minister of the interior was privately dubbed "the villain."[30] For his part, Sifton has no respect even for Minto's abilities, and he considered that the governor general was little more than an irritating relic from

Canada's colonial past, certainly not adapted to the needs of self-governing dominions. The governor general ought to recognize his constitutional limitations and be bound by the views of his constitutional advisers. It is doubtful whether Sifton knew fully of Minto's belief that he was corrupt. In the past, nevertheless, he had been angered by Minto's open interest in criticism of the government while in the Yukon; by his obvious sympathy with the imperial aims of Chamberlain; by his friendship with Senator Kirchhoffer; and by his gratuitous interference in the administration of Indian affairs. In 1901 the governor general compounded these errors. When the Duke of Cornwall toured Canada in that year, he went shooting near Portage la Prairie, and Minto put Kirchhoffer in charge of the arrangements.[31] A further dispute arose in the cabinet over the question of titles and who should determine the honours list. Minto believed that ultimately the prerogative lay with him; politicians like Sifton considered that titles were properly the gift of the cabinet. Most important was Minto's insistence that T.G. Shaughnessy, the CPR president, receive a knighthood. Given the CPR attitude during the 1900 general elections and the general state of strained relations then existing between the government and the Company, in Sifton's eyes such a reward was unthinkable.[32]

J.W. Dafoe went east shortly after Shaughnessy's choice was made public and discussed matters with Sifton. The result was a series of important editorials in the *Free Press*, beginning with a personal attack on Minto as a second-rate man and expanding into full-blown discussions of the nature of Canadian loyalty, the office of governor general, and the implications of the British connection.[33] Minto ignored the personal attack but took umbrage at the "studied attack" in a government organ upon the office he held. Laurier was annoyed at Dafoe's editorials, though he probably suspected that they had been inspired by Sifton. At any rate, Dafoe soon told Sifton, "My attack has evidently struck home as I am in receipt of a long confidential letter from Sir Wilfrid begging me, in effect, to let up for God's sake."[34] Relations between the minister of the interior and the governor general remained decidedly frigid.

The first issue to affect the complexion of the Laurier cabinet was the persistent problem of the tariff. The divisions in the government reflected the divergent interests of the country, although on this occasion the issue was raised by industrialists and manufacturers, mainly of central Canada, who sought higher levels of tariff protection. The plain meaning of the tariff plank of the 1893 Liberal platform had been that a Liberal government would abandon protection as a principle, opt for a revenue tariff, and wherever possible seek freer trade with Britain and the United States. The policy was intended by the Liberal leadership to moderate the drastic

Unrestricted Reciprocity policy of the years 1888 to 1891. It was vital if the party hoped to gain power to make some concessions to the protectionist business interests, and so the careful qualifications in the 1893 resolutions permitted the Liberal government after 1896 to wriggle out of the apparent commitment to abandon protection. Westerners, by and large, did not appreciate these subtleties. They adhered to the 1893 platform; it called for dramatic changes; since 1896 a Liberal government had introduced no dramatic changes that significantly reduced the cost of farm machinery or other consumer goods. Increasingly western audiences demanded to know why.

After 1900 Sifton was still trying to convince them that the average decrease in the tariff of less than two per cent was significant, that many items had been lowered much more, and that westerners must be broad-minded enough to look at the situation from a national, and not merely a regional perspective. When Dafoe came to the *Free Press* a strenuous campaign was launched to persuade them of the virtues of Grit policy. Change, he argued, was unlikely, but if it did come the trend would be toward lower, not higher tariffs.[35] Campaigning against Richardson in 1902, Sifton faced an opponent who championed the obvious meaning of the 1893 platform. Constantly the minister of the interior found that he had to defend the tariff. He explained, for example, that removal of the duty on agricultural implements would destroy the Canadian industry, and then farmers would be totally at the mercy of American manufacturers. Speaking at Miami, Manitoba, on 8 February, Sifton claimed that he had been on the committee that had drawn up the 1893 tariff plank. He recalled "that the expression in the platform, 'with due regard to all interests of the community,' was put in, that no industry, in which men were employed and capital invested because of a protective tariff, that is no industry that existed through the artificial tariff, should be wiped out."[36] Taken at face value, these remarks would characterize Sifton as a defender even of inefficient industry, so long as it created Canadian jobs; in practice, he was not prepared to go quite so far. Whatever his explanations, however, he increasingly was identified in the West either as a proponent of protection, or as a defender of a government controlled by eastern protectionist interests.

Six or seven months after the Lisgar contest Sifton was cast in a dramatically different role. He would be charged by many in central Canada with being no more than a raving free trader and an unthinking mouthpiece of narrowly regional interests. For reasons still not fully understood the minister of public works, Israel Tarte, undertook a vigorous campaign for higher protection with the ecstatic blessing of the Canadian Manufacturers' Association. Laurier was absent in England and Europe and ill to boot. Tarte took the opportunity to give over one hundred addresses in support of his ideas, without the approval of his colleagues. Some at the time and later believed that he was building up a constituency of support to enable him to succeed the prime minister as Liberal leader.[37] The evidence that such were his ambitions is very slight, notes H.B. Neatby, who points out that "to his contemporaries it was merely Tarte being carried away by his convictions again."[38]

Tarte believed that the Liberals must adopt a higher tariff or suffer defeat at the hands of a protectionist party.[39] His "convictions," then, were essentially political necessities as he saw them. True, he had long espoused protection, but he saw no necessity to act independently before 1902. Why? Probably in part because since 1901 the CMA had been mounting a propaganda campaign in support of more protection, and it had begun to strike home in Tarte's bastion of Quebec. In 1901 Laurier had remained distinctly cool to the protectionist overtures, but they were causing anxiety in the West. As Dafoe told Sifton, "It is a tough enough job to defend the tariff as it stands up here: and an increase would have a tendency to put us out of business in a political sense."[40] In 1902 the CMA pressure mounted, and the business interests knew how to apply the screws where the Liberal organization was most vulnerable. Moreover, as Laurier's illness persisted, businessmen worried about who might succeed him.[41]

With pressure mounting through the summer of 1902, Sifton maintained a steadfast silence on the subject. He and the rest of the cabinet hoped that Laurier would return quickly from the Colonial Conference or at least order Tarte to hold his peace. But the conference extended interminably; the prime minister's health deteriorated, necessitating a European holiday; and no order came to curb Tarte. Finally, with western Liberals frantic with worry, and Opposition Leader Borden about to undertake a western tour, Sifton made his move. Early in September he gave the *Globe* correspondent a short interview. Tarte spoke solely for himself, said Sifton, and not for the Liberal party, on the question of the tariff. He also claimed that all western Liberals, and probably the majority of the Party, would oppose increased protection.[42] That was all that he said publicly prior to Laurier's return. But it gave Dafoe the freedom to let the *Free Press* at last take up Sifton's views.[43] And it relieved the pent-up feelings of both western Liberals and Sifton's cabinet colleagues. "Your interview has done good and is useful as a counterblast to Tarte's declamations," wrote Sir Richard Cartwright.[44] The cabinet crisis was resolved only when the prime minister returned in October and asked for Tarte's resignation, on the proper ground that independent action on the subject by a member of the cabinet was unacceptable.

The decision, though correct, was not easy. Laurier had valued Tarte as a colleague and organizer, and he knew that the ex-minister's campaign had been popular in large parts of central Canada. The business community was angry at his decision. One Ontario Liberal businessman told Laurier, "I do not know what the effect will be to our party but it does appear that the time has come that the two great provinces that have to bear the brunt of the burden, shall put their heads together and form a business policy such as will develop the industries in their own province. Mr. Fielding has secured a good duty on coal, and a mighty high one on iron. Mr. Sifton is howling because he has six uncertain seats to control, peopled mostly by foreigners, who are as uncertain as the weather, and expects all sorts of money to be raised and expended for the benefit of the West, and at the same time to have them contribute as little as possible to the cost." Revising the tariff in the manner suggested by Tarte would "invite not only millions of money, but millions of people to come here, and do what they have done in the country to the South."[45]

In the West, by contrast, the reaction to Tarte's departure was one of joy. Dafoe reported that it "has put the Liberals out here in a great humour: it has no doubt strengthened us very much." J.D. Cameron considered that it "clears the atmosphere a whole lot." To a similar sentiment from Walter Scott, Sifton replied, "I am glad to know that the Government has at last done something that pleases the North West."[46] Ironically, although Sifton's views on the tariff had not changed, his public image had. Suddenly he appeared to be the champion of free trade interest. Lord Minto accurately reflected the mood when he portrayed the contest as between "Tarte advocating higher protection for the sake of Canadian industries, & Sifton supporting Free Trade doctrines for the sake of the farmers."[47] This confusion about Sifton's views was not based upon any of his public statements, yet was astonishingly persistent until 1911.

Beneath the public issue of the tariff apparently lay a bitter personal feud between Tarte and several of his former colleagues, particularly Sifton. The most important evidence of the dispute lies in Minto's notes of conversations he had with Tarte and Laurier, though it is difficult to evaluate the accuracy of Tarte's statements. At the very least his remarks to the governor general were those of an embittered man; at worst, they seem close to the babblings of an overworked imagination. Tarte did reveal that there were deep cleavages in the cabinet in 1902 over transportation policy (Tarte favouring the CPR). He also claimed that there was excessive corruption, most notably on Sifton's part. As before, Minto eagerly copied down every scrap of evidence of the latter's alleged corrupt activities, remarking snidely that "Sifton has risen from a small surveyor [*sic*] to the position of a rich man with a house on the St. Lawrence & one of the finest steam yachts on the Lakes." Tarte also confessed to Lady Minto "that his colleagues were a gang of corrupt scoundrels and thieves, he said there was the Sutherland, Sifton gang, to whom Sir Wilfrid had made over Manitoba and the North West, and Yukon and that Sifton had received a million dollars in hard cash and that Sir Wilfrid's hands were not clean, as he had accepted money from them." Minto concluded, "we seem to be back at the days of the old Quebec 'intendants' and the '100 associates'—we have I find even got our Madame de Pompadour!" "It is," he added, "very interesting, and very disgusting."[48]

He told Laurier all of the stories about Sifton and also of reports from Comptroller F. White of the NWMP about Sifton's manipulation of the Police in the Territories. Laurier apparently discounted the latter, but he did admit that "discreditable rumours" existed about Sifton which "should be cleared up" or the minister of the interior would have to retire. Yet the prime minister added that Sifton already had submitted his resignation, but he would not accept it on the basis of "unsubstantiated reports."[49] Just what action Laurier did take, if any, is unknown. The internal rivalries and suspicions within the cabinet were worsened by his inability to provide decisive leadership, his reluctance to reconstruct the cabinet, and his failure to restore harmony.

Once Tarte was out of the cabinet, Sifton was at some liberty to expand upon his views in public. Early in 1903 he assured a Winnipeg audience that Tarte had not originated the episode. Rather, it was a plot hatched "by interested manufacturers for the purpose of extracting illegitimate and enormous profits." It was utter nonsense in his view to suggest that higher tariffs would result in more investment in the country. Not only was business booming in 1903 without any increase in the tariff, but there had been great growth since 1896 with a tariff slightly lower than before. Such industries were "natural to Canada, and have not been built up upon an excessive tariff, nor do they extract from the consumer a price he should not be called on to pay."[50] In maintaining its low and reasonable tariff, argued Sifton, the Liberal government had never departed from the principles of 1893:

> In all revisions of the tariff by the government there had been three cardinal underlying principles. The first was, to lower the duties on staple articles of general necessity as much as possible. The second was, to give a preference to the British manufacturer in the Canadian market, and the third, wherever it was possible, to reduce the duty on the raw material for the manufacturer, thereby lessening the cost of the article to the consumer.[51]

Sifton added that by no means was he doctrinaire on low tariffs. Only a flexible policy could meet the changing and varied needs of the country. Lower tariffs were naturally preferable, "but if he saw a legitimate Canadian industry suffering through foreign competition, when a slight change of 4 or 5 per cent. would save it from being wiped out, he was not prepared to say that he would not consider a case of that kind, and consider it favorably."[52]

It should be added that Sifton's view of the future development of the prairie West was largely agricultural. He would have liked to see the tariff encourage "the establishment of some small industries in the North West," but there is no doubt that he believed that central Canada would remain the industrial heartland. "We all desire — every patriotic Canadian desires," he told a Winnipeg audience in 1904, "that the great trade of the prairie shall go to enrich our own people in the east, to build up the factories and the workshops of eastern Canada, and to contribute in every legitimate way to its prosperity."[53]

In the wake of the cabinet upheaval, the government decided in 1903 to postpone any revision of the tariff. The wounds of division were too fresh, the factions in the country too sensitive to risk a debate. Furthermore, the Canadians desperately wanted not to appear, by sins of omission or commission, to be interfering in the British debate on tariff preference. Finally, there were feelers from some American groups on the possibility of reopening talks on reciprocity. Sifton believed that they had a long way to go simply to prepare their fellow Americans, without engaging Canada in a debate. It was best, he counselled Fielding, to go slow, because reciprocity was "distinctly unpopular" with Canadian manufacturers, and "not too popular" with consumers.[54]

The Liberals realized that some revisions in the tariff schedule were overdue and must be undertaken in 1904. Rather isolated from western sentiment during much of 1903, Sifton professed to believe that the tariff would not "cut any figure" at the next election, although the Liberals could not afford to be perceived to be protectionist. Yet he also thought that protectionist sentiment was rapidly rising.[55] In his opinion the Liberals should point out that the Tories supported a near doubling of the tariff to the American level. That in itself should convince voters that the Liberals were the more reasonable and low-tariff party, without confining them to a narrow ideology. Flexibility was the key to adjusting the tariff. Indeed, despite their professed devotion to a revenue tariff or free trade ideology, Sifton believed that western farmers too wanted protection on some items. Scrub horses, for example, should not be allowed entry from the United States, and the British Columbia market must be preserved for prairie produce. "It is most unsatisfactory," he told Dafoe, "to be tied down as we are at the present time to a declaration which practically amounts to a statement that we cannot do anything."[56] Dafoe balanced Sifton's perception of increasing protectionist sentiment by reminding him of the persistence and strength of low-tariff sentiment in the West. "I run across from time to time Liberals," he wrote, "who make no bones of saying that they voted Tory last time [1900] because they thought our policy less radical than it should be."[57]

The principle of moderation and flexibility was easier to determine than what specific duties ought to be. There was, for instance, pressure from British Columbia for protection of the forest industry. To this Sifton was flatly opposed: "there will be no duty put on settlers' lumber while I am here. If British Columbia cannot compete with Puget Sound in lumber business it had better get out of the business." He was "prepared to fight the lumber duty from beginning to end. I have been up against the lumbermen ever since I came down here, and they understand who their enemy is on the subject of the duty." Obviously it was one thing to force BC lumbermen to eat prairie produce at protected prices and quite another to force prairie farmers to purchase BC lumber with similar protection. Sifton also sought protection for western wool producers.[58] He supported anti-dumping laws against American goods and prohibiting entry of cheap buggies and horses. Sifton formed his views in close collaboration with Dafoe and then passed their ideas on to the cabinet. Probably one of the biggest factors in minimizing tariff changes in 1904 was Dafoe's fear that they would jeopardize the position of the Liberals in the forthcoming election.[59]

When Finance Minister Fielding announced his budget in 1904, it was obvious that an election was in the offing and that Sifton had largely had his way. A record surplus of $16,500,000 was announced, out of revenues of $71,000,000. He introduced anti-dumping measures, raised the duty on woolens to 30 per cent, and reduced the duty on coal oil — a long standing western grievance — by 50 per cent.[60] Many Liberal businessmen remained angry, however, at the failure to increase protection. One irate senator told Laurier that Ontario ministers had no influence on tariff policy: "Fielding in the Maritime Provinces and Sifton in the West and Manitoba, apparently control all tariff legislation. This is the feeling in Ontario and there is a lot to justify the conclusion."[61]

The criticism was hardly fair, though Sifton's great influence was undeniable. He was trying to reconcile the diverse needs and interests of the country as far as possible for the general good as well as for the political interests of the Liberal party. To have followed the CMA cry would have been to write off the West; to have followed western demands would have been to write off Ontario and part of Quebec. Maintaining tension and balance in the reins of power was a tough job, and Sifton was recognized by his colleagues to be one of the most adept among them. The short-run advantages of accepting Ontario's demands were tempting; the long-run results for country and party could have been most serious. When the temptation to choose one side became too great, as it would in 1911, the results were disastrous. By then, however, Sifton was no longer party to the government's decisions.

His record makes it abundantly clear that he was not a high protectionist. His was a nationalist, pragmatic policy of development: a moderate tariff, adjustable in any direction or sector to promote national progress. Like most Canadians of his day, he believed that American investment should be encouraged. But higher tariffs were not the proper means. Rather, it would be attracted more readily by an expanding, dynamic economy, an efficient transportation network, and a moderate tariff. There were many other ways to encourage such investment than through manipulation of the tariff. For example, he strongly supported government aid to establish the Clergue Steel interests at Sault Ste. Marie by guarantees of purchases of steel rails for the Intercolonial Railway.[62]

If he opposed high protection, Sifton also questioned the desirability of reciprocity. The journalist E.W. Thomson conducted a series of interviews with members of the cabinet in 1904, in which the positions of 1911 are fascinatingly anticipated. Laurier and Fielding, Thomson revealed, favoured reciprocity in natural products and raw materials, if there was a reasonable guarantee of American agreement. Sifton did not concur (though his view was said to be somehow "reconcilable" with that of Laurier). Even the West, declared Sifton, was not a unit on the subject of reciprocity. If it were in Canada's interest, a measure of freer trade might be acceptable, but only with guarantees that the arrangements would be long-term and that they could not readily be abrogated. Sifton was worried that reciprocity might divert trade patterns from the national transportation system which was then being expanded. The east-west channels of trade, he pointed out, were better adapted for exploiting the British and European markets than that of the United States. Furthermore, what would become of the British preference under reciprocity? Canadians had accepted the necessity of a tariff to promote development. The country was prosperous, and "we are not going to throw any good thing away" unless reciprocity were "tendered on conditions that we can honorably and profitably accept." Sifton later disclaimed responsibility for the article, but probably more because it constituted a rather racy resume of his ideas than because it was substantially inaccurate.[63]

No aspect of the history of the Laurier government more closely demonstrates acceptance of the principles of the national policy than the subject of transportation. As had been the case twenty years earlier when the Tories had promoted the Canadian Pacific Railway, Liberal policy was predicated on developing east-west, all-Canadian trade and on the need of transportation for national development. At the same time there emerged the need to provide competition for the CPR. Competition, it was hoped, would stimulate development while lowering costs of transportation.

The new century began with a vigorous quarrel between the government and the CPR; also involved were the Crow's Nest Pass Coal Company and the Great Northern Railway. When the CPR undertook to build the Crow's Nest Pass Railway in 1897, it made two other important agreements. One was the acquisition of certain smelter and mining properties in southern British Columbia, the foundation of Cominco. The other was an agreement with the independent Crow's Nest Pass Coal Company (controlled by Liberals Robert Jaffray and Senator G.A. Cox) under which the coal company would control most of the coal lands in the district in return for guaranteeing a sufficient supply of coal for the CPR smelter operations. Owing to operating problems the CPR shut down its smelter for a time in 1900, and the coal company understandably began to look for new markets. They found a ready buyer in James J. Hill, the American railway magnate, who wanted to secure enormous quantities of Canadian coking coal for proposed smelter operations in Montana. The Great Northern proposed a railway extension to move the coal directly down the Kootenay River valley and requested a charter from Parliament. The CPR opposed the charter because upon reopening its smelting operations it found difficulty in obtaining sufficient coal. The Canadian railway charged that the coal company was violating its agreements and discriminating both in prices and priorities in favour of American customers.[64] It should be added that the dispute was part of an ongoing conflict between J.J. Hill and the CPR and that the proposed line would be but one of four Great Northern extensions into southern British Columbia, a region jealously guarded as a private preserve by the Canadian line.[65]

Clifford Sifton defended the agreement between the coal company and the Great Northern on two grounds. One was that, while he desired to see the CPR have first opportunity to open up and exploit the district to strengthen east-west trade, it could not reasonably expect its monopoly to be extended indefinitely. After four years it had had sufficient time to establish itself and must now be prepared to face competition which would generate further development of the region. The second point was that the Canadian market for coal had been small and so unstable that the coal company had not been able to borrow the necessary capital to begin large-scale operations. With a sizeable guaranteed market, the capital would be available and would permit production of a sufficiently large volume that the price to the Canadian consumer ultimately would be reduced. The Winnipeg *Tribune* (which Sifton believed to be under CPR influence) had denounced the deal as a sellout to the Americans. This infuriated him, and he told A.J. Magurn, "The idea of attacking a man [Hill] who comes to buy a thousand tons of our coal a day while we are sending trade commissioners all over creation to find a market for our products only needs to be stated in order that its absurdity may be made clear." In April 1901, Laurier, Tarte, Blair, and Sifton met with CPR and coal company officials to hear their arguments. The CPR greatly feared that Hill would come to control the coal company—which he eventually did—and would then contrive to put the CPR smelting operations out of business unless conditions were written to the charter.[66] There was force in both sides to the argument, and a compromise resulted in a requirement that the coal company would be restricted in selling its coal at $2.00 per ton, so long as there was no competition. The capital stock of the company also was increased by one-third to $2 million.[67]

This dispute contributed significantly to a serious falling-out between the government and the CPR. For Clifford Sifton the reversal of his former attitude to the railway was particularly acute. In Winnipeg after 1888 and in Ottawa after 1896 he had been one of the few westerners willing to shed a reflexive suspicion or hatred of the corporation, preferring to co-operate with it on a frankly business basis. There is little evidence of any motive of personal gain in this relationship. Rather Sifton had sought to work with the CPR in policies of development that also would be politically advantageous to the Liberal party. In the building of branch lines, in the Crow's Nest Pass agreement, in movement of immigrants, in policies concerning the movement of grain, there was a significant degree of co-operation, despite occasional minor tensions. Even Sifton's acquisition of the *Manitoba Free Press* from the CPR appears to have been a straightforward business deal; suspicions that more was involved never have been supported with hard evidence. He and Sir William Van Horne had shared a pragmatic, aggressive attitude to policies of development and a mutual respect. T.G. Shaughnessy, by contrast, was a more private, less openly aggressive man. The company expanded dramatically under him, but less now to open new country than to protect CPR interests against vigorous competitors strongly supported by the government. He entered the presidency in 1899 at a time when pressure on the government to provide competition began to coincide with evidence of a strong diversifying and growing economy. For politicians like Sifton, the CPR was no less necessary than before, but a second transcontinental line appeared both necessary and economically viable. Added to this was the reluctance of the CPR to settle the outstanding land problem in the West and Shaughnessy's decision to work against the government—especially against Sifton—in the 1900 election.

Sifton was astute enough not to burn his bridges and create a permanent rupture, but as the year 1901 began it was obvious that a kind of guerrilla war of retaliation was under way. The report of a royal commission investigating the CPR's townsite deals at Virden, Moose Jaw, Regina, and Qu'Appelle was made public.[68] Sifton encouraged Magurn to play up the embarrassing aspects of the report and to "devote a little attention to Mr. E.B. Osler," MP for West Toronto, for his involvement in the deals. Osler, added Sifton, "is a disciple of the esteemed Pecksniff and a brother of the pharisee who thanked God that he was not as other people."[69] He vigorously attacked a CPR decision to close down an unprofitable branch line during the winter. He was vigilant in checking increases in freight rates on the Crow's Nest line. He refused to accede to CPR demands regarding selection of coal lands in the Crow's Nest Pass.[70] He opposed extension of CPR control of the Great Northwest Central Railway charter, arguing that the company had had it for twenty years and had done nothing with it.[71] Great pressure was put on the CPR to settle its land patents and, as seen, court cases against the company were prepared on taxation issues. The animosity gladdened the hearts of western Liberals, one of whom wrote, "I am extremely pleased to find that the C.P.R. and the Government are not on friendly terms. I think that is of more benefit to the party than half a dozen News Papers and I have no doubt it is in the interests of the country."[72]

The minister of the interior was well aware of the political benefits of opposition to the CPR, both for himself and for the *Free Press*. It was more important in his estimation, however, to be seen to be supporting competition for the CPR than merely to foment a useless and destructive quarrel. Quite apart from merely political motivations, he had concluded that the time was ripe for effective competition, both regional and transcontinental, and began to promote the concept of "free trade in railways." By allowing anyone a charter who desired it, he hoped to induce American capital to develop the country, as was being done in BC, and to open up ways of exploiting the American market.[73] That of course would be done without the government aid that was necessary to construct and maintain the east-west national trading patterns. A decade earlier Sifton had opposed the introduction of a railway commission, but the idea of a regulatory governmental agency remained popular in the West, and Sifton, after years of discouraging the concept, decided to support it.[74] In general, he supported what he termed a "uniform" railway policy, including free access to charters and greater government supervision.[75] This last point is significant. Well before the grain blockade of 1901 he had come to the conclusion that railways operated too much in their own interest and failed to live up to their public responsibilities. Only government supervision and requirements exacted in charters and contracts could force the companies to serve the public interest. Nevertheless, this was a concept sharply distinguished in his mind from any proposal for government ownership.

By 1902 few public men in Canada would have disagreed with the idea of a second transcontinental, all-Canadian railway. The CPR could no longer meet the requirements of the expanding economy of central and western Canada. To open up new districts for settlement and resource exploitation, to move the large volume of grain, lumber, mineral ores, and other products, and to tie it all into the context of a strong east-west economy, such a line was essential. The basic points at issue were, by whom would the new railway be built, and under what terms? Unhappily the Laurier government was ill prepared to face these basic issues. Within the cabinet were supporters of government ownership and free enterprise, of the Canadian Northern, Grand Trunk, Intercolonial, and other lesser interests, of politically expedient rather than economically sound routes, and all led by a man who was unwell, politically astute but devoid of business sense, and spineless in dealing with vigorous railway magnates.

An omen of pending difficulties lay in Laurier's relationship with his minister of railways, Andrew Blair. Apart from permitting the extension of the Intercolonial to Montreal, Laurier had scarcely trusted Blair or followed his advice since 1896. Blair was an advocate of government construction and ownership and of a powerful government-controlled regulatory commission for railways; Laurier believed in neither, certainly prior to 1903. Blair's advice concerning the Crow's Nest Pass line in 1897 and the "all-Canadian" route to the Yukon in 1898 had been rejected in favour of Sifton's policies. As late as April 1902, Laurier wrote, "My impression is that there is at this moment, no discontent with the administration of any of the Departments, with the single exception of the Department of Railways and Canals."[76] Despite the prime minister's obvious lack of confidence in him, Blair had stubbornly clung to his department. In February 1902, as seen, he had refused to be moved to Justice, and Laurier had lacked the courage to insist. The result of this poor relationship was that during Laurier's absence and illness in 1902 no initiative was taken by the government, while the two major contenders for transcontinental status, the Grand Trunk and Canadian Northern, jockeyed for the advantage.

The more aggressive was the Grand Trunk. Since a reorganization of the company in 1895 and under the dynamic leadership of the general manager, Charles M. Hays, the line had become both profitable and ambitious. Its main lines ran from Chicago in the west through Sarnia, Toronto, and Montreal to Portland, Maine. Its extensive holdings and branch lines in Ontario and Quebec made it confident that the majority of cabinet ministers and MPs must favour its case. After six or seven months of behind-the-scenes manoeuvering, Hays told Sir Charles Rivers Wilson, the chairman of the Grand Trunk board, "I think we have the support of all the Ministers, with the possible exception of the Minister of Railways, Mr. Blair, who advocates extension of the Government Road [Intercolonial] to the Coast, and the Minister of the Interior, Sifton, who is supposed to be in some way identified with Mackenzie and Mann."[77] Essentially the Grand Trunk scheme was to create a subsidiary company, the Grand Trunk Pacific, to build west from the GTR terminus at North Bay to the Pacific coast with substantial subsidies in cash and land.[78] Late in December Hays wrote that Sifton had said in an interview that "any assistance given...in aid of our

[GTR] proposed trans-continental line will be subject to the condition that its terminus must be a Canadian port and that its trade must be exported through Canadian channels.'' Such a policy, agreed Hays and Rivers Wilson, ''would be the veriest claptrap and merely obstructive.''[79] Perhaps; but unhappily for the Grand Trunk, Sifton regarded an all-Canadian route as central to any policy, and he had the strength in the cabinet to insist upon his views.

Sifton was also recognized as the principal supporter in the cabinet of the Canadian Northern. By 1902 it had lines west from Port Arthur past Dauphin to the northwest corner of Manitoba. It was still very much a regional railway, inclined to view transcontinental expansion as a long-term project, and it was more immediately interested in expanding its prairie base with possible extension to the Pacific.[80] Its popularity in the West was founded largely on the lower freight rates and government control of rates negotiated by the Roblin government. Hays believed the Grand Trunk could swallow or crush the upstart western line; he reckoned without the will of Mackenzie and Mann to survive and even expand their line, fear of the westerners that control of rates would be lost, and the singular strength of Sifton in the cabinet.

As luck would have it, however—or perhaps as Laurier intended it— Sifton's strength would be lost during the crucial period of negotiations, because he was sent off to London to defend Canada's interest in the Alaska boundary dispute. Nevertheless, before his departure he attempted to shape the government policy in two ways. First, and most successfully, he secured the future of the Canadian Northern by pledging the government to pass a bond guarantee of $13,000 per mile for 620 miles of line via Prince Albert to Edmonton. Introduced in his absence, and passed upon his return in July, the guarantee secured by Sifton foiled Hays's ''attempt to starve the Canadian Northern into submission.''[81]

Saving the Canadian Northern was much less ambitious than the second stage of Sifton's plan. He wanted to introduce rationality and global planning into developing a comprehensive national transportation policy, of which the new transcontinental railway would be but a single component. Of all the cabinet he had by far the broadest grasp of the issues at stake. Few saw beyond a competition between two companies for government support for their expansionist fantasies. Mulock went a bit further when he suggested that the new line not only would stimulate east-west intercourse but would promote the nationalization of the ''foreign element'' then populating the West.[82] But Sifton, in public speeches, in his memorandum to Fitzpatrick of 1902, and in memoranda for Laurier in 1903,[83] constantly placed the issue in terms of Canada's total transportation requirements. He held to his belief that the government needed far more detailed and expert information if it was properly to rationalize transportation policy. Advocating a commission to investigate, he put the problem succinctly: "The object to be attained is the transportation of Western products by Canadian railways and transportation agencies from the place of production to the markets in Europe." This involved three phases: transportation to the Lakehead; from there to Canadian seaports; and from there to Europe. Three countervailing forces had to be met: American railway competition from the North West; competition on the Great Lakes to Buffalo; and diversion of traffic through Boston and Portland. "The prime consideration to be borne in mind is that everything affecting the cost of getting the grain to market must be considered. The grain will go by the cheapest and easiest route. The object, therefore, must be to make the Canadian route cheapest and easiest." The commission should look into storage and water transportation facilities as well as railways.[84] At the same time Sifton had become avidly interested in the possibilities of a fast Canadian Atlantic steamship service as an extension of railway policy.[85]

By the time Sifton was ready to depart for England it was clear that no such broad approach would be undertaken. The cabinet was determined to announce a dramatic railway policy in 1903, undoubtedly with an election in view. Prior to his departure Sifton addressed himself to the new situation. The government, he wrote, should "require" the Grand Trunk and the Canadian Northern to co-operate, the former to build a line from Quebec to Port Arthur, and the latter from the Lakehead to the Pacific at Port Simpson. The companies would be bound in a perpetual traffic contract. Each railway would undertake a steamship line from its respective coastal ports. Such a scheme would minimize public expenditure and duplication of services. He believed that such a scheme would be advantageous to both railways and that two separate companies would result in "more effective management." The CPR, he argued, was too big for efficient management from Montreal, with the result that it was "unable to appreciate the requirements of the country and we see a breakdown in the West such as we had last year." He supported the CN bond guarantees to facilitate needed construction in the West in 1903 and the completion of surveys of the transcontinental route during 1903. Then in 1904, "after the public have had time to digest the proposals," the government could "come down with a moderate proposition for completing the whole system." With a full year to prepare, "we would have the advantages of exact surveys, we would know exactly what the route was going to be, and we would know within a fraction of the cost." Sifton also supported Blair's proposal of 1903 to create a railway commission with power to control rates. Taken together, he argued, this broad proposal would win popular acclaim. "The only objection," he added prophetically, "is the sentimental ambition of the Grank Trunk people to own a transcontinental line, but if they find out that an arrangement which will be extremely profitable for them is open to them and that the arrangement which they propose and which in my judgment would for many years saddle them with an unprofitable property is not open to them they will come to time.''[86]

Of all the proposals made for purely private construction, this probably had the most to recommend it. Yet Sifton's scheme also had its weaknesses. Simply coupling the two lines as they existed, however economically efficient, would result in most of the ocean port business going via Portland; it would be difficult for the government to force the GTR to use Quebec City via Montreal or a Maritime port via the Intercolonial. A Canadian port was essential for the political success of the scheme and to maximize the economic benefit to Canada. Both Laurier and Fitzpatrick, representing Quebec City, were determined to strengthen their city as a rival to Montreal by a direct line from the Lakehead. Unfortunately such a line would be costly and inherently unproductive, so there was little benefit for the GTR in Sifton's scheme, though he seemed to believe that the sheer volume of traffic to and from the West via the CN would make it profitable.

Laurier might have been interested in Sifton's proposal had the railways been willing to co-operate. Sifton optimistically set off for England, where he interviewed Rivers Wilson and A.W. Smithers, a director of the Grand Trunk, trying to persuade them of the merits of his scheme. ''They talked at me a good deal,'' he told Laurier, ''but I took a pretty firm & independent stand with them.'' His scheme, he said, would result in immediate profits; the ambitious plans of Hays would not. ''They were a bit staggered,'' thought the minister of the interior, and considered his plan seriously. ''They don't take quite such a lofty stand as Mr. Hays & will be much easier to deal with.''[87] He overrated his influence. When Rivers Wilson and Smithers visited Canada and talked with Hays, they were readily won over to his transcontinental ambitions. Neither the CN nor the GTR would compromise willingly, and Laurier was unwilling to force them to co-operate. Perhaps he was merely unwell, but the negotiations were almost directionless in April and May. Blair was being ignored; no other minister stepped into the void; and wearily Laurier requested Sifton to return from England for ''the heavy work'' of the parliamentary session.[88]

At the end of March a private member's bill to incorporate the Grand Trunk Pacific was introduced and subsequently debated by the railway committee. The route was especially controversial, and in June, under pressure from Maritime MPs, the bill was amended to extend the line from Quebec to Moncton. More and more the scheme was taking on the appearance of a ''something-for-everyone'' election measure rather than a coherent, logical, economically sound policy. Desultory negotiations were continued between the CN and GTR until early June. They were broken off when the government indicated that it was going ahead with the CN bond guarantees for the West, leaving the government and Grand Trunk to wrestle over details of the GTPR scheme, particularly the portion of the route from Winnipeg to Quebec and Moncton. Late in June, shortly before Sifton's return, two proposals were being debated by the cabinet. One provided for the Grand Trunk to build the entire transcontinental line, with heavy government subsidies. The second would see the GTPR build from Winnipeg to Port Simpson and the government construct and own the eastern portion of the line, leasing it to the GTPR. This scheme was supported by Mulock and Blair; the former, by most of the rest of the cabinet. Hays believed that the former was about to be adopted, when Sifton arrived on the scene. The minister of the interior promptly threw his weight behind the Mulock-Blair scheme; and a perfect indicator of his influence, and of the indecision of the rest of the cabinet, was Hays's message to Rivers Wilson that the Sifton-supported scheme would "be carried at once unanimously" if the GTR agreed, while insistence upon the other would defer the project. The presence of Sifton, added Hays, gave to the supporters of government ownership "another ally, with, I think I may say, more force and cunning than existed in his absence."[89]

By no means was Sifton a convert to public ownership, per se, though it is worth remembering that he had told Fitzpatrick only months before that if expert opinion recommended extending the government system, he would do it. At this stage, however, there is evidence that he was employing tactics to gain time, to delay operations in 1903 to give the Canadian Northern a greater edge as their construction went ahead. Equally important, as a pragmatic politician Sifton did not believe that the public, particularly in the West, would approve the outright donation of $75,000,000— a minimum cost in all likelihood—to a private railway. If the government was going to expend that money, he believed it better to own the road from Winnipeg to Moncton, lease it to the GTPR, but reserve running rights for other lines such as the CN. He did not believe that Canada could afford two more lines across northern Ontario and Quebec.[90]

Early in July the basis of a compromise was established, one which seems to have pleased very few people. The Grand Trunk Pacific, a wholly owned subsidiary of the GTR, was to construct a line west from Winnipeg to Port Simpson (moved later to Prince Rupert), with substantial bond guarantees by the government. The eastern section, from Winnipeg to Quebec and Moncton, now called the National Transcontinental, was to be built by the government and leased to the GTPR for fifty years, the annual rental to be 3 per cent of the cost of construction.[91] Throughout the negotiation Hays assured Rivers Wilson that the NTR proposals were largely window-dressing for an impending election. He doubted that it would be built. If it were, the GTPR probably would not have to use it very much, because rates could be so adjusted as to force traffic out via the main

GTR lines to Portland.⁹² During July Sifton was intensely involved in the negotiations of the details of the project, though precisely what provisions were the product of his influence is impossible to say. On 29 July the contract was signed; on 30 July Laurier announced the terms in the House of Commons; early in August the GTPR bill was amended in accordance with the contract and shortly passed.⁹³ The debate over the NTR proposals would be much more extended.

It should be emphasized that the Liberal party in these months was by no means united upon the wisdom of the proposed measures. Indeed, it was divided and pessimistic. For Sifton the procedure was not at all the orderly affair he had envisaged. Both government and railway were negotiating without full particulars, the former with an eye on forthcoming elections and the latter with an eye on its nervous British shareholders. Railways Minister Blair had resigned in mid-July, citing among other things a lack of pertinent information on the part of the government. Certainly Sifton must privately have agreed: the government simply did not know what it was getting into.⁹⁴ The loss of Blair also was a blow to Liberal popularity in the West, both because of his general support of government ownership and because of the eminently sensible plea for caution contained in his resignation.⁹⁵ Probably Sifton would have agreed with all but one or two points in the ex-minister's case for resigning. But Blair was the responsible minister, and Laurier had casually ignored his views. Sifton was not directly responsible, and for the time being could hold his peace. Many years later he admitted that the GTPR contract had been "unwise" and the NTR "unnecessary," but he had decided nevertheless to support the government loyally and work for a better contract. "Whether I was justified in waiving my opinion and supporting Laurier's scheme or not I have never been able to decide, but I acted to the best of my judgment."⁹⁶

Upon Blair's resignation, rumours sprang up that Sifton would be his successor. Although circumstantial evidence would suggest that he had wanted it until early in 1903, there is no evidence that he actively sought it in the summer. It is highly unlikely that he would have wished to be made responsible for defending and executing a policy with which he so profoundly disagreed. The possibility nevertheless raised vigorous opposition both in Ontario and in railway circles. Ontario Liberals were acutely sensitive to Sifton's dubious reputation in administering the West and the Yukon. Grand Trunk officials considered that Sifton's appointment would be tantamount to "throwing us over for the Canadian Northern Railway."⁹⁷ Laurier, however, procrastinated. He named Fielding as acting minister, and not until early 1904 did he select the weak and unstable H.R. Emmerson of New Brunswick to fill the vacancy.

The policy having been forced through by Laurier, the ministry had to make the most of it. The Liberal propaganda network swung into action.

The *Free Press* declared that the scheme was the "crowning achievement" of Laurier's political life.[98] Sifton dutifully spoke at length in support of the NTR proposals before departing once more for England and the last phase of the Alaska boundary hearings. The growth of the West and of Canada, he assured the Commons, would certainly make the GTR-NTR scheme a paying success. Prior to his speech the Geological Survey had been scoured for all available scraps of information about the country through which the line was to pass. Skilfully using this data to make it appear as if the government had a fairly clear picture of the situation, he blithely promised the House that a more detailed knowledge of the country could be obtained during construction. Doubtless; but at what cost? He did remind the House that, in spite of excellent surveys, the CPR route had been changed during construction after the contract was approved. There was a clause in the contract to allow other lines, such as the Intercolonial, to use the NTR should they so desire. He argued that the project was popular and would generate a great deal of business throughout its route. It was all pretty thin stuff. Sifton avoided squarely addressing the contract itself, and generally his speech was contrived and unconvincing.[99]

The contract also had to be ratified by the Grand Trunk board. They did not like all the proposals and insisted upon modifications. Probably Sifton had only a limited role in the renewed negotiations. In February 1904, during a brief vacation in the southern United States, he wrote the prime minister, "I am more & more thoroughly convinced that we cannot now make anything of dealing further with the Grand Trunk & that further attempts will result in further discredit." He quoted an old political maxim, "Find out what you would not like your opponent to do if he were in your place & do that." "If I were Borden," he continued, "the last thing I would want you to do would be to take hold of this railway as a national project, put it under a strong commission & push it through."[100] Probably a combination of growing western demands for a government-owned system, combined with difficult negotiations with the GTR had brought him finally to a position of full-fledged government construction and ownership. But the prime minister had already signed a new contract more favourable to the Grand Trunk a few days earlier. Once more when he returned Sifton loyally supported the government and publicly opposed government ownership. When the Opposition supported the latter policy, the *Free Press* denounced the Tories as "coquetting with Socialistic fads." In his own speeches, however, Sifton avoided the subject whenever possible, telling his western supporters that nothing in Borden's speeches committed the Opposition to build the line, while the government was firmly pledged.[101]

During the 1904 parliamentary session Sifton, whom Borden described as the "strongest debater" on the government side, gave a speech of much greater power and conviction than he had the previous August.[102] He was at great pains to defend the financial terms of the contract, after which he addressed himself to the question of government control. As he had done so often in the past, he contended that by exacting certain terms in contracts, beginning with the Crow's Nest Pass Railway, the government had achieved the essential values of public ownership without being put to the expense of constructing and maintaining the railways. It was the merest "humbug" and "delusion" to imagine that the government could begin to afford to build the lines needed all over the North-West. The framework of his speech was nationalism: the policy was a national undertaking which would help "to prevent the life-blood being sucked" from Canadians "by the efforts which are being made to take the traffic to the south. It is true that we cannot change the geography of our country, but we can fight against its disadvantages, and to some extent we can overcome them." This project, combined with waterway improvements, would "practically revolutionize the conditions of transportation in Canada." "Surely," he concluded, "in the presence of the unbounded prosperity of Canada, we cannot afford to say that we will not avail of this opportunity: surely we should push forward to accomplish the successful completion of this great national enterprise."

Therein lay the heart of the case of the Laurier administration. It was built, not on logic, but on emotion. Times were prosperous; prospects for development seemed illimitable; and surely the expanding Canadian economy would support any burden, including two new transcontinental lines, frequently paralleling and duplicating one another's services. For there would be two lines: in light of the government's policy, the Canadian Northern knew it must quickly become transcontinental or perish.[103] Weak and divided in devising policy, the government was imaginative and aggressive in selling it. They were the true prophets of prosperity, the engineers of progress, while the Opposition were men of little faith, pariahs of limited vision. The reality was, however, that when the times cried out for a bold and carefully conceived plan of development, based on sound knowledge and business principles, Laurier had produced only an amalgam of political compromises. Only the prosperity of the times enabled him to foist this policy upon the Canadian people, in the name of faith in the inexhaustible prosperity of the Canadian future.

Nor was it Clifford Sifton's finest hour. His defence of the contracts revealed more about his partisan loyalty than his true sentiments. Probably he saw no reason to resign over a policy the basic features of which he had no part in making. He had tried to influence Laurier to accept a more rational plan; having failed, he concluded that the policy could be sold and that the advantages of power outweighed the very obvious failings of the scheme. The episode also constituted another step in the gradual estrangement between the minister of the interior and the prime minister.

Once again a policy vital to the West and to the nation had been determined principally by the political necessities of central and Maritime Canada. Equally important, while Sifton had gained some minor victories, Laurier plainly was intending to exclude him from the one area of government policy outside his own department in which he had evinced steady and public interest.

5

Defending Canada's Honour:
The Alaska Boundary Tribunal
(1903)

In the midst of the railway negotiations early in 1903 Clifford Sifton was
abruptly thrust into a strange position. He was selected by Sir Wilfrid
Laurier to supervise the drawing up and presentation of the Canadian case
on the Alaska boundary to a Tribunal called to make a final decision on the
vexed issue. For four years he had had almost nothing to do with the negotiations following the failure of the Joint High Commission of 1898-99.
Furthermore, he had been highly critical of this method of setting the dispute, in which the cards appeared to be heavily stacked against the
Dominion. Choosing Sifton proved to be a brilliant strategy on the part of
the prime minister nevertheless, for he knew that the minister of the interior
would take his role as British agent seriously, prepare thoroughly, and
present the Canadian case with such conviction that no one could charge
weakness or timidity in upholding Canada's honour.

In fact, honour was about all that Canada had left to defend in the region.
After 1900 the Yukon rapidly died as a centre of interest to most Canadians.
News from the Territory captured few headlines. People were leaving in
droves, going to rumoured large gold finds at Nome or Atlin or Tanana, or
just simply getting out altogether. Late in 1903 one news despatch from
Dawson reported that the trail to Whitehorse was "black" with departing
people. [1] When agreeing to settlement of the boundary dispute by judicial
tribunal, therefore, the dominion government was more concerned with
saving national honour than achieving the economic ends that had so

preoccupied her in the years 1897-99. The boom that had produced the earlier crisis had passed, and the Americans remained firmly in control of the important areas under dispute. There now was little of practical economic importance to be gained; even if there were, there was almost no chance for success. Could the Tribunal save even national honour for Canada?

With the failure of the joint high commission in 1899, the British and Canadian governments recognized that the boundary dispute would probably be resolved only by some form of international arbitration. This realization materially changed the Canadians' approach to the problem. During the sittings of the commission they had persistently hoped that a suitable compromise could be reached by bartering concessions in other areas. For example, to take Sifton's suggestion at the time, perhaps the United States would give Canada a port on the Lynn Canal and direct access to Canadian territory in return for Canada giving up her claims with respect to pelagic sealing in the Bering Sea. Under such circumstances a detailed legal case documenting Canada's claims seemed almost superfluous. Success or failure depended only slightly on the legalities of the situation, and heavily on political and diplomatic give-and-take.

An arbitration, at least in theory, would reverse the situation. A well-documented case was essential. In June 1899 Laurier asked Joseph Pope, under-secretary of state, to draft a memorandum setting out Canada's claims. Two or three weeks later a dismayed Pope complained to Sir John Anderson, the Colonial Office official in charge of Canadian affairs, "it is a case of making bricks without straw. I find the greatest difficulty in collecting the papers necessary to a proper understanding of the case." Could not the basic published documents be sent to Canada? "Alaska matters," he added, "have been always referred to the Minister of the Interior, and though I say it with bated breath, never properly dealt with. We sadly lack system here."[2] In fairness to Sifton, it ought to be noted that what Pope wanted was chiefly Foreign Office material of the sort that the dominions had had little cause (or right) to consult up to that time.[3] Neither Canada nor the United States had developed their case by 1899 with the care and detail that they would use thereafter.

When it was necessary in the fall of 1899 to send a member of the government to London to assist in making a case at that stage, Laurier chose, not Sifton, but Sir Louis Davies, minister of marine and fisheries and a member of the recently failed commission. Davies found that Canada was already in an awkward corner. The Americans offered the dominion a lease of land for a port and railway from Pyramid Harbour on Lynn Canal to Canadian territory; the offer was as far as the United States could go, but the Canadian government knew that anything short of outright sovereignty would be politically dangerous.[4] Consequently, the offer was rejected. When an arbitration was suggested, Canada found that it would not be acceptable to the United States unless continued possession of Dyea and Skagway be guaranteed in advance, with possible monetary compensation should the Canadian contention be upheld. Canada countered, somewhat unrealistically, that she should similarly be guaranteed in advance possession of Pyramid Harbour; since the Americans already controlled the harbour, the case was clearly different and the Canadian offer naturally was spurned. Again for Canada it would have been politically impossible to accept an arbitration in which the basic decisions had been made in advance and contrary to the Canadian contention. Finally in October 1899 a modus vivendi was agreed upon, setting a temporary boundary at the summits of the White and Chilkoot passes and at the confluence of the Klehini and Chilkat Rivers on the way to the Chilkat Pass.[5]

Canada had been altogether excluded from the Lynn Canal. Laurier hoped that time would work out a more satisfactory (or politically less dangerous) solution. The British were angry at what they took to be Canada's lack of realism in refusing the lease. The Americans were going to hold fast to what they possessed, regardless of the legal niceties, and the Canadians ought to realize and accept this, despite what they believed their legal rights to be or the political risks entailed. The next two years saw prolonged and difficult negotiations over a satisfactory form of arbitration. Laurier agreed reluctantly in 1901 to the principle of an even-numbered tribunal. He was under pressure to reach a settlement, and the British were attempting to persuade him that the Canadian case was weak in the Lynn Canal area, but reasonably strong on the southern boundary along the Portland Canal. However Canada still requested that at least one arbitrator on each side should be from a neutral country, asked for several modifications in the language of the proposed draft treaty, and wanted the arbitrators to resolve six issues: 1. the southern point of commencement of the boundary; 2. the location of Portland Canal; 3. the boundary between the southern tip and the mouth of Portland Canal; 4. the boundary north to the 56th parallel; 5. which mountains constituted the chain of mountains parallel to the coast, referred to in the Treaty of St. Petersburg; 6. whether the boundary followed the general outline or the sinuosities of the coast.[6]

Negotiations dragged on, but from the fall of 1901 in a drastically changed atmosphere. The assassination of President McKinley brought Theodore Roosevelt to the American presidency. His forthright aggressiveness, his known impatience with Canada for pushing its weak case, his obvious willingness to march in troops to back up American claims in disputed territory, all made a quick solution seem imperative. In May 1902 Lord Minto privately told an American correspondent that his ministers had given up any hope of a salt-water port, and "would I believe be satisfied with any small concession to save their 'amour propre'..this cd. probably be most easily obtained at the Portland Canal end of the frontier."[7] Probably this was true enough; the issue for the Canadian government was how to give way to the Americans while saving Canada's face.

Evidently Sifton and four or five of his cabinet colleagues told Laurier before he left for the coronation of Edward VII and the colonial conference in 1902 that he must hold firm for an arbitration commission with an odd number of members, one of whom would be a neutral "umpire" capable of casting a deciding vote.[8] Whatever his pledges to his ministers before departing, Laurier made a complete about-face from his position of the preceding three years while he was in London. In effect, Lord Lansdowne, the British foreign secretary, told the American ambassador that Canada did not now want a port on Lynn Canal and that she would accept the American formula for a tribunal—essentially three British and three American jurists who would fulfil a more judicial than arbitral function.[9] Sifton and his colleagues felt betrayed. Yet given the difficulty with Israel Tarte, the poor state of Sir Wilfrid's health, and pressing domestic matters, they concluded that it was not possible to stage a revolt without endangering the government. For several weeks, nonetheless, they badgered Laurier unsuccessfully to fight for more favourable terms.[10]

On 24 January 1903 the Hay-Herbert Treaty was signed by the American secretary of state and the British ambassador to Washington. It called for each side to select three "impartial jurists of repute," who would decide by majority vote the questions put before them. The questions proposed by Canada in 1901 were used with some modifications, but the jurists were also to decide the basic problem of whether or not the United States was entitled to a continuous *lisière* along the coast.[11] The two sides were to exchange cases within two months of ratification, counter-cases within a further two months, and then to have opportunity to argue and clarify their cases before the tribunal within yet a further two months. Each side also would have an agent to supervise the preparation and presentation of its case.

Laurier had scarcely begun to think out the composition of the British side. Minto, characteristically, considered that there was "no one big enough in Canada" for the task of British agent, and he suggested the British Lord Chief Justice, Lord Alverstone. Laurier also seemed inclined to accept two British arbitrators and only one Canadian.[12] Eventually Alverstone became the sole British arbitrator, and two Canadians were selected, Sir Louis Jetté, a former judge, and Justice George Armour of Ontario. No decision was made about the agent until early March, when with little forewarning Laurier chose Sifton.[13]

The minister of the interior could not have been chosen for his diplomatic qualities or his sympathies with the proceedings. Less than two weeks after the signing of the Hay-Herbert Treaty he bluntly told Dafoe:

> The British Government deliberately decided about a year ago to sacrifice our interests at any cost for the sake of pleasing the United States. All their proceedings since that time were for the sake of inveigling us into a position from which we could not retire. I am bound to say that we have been pretty easy prey but the result probably would have been the same in any event, as it simply gets down to a very narrow question. The United States would not recede, and England would not take any chances of a quarrel.
>
> It is, however, the most cold blooded case of absolutely giving away our interests without even giving us the excuse of saying we have had a fight for it which I know of, and I do not see any reason why the Canadian press should not make itself extremely plain upon the subject. My view in watching the diplomacy of Great Britain as affecting Canada for six years is that it may just as well be decided in advance that practically whatever the United States demands from England will be conceded in the long run, and the Canadian people might as well make up their minds to that now.[14]

His bitterness, and that of the government, redoubled when the American arbitrators were announced. President Roosevelt had never accepted the idea of a truly impartial arbitration, and he had been forced to make highly partisan choices in any case to secure senate approval for the treaty.[15] Senators Henry Cabot Lodge and George Turner were already strongly and publicly committed in favour of the American case, while Elihu Root, secretary of war, naturally was expected to uphold the position of the administration. Such choices made an utter mockery of the judicial process and sparked Canada's near withdrawal from the proceedings. As seen, the Laurier government did not anticipate winning much in any event, and the entire procedure had validity only insofar as it would create the impression that Canada was losing by fair and impartial decision. But Roosevelt's prejudiced appointments removed even this face-saving feature. Sifton and Fitzpatrick each drafted strong replies to the American procedure — so strong that in Laurier's opinion the result of using them would have been Canadian withdrawal. In light of the fact that the British had ratified the Treaty before announcing the identities of Roosevelt's arbitrators and because he believed that the dispute must be terminated even at the loss of some national pride, Laurier concluded that Canada must fulfil her part of the agreement.[16] Such, then, were the circumstances when Sifton assumed the post of British agent; he was determined to make the strongest possible fight for the Canadian case.

The circumstances also made it essential that the Canadian public not entertain too high hopes about the result. Just prior to leaving New York for London, Sifton mailed a carefully written news story to be printed in the *Manitoba Free Press*, Toronto *Globe*, and Montreal *Herald*, and subsequently throughout the Liberal newspaper network, with the purpose of conditioning the public reaction. Three basic questions were said to be at stake: the boundary at the Portland Canal; the width of the American coastal strip; and the ownership of the heads of large inlets, particularly the Lynn Canal. Canadian and American claims were set out with admirable clarity and brevity. The issue about the location of the Portland Canal boundary was said to be important because of the strategic location of the disputed Wales and Pearse Islands, commanding Port Simpson and Observatory Inlet where the new transcontinental railway was expected to terminate. The width of the lisière along the coast was important because of the possible discovery of gold or other minerals in the disputed territory. The question of Canada's claim to the heads of inlets, Sifton admitted with surprising candour, had "been to some extent compromised by official neglect and indifference and also by acts of jurisdiction and occupation on the part of the United States. It will unquestionably be most difficult to secure recognition of our view of this claim, but it will be fully pressed and argued before the Tribunal."[17] With its very neutrality on the first two questions, and admission of Canadian weakness on the third, the article left serious doubts about the Canadian chances of success.

Sifton and his party sailed for London on 24 March aboard *Kronprinz Wilhelm*, arriving a week later. Immediately the Canadians, aided by Sir John Anderson and British counsel, plunged into the task of preparing the case. Rapid progress was made, and Sifton wrote to Laurier, "The staff I brought are working excellently. None could do better. The British people (officials) have done every thing possible to help us....We have a desperate time to get ready within the time limited [sic] but shall succeed no doubt if everyone does not collapse from overwork before it is done." The only personnel problem was Edward Blake, former Canadian Liberal leader, now residing in Britain where he was an Irish MP and an eminent London barrister. Canada undertook to pay a high fee of $30,000 for his brilliance and prestige, but he was both difficult and unwell. He was "by turns excessively courteous & considerate and overbearing and intolerable," reported Sifton. "He is an impossible man. I am handling him as diplomatically as possible."[18] Despite the pressure, the Canadian case was filed within a month, on 1 May 1903.[19]

The compliments were returned by those who worked with the British agent. "No man could have done better than Mr. Sifton," wrote Joseph Pope some years later.[20] Sir John Anderson told Lord Minto that Sifton was "very capable and an excellent man for business, and we are getting along well together."[21] Minto replied that he considered Sifton "to be the ablest man in the Cabinet" and growing in influence. "I have always found him well worth listening to on any subject—& he decidedly knows his own mind," added the governor general, "but of the Yukon & the N.W. I think you know!"[22] Indeed, Minto seems to have done everything possible to ensure that Sifton would receive a cool reception in British society. "I wonder if you met Sifton," he asked his brother Arthur Elliot; "I see he has been made much of—as was quite right...he is very able...but absolutely unscrupulous." Perhaps as a result of these reports Sifton was distinctly snubbed; the Prince and Princess of Wales invited Joseph Pope to lunch and were "intimate" with him but they "would not see" Sifton.[23]

The Canadians did not receive the American case until 11 May, when once more they plunged into feverish activity to prepare the counter-case, due to be filed early in July. At this point the failure of the Canadians and British to prepare adequately over the previous years became painfully obvious. No one on the British side matched the diplomatic experience or the close connection with the question over five years that at least three men on the American side possessed. More significantly, when the American case was presented, the Canadians demanded the right to photograph and examine the originals of nearly 40 per cent of the American documentation — a sad commentary on the work of the previous four years. The request irritated the Americans, who refused to allow any extensions of the time limit as provided for in the treaty and requested by the Canadians.[24] In the final analysis these problems probably had little effect on the final decisions of the tribunal; they do suggest the inexperience of Canada and the limited interest of Britain. Very revealing too was the attitude of Sir Wilfrid Laurier, who wrote Sifton in late May, "I took a look into the American case some few days ago. There is nothing in it, very new, very exciting or very strong. Your reply will be comparatively easy work, & as soon as you have got through it, I would want you to hasten your return home."[25]

Comparatively easy work! The prime minister, so distant from the scene, had little perception of the frantic pace of the Canadians and British as they checked and double-checked each comma and period of the American case, each syllable of translations from Russian documents, probing for even slight weaknesses and advantages. A momentum developed, a belief in the soundness of the Canadian case, almost an exhilaration in the conviction that it was stronger and the American case weaker than they had at first dared hope. This would be especially true if they could persuade the tribunal, or at least Lord Alverstone, that the decision should be based on an interpretation of the Treaty of St. Petersburg of 1825 and subsequent diplomatic documents and that "extraneous" items such as possession of disputed territory or various maps showing one claim or another were irrelevant. But such factors were not irrelevant, nor was the Canadian interpretation of the treaty as indisputable as they hoped. The Canadians realized that they had practically no prospects of persuading the Americans. Was there a chance that Alverstone would accept the dominion arguments and force a drawn Tribunal? "In that case," wrote Sifton, "the United States Government would have a fair reason to present to the Senate for some kind of compromise, after which, if we wanted reciprocity discussion we could have it."[26]

It was the mentality of 1898-99 cropping up again. Sifton was not seeking reciprocity per se; he mentioned it because it was a topic of public debate at the time. He wanted some significant concession in return for what he knew was the inevitable conclusion that the Americans would not be moved from territory that they occupied. What he did not know — indeed, what no Canadian apparently realized until well after the proceedings — was that President Roosevelt had already decided against any compromise and had begun a vigorous diplomatic initiative to ensure a favourable decision. The legal niceties of the argument would appear to have been more and more irrelevant.

Sifton nevertheless remained in London until the first draft of the counter-case had been completed, departing for Canada on 17 June. Junior Counsel F.C. Wade was left in charge of preparing the final draft and, once it had been submitted, beginning work on the analysis of the American counter-case and preparation of the argument to be made to the Tribunal.[27] Sifton was in Canada scarcely two months before it was necessary to re-embark to supervise the final preparations and the argument itself. It had not been an uneventful summer, so far as the Alaska boundary question was concerned. Following the death of Justice Armour, Sifton recommended the appointment to the tribunal of Allen Aylesworth. The latter was chosen partly because he was already in England and partly because Sifton regarded him as "no doubt the foremost lawyer in Canada at the present time."[28] Also during the summer Roosevelt stepped up his diplomatic offensive, bluntly threatening in a private letter that should the tribunal fail to settle the boundary, he would "run the line as we claim it...without any further regard to the attitude of England and Canada."[29] This and other evidences of the American president's belligerence were passed on to the British authorities, ultimately reaching the ears of Alverstone himself, as was intended. The Canadians too were trying one way and another to persuade him that it was practically his imperial duty to side with the Dominion. Of course Canada could not wield as big a stick as the United States; yet it is arguable that Alverstone resisted the pressure from both sides in his search for a realistic and fair compromise.[30]

For it *was* compromise, not a judicial decision between two contending

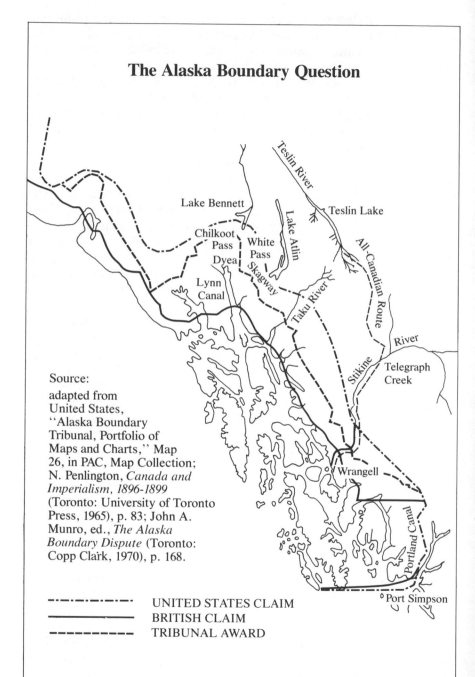

The Alaska Boundary Question

Source:

adapted from United States, "Alaska Boundary Tribunal, Portfolio of Maps and Charts," Map 26, in PAC, Map Collection; N. Penlington, *Canada and Imperialism, 1896-1899* (Toronto: University of Toronto Press, 1965), p. 83; John A. Munro, ed., *The Alaska Boundary Dispute* (Toronto: Copp Clark, 1970), p. 168.

—·—·—·—·—·—·   UNITED STATES CLAIM
——————————   BRITISH CLAIM
— — — — — — —   TRIBUNAL AWARD

sides, that Alverstone had decided would provide the key to a solution. Five days before the oral argument began on 18 September, he asked Pope confidentially what Canada would accept. Would she accept a favourable decision on the Portland Channel and a "mountain line" if she lost on the question of the heads of inlets?[31] Pope thought not, reflecting Sifton's preference for an evenly divided tribunal. A few days later, however, Pope did tell Alverstone that such a solution would be acceptable, for Canada would be able to claim nearly as great a "victory" as the United States.[32] The rumour mill was working overtime as the argument commenced, and Sifton believed that Alverstone had conceded the American case on heads of inlets in advance "and that this concession would enable the Americans to hold out for the mountain range and Portland Canal."[33] He told Anderson that Alverstone must be instructed either to bring about a deadlock or to seek a postponement of the hearings until after the next American election. Anderson quite properly resisted issuing orders to Alverstone, but he did approach him to assure him that Sifton would be satisfied with a favourable decision on the Portland Canal and a compromise mountain line. Alverstone reportedly replied, "I can do much better for him than that."[34] Sifton was placated. He also was very happy with the efforts of the British counsel arguing the case: "Nobody need have any fear that everything that it is possible to say on our side is not going to be said and in, I think, the best way."[35] So sure of the soundness of the Canadian position was he that he told Laurier, "If we had an impartial tribunal we should certainly win."[36]

Early in October Sifton began again to believe that Alverstone intended to side with the Americans; he told Laurier that Jetté and Aylesworth were so "exasperated" that they were considering withdrawing.[37] At once Laurier replied that withdrawal was unthinkable and that they should fight at least for Canada's contention on the Portland Canal. He concluded, "If we are thrown over by Chief Justice, he will give the last blow to British diplomacy in Canada. He should be plainly told this by our commissioners."[38]

During these difficult days Alverstone was subjected to a barrage of American pressure, but he refused to allow the full American claim on the lisière. Faced with his intransigence on this subject, the Americans began to press for a compromise on the Portland Canal. They knew that the two large islands, Pearse and Wales, must belong to Canada, but the two smaller western islands, Sitklan and Kannaghunut could be used as a "make-weight," according to Roosevelt. Finally, much to the shock of the Canadians, Alverstone accepted this compromise of a boundary along Tongass Passage, dividing the western and eastern islands on Portland Canal. Only a few days previously Alverstone had assured the Canadians in writing that all four islands would be Canadian. Now he accepted a boundary for which no one had argued in the cases, counter-cases, or oral arguments. In the one area where Canada had hoped to claim complete victory she had been rudely denied. Directly Sifton concluded that the decision destroyed the strategic value of Wales and Pearse islands and that the verdict was "wholly unsatisfactory." It was, agreed Laurier, "one of those concessions which have made British diplomacy odious to [the] Canadian people and it will have [the] most lamentable effect."[39]

What, finally, did the tribunal decide, and how did it affect Canada? First, in the north, Canada was wholly excluded from Lynn Canal. The modus vivendi of 1899 was maintained at the White and Chilkoot passes, but on the Chilkat River the line was moved twenty miles farther inland—a substantial concession to the Americans. Also, in a major victory for the United States, the tribunal concluded that the Americans possessed all the heads of inlets along the coast and were entitled to an unbroken lisière, though not all the details were filled in between the Stikine River and the Taku River. Yet, even though there was no clearly defined chain of coastal mountains, the tribunal accepted the idea that the boundary should follow the summits of the mountains nearest the sea—a partial victory for Canada. At the south end, the Canadian contention that the Portland Canal ran north of the islands was basically accepted, despite the decision to run the line along Tongass Paasage, thus granting Sitklan and Kannaghunut as sops to the Americans.[40]

Looked at objectively, and with the benefit of hindsight, the decision may be regarded as fair under the circumstances. The Americans did not obtain the extreme version of their claims, yet the award favouring them probably constituted a reasonable interpretation of the Treaty of St. Petersburg. Even though there might have been room for other views, Canada's case had been weakened, as Sifton himself had admitted, by "official neglect and indifference" and by inexperience. Canada did not have to give up as much land along the lisière as she might have expected, and she did gain uncontested title to Wales and Pearse islands. More important, the danger of continuous friction with the United States was removed, to the relief of officials in all three countries involved.

That, of course, was not how the award appeared to Canadians in 1903. They objected strenuously both to the award itself and to the method by which it was decided. The claim about the strategic value of the two lost islands was indefensible, and before long the government was soft-pedalling that aspect of the protest.[41] The concession of the two smaller islands nevertheless prevented Canada from being able to claim total victory on any of the issues under dispute. This was especially hard to swallow because the Americans had secured everything basic to their claim. The decision on the islands symbolized the general sense of defeat for Canada. It was not a judicial decision, but a political compromise.

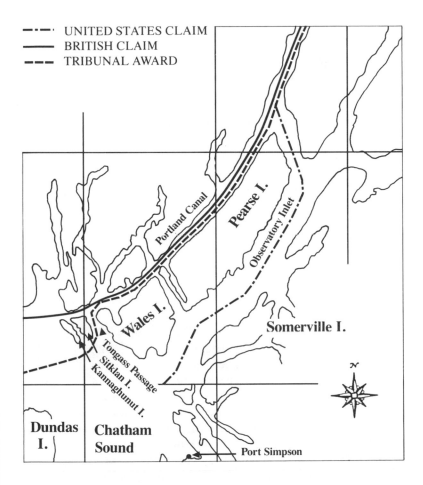

The Portland Canal Question, 1903

--·--· UNITED STATES CLAIM
———— BRITISH CLAIM
--- -- TRIBUNAL AWARD

Portland Canal

Pearse I.

Observatory Inlet

Wales I.

Somerville I.

Tongass Passage

Sitklan I.

Kannaghunut I.

Dundas I.

Chatham Sound

Port Simpson

Source: adapted from United States, "Alaska Boundary Tribunal,
    Portfolio of Maps and Charts," Map 30, in PAC, Map
    Collection.

Alverstone was perceived to have capitulated to diplomatic pressures, to have gone back on his word, to have sold out Canada to placate the greedy, grasping Americans. His compromise became an excuse for venting the pent-up sense of helplessness and outrage that developed as Canada was gradually manoeuvred by the two great powers into accepting the tribunal. Certainly the government took a strong stand, claiming that Canada could better look after her interests abroad than could Britain. This undoubtedly was partly for political effect. Yet for Sifton, and for many who agreed with him, the colonial mantle was beginning to feel more like a straightjacket. "The decision," he wrote, "unfortunately appears to have been a foregone conclusion."[42] To his old friend Isaac Campbell he observed, "My impression is that we were entirely given away before we started, perhaps not deliberately but in such a way as to bring about the same effect. The intention was, no doubt, from the English standpoint, to see that there was an award that would be binding, and would thus get the question out of the way of British diplomats." In a subsequent, more mellow mood he added, "The net result of the Alaskan business is that we have two islands which we would not have had if we had not arbitrated. Nevertheless the way Lord Alverstone acted was very exasperating."[43]

Upon his return to Canada, Sifton was interviewed by Lord Minto. He told the governor general that he had taken great pains to inform Alverstone that Canada did not want "an award and...a final settlement" at any price. Diplomacy, he had assured the lord chief justice, could be expected to resolve the question in the event of failure of the Tribunal to agree. Sifton thought that while Alverstone had listened courteously, he "set no value" upon these views.[44] Thus it may be seen that Sifton had at least remained consistent. Almost certainly Laurier did not agree with him, and Alverstone understood this very well. The British government believed that Laurier was anxious for almost any settlement. Lord Minto's earlier conversations with the prime minister in the latter part of 1902 and early 1903 suggest this strongly, confirming the impression Laurier had made while in Britain during 1902. He was worried about Roosevelt's belligerent mood and the potential difficulties should gold be discovered in disputed territory. All this information Minto faithfully passed on to London and to the British ambassador in Washington. So it happened that Laurier was willing to accept a tribunal on terms which he had formerly rejected and to accept under protest American abuse of the intended judicial nature of the tribunal. While he subsequently denied his ready compliance with these conditions, placing the blame with British diplomacy, there can be no doubt that both American and British authorities understood that Laurier wanted virtually any settlement, preferably in a form justifiable to the Canadian public. Joseph Chamberlain may well have been correct when he later suggested, "My own belief is that Sir Wilfrid wanted to settle almost at any price, but he wanted at the same time to throw the blame of any concession on to our shoulders."[45] In this, Laurier succeeded.

Sifton, by contrast, had been for a hard line. He had not fought the case as hard as he did in the expectation that Canada need lose everything. His reaction to the award was more than posturing; he was honestly irritated at Canada's colonial situation, the British attitude, and American aggressiveness. Canada was powerless, the British for their own interests were anxious for a settlement, and the Americans were simply out to grab territory wherever they could. To one correspondent he wrote:

> It is beyond a question that the cold blooded and somewhat super-cilious conduct of our English friends has had a profound effect upon Canadian opinion. There has not been much said that was not fully justified by the facts....I regard it as out of the question that the representatives of Canada as it exists today will be content to do business in the way in which it has been done, and...a somewhat radical readjustment will be required before a great while. I do not see why the aspirations of the young men of Canada for independence should be either suppressed or ridiculed. There are many countries much less strong in population and resources who find no difficulty in managing their own affairs.[46]

In a strongly worded speech to the Ottawa Canadian Club on 7 December, he spoke of the need to improve Canadian defences because in future Britain could not be relied upon. In a letter to Dafoe he added that this was the only way Canada could resist being forcibly annexed to the United States. "The Yankees have simply got a lust for power territory & expenditure," he warned, "& they are going to be the biggest bully the world has ever seen."[47] He had to be guarded in his own public remarks, he told Professor Adam Shortt of Queen's University. But Canada was "able to navigate commercially alone," and it was important to make Canadians realize that she could be self-reliant. "I should be very glad," he wrote, "to see those who are in a position to speak freely on the subject without being misunderstood give a decided lead in that direction."[48]

The experience of the Alaska Boundary Tribunal was a turning-point in Sifton's thinking about Canada's destiny in the British Empire. Previously he had exhibited only vague opinions, being annoyed at Lord Minto's pretensions, for example, or privately cynical about imperial enthusiasm during the Boer War. He had believed in the imperial connection only insofar as it was of practical advantage to Canada. In 1903 he experienced first-hand what he considered to be a calculated sacrifice of Canadian interests on the altar of Anglo-American amity. It was not the award itself that was so serious; while fervently hoping for more, Sifton must have understood the likely outcome from the beginning. It was what the method and attitude symbolized which was of concern. Canada could not count on Britain. She would have to begin active preparations to enable herself to look after her own interests. The British connection must become much more informal, a thing of self-interest and sentiment, in no way binding or constricting Canadian growth.[49]

Certainly Sifton saw danger in the British connection. Yet he was equally uneasy about Canada's relations with the United States. Experience had shown that the Americans could not be trusted. They were power-hungry bullies, snatching territory wherever possible. The Canadian position on the Alaska boundary question and the final award, and indeed much of the Yukon administration, cannot be understood without taking this sentiment into account. Citizens of the Dominion may have envied and copied much in the American experience, but they disliked and mistrusted what they conceived to be the essential American character. Between 1897 and 1899 Sifton's anti-Americanism had hardened substantially. The United States had undermined Canadian trade with the Yukon and the possibility of an all-Canadian route. She had controlled, illegally in Sifton's opinion, the ports leading to the Yukon and insisted upon an unjustifiably extreme version of the boundary. She had tried to press the boundary back over the White Pass, a course only narrowly averted by Sifton's decisive action. It had been necessary to take a strong stand to protect Canadian interests during the meetings of the Joint High Commission. It would be so again.

Sifton had much stronger anti-American sentiments than did the prime minister. He could agree with Laurier's stand on the British connection. But when the prime minister appeared cowed by American bluster and threats, Sifton stood firm for asserting Canadian rights. He probably was the strongest apostle of nationalism in the cabinet, though others— Fielding, Blair, Davies, Mills, Tarte, and Fitzpatrick—frequently agreed with him. It is probable that Laurier would have reached an accommodation with the Americans in 1898-99 had it not been for Sifton, who organized the cabinet resistance. Laurier himself told Minto that he had only succeeded by a hair's breadth in overcoming cabinet opposition, led by Sifton and Fielding, to proceeding with the tribunal in 1903.[50]

Behind this cabinet crisis lay a background of continuing friction between the two countries. Late in 1901 reports reached Ottawa that attempts were being made to foment an uprising among American miners, who predominated in the southern Yukon. The NWMP, first alerted in September, were convinced by November that a conspiracy did indeed exist, inspired from Skagway. Sifton took immediate measures to strengthen the force. Officially the stories that reached the press were discounted as rumours, but a large supply of guns and ammunition was quietly rushed in, and the number of police in the Whitehorse and Dalton Trail areas was doubled. Every effort was made not to antagonize American officials as arms and men were sent in. Perhaps the mere knowledge of Canadian preparedness discouraged any more trouble.[51] Subsequently, reacting to reports of unrest among the miners in southern Alaska, President Roosevelt moved troops into the panhandle region in March 1902, intensifying the tension along the border.[52] Discovery of American storehouses erected on Wales and Pearse islands also angered Canadian authorities, since the islands were still in dispute.[53]

These experiences caused Sifton to become anxious about Canada's title to the Arctic islands, where for years American whalers had been operating, wintering, and trading with the native people.[54] In 1902 a plan for sending police down the Mackenzie River and into the Yukon was abandoned at the last minute because of other priorities for the force. It was revived late in the year, this time with the express object of establishing a permanent post in the Mackenzie delta region, showing the flag and confirming Canadian sovereignty. A report submitted to Sifton by Smart, Comptroller F. White of the Police, Commissioner McDougald of the Customs Department, and Dr. Bell of the Geological Survey led him to conclude "that it is necessary for this Government to take immediate steps to establish such posts as may be necessary for the assertion of its authority, over the territory in question[,] respecting the right to which there is of course no dispute." He recommended the preparation of two expeditions, one each in the eastern and western Arctic, to establish permanent posts and customs collection. He outlined a detailed plan of action, suggesting that the expeditions "should be conducted by the Marine & Fisheries Department as part of its Coast service." As soon as possible in the spring of 1903 the expeditions should set out.[55] Before sailing for England in March 1903, Sifton told Smart to see that the government obtained the co-operation of the opposition so that the appropriation would not be questioned and the operation could be carried out quietly. He also prepared an innocuous press release to ensure that no embarrassing questions would be raised about the real intent of the expeditions.[56]

During the voyage to Britain, Sifton became more concerned than previously. Conversing with W.F. King, the official who had done much of the research on Canada's claim to the Arctic islands, he discovered that her title was more tenuous than he had believed. "Extreme care must be taken to make the whole work as thorough and complete as possible," he wrote upon his arrival in London. "Herschell Island near the mouth of the Mackenzie also requires attention. American whalers are there and unless decisive action is taken very soon we shall run up against another boundary question along these waters.''[57] With the ready co-operation of the opposition, the project was quickly passed by Parliament, and the expeditions set forth as Sifton had directed.[58]

Upon his return from England in the fall, he received a report on the season's operations. He then asked Comptroller White to make recommendations concerning possible further actions.[59] Meanwhile a friend of Sifton on the Geological Survey, H.M. Ami, set about writing to Laurier and Fitzpatrick, suggesting that the only way to ensure Canadian sovereignty in the far north was for Britain to make a full and detailed declaration. Laurier disagreed; the best way, in his opinion, was for Canada to quietly establish a presence there before issuing any proclamation.[60] The prime minister feared that the Americans might have had posts established for years on Canadian territory quite unknown to the government; he also was apprehensive that the United States might take offence at the collection of customs duties in the Arctic.[61] Sifton concluded that a thorough review of the situation was essential, and he asked King to prepare ''an exhaustive report upon the title to all our Northern Islands.'' He added, ''After the experience that we had in connection with the Alaska Boundary you will know without difficulty what I require.''[62] Sifton also requested another increase in the size of the NWMP to handle their expanding duties in the north. He found, however, that Laurier was not seized with the urgency that he felt and had to be prodded several times in 1904 before anything was done.[63] Sifton can be credited nevertheless with making some of the earliest attempts to establish a credible, continuous Canadian presence in the far north.

6

Concessions in the Klondike
(1901-1905)

The appointment of James Hamilton Ross as Yukon commissioner was a masterstroke. For the first time Sifton enjoyed a brief respite from the harping chorus of complaint emanating from the gold fields. The new commissioner's rapid grasp of the issues and his clear and full reports to Sifton demonstrated an uncommon ability. Ross could make independent judgments and was not easily swayed either by popular opinion or by pressure from above—including Sifton. He weeded out and reorganized the bureaucratic structure, suggested many reforms in mining legislation, exhibited a remarkable flexibility in administering the law, and demonstrated an appreciation of the unique frontier character of the community. Yet his term in the Yukon was one of personal tragedy: in August 1901, his wife, child, and niece were drowned in a boat disaster off the British Columbia coast. Eleven months later he suffered a partially paralytic stroke while travelling from Dawson to Whitehorse, from which he never fully recovered and which forced him to resign in the fall of 1902, only eighteen months after he had assumed his new post.[1]

"It is a pleasure to be able to say now that the laws are neither 'old nor obsolete,' but are a credit to the Canadian government," wrote H.J. Woodside, a Yukon journalist, to Laurier shortly before Ross arrived. "We seem to be entering another era of greater development and prosperity, and everyone here now is an optimist. Since the country and claims have been thrown open, it has been almost one steady stampede to the old and new creeks."² Undoubtedly, the happy reception of Ross was stimulated by the halving of the royalty on gold announced early in 1901, by the sense in the previous months that Ottawa at last was beginning to respond to Yukon grievances, and by the fact that Ross was known to have Sifton's ear. From the beginning the minister of the interior backed the new commissioner. He asked that all government business be conducted through the commissioner because he was "the Chief Executive Officer of the Government, not of the Department of the Interior alone but of every Department, and he is responsible for the carrying on of the business of the Government in every Department."³ To aid in the bureaucratic reorganization Sifton sent one of his most trusted officials, W.W. Cory; and he secured an expert, A.L. Beaudette, to assess mining and engineering problems.

After three years of Ogilvie's lax control, Ross found that his first task upon arriving was to persuade the local civil servants to follow policy set out by Ottawa rather than devise their own. He believed that the service was overmanned and, moreover, not of the best quality. The staff had remained large while the population declined sharply, and patronage had been for too long the overriding factor in appointments. Ross also complained that "very many of the officials have been at all times largely mixed up in mining property," an undesirable practice that he wanted curtailed.⁴

The most distressing discovery was that, despite Sifton's directive to Ogilvie to clean up the gold commissioner's office "at all costs," nothing had been done. Indeed the assistant gold commissioner, J. Langlois Bell, who ran the office, was a distinct embarrassment to the government. Records were badly kept and poorly indexed, clerks were found freely altering the records, business was conducted inefficiently, and officials were giving advice on matters "with regard to which applicants should not have been advised by the Office." Bell exceeded and altered his orders regularly, selling claims which he was not authorized to sell, causing later embarrassing cancellations. He actively supported individual miners opposed to the large mining concessions established by the government, encouraging them to stake and record claims on concession properties. Finally, he had made no serious effort to enforce the royalty on gold production because he believed it was a badly framed law. "Although reputed to be a strong man intellectually and morally," commented Sifton some time later, Bell "was not able to stand the temptation which was placed in his way, and I was compelled to retire him summarily."⁵

The dismissal of Bell was merely the most dramatic of the changes in the Yukon civil service, changes that brought home to the officials the fact that Ottawa would no longer tolerate deviations from declared policy. Ross was not merely engaged in firing the incompetent. He can only have improved morale by supporting demands for higher allowances for those who deserved them to help combat the very high cost of living in the Territory.⁶

And neither he nor Cory failed to be blunt in their comments to Sifton when occasion demanded it:

> I am of the opinion [wrote Cory] that the present Mining Inspectors have not had the technical teaching and experience necessary to properly fit them for the position they occupy. For instance, the proper timbering of drifts and shafts is of the utmost importance in respect to the safe-guarding of the lives of those working in them. I think I am safe in stating that not a single man, now holding the position of Mining Inspector in the Yukon, ever saw a shaft or drift properly timbered. Several lives have been lost in the Territory already owing to defective timbering. Then, again, the matter of underground engineering; none of the present inspectors have any knowledge of this at all. [7]

It must have taken some courage to write in such language to a minister who had not hesitated to appoint a rancher and a whaling captain as mining inspectors. The statement stands as a damning indictment of the principles of the government in appointing unqualified political supporters to posts of such vital importance to the lives and welfare of people in the Yukon. Lord Minto had commented acerbically in 1900, "The Dominion Govt. seem to have looked upon the Yukon as a source of revenue, as a place to make as much out of as they could, & have used the proceeds largely for political corruption instead of the development of the country, & in so doing are in a fair way to kill the goose that laid the golden egg." [8] Even if the ministry itself was not benefitting as much personally as Minto suspected, the attitude to the appointment and behaviour of officials certainly bears out his sentiments.

Ross presided over a reorganization of the Yukon government, including the incorporation of Dawson as a city. He personally carried to Ottawa appeals for reform, including increased elected membership in the Territorial Council and representation in Parliament. Sifton conceded both during the 1902 session, also giving more authority to the commissioner-in-council, including control of the liquor traffic. [9] Ross also was instrumental in persuading Sifton, as no one else had been able to do, to abandon the royalty on gold production. Halving the royalty had only been welcomed by Yukoners as a sign of government responsiveness. As Ross found, it did not produce more revenue, for miners already in the habit of "beating" the government by false declarations were unlikely to change their habits. He recommended an export tax of 3 per cent as much easier to administer and less likely to be resented. Cory concurred with Ross, and finally Sifton yielded, setting a 2.5 per cent export tax in 1902. [10]

Strangely for a man who had made so much of the need to secure a portion of the profits of Yukon mining for Canada, Sifton had done nothing to keep the gold in Canada. There was, prior to 1901, neither an assay office nor a mint to process the gold. The result was that almost all of the gold mined in the Yukon in those years went to the United States, where assay offices were readily available in Seattle and San Francisco. Yukoners had been demanding an assay office in Dawson for some time, but perhaps owing to countervailing pressure from the chartered banks[11] and to agitation in Vancouver, for location of the assay office there, Sifton announced in 1901 that an office would be located in the west coast city. In the same year Parliament at last provided for a mint.[12] To induce miners to take their gold to Vancouver Sifton proposed a 1 per cent rebate on the royalty, but this had almost no effect. Therefore in 1902 free assay services were provided for miners who had paid the royalty or export tax.[13]

The mellowing of Sifton's views since the summer of 1900 also was apparent in the area of public morality. As seen, he finally abandoned control of the liquor traffic to the Yukon Council. When he postponed the closing of the dance-halls and gambling houses until 1 June 1901, Sifton predicted that "in the course of three or four months the evil will practically be removed, and will be done in such a way that there will be no reactionary agitation started."[14] He was correct. Ross was directed formally to enforce the order, but in fact he was permitted to use his discretion and phase out milder forms of gambling and dance-halls into 1902. The effect on Dawson was not traumatic. As Z.T. Wood told Lord Minto, "the closing of the gambling houses and dance halls on the 1st drove a large portion of the undesirable element to Nome, and while all kinds of dismal forebodings were indulged in by business men, as a result of the closing, the change has not had the disastrous effect they predicted."[15] Dawson decided to clean up its own red-light district; the result was to drive the prostitutes across the river to Klondike City where they remained, in the opinion of F.C. Wade, a "menace to the morals of every child in Dawson."[16] Despite such occasional comments or the indignation of the clergy in Dawson,[17] most of the Territory's citizens seemed resigned to the inevitable changes and developing respectability. Canadians could rest assured that the government was supervising the transition from a wild frontier mining community to conformity with the standards of the more settled parts of the Dominion.

Underlying the apparent harmony of the early months of Ross's administration was a thinly veiled disquietude over the government's hydraulic mining concession policy. What would it mean for the future of the Yukon? The applause that should have greeted Sifton's changes in policy and easing of regulations never materialized, forgotten amidst the controversy beginning in 1901 over the so-called "Treadgold Concession." It was, according to one historian, "the most significant political issue ever to appear in the territory," an issue that once again brought Yukon affairs briefly to the fore in national politics.[18]

The optimism of which Woodside had written to Laurier in 1901 was born of the hope of Yukoners that an easing of government red tape and taxes would renew the prospects of the placer miners. Gold production had been $10 million in 1898, $16 million in 1899, over $22 million in 1900, falling to $17 million in 1901, and less than $12 million in 1902. The figure for 1900 reflected the production of the 1899-1900 season; by the summer of that year easily recovered gold was gone on most claims, and discouragement was setting in. Increasingly miners found that a sizeable capital outlay in mechanical equipment, transportation, and hired help was necessary to work their claims. They were certain that if only the government would relax its grip, open reserved claims, and prevent large tracts of land from being tied up in concessions, the placer miners' future would be assured. The very granting of concessions ran against the grain of the community. It prized a vigorous individualism and believed in the idea of a free and equal chance at wealth for everyone who was willing to make the effort to locate and work a claim. In such a community the privileges conferred on a few by the patronage system, or by the manipulation of laws and regulations on behalf of those with connections or wealth, was always resented. Such abuses could be tolerated, however, so long as they did not attack the basic individualism of the mining system. In the spring of 1901 they hoped that their view was beginning to prevail.

Those who were more realistic, however, could see the writing on the wall. Commissioner Ross put it succinctly to Sifton: "Conditions in respect to mining have largely changed here. There are no more Bonanzas or Eldorados and it is down to a business proposition—low grade ground and only by the assistance of machinery are they able to make it pay."[19] That, of course, had been the prediction of astute men since 1897: that before long the easily recoverable gold would be gone, but that large tracts of low-paying gravel could be worked profitably by mechanical means. Only the guarantee of large tracts of land and other conditions could attract the capital necessary to fund such a venture. The first application for a lease of this nature was made in August 1897 by a California dredging company; the first granted was the Anderson concession, a British-backed enterprise, in January 1898. By August 1904 forty-four concessions would be granted, the largest and most controversial of which was that proposed by a diminutive, energetic Englishman, A.N.C. Treadgold.[20]

Regulations of 1900 were intended to ensure that grantees would not find themselves in conflict with the placer miners. Their leases were neither supposed to hinder existing placer mining operations nor to contain land suitable for placer mining. Concessions could be from one to five miles long and a mile wide. Leases were for twelve years, with rent set at $150 per mile per annum. Royalties on gold production exceeding $25,000 annually were at the same rate as for placer mining. Lessees were to begin work within a year of being granted the lease, and to invest at least $5,000 a year in the operations.[21] Inevitably there were many complaints: disputes arose over whether some of the land so leased was suitable for placer mining; some leases in practice limited water available to free miners; some lessees did not live up to their agreements and work the land; some exceeded their legal rights, restricting access to placer miners or selling timber from their lands; and almost all leases were gained chiefly by political influence or lobbying at Ottawa, so that rarely was compliance with the regulations enforced.

In their wildest dreams, however, none of the other concession holders thought on the grand scale of Treadgold, whose proposals exceeded all others both in size and daring. He proposed to harness several of the richest creeks and water diverted from the Klondike River into a complex system to provide water for mining hill and bench claims back from the streams. With extensive British backing and Sifton's evident blessing, he set out to buy up the placer claims in other names, spending some $219,000 in 1899 in this way. This, it was hoped, would eliminate any problem about interfering with placer mining. At the same time he sought to buy out, or purchase an interest in, several of the larger concessions.[22]

The enormous scope of Treadgold's plan was revealed in a proposal submitted by Sifton for cabinet consideration early in 1900.[23] It was sheer monopoly. For twenty-five years the grantee would have the sole right to divert water from the Klondike River, to a maximum of 25,000 miner's inches (or 37,500 cubic feet per minute) for power, pumping or mining purposes to serve the several creeks and their tributaries not already controlled by free miners; the right to construct works and establish reservoirs anywhere in the area, crown lands being available free of charge; the sole right to generate and sell electric power; the right to purchase any crown lands at a price not exceeding $10 per acre; right of way on all private lands; the right to all unoccupied lands or abandoned claims in the district, free of charge; exemption from all taxes on property, and lower than normal royalties; the right to take from crown lands all timber required for its works; and the first right to enter claims on any mineral ores discovered as a result of the operations of the Company. In return, for ninety days a year the grantee was to provide 1,000 miner's inches (or 1,500 cubic feet per minute) of water to meet the applications of free miners for water; free miners were to be allowed specified amounts of water necessary to work their claims, and to be compensated for any damages caused by the grantee; and the company was to sell excess water to miners at a rate not exceeding one dollar per miner's inch per hour. Writing some weeks later to Laurier in justification of the proposals, Sifton commented:

So far as the general details are concerned, I do not think it ought to be looked upon in too academic a way. The whole future of the Yukon depends upon the inauguration of such a scheme as this. The promoters have been working now for two years, and they are the only substantial people who really understand the question and believe in it sufficiently to put in from $5,000,000.00 to $10,000,000.00 as will be required. It is the chance of a lifetime to have the country put upon an enduring basis and development started upon a scale hitherto unknown in mining in Canada. Too much hypercriticism of details will wreck the whole plan, and if it fails the production will gradually fall off until some similar scheme is brought up again, probably some years from now.

I think it is of great importance to have it put through. Practically the only thing that is being asked for is the use of the water in the Klondike River. All the other matters referred to in the application are mere matters of detail which almost necessarily follow from the granting of the franchise and the necessities of the enterprise.

The best consideration that I can give to the whole subject leads me to recommend that the scheme be adopted without any very material modifications.[24]

The audacity of this statement is astonishing. Mere matters of detail! Even the Laurier cabinet could grasp the fact that the granting of such a monopoly, especially in the midst of all the charges of corruption in the Yukon, would be politically disastrous. The proposal, as later protests pointed out, involved 350 square miles of territory, or two-thirds of the gold-producing area, including the richest of the creeks.[25] No action was taken while Sifton was absent in Europe in 1900; a modified charter was passed in October, but it was never proclaimed because Treadgold's backers refused to accept the changes. Finally in June 1901 an acceptable charter was passed, and it was proclaimed in the Yukon in mid-July.[26] The original proposal had been subjected to modification nevertheless. No longer did the Company have the exclusive right to relocations or abandoned claims; it was required to expend $250,000 within eighteen months; within four years it was to be prepared to provide the required 1,000 miner's inches of water to free miners; it had to pay school taxes on its property; and numerous regulations had been added to protect miners' rights.[27]

The Treadgold Concession was instantly unpopular and opposed by virtually everyone in the Territory from Commissioner Ross on down. On 30 July, two weeks after the scheme was announced, a public protest meeting was held, calling for repeal of the scheme. In succeeding weeks a picture of administrative confusion began to emerge. It became clear that no over-all planning had governed the granting of concessions. Sifton him-self confessed that they had "been granted a little too freely."[28] They were supposed to be worked by hydraulic means, but a number of them were located in places where the requisite amount of water was unavailable, so they could only be worked by placer methods.[29] The Treadgold scheme appeared to be superimposed upon these other concessions with no clear idea of how they were to mesh. It is true that the prime purpose of the monopoly was to induce a large block of capital to invest in supplying water to the hill and bench claims above the creeks. It would require skilled engineering and many miles of conduits and flumes. Water would be diverted from the Klondike River to reservoirs at high levels to ensure an adequate supply for the summer washing of the low-grade gravels. Without such a scheme much of the gold could never be recovered. It was also true that water was scarce on the creeks and miners would have welcomed a reasonable scheme to ensure a reliable supply. But the Treadgold Conces-sion both created a monopoly and proposed to charge outrageous prices for a very limited amount of water. Sifton's own cousin, Orange H. Clark, told him that a reasonable price would have been 5 cents per miner's inch, not the $1 proposed.[30]

Added to this was confusion over the company's right to automatically control abandoned claims. Not until September did Sifton ease public concern by explaining that the company only had the right "to stake and enter for the abandoned claims in [the] same way as any other free miner."[31] Public concern uneasily subsided.

Then on 7 December 1901 Sifton had new amendments to the Treadgold charter passed. He doubled the amount of water the company was to supply to 2,000 miner's inches and reduced the price to 25 cents. At the same time, however, he guaranteed their automatic right "to obtain entry for and work all mining locations now or hereafter abandoned on Bonanza, Bear and Hunker Creeks and their tributaries," effective 1 January 1902.[32] When these new regulations were posted in Dawson in February, there was an instantaneous hostile reaction. All the fears of the Yukoners were realized. The true colours of the company and the real purpose of government policy were now exposed. The concession was a frontal assault on placer mining. It must be destroyed, root and branch. No delaying tactics, halfway measures, or obfuscating amendments could be allowed to divert Yukoners from that objective. To many, writes one authority, the Treadgold Concession was seen "as a conspiracy to destroy the prevailing economic system, and, with it, their livelihood."[33] The Dawson postmaster perfectly reflected the sentiment of the day when he wrote bluntly, "All concessions are a curse as not one of them are doing any work. Cut them out and then we will have the finest mining country on the face of the Globe."[34]

Sifton had anticipated the storm. Writing to Ross, he emphasized the increased amount of water and lower price. The only concession to the Treadgold people was the guarantee of title to "abandoned locations": "I do not, however, consider that this is any particular grievance, as the people have had all summer to make entries on any portions of these creeks which they desire." The important thing to remember was that "there is a strong possibility that these people [Treadgold and his backers] will go ahead and do this work, and from all that I can learn if they do it will probably result in the introduction of a very large amount of capital into the Yukon Territory." Sifton had gone over the amendments very carefully, believed they were for the best, "and I rely upon you to stand *by my action and see the thing through*."[35]

Publicly Ross pooh-poohed the agitation in the Yukon as "chiefly hot air," but he already was on his way to Ottawa where he would strongly oppose the concession. Even the staunchest Liberals in the Territory were stampeded. Several joined in cabling Sifton, "Publication of Treadgold order in council regarding abandoned claims has ruined the Liberal party here; most intense indignation universally expressed."[36] Orange Clark added in a letter that "the movement became so general that a few of the faithful thought it best to form in with it, on the principle of Lord Beaconsfield, that if you cannot stem the tide of public feeling lead it. So we went to mass meetings, were appointed on Committees &c." Nevertheless, "I think you have made a mistake in this contract."[37] So intense was the reaction that once more Sifton reversed his field. On 21 April the government rescinded all the previous orders in council respecting the Treadgold Concession and substituted one with far fewer privileges. Again abandoned claims were thrown open to the public, generating a mini-stampede. The company would only have the right to such claims after it had completed the work to deliver the required water. On the other hand, the company was given six years to complete the work, with no specification of work to be done each year; and there was now no specified price for water.[38]

This time, however, the Yukon population refused to be placated. Not only the Treadgold, but all other concessions must go. This sentiment fuelled public meetings, delegations to Ottawa and the formation of a distinctive political opposition in the Territory. Sifton's officials concluded not only that most of the grantees were not performing the work stipulated in their leases, but also that improving technology meant that substantial portions of the leases now could be worked by individual miners. Sifton appeared to be disposed to rectify this grievance too, and he did cancel some of the concessions. However, he found great difficulty in dealing with the larger and more privileged leases because of substantial British investment in them. The result of cancellation, predicted Sifton, would be a serious attack in the British press and damage to Canada's reputation.[39]

Then again, even Ross caused him embarrassment, inexplicably allowing individual miners to stake and register claims on a concession, claims that Sifton had directed him, and Ross had agreed, to reserve. The result was a court case and unnecessary acrimony.[40]

The decision to call a by-election in the Yukon could hardly have come under less auspicious circumstances. Although the Territory was entitled to representation in the House of Commons, the government had delayed the election, ostensibly to permit Yukon affairs to become more settled, but actually to ensure the return of a Liberal member. Following Ross's stroke in July 1902, Sifton sent Deputy Minister James Smart to Dawson to supervise a reorganization of the staff to allow the administration to carry on and to see what could be done to salvage Liberal prospects. Smart quickly concurred with prevailing opinion among friends of the government that there was only one man popular enough to carry the constituency: Commissioner Ross. Clearly Ross could not continue in his official capacity, and so he agreed from Victoria, where he was slowly recuperating, to accept the nomination.

The writs were issued in September, the election date set for 2 December. The Liberal electoral machinery creaked into motion, belatedly appointing French Canadians to civil service posts to ensure their support, and — according to Israel Tarte — spending as much as $30,000 in sundry ways to ensure victory.[41] The Grits also were fortunate in Ross's opponent, the demagogic Joseph Clarke, one of the leaders of the agitation in the summer and a man given to extreme, libellous statements. So distasteful was Clarke to political moderates that many Tories joined in support of Ross. That latter step was only made possible, however, by a platform highly critical of Sifton's policies and demanding immediate cancellation of the Treadgold Concession, strict interpretation of the terms of other concessions, and government construction of the water supply system. Even his great popularity, Ross's supporters unanimously agreed, could not have resulted in victory had that plank not been adopted. One of the leading Yukon Liberals, F.T. Congdon, told Sifton:

> You have no idea of the intense hostility to the Govt here. Liberals are compelled largely to fall back upon a defence akin to the ground upon which charitable Catholics base their generous hopes of the ultimate salvation of Protestants, their impenetrable ignorance, which in the case of the administration will be more successfully enlightened by Mr Ross than by Mr Clarke. Please do not take offence at this course and do not interfere with our line or we are gone beyond redemption.[42]

Sifton took the advice. The final results were: Ross, 2,971; and Clarke, 2,079. Such was Ross's margin of victory that Sifton noted with disgust, "It seems quite clear that our friends were trying to frighten us into 'loosening up'.''[43]

For a normally astute politician, Sifton gravely misread the mood of the Yukon populace. They were now fighting for a principle. The Treadgold Concession not only was evil in itself, it also came to symbolize the big business, the grafters, the Ottawa corruption, all combining to crush the individual miner. Sifton himself was widely believed to have an interest in the concession; how else could his continued defence of it in face of popular protest be explained? They could not understand Sifton's conviction that their method of mining already was passé, that they must give way to the forces of progress. They certainly could not be expected to appreciate how the sheer scale and magnitude of Treadgold's scheme appealed strongly to the minister of the interior. All abandoned claims, however unprofitable if worked individually, became in the eyes of the protesters possible sources of livelihood for miners.

The absence of Sifton during the spring of 1903 and the continuing agitation in the Yukon provided the Opposition with an excellent opportunity to score some political points. Despite the cancellation plank in his platform, Ross suggested to Laurier that nothing be done on the Treadgold Concession until Sifton's return. Meanwhile, an engineer should be sent to the Yukon to produce an independent report on water supply.[44] Laurier agreed. To quell the Yukon protests in the interim Ross also wanted some of the other concessions cancelled which were not fulfilling the regulations. One of Sifton's officials, J.G. Turriff, wrote to him for instructions, and received a testy reply:

I have a very clear and definite opinion on the subject of the concessions. I think we have been making an entire mistake during the last two years in the Yukon in giving way to the clamour which was raised. I think we made a mistake in increasing the number of elective members [on the Yukon Council], and also in giving them representation [in Parliament]. There is nothing in the concession question which is causing any reasonable difference and the legitimate miners are not paying the least particle of attention to it. There are five or six thousand abandoned claims for the people to prospect if they wish, almost any of them would present more promising ground than the hydraulic concessions to which reference is made. The row is being kicked up by professional agitators and our fellows, including Mr. Ross and Mr. Congdon, have allowed themselves to be more or less intimidated by them....If the matter comes up in the House my colleagues will have to make the best answer they can in the meantime and tell the opposition that if they want the matter fully discussed they can bring it up when I return. My impression is that if the policy of gently putting off is adopted (in respect to which Sir Wilfrid needs no education) there will never be a discussion which will cause the Government any embarrassment.[45]

Turriff showed Sifton's letter to Laurier, who replied, "Tell Mr. Sifton that I have read his letter and have looked into these concessions, and that I am not at all scared about them and think I can manage the matter."[46]

However, Laurier and Sir William Mulock, acting minister of the interior in Sifton's absence, bungled the issue badly when it was raised in Parliament. Already concerned about the Yukon agitation, lacking in a basic understanding of the concessions, and devoid of expert knowledge about engineering and water requirements, they fumbled opposition probes woefully, claimed that the agreement with Treadgold had no legal effect (on the technicality that the order in council agreed to had not yet been proclaimed), and finally caved in and appointed a royal commission to consider concessions generally, and the Treadgold Concession in particular. Even this was subject to criticism because of the selection of Justice B.M. Britton, until shortly before a violently partisan Liberal MP, as chief commissioner. All this was done in Sifton's absence and without his consent.[47] Public Works Minister James Sutherland, on whom Sifton had counted for support, weakly pleaded overwork for his failure to come to his absent colleague's defence. Nevertheless, he was probably responsible for ensuring that the second member of the commission would be the sympathetic B.T.A. Bell, secretary of the Mining Institute and editor of the *Canadian Mining Review*. Sutherland also delayed the departure of the commissioners until after Sifton's return to Canada so that they could be fully briefed.[48]

Sifton was thoroughly disgusted. Not only was the capitulation of the government a demonstration of lack of confidence in his administration, but the appointment of the commission precluded any further debate in which he could defend his record. Moreover, the action came at a crucial time for the Treadgold interests. The agitation in the Yukon meant little to them so long as they had strong government backing. In spite of his various retreats and limitations of their privileges, Sifton's presence had always guaranteed that requirement. The company had overcome several reverses and had almost closed a deal for the capital required to commence the work when the parliamentary debate occurred. The statement of Mulock and Laurier to the effect that the order in council establishing the concession was not legally in force destroyed the confidence of the English backers. "It seems to me the weakest flop over I ever saw and the least excusable," Sifton commented sourly to Sutherland.[49]

The Treadgold scheme was effectively killed, though it was another year until the promoter finally withdrew and the cabinet rescinded the order in council. Its death was the direct result of poor planning, popular agitation, and governmental weakness. Sifton, however, believed another cause responsible. Writing to one of the investors in the scheme, Malcolm H. Orr Ewing, and hoping to reassure those who had put money into it, he stated that Treadgold, although "honest & honorable," had been the cause of his own misfortune.

> What might have been a magnificently successful enterprise known all over the mining world & of the greatest benefit to Canada drifted into his reach...I being overloaded with public business could give no attention to the details and assumed (too hastily) that he probably had the capacity to succeed. The complete failure to make it go, & the antagonizing of the whole community are due to Treadgold's stubborn narrowness & complete incapacity for business on a large scale. He is *hopelessly* out of his class (as a businessman) in dealing with such matters. His spirit is admirable, his judgment is a negligible quantity. I have done the best I could to put his backers in a safe position to save their money solely out of regard for the fact that they were & are innocent investors....
>
> Such an enterprise cannot succeed in such hands. I am writing you simply in a friendly way to say that your company's claims & franchises as they now exist should—properly handled—without any Government assistance much more than pay you back all you have, but playing golf & skating around Ottawa will not produce the results. You need a first class business & mining man to take hold & you should be at his elbow to see that he does his work.[50]

While Orr Ewing at first protested this harsh assessment, some years later he was forced to acknowledge that Sifton had been correct after all, as Treadgold managed to raise and lose another small fortune in the Klondike.[51]

While it seems unlikely, given his attitude between 1902 and 1904, that Sifton had a direct interest in Treadgold's scheme, it is impossible to state whether or not he was involved in any of the smaller concessions. It appears that some of his colleagues, such as Sutherland and Sir Frederick Borden, had invested, as had other Liberal MPs and party supporters.[52] A large proportion of the grantees had no desire to work the concessions, regarding them as potentially profitable speculations, and they were sold, often quickly, to larger interests. A number, probably about fifteen, were granted in the months preceding the 1900 election. Hence Sifton's reluctance to countenance wholesale cancellation of leases. Some of the concession holders probably were waiting for the Treadgold scheme to be completed in order to obtain an adequate supply of water to work their holdings. Had Treadgold succeeded, the other concessions would instantly have increased in value, whether sold or tied in to the larger syndicate or worked separately.

Sifton did everything he could to encourage large-scale mining as the way of the future in the Yukon. Official reports of the commissioner annually reiterated this fact. Sifton asked anyone likely to support this view to write for newspapers or journals. Probably B.T.A. Bell was of this group. Another was S. Morley Wickett, Ph.D. and lecturer at the University of Toronto, who reported on trade conditions and prospects in the Yukon to the Canadian Manufacturers' Association late in 1902.[53] Also encouraged and assisted was Henry A. Miers, Waynflete Professor of Mineralogy at the University of Oxford, who visited the Yukon in August 1901. In return for Sifton's aid, Miers produced a report which he let the minister censor before publication. For example, in the course of his draft report, which predicted a great future for large mechanized operations and a decline in placer mining, the professor wrote, "The judicious granting of concessions is no doubt paving the way towards larger and more systematic operations; it is only to be hoped that they will never be allowed to assume the character of monopolies, for this would deprive the Territory of precisely what it most requires — free competition." The statement was excised, as was anything slightly critical.[54] The Britton Commission report, which appeared at the end of July 1904, predictably reached the same conclusion, adding that some scheme such as the Treadgold one would ultimately be necessary. It observed, however, that popular resentment in the Yukon would make it inadvisable to proceed with such a policy.[55] Inexorable forces proved Sifton correct, and "by 1906 the supporters of the large-scale methods had emerged triumphant."[56] Nevertheless, difficult as the transition inevitably was as the dramatic hey-day of the gold rush gave way to the settled, dully efficient mechanized mining era, it might well be argued that much of the tension of the era need never have occurred. Had Sifton taken the trouble to go to the Yukon and investigate for himself, had he not been so ready to dismiss those who opposed his plans as "loafers" and "scalawags,"[57] had he been willing or able to spend more time dealing seriously and diplo- matically with Yukon affairs and limiting the excesses of the patronage system, much trouble might have been avoided.

The tragedy of James Ross continued to cast a shadow over Yukon politics. During his tenure as MP for the Yukon he was but a feeble reflection of the politician he once had been. He rarely appeared and almost never spoke in the House of Commons and was mercifully appointed to the Senate in 1904, where he languished until his death in 1932. His failure to realize most of the promises made on his behalf in 1902 convinced many Yukoners that voting for a government candidate, regardless of his platform, was futile.

Moreover, when Ross vacated the Yukon commissionership, he left an outsized pair of shoes that the government had trouble filling. As Sifton and his colleagues cast about for a suitable replacement, Major Wood of the NWMP served for several months as acting commissioner. There was much pressure to appoint someone who had lived in the Territory and understood its problems, and of course the appointee would have to be a Liberal of some standing. One name came constantly to the fore: Frederick Tennyson Congdon, a Nova Scotia lawyer and ally of W.S. Fielding; he had been appointed as legal adviser in 1901, and shortly succeeded F.C. Wade as crown prosecutor and assumed Wade's lucrative law practice. He was a leading light in the Yukon Liberal Association, became a close confidant of Ross, and had his eye on the federal Liberal nomination before Ross suffered his stroke.[58] Letters supporting Congdon reached Sifton from men whose judgment he trusted, such as Ross, Cory, and Smart. He was one of the few English-speaking Liberals who was sensitive to the French-Canadian community and enjoyed their support. He was variously described as capable, honest, intelligent, and warm-hearted, although one correspondent added, "He has a great fault which is unpardonable for this country, he don't drink; not only he don't drink but he has no liquor in his house and of course in the eyes of some people it is a crime. Not so much now; for two years ago it would have been a capitol [sic] crime."[59] Undoubtedly that appealed to Sifton. Furthermore, Congdon set aside his own ambitions and not only loyally supported Ross's candidature but zealously headed the Liberal campaign at some financial sacrifice.

That sort of commitment demanded reward, yet Sifton and his colleagues seemed strangely hesitant to act. Only in March 1903 did Congdon receive the commissionership, more than eight months after Ross's stroke and four months after the election. Events would prove Congdon to be a poor choice, unable to be an effective leader, being instead a divisive force in the Territory generally and in the Liberal party in particular.

In many respects the Yukon elections of 1902 and 1904 could be the subject of a rollicking farce. Canada has had many carnivals of corruption at election time, but it is doubtful whether many can match the openness and exuberance of these northern events. In neither election did great issues divide the contending parties: in 1902 both sides agreed that the Treadgold concession should be abolished; in 1904 it had disappeared, and the issue was one of personalities. Patronage was a major factor, Yukoners being at least as susceptible to this vice as Canadians elsewhere. Sifton's administration had not endeared the Laurier government to the populace, but there were ways and means of getting around mere unpopularity.

Commissioner Congdon was the central figure in both elections. Subtlety of organization was not his strong point. He had an uncommon gift for alienating even loyal Liberals in his ham-fisted tactics and cast a blind eye toward the unsavoury activities of some of his followers. There were diverse supporting actors. T. Dufferin Pattullo, a future premier of British Columbia, had been employed in the Yukon civil service since 1897; he saw himself as a man of principle and reform among Liberals, but he was angry at Congdon because of a $2,500 debt for a printing contract and angry at Sifton because he had not received a promotion and salary that he believed he deserved. Pattullo was instrumental in establishing a rival Liberal organization. Another character, who repeatedly assured Laurier and Sifton that he was a good Liberal, was the Reverend John Pringle, Presbyterian divine, moralist, and gossip par excellence, who delighted in denouncing lewd women, dancing and gambling, and the general conduct of the government. The rabble-rousing Joe Clarke, a third-rate politician of frustrated ambition, was chronically opposed to any and every government policy. His counterpart among the press was W.A. Beddoe, scheming newspaper editor, who would support or attack anything if the price was right. On the government side were such gems as William Temple, alleged diamond drill expert, but actually an ex-railway brakeman from Nova Scotia; ostensibly sent to aid the miners, experience showed that he hardly knew which was the business end of the drill. His chief function was to create a political organization for Congdon, which he attempted to do through bribery and threats. There also was the notorious "Pickles" Falconer, detective embarrassment to the NWMP. He was forced upon the Police by the government, was paid more than Major Wood who headed the force, and seems to have done little but collect protection rakeoffs for the Congdon machine from local gambling and dance halls. Among this unsavoury crew, the most upright seems to have been Major Wood himself, mainly preoccupied with the thankless task of keeping his force out of politics, retaining its dignity, and preserving the frequently disturbed peace.

The crowd and props would include an enormous "slush fund" — possibly as much as $10 for every voter in the Yukon. There was a corps of prostitutes and dance-hall girls, paid to keep opposition voters occupied on election day, but otherwise usually in tow to government officials and businessmen. A small army of unemployed miners was paid just before the elections for constructing roads and other works which they never saw. There was a reserve force of aliens (mostly Americans) who were paid and voted illegally at distant polling stations on the creeks. Various companies and interests controlled blocks of votes, through not always supporting the government. There was, finally, an irate force of police, who normally voted for the government, but were so offended at Congdon (who insisted on red-coated policeman servants) that Wood doubted that the commissioner would receive a single police vote.

The various scenes have excellent dramatic possibilities. A crowd of aliens who voted in 1902 were not paid and staged a memorable rampage. In 1904 the voters' lists were withheld by carefully instructed enumerators until 11:30 p.m. on the last night of the legal limit; the lists were posted a few minutes and then removed, the enumerators claiming they were stolen. Later irate opposition supporters got together a mob to ferret out the enumerators. They discovered one official, J.E. Girouard, registrar of land titles, at the cabin of one "Montreal Marie," who diverted their attention until he was spotted scurrying out the back door and up a hill. The howling mob chased him and haled him, still not fully dressed, back into town. The only real violence occurred when one enumerator, to the horror of Congdon's supporters, turned out to be impartial in preparing his lists; he was pursued and beaten, and but for the last-minute intervention of the police, would have had his lists stolen. Another telling scene occurred when Congdon came to deliver an address to the police and not a single constable would volunteer to hear him.[60]

While Sifton and Laurier were not direct participants in the elections, they cannot be excused as either innocents or dupes. They knew what was going on, as their bulky correspondence makes clear. They appointed several of the most corrupt officials, provided other patronage, and it is inconceivable that they did not know where the money came from or in a general way how it was spent. They were ultimately responsible for what took place, and they condoned it. In a sense the very success of Congdon in electing Ross in 1902 laid the groundwork for failure in 1904. "Was there ever such a dirty campaign in the interest of a good man?" asked John Pringle of Sifton.[61] Ross's popularity, the offensiveness of Joe Clarke, and the anti-Treadgold plank should have been sufficient to ensure his victory. Instead Congdon exploited every resource and device, overspent even his generous "slush fund," and could not pay off his political debts. His high-handed methods sowed seeds of future discontent.

Following the reverse of 1903 on the Treadgold Concession, Sifton seems to have lost interest in the Yukon. Major decisions and most details were left to Congdon, while Sifton merely brushed aside criticisms of the commissioner. Laurier too dismissed complaints, perhaps because Congdon was popular with the French Canadians, although this alienated many of the English-speaking Liberals in the Territory. Congdon himself ran as the Liberal candidate in 1904; but the issue then was not for or against the Laurier government, but for or against Congdon. All those whom the commissioner had alienated united to support Dr. Alfred Thompson, a former Conservative who ran as an Independent. Even with the many devices he had arranged in his own favour, Congdon lost by 600 votes.

Despite the renewed flourishing of gambling and dance-halls in the summer before the election and unassailable reports of Congdon's corruption and incompetence, neither Laurier nor Sifton lifted a finger to interfere. On the other hand, once Congdon had been defeated, there was no chance that he would be reappointed commissioner. Only electoral success could have justified his record in the eyes of the Liberal government. No new appointment was made, however, before Sifton himself resigned in 1905.[62] A sure sign of the changing times was the dismissal of thirty government employees after the election. Months before, Sifton had drastically cut Yukon salaries by between 30 per cent and 40 per cent. Now redundant offices were abolished and others amalgamated in the first serious, if belated, move toward efficiency in several years.[63] The army of grafters were receiving their deserts for electoral failure.

Fortunately for the Liberal government, the inefficiency of the party machinery and the state of public opinion in the Yukon was not typical of the rest of the country. The state of the party was indeed one of Sifton's major preoccupations, one that helped to push Yukon affairs increasingly into the background.

7

The Liberal Machine
and the General Election of 1904

The power that Clifford Sifton wielded in the Liberal government stemmed not only from the strength of his intellect and the breadth of his grasp of the issues confronting the administration; it was firmly rooted in his mastery of both tactics and the strategy of political organization in Ontario and the West. Not for him was the nonchalant indifference to organization exhibited by some of his colleagues, and they willingly deferred to his energetic combativeness. It was impossible to keep the rank and file in a constant state of battle readiness between elections. During that period a skilfully manipulated Liberal press was more important. It could sustain party morale, counter opposition thrusts, and keep a positive image of the Laurier government constantly before the public.

Such a press network had to be provided with material, and Sifton was one of the earliest and most efficient exponents of a national party propaganda system. In fact, his "Press Bureau" at Ottawa was so successful that early in 1902 the Conservatives decided to establish one of their own.[1] Details of the Liberal operation appear not to have survived. It is clear, however, that the principal organs in the English-language network were the Montreal *Herald*, the Toronto *Globe*, and the *Manitoba Free Press*. Of all the papers, the *Globe* carried most weight. The Toronto *Star*, purchased by the Liberals before the 1900 election in hope that it would be a more tractable organ than the *Globe*, still had a minor impact on public opinion.[2] Sifton often used the technique of making announcements first through the *Globe*, probably to avoid being too obviously identified in the public mind with the *Free Press*. After J.S. Willison left the *Globe* for the Toronto *News* at the end of 1902, however, Sifton grew distinctly cool in his attitude toward it. The sentiment was reciprocated by the *Globe*'s owner, Robert Jaffray, and the new editor, J.A. Macdonald. Sifton remained fairly friendly with J.S. Brierley, proprietor of the *Herald*, but it was declining in influence in face of the immense popular success of the Tory Montreal *Star*. The "Press Bureau" at Ottawa kept the party organization thoroughly informed about press opinion across the country and opinion in important foreign papers as well. It also composed editorials and carefully slanted news stories for the press network and prepared speakers' handbooks and pamphlets for public distribution at election time. At all times Sifton personally read a large number of newspapers. Even when on holiday he had no less than seven papers sent to him regularly.[3]

Central to his political plans in the West was the *Manitoba Free Press* and, as time went on, its editor, John W. Dafoe. Sifton always considered the paper to be as much a financial as a political investment. Either way, its success was undeniable. Its average daily circulation stood at 11,379 in 1899, 14,680 in 1901, and 22,375 in 1905, consistently exceeding the combined circulations of the rival *Telegram* and *Tribune*. In 1901 the weekly edition was only about 7,000, trailing far behind the *Tribune*'s 11,500; but four years later the *Free Press* weekly circulation stood at 15,261, while the *Tribune* was unchanged.[4] There is little doubt that Sifton aided his paper's progress by using his position to keep the opposition papers weak and divided, while judiciously granting patronage to the *Free Press* and using the Liberal organization to broaden the readership. He worked to prevent a rumoured sale of the *Telegram* to the Southams.[5] There also were rumours to the effect that, had the Tories lost the Manitoba election of 1899, the *Telegram* and the *Tribune* would have been merged. The Conservative victory, however, allowed the *Telegram* to survive by heavy infusions of provincial patronage. Even so, the paper was still losing $20,000 annually at the end of 1900.[6] The *Tribune* was in even more precarious circumstances, providing a living for R.L. Richardson and little more.[7]

Sifton was determined to control every possible share of Free Press Company stock. Although he had purchased 1,127 shares in 1897-98, there were still outstanding more than 200 shares with a face value of over $20,000. Securing them was not easy, because 100 were owned by W.F. Luxton, the former proprietor who had been ejected by Sir William Van Horne and Sir Donald Smith in 1893 and who still harboured a hatred for the CPR and the Sifton Liberals. Another 100 shares were controlled by Alexander MacDonald, a friend of R.L. Richardson and a shareholder in the *Tribune*. By the patient collaboration of H.M. Howell, Sifton's lawyer in Winnipeg, and conveniently a friend of Luxton, the purchase of the shares was slowly consummated. Claiming that he was acting for Walter Barwick, the Toronto lawyer in whose name the bulk of the stock was then held for Sifton, Howell presented Luxton with a carefully doctored picture of the Free Press Company's financial situation, designed to make fore-closure seem inevitable and the stock almost worthless. Both Luxton and MacDonald were persuaded by early 1902 to part with their shares at 25 cents on the dollar, which Sifton complained was "an excessive price."[8] The two or three other outstanding shares were then quickly purchased at a similar price, and all were placed in the name of John Mather, president of the company, though Sifton actually held the certificates and complete control. To comply with the provisions of the Joint Stock Companies Act, Mather owned three shares, and E.H. Macklin, J.W. Dafoe and J.W. Sifton one each.[9]

Sifton's financial grip was extended in other ways, all designed to maximize his income from the newspaper and to prevent its being tied to banks or other lending institutions. For example, when a press and lino-type machine were purchased, Mather bought them in his own name using $4,000 provided by Sifton. The company then purchased the machinery from Mather with another $4,000 provided by Sifton and secured with a lien against the company. The result was that while his name was not involved formally in the purchases, Sifton had paid for the machinery and the Company was making payments at a then comfortable 6 per cent interest to him.[10] At the end of 1901 he arranged, through some shrewd legal manoeuvres, to have the company declare that it was unable to clear its first mortgage, taken in 1898, and the whole thing was renegotiated in a new mortgage at then extraordinary rate of 12 per cent. The new mortgage was to include "*everything*, plant, franchise, goodwill of the newspaper, book-debts, and everything of that kind except the machinery, which is com-prised in the lien agreement."[11] Despite these heavy obligations, the paper did well enough that early in 1903 Sifton arranged for payment of an 8 per cent dividend upon the capital stock, payable quarterly.[12] These arrangements, at a rough calculation, must have produced an income of at least $20,000 a year for him.

In 1901 Sifton was able to find work for his sixty-seven-year-old father, who had been unemployed since the Conservatives had relieved him of his inspectorship of public institutions. He was to aid in the audit of the Free Press Company's books and then to act as an overseer of bookkeeping for the business. For these light duties Sifton directed that he be paid $150 per month.[13]

In 1903, when the company was forced to find a new site upon which to erect expanded facilities, Sifton decided that he would "have a company in-corporated to own the property and building, and the newspaper company can pay a rental agreed upon when they go into occupation. It is not desirable to have the Free Press Company tangled up with the financing of the building."[14] The Free Press Building Company, as the new company was called, was incorporated at $130,000. Sifton carefully scrutinized the structural plans from Ottawa, correcting various interior details, and flatly refusing to have a proposed solid stone exterior. Instead he wanted a facing of "the best quality of white brick, windows and doors trimmed with stone and possibly a coping stone at the top." That would save at least $5,000; "no money," he directed, should be "spent on the outside of the building that will not earn a dividend."[15]

The philosophy of cutting unnecessary expenditures preoccupied Sifton. He was not involved in the day-to-day operations, did not know the employees, or face the real problems of selling the paper. He told his father that "of course the object in the business, as in every other business where anyone is trying to make a profit is to keep down expenses."[16] That was all very well, J.W. Sifton commented a year later, but if the paper was to maintain its relative position in an expanding economy, some expenditure would have to be tolerated. The local government, for example, was taking 10,000 copies of the *Telegram* every two weeks to pass out among immigrants; to compete, the *Free Press* had to distribute 20,000 sample copies between January and April 1902. To help push the weekly, J.W. Sifton had written to each postmaster in the North-West Territories and Manitoba and to some in British Columbia and northwestern Ontario, obtaining the names of prospective subscribers and sending out about 500 free copies a week. The response was good, but the plan was not cheap.[17] There were costs, too, in some of Macklin's promotional schemes for the daily: in 1902, the offer of a "thermometer and weather glass" to subscribers; in 1903, twenty-four colour reproductions of paintings.[18] Moreover, Dafoe found when he arrived in 1901 that the paper was understaffed, and the staff underpaid. He immediately gave sharp increases in salary and told the employees that they would receive "fair incomes in the course of two or three years."[19] A good staff with high morale would not come cheaply either. Ultimately Sifton accepted the judgment of those whom he had put in charge of the paper and chose not to insist upon his cost-cutting philosophy.

There was no gainsaying the success of the efforts of Dafoe, Macklin, and J.W. Sifton as they took advantage of the phenomenal western growth of the early twentieth century. "I confess it makes my head swim trying to keep tab on the development that is going on," Dafoe told Sifton in 1902.[20] A year later, his confidence brimming, he predicted that within five years he could make the *Free Press* the best newspaper property in Canada, possibly excepting the Montreal *Star*. "I want you to simply outclass the other papers, east as well as west," replied Sifton, "but on *strictly business lines*."[21]

The close relationship between Sifton and Dafoe seemed to be established extremely rapidly. The editor became the politician's chief western contact, his sensitive feelers, his diplomatic bridge to local Liberals, his reminder of the realities of regional and agrarian sensibilities. From the beginning Sifton trusted his editor. His frequently proffered advice on editorial policy was rarely couched in peremptory terms: often there was a comment such as, "You need not pay any attention to this information if you do not wish to"; always there was room for Dafoe to make his own decisions.[22] Excellent as the *Free Press*'s coverage of political news was, the average reader did not wish to be overwhelmed by it. "I often think," he suggested, "that a really first class up-to-date report of a football match is better than any possible editorial as a means to reach the heart of the public." These things should be done, however, without losing any of the "ginger" in the paper's political views.[23]

Under Dafoe the *Free Press* took for its constituency the entire West. Regular reports were published of affairs in smaller centres from the Lakehead to the Rockies. Feature articles on various towns and industries appeared almost weekly. Any sign of progress or growth was noted, and articles appeared on forestry and tree planting, mining, ranching, hydroelectric power, railways, and any industrial development. The most notable change was in the paper's attitude to the farming community. Both Dafoe and Sifton perceived that farmers' movements were gaining momentum after 1900; indeed, it was often Dafoe who had to educate his employer on the subject. No longer would a policy of confrontation be acceptable, either politically or from a business point of view. Much more complete reports of agrarian meetings were published than previously, and wherever possible—as, for example, with the contentious issue of the movement and storage of grain—the farmers' views were championed with vigour. The old hard line on government ownership was now softened in editorials that claimed that however desirable such policies might be, they were not politically possible.[24] Annual exhaustive crop forecasts for the entire West were also undertaken, and regular reports on the grain situation appeared during the growing season.

This hardly meant that conflicts between the views of Sifton and those of the farming community did not occur. As always, he never hesitated to express his opinions forthrightly when the need arose, and he was invariably supported by his editor. The society they promoted was rigorously individualistic, oriented to hard work and progress. The duty of government was to facilitate progress by striking a balance between the requirements of capital and those of producers, labourers, and consumers.

Gradually Sifton and Dafoe came to realize that much more would have to be done to accommodate the latter groups. Dafoe's success in coping with this issue helped to make the *Free Press* a great newspaper. Sifton, as it turned out, did not have so long to adjust in politics; yet it is clear that he recognized the legitimacy of many popular demands in the West prior to his resignation.

Dafoe could never forget that he and the *Free Press* constituted the heart of the western Liberal press network. By 1904 some thirty-five papers in Manitoba, twenty-two in the Territories, and sixteen in British Columbia were on the Liberal patronage list.[25] Included in this group was a growing number of papers directed at ethnic groups — Scandinavian, German, French, and Slav. In 1902-3 Sifton appears to have assumed control of a Ukrainian-language paper, the *Canadian Farmer*; and he did purchase 51 per cent of the stock of *Der Nordwesten*, a floundering German paper. The stock of the latter was held nominally in his father's name and later transferred to Macklin.[26] As the election of 1904 approached, the Manitoba Conservatives tried to buy the German paper, offering $25,000. Its editor and former proprietor would gladly have sold. But the Tories were unaware of Sifton's control, and their persistent efforts were encouraged, to "keep them on a string" and prevent them from establishing their own paper until it was too late to do any good.[27]

A good example of Sifton's methods occurred when a German Catholic colony was about to be established in 1904 near Quill Lake, under the auspices of the Saskatchewan Valley Land Company. "The German movement is already large, and it is our aim to encourage it to the utmost possible extent as they are the best settlers," Sifton told Dafoe. The people were coming from the United States, "were nearly all low tariff men, and strong on the policy of anti-monopoly. Their tendency will naturally be Liberal. I think you ought to make a study of the whole question," particularly their interest in having a paper of their own.

> In the first place, any and all papers that are started to circulate there ought to be printed in our office if possible. They are bound to grow because the people are thrifty and prosperous, and you will always know what is going on. In the next place you ought to consider what is [the] best way to get hold of the circulation amongst these people. If they will not take an English paper like the Free Press then I think an attempt ought to be made to make Der Nordwestern [*sic*] acceptable to them if it can be done without offending the present subscribers. If not, you should consider whether another publication is necessary.
>
> You will see from the fact that there is the possibility of a solid settlement of 25,000 or 30,000 people or perhaps more collecting there that the question requires careful attention.[28]

The same attention to detail and supervision of editorial content was undertaken with other ethnic papers, always trying to ensure Liberal dominance among the non-English population.[29] Thus when election time approached, the Liberals had in place effective and responsive propaganda machinery.

Sifton was a firm believer in the virtues of democratic partisan politics and strongly disagreed with those who claimed that "everything is going to the dogs through partyism." Addressing the Young Liberal Association of Winnipeg in 1901, he adjured them to remember that "nearly all the civil and religious liberties we enjoy were won under the system of party government." This system under the British constitution had done more than any other "to relieve humanity, to make men free and equal, and to give men the liberty of enjoying life." Only under a system "of one party pitted against the other can the rights and privileges of the people be properly safeguarded." Only as young people became involved in the political process, educating themselves about the issues of the day and the functioning of the constitution, could the political process be both protected and regenerated. A young man, he declared, should join one party or the other, and "work in that party to bring about the triumph of those ideas he believes in and to bring the politics of the country to a higher moral plane."[30]

While it would be difficult to show that Sifton's record helped to raise the moral plane of Canadian politics, there can be no doubt that he fought hard for his beliefs, that he relished a strenuous partisan contest, or that, at bottom, he accepted the basic premise of the democratic system that the voice of the people as expressed in elections was the decisive arbiter between the parties. Influencing the electorate was a serious game in which the rules were stretched to the limit, and occasionally beyond, in which every advantage must be seized to outflank or outmanoeuvre the other side. Both sides used dubious tactics, accepted the practices as part of the realities of the game, and ultimately co-operated with each other to prevent full-scale investigations of their procedures.

The preparations for the dominion election of 1904 reveal Sifton at the peak of his form and powers. The government was riding high in popular esteem in the West, and indeed in most of Canada. The GTPR and the expansion of the CN were widely approved, the government had recognized many of the legitimate grievances of the farmers, prosperity was breeding a general optimism, and the success of the government's immigration policy was undeniable. Laurier, now the experienced statesman, was quite highly regarded in the West.

By contrast, the Tories were not well liked. They were perceived as the party of high protection. Opposition leader Robert Borden's railway policy, undoubtedly more realistic than that of Laurier, was an undramatic patchwork that utterly failed to grip the western imagination or to shake the image of the Tories as being tied to the CPR. Borden himself toured the West in 1902, but Sifton was confident he would have little impact. "I have no doubt that Borden would make a personally favourable impression," he observed later, "as there was nothing for him to do except to make a pleasant speech on the stock subjects of discussion. My own judgment, however, was that he entirely failed to strike any new note or excite any enthusiasm."[31] The Grits' greatest worry was that western Tory candidates would not run openly on the Borden platform of protection, and "we will have our old experience of Conservative protectionist candidates strongly advocating free trade."[32]

The Liberals aided their prospects in 1903 with the first major redistribution of seats since the famous Tory gerrymander of 1882. Laurier evidently had wanted to have an impartial judicial review, but partisanship won as his caucus forced him to agree to a Select Committee of the House of Commons, where ultimately the Liberal majority could prevail. Even so the procedure was not as blatantly one-sided as some Liberals had hoped. Cartwright told Sifton in 1902, "I am preparing a stiff dose of their own medicine for our Conservative friends in Ontario re distribution. I will want to discuss my plans with you shortly. They are pretty far reaching."[33] He wanted Sifton's support, but the minister of the interior was in England in 1903 when the basic decisions on procedure were made. Still, there is no doubt that the Liberal redistribution appeared to be much fairer than the earlier Tory one, and the Opposition was consulted. Based on the average population of the sixty-five Quebec constituencies, the "unit of representation" was 25,367. This raised the number of constituencies in Manitoba from seven to ten and in the Territories from four to ten.[34] The basic constituency boundaries were worked out in Sifton's absence, but there was time for him to do a little fine-tuning upon his return in the summer of 1903, when, for example, he carved up R.L. Richardson's former base of support in Lisgar, and hived as many of the Tories of southwestern Manitoba as possible into the new Souris constituency.[35]

Laurier expected to follow the redistribution and railway legislation with an election in the fall of 1903. Probably anticipating such a strategy, the Opposition protracted debate, and the session did not end until well on in October, ruining the prime minister's plan. Sifton, however, seems to have expected no election, for he certainly took few pains to stir the Liberal machine to action during the summer. The only precaution he took was to hire an organizer, E. Blake Robertson, to work in Brandon at $100 per month.[36]

While in England for the Tribunal hearings, Sifton heard disquieting

Manitoba Constituencies, 1904

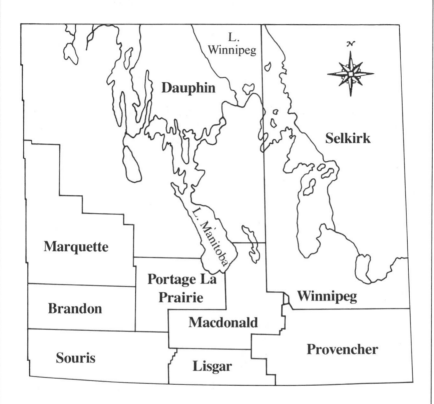

Source: *Electoral Atlas of the Dominion of Canada as Divided for
the Tenth General Election Held in the Year 1904*,
Ottawa: Government Printing Bureau, 1906.

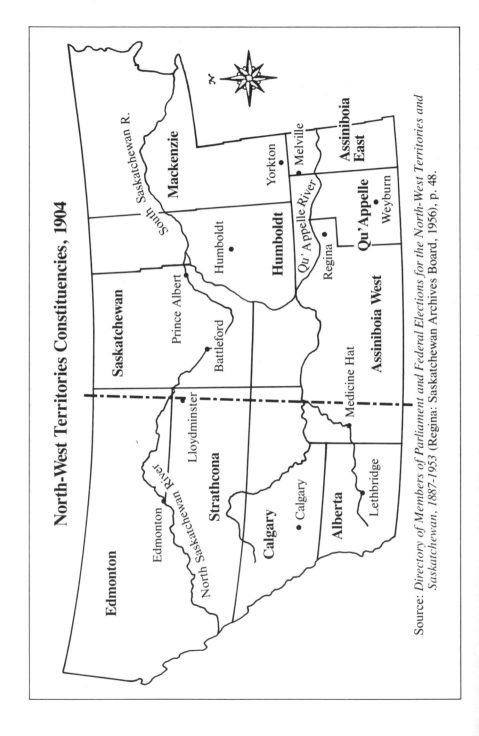

North-West Territories Constituencies, 1904

Source: *Directory of Members of Parliament and Federal Elections for the North-West Territories and Saskatchewan, 1887-1953* (Regina: Saskatchewan Archives Board, 1956), p. 48.

rumours about Tory election strategy. The CPR, Mackenzie and Mann, and the CMA were all supposedly behind Borden, and the Conservative campaign coffers were said to be in excellent shape, with over $1 million, of which the CPR contributed $250,000, and Senator Drummond of Montreal another $100,000.[37] Sifton immediately wrote Laurier that he "should at once see Shaughnessy yourself and put the matter to him straight." In that case the CPR would probably pledge neutrality and could not "go back on it, openly at least." Laurier "should also see Dan Mann....Tell him that we rely on their active support and make him promise it. I will see Mckenzie [*sic*] here [London] in a few days."[38] Reports also surfaced that Israel Tarte had agents working against the Liberals among the French Canadians of Manitoba; they were even supplied with introductions to Premier Roblin. Sifton ordered that they be "neutralized" at all costs. He asked Sydney Fisher, minister of agriculture, to get "a good reliable Frenchman...to be detailed to keep track of everything he [Tarte] does and in order to accomplish this he ought to get as close as possible to him." Sifton added that "somebody in Montreal should also be deputed to take the temperature of the C.P.R. and keep track of what they are doing."[39]

The prime minister was leaning toward an election date early in the new year, perhaps in February. Even as he waited impatiently for the Tribunal proceedings to wind up, Sifton began to press the Liberal machine into action. A good example of the detail of political planning was the attention given to French-Canadian voters in Brandon constituency. Sifton hired a special agent, J.F. Prud'homme, who spent three weeks canvassing each of the 113 French-speaking voters and reported that seventy were Liberal, twenty-nine Conservative, one Independent, and thirteen doubtful. He gave particular attention to two priests, favourably impressing one of them with the promise of a post-election trip to do colonization work near his home town in the Rimouski area. The other priest was suitably influenced by the promise of land for grazing purposes near his mission; at a cost of $64, reported Prud'homme, the land could be purchased for the priest, and the result would be several more votes for Sifton.[40] Appropriate newspapers were being sent to each voter to counter the influence of Tarte's *La Patrie*, and Prud'homme recommended sending to all of them "a large good portrait (steel engraving) of Sir Wilfrid Laurier." An unexpected benefit of Prud'homme's work was intelligence about Tory plans. He encountered some Tory organizers and, without identifying himself, encouraged them to talk. They even supplied a list of all their meetings, and revealed that "prospects were not good for the Conservative Party in the N.W.T., and they were abstaining at their meetings to mention the G.T.R. as everyone is in favour of the new railway."[41]

Upon his return from England, Sifton began intensive preparations for an election. Detailed plans for selecting candidates and preparing and sending literature began to fly back and forth. The frantic pace was reflected when, concluding a list of orders to his assistant private secretary, J. B. Harkin, Sifton declared, "It should be done immediately, in fact everything should be done immediately."[42] The western organization may be outlined briefly. Since Templeman's appointment to the cabinet in 1902, Sifton had been relieved of direct responsibility for British Columbia. His principal concern was the twenty prairie seats of Manitoba and the Territories. From Ottawa he directed operations, assisted, as in 1900, by his private secretary, A.P. Collier; when the latter resigned in 1904, he was replaced by Harkin. A former journalist, Harkin oversaw the preparation, printing, and distribution of propaganda, the pamphlets, newspaper articles, and literature directed at particular ethnic or other religious groups.

In the west, Senator Finlay Young supervised Manitoba organization, and G.H.V. Bulyea did the same in the Territories. Immigration Commissioner, J. Obed Smith, was charged with organizing the ethnic vote. Individual organizers were appointed for each ethnic group, as with Prud'homme among the French Canadians. John Dafoe acted as a kind of special agent, with an extraordinarily broad grasp of the situation, and a remarkable rapport with Liberals at every point, enabling him to feed a steady stream of important information to Sifton. The *Free Press* handled as much of the printing of literature as it could, but the demand far exceeded the capacity of its plant, and much was done in Ottawa. Each constituency had a full-time organizer, paid $100 per month. Another was given the task of naturalizing the "foreign vote," and yet another of organizing the Orange vote. The Liberal candidates in the provincial election of 1903 were involved in the riding executive in each constituency to ensure the co-operation of the provincial Liberal organization. Bulyea estimated that it was costing a minimum of $3,000 or $3,500 a month to run the territorial organization, and it must have cost at least as much for Manitoba, apart from special organizers and literature.[43] At a rough estimate, Liberal campaign costs for Manitoba and the Territories from September or October 1903 through January 1904 must have been running near $10,000 per month, considering all forms of expenditure.

"I am working like a beaver to get ready for the election," Sifton told Dafoe.[44] But everything depended upon the negotiations over the Grand Trunk Pacific. Sifton observed to Walter Scott that "It will be impossible to dissolve before a [Parliamentary] session unless Mr Hays is able to show us such facts in connection with the authority of his directors and shareholders as will enable us to pledge ourselves to the people that the project is going ahead at once. We cannot take any chances of making such a pledge unless we know that it will be carried out in good faith. Obviously it would be much better to wait and put it in shape." Personally Sifton wanted another session, but Laurier was equally anxious for a February contest. An important factor against such a choice may well have been the fact that "the party workers generally throughout the country are simply in terror of a winter campaign."[45] Early in January, Laurier finally decided to postpone the election and recall Parliament. The election machinery was quickly wound down, most of the organizers being released once conventions were called and candidates announced.

Inevitably these uncertainties produced tensions within the party. Rumours reached Sifton of another incipient rebellion in the party; as it turned out, they were largely unfounded, reflecting merely minor discontents. Sifton, however, was in no fit state to face another revolt in the ranks. He had exhausted himself in the preparations for the election, and his insomnia and tension had recurred. He wrote an extraordinary outburst to D.W. Bole, a druggist and former president of the Winnipeg Liberal Association, who was to be the Liberal candidate in the city. Bole and W.F. McCreary, MP for Selkirk, had been among those said to be dissatisfied with Sifton's leadership.

I have never sought office at the hands of my party. When I first became a candidate for the legislature it was to fight a forlorn hope for the party in what was regarded as a Tory hive. When I entered the local government and afterwards when I entered the Federal Government it was the first time on the insistent demand of the leader Mr. Greenway and the second time after Sir Wilfrid had informed me that he would not take in Mr. Martin on any consideration and that if I did not come in there was no one else from Manitoba available.

Since I have been here I have devoted myself with unceasing labor to carry out a policy which would lift the West from the stagnation and dullness which existed in 1896 and send it forward. You can judge of my success. What perhaps you cannot so well judge is the fact that I have had to initiate and carry through this policy in the face not only of the vicious and bitter opposition of the Tories but with absolutely no help from anyone on our own side. I have had to fight a persistent and malignant system of slander by the Tories and an equally malignant and persistent system of throatcutting by alleged friends many of them in receipt of constant favors and benefits from the Government on my own recommendation.

After the Lisgar by-election feeling that incessant labor anxiety and worry were slowly but surely undermining my health I earnestly solicited Laurier to allow me to retire. He emphatically refused, declaring that he would not hear of it and even said that if I left him he would probably go out himself. This of course I did not take seriously but his refusal for the time being put the matter off. Then came

Laurier's illness, Tarte's deliberate treachery and now we are within sight of a general election.

I am where I am because of my loyalty to my chief and party not because I desire to remain in office. I am prepared to help pilot the party through a general election with all its attendant anxieties and labors but only one condition, i.e. that the party desire me to do so and is prepared to be loyal to me. If the party represented by leading men like yourself desire a change you have only to say so: if you say so I shall take immediate steps to bring it into effect but I have a right before we go any farther to know whether or not I can rely upon the absolute loyalty and fidelity of the leading members of the party.

The burden of carrying the affairs of the West is a heavy one to say nothing of the enormous mass of departmental work and political details which are forced upon me at every turn. No one should be charged with this duty in whom the party has not implicit confidence. This is very obvious.[46]

For a man usually so reserved and self-possessed as Sifton, this emotional and sometimes self-serving document was an indicator of the severe stress under which he had worked for over a year. Directly after mailing the letter he went south for a two-week vacation. Upon his return, he found a reply from Bole emphatically pledging his loyalty to Sifton and the Liberal Party.[47] Perhaps this reassurance helped. Sifton resumed his management of the party machinery, but he was not prominent in the House of Commons during the session, certainly compared with his active role from 1901 to 1903.

In February, he predicted a July or (more likely) a fall election. He would have preferred a June contest, "but notwithstanding what Tarte says I am not complete boss, that is to say, there are others!"[48] In the interim, Manitoba Liberals, with Sifton's support, conducted a strenuous campaign to persuade Laurier to change the law that left preparation of the electoral lists in the hands of the local government. The Dominion Franchise Act of 1885 had placed preparation of the lists in federal hands, over the loud protests of the Liberals, who contended that the provinces should have the responsibility. Upon attaining power, Laurier acted on this policy—which was fine so long as the provinces had Liberal regimes. In Manitoba, however, Roblin and Rogers were not above manipulating the lists in the Tory interest. When preparing for the provincial election of 1903 they arranged in effect to disfranchise the "foreign vote," the Slavs in particular, since they were predominantly Liberal. Under the Dominion Franchise Act, however, *classes* disfranchised by provincial legislation could take an oath and vote in federal elections. To get around that loophole, Roblin and Rogers restored the vote to the Slavs, but made it virtually impossible for them to be registered. Courts of revision sat for a few hours on one day at points from twenty to sixty miles away from the Slav colonies, and the voters had to register in person. As D.W. Bole told Laurier, "not being registered they cannot vote, neither can we swear in their vote, because forsooth they are *not legislated against*. We can prove to you that as many as 500 in one constituency were deprived of their rights, and cannot vote for the reason named."[49] All the work of naturalizing the "foreign vote" would, it seemed, be for naught.

Since 1903, the battle had been waged with an unsympathetic prime minister who, with many of his eastern colleagues, regarded provincial control of the franchise as a constant Liberal principle since 1867, and standing proof that the Grits were the true party of provincial rights. "How," demanded L.G. Power of Laurier, "can we advocate respect for provincial rights and provincial sensibilities in the matter of education if we disregard them when it is a question of the franchise?" Surely a change in the legislation would hurt the Liberals in the rest of Canada.[50] All that Laurier could reply to the westerners was that the Manitoba law would "work both ways and to the prejudice of both parties," while admitting that the Liberals might be hurt more.[51] Reflecting the near paranoia among Manitoba Liberal candidates and the belief that sinister motives must have underlain Laurier's intransigence, Dafoe asked Sifton, "Is it not possible that they feel so safe in the east that they would just as soon not have too many western supporters? I do not imagine they like our style any too well."[52]

Great gloom settled over the western camp, and undoubtedly Sifton too was exasperated at the decision. But he had foreseen the probable outcome and did not become depressed. He had earlier advised the westerners to take full advantage of the courts of revision, and he did so himself in Brandon. The others generally did not, so convinced were they that Laurier would admit the cogency of their case and provide the required changes in the law.[53]

The federal Liberals were not without advantages of their own. Grit sensibilities about provincial rights were much greater than their worry over the abandonment of another historic Liberal principle, economy in government. That was hastily cast aside as the election came into sight. Not only did Fielding produce a strong election budget and a huge surplus, but the cornucopia of public works was opened on an unprecedented scale. Brandon received a new drill hall; $341,000 worth of public works were slated for Winnipeg; and (acting on a suggestion of Dafoe) $50,000 was granted to hold a Dominion Exhibition in the Manitoba capital in July.[54] Poor old Sir Richard Cartwright, who for so many years had exhorted governments to economize, was aghast. Appealing futilely to Sifton for support in demanding a limit, he noted that the government was asking "for something over nine millions for Public Works'' for 1904-5. In 1896, the Conservatives had only asked $1 million, and had previously averaged $2 million annually, so that the 1904 expenditure ''is sure to expose us to most severe criticism.''[55]

The tide was running in favour of the government and expansive, dynamic programmes, as Sifton well knew. In May, he had confidently written, ''So far as I can see there is no possibility of the Conservative Party winning the next election by any possible consideration.''[56] When Laurier finally called the election at the end of September for 3 November, the main problem for Sifton was to ensure that the embarrassment of 1900 for the Liberals in Manitoba would not be repeated. His success was convincing: the Liberals carried seven of the ten seats in each of Manitoba and the Territories, and swept British Columbia. Across Canada, the government carried 138 seats, to 75 for the Tories, and 52 per cent of the popular vote. Among the provinces, only Prince Edward Island and Ontario gave a majority of seats to the Opposition.[57]

The western campaign had been uneventful. In Brandon, Sifton's opponent was none other than R.L. Richardson. As in 1900, numerous candidates for the ''sacrifice,'' as Sifton smugly put it, were suggested, ranging from Roblin and Hugh John Macdonald on down. However, Richardson appears to have forced himself on Roblin and Rogers (who were running the Tory campaign) by threatening to run in Souris as an Independent, splitting the vote and endangering what was considered a safe Conservative seat. As a result ''the farmer's friend,'' as Richardson styled himself, was nominated as an Independent Conservative for Brandon.[58] The *Free Press* immediately condemned the nomination as ''a job'' and turned Richardson's tactics upon himself by denouncing him as ''the machine candidate.''[59] Hugh John Macdonald was brought in to allay the fears of straight Conservatives, who were unenthusiastic about the publisher of the *Tribune*. Sifton and Richardson met in traditional platform debate on 28 and 31 October. The voters at least were able to choose between the government ownership-low tariff Toryism of Richardson, and Sifton's defence of the government record. ''I believe,'' Sifton declared in debate, ''that government ownership on general principles tends to kill private enterprise and energy.''[60] There was now no hint of his private willingness to consider expanding public ownership of railways if it were shown to be in the public interest.

Sifton's victory margin of 821 votes seemed convincing, but Richardson believed that he had left little to chance and duly entered a strong protest. Sifton responded with a counter-protest, attacked Tory seats with as many protests as possible, and determined to make the contest against his election as troublesome and expensive for the Conservatives as possible.[61] Most of the protests were, as usual, eventually sawn off. Still, Sifton had

had some dubious tricks up his sleeve during the campaign. A secret deal certainly had been arranged to reduce the Tory vote in north Winnipeg, helping to bring about a Liberal victory in the city.[62] He told a victorious MP in British Columbia, ''We did pretty well in Manitoba and the Territories. We kept our hand concealed and I don't think the other fellows ever got any idea of what we expected to do. A couple of our candidates developed unexpected weakness or we should have two more seats.''[63]

Still, he really could not complain. The seven seats in Manitoba were particularly satisfying, obliterating the losses of 1896 and 1900, proving the effectiveness of his organizing skills, and seemingly justifying his record. Former Lisgar MP, D.A. Stewart, quoted scripture to Laurier on the victory: ''While the righteous are in authority the people rejoice.'' Undoubtedly more apt, however, was Cartwright's scriptural allusion in congratulating the minister of the interior: ''You certainly smote the Philistines hip and thigh.''[64]

Late in 1904, Sifton seemed to be at the apex of his power. He was widely regarded as the most influential of Laurier's colleagues, and his impact on the electoral victory was generally believed to have extended far beyond the prairie West. The appearance, nevertheless, was far from the reality. He was not, as he knew and often pointed out to others, the master of the administration. Laurier preferred men who thought as he did and who were less likely to rock the boat. Sifton not only radiated power and authority, and inevitably appeared to be a rival, but he also had his own pronounced ideas and attracted controversy. Moreover, for all his strengths, he never succeeded in penetrating the French-Canadian and Roman Catholic mind. It had been apparent for some time that his ambitions, his idea of the role of government, and his conception of the nature of Canada were not compatible with Laurier's views. Tensions that had been building up for several years shortly would come to a head. Few would have guessed that less than four months after the victory of 1904, Laurier would have lost the man who had been a principal architect of his party's success.

8

Resignation
(1905)

The elections over, almost the first order of business for the freshly sustained government was provincial autonomy for the North-West
Territories. Laurier had bowed to the increasingly strident demands of the
territorial government when, at the end of September 1904, he had
promised to introduce an autonomy measure at the next session of
Parliament if his government were sustained in the elections.

As the western representative in the cabinet, Sifton had never considered it his duty to automatically support all the demands of the region's
popular leaders. His seeming indifference to the economic plight of the
local government and the resultant demands for autonomy were a case in
point. It certainly baffled F.W.G. Haultain, the territorial premier. In 1896
Sifton had grandly declared that he would end "the swaddling clothes plan
of treating the North-West"; in 1897 he had been instrumental in granting a
measure of responsible government to the Territories. Since then he had
exerted himself mightily to get the Territories settled as quickly as
possible. Yet he refused to permit any devolution of power (as the local
government found, to its sorrow, when it tried to regulate the liquor traffic
in the Yukon), nor did he exert himself to relieve the financial embarrassment of a government expected to provide basic services—roads,
bridges, schools—for the tens of thousands of immigrants pouring into the
West each year. The territorial government was expected to provide most

of the same services as any provincial government, but without equivalent powers or tax base.

During the fiscal year 1899-1900, for example, less than $42,000, or approximately 10 per cent of the territorial revenues, was raised locally by fees, licences, and other taxes; the federal grant stood at some $283,000; and other monies, such as interest from school lands funds, made up the remainder. Even so, the local government was about $120,000 short of its anticipated expenditure requirements of $535,000.[1] When territorial officials desperately pleaded for a supplementary grant of $50,000 so that educational expenditures would not have to be curtailed, Sir Wilfrid Laurier curtly refused "to add a single cent to the present Estimates."[2]

It was such repeated refusals by Ottawa to respond adequately to territorial demands that led the local assembly to pass unanimously on 2 May 1900 a resolution requesting provincial status as a solution to the outstanding difficulties.[3] The resolution was officially transmitted to Ottawa in July, but with a fall election in the offing, it received no more than an acknowledgement. Early in January 1901 Haultain wrote directly to Sifton, urging him to proceed with provincial status. The minister of the interior appeared to give territorial officials some ground for cautious optimism as he replied, "Without at the present moment committing myself to any positive statement I am prepared to say that the time has arrived when the question of organizing the Territories on the Provincial basis ought to be the subject of full consideration."[4] Indeed, a few days earlier he had told the House of Commons that "the people of the Territories are as capable of self government as any other people in Canada."[5]

On 25 October 1901 Haultain and A.L. Sifton of the territorial cabinet met in Ottawa with Clifford Sifton, Laurier, and four other federal ministers. By this time the government was beginning to have second thoughts. The minister of the interior, in unusually opaque language, declared that the meeting was being held "with a view in the first instance to an informal interchange of views which will furnish material for consideration pending a more definite discussion at a later date." Haultain accordingly was invited to submit a more detailed proposal for the consideration of the federal cabinet. He did so early in December, only to have Sifton scotch provincial autonomy late in March 1902. The population of the Territories was still sparse, argued Sifton, while the rapid influx of immigrants pointed to a fluid rather than stable set of circumstances for which to devise government institutions. Furthermore, he alleged that the people of the region were not agreed as to whether there should be a single large province (as Haultain desired), or more than one.[6] Haultain promptly had the Assembly pass a resolution regretting the federal decision and then called an election on the issue in which he was strongly sustained.[7]

Meanwhile in the House of Commons there occurred a debate in which several western MPs advocated at least more generous financial treatment of the Territories, if not outright autonomy. In his reply Sifton alluded to the complexity of governing so vast a region, suggested that the issue had only surfaced recently, and maintained that westerners were characteristically impetuous and impatient in their demands. No hurried ad hoc solution would do; a permanent solution would require time and care; and "if they get such a settlement within three or four years I should feel very well satisfied indeed, and I should feel that we have accomplished that result in a comparatively short time."[8]

However valid these reasons might have seemed, they were only a partial explanation of the delay. Opposition members suggested that the government was seeking political advantage and that it was afraid of the separate school issue. Sifton flatly denied both charges, adding that "my own view is that the school question is settled so far as the North-west Territories is concerned." Both the Catholics and the Protestants "feel that they have a satisfactory compromise and that there is no necessity for difficulty or agitation upon the question."[9] Yet as events unfolded there seemed to be some substance in the Opposition's suspicions. There also was a much larger problem before the government in its plans to support railway expansion in the Territories. It would be undesirable to devolve greater powers to the local government and alienate public lands from federal control — as Haultain's scheme demanded—until the main lines of federal policy were in place.

Both the federal Liberals and Conservatives recognized that autonomy for the Territories could not long be postponed, and they began to man-oeuvre for partisan advantage. Opposition leader Robert Borden moved first. Anxious for a popular cause to offset his unpopular defence of high tariff protection during his western tour in 1902, he clambered aboard Haultain's autonomy bandwagon. Subsequent events suggest that the issue did little to aid the Tories except to ensure that Haultain would identify himself firmly as a Conservative.[11] This was confirmed at a convention of Territorial Conservatives in 1903 where Haultain became honorary president of the association, although he personally disapproved of a resolution to abandon non-partisanship in local politics.[12]

Borden's endorsement of Haultain's scheme, and the latter's embracing of the Tory cause, made it politically impossible for the Liberals to accept the scheme as it stood. While recognizing that probably a majority of citizens of the Territories favoured autonomy, Sifton knew that there was room to manoeuvre on the terms. He also believed that the provincial rights sentiment had its origin in financial grievances. As Walter Scott told Sifton, the autonomy question could be minimized as a political issue "so long as schools & roads & bridges requirements are being met."[13] Accordingly, the federal grant was raised from $457,979 in 1902 to $707,979 in 1903. In addition, the government granted $250,000 to cover the deficit of the previous year and offered a capital advance, or loan, of $250,000 at favourable rates.[14] Haultain easily saw through the stratagem for delay, pointing out that the grant for 1903 was still $300,000 short of what was required. Moreover, he scoffed at the notion of borrowing $250,000 from a federal treasury that had enriched itself by at least $1,000,000 from western lands— "our money," as the *Calgary Herald* put it.[15]

Embarrassing as Haultain's refusal appeared, and despite some apparent support for Haultain from the Liberal members of the local Assembly, Sifton was confident that he could succeed. The territorial MPs, who earlier had supported autonomy in varying degrees, now were ranged solidly behind the government. Other issues more favourable to the Liberals would probably dominate an election campaign in the West, unless the government tripped up and allowed Haultain to make autonomy the central issue. Realizing that the matter would be raised in Parliament while he was absent at the Alaska Boundary Tribunal hearings, Sifton carefully instructed W.S. Fielding "not to antagonize [the territorial government] or take an attitude of opposition."

> I would like you to make the following statement in substance on the subject of Provincial Autonomy;—that the Government have no desire or disposition to put off for any length of time the settlement of the question of Provincial Autonomy for the North West Territories; that the rapid settlement now going on and the considerable increase in population which has already taken place have created a necessity for dealing with the subject with very little delay. So soon as the pre-liminary difficulties such as the [CPR] tax exemption question which is now before the courts are out of the way the Government will be prepared to deal with the question.
>
> You will observe that the purpose of having the matter stated in the above way is to make it so that the opponents cannot take the ground that we are opposed to granting Autonomy or wish to put it off indefinitely.[16]

Shortly after Sifton's return from England, he heard through various intermediaries that Haultain desired a judgeship and retirement from politics. Seeing the political advantages of removing the territorial premier, a position was quickly found, only to be turned down by Haultain after some indecision early in December.[17] Western Liberals were both disappointed and bitter at this turn of events, for they had been increasingly frustrated under Haultain's leadership. Bulyea in particular, the only

Liberal in the territorial cabinet after A.L. Sifton's elevation to Chief Justice of the Territorial Supreme Court, found life with Haultain nearly intolerable. As commissioner of public works he had questioned certain features of the proposed federal capital advance,[18] but in light of the heavy demands upon his department he had wanted to accept it. Only great pressure from western Liberals prevented his resignation when Haultain spurned the federal offer. His presence in the cabinet, and continued local Liberal support of Haultain's autonomy resolutions, were deemed vital to preventing the premier from succeeding in making it a partisan issue of major proportions.[19]

In 1904 the federal authorities increased the subsidy by $200,000 to $909,979—"for the first time," in the opinion of C.C. Lingard, "what might be termed 'a liberal response.'"[20] But no amount of financial liberality was now going to satisfy Haultain. On 1 June he again demanded that Laurier grant provincial status on an equal basis with other provinces, including local control of public lands and compensation "for that part of the public domain alienated by the Dominion for purely Federal purposes."[21] Throughout the summer the prime minister did not even bother to acknowledge the letters. At the beginning of September, however, Walter Scott told Sifton that Laurier must write an official letter undertaking to negotiate with the Territories the terms of provincial status. This was vital for the Liberals during the fall session of the territorial Assembly.[22] Having dissolved Parliament, and unable or unwilling to procrastinate any longer, Laurier finally assured Haultain,

> should my government be sustained, we will be prepared immediately after the election to enter upon negotiations for the purpose of arriving at a settlement of the various questions involved in the granting of provincial autonomy, with a view to dealing with the question at the next session of Parliament.[23]

The firm resolve of his language notwithstanding, the prime minister remained uneasy. It was not Haultain who troubled him, but the spectre of renewed racial and sectarian discord over the school issue. For two decades political life for Laurier had turned on the disputes of French and English, Catholics and Protestants: from the North-West Rebellion and the execution of Louis Riel in 1885, through the Jesuits' Estates and Equal Rights agitation, to the Manitoba school question and the South African War. Even when there were no great issues to keep the pot boiling, there were plenty of smaller disputes to keep it at a steady simmer, ranging from patronage in the Montreal post office to accusations of discrimination in the Yukon.

Above all, Laurier was acutely aware that the school issue had not disappeared after the compromise of 1896. Three more years of constant delicate negotiations had bought some relief for the minority in rural Manitoba, but Winnipeg remained both unsettled and sensitive. During the spring and summer of 1903 there had been some hope of resolving the conflict there, but intensive negotiations failed amidst recriminations and charges of bad faith. Laurier chose not to use Sifton during the negotiations, preferring to treat directly with Premier Roblin.[24] This episode had a bearing on the subsequent territorial school issue because of its profound impact upon the papal delegate to Canada since 1902, Monseigneur Sbaretti, archbishop of Ephesus. To him, zealous for the Catholic cause and unfamiliar with the realities of Canadian politics, it should have been a simple matter for a Catholic prime minister and a premier who professed sympathy for the plight of the minority to resolve the issue with some concessions for separate schools.[25] Disillusioned, he resolved to fight for restoration of more extensive Catholic privileges in the Territories when provincial status was granted.

The school issue in the Territories had a certain sensitivity as well. Unhappily, the small French Catholic minority was scattered or isolated and it was being overwhelmed by the heterogeneous flood of settlers. Bishops Legal and Grandin were not figures of national stature who could command the active support of fellow Catholics in other regions, particularly in Quebec, as Taché had done for the cause in Manitoba. Certainly Laurier felt no compunction over his failure to press the Haultain government for any of the concessions he was working so assiduously to secure in Manitoba. When Grandin complained to Lord Minto of the treatment suffered by Catholics, Laurier promptly dismissed "dear old Bishop Grandin's letter." Prime Minister Thompson, himself a Catholic, had said in 1893-94 that nothing could be done for the territorial Catholics, and Laurier concurred, except to add that "a Roman Catholic [school] inspector...would be a reasonable concession." But nothing was done.[26]

When Sifton stated in 1902 that the existing system of schools in the Territories was satisfactory, he presumably spoke for the government, insofar as it had considered the question at all, and there was no contrary opinion expressed in the Commons. Haultain tried to introduce the school question into the territorial election in 1902, but the government refused to be drawn into debate. By himself, Haultain could not make the issue into a national question.

Then Sbaretti entered the picture. He was one figure who could rouse Catholic support for the minority cause in the North-West. Because of the failure of the Manitoba negotiations in the summer of 1903, and aware of the autonomy agitation in the Territories, he asked Legal for information about schools in that region. He was told that the North-West Territories Act of 1875 had stipulated the establishment of public and separate schools and that in 1884 the first school ordinance established a "just, impartial and loyal" dual system in which Catholics and Protestants had practically complete control over their own schools, independent of each other. Almost immediately, however, the process of chipping away at French and Catholic privileges had begun, eventually leaving the Catholics still in possession of their own schools, but now thoroughly under government control and regulation of an increasingly Protestant flavour. These changes were consolidated in territorial ordinances of 1892 and 1901. At a minimum, thought Legal, the Catholics should be able to insist upon Catholic-approved textbooks, French Catholic inspectors, flexibility with respect to the timing of religious instruction, and some use of French as a language of instruction. Furthermore, the Catholics desired concessions with respect to normal school regulations,.the method of organizing school districts, and the law governing assessment for school taxes.

> As a conclusion it can be affirmed that for several years there has been a continued tendency to encroach on the advantages which a system of separate schools gives to Catholics. If they have not dared to suppress them by law, they have tried in fact to diminish as much as possible the efficacy of this system.
>
> In the agitation which is being carried on at the present time with respect to the future organization of the Territories into regular Provinces, the question of schools is especially aimed at; they do not fail to claim for the new province or the new provinces the absolute control of the schools, with the intention, scarcely disguised, to impose on us a system of schools similar to that of Manitoba, by suppressing the principle of separate schools.
>
> The results of such a measure would be even more disastrous here than in Manitoba. In Manitoba there are groups of people, perfectly distinct, some entirely Catholic, others entirely Protestant, except in the somewhat important towns; but throughout the whole extent of the territories the different peoples are almost everywhere mixed together, so that everywhere the schools would be found to be in fact Protestant schools.
>
> An energetic and decisive action on the part of the Government of Ottawa is necessary to shelter us in this regard from the encroachment and tyranny of the Protestant majority.[27]

It was a plea that Sbaretti could not refuse. At the beginning of March 1904, he asked Laurier to pledge on behalf of the government that the Catholics would be guaranteed "the system of separate schools." The prime minister replied that he believed that the original reasoning of the Fathers of Confederation still held, that minorities should be guaranteed the privileges that they possessed at the time of Confederation. "My opinion is very clear," he added, "that when the territories are admitted as a province, the minority should not be placed in a worse condition than it is today; that its schools ought to receive the same degree of protection as is granted to the minority in Ontario and Quebec where separate schools existed at the first establishment of Confederation, and that the act of admission of the territories into confederation should especially provide that the system of separate schools now in existence shall be secured and beyond the power of the provincial legislatures as provided by section 93 of the Constitution, either to abolish or even prejudicially affect such schools."[28] Whether inadvertently or by design, Sbaretti persisted in slightly twisting Laurier's words into a promise "to guarantee to the Catholics...the system of Separate Schools, as enjoyed by the minority in the Provinces of Ontario and Quebec, beyond any interference of the Provincial Legislatures."[29] This could be taken to mean considerably more privileges for the minority, and Sbaretti repeatedly pressed Laurier for details and clarification. Prior to the 1904 election, nevertheless, Laurier simply continued to affirm only that existing privileges would be protected.[30]

By mutual agreement, the Church and the Liberals agreed to discourage discussion of the school issue in the press, a "conspiracy of silence" that was maintained through the elections and for some time afterward.[31] Indeed, with Laurier's public promise of autonomy and private assurances on schools, the problem of provincial status was a mere footnote in the election campaign. Laurier then left the preparation of a draft bill to Justice Minister Fitzpatrick, while he left for a California vacation. No less exhausted than the prime minister, Sifton nevertheless felt obligated to record his views before taking a short holiday. He used Haultain's draft bill as a guide, leaving written notations and a memorandum of his views for the minister of justice.[32] Subsequently Fitzpatrick told the House of Commons that Sifton had noted, "Make memo of present provisions in law relating to the Northwest Territories Act as to public schools and provisions in the other constitutional Acts."[33] The minister of the interior had no doubt that his views were well known: as in 1902, he was prepared to see the existing system perpetuated. But before an education clause was drafted he anticipated being closely involved in the final drafting of any bill. Having at last cleared his desk of the most pressing matters, Sifton left at the end of December, seeking relief from continuing severe insomnia and nervous tension.[34]

Early in January 1905 Laurier and several cabinet ministers met with Haultain and Bulyea in Ottawa, the negotiations continuing over several weeks. Meanwhile the parliamentary session began on 12 January. Initially

Sifton had intended to be absent only two weeks, but his nerves were so spent, and the "mud and lithia water baths" of Mudlavia, Indiana, so relaxing and beneficial, that he extended his stay. (The baths, stated the promotional literature, were excellent "for all forms of Rheumatism, Gout and all diseases of the Kidneys, Blood, Skin and Nerves.") Laurier consequently found it advisable to write him about certain points at issue, while assuring him that all was well in Ottawa and "rapid progress" was being made on "the North West bills."[35]

The prime minister was most concerned about the question of control of public lands and of irrigation. Haultain had been particularly insistent upon the principle of provincial ownership of the lands, as existed in all other provinces except Manitoba. Sifton's response was unequivocal: the Dominion must retain control. He also rejected provincial control of grazing lands, a compromise suggested by Haultain.

> I think it is impracticable. It would be found absolutely impossible to say what were and what were not to be regarded as grazing lands. As to the other lands, giving them to the Provinces would be ruinous to our settlement policy and would be disastrous to the whole Dominion. The mere report that the lands had been handed over and that there might be a change in the policy of administering them would cost us tens of thousands of settlers in the next two years to say nothing of the more distant future. The continued progress of Canada for the next five years depends almost entirely on the flow of immigration.

Similarly, with respect to provincial control of irrigation, Sifton believed that control must finally rest with Ottawa. "In regard to every stream of importance interprovincial questions will arise and in regard to some international questions will arise....By retaining the plenary power at Ottawa you ensure the fact that a central body which for its own interest is bound to try and do justice to all parties will be able to adjust difficulties as they arise."

Evidently the decision that there would be two provinces had already been taken. When Laurier asked Sifton his views on the names for the new provinces, he stated that Alberta would have to be retained for the western province, which would be dominated by the old provisional district of the same name. The eastern province would be more complicated, for the Districts of Assiniboia and Saskatchewan both had strong claims. While Sifton preferred Assiniboia, "I do not think it matters much; both names are identified with the history of the territories." He also noted that Laurier had not mentioned "anything about the school question & I assume that you have not as yet discerned any serious difficulty in dealing with it." His holiday was proving so beneficial, he added, that he wished to remain until

15 February. "I found my nerves in a much worse state than I had thought and it is essential to get them thoroughly steadied before I return to work. I have never found a better place to rest. It is completely out of the world so far as Excitement is concerned."[36]

In Ottawa, Haultain was fighting a losing battle.[37] He wanted one large province; the federal government decided upon two. He wanted provincial control of public lands and irrigation; the Dominion, at Sifton's instance, decided to retain control. He wanted complete provincial control of education; the Dominion intended to place certain restrictions in the provincial constitutions. Whatever the explanations, the determination was that the settlement should be a Liberal one. The western members assured Laurier that with a generous subsidy the failure to gain provincial control of lands would not be a serious issue. Important as these political considerations were, however, it is clear that the decisive factor in determining continued dominion control of lands was national policy. For Sifton, the question of immigration and settlement was a national enterprise, too important to leave to uncertain and parochial local administrations.

National considerations as understood by Laurier had already determined the policy upon the school question.[38] That the nature of Canadian Confederation demanded recognition and federal protection of minority rights was a self-evident proposition to the prime minister. A spirit of compromise, he believed, lay at the heart of the Canadian experience. Protection for minority school privileges had both historical and moral justification. "The only thing to do, is the right thing, and take the consequences," he told J.D. Cameron, ex-attorney general of Manitoba. "I would not impose separate schools to-day upon the Territories, if they had not been therein introduced in 1875, with the avowed statement that they were to be part of the system of separate schools as organized at the time of confederation. At the time of Confederation it was settled that in every Province coming or to come later on into the Union, and in which there was a system of separate schools, the local Legislatures of such Provinces would be bound to respect them."[39] Mindful of the unhappy failure of the Manitoba Act to protect separate schools, both Laurier and Sbaretti desired to create the most ironclad protection possible for Catholic schools in the new provinces. To this end, lengthy and tedious negotiations went on between Laurier, Sbaretti, and Fitzpatrick, an Irish Catholic of like mind.[40]

Meanwhile Laurier wrote back to Sifton, near the end of January, that the school question was slowly being worked out. "I am satisfied with the progress which we have made on it," he added apprehensively, "though everybody fears it." Still, he did not ask for Sifton's views on any of the several draft proposals then available. Instead, he requested Sifton's opinion on financial compensation for the failure of the provinces to obtain control of public lands.[41] The minister of the interior answered quickly. Senator J.H. Ross had proposed setting up the revenues from the lands as a trust fund for the provinces. To this Sifton was entirely opposed. It would mean the establishment of "an elaborate and untenable fiction" that "the Provinces were or ought to be constitutionally owners of the land. This is wholly untrue. The original provinces owned the crown lands. The Dominion owns these lands & decides now to erect provinces—It is for the Dom. to say upon what terms." The proposals would lead to "perennial agitation" and "interminable argument" in the future. He proposed instead a fixed allowance for government, a periodically adjusted per capita grant, debt capital of $32 per capita based on 250,000 population for each province, "$200,000 in lieu in lands per annum," and "about $50,000 per annum as compensation for assuming the administration of justice in the northern and unoccupied territory."[42]

For nearly three weeks there was no further correspondence. Laurier had not indicated any great urgency—indeed, quite the reverse—and, as the *Manitoba Free Press* had reported, it was widely assumed that the bills would not be finally settled until Sifton's return. Still not feeling fully recovered, he postponed his return for another week beyond 15 February.[43] Suddenly on Monday, 20 February Laurier wired Sifton that the bills would be introduced into Parliament the next day.[44] This was extraordinary, because he mentioned that the financial terms were not completed, and it is also known that the schools clause did not reach its final form until the morning of 21 February.[45] Sifton wired in reply, "I shall be home Friday morning [24 February]. If any serious difficulty it might be well to postpone final action until then."[46] The next day Laurier answered, "Important Bill should be introduced immediately to direct to public opinion [*sic*] which is being worked against us though not injuriously so far. Do not hasten your return. First reading to-day but cannot come up for discussion for at least a week."[47]

It is difficult to accept Laurier's explanation for his precipitate action at face value. Sifton indeed had twice postponed his return, but evidently with Laurier's blessing. Public opinion, by the prime minister's own admission, was not so roused as to endanger the government. Financial and school arrangements were barely complete, and Laurier made no effort to seek the approval of Sifton or Haultain on the final product. Given Sifton's position, his past connection with school legislation, and his proven skill at construing such legislation, it should have been expected at the very least that Laurier would have wanted his prior agreement. Leaving aside the subsequent dispute over the wording and intent of the education clause, in terms of political tactics one is left with two possible conclusions about his procedure. Either he panicked in face of some anticipated shift in public opinion against the government and in the process blithely assumed that the legislation was substantially in line with Sifton's views; or he anticipated the disagreement of Sifton, and possibly others, and hoped to forestall future divisions by a fait accompli. Whatever the reason, he plainly blundered. [48]

Better than his word, Sifton returned to Ottawa a day early, taking his seat in the House of Commons on the evening of Thursday the 23rd to "the astonishment of everybody," his health apparently largely recovered. [49] The next day he conferred with the western members and with the prime minister. He told J.W. Dafoe that Laurier "spoke at some length of the difficulties which he had had. He did not ask me my opinion or what my views were. Sir Wilfrid's proceeding in matters of this kind is always to assume that everyone agrees with him until they insist upon quarrelling. He finds this much the easiest way of getting on." [50] On the 25th he advised Dafoe of his disagreement with the bills as they stood. On the 26th he told Laurier that he contemplated resignation; a further conference that evening did not resolve their differences. On Monday the 27th Sifton submitted his resignation, which was accepted the following day. [51] Laurier apparently made no serious effort to seek a compromise or to persuade Sifton to remain in the cabinet.

Apart from a small quibble on the method of compensation for public lands, [52] Sifton's disagreement was based upon clause 16 (the education clause) of the provincial autonomy bills as introduced by Laurier on 21 February; and upon the general context in which the prime minister had placed the school issue in the course of his address. The offending clause [53] attempted to protect the separate schools in several ways. It applied the remedial provisions of the British North America Act, section 93, to the new provinces by establishing the legal fiction that the Territories should be considered already provinces at the time of union. It reaffirmed the principle of separate schools found in the North-West Territories Act of 1875, establishing the right of a Protestant or Catholic minority in a particular school district to establish separate schools. Finally it attempted to ensure an equitable distribution of public money to the respective school systems. In several respects the clause seemed ambiguous. Were the modifications of 1892 and 1901 included in the definition? Was the public money to be distributed according to the number of schools organized, or by some other formula? Doubtful as he was about the meaning and intent of the clause, Sifton found himself strongly opposed to Laurier's analysis of the situation. Subsequently explaining his resignation to the House, he recalled that "immediately" upon his return to Ottawa he had read Laurier's speech, and "I regretted that in the right hon. gentleman's address I found some principles enunciated with which I am unable to agree." It was then that he read the bills, discussed the question with

Laurier, and "as a result of such consideration I determined that I could not endorse or support the principle of the education clauses."[54]

Laurier had spoken of the educational provisions as being "perhaps under existing circumstances the most important" question connected with provincial autonomy.[55] Thus he suggested, both in this statement and in the emphasis on the subject in his speech, that he anticipated a major battle on it. He stated that he would not deal extensively with the specific provisions of the bill, preferring to lecture the House on the nature of Confederation and the need for tolerance and compromise. He reviewed the history of separate schools in Canada and praised George Brown's spirit of compromise on the education issue in 1864. Unfortunately, he did not entirely understand Brown's views and stumbled badly in trying to explain away Brown's opposition in 1875 to the establishment of separate schools in the Territories. Brown's view then had been that education ought to be a matter of provincial, or local, decision. Almost certainly he would not have agreed that the compromise of 1864 between Canada West and Canada East must be applied to every future province. Laurier contended, however, that the meaning of Confederation, of the Manitoba Act, and of the North-West Territories Act was that separate schools for the minority should be protected by the federal government in every province.

Sifton, by contrast, believed that the separate school issue had been inappropriately fastened on the Territories in 1875 because of central Canadian experiences and not as a result of demonstrated need. In principle he believed that the new provinces should be able to determine their own educational system free of the pressures of central Canada. He was, however, both sensible and realistic enough not to be drawn into the hue and cry in favour of that position raised, among others, by the Toronto *News* and *Globe*. Political necessity in central Canada still required living with the existing separate school system, but in Sifton's view the freedom of the provinces to control their own systems should be restricted as little as possible.

Imperceptive and superficial observers, both at the time and since, have claimed that the whole issue between Sifton and Laurier was one of mere semantics, even artificial or manufactured, and that there was no sub-stantive difference between the clause proposed by Laurier in February and that accepted as a compromise by Laurier and Sifton in March. Did not both preserve the existing system and ensure a fair distribution of public money? Surely, they note, it is clear that neither offered local control of education, as much of the Protestant press was demanding, and as Sifton was known to prefer. Did Sifton's resignation have any real point to it?

Such comments miss the real issues at stake. Local control of education never was an issue between Laurier and Sifton. It could equally appro-

priately be pointed out that Laurier's personal preference was for substantially extended rights in law for the minority, an equally unattainable
objective. The two sides in fact were fighting for the advantage in a much
more restricted field. There was a little room for disagreement as to what
constituted the existing system; and there were differences on how to
preserve it. Laurier probably, and several of his Catholic advisers certainly,[56] wished to maximize the advantage to the minority, perhaps leaving
the door open for more gains in the future. Sifton wanted to define the
restrictions specifically and narrowly, leaving as much flexibility as
possible for the provincial governments. The howls of "betrayal" from the
Catholic side when Laurier capitulated to Sifton's demands bespeak the
gravity with which the principals regarded the issues in dispute.[57]

What was the "existing system" which Laurier claimed he wished to
perpetuate? He wrote to one correspondent after introducing the bills, "We
do not want to introduce a new system in the Provinces, and the only thing
that we have provided for is the continuance of the system which has
existed in the Provinces for the last thirty years and which, as I understand,
has given satisfaction."[58] What did this mean? The system had hardly
remained the same for thirty years, as Laurier well knew. The *Catholic
Register* had no doubt of Laurier's intention to "maintain every right
guaranteed by the Parliament of Canada in 1875 to the minority in the
North-West Territories."[59] The spirit of the 1875 legislation was identified
in many Catholic minds with the dual system established in 1884, not with
the more restricted privileges that later evolved. Laurier's reference point
was always obscure: was he referring to the original system, or to the
approximation of a national school system realized under ordinances of
1892 and 1901?

It is fairly certain that those drafting the school clause—Fitzpatrick,
R.W. Scott, Henri Bourassa, and very probably Laurier—knew exactly
what they were doing. Two years later Scott recalled the "honest effort to
secure for the minority the unconditional school privileges to which I think
they were entitled" and spoke of "our attempt to re-enact the legislation of
the former period." The ministerial crisis precipitated by Sifton's resignation had made it necessary instead to "practically adopt the law as it then
stood in the Territories."[60] Laurier could never admit as much publicly or
on paper and his natural instinct was to cloud the issue. The most logical
conclusion is not that the prime minister did not know what was intended.
Rather, it would appear that he was absolutely and irrevocably committed
to protecting the limited privileges of the minority as they existed in 1905,
and beyond that that he was willing to try to secure further privileges via the
back door, if possible.[61] When he spoke of the "existing system," he never
made reference to the ordinances of 1892 and 1901. His point of reference
was the much more ambiguous legislation of 1875. What did that cover in

terms of subsequent school laws? Neither the Catholic leaders nor Sifton could have pinned him down. Technically he could argue, as he did in accepting Sifton's resignation, that "the differences between us, were more of words than of substance." [62] If that were true, he could as well have accepted Sifton's proposed changes in February without a resignation, as he could in March facing a ministerial crisis. In his heart Laurier knew, as did Sifton, that their differences were both substantial and fundamental.

For his part, Sifton at least had the virtue of being more straightforward. He had agreed to continue the system as it existed after 1901. Writing to Dafoe he stated his position with admirable clarity:

> what I agreed to was that the present system of separate schools in the North West Territories should be perpetuated. In my judgment the present system is substantially unobjectionable. That is to say, while theoretically there is some objection to it in practice the objection is of no real or substantial moment, and from every standpoint I regard it as most desirable that the question should be settled by simply adopting the principles of the system as it exists now.
>
> Walter Scott was of the same opinion, and in discussing the matter a year ago we practically agreed upon this. As I understand it the North West members are unanimously of the same opinion, that is to say, they are willing to be bound by this conclusion.
>
> As the clause in the Bill is drawn, however, it seems to go further and it seems to be vague. I do not myself with all my experience in construing and arguing clauses of this kind profess to know what it means, and the fact that it was drawn by Fitzpatrick does not add anything to my confidence that the draftsman had in mind the same intention that we had. I do not accuse him of intentionally deceiving anyone, but he makes no secret of the fact that he is desirous of meeting the views of the Church.
>
> There are two points that seem to me to be of difficulty in the present draft. First, it does not seem to me at all clear that the central authority will have the power to regulate the separate school, prescribe text books and qualifications of teachers, and these powers are admitted by everyone to be essential. Laurier does not dispute this.
>
> Another and serious difficulty is as to the last clause which provides for a sharing up of the proceeds of the public school lands. This question was never discussed before, it has never been discussed at all between myself and any other Member of the Government, and the contents of the clause as it stands now in the Bill are altogether new to me. I have not had time to form an opinion upon it, but...I am disposed to be very much opposed to it, at least in its present form. [63]

Sifton's theoretical objection to the existing system was that it contained separate rather than national schools. In practice, however, it more closely approximated the national school concept than did the Manitoba system. It was the financial provisions that caused him most concern. "The proposition made," he told Laurier after further contemplation, "would constitute a most colossal endowment of sectarian education from public property. I am wholly and unalterably opposed to any such measure."[64]

Thus were the positions defined when Sifton submitted his resignation. Laurier had refused to alter the clause in any way and threatened to resign if Sifton did.[65] From outside the cabinet Sifton was quickly able to organize enough opposition to the measure that the prime minister was forced to join in the search for a mutually acceptable compromise to avoid divisions in the government ranks. The governor general, Lord Grey, appears initially to have played a mediating role. Very rapidly Sifton and the North-West members drafted an alternative clause, offered to the government on 3 March.[66] It reflected their interests accurately: the point of reference was not the North-West Territories Act of 1875, but the North-West Territories Ordinance 29 of 1901, which organized the school system under the central authority and spelled out what limited privileges were retained by the minority. Section 93 of the BNA Act was not applied, though there was a remedial provision. Finally, nothing was said about distribution of public funds. Reluctantly, Laurier agreed to the clause, provided that Sifton would include in it Ordinances 30 and 31 of 1901, which governed financial matters.[67]

The Catholic minority rejected this compromise, however, and a week of intense negotiations followed. Sifton was in constant contact with Dafoe, both for advice and to keep in touch with the pulse of western opinion. Between them they worked out a proposal which was substantially accepted. The minority fought first to have section 93 of the BNA Act applied, believing it would provide a stronger constitutional guarantee of their rights than the remedial clause of Sifton's proposal. The second point at issue concerned the distribution of money from the school lands fund. "This is in reality where the conflict was hottest," Sifton told Dafoe. "They did not expect to get much more in the way of separate schools than they have now, but they expected to get a declaration in the Constitution which could not be repealed, and which would give them a vested interest in the proceeds of the school Lands which would be an inducement to the Catholic people to organize as many separate schools as possible."[68]

The final version of the education clause[69] was introduced by Laurier on 22 March, a full month after first reading.[70] The protection of section 93 of the BNA Act was extended only to those minority rights spelled out in the ordinances of 1901. And in the distribution of public money, it was only stated that "there shall be no discrimination against schools of any class described in the said chapter 29." This allowed the local governments more flexibility than the original clause which, in Sifton's view, would have required distribution of the money according to the number of schools, thus encouraging the Catholics to build more schools. Laurier, as might have been expected, claimed that the new clause was simply a redrafting of what the government had intended from the very beginning. It was plain to everyone, nevertheless, that he had been forced into an embarrassing compromise, if not a defeat.

Sifton spoke two days later—his only participation in what would prove a long debate—and made it clear that for him acceptance of the final version meant a compromise of his principles.[71] He had been one of the major architects of the government's policy on provincial autonomy and defended the bills generally. The education clause, which had caused his resignation, now could receive his reluctant acceptance. It firmly established the school system as defined in 1901, and under its provisions the minority could only receive public funds for properly efficient schools. He supported the compromise "because I believe that the essential principles of a first-class, thoroughly national school system are not impaired, and the taint of what I call ecclesiasticism in schools, and which in my judgement produces inefficiency, will not be found in the school system of the Northwest under this legislation."[72]

Despite his resignation, Sifton had no desire to break up the Laurier administration. Certain ministers, notably Mulock and Fielding, were much distressed when Sifton revealed to them the possible ramifications of the original clause. He had prevailed upon Fielding not to follow his course in resigning, believing that "one resignation will accomplish the desired result."[73] He also was busy organizing western public opinion behind his stand, opposing equally the Laurier position and the vigorous provincial rights stance of many in Ontario. In this, of course, Dafoe and the *Free Press* played an important role. After initial embarrassment caused by Dafoe's assumption that Sifton supported the bills which Laurier had introduced, the editor of the *Free Press* righted the ship and skilfully manoeuvred it in support of Sifton. *Free Press* readers were constantly reassured that "there are no church schools in the Territories" and that Territorial separate schools were in no way inferior to public schools because they were directly under state control. The situation was very different from that in Manitoba in the 1880s.[74] Additionally Dafoe was asked to ensure that the Methodist, Presbyterian, and Baptist clergymen of Winnipeg were canvassed prior to announcement of the final clause, every effort being made to secure their support. "If...the clergy of Winnipeg support it," declared Sifton, "I am not afraid of anything else. When the proposal is published from here [Ottawa] it will of course be very desirable to get *as many as possible* of them to express themselves for publication."[75]

Finally there was the problem of ensuring the support of the western Liberal members, several of whom were inclined to prefer Haultain's demand for complete provincial control of education. Sifton mentioned particularly T.O. Davis, Robert Watson, Thomas Greenway, and "to a slight extent" Walter Scott as giving some trouble, but "the sentiment has been too strong for them and they will, I think, have to drop into line." Of them all, Greenway was the least predictable.[76] In the result, however, the government did not have too much trouble in exercising its control over the western members.

Why, in the final analysis, did Sifton resign, and what did he accomplish by so doing? Human motivation is notoriously complex, and undoubtedly there was more to his action than the 1905 crisis, though not, perhaps, as much as some suspected. To those who disliked Sifton or disagreed with him, to many who could not distinguish the subtleties of the education issue, there had to be some dark and hidden secret, a source of dubious profit or a seamy scandal, that would account for the abrupt departure of so powerful a politician.

To deal first with the obvious, Sifton felt snubbed by the prime minister who had rushed ahead without consulting him as the responsible minister and who had refused seriously to discuss changes prior to his resignation. It was a process that Sifton had seen often enough before when Laurier wilfully held to a policy, even to the point of humiliating the responsible minister, as had happened with A.G. Blair. As minister of the interior he was too proud to tolerate such treatment.

Then too Sifton had strong sentiments about the schools, however frequently he was accused of being unprincipled or inconsistent. He believed in a national school system controlled by the local government. Such a system was essential, in his view, for Canadianizing the ethnically diverse West. He believed that Laurier's original proposal potentially endangered these principles.

Numerous other factors doubtless contributed to the state of mind in which he returned to Ottawa and resigned. His health had been poor, and his lengthy convalescence had given him time to reflect on just how taxing his political life had been. He also was tired of his work. As Walter Scott told a correspondent, "I am pretty sure that it has been for some time his wish to get free from the Interior Department for the reason that the work was beginning to tell on his health."[77] Scott was correct. Administering the Interior Department held no more challenge for Sifton. The heavy workload combined with running the party machinery had exhausted him, and he had little enthusiasm for continuing. Laurier had overlooked him in the past, refusing him a different portfolio, preferring Fitzpatrick and concentrating his strength in Quebec. The partnership of the minister of justice and the prime minister was not congenial to Sifton. He had achieved what he had come to Ottawa to accomplish. When Laurier refused his advice on transportation, his other major interest, and did not consider him for the railways portfolio, there was little left to hold Sifton at Ottawa except a sense of loyalty to the party. He was an ambitious man, but he had never sought power for its own sake.

Those who thought that the school issue was merely a front for other, more tantalizing causes of his departure from the government, focussed essentially on two stories. One was that Sifton had become deeply involved in corruption and shady deals which supposedly were about to be made public. He resigned, it was said, to preclude this public embarrassment. It must be remembered, however, that the Tories circulated many juicy stories and allegations which they never had the courage to state publicly. Such accusations as they did make in the Commons were never sub- stantiated.[78] Every indication suggests that Sifton never feared to face such charges when they surfaced; it seems highly improbable that he would have resigned from fear of imminent censure from the Tories. The second main story concerned an alleged liaison with the wife of a millionaire lumberman named Mackay. The lurid details also were supposed to be on the verge of being divulged when Sifton hastily retired. The tidbits of gossip in this case were published in the sensationalist Calgary *Eye-Opener* and sedulously circulated at Ottawa, where they created much excitement. The general consensus, however, seemed to be that nothing had been proven and that such behaviour from Sifton was unlikely. As had been his life-long practice, Sifton utterly ignored the rumours; the absence of legal action or denials proves nothing. Without more substantial proof than rumours and gossip, it is impossible to accept either of these popular contemporary explanations of Sifton's conduct.[79]

In the back of his mind early in 1905 the attractions of resignation must have been considered. Scarcely a year previously he had been on the verge of resignation because his nerves were spent and he had believed that western Liberals were plotting against him. Having helped to pilot the Liberals through the election of 1904, he had discharged his duty to the party. He had faced several plots against himself in the past, and suspected more. It was not difficult for him to read "plot" into the events of February 1905: the fact that Laurier apparently consulted only Catholics on the school clause; that he rushed the bills into Parliament for no obviously pressing reason; that he seemed to anticipate, and possibly desire, a confrontation on the issue by drawing attention to it in his speech; that he seemed intent upon antagonizing many English-speaking members, given the tenor of his remarks on the nature of Canada; that he refused any compromise with Sifton upon the latter's return to Ottawa. This whole exercise was unnecessary if Laurier's object had been only what he claimed it to be, namely, the continuation of the existing system. Such gross and blundering stupidity was not characteristic of him. Perhaps Sifton was overly suspicious. Yet he had closely observed Sir Wilfrid's skilful political manoeuvres for many years and might be forgiven for believing that in this as on so many other occasions, the prime minister was in Dafoe's words, "a man who had affinities with Macchiavelli as well as Sir Galahad."[80]

As it was a school question that had first involved Sifton in national politics and led to his entry into the federal government, so it was a school question that caused his departure. In both cases he has been seen as an uncompromising hard-liner. Certainly in 1905 he did not see his course in that light. "No one knows better than I do that the simple course in politics is not to compromise anything," Sifton wrote during the negotiations for a revised education clause, "but unfortunately it is not the road to practical progress."[81] He would not insist upon full provincial rights in education because of political realities. To the Reverend Charles W. Gordon, who opposed the constitutional establishment of separate schools, he wrote:

> You will readily understand that I do not wish to do anything which those who think and believe as I do will not approve of. We are face to face with an impasse. I simply do not believe that a constitution for the new Provinces can be passed in the present parliament without some limitation, and at the present stage in the affairs of Canada to have a complete smash-up followed by dissolution and a recasting of the parties on religious and racial lines presents the prospect of a national disaster of such an extent that it is impossible to contemplate it with any degree of equanimity....
>
> There is just a bare possibility that the Catholic party might be able to convince Sir Wilfrid that he could carry it over our heads—I doubt it but he might. In that case the damage would be irreparable.[82]

In retrospect, Sifton believed that a workable compromise had resulted from his resignation. It at least had the virtue of being specific and likely to prevent future wrangling as to meaning and intent. The compromise also was perceived, certainly among French Catholics, as a victory for Sifton's view of the nature of Canada, in which an Anglo-Saxon Protestant society would be the norm outside Quebec. Their hopes of tolerance and understanding for the Catholic and French fact, raised so eloquently in Laurier's speech, seemed dashed. Those goals were no more appreciated by Sifton in 1905 than they had been a decade earlier. Where Laurier appeared to view cultural conflict as the principal problem facing Canada and favoured a laissez-faire approach to many of the other problems affecting the country, Sifton tended to view cultural conflict as an annoying political necessity that detracted from the urgent requirement to transform government into a dynamic, efficient, businesslike operation geared to promoting national development and prosperity. The frustration of fighting for so long with but limited success for his views had taken its toll, and was reflected in the tremendous sense of release that Sifton felt once the hurdle of resignation had been crossed and the compromise effected. It was unfortunate, nonetheless, that his departure had been so surrounded by controversy, leaving a long legacy of bitterness.[83]

Plate 11. Sifton supported development of grain elevators and of the Canadian Northern, but both would embroil him in political controversy.

Plate 12. Entitled "Old and New Homestead," this picture taken near Moose Jaw in 1905 shows the solid material prosperity to which the homesteader aspired, the original home becoming a mere annex to the new.

Plate 13. Clifford Sifton and his family, 1910.

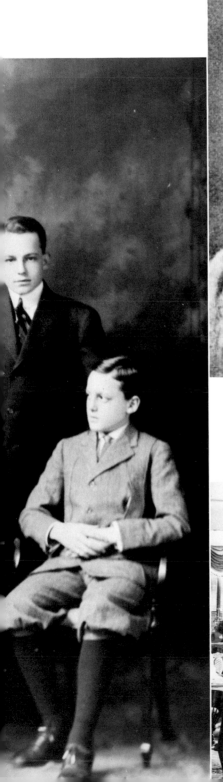

Plate 14. Mrs. Sifton, ca. 1903.

Plate 15. An interior view of the Sifton's Ottawa home, 1903.

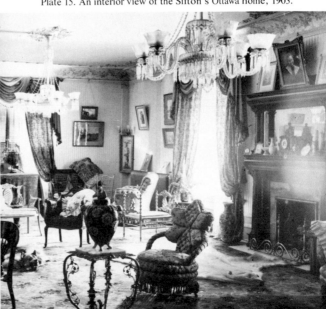

Plate 16. Attracting domestic servants to Canada was a significant concern of immigration policy prior to World War One. This group arrived at Quebec in 1911.

Plate 17. The interior of the Manitoba immigration office in St. Paul reflects the image of the prairies that was projected abroad in Sifton's era.

9

Private Member
(1905-1911)

The debates of Canada's tenth Parliament, elected in 1904, were frequently among the least edifying since Confederation. The creation of Alberta and Saskatchewan for all its attendant bitterness could well be regarded as the high point of legislative accomplishment. Some legislators undoubtedly would have selected the Lord's Day Act of 1906 if asked to single out a legislative highlight; the victory of the sabbatarian lobby indeed was both remarkable and symbolic at a time when even the forces of moral reform seemed mired in the deadening muck of corruption that pervaded the public life of the country.

The "Laurier boom" continued unabated. The flood of immigrants and the settlement of the West; the rapid expansion of Canada's cities and industrial capacity, and of the transportation network and service sector; the rapid growth in exploitation of the Dominion's natural resources and in her exports: all meant unprecedented prosperity—and, given the political morality of the day, unprecedented opportunities for self-enrichment by those who held public office. By 1906 the sometimes outraged, sometimes envious Opposition was convinced that not only had the government exceeded the extraordinarily generous bounds of public tolerance, but that they had the evidence to destroy the careers of several leading Liberals, if not the government itself. And the Tories did enjoy some success. In 1907 both H.R. Emmerson, minister of railways and canals, and Charles Hyman, minister of public works, were forced to resign as a result of opposition disclosures and election irregularities. A third member of the government, Joseph Préfontaine, minister of marine and fisheries, who had died in office late in 1905, was shown to have abused his powers, and several of his officials had to be dismissed.

Achieving these victories over a government which previously had been impervious to opposition censure was some consolation. But to the Tories, the officials and politicians implicated were small fish. The man they desperately wanted to bring down was Clifford Sifton. No one else so symbolized the corruption of the government—though without a conclusive case ever having been made against him. Sifton seemed vulnerable now, outside the cabinet, without the vast resources of his department to buttress his case, perhaps without the solid backing of the government. He still was regarded as a power in the Liberal party; it was possible that he would return to the government; and the Tories were anxious to repay him for his aggressive political tactics. In fact, his reputation was such that even many Liberals were glad to see him leave the cabinet. "I cannot but rejoice that Mr. Sifton has resigned," Howard Duncan of Vancouver told Laurier. "Apart from the great qualities he undoubtedly possesses he is wanting in the spirit and tone of character which creates and maintains respect. I may express it best by saying he is not to the manner born and has failed to acquire the ideals of high office."[1] Henri Bourassa was more blunt, denouncing Sifton as "a barnacle on the government ship" who "should be treated with an iron hand."[2]

Most of the Conservative charges related to well-worn issues: the North Atlantic Trading Company, the Saskatchewan Valley Land Company, assorted timber and land deals. Always there was the suggestion that Sifton had both profited personally and rewarded his friends; typical were George E. Foster's remarks during the debate on the North Atlantic Trading Company:

> [The] Siftonian cult....is a kind of a modern Pilgrim's Progress—not to a spiritual but to a material Paradise. Your novice enters it a pauper— he comes out a millionaire. He goes in a poor pilgrim, leaning on his staff and with modest garments, he comes out a pampered prince, clad in fine raiment, riding in liveried chariots. Whiskey permits, Treadgold concessions, claim lifting in the north; land looting, timber, coal scrip, wire fence graft in the middle areas. Immigration frauds everywhere— crowned by a million dollar contract with a headless, houseless, homeless monstrosity [the NAT Co.], a sort of a fugitive maw into which the Siftonians pour Canada's hard earned taxes.[3]

The very breadth and vagueness of these insinuations suggest the weakness of the Tory case. When it came to the crunch, they had neither the character, the evidence, nor the skill to overcome Sifton.

As to character, many of the Tories were still associated in the public mind with the scandal-rocked Conservative government of fifteen years previously. Furthermore, the Liberals easily demonstrated that many leading Tories as well as Liberals had benefitted from speculation in western lands during the recent land boom. And Foster and several other Tories were revealed to have been involved in scandalous land deals and manipulation of trust company funds.[4] To most Canadians, then, the Conservative charges were nothing more than another tiresome case of the pot calling the kettle black.

Sifton played the whole episode with a supreme confidence, not to say audacity, which appears to have unnerved the opposition. Most of the time he did not trouble himself to attend the debates, instead travelling in connection with his own business affairs. Periodically he would appear to make a brief denial of a specific charge made earlier or have the Prime Minister make the denial in his absence.[5] The government tended to fall to the opposition's level, debating niggling details of policy or responding with muckraking of its own.

When Sifton did decide to address the House, on 31 May 1906, he delivered one of the greatest debating speeches of his career.[6] Rather than denying many of the major points being made by the Opposition, he proudly accepted them and turned them into an impressive defence of his record as minister of the interior. Opposition leader Robert Borden had attacked the centralization of lands administration prior to 1905. Sifton pointed out that every amendment to the Dominion Lands Act had been passed by Parliament without division. He recalled that before 1896 the Department of the Interior had been ''a department of delay, a department of circumlocution, a department in which people could not get business done, a department which tired men to death who undertook to get any business transacted with it.'' Whatever their views of his administration, few people made such charges while Sifton was minister. Centralization minimized duplication of effort, and increasing ministerial discretion meant more rapid decision-making. At the same time, the minister had to delegate responsibility. ''There are hosts of matters arising constantly in the Department of the Interior about which council [i.e., cabinet] cannot know anything, and as to the details of which the minister himself can know very little. They come before the minister on the recommendation of his official; he takes the word of his official that the proper formalities have been complied with. The business of the department could not be carried on for a week if that were not done.''

Sifton did not deny that he had used his powers to lower the price of government lands for persons otherwise unable to qualify for a homestead, such as those who had failed on their first patented homesteads. Allowing such men to purchase lands at $1 or $1.50 an acre, it was said, was an abuse of ministerial discretion, robbing the government of legitimate revenue. ''I say,'' retorted Sifton, ''that my policy was never to get the highest possible price for the land. It was rather to settle the land, believing that was the best policy for promoting the prosperity of the country.''

He also defended his policy of issuing long-term closed grazing leases to ranchers on the southwestern plains. He recognized that there was a conflict of opinion between the ranchers and homesteaders in the region which made policy decisions difficult. Siding with the large ranchers against the little homesteaders was easily represented as an anti-populist, pro-big business policy. The fact, maintained Sifton, was that the land in question was mostly unsuited for homesteading. It was too dry, the homesteaders would fail and in the meantime would destroy the prairie sod that made a natural pasturage. ''And then you will have a vast area, such as Montana has, absolutely fit for nothing.'' It was time to recognize that lands in different regions were suited to different uses. And it was time to recognize that the rancher was not a ''criminal,'' but played as important a role in building up the country as anyone else.

The Saskatchewan Valley Land Company provided much ammunition for the Opposition. A.J. Adamson, the principal organizer of the project in 1902, was the brother-in-law of J.G. Turriff, then the land commissioner in the Department of the Interior. The arrangement allegedly netted as much as $1 million in profits, and both gentlemen were subsequently elected as members of Parliament in 1904.[7] It was always implied, but never proven, that Sifton himself had profited from the deal, an allegation that he flatly denied. But he refused to deny that others had profited—in his opinion, legitimately. The land which they had settled had lain unused for twelve years since 1890 along a railway line north from Regina. The railway company itself had no faith that the region ever could be productive, and in 1902 many had sympathized with the ''guileless'' American backers of the project who had sunk their money into worthless land.[8] But they prospered: ''They wanted to make some money out of it if you will—and that is a proper ambition on the part of anybody; I may say it is the ambition that most people have when they go west.'' A tremendous and costly campaign was undertaken by the company to attract settlers, with great success. ''In going through this tract a year ago this month,'' Sifton told the House in the course of his 1906 speech, ''I saw on that land which in the Spring of the year 1902 was an absolute desert without anybody on it without means of subsistence for man or beast; I saw in that tract last year, villages, elevators, stores, hotels, and the largest wheat field I ever saw in my life. That is the result of the operations of this company.''[9]

Triumphantly proceeding from this point, Sifton compared the settlement policies of the Conservative and Liberal governments, noting the
complications that Tory land grants to railways had created. In eighteen
years, he pointed out, the Tories had given away nearly 32 million acres to
"corporations and speculators," and less than 8.5 million in homesteads
and pre-emptions. In less than ten years, by contrast, the Liberals had
given away but 2 million acres to persons other than settlers (for irrigation
projects, the Saskatchewan Valley Land Company, half-breed scrip, and so
forth), and 20 million acres to settlers. Such figures "in my judgment
conclusively [vindicate] the claim that this government carries out the
policy of the land for the settler."

There was nothing to apologize for, concluded Sifton, in any of the issues
raised by the Opposition:

> I have given my version of the matter as it has appeared to me; I have
> placed the facts before the House to the best of my ability, and I shall
> be content when the history of this country shall be written to have the
> history of the last eight or nine years, so far as western administration is
> concerned, entered opposite my name.

It was unquestionably a brilliant debating performance. Having considered
the speech, and the various indicators of western growth and development
from 1896 to 1905, John W. Dafoe concluded that it was Sifton's "vision
...and practical sagacity," his "courage and imagination," that were
largely responsible for turning "a wilderness with a handful of depressed
people into a great community of busy thriving hopeful men." Sifton might
well have declared, wrote Dafoe, "Si monumentum requiris circumspice."
"If you seek my monument look around."[10]

Although the contrast was a bit overdrawn, the evidence of growth was
undeniable. For its part, the Opposition was not much interested in
debating whether Sifton was taking too much credit for the propitious times
in which he held office. They were convinced instead that they could prove
that he had directly benefitted himself by issuing a long term closed lease to
a ranch which he owned, or came to own immediately after his retirement.
Evidently George Foster was to make the charge in following Sifton, but,
claimed one observer, "he was noticeably cowed by Sifton, whose speech
contained the most scientific vituperation I ever heard."[11] The best Foster
could do was to imply that Sifton controlled a 60,000-acre ranch along the
international border and to point out that Sifton's friends had been the main
beneficiaries of closed leases.[12] The following day, 1 June, another
Conservative, M.S. McCarthy, approached the accusation, skirted it
warily, and backed off. The frustrated Tories, it seemed, could find no one
to bell the cat until on 5 June Herbert Ames baldly stated that Sifton had

acquired control of the Milk River Cattle Company and of the Grand Forks Cattle Company, both closed leases of great size. Sifton at once flatly denied that he or any member of his family had any direct or indirect interest in the ranches in question or indeed in any grazing lease. Ames meekly replied that he was content to accept Sifton's word. [13]

The Opposition nevertheless were utterly certain that the charges made were true and hoped in the absence of conclusive evidence to bluff Sifton into a slip or confession; instead, they were outbluffed. "Do not forget," J.S. Willison told his Ottawa correspondent, "that Sifton is very shrewd and very able. If it be true, as charged, that he has made money improperly he will not easily be detected or convicted." [14] Of course Sifton's denial might have been the truth. Either way, however, the Conservatives had used poor tactics, focusing on a poorly chosen issue in the hope of destroying Sifton and being forced to retract the accusation. This in turn blunted the edge of their many other well-substantiated charges concerning such matters as patronage and the corruption of lesser officials. The real thrust of their argument, so often obscured, was that while the West had prospered, so too had Sifton's friends to an undue extent, and at the expense of others—especially the homesteaders struggling to get themselves established.

Sifton did not appear at all during the 1906-7 session of Parliament, despite continued revelation of corrupt or questionable dealings by his former officials. During the 1907-8 session, however, the Conservatives renewed their attacks on his timber administration, a subject which had exercised them from 1899 through 1906. They were correct in guessing that the ex-minister of the interior was vulnerable on this issue, principally through the benefits bestowed upon T.A. Burrows, his brother-in-law. Sifton felt constrained to reply to their charges on 6 February 1908.

The Tory contentions may be boiled down essentially to three points. The first was that in 1903 Sifton changed the regulations, which required yearly renewal of timber leases, to practically permanent leasehold as long as there was merchantable timber on the lease. This, argued the Tories, greatly enhanced the value of the leases which otherwise could be cancelled at any time. Sifton's reply was that this was perfect nonsense. In practice, he pointed out, it had to be understood that the yearly leases were to all intents and purposes perpetually renewable; otherwise no capitalist would trouble himself to erect a mill, and undertake the other investments in development and transportation. Sifton argued that he simply had regularized existing practice to satisfy foreign investors who did not recognize the security that Canadians had understood to be inherent in the system of annual renewals. The long term leases had an added conservationist benefit, in his opinion, because they would encourage greater care of the forests.

The second charge was more serious: that the advertising of the sale of timber limits was manipulated to benefit government favourites. For example, one limit was advertised late in October for a December deadline, but in the knowledge that ice conditions on the northern lakes in November would make travel impossible for those wishing to assess the limit and make a bid. The result: T.A. Burrows, who of course had previously assessed the proposed limit, was the only bidder. Sifton replied that he simply followed the same rules and practices established by the Tories in 1889 (and which had been used to benefit Conservatives until 1896). However, a *tu quoque* argument carried little force in light of a well-documented case.[15]

Most serious was the third charge, that the system of sealed bids had been corrupted, Liberal favourites mysteriously learning about the amounts of other bids. Naturally the Tories were unable to persuade any officials to admit that they had been suborned, but a remarkable series of coincidences was compiled none the less. For example, T.A. Burrows bid on berths nineteen times between 1902 and 1905; he was the successful bidder eighteen times, usually by a very narrow margin. In the case of a timber limit on Moose Lake, Manitoba, A.W. Fraser, a Liberal Ottawa lawyer, bid nominally $1,000. Late in the morning of the day the bids were to close, another company bid $6,420. T.A. Burrows the same day went to Fraser and arranged for him to enter another bid for $7000 under the fictitious name of W.H. Nolan. How did Burrows know that $7,000 would capture the limit?

Not insignificantly, the Moose Lake limit passed to the control of the Imperial Pulp Company. This business, the Tories discovered, was essentially speculative, acquiring, holding, and selling timber leases, but never working them. It had no office, only a Winnipeg post office box. No list of officials or shareholders was available, though eventually it was determined that D.H. McMillan was president and Burrows was managing director. Unquestionably the Conservatives would have been much more agitated had they known that before long Sifton himself would surface as managing director of the concern.[16] Between December 1902 and February 1904 the company bid upon nine timber limits and obtained every one, some 417 square miles for $54,975. Remarkably, this was only 6 per cent higher than the total of the next highest bids on each limit. The Tories estimated that the value of these berths by 1908 was at least $1 million; indeed, according to one source, "three lots which cost in the aggregate $12,500 are held and offered at $1,500,000."[17]

One case of several cited by the Tories should illustrate the typical proceedings. In the summer of 1902 an Edmonton company explored a timber stand west of the city on the North Saskatchewan and applied for the government to put some 118 square miles on the market, which they wished to begin cutting immediately. The government of course, sent its own inspector to report on the timber—a normal, proper proceeding, but one which also gave Ottawa officials full information on the value of the timber. On 19 November the entire block was put up for bids, to be opened 31 December. No announcement appeared in Edmonton until 1 December. Various appeals to extend the time limit were ignored. When the bids were opened on 31 December, it was found that T.A. Burrows had made a token offer of $6,057, the Edmonton syndicate a bid of $17,010, a company called McDonald & Frith some $31,161, and Imperial Pulp Company, $31,575. What was doubly remarkable about the Imperial Pulp offer, however, was that it had come in two instalments. The first was for $17,575, just large enough to outbid the Edmonton syndicate. When the McDonald & Frith bid arrived shortly before noon on 31 December, a further cheque for $14,000 mysteriously enlarged the Imperial Pulp Company's offer. Both cheques were handled from the Ottawa branch of the Bank of Ottawa, where coincidentally (although the Tories did not know it) Sifton often did his banking. No one could prove that the sealed bids had been illegally opened, or that anything but a fantastic series of coincidences had occurred. Still, the timber limits in question were estimated to contain approximately 75 million board feet of merchantable timber, worth perhaps $250,000 in 1908.[18] All told, Burrows gained over 351,000 acres, the Imperial Pulp Company almost 269,000 acres, and other Liberals some 896,000 acres of western timber lands while Sifton was in office.[19]

The Liberals attempted to defend themselves first on the basis of rapid expansion of the timber industry. The Tories had issued leases for 30,000 square miles of western timber, and in 1896 only 34 million board feet of lumber were produced. Most of the leases had reverted to the government undeveloped because of lack of markets. The Liberals, by contrast, had alienated only 8,000 square miles, and in the nine months ending in March 1907 some 141 million feet were produced.[20] The reality was, however, that most of the Liberal leases remained undeveloped, held as speculations.

Sifton himself was not very convincing in his own defence. He contended that the opposition was greatly exaggerating the worth of the timber limits and that such limits in the West could not be compared in value with those in central Canada or in British Columbia. There was less timber, acre for acre, in the west, and less than half the timber land had been leased, keeping the value down. Furthermore, in his words, there was "an absolutely illimitable supply" of lumber in B.C., which also undercut the value of leases in the prairie provinces. As to Burrows, he pointed out that his brother-in-law had been in the timber business for fifteen years before the Laurier government assumed office. "Will anybody suggest that because I became Minister of the Interior, my brother-in-law was to go out of the business he had followed for fifteen years?"[21]

His speech pleased his Liberal friends. "As usual," McMillan told him, "you wiped the slate clean. I don't begrudge the Opposition any comfort they can get out of their charges after you get through with them."[22] Many Canadians, however, were less certain. If nothing had been pinned on Sifton, the investigations of his administration left a strong stench. The Tories were happy with the ambiguity, regularly pointing out that he had acquired his wealth, not as a captain of industry, but while in politics, the inference being clear. "What a wonderful revolution has taken place in the hon. gentleman's own history," commented W.J. Roche acidly, when following Sifton in the timber berths debate. "Had he been as conscientious in the discharge of his public duties and as good a financier, in the interests of our country, as he has been in his own interests, would it not have paid us to have had him as Finance Minister?"[23]

One other scandal under Sifton's administration was uncovered before the session was over. In mid-July, in Sifton's absence, the Tories charged that certain Indian lands with valuable timber in Algoma had been sold in 1900, without public tender or auction, to three of Sifton's friends from Brandon: W.F. Wilson, A.E. Philp, and D.A. Reesor. The three acquired the lands for $9,987.75, and resold them in 1906 to American timber interests for $101,830. The facts were basically correct, except that Philp claimed the resale price was only $68,000. The evidence would suggest that in fact this was a transaction that Sifton had not been aware of after the original sale, and its revelation was a surprise to him.[24]

Sifton's record, then, remained as controversial after his retirement as when he was in office. No one could ignore the magnitude of his achievement, which his great speech of 1906 had so boldly summarized. At the same time, while the Conservatives had been unable to demonstrate specific personal corruption, Sifton had not succeeded in cleansing himself of the sordid administrative muck that the Tories were so industriously smearing around. It remained to be seen how seriously this would affect his personal and political future.

The transition from the power and influence of a cabinet post to the impotence of the backbenches is difficult for any person. It was complicated for Sifton by the fact that, as J.W. Dafoe put it, he "never could interest himself in the small change of politics."[25] He could read the political stars as well as anyone. Laurier had made no effort in 1905 to compromise on the autonomy bills or to offer concessions in order to persuade him to remain in the government. And for at least two years the prime minister showed no serious interest in bringing him back. The sense of rejection and exclusion was reinforced by the choice of Frank Oliver to succeed him as minister of the interior. No one within the Liberal party had been so severe a critic of Sifton's policies as Oliver; and Sifton realized at once that his influence in his old department, even in the day-to-day concerns of his constituents with respect to land administration, would be exceedingly limited. The changes in policy came quickly. Oliver cancelled the North Atlantic Trading Company contract in 1906, despite a strong plea from Sifton to Laurier to maintain it.[26] Also in 1906 the Immigration Act was amended to give the minister more discretion to reject and deport.[27] Oliver, not unexpectedly, was far more inclined to limit continental European immigration, while being less selective in the kind of British immigrants who were encouraged. In 1908 Oliver's capitulation to the demands of the homesteaders, already seen in his policy on grazing leases, was further demonstrated in amendments to the Dominion Lands Act to restore pre-emption and second homesteading privileges, which Sifton had always rejected. Once again his protests to the prime minister availed little.[28]

Sifton's papers for this period—or such of them as survive—are full of correspondence on minor patronage matters, sometimes from people outside his constituency who imagined that Sifton's views still carried weight. Under the circumstances, however, he was not often inclined to exhaust his limited fund of goodwill by pressing too hard on small issues. It is clear too that he remembered well the frustration while minister of dealing with constantly importuning backbenchers. His declining influence might perhaps be measured on the question of getting the Grand Trunk Pacific Railway to serve Brandon. In August 1905 Sifton represented to the cabinet his constitutents' demands that the GTPR should have its main line serve Brandon as competition for the CPR. The CPR, of course, strongly opposed this route. The GTPR had proposed to build northwest from Portage la Prairie to the Touchwood Hills region, rather than west to Brandon, and finally consented with government approval to build a branch line to Brandon within six months of the time that the main line passed to the north of the city. As the Grand Trunk people came to appreciate Sifton's loss of influence, they found one excuse after another to avoid building the branch line, demanding various tax concessions, bridges, land, and so forth as preconditions. Four years later the line remained unbuilt, despite repeated efforts by the member for Brandon. It was the same kind of branch line that he had succeeded so often in getting built while in the cabinet.[29]

Sifton also showed little interest in western politics generally. In 1905 he did advise Walter Scott, premier-designate of Saskatchewan, on the size and composition of his cabinet—advice which was heeded. He also contributed heavily to the Liberals' campaign funds that year.[30] These, however, were exceptional gestures for a politician whom he liked. For two years before his resignation, by contrast, he had refused to become involved in the local politics of Manitoba, even largely resisting appeals for aid in the 1903 provincial election. Out of office and with far less influence, Sifton declined altogether to interfere apart, of course, from ensuring that the *Free Press* was solidly aligned behind the local Liberals. Premier Roblin's Conservatives swept to victory again in 1907, much to Sifton's disgust. In Brandon, he later commented sourly, "the one thing that was apparent was that the petty patronage which was being distributed throughout the town has pretty nearly chloroformed the whole community," and the same thing was applicable to the whole province.[31] Manitobans, nevertheless, would have to effect their own salvation, for the Laurier government was not supportive and Sifton's interest now mostly lay elsewhere.

The one important public question to engage his attention in these years was the All-Red Line scheme. It was a project designed to establish a fast steamship and railway service from Great Britain to New Zealand and Australia via Canada. Imperialists noted that existing routes via the Suez Canal, via Europe, or, in some instances, via the United States, were vulnerable to enemy interference; a route via Canada would be safe and dependable, all parts of the route being within the British Empire, coloured red on contemporary maps. Even more desirable would be the strengthening of sentimental and commercial ties within the Empire. Sifton, however, was influenced less by such patriotism than by the conviction that it would be an excellent stroke of business for Canada.

It is not clear exactly why the project should suddenly have captured public attention in 1907 and 1908. In the nineteenth century the term "All-Red Line" had referred to the linking of the major components of the Empire by a telegraph cable.[32] A shipping link perhaps seemed a logical extension of the completed telegraph; at any rate, men like Lord Strathcona had long professed belief in some such scheme. In 1907 a group of British investors, led by Sir Thomas Troubridge, proposed to develop such a shipping scheme out of Blacksod Bay on the northwest coast of Ireland. Canada, declared a supporter of the project, "would become the central province of the Empire and the carrier of all the traffic between the Australian Colonies and the Mother Country, and in addition could pour the contents of her granaries into Ireland, Scotland and England at the minimum expense and loss of time."[33] Robert Bickerdike, Liberal MP for St. Lawrence, Quebec, approached the Canadian government in January 1907 for a $1 million annual subsidy, and it was expected that the concept would be raised at the Colonial Conference scheduled for April and May.

It transpired that the Blacksod Bay promoters were but one of several organizations anxious to obtain approval to run the service. Sifton was in England on private business in the spring of 1907 when Strathcona asked him to use his influence with Laurier to have at least the concept of the All-Red route approved by the Colonial Conference. The Canadian prime minister in turn evinced interest, and on his initiative the conference passed the following resolution:

> That in the opinion of this Conference the interests of the Empire demand that in so far as possible its different portions should be connected by the best possible means of mail communication, travel and transportation; that to this end steps should immediately be taken to establish a fast service from Great Britain to Canada, and through Canada to Australia and New Zealand, and also to China and Japan; that such service upon the Atlantic Ocean should be carried on by means of steamships, equal in speed and character to the best now in existence, and upon the Pacific Ocean by steamships of a speed of not less than 18 knots, and in other respects as nearly equal to the Atlantic ships as circumstances will permit; that for the purpose of carrying the above project into effect, such financial support as may be necessary should be contributed by Great Britain, Canada, Australia, and New Zealand in equitable proportions.[34]

In a memorandum drawn up for Laurier's use, Sifton had contended that Canada was obtaining little but tourist traffic on both the Atlantic and Pacific services. Most Canadians travelling to England went by New York because of the faster and better quality service. On the Pacific coast, although the Canadian Pacific steamships had captured some of the trade between Vancouver, Yokohama, and Hong Kong, "information is to the effect that most of the British passengers are tourists and it can hardly be claimed that as yet this route has made any serious impression upon the business traffic." Replacing the thirteen-knot CP vessels with an eighteen-knot service would reduce travel time between Vancouver and Sydney from twenty-three to fifteen or sixteen days, to Yokohama from thirteen to ten days, and to Hong Kong from twenty-one to fourteen and a half days. The Canadian government would have to undertake to improve port facilities and the transcontinental railways, with a view to improving the four and a half day journey from Halifax to Vancouver. In addition, he projected substantial subsidies for both the Pacific and Atlantic services. On the latter ocean, ships of the class of the recently built *Lusitania* and *Mauretania*, capable of twenty-five knots, would be used, to reduce the crossing to four days. The project, claimed Sifton, would "bring about the greatest revolution in travel and in the formation of lines of communication that has taken place for many years."[35]

Before returning from Britain in July, Laurier told the Imperial government that Strathcona was prepared to form a company to operate a twenty-four-knot service on the Atlantic. It would require an annual subsidy of £450,000 for ten years, of which Canada would meet half.[36] The prime minister professed enthusiasm in September when he told the Canadian Manufacturers' Association, "This project shall and will succeed."[37] The late fall found Sifton in England once more, at Laurier's "earnest solicitation," to work on the proposed company and to try to persuade the British government to support it. The British made it clear that if they were to look at all favourably on the scheme, it would have to be a total package for Atlantic and Pacific, and not just a partial Atlantic service. Unfortunately, there was a misunderstanding between Sifton and Laurier, the former believing that he was acting as an agent of the Canadian government with power to negotiate, while Laurier had authorized no more than informal discussions. When he discovered his true status, Sifton angrily broke off negotiations and returned to Canada.[38]

Before he left, however, he addressed the Liberal Colonial Club in London. He claimed that while mail took thirty-eight days to reach Australia and New Zealand via Suez, it could travel via Canada in 25 days under the All-Red scheme. It would have naval and military advantages in the development of Canadian ports capable of handling the largest vessels. Britain's food supply would be ensured by wholly imperial sources and shipping routes, and supply from Canada would be safer than any other in time of war. Furthermore, he claimed that the proposed vessels could be constructed to meet Admiralty requirements and be fitted to carry heavy guns. This was a meaningful way for the colonies to assist Britain in maintaining naval supremacy.[39]

Upon his return to Canada, Sifton conferred with Laurier, who assured him that he was, "if possible, more than ever favorable to the project." Sifton thereupon supplied the prime minister with definite cost estimates, calculating that about £6 million would be required to place four vessels on the Atlantic service, and five on the Pacific. This would necessitate an annual subsidy of £1 million, half to be paid by Great Britain, £325,000 by Canada, £100,000 by New Zealand and Fiji, and £75,000 by Australia.[40] The prime minister, however, appeared to be disinclined to put the proposals before Parliament, so Sifton took the initiative on 20 March, during the budget debate. The figures, he told the House, were not as shocking as they appeared at first glance because Canada already was paying subsidies totalling $680,000 for the Atlantic and Australian mail services. The existing subsidies would be subsumed in the proposed All-Red Line subsidy, leaving an additional cost of $900,000 to $950,000 above current levels. Britain and the Dominions, he declared, had "now arrived at that state which justifies the people of those countries in coming to the conclusion that they are entitled to the best service, the best method of communication that modern skill and modern science will enable them to have." Under current conditions, "so far as travel and transportation are concerned, Canada is on the side street instead of on the main thoroughfare. What this proposition means is that Canada shall be put upon the thoroughfare instead of upon the side street....All the great social, political and commercial advantages which come from being on the main avenue for this traffic would come to Canada if this scheme were carried into effect."[41]

It was not long, however, before an array of disparate forces dramatically slowed the momentum that Sifton and Strathcona were trying to build. First, only two of the necessary partners in the project—Canada and New Zealand—appeared at all enthusiastic. The Australians had first expressed interest, but when detailed investigation showed that the All-Red route could offer only marginal improvements in speed of mail and passenger service, and virtually no improvement in freight service—particularly chilled freight—the Australians realized that they would be paying £75,000 for sentiment. Admirable as it might be to encourage trade in all-British channels, the Australians were dubious, particularly in view of the fact that the Panama Canal was then under construction and would, when completed, render such a subsidized route via Canada obsolete. The British government also was cool to the project, but officially took the position that if a definite proposal supported by the three dominions were submitted, they would seriously consider it. Australia's attitude naturally meant that a firm proposal was impossible.

British coolness stemmed from several sources. Treasury officials pointed out that Britain already subsidized the Cunard service to New York to the tune of £5 million, and another transatlantic service was not required. Two transshipments, at Halifax and Vancouver, would add to the cost and almost certainly contribute to delays not allowed for by Sifton and others. Furthermore, British insurers were convinced that the proposed Canadian route, to Quebec in summer and Halifax in winter, was far too risky compared to the New York route and that higher insurance costs would undermine the route's competitiveness. Sifton was at especially great pains to counter this propaganda, claiming that actual figures proved that there was twice the risk of fog on the American route; that ice was not a serious hazard; and that between 1880 and 1907 only five passenger vessels were lost on the Canadian routes in question, only one of which was attributable to the dangers of the route, the remainder resulting from navigational error.[42] It was argued that to increase the speed of the vessels beyond a certain level would mean an enormous increase in size and expense, to a degree beyond the capacity of the Canadian route to sustain. According to one estimate, while vessels of 10,550 tons could maintain twenty knots, it would take a vessel of 32,500 tons to contain the powerful engines required to maintain a twenty-five-knot speed. Sifton countered with figures from British ship builders purportedly showing that a twenty-five-knot vessel of only 20,000 tons could be built, but apparently this was not widely credited.[43] A final factor in dampening British enthusiasm was the outcry of the vested interests controlling the profitable New York route and also the P & 0 Steamship Line.

In Canada there was an outcry from some vested interests as well. The most notable was the CPR. Strathcona's plan evidently was to remove the CP vessels serving the Atlantic to the Pacific, where they would provide the required eighteen- to twenty-knot service. Strathcona's own company would operate the Atlantic service with the costly new vessels. CPR president T.G. Shaughnessy was not about to surrender the profitable Atlantic end of the route and even journeyed to England to tell the British cabinet committee looking into the project that the CPR already operated an "All-Red" service. The big boats, he contended, were much too costly for the Canadian route, and in any event they could not be operated at maximum speed during much of the winter."[44] The Tory opposition in Canada also underscored the lack of ocean freight capacity in the proposed vessels and the lack of cold storage facilities. Robert Borden claimed that 75 per cent of Canadians "were more interested in a cheaper freight service than in a faster passenger line."[45]

He may have been right. Despite evidence of countervailing support for the scheme from Canadian manufacturers, the All-Red Line clearly lacked a broad appeal. When the prime minister finally introduced a motion in Parliament to authorize the government to negotiate, his heart was not in his flat and cursory speech. Once again Sifton tried to rouse some interest. He denied having any financial interest in it and portrayed his role as that of a patriotic citizen furthering his country's interests. The Atlantic vessels could carry up to 1,000 tons of freight, and the Pacific vessels up to 3,000 tons. That was a small amount, but a fast passenger and mail service would increase general trade and advertise the efficiency of the St. Lawrence route and Canadian channels of trade. Canadians, he declared, should not continue to rely on "the courtesy and good will of our neighbours to the south....It seems to me the time has come when Canada can afford what is, in this respect, a necessity for her national growth and development."[46] The prime minister's motion passed on a routine party division, but public interest had subsided, Australia could not be enticed to lend active support, and the scheme was allowed to die quietly in succeeding months.

Considering the strenuous efforts Sifton had made on behalf of the project during the course of twelve to fifteen months, he did not appear particularly embittered at its failure.[47] Its appeal to him lay in the potential of the plan to strengthen Canada's eastern and western transoceanic trade, to divert some Canadian trade back from American channels, and to render Canada stronger and more independent of the United States. The imperial connection could appear practical and profitable under such circumstances. Perhaps with time he came to understand the limitations of the scheme. Certainly his own patriotism never overcame practical realities, and he continued—as he had always done—to sail to England via New York because it provided the best available service.

Not insignificant in spurring Sifton's interest in the project was Sir Wilfrid Laurier's request that he support it. It was part of an attempt at rapprochement with his former minister of the interior. By 1907 Laurier was deeply conscious of the weaknesses of his cabinet, of the failings of his railway policy, and of the approach of another election for which his government was not well prepared. Sifton's strength was desirable, and he determined at last to open the door and make Sifton an offer. As for Sifton, he could be tempted. There was so much that the government could do, needed to do—yet, would he be in a position to ensure that his views would be acted upon? His two years out of the cabinet had given him perspective and appreciation of the relative freedom from public pressure. There would have to be generous terms to entice him back, particularly guarantees of significant influence on government policy. John W. Dafoe, by this time a close confidant of Sifton, paraphrased his remarks on Laurier's style: "I was not Sir Wilfrid Laurier's colleague for eight years without finding out that he is, despite his courtesy and gracious charm, a masterful man set on having his own way, and equally resolute that his colleagues shall not have their way unless this is quite agreeable to him."[48] Such a state of affairs would not be acceptable to Sifton should he return to the cabinet.

From the time of his resignation in 1905 Sifton had received letters supporting his return to the government, though those who knew him well were pessimistic. Walter Scott's views were, perhaps, representative, when he said, "I do not think that he will go back, which is a pity because, without minimizing his faults, he is certainly a great administrator and we have no man approaching his class to replace him."[49] In 1906 the pressure on Sifton to re-enter the ministry began to mount. After a year without his political leadership in the West, the Liberal MPs from Alberta, Saskatchewan, and Manitoba gathered to request that an additional western representative be taken into the cabinet and that Sifton should be the man. Laurier promised to accede to the demand, declaring "that he was the most anxious man of us all" to have Sifton return.[50] Still, however, the prime minister made no direct contact on the subject. When C.S. Hyman was expected to resign late in 1906, requests flooded in on Sifton to let his name stand for the vacant public works portfolio. Horace Chevrier, a Liberal Franco-Manitoban, told Sifton, "we are now at a point, where the quick construction of a country commercially, financially and agriculturally can be gotten under way. You alone know intimately all the elements lying at hand. The position seeks the man. We beg you to accept it." At least as important a factor in the western Liberal pressure on Sifton was revealed in

Chevrier's further comment: "I cannot express the orphaned feeling we have known since you retired. The impetus your policy gave the West is disappearing, the party is losing its snap and go, the Provincial outlook is disheartening. The immediate reversal of this situation is urgent. It can only be done by you."[51] In June 1907 the Liberal executive of Manitoba urgently requested that Laurier take Sifton once more. Thomas Metcalfe, the president of the Manitoba organization, bluntly told Sifton, "I am stating the matter mildly when I say that if you do not return to the Cabinet we are practically lost in so far as Manitoba is concerned at the next General Election."[52]

Still there was no direct approach from Laurier. Public works held little appeal for Sifton; still less did a return to political organization attract him. The policies of the cabinet, particularly those of Oliver, would have made him uncomfortable. "I have no desire whatever to return to official life," he replied to Metcalfe, "and my disinclination in that respect has been decidedly strengthened by a number of circumstances which have transpired during the last year."[53]

Late in August Laurier finally made up his mind to call William Pugsley of New Brunswick and Sifton to take up the vacant portfolios of public works and railways and canals. Failing Sifton, he would call on George P. Graham, leader of the Ontario Liberal party. When the prime minister informed Governor General Lord Grey of his decision, Grey noted, "Sir W. again dwelt with emphasis on the importance of securing brains—he appears to attach more importance to brains than character." Grey warned him that Sifton's appointment would be subject to severe criticism. "He replied that all that had been considered & that they were prepared to face the music. The woman scandal with wh. Sifton's name had been associated was not a public scandal—there had been no proceedings before the Court—that the Yukon charges were the unproved allegations of reckless partizans. Sifton had made money—in CPR & Canadian Northern—He had challenged his assailants to make good their charges against him—and they had not done so. He was the ablest business man in politics—& he did not believe there was any truth in the party charges."[54]

It was hardly a ringing endorsement of a prospective cabinet member, but there was little doubt that Laurier wanted Sifton's ability in the government. After an inconclusive meeting with the prime minister, Sifton returned to Assiniboine Lodge to consider the offer. Sydney Fisher, minister of agriculture, visited him to add his encouragement, and Sifton may have had another direct meeting with Laurier before finally declining. He offered a fascinating explanation of his decision to J.S. Willison:

> It may interest you to know that I have finally given a negative answer
> to Sir Wilfreds [*sic*] proposals. His wish was for me to take the Railway

Dept and be sworn in at once & he urged it so strongly as to make refusal very difficult.

It was however perfectly clear

1st That Pugsley was to come in

2nd That my reentry was to be regarded as sufficient as to meet the present situation &

3rd That no further reorganization was contemplated or in fact seriously considered.

I did not make my acceptance bluntly conditioned upon a reorganization which would involve the withdrawal of some of the present ministers. I did not think I was called on to do that. Such a course would have precipitated an internal conflict in which I should have been regarded as the aggressor. I went as far in the direction of suggesting the desirable as I could but there was no encouragement whatever. Even the slight change of replacing the most aged member [R.W. Scott, then 82 years old] seems to be abandoned for the present.

I sent my final reply by letter yesterday [26 August]. Have not heard since & do not know that I shall do so.

I am quite aware that what I have done probably shuts the door so far as political life is concerned finally. The demand for any man is bound to cease after somewhat repeated refusals to meet it favorably. The fact is however that acceptance practically meant that I should take the responsibility for what is euphemistically called "political management" not because that was directly intended but because no one else would be allowed to do it while I was there. That was a phase of the affair which I positively cannot face. It is too distasteful and life is not worth living at the price.

There is a perceptible relief visible in my family circle. The only difference I feel is that I have a bad headache—the sure result of a couple of weeks of strenuous mental strain.[55]

It was essentially the same account that Sifton had verbally given Dafoe, then vacationing with the Siftons at their summer home.[56] His demands had been extraordinary. In addition to Scott, he probably also desired the replacement of Sir Richard Cartwright, the seventy-one-year old minister of trade and commerce; and perhaps of William Paterson, the sixty-seven-year old Minister of Customs. Laurier, himself sixty-five years of age, declined, recalling that "they had been...colleagues in the old barren days of opposition and he couldn't ship them off in the days of success." The sentiment, commented Dafoe, "was magnificent, but not politics."[57] Undoubtedly Sifton was tempted by the chance to bring order out of the chaos that had characterized the railways and canals department and to use it as a base to realize his vision for Canadian transportation development.

Yet he recognized too that he would be entering a failing, faltering administration. The suggested changes would be a signal that Laurier was serious about rejuvenating his cabinet. Still, for Laurier to have accepted Sifton's terms would have been almost impossible. Sifton would have become, as Dafoe correctly observed, "second in command of the party, the inevitable successor to Sir Wilfrid."[58] Laurier would have had to be prepared to give great weight to Sifton's views on policy, and their ideas were not sufficiently similar to make that a workable proposition.

Never again would Laurier make so serious an effort to obtain Sifton, though he pointedly remained friendly to him both in public and in private. In June 1908 a series of meetings between the two men gave rise to considerable speculation; and there is some evidence that in August, with a general election in sight, Laurier made another approach, possibly offering Trade and Commerce as an inducement.[59] Once again the negotiations—if, indeed, they were such—came to nothing, and Sifton would have to decide whether to run again as a private member.

In case there was any doubt about Sifton's continuing abilities, he intervened in the budget debate in 1908 to deliver within one speech a series of pronouncements on public questions of the day. In retrospect the speech does not stand as one of his most effective, partly because of its diverse subject-matter. He defended the moderate protective tariff, urged the aggressive promotion abroad of Canadian products, advocated throwing lands formerly held as railway reserves open for homesteading, suggested reserving three million acres of these lands to sell to finance a Hudson Bay railway, and, as seen, promoted the All-Red-Line.[60] It was a short section of his speech, however, which caught public attention: reform of the civil service. The topic was not new. Various reformers had exerted themselves for years to persuade the government to abandon the patronage system which most politicians still believed was vital in maintaining political power and organizations. In 1907 the government had appointed a royal commission to consider the subject, and Opposition Leader Borden had climbed on the bandwagon in urging reforms as well. Three days before Sifton's speech of 20 March 1908 the commissioners submitted their report to the government, excoriating the existing state of affairs, and recommending a civil service commission, examinations for civil service posts, and so forth. Many of the recommendations were duly adopted during the session by the government in the Civil Service Amendment Act.[61]

Perhaps what struck people about Sifton's speech was that one of Canada's politicians who had been most diligent in the application of patronage and manipulation of the civil service had now seen the light of reform. He agreed with Borden that the principle of patronage should be removed and the civil service placed "on a higher plane." He declared that patronage was no advantage either to the government in power or to the individual MP. Rather, it was "the greatest nuisance in public life." Canada was outgrowing the system, "and it is the duty of a progressive parliament to anticipate the enlightened sentiment of the country and put these reforms into practical shape before they are forced to do so." He noted the close connection in England between university graduates and the government service, a situation not developed in Canada. Instead, many Canadian university graduates were being forced to seek employment abroad. If the public service could absorb the graduates, it would establish a close linkage that would be mutually beneficial to the public service and the universities. "We are now passing from the condition of a simply pastoral community and we have questions arising of the most complicated character in connection with our affairs," necessitating specialist knowledge, "and it is in the highest degree desirable that between the educational institutions and the government there should be a close and intimate relationship established."[62]

The sentiments were commendable and timely, if not original, and very few of Sifton's speeches excited so widespread and enthusiastic a response. C.F. Hamilton had observed a few weeks previously that Sifton's "sheer ability in speaking fairly intoxicates me. It is such an intellectual pleasure to see a mind like that at work." The budget speech, he subsequently wrote, "made a tremendous impression on me; it is so wonderful to see a man in Parliament get up, say something important, & sit down."[63] J.W. Flavelle, a somewhat prickly moralist and successful businessman, told Sifton, "The dead level of the ordinary in party strife and debate was thrown into sharp contrast by the broad, large, and common sense series of propositions presented by you....It is too bad, too bad, that such constructive talent cannot be used in a government so lacking in moral and intellectual force, and business grasp." Not unexpectedly, Sifton's speech also generated enthusiasm from some university professors.[64] It is true that, being free of the necessity of administering patronage, Sifton could more readily support reform. Yet it also must be admitted that he had always found the pressures of the patronage system trying while in office. He was perhaps more willing than many of his colleagues to recognize that the complexities of an urban industrial society could no longer be handled by a corrupt and ill-trained public service. Finally, as will be seen, there was within Sifton a reform streak which surfaced more frequently when he was freed of the responsibilities of political office.

The eleventh general election in Canada, held 26 October 1908, brought the debate on corruption to a climax. The Liberal slogan was "Let Laurier Finish His Work," to which the Tory newspapers gleefully responded with cartoons of Laurier smashing his platform of election promises, and bloated grafters with fat cigars making off with wheel barrows and bags overflowing with the taxpayers' hard-earned dollars. Clifford Sifton remained the central target of the campaign of vilification, especially in the West; but also, as he later was told, even in Ontario, where "one would think you were the whole Liberal party."[65]

Unable to lay their hands on concrete evidence of Sifton's personal corruption that would stand up in a court of law, the Tories were determined to carry their case beyond the House of Commons and its committees to the court of public opinion. There the remarkable coincidences, the timber berths, the land and grazing deals, and Sifton's personal wealth, would all be aired fully and repeatedly. The Conservative efforts outdid even those of 1900 when the Tuppers had tried to bring down the young Napoleon with the ammunition of the Yukon charges. Herbert Ames went so far as to tour the country lecturing with a stereopticon and slides illustrating the Liberals' abuse of power. He played to a packed house in Winnipeg. Afterwards the *Winnipeg Tribune* commented that Sifton "apparently bears a charmed political life. He has been responsible for transactions and policies that would discredit and drive to oblivion a dozen Governments, and yet in his smug style he returns, discusses the monstrosities in his unique way, concealing this point and that and actually taking credit to himself for being a philanthropist and a statesman." Meanwhile, at Ottawa graft and corruption had become "a dangerous canker in the vitals of the national existence."

> At the present election Canadians are now at the parting of the ways: Canada has now to decide once and for all whether she will allow her political life to descend to the lowest level of Tammany Hall and to be controlled by "bosses" and "grafters"...or whether she will make a strenuous and determined effort to cleanse the Augean stables at Ottawa and endeavour to emulate if not attain to the almost Puritanic virtue of the motherland's politics.[66]

The Conservative campaign was fuelled by more than the conviction that Sifton was the principal villain among Laurier's crew of grafters. He was still perceived to be a major influence in the Liberal party, the principal organizer of the government campaign, and a strong candidate for a cabinet post should the Laurier government be sustained. Some Conservatives reportedly believed that they were unlikely to win the election, but that "if they defeated you [Sifton] they had the Laurier Government half defeated."[67]

Sifton's original intention was not to run in the election. He had rejected Laurier's overtures and was increasingly unhappy with the direction of the government. "My present impression," he told one of his supporters in December 1907, "is that I shall not be a candidate and I may add that if I were willing to become a candidate I doubt if I would feel at liberty to accept nomination as a straight supporter of the Government." He was particularly unhappy with the failure of Laurier to extend Manitoba's boundaries and to increase provincial subsidies.[68] A month later he had changed his mind, probably as a direct result of the renewal of Tory attacks on his administration of timber berths and furious cries for an investigation. Refusal to run again might appear to be an admission of guilt, a fear of seeking vindication at the hands of the public. Quietly the Brandon constituency organization was geared up. A man was hired in April at $2.50 per day to canvass each voter and prepare a card on each one's political views. A second organizer was retained at $100 per month.[69]

Although he visited Brandon late in March, Sifton seemed to be content to leave most of the details of organization to local Liberal officials. There is no evidence of the sort of careful supervision and cultivation of the constituency that always prevailed while he was in the government. Instead, he worked on his own business affairs, appeared occasionally in Parliament, and then devoted his attention to the fight in Ontario. As in many other federal elections, the parties recognized that Ontario could decide the result. Laurier's large majority in Quebec was almost taken for granted. In Ontario the Tories enjoyed a small majority, but now the Grits appeared unusually vulnerable. Corruption charges had played a significant role in James Whitney's Conservative victory in the province in 1905, ending over thirty years of Liberal rule. Would the story be repeated in the federal elections, when the Liberal organization was demoralized and the Tory organization finely honed and backed by the Whitney government?

Most of the Liberal resources were thrown into stemming the hemorrhage of popular support in Ontario. Well before the dissolution of Parliament Laurier began a major tour of the province, and Clifford Sifton undertook to shore up the Liberal machine and devise strategy behind the scenes. They produced, claimed J.W. Dafoe, "the most efficient organization that had ever been known in the province in a Dominion election." Few details survive, apart from some directions on the distribution of literature and the secret reports of a Liberal "operative" in Toronto who was trying to infiltrate the Tory organization and reporting daily to Sifton. The Liberals particularly wanted to know whether the Tories had a "war chest" for the buying up of votes. At first all such enquiries elicited negative responses, the Tories asserting that the federal party had only enough for legitimate expenses. Anything more would have to be raised locally. As election day drew nearer, however, plenty of evidence of the purchase of votes began to emerge, the money being passed to voters by means as diverse as stuffing it in a turkey or passing it during a casual handshake. In Toronto a number of houses were turned into free bars well supplied with liquor, while the police inspector was bought off for a consideration. In addition, the operative supplied useful reports on the Tory organization and campaign plans.[70]

Once Parliament was dissolved on 16 September, Sifton could no longer afford to neglect his own constituency. The Manitoba organization had fallen on hard days since Sifton left office. Without his direction, as Dafoe put it, the local machinery "virtually went to pieces." The Roblin-Rogers Tory organization, by contrast, was aggressive and almost unopposed. As in 1904, the local Liberals believed they were seriously disadvantaged by the Dominion Elections Act, which allowed the provincial government to draw up the voters' lists. Undoubtedly the lists were rigged to some degree, and to meet the party protests the Laurier government agreed to amend the act to provide for some federal control of the lists in British Columbia, Manitoba and northern Ontario—all under Tory governments; and in northern Quebec. The Conservatives naturally were enraged, set in motion an effective filibuster during the spring of 1908, and eventually forced Laurier to withdraw the amendment in July and substitute limited judicial supervision of the lists in Manitoba and Ontario.[71] The eventual compromise was not dissimilar to one proposed by Sifton in May; as in 1904, he was much less convinced than the Manitoba Liberals that the election would be won or lost on the basis of corrupt lists.

When Laurier finally capitulated to the opposition demands, Dafoe angrily told Sifton that the decision did not surprise him, and added, "We're not Liberals because we support Laurier but we support him because we are Liberals; he is a mere incident while the party goes on." The local Liberals were so exasperated that "the use of Laurier's name as a shibboleth is no longer advisable."[72] The compromise had been too little too late to be of any use in the forthcoming campaign. Beyond that, Dafoe believed that Laurier's response was symptomatic of a leader who had ceased to listen seriously to the plight of his western followers and whose actions were causing increased alienation. Sifton did not dissent, telling Dafoe that his letter "embodies a very sensible view of the situation and I cannot suggest anything better."[73]

As the campaign in the West developed, Sifton relied heavily on Dafoe and the *Free Press* to provide general leadership. Certainly what the *Canadian Annual Review* termed the "slashing, clever editorial work" of the newspaper was the most effective feature of the Liberal campaign in the province. Although Sifton spoke a few times outside his constituency, he was forced to confine his major effort to Brandon, where the atmosphere had become notably unfriendly. At every turn he had to contend with the corruption charges, so that much of the time he appeared to be on the defensive. But there were additional difficulties. His failure to get the Grand Trunk Pacific to build into Brandon told heavily against him. During the campaign there was a strike by CPR workers, who became very hostile to the government because of its failure to support the men. The fact that Sifton had not lived in the constituency for twelve years was played up, despite the fact that his opponent, T. Mayne Daly, had for some years been resident in Winnipeg. The Tories calculated that in the late session of Parliament Sifton had been absent from the House for 147 of 159 sitting days, supposedly proving that he was more concerned about his own affairs than those of his constituents.[74] And finally, Sifton no longer had his cornucopia of patronage with which to influence the voters.

It was widely understood, of course, that Sifton was not without other means of persuasion. This was underlined by Daly who, in accepting the Conservative nomination, pointedly—and a bit piously—remarked, "This constituency is looked upon as the most corrupt in Canada, but I come to you without money and without price and I believe you electors will redeem yourselves and place this constituency rightly where it belongs." Sifton's "operative" in the Tory camp confirmed that they expected to win with "clean methods," despite some evidence of Tory boodle. But the Conservatives also claimed that there was a great deal of Sifton money on the streets. One reportedly said "he would bet that at least a dozen Grits would be in jail for bribery before noon on election day." Furthermore, some intimidation if not blackmail could be used. The "operative" reported that two owners of a livery stable had permitted a prostitute to use a room for immoral purposes, and this information could be used to prevent the two Tory gentlemen from voting.[75]

Daly proved to be a wily, experienced opponent. Sifton tried repeatedly to meet him in a public debate, but Daly always declined, or sent a representative to Sifton's meetings. He was not above playing on the nativist sentiment of Brandonites, contending that, while the Tories had followed a selective immigration policy, "the jails and asylums of Canada are to-day crowded with the class of settlers which Clifford Sifton had brought to Canada."[76] Once again Sifton had to fight back with a thorough canvass of his constituents, meeting as many as possible individually, speaking as widely as possible. In one twelve-day blitz he scheduled eighteen meetings outside Brandon city. Apart from defending his own administrative record and that of the Laurier government, he hoped that a definite commitment by the prime minister to build the Hudson Bay railway as a government work would offset disappointment regarding the GTPR.[77]

The most important single meeting of the Manitoba campaign, nevertheless, took place in Winnipeg on 21 October, where Sifton and other prominent Liberals appeared on behalf of D.C. Cameron, the Grit candidate. The newspaper accounts of the event differ widely, but it is clear that Sifton met with an unprecedented display of hostility. According to the *Tribune*, the outbursts, catcalls, and fistfights which disrupted proceedings were the expected result of public fury at Sifton's personal corruption and machine politics. The *Free Press*, by contrast, reported that "hundreds of hoodlums" organized by the Tories had stimulated the interruptions. The paper alleged that "the scourings and riff-raff of the lowest dives and bar-rooms in the city" had arrived at the meeting drunk, shouting "filthy epithets and obscenities," and were supplied with written questions with which to disrupt the meeting. The *Tribune* contended that Sifton had become angry and was eventually forced to give up his speech after two hours; the *Free Press* printed a verbatim report to prove that he had in fact finished his speech. It is clear that much of whatever was said from the platform went unheard by the 3,000 people crowded into the Walker Theatre. The meeting, as the Tories must have hoped, turned into a public relations disaster."[78]

In the course of his remarks, Sifton defended his administration of the timber berths by pointing out that even examination of documents and officials by the Public Accounts Committee had turned up no evidence upon which charges could be laid. "I make the statement...that no lawyer in the Dominion of Canada would face a court with that evidence and upon it ask the court to conclude that there was any impropriety or any fraud in conjunction with the transactions." "What," he demanded, "would the Conservative Party have done in this election if I had had no brother-in-law?" T.A. Burrows had obtained only nineteen or twenty berths out of more than 1,000 offered, and "a company in which he was interested got seven or eight or nine more. That is not a very considerable proportion."[79]

Sifton dwelt on the government's record of labour legislation, particularly the establishment of the Department of Labour, of the *Labour Gazette*, and of fair wage clauses in government contracts. The latter, he declared, was "a work of humanity, which is a distinct credit to the government of the Liberal party....We have by that legislation discharged our duty to humanity, by seeing that the class of the population, who are least able to protect themselves are properly protected by this legislation." He was at pains to defend the Industrial Disputes Investigation Act (or Lemieux Act) of 1907, though admitting that he had little sympathy for the principle of compulsory arbitration and also that the act had done nothing for the striking CPR employees.[80] Finally, there was the establishment of the Railway Commission, empowered to regulate railways, telegraphs, and telephones on behalf of the citizens of Canada. "Is it a matter of no importance that the poorest citizen of Canada can have his grievance against the greatest corporation in Canada redressed by an impartial tribunal at public expense? I don't think that any man who believes in Liberal principles, who believes in legislation by a parliament for the benefit and protection of the individual, will think it a matter of no importance.''

The speech also bestowed much of the credit for prosperity since 1896 upon the transportation and immigration policies of the government. But the emphasis on labour legislation, rare among Sifton's speeches, drew attention to Liberal concern about an increasingly hostile labour vote.

So serious had the personal attacks on Sifton's wealth become and so rife was the political atmosphere with scurrilous rumours about how he had acquired it, that for the only time in his public career Sifton apparently permitted a few facts about his private fortune to be announced. Most notable was an article in the *Boston Transcript* by its Canadian correspondent, E.W. Thompson, who was especially sympathetic to Laurier. Friends in Brandon were quoted as stating that Sifton had been "a man of property and considerable wealth" while living in that city and also possessed of a large professional income. He was not the poor man when he went to Ottawa that the Tories loved to portray. It was also understood that he "made large sums by investment in the stock of the Canada North-West Land Company and...he made $160,000 profit by buying and selling Northern Pacific Stock." During the campaign William Templeman stated that he personally knew of two stock speculations in which Sifton had made $360,000 profit. He went on to affirm, "There is no clearer-headed, bolder speculator in Canada" than Sifton.[81] It was very far from a full financial disclosure, but Sifton probably hoped it would be enough to convince the public that his fortune had been legitimately acquired.

That was probably a miscalculation. It whetted the public appetite for more information, drew attention to his personal interests, and encouraged the opposition to dig up more charges. The most troublesome of these was the story that Sifton had profited heavily from deals between the International Marine Signal Company and Shawinigan Carbide and the government. It was claimed that Sifton held $850,000 worth of shares and control of the former company and that he was one of the owners of the latter. He directed Dafoe to print a denial in the *Free Press* that he had any stock in either concern. He had earlier held stock in the Marine Signal Company, but "sold it for what I paid for it and 6% interest, made no profits of any kind out of the Government." A judicial investigation in Montreal had specifically exonerated him of any wrongdoing.[82]

On 26 October the Laurier government was sustained with 135 seats, three fewer than in 1904, while the Conservatives won eighty-five seats, a gain of ten. Across the country, the government lost only 1.5 per cent of the popular vote; the Tories gained but 0.5 per cent. The campaign of calumny and corruption had not appreciably affected the voting public. The biggest surprise was Ontario, where the Conservatives made no gains whatever. There the strenuous Liberal efforts to save the province had paid off. In the West, however, growing dissatisfaction with the government was evident. The two parties each gained seventeen seats in the four western provinces, compared to a twenty-one to six margin in favour of the Liberals in 1904. In Manitoba the Tories were elected in eight of ten seats, with 51.5 per cent of the popular vote, up 10 per cent from 1904. Sifton barely held Brandon by a plurality of sixty-nine votes in a total poll of 7,162. One of Sifton's old-time friends since 1881, Philip McKenzie, later recalled the election night: "Returns coming in the 1st Hour looked *bad*. guess I was feeling blue. He came down to where I was, & said *Phil* I have been watching your face, and if it is any indication of the results, I had better go home but *cheer up* the best is yet to come." The only other Liberal victory was in the Franco-Manitoban riding of Provencher. In Dauphin, T.A. Burrows, who had been running to vindicate himself, was defeated.[83]

It was a victory that gave Sifton little satisfaction. The margin was too narrow to serve as a convincing rebuff to his critics, and there were instant charges that "the archdebaucher of public life and the seducer of Liberalism" had once more bought up his constituency. [84] As might have been expected, Daly protested the election, Sifton responded by protesting all the Tory victories, and after a few months' wrangling the parties as usual agreed to saw off the protests. Sifton publicly declared that "the adverse result in Winnipeg and Brandon" was mainly attributable to "stuffed voters' lists." Privately he engaged in few post mortems, telling F.C. Wade, "We had an old time battle in Manitoba and we were handicapped beyond any possibility of success by the Voters lists and the fact that the Railway men were stolidly [*sic*] against the Government on account of the Lemieux Act."[85] There were no victory celebrations on this occasion. Sifton quietly slipped into Winnipeg for a few days with his parents before returning to Ottawa.

The visit with his parents, as it happened, was possibly the last time that Clifford saw his mother alive. After a very brief illness, Kate Sifton died on 19 March 1909, aged seventy-six years. She had immigrated to Canada from Ireland as a girl; little is known of her life or personality except that she was devoted to her family, and her sons were deeply attached to her. Both Arthur and Clifford were present in Winnipeg for the small, private funeral.[86]

Ironically, it had been the poor health of John Wright Sifton that had caused the most concern in recent years. He appears to have been subject to depression, both because of his advancing years and infirmity and because of increased sensitivity to his separation from his two sons. In the summer of 1908 he was diagnosed as suffering from neuritis. Aware that Sir William Mulock had been successfully treated for the same disease, Clifford arranged for his father to travel to the Rochester clinic for the same treatment, producing significant improvement within weeks.[87]

Among the greatest blessings of freedom from administrative responsibility after 1905 was opportunity for more time with his family. Sifton now took extended vacations at Assiniboine Lodge on the St. Lawrence or combined business trips to England with vacations for his family. They would join him at country estates for fox hunting, be introduced to assorted British political and financial leaders, and tour the continent. One British friend assured Sifton that his sons were "all very bright and the two older ones about the keenest young men on public affairs that I have ever met."[88]

He was also fast becoming a leader in Canadian equestrian circles. His interest was not principally in racing horses, but in horses for the hunt, for polo, and the aspects of show and competition that derived from those sports, such as jumping. Although he naturally maintained a staff to care for his stable, he himself became an expert on the selection, breeding, care and training of horses, and with his sons usually rode his own horses in competitions and shows. It was not without peril: at the end of February 1909 Sifton fell and broke his collar bone during a competition in Washington; the following year Winfield was injured at the Montreal Horse Show, and Clifford junior's horse fell on him during a show in New York. According to reports of the latter incident, Sifton and his wife were watching from a box, and he leaped the railing and knocked down several people as he frantically rushed to reach his fallen son. Fortunately, on that occasion no serious injury occurred.[89] Within Canada Sifton's horses enjoyed marked success; as he proudly told a friend, "they have been doing extremely well, and have practically cleaned out all the shows where they have been shown this fall [1910]."[90] He did admit that in New York the competition would be stiffer, but he exhibited his horses not only in the eastern United States, but in Britain as well.

His principal business interest remained the *Manitoba Free Press*, though as it prospered under the direction of Dafoe and Macklin, and because he was no longer in the government, the need for Sifton's detailed, close supervision was minimized. When in 1906 John Mather died, John Wright Sifton succeeded to the presidency of the Free Press Company, a position he would retain until his death. The position was largely honorary, as befitted the elder Sifton's declining years, but the new president did appear at his offices regularly and concerned himself with the paper's fortunes.

Neither the owner nor the president could find much of concern in the *Free Press* of those years. Figures of 1907 show that the average daily circulation of the paper, 36,015, was practically as large as that of the

Telegram and *Tribune* combined. The average circulation of the weekly, 22,941, exceeded that of the *Telegram* by over 9,000.[91] The figures are probably typical of the proportion of the market controlled by the *Free Press* during most of the years after 1905. The paper was readable, lively in appearance and subject-matter, and crammed with advertising. It was far more attractive than, for example, that staid old flagship of Canadian Liberalism, the Toronto *Globe*, and was marketed with flair. Dafoe and Macklin were active in the founding and direction of the Western Associated Press and the Canadian Press organizations from 1907.[92] The editor already was recognized as a figure of regional and national influence, well connected with the government at Ottawa, and was one of fifteen delegates chosen to represent Canada at the Imperial Press Conference in London in 1909.[93]

The growing prestige and authority of his editor must have influenced Sifton as he relaxed his grip and more and more relied upon Dafoe's judgment. Indeed, Dafoe was emerging as the closest thing to a personal confidant that Sifton ever had outside his immediate family. He was often a visitor at Assiniboine Lodge or at the Siftons' Ottawa residence. Between visits the two men conducted an extensive correspondence discussing public affairs of the day.[94] A measure of how far Sifton had shifted his views on the role of a newspaper since he had left office, and certainly since he had debated the issue with J.S. Willison in 1901, is a letter to Dafoe of 1910. He was referring to the paper's attitude on a municipal election in Winnipeg when he wrote:

> It cannot be made too clear that in all these matters of violent agitation in a City like Winnipeg it is wholly outside the province of a great daily paper to undertake to champion one side or the other. The day is past when the daily paper is expected to direct the community. What the community has a right to expect is that the facts and the arguments on both sides of every important discussion should be set before them so that they can form their own opinions intelligently. There will always be extremists in every violent dispute, who will desire to have the backing of the editorial columns, but it will not be very long before the solid sense of the community will find extreme relief in the conviction that no matter what kind of a dispute arises they will be able to find in the columns of their paper fair and impartial statements of the facts on both sides instead of hot headed partisanship.[95]

On another occasion Sifton told Dafoe that "the only strength that the Free Press can have will be its independence and freedom from corporate influence."[96] None of this meant that Sifton was espousing a non-partisan, impartial approach to journalism. It did mean that the *Free Press* must be less willing to suppress the views of its opponents and more selective about those issues on which it would take a decisive stand. It must be seen to support policies because they were in the public interest, or the interest of the region or nation, and not merely because they were supported by the Liberal party or some corporate interest.

A case in point is that of the Hudson Bay railway. Public opinion in the West strongly favoured government construction and ownership, a principle which Sifton had habitually opposed. In the early spring of 1908 he had declared, "I regard the craze for public ownership of everything as one of the most serious menaces to the industrial progress and general prosperity of Canada."[97] It was a philosophy that Laurier held, if anything, more strongly, and the resulting differences in opinion between western Liberals and the government probably contributed to the delays in beginning construction. Despite Liberal promises of construction during the 1908 election campaign, nothing was done in 1909 or 1910, and Laurier was repeatedly reminded of his promises when he toured the West in 1910. The prime minister personally favoured giving the project to the Canadian Northern Railway to build, a proposal westerners believed would doom the line to failure. No east-west transcontinental would wish to divert significant amounts of traffic to Hudson Bay; while an independent private company would still have to make deals with, and in fact be controlled by, the large transcontinentals. "There is nothing for it," Dafoe told Sifton, "if the new road is to be worth anything to us, but for the road to be built and operated by the Government." "The West," he added, "in view of its political strength cannot reasonably hope to be more than a modifying influence in determining the tariff policy of the Dominion, but this Hudson's [*sic*] Bay matter is almost exclusively western, and western wishes should determine the policy of the Government." Replied Sifton: "I am quite of your opinion."[98] He had recognized the logic of the argument and the force of public opinion as Laurier had not. Equally important, Dafoe's exceptional sensitivity to the currents of western and national opinion enabled him to continually place the *Free Press* in a position of leadership and influence.

Owner and editor were not, however, always in agreement. Sifton once wrote a stinging letter attacking the staff of the paper and its allegedly poor coverage of certain events, especially sports. Dafoe replied diplomatically but firmly, reassuring Sifton that he had often profited from the owner's forthright views. However, he continued, "I should like...to disabuse your mind of one idea that appears to be rooted there—that the staff is made up in part of old pensioners who do their work in a more or less perfunctory manner and that this...coupled with their party regularity enables them to retain their positions by virtue of my good nature." This was neither fair nor just. The staff was "on the whole a good one." It was also an underpaid staff, and "every man on it gives value for his money." Of course there was room for improvement, but only higher salaries could attract better people. After perusing Dafoe's lengthy and detailed defence of his staff and procedures, Sifton commented, "Anybody who can write so extremely good natured and explanatory a letter in reply to the kind of a letter I wrote you is worthy of better things than running a daily paper."[99]

It was a remarkable relationship. Dafoe was sure enough of himself to hold his ground, to evaluate Sifton's often impetuous and blunt outbursts, to adopt that which was useful, and ignore the rest. But every comment from Sifton received a serious reply. For his part, the publisher respected a man who was able, confident, successful, and not readily intimidated. The strong roots of mutual admiration and trust developed since 1901 were probably the only reason the relationship survived the extraordinary stress of the reciprocity election of 1911.

The *Free Press* may have been unique, or nearly so, among Sifton's investments in the sense that it was an operating business. His fortune arose principally from speculation, not from companies actually engaged in productive development. An illustration of this attitude occurred in 1908 when he and D.C. Cameron, a Winnipeg lumberman, were considering the formation of a company to hold some timber leases which they jointly owned. He made it clear that he did not want to be involved in a company which was empowered to run a lumber business, "as I have sufficient to occupy my time without going into such an enterprise, to which I should be unable to give personal attention." The company should merely be empowered "to hold, and ultimately, when it is so desired, to sell" the limits.[100] Typically, Sifton appears to have made most of his money from speculations in lands, and in stocks and bonds, at least up to 1905.

Once he had left the government, however, Sifton began to examine the possibilities of investment outside Canada, particularly in Latin America— in Mexico, Colombia, and even Brazil. He acquired control of the Atlantic Oil Company, formed for the purpose of exploring for oil in South America. In the fall of 1907 it was engaged in drilling in Colombia and later in Mexico. Despite widespread rumours that Sifton was making a fortune in oil, the reverse appears to have been the reality. Almost no commercial oil was found.[101] In May 1908 Sifton went to Mexico to examine a timber berth known as the Esperanza Tract, in Chiapas state, near Guatemala. Covering 154,000 acres, the tract was supposed to have some 500,000,000 board feet of top-grade mahogany and 1,000,000,000 feet of other timber, including cedar. The asking price was $400,000 U.S. As was his custom with major investments, Sifton wanted to see the property for himself. After a five-hundred-mile train trip from Mexico City, he had to travel for five days on horseback, returning downriver by canoe. His impression was favourable, though he thought it unlikely to produce as much as predicted. Upon his return to Canada he decided to send professional Canadian forest rangers to assess the tract; when they reported that only 61,000,000 feet of mahogany was available he cancelled the deal. [102] Such experiences soured him on Mexican investments, particularly in light of developing economic nationalism in the country. [103]

Sifton's record for investment in Canada was by no means uniformly successful either. He had been greatly impressed by the immense profits realized by M.J. O'Brien in mining speculations in northern Ontario. Mining claims were generally not significant in Sifton's pattern of investments, but he persuaded O'Brien to let him buy a 30 per cent interest in a certain claim. O'Brien sold him the partnership for $12,000, which was what O'Brien and another partner had originally paid for the claim. Sifton decided that he must see the claim, enduring a bitter sub-zero trip of thirty miles from the closest railway line. By the time he arrived at the mine he was in a foul mood and assumed a peremptory tone in dealing with the mine manager. The manager as a consequence did not prove very forthcoming about the prospects of the mine. Disillusioned, Sifton decided to get out of the company, but retrieved only $10,000 of his original investment. A few months later, in the fall of 1910, the claim "shipped what was described as the richest ore, for its tonnage, ever moved out of Gowganda." [104] There is evidence that Sifton had other dealings with O'Brien, but how profitable he found them is unknown.

He did invest small amounts in a wide assortment of companies, for example, the Crown Bank of Canada, the Lake Superior Corporation, North American Oil and Gas Company, even the Pioneer Fire Insurance Company. He held securities issued by the city of Port Arthur. He purchased $55,000 worth of interest in the Knox and Hamilton group of hill claims on Bonanza Creek in the Yukon. In 1906 he invested $10,000, or almost a 20 per cent interest, in a consortium which included Sir Frederick Borden and Robert Borden, to purchase Parc St. Denis in Montreal. [105] None of these account for any significant portion of Sifton's wealth, and the available papers do little more than throw out some tantalizing hints.

The hints tend to confirm the general impression that Sifton made a good deal from speculation in timber berths. For example, in 1909 he and D.C. Cameron were offered $750,000 for two tracts that they owned. Sifton refused the offer, believing that within two or three years they would considerably appreciate in value. The precise berths in question are not known, though in 1907 the two had purchased a single berth for $1,526. [106] Most timber berths when sold by the government realized no more than $5,000; a very few went for $20,000 or more. It is clear that the price offered in 1909 for two would have represented an enormous profit. And Sifton had a ready eye for such opportunities. In 1908 he was considering purchase of a tract just west of the Yellowhead Pass along the projected route of the

Grand Trunk Pacific, some 281 square miles of timber which he believed could be purchased from a private concern for $400,000 or $500,000. Because the GTPR would require great quantities of timber for bridging purposes, sizeable profits could be realized. [107]

As a businessman, Sifton adhered to a certain moral code. Even as a young lawyer in Brandon he had established a reputation for meeting his commitments. When Arthur Sifton left for Prince Albert, and the brothers' law practice was dissolved, Sifton was left with heavy obligations from a farm investment. He eventually paid off thousands of dollars' worth of debts in the 1880s before he could look after his own security and future. [108] In later years, he was careful to advise others against risky investments. When a correspondent expressed interest in purchasing stock from a minority shareholder in the Atlantic Oil Company—a purchase which might have increased the value of Sifton's own shares—he discouraged the idea, "knowing that the value of the stock was purely speculative, and should not be offered to any person as an investment." [109] As it turned out, it was good advice. Perhaps the clearest statement of Sifton's views arose from a dispute with Premier Walter Scott of Saskatchewan. Acting as an agent for British investors, Sifton believed he had reached an understanding with Scott and J.A. Calder of the provincial government on the sale of provincial bonds. It was a verbal understanding that Scott apparently broke. When the premier sought a reconciliation, Sifton retorted:

> I entered into a straight business arrangement with you and Calder not asking, receiving or desiring any favor of any kind whatever. You broke your word and violated the elementary principles of business honor....
>
> It has been my one determination in my very strenuous political and business life to act so that no one should be able to say that I had treated him in any manner except with transparent good faith and straightforwardness. So far as I know I have kept this principle good. [110]

Of course Sifton had his own peculiar way of defining and rationalizing his principles, but a reasonable adherence to the unwritten moral code of the business community was important in establishing his influence and success.

His success both in business and in politics no doubt motivated the New York State Chamber of Commerce to invite Sifton in November 1908, along with B.E. Walker and J.J. Hill, to address it on the Canadian situation. He began with a history lesson, to show that Canadians, like Americans, had struggled with natural obstacles to develop the country, but also that Canadians had chosen the path of evolution rather than a revolution to change their form of government "from the crude and somewhat despotic status of the Crown colony" to a system "suitable for an expanding nation and giving the fullest opportunities for self-government.'' The United States had also played a role in the development of the Canadian nation. The American refusal to extend or renegotiate the reciprocity agreement of 1854 had forced Canada to strengthen her east-west trade linkages in order to survive. But, in Sifton's view, this had led to a lengthy period of disappointingly slow growth and the loss of hundreds of thousands of young Canadians who had been unable to find work at home. It was during this period that Canada established her transcontinental trading patterns, secured the domestic market, and began to expand the east-west trade across the ocean. ''Looking back now,'' asserted Sifton, ''it is beyond question that nothing better could have happened to Canada than the refusal of liberal trade relations with the United States, because by being thrown upon her own resources she has been forced to fight her way through to ultimate success.''

Americans should not imagine, in his opinion, that Canadians wished either independence from the British Empire or closer association with the United States. Rather, Canada would remain part of the Empire, ''one of a sisterhood of self-governing nations centred around the British Crown.''[111] As for her trade relations with the United States, Sifton made it clear that Canada would look to her own advantage, as he was sure the Americans themselves would do. Friendship and sentiment ought not to be allowed to interfere with good business principles, and each side ought to recognize the right of the other to pursue its own advantage. ''You are perfectly able to get along without making trade arrangements with Canada,'' continued Sifton, ''and Canada has shown itself perfectly able to get along without making trade arrangements with the United States. We sought reciprocity with you for many years. We are not seeking it now ....We are perfectly satisfied with matters as they stand.'' In future mutually beneficial proposals might be considered, ''but with the clear understanding that no proposals will be accepted upon either side which are not considered to be of advantage to that country which is asked to adopt them.'' Canada was at the point where she could work out her own destiny, assured of rapid development of her natural resources. The Dominion, he told his audience with breathtaking assurance, ''has no racial or social problems which threaten its stability. It has no large masses of population living in poverty and want. Peace, plenty and prosperity are within its borders.''[112]

Both the prime minister and the governor general wrote to commend Sifton for what Grey termed ''your courageous & opportune speech.''[113] It certainly reflected the tremendous optimism about Canada's future, the positive sense of nationalism that had become prevalent during the previous decade. It was also a speech that appeared to be quite apolitical, a stance that Sifton was beginning to enjoy. He could command national attention on almost any topic that he chose to speak upon, and such speeches and interviews could become an indirect influence on public policy. The partisan excesses of the late election campaign, the identification of prosperity and progress with the Laurier government, had been exceptional, and they did not reflect Sifton's growing dissatisfaction with the federal government.

Normally he restrained his desire to criticize the ministry publicly, though once he irritably replied to a critic of the Department of the Interior, "I beg that you will not hold me responsible for the fact that Providence put an incompetent mischief maker in the position to do a great deal of mischief."[114] Rather it was his aloofness, his unwillingness to defend the ministry, and indeed his isolation from the normal activities of politicians that led some observers to conclude that he might even end up in the Tory camp.[115] As before 1908, he attended the House of Commons infrequently, made no partisan speeches in 1909 or 1910 and, by his own admission, never attended the meetings of parliamentary committees."[116] To be fair, in 1910 he was heavily involved in the activities of the Conservation Commission,[117] but that simply reinforced his determination to avoid partisan positions, at least in public.

A case in point occurred during the debate on naval policy in 1909. The revelation that the supremacy of the Royal Navy was under serious challenge from Germany led to a flurry of promises from various parts of the Empire to support the British and contribute to naval defence. A resolution unanimously passed the Canadian House of Commons calling upon the government to fulfil its pledge, originally made in 1902, to construct a Canadian navy, and to do so "speedily." The resolution papered over not only partisan differences, but differences among those imperialists who wanted an immediate, substantial contribution to the Royal Navy, those supporting a Canadian navy, and those who wanted Canada to avoid all naval commitments. Sifton quickly received a letter from Lieutenant-Governor McMillan of Manitoba complaining that "the promises are too indefinite and the contemplated action too far in the dim and distant future." The immediate contribution of a couple of Dreadnought battleships followed by a Canadian naval programme would have been better received in Winnipeg. Replied Sifton, "I fancy that my views and yours are precisely the same." He had not spoken "because I was afraid I would say what I thought, which would probably have made a commotion and the consequences would have been hard to foresee." In any case, he added, Quebec opinion warranted restraint by the government, and most "jingo sentiment" was probably Tory.[118]

During the first two sessions of the eleventh parliament, in fact, Sifton addressed the House only once on a topic not connected with conservation. The sole issue to seize his interest was a proposed amendment to the

Criminal Code introduced late in 1909 to eliminate all forms of organized betting on horse races in Canada.[119] The occasion permitted him to express his views on matters he rarely touched on publicly. He professed sympathy with those who promoted moral and social reform in the country. He declared that he was free of any sympathy with gambling, never having bet on a race or taken part in any game of chance where money was at stake. However, "I cannot plead that my freedom comes from any deep-rooted feeling that gambling is immoral. It has rather seemed to me to be an exhibition of stupidity, and I have not felt it necessary to indulge in that particular form of stupidity." He had decided to oppose the measure for different reasons. The extended debate on the subject, he declared, had shown, first, "that the English thoroughbred horse is the basis of the improvement of all light horse breeding throughout the whole world"; second, "not only that racing has developed the English thoroughbred, but that racing alone will keep him in his present condition and quality"; and third, that "stoppage of bookmaking" would do away with racing "by men of means." Then racing would fall into the hands of the disreputable. In other words, to eliminate betting would undermine the sport of gentlemen, and without races there would be no incentive to maintain or improve the quality of breeding stock.

There were, admittedly, some obvious evils, including advertising of betting, off-track betting, and extended racing seasons which become more than trials of speed and "are simply devices for the purpose of furnishing gambling facilities." Remedying these evils was, he judged, as far as the proposed legislation should go. Given this situation, what course should the House take?

> What is the principle upon which criminal legislation, under the British system is based[?] The principle of all our criminal legislation is this, that it is the crystallized or, if you may so call it, the sanctified common sense of the community. It is the expression of the general assent of the community that such and such an act ought to be condemned....Under the British system what we may call freak legislation is unknown. It never has been admitted that it is the duty of a British legislature to decide moral questions for the British people....It is the right of the individual, the liberty of the individual, and the only way he can develop character is by exercising his right to decide moral questions for himself.

He believed that acts "commonly indulged in by a large and respectable section of the community" ought not to be declared criminal by a narrow majority of Parliament. If there was not widespread support for the law, the result would be to "bring the law into contempt." The proposed legislation "practically confiscates a large amount of private property and brands as criminal acts which are constantly being performed by some of the best citizens of the Dominion."[120]

The speech is interesting on at least two levels. First, it shows an ability to rationalize a behaviour of which Sifton personally disapproved because its elimination would have an adverse effect upon his favorite pastime, equestrian sports. Second, it is an interesting case of the class bias behind at least some contemporary morals legislation.[121] Vagrancy, prostitution, and public drunkenness were widely assumed to be lower-class activities and were readily proscribed by a righteous middle-class legislature. But when the issue struck closer to home, it was more difficult. The emphasis in Sifton's speech was on "respectable, reputable citizens," "some of the best citizens of the dominion." He might not have approved of gambling, but these people were not in his mind criminals and ought not to be branded as such. Put another way, the liberty of the individual to decide moral questions for himself was understood to exist within certain clearly understood limits. He was quite consistent, in this sense, with his statement in 1890 that it was "the respectable element in his constituency" that supported strong measures of prohibition.

In only one area after 1908 did Sifton make a serious gesture toward partisan politics, an attempt to revive the demoralized Manitoba Liberals. Narrowly defeated by the Tories in 1899 and twice crushed by Premier Roblin in 1903 and 1907, they had been unable to provide much assistance in the federal campaign of 1908. Perhaps Sifton was spurred to assist his old allies after witnessing their condition in 1908. Possibly he wanted their assistance in the post-election protests. The death of Thomas Greenway in October 1908 might have symbolized for Sifton the passing of the old guard and the opportunity to regroup under new leadership. Whatever the reasons, he took a much greater interest in the welfare of the party than at any time since 1903. He personally financed the protests, some by-elections, and the party headquarters, as well as looking after organizational details and urging members to public activity.[122] At the beginning of 1909 he undertook to pay the local party $5,000 a year for two years; by early in 1910 he had already paid $10,776 for organization and administration, and was facing calls for even more.[123] He believed that the organization was much improved by 1910, but in provincial elections in June the Liberals were defeated by the same margin of twenty-eight to thirteen as in 1907. Sifton's enthusiasm for aiding the party dropped sharply. In refusing a request for more funds from the party executive, he commented that "under present circumstances, I am not disposed to contribute anything whatever."[124]

The "present circumstances" in all probability referred less to the condition of the Manitoba party than to Sifton's general relationship to the Liberal government in Ottawa. The gulf between him and the party establishment had been perceptibly deepening since the last dominion election. Illustrative of his disillusionment was a comment about Laurier made to Lieutenant-Governor McMillan in 1909:

> In the course of thirteen years I have not on any single occasion known him to stand firmly when the interests of the Liberal Party in Manitoba required it. Practically we have been thrown down on every occasion upon what I have conceived to be very flimsy excuses. It is quite surprising how weak an argument he will accept when it is in accordance with his views and how impervious he is to reason, even of the strongest kind, that points in a direction which he does not want to follow. [125]

By the summer of 1910 Sifton's concern was not with the welfare of the local Liberals, but with the welfare of the country. It was already well known that the Laurier government was involved in trade discussions with the United States. If, as rumoured, reciprocity was under serious consideration, Sifton knew that it would call into question his entire relationship with the Liberal party.

10

Reciprocity
(1911)

Reciprocity had long been the Liberal dream. No concept was more central to nineteenth-century liberalism than the laissez-faire state, particularly an economy freed of artificial encumbrances on trade. It was an article of faith among Canadian Liberals after Confederation that no policy could so ensure the prosperity of the country as a renewal, in some shape or form, of the reciprocity treaty with the United States that had been abrogated in 1866. The protectionist star was in the ascendant in America, however, and the Conservatives under Sir John A. Macdonald retaliated in 1879 with Canada's own National Policy protective tariff. It was both a response to Canadian nationalism and a stimulus to Canadian industrialization, in turn strengthening the protectionist forces in the country. Stubbornly, however, the Liberals held the faith and marched to three consecutive electoral defeats before realistically coming to terms with the business community in the early 1890s. In return for private assurances that protection would not be abandoned, many businessmen supported Laurier's Liberals in 1896 and were rewarded with the Fielding budget the following year.

Already the principal locus of free trade sentiment was shifting westward, a trend accelerated during the Laurier boom as the prairies were settled and powerful agrarian organizations began to lobby for the interests of their constituents. They firmly believed that access to the American market would give them higher prices for their produce, and that reciprocity also would lower the price of farm machinery and consumer goods generally. The effectiveness of the lobby was demonstrated when, from 7 July to 3 September 1910, Prime Minister Laurier undertook his first political tour of the West in sixteen years. At every stop he was confronted by delegations of grain growers armed with long recitals of the farmers' grievances and demands. On 18 July at Brandon, for example, they told him that "there are no trade relations our Government could enter into with any country with better advantages to the farmers of the West than a wide measure of Reciprocity towards the United States including manufactured articles and the natural products of both countries."[1]

Laurier's vague replies and assurances that he too had always favoured free trade and reciprocity if an equitable agreement could be achieved did not satisfy the westerners. They knew that in the spring of 1910 the United States had offered to open talks on the subject of reciprocity. They also knew that the industrial community and other interests were alarmed at the prospect. Always in the past the government had been able to claim that American disinterest made the pursuit of reciprocity futile. That excuse no longer obtained; would the government seize the opportunity to implement historic Liberal doctrine? Or would the lobbies of the business interests prevail? The farmers knew that Laurier's western tour of 1910 was an important phase in influencing the government.

However, the resurgent West was not the only new reality in Canadian politics. The boom that had settled the prairies had also accelerated the industrialization and urbanization of central Canada and strengthened the east-west transportation system. The manufacturing and transportation interests were not only mostly protectionist in sentiment, but also sensed that they had been thrown on the defensive by the aggressive and often successful tactics of the farm organizations in recent years. They also were suspicious of the government which had seemed to them predisposed to heed the farmers and indisposed to sympathize with the plight of business. The announcement that reciprocity negotiations might take place sent tremors of dismay throughout the business community of central Canada. As early as June 1910 William German, Liberal MP for Welland, and Lloyd Harris, Liberal MP for Brantford, informed Finance Minister Fielding of their opposition.[2] In the summer the Canadian Manufacturers' Association was at pains to dissociate itself from the government and warned that the partisan loyalty of Liberal businessmen ought not to be taken for granted.[3] Late in September Sir George W. Ross, former Liberal premier of Ontario, wrote two articles for the *Globe* denouncing reciprocity and led the Toronto Board of Trade in opposing it on 3 November, just before the Canadian and American commissioners met to open discussions in Ottawa.[4] The Toronto *News* and the *Montreal Star* had already taken a strong lead in the anti-reciprocity campaign, and on 8 October *The News* published no less than eighteen reasons for its opposition, which anticipated most of the arguments of the subsequent battle.[5] Given the strength of the business lobby, it was small wonder that the Canadians immediately informed the Americans in Ottawa that the "comprehensive inclusion of manufactured articles" in a reciprocity agreement would be unacceptable.[6]

The business challenge could not be ignored by the farmers, determined to strengthen the hands of the pro-reciprocity forces. Late in October Laurier consented to receive a delegation of farmers, and on 15 December nearly one thousand of them descended on Ottawa. It was the largest such group ever to wait on a Canadian government to that time, and it left no doubt about the determination of many farmers in Ontario as well as the West to secure reciprocity. Laurier responded that the government was indeed negotiating for better trade relations in natural products, but it was unable to do so with respect to manufactured products.[7] The manufacturers were not reassured. They had been anxious observers as Laurier met the farmers and concluded that they needed to step up their own campaign. T.A. Russell of the Canadian Cycle and Motor Company of Toronto told the local Canadian Club on 29 December that the farmers' movement was selfish and controlled mainly by men who were new Canadians, not imbued with the history and aims of Canada, the principles of Canadian nationality, or the aspirations of British subjects. They had fallen heirs to a rich and easy heritage won and held only by a century of struggle, suffering, privation, taxation and development in the East. The men of the West were prosperous, a situation built by protection which developed Canadian industry and a domestic market for agricultural products. A little education, declared Russell, would soon have the farmers thinking along the right lines.[8]

The issue was deepening the conflict between East and West, and between farmers and businessmen. The government was apparently on the horns of a dilemma. To give in to the American demands of November, that manufactures should be included, would be impossible, for it would alienate all the powerful urban and manufacturing regions. To abandon reciprocity would be to write off the western farm vote. Laurier's response to the farmers in December pointed to the ideal way out, giving something to both sides, but would the Americans be accommodating? In fact, as negotiations resumed in Washington in January, it was clear that the administration of President Taft had become much more flexible. Probably the swing to the low-tariff Democrats in the November elections had convinced Taft and his advisers that they must seek an agreement quickly. The result, announced by Fielding in the Commons on 26 January 1911, was virtually everything for which the Laurier government could have dreamed. The first schedule of the agreement eliminated the duty in both countries on a wide range of agricultural products, including grains, live animals, poultry, dairy products, fresh fruits, and vegetables; and also on fish, timber, some minerals, pulp wood, and wood pulp. Thus the farmers would have access to their coveted American markets. Other schedules lowered existing duties on many processed items and a very few manufactured items, yet left most of Canada's manufactures well protected.[9] The respective countries were to implement the agreement by concurrent legislation. Both the gleeful Liberals and the doleful Conservatives were convinced that Laurier had once again miraculously pulled a rabbit from his magician's hat. Once again his policy of adhering to the middle of the road and offering something to everyone had succeeded. His aging government would have a new lease on life, a triumphant election issue.

Clifford Sifton was among those who believed differently. He was one Liberal for whom reciprocity had long since ceased to be a dream. In 1897 he had declared that the sudden wholesale implementation of free trade doctrine would put at risk hundreds of businesses and thousands of jobs created during the previous eighteen years under the protective tariff. Experience since then had reinforced his views. A moderate, flexible policy of protection remained his ideal, one which would treat the different regions and economic sectors equitably, while preventing undue exploitation of the consumer. Since 1902 he had often publicly declared that Canada was prosperous and had no need of reciprocity, that she was better off free to pursue her own economic goals. He had always left the door open to consider a fair and favourable offer from the United States, but he instinctively mistrusted the Americans and did not believe that they would agree to anything that would prove good for Canada. During the negotiations of 1910 he refrained from any public pronouncement on the subject, though his private conversations and correspondence left no doubt as to his opposition. Then on 9 January 1911, while the talks were proceeding in Washington, he went farther than ever before. Even an apparently good and fair agreement, he told the Montreal Canadian Club, would be disadvantageous. Would not Canadian and American business become intertwined, "so that we shall become increasingly dependent upon them with the usual ultimate end of political union?" Those opposed to reciprocity did not oppose good relations between the two countries: "On the contrary, my view is that the best way of continuing good relations between Canada and the United States is that each should do its own business independently, and have no entanglements—nothing in the world to quarrel about."[10] Thus when Laurier subsequently expressed surprise at Sifton's opposition he was simply overlooking his former colleague's long and remarkably consistent series of pronouncements on the subject.[11]

In an apparent attempt to postpone or avoid the division with the Liberal leadership which now seemed imminent, Sifton persuaded five other Grit MPs to join with him in appealing to Laurier on 1 February not to proceed with the reciprocity resolutions until they had been ratified by the United

States Congress. Evidently Sifton's assumption was that the agreement would never receive congressional approval. The prime minister, however, ignored the request, and the next day it was announced that the government was determined to press ahead with the resolutions as priority business.[12] From that time Sifton's break with his former colleagues became inevitable, although meanwhile there was lively public speculation as to what course "the Sphinx," as he was sometimes called, would take.[13]

Before he would take a public position, Sifton was determined to confront John W. Dafoe concerning the policy to be followed by the *Manitoba Free Press*. The editor had always been more sympathetic to free trade notions than his employer, and more inclined to believe that such notions were prevalent in Manitoba and throughout the West. In August 1910 Dafoe had told Sifton:

> I think there is much more lower tariff sentiment in the West to-day than there was three or four years ago. The people who made the trouble on this score formerly were a handful of disgruntled Grits who felt that the pre-election promises of the Liberals had not been fulfilled by Laurier. They were not numerous enough to do us very much harm although, here and there, they cost us a constituency. My opinion is that a much larger section of the electorate are now disposed to quarrel with the Government over the tariff. We have had a very large immigration of men from England and Scotland, many of whom are convinced freetraders, and, though it may appear strange, a great many of the Americans since crossing the boundary, have modified their views on the question of the tariff....Then the Grain Growers, who now number nearly 30,000 in the West, are busying themselves in this matter of the tariff and are helping to crystallize public opinion.
>
> At the same time, I do not think the question one of prime importance. I think that they all recognize that free trade is out of the question in Canada. They hope, however, certainly to prevent any increase in the tariff, and possibly to get some concessions which appeal to them particularly.

Sifton generally agreed with Dafoe, but he noted that western towns and cities were "Protectionist at heart, and what you regard as free trade sentiment is confined to the rural population."[14] During 1910 Dafoe took the position that there would not be "one chance in a hundred" of reciprocity being achieved, that no one seriously expected the negotiations to succeed; and thus any conflict with Sifton was postponed.[15]

Understandably Fielding's announcement in Parliament staggered Dafoe every bit as much as the Tories. Gloomily he went home that night to inform his wife that he probably would have to resign his post because of inevitable differences with Sifton. On 27 January the paper carried an editorial cautiously approving the government resolutions. And then—the exact date is unknown, but most likely early in February—Sifton summoned Dafoe to Ottawa. For almost a week, Sifton's son Clifford later recalled, the two men argued vigorously and tirelessly, in Sifton's carriage, in the parlour, but always privately. Undoubtedly Sifton exhaustively rehearsed the economic, political, and social disadvantages of the scheme, the reasons for his mistrust of the Americans, his belief that Canada's survival was at stake, that the paper had a protectionist, nationalist, even imperialist constituency in Winnipeg to which to appeal. Dafoe probably replied that not only did he believe that the agreement would be good for both the West and for Canada, but that in the West the agreement was viewed as a long-overdue attempt to put historic Liberal doctrine into effect, to offset some of the regional disadvantages of the National Policy. He certainly would have argued that the appeal of the *Free Press* was much broader than Winnipeg, that it was an influential voice across the West, not only through the weekly sent to farmers, but as a paper which set the tone for many others across the West. To oppose reciprocity, to abandon the faith, would destroy the pre-eminence of the *Free Press* and would have a catastrophic effect on both its readership and its advertising. It is unlikely that Sifton would have been swayed by theories about freedom of the press and the ideal of the proper independence of editors; it is much more likely that an argument about the future of the newspaper carried most weight.[16] In the event, however, the two men had to agree to disagree: Dafoe would be free to give vigorous leadership to the pro-reciprocity forces in the West, while Sifton determined to throw himself heart and soul into the campaign to defeat the scheme. This period constituted the severest test of the relationship of mutual respect that had developed between the two men over almost a decade.

Opposition to the agreement was evident almost from its first announcement. On 30 January the Montreal Produce Merchants' Association condemned it, followed on the 31st by the Montreal Board of Trade. On 1 February the Toronto Livestock Exchange declared against it, while on the 3rd a return to Parliament listed nine Ontario Boards of Trade opposed. The Dominion Millers' Association took action on the 7th, while on the 10th a delegation of 2,000 fruit growers descended on Ottawa to protest the effects on their industry. On the 11th William German declared his antipathy to the agreement; on the 16th the Toronto Board of Trade voted 289-13 to condemn it.[17] As the protests developed and then accelerated, those opposed to the agreement began to take heart. There was indeed a constituency which believed the agreement disastrous, but it would need organization and effort to be effective. As Borden told Premier Whitney of

Ontario, "If the business interests of the country believe that the crisis can be met by a few casual meetings and occasional vigorous protest they are living in a fool's paradise. We have got to fight and fight hard."[18]

Quickly signs of effective organization became apparent. On 20 February eighteen Toronto Liberal businessmen published a Manifesto in the *Mail and Empire* opposing ratification. There was distinct evidence that Sifton at least was consulted about this gesture.[19] On the same day Sifton informed the prime minister of his intention to oppose the resolutions in the House of Commons:

> Such action, I need not say, I deeply regret the necessity of, involving as it will, the breaking off, of political relations with friends of a lifetime. I see no help for it, however, though I have tried diligently to find some other way of satisfying my views of what the circumstances demand.
>
> So soon as it can conveniently be done I shall turn over the patronage of my county to a committee in which the government can have confidence.[20]

When rumours that Sifton would oppose the scheme reached his supporters in Brandon, they desperately appealed to him to abstain to avoid giving the Tories ammunition. He refused, wiring in reply, "I am unalterably opposed to the whole arrangement believing it against commercial interests and inconsistent with national interests of Canada."[21]

Probably no speech of Sifton's had evoked such intense anticipation and speculation as that which he delivered on 28 February. Even *The Times* of London had taken the trouble to obtain a synopsis in advance.[22] No more important issue, he declared, had come before the House since he had become a member of Parliament. He chided the government for not placing before the House a detailed report on the probable effects of the tariff changes, observing "that either our hon. friends in the government have not made the investigation and do not possess the facts, or else that the facts do not bear out the contention which they put forward." Furthermore, since the failure of the Joint High Commission of 1898-99 reciprocity had not been part of the Liberal party's platform and the government had no mandate whatever to "commit the country to a radical change of fiscal policy." He had come to believe that the tariff of 1897, "which embraced the principle of moderate protection applicable to all classes of the community," remained basically the best policy for Canada.

The country was enjoying unprecedented prosperity, and no class had benefitted more than the farmers. In the decade 1900-1909 average prices for farm products had increased by 35.7 per cent over the previous decade, compared to an average increase of 14.3 per cent for the manufactured goods most commonly purchased by the farmer. "There you have proof of the fact that the urban community is not living at the expense of the farmer, but the farmer himself is getting more than his share of the general prosperity of the community." It was a prosperous, sound, and independent economy wherein the domestic market absorbed 80 to 90 per cent of the farm produce, and there was a ready market in Britain for the surplus. The government's policy would lead to the destruction of several Canadian industries. The meat packing industry would be ruined by the American meat trusts. The fruit and vegetable growers would be ravaged by American competition. American branch plants in Canada would in many cases shut down or curtail their Canadian operations, and the flow of American capital for industrial development would shrink. Timber and farm products would be shipped in their raw form to the United States, endangering processing jobs in Canada. At the same time, efforts at stimulating conservation practices both in the forest and on the farm would be undermined. As for the farmers who expected to get 4 cents or 6 cents per bushel more for their grain under the agreement, the American price of wheat had fallen 12 cents in the month since the announcement of the agreement, in consideration of the competition from Canadian grain.

But the agreement had deeper, more sinister implications. First, it would not stop at free trade in natural products. Before long there would be pressure to eliminate the tariff on agricultural implements and other manufactured goods, resulting practically in "commercial union with the United States." Second, rather than binding the regions of the country together, it would bind the regions to the neighbouring States, fragmenting the country. The thrust of the transportation policies of both the Macdonald and Laurier governments had been to forge trans-Canadian channels of trade. Now the government proposed to abandon this historic policy. Third, "I do not believe that if this treaty goes into effect there will ever again, so long as it goes on ...be a revision of our tariff in which United States interests, United States lobbyists, and United States pressure will not be brought to bear on this parliament....The only possible effect is domination of the smaller by the larger." Canada was just reaching the point where she could be of some use to the British Empire "that has given us our liberties and all the traditions of our citizenship." Why should Canadians be asked "to turn from the path that leads to the capital of the empire, and to turn towards the path that leads to Washington?" The Americans themselves had made the point when President Taft had stated that Canada was at the parting of the ways; and when Champ Clark, speaker of the House of Representatives, had supported the scheme because he believed it would lead to the annexation of Canada. That was a price too great to contemplate.

Sir [concluded Sifton], I oppose these resolutions, because, in my judgment, they reverse the great and successful policy under which the people of Canada, fighting against poverty, against natural obstacles, against geographical conditions, have made of their country one of the most enviable in the world. These resolutions, in my judgment, spell retrogression, commercial subordination, the destruction of our national ideals and displacement from our proud position as the rising hope of the British Empire.[23]

To tumultuous cheers from the opposition benches Sifton sat down. He had, as they hoped and Liberals feared, provided with incisive clarity a textbook summary of the arguments upon which opponents of the agreement would draw frequently in the months ahead. Liberal reaction was understandably heated. "A complete moral degenerate," insisted one; Sifton should be purged from the party, demanded another. Laurier was more measured. Sifton's speech he told the governor general was "not so strong...as I expected but an absolute & irreparable breach. Politically it means the accession to the opposition of an active, clearsighted strategist & organiser."[24]

The prime minister knew well whereof he spoke. On 1 March, the day after Sifton's speech, JS. Willison, Lloyd Harris, and Zebulon A. Lash, KC, met in Sifton's office to consider how they could best oppose ratification of the reciprocity agreement, defeat the Laurier government, and "arrange a basis of co-operation with Mr. Borden, Leader of the Conservative party." It was an influential group. Willison, formerly editor of the *Globe*, had moved to independent Conservatism with *The News*. Harris represented a wide range of business interests, including Massey-Harris, Steel Company of Canada, and other assorted manufacturing, banking, insurance and trust companies, and was prominent in the CMA. Lash, a Liberal lawyer, represented the Canadian Bankers' Association, the Canadian Northern Railway, National Trust, and the Bank of Commerce. He probably had been the moving force behind the revolt of the "Toronto Eighteen" and appears to have been substituting at the meeting for Sir B.E. Walker, president of the Bank of Commerce and one of Canada's most distinguished financiers.[25]

As the price for their support in the campaign, they agreed that Borden must consent to seven conditions. Although he should not discriminate against Roman Catholics or the province of Québec, he must "not be subservient to Roman Catholic influences in public policy or in the administration of patronage." Canadian fiscal policy and natural resources must be held independent of the United States, with policies "to preserve and strengthen Canadian nationality and the connection with the Mother Country." Borden must consult Walker, Lash, and Willison when forming his cabinet to ensure "the effective adoption and application of this policy," and "representation...of the views of those Liberals who may unite with the Conservatives against the policy of Reciprocity." The Conservative leader must pledge himself to extend reform of the civil service to the outside service by placing it under the Civil Service Commission. He must strengthen the Department of Trade and Commerce to expand Canada's foreign trade. Where necessary Borden must be prepared to seek strong cabinet members from outside Parliament "in order to give confidence to the progressive elements of the country and strength and stability to the Government." Finally, he must promise the appointment of a tariff commission. Sifton acted as spokesman for the group, and the Conservative leader readily accepted the conditions.[26] Borden later recalled that he had offered to resign as leader of the Opposition if the others thought it would help to ensure success: "Sifton reflected for a moment and then expressed a decided opinion that it would be unwise to make a change."[27] It was a sensible decision. Borden was not widely regarded as a strong leader, but he did have a reputation for integrity and an influential constituency of support among some Tories. To change leaders in the midst of what appeared to be a developing electoral battle would be risky enough; to seem to do so at the instance of Sifton would seriously divide the anti-government forces.[28]

In the weeks that followed most of Sifton's work was done quietly behind the scenes. In Montreal on 26 February a branch of the Anti-Reciprocity League of Canada was formed in which he might have played some role. Following a successful anti-reciprocity demonstration at Massey Hall, Toronto, on 9 March the Canadian National League was formed with the express purpose of conducting a propaganda campaign against reciprocity. Lash was chairman; but, claimed the secretary, Arthur Hawkes, it was Sifton who "was the rock on which the secretary most surely relied. He was there at every call. When others were in perplexity he was in his element."[29] Indeed he was. Probably no one surpassed his knowledge of the effective production and distribution of literature to select audiences, making use of voters' lists. Sifton's own parliamentary address was reprinted, with a foreword and afterword, and distributed by the hundreds of thousands, including a copy to every voter in his constituency. He encouraged the collection of statements by Americans and others that could be interpreted as encouraging annexation through reciprocity; it was published as *The Road to Washington,* an immensely successful propaganda instrument. When Hawkes wrote a newspaper article, "Appeal to the British-Born," Sifton immediately recognized its effectiveness and urged Hawkes to produce it as a pamphlet that could be distributed especially in Ontario constituencies of mainly British background. Closely co-operating with the Canadian National League was the Canadian Home Market Association, an offshoot of the CMA and also formed to conduct a propaganda campaign. The CHMA alone blanketed the country with over ten million pieces of literature during the election. "Clifford Sifton," claims one authority, "was kept aware of the collaboration between the two organizations and in many ways seems to have been the *éminence grise* behind much of their work."[30]

When he did speak publicly, at Hamilton on 16 March and Windsor Hall, Montreal, on 20 March, Sifton had little to add to his previous remarks. The latter occasion was chiefly notable for a riot of McGill University students who turned Sifton out of his carriage, set it ablaze, and dragged it through the streets, smashing windows and pulling down trolley wires. The motivation behind the attack remained obscure, though it might have been some Liberal-inspired harassment that got out of hand. Whatever the case, the incident attracted more attention and sympathy to Sifton's speech than it otherwise might have received.[31]

The Liberals naturally were at pains to undermine Sifton's credibility, using arguments already well tested by the Tories. "When he was a member of the Manitoba Legislature," declared a pamphlet produced by the Ontario Liberals, "Mr. Sifton felt for the settler and was heartily in favor of freer trade with the States. He continued in that frame of mind until he waxed rich and became an investor in manufacturing enterprises. Now he considers reciprocity base and disloyal, self-interest being an inexhaustible source of convenient illusions." When the Ottawa *Free Press* charged that, as a manufacturer, Sifton's "political spectacles" had become "clouded," he retorted with a rare letter to the editor: "I am not a manufacturer. I have no money invested in manufacturing in any way that can possibly be affected by the tariff policy. My political spectacles have not become clouded, on the contrary they never were so clear."[32] If familiar, the charges mattered little in 1911. Sifton was wealthy and had taken the side of the financial and manufacturing interests, and regardless of the truth of his response, his enemies would easily assume that his course was only to be expected.

The Opposition in Parliament, buoyed by the surge of popular and business support, was determined to prevent passage of the Fielding resolutions. The government eventually sought a two-month adjournment to enable Laurier to attend the Imperial Conference and Coronation of George V, which seemed only to confirm that the momentum was passing to the Opposition. Sifton too sailed for England late in May, intending to return in September. He was jauntily confident that an election sooner or later would be forced on the government, and "when the fight comes it will be eighteen seventy-eight over again." Early in July, however, he mysteriously reappeared in Canada, telling Hawkes, "The government will call the election within three weeks. I know the signs." Seventeen days later, on 29 July, he was proven correct.[33]

The most painful responsibility now before Sifton was a final, formal break with his Brandon supporters, some of whom had backed him for twenty-three years. Of course his parliamentary speech in February marked the actual break, leading the local Liberals to reaffirm their support of Laurier, and of reciprocity, and to declare that "the views expressed by our representative the Hon. Clifford Sifton do not represent the sentiments of his constituents."[34] That did not make the final dissociation less difficult. In his letter formally advising the Brandon Liberals of his decision not to run again, he noted that ever since he had left the government in 1905 he had believed that it was inappropriate for the constituency to be represented by a person resident in Ontario; before that, the pressures of office had justified it. He reminded them that he had only reluctantly accepted the nomination in 1908 and had "let it be understood that I should not again contest the riding under any circumstances." Certainly he had never anticipated that his retirement should be so surrounded by controversy that would embitter his former friends and associates. Nevertheless, he re-affirmed his opposition to reciprocity, a question which in his view transcended the issues of partisan loyalty. The country, he insisted, would gain little economically, while risking her national existence.[35]

Sifton then vigorously entered the fray, not only providing his invaluable advice on strategy and tactics, but putting himself at the disposal of the Tory machine for a busy speaking schedule. He did refuse to campaign directly against his former Liberal associates in Brandon or in the ridings of any of his former colleagues in the Laurier cabinet.[36] Between 22 August and 16 September he addressed at least twenty election rallies in Ontario, New Brunswick, and Nova Scotia. As an orator, his voice was unremarkable; though it carried well, it gave evidence of his deafness. He spoke without gestures, with little facial expression, and usually without notes. He never strove for eloquence or artificial effect. Arthur Hawkes recalled that "he reasoned as impersonally on the platform as he did with a book before him in his library." Occasionally he would make a light-hearted reference to his hearing disability, but humour was rarely part of his style. The impression, rather, was one "of faultless sequence of argument," solidly founded on facts, and it was this characteristic that intensified audience interest.[37]

Once, at Tillsonburg, Sifton faced that nightmare of every public speaker, a bumbling local official with faulty memory. Joe Thompson, the mayor, grandly introduced him, but could not for the life of him get Sifton's name straight. "We have with us tonight," he declared, "the Honorable Clifford Stanton—Stinton, Stifton." Reported *The News*, "he was getting closer to it with every trial but he finally gave up in despair and turning to the stalwarts seated on the platform behind him asked: 'What's his name?'''[38] At St. Thomas, not far from where Sifton had spent much of his childhood, a blacksmith named Frank Hunt introduced him by recalling that some forty years earlier young Clifford had sneaked mischievously into his premises and ruined a new set of tongs in the forge. Hunt caught him, spanked him, and promptly plunged him into the tub of water used to cool forging irons. As he rose to speak, Sifton ruefully admitted that he recalled the incident all too well.[39]

By this time in the campaign there were few new arguments to be made on either side of the reciprocity issue. Sifton did claim that the chief object of the agreement was to give the United States access to Canadian forests, and that all processing of Canadian lumber would be carried on in the United States. Any country which shipped its raw products abroad unprocessed, he insisted, would be reduced to poverty. As traffic was diverted increasingly to north-south channels, there would be fewer jobs and less investment in Canada and a shrinking home market. In past years the great public expenditures on both railways and the St. Lawrence waterway had been undertaken both to keep Canadian trade in Canadian channels, and to bind the diverse parts of the country together. The agreement would render these expenditures futile. In Canada, he claimed, there existed "no unemployment, no poverty, no soup kitchens, no demand for public relief," but reciprocity would ruin all that.[40]

The election on 21 September provided almost an exact reversal of the verdict of 1908, returning 134 Conservatives to eighty-seven Liberals. Ontario had made the largest contribution to the victory, seventy-three seats to thirteen, reflecting a voting shift of 5 per cent to the Tories, compared to the vote in 1908. But even in Québec some twenty-seven Tories were returned, reducing Laurier's margin in that province to eleven seats. Manitoba produced an almost identical verdict to that of 1908, with eight conservative seats to two Liberal; but this time Brandon fell decisively to the Tories, a result at which Sifton expressed himself "very much gratified."[41] From Brandon, from Frank Cochrane (the Tory organizer in Ontario), to the prime minister-elect, Sifton was showered by Tory compliments and gratitude for his contribution to the victory. Twenty years later Borden went so far as to acknowledge that "beyond question, Sifton's support...was a most powerful factor and I am prepared to agree that without it we might not have won."[42]

What did the Conservative victory mean to Sifton? He saw it, first, as proof that "the country has outgrown the policies of the past." The Laurier government had not sufficiently realized "the changed conditions of commerce and industry as a result of what had taken place during the previous eighteen or twenty years. There was a time, for instance, when the cry of "free fish" would have swept the Maritime Provinces and when the cry of an enlarged market for hay, potatoes, barley, cattle and dairy products would have swept Ontario and Québec, but conditions had changed in twenty years and the case had to be argued from new premises altogether." The old appeal was no longer effective because of the greater complexity and development of the Canadian economy.[43] He contended that Canadians had simply voted in their own economic self-interest, an argument scoffed at since by many apologists of the agreement, but sustained by a recent economic analysis.[44]

Second, Sifton saw the election result as a blow struck for Canadian nationalism, for survival and independence in North America. He had been a severe critic of the British in the past, but he believed that it was in Canada's self-interest to remain part of the Empire. Britain was more than a huge market for Canadian goods and a vast well of development capital. He had asserted often that she also was the source of Canada's parliamentary and legal traditions and freedoms, a principal contributor to that social fabric and outlook which differentiated Canada from the United States. She was an effective counterweight to the pull of America, yet was far enough removed to remain non-threatening. The reciprocity agreement had put this relationship at risk. A vote for it would have chanced the loss of the British market, made British capital nervous, and struck a psychological blow at the ties of tradition. It would be a major step toward the integration of the Canadian and American economies. Canada would, in his view, become little more than a hewer of wood and a drawer of water for the Americans, drawn inexorably into the American economic and political orbit. He denied that Canadians who opposed the agreement intended to exhibit any "hostility or unfriendliness to the United States." They understood the Americans to have offered very liberal terms. Many Americans might not have consciously sought to dominate Canada, but it could not be avoided simply because of the disparity in size between the two countries: "the judgment of the businessmen of Canada was that the reciprocity agreement, if carried into effect, would mean a commercial alliance which would of necessity have to be carried further, and that as a necessary result of such an alliance the United States, being the greater, wealthier, stronger and more populous country, would dominate Canada's commercial policy and development." This in turn would "interfere with her national independence"[45]

Sifton also believed that the election had finally killed reciprocity as a serious political question. Only a peculiar, perhaps unique, conjunction of circumstances could, in his opinion, have allowed Congress to pass such an agreement. Similar circumstances would not likely recur. In Canada the election result would make any national political party very cautious about tariff questions in the future, particularly what he viewed as so sudden, sweeping and revolutionary a policy. Although the western farmer would continue to favour free trade, "these sentiments will be modified by the knowledge that no one section of the country can have its own way entirely and that fiscal policy in a country of great extent and diversified interests must of necessity be a matter of compromise."[46]

The election of 1911 marked the end of a political era. Sifton had played a significant role in the defeat of Laurier, whom he still could describe respectfully as "perhaps the most striking and brilliant personality in the British Empire."[47] He knew that politics at Ottawa would not attain the same glamour under Borden. The election also concluded twenty-three years of active politics for Sifton himself. Once again the quiet retirement that he had anticipated had eluded him, and his departure from political life was surrounded by controversy of major proportions, as had so often involved him in the past. His retirement certainly would change the political scene, for better or for worse. He was abandoning politics at age fifty, a time when many men were just beginning a public career. The years had taken their toll, nevertheless, and Sifton gave little evidence of regret as he resumed a more private life. Yet he was not without a public platform. Remarkably—some would have said, miraculously—he had retained his position as chairman of the conservation commission, a situation that would enable him still to speak out on matters of national significance.

11

The Commission of Conservation
(1909-1921)

The creation of the Canadian Commission of Conservation in 1909 marked a new departure for the Laurier government and the beginning of an extraordinary yet isolated chapter in the history of conservation in the Dominion.[1] The government had never evinced a broad interest in conservation prior to 1909, although a few specific cases of action can be found. While minister of the interior, Sifton had established the forestry branch of the department and encouraged conservation measures in areas under federal jurisdiction. In August 1905 Laurier had called for a national meeting to consider problems of forestry. When the ensuing conference met in January 1906, it was addressed by leading politicians including Laurier and Borden, by leading scientists, and by the eminent American forester and conservationist, Gifford Pinchot.[2] The conference at first tended to focus somewhat narrowly on the problems of silviculture, but the discussions broadened to include the relationship between forest conservation and maintenance of water resources and the interconnections between forestry, agriculture, and irrigation.[3] Such concerns, of course, had been of interest to Sifton and his officials for some years previously, but they now received an unprecedented public impetus. The federal and several provincial governments made subsequent gestures to implement some of the recommendations of the conference, including expansion of forest reserves, creation of provincial forest services, and establishment of schools of forestry at the universities of Toronto and New Brunswick.[4]

Important as these beginnings were, however, Canadian conservationists remained few in number, the movement had generated little but a stumbling momentum, and government action remained narrowly focused on forests and, to some degree, water resources. In fact, the Canadian movement had always been substantially derivative, its interests and concerns usually reflecting those of the more powerful American conservationists. The latter had long concentrated on forests and water as well, but in the twentieth century the lobby became more confident and influential, and more inclined to recognize that the problem of how the public viewed and used natural resources needed to be attacked from a very broad perspective. People had to be informed that the vast natural resource potential of North America was not unlimited, that the ravages of uncontrolled exploitation were destroying their birthright and undermining the quality of life of millions, not only then but for future generations.

Few conservationists in the United States, and fewer in Canada, believed in preservation, the so-called sentimental desire to protect nature for its own sake, or for the future. The great majority were firmly in the progressive liberal tradition which believed that resources were there to be developed and that principles of scientific management could lead to their efficient exploitation and the elimination of wasteful practices.[5] This would lead to better financial returns both in the short and the long run. That was the basis on which conservation was to be sold. Concern for conservation also was part of the reform sentiment of the era. By application of utilitarian theory, scientific research, some government regulation, and moral suasion, it was thought that the machinery of society and government could be cleansed and renewed, while corruption, slums, greed, and waste were controlled or eliminated. A clean, productive natural environment was essential for the proper functioning of the social—particularly the urban—environment.

To begin the achievement of some of these goals, President Theodore Roosevelt called a national conference on conservation to meet in the spring of 1908. It recommended a national inventory of natural resources, the creation of conservation commissions in each state and by the federal government, and co-operation between the levels of government. In June, Roosevelt appointed the National Conservation Commission, divided into four sections: waters, forests, lands, and minerals.[6] Following a further conference later in the year, the president wrote to the Canadian and Mexican governments on 24 December, proposing a North American conference on conservation. The governments readily accepted, and delegates from the three countries and Newfoundland met at the White House on 18 February 1909.[7]

As the Canadian delegates, Laurier selected Sydney A. Fisher, minister of agriculture,[8] Dr. Henri S. Béland of Québec,[9] and Clifford Sifton.

Although he had not been notably active in conservation matters since he left office, Sifton had certainly evinced the greatest interest in the subject of anyone in the cabinet before 1905. Perhaps his appointment was a plum offered in gratitude for his efforts in the 1908 election. In any event, Lord Grey assured the British ambassador in Washington, James Bryce, that Sifton was "the ablest business man in politics. Notwithstanding his deafness, from his ability and knowledge he will be able to hold his own at Washington." [10]

The declaration of principles which emanated from the conference recognized that international co-operation in conservation was desirable and recommended the concurrent adoption of conservation measures by each country represented. It continued:

> We recognize as natural resources all materials available for the use of man as means of life and welfare, including those on the surface of the earth, like the soil and the waters; those below the surface, like the minerals; and those above the surface, like the forests. We agree that these resources should be developed, used, and conserved for the future, in the interests of mankind, whose rights and duties to guard and control the natural sources of life and welfare are inherent, perpetual, and indefeasible.

The declaration recommended measures to protect public health, especially legislation against pollution. It contended that forests were "indispensable to civilization and public welfare"; that those who owned forests needed to recognize a public responsibility; that more study of forest resources, their rates of depletion and reproduction should be made; that fire protection measures be made effective; that forests along streams and rivers, especially the headwaters, were essential for maintaining a steady flow of water, and should be especially protected. Waters were a "primary resource," required for domestic and municipal supply, irrigation, navigation, and power. These were "interrelated public uses, and properly subject to public control." Land needed to be made more productive, with training for farmers in crop rotation, fertilization, and "improved methods in farm management." The role of government should be to prevent large land monopolies, and to engage in agricultural research. Wastage of mineral resources, particularly those used as fuels, should be controlled. Separation of surface ground rights and subsurface mineral rights would permit more public control over mineral exploitation. More stringent regulations for mine safety should be rigorously enforced. Game protection was urged, along with game preserves. Each country was exhorted to establish its own "permanent Conservation Commission," which in turn would provide a means for exchange of conservation information and co-operation. Finally, it was hoped that in the near future a worldwide conference would be held, at the invitation of the president of the United States.[11]

The thrust of the White House conference was, first, to insist upon the interdependence of natural resource conservation concerns and upon the interdependence between society and natural resources. Second, it was opposed to private monopolies in any resource field because the private sector would not readily operate in the public interest. Only government could reflect both the short- and long-term public interest. Therefore, third, there must be an expansion of the role of government, both to regulate and control the private sphere and to conduct research and disseminate information. The private sector would have to recognize its public responsibilities, accept more controls, and even give way when necessary for the good of society.

It was one thing to adopt such proposals under the encouragement of enthusiastic conservationists and with the vigorous support of Theodore Roosevelt, just weeks before he retired from office. It was another to contend with the political realities in each country: the divided jurisdictions over natural resources, the vested private interests who resisted any controls, and the politicians who for various reasons lacked a commitment to conservationist principles. In the United States, for example, the National Conservation Commission did not long survive the end of the Roosevelt era. In Canada, most control over natural resources, except in the prairies and the north, lay with the provinces. Laurier, as so often seen, did not believe in a strong interventionist or regulatory role for government in any case. While there was apparently a favourable public disposition toward conservation measures, any solution adopted would inevitably be a compromise. In these circumstances, it was perhaps remarkable that it was Canada, among all the countries represented at Washington in 1909, that would come closest to realizing the objectives of the declaration.

In early February, shortly before the conference convened. Opposition Leader Borden had hurriedly jumped on the conservationist bandwagon, proposing a select standing committee of the House of Commons on natural resources to be concerned with both conservation and development. Laurier had responded with a suggestion to set up separate committees on such subjects as fisheries, mines and minerals, and forests and waters.[12] The recommendations of the Washington conference, however, caused the government to rethink its approach, and in April and May Parliament passed an act drafted by Sifton to create a "Commission of Conservation."[13] No mention of Sifton's role was made during the debate, however, and he himself kept a very low profile. Apart from one member, Haughton Lennox of Simcoe South, who insisted that the commission was an unnecessary extravagance, the measure appears to have had the general support of both sides of the House. Sydney Fisher, as the minister through whom the commission would report to the House, was at pains to stress the non-partisan nature of the commission, and the small projected costs of about $22,000 for the first year. Section 10 of the act sweepingly stated that "it shall be the duty of the Commission to take into consideration all questions which may be brought to its notice relating to the conservation and better utilization of the natural resources of Canada, to make such inventories, collect and disseminate such information, conduct such investigations inside and outside of Canada, and frame such recommendations as seem conducive to the accomplishment of that end." Fisher interpreted this in a somewhat limited way when he declared that publicity would be the important function of the commission.[14] Not one MP felt constrained to make a passionate plea for an activist policy; no great statement of conservationist principles was even attempted. To read the debate and the act might well be to conclude that the government was hastily establishing an innocuous, inoffensive, and possibly ineffective body to satisfy the importuning conservationists.

Such an impression would be deceiving. Scarcely two weeks after the bill was debated Fisher advised Sifton that the cabinet had decided to offer him the chairmanship of the commission.[15] Probably his appointment had been contemplated from the start in recognition of his experience as minister of the interior, his knowledge of resources and interest in conservation, and his reputation as a practical and successful businessman. And, again, it might have been a partial reward for his services in the late election. Whatever the reason, the Laurier government can hardly have expected Sifton to take a post in which he could do next to nothing; he could never be a mere publicist for the conservation movement. If, to Fisher, section 10 was susceptible to a limited interpretation, Sifton had drafted it in such general and vague terms that it also had enormous possibilities for an energetic, skilful, and determined individual to exploit. Temperamentally, he naturally would interpret his powers in the broadest manner possible. The fact must be underlined that the question of the intended purpose of the commission was not merely academic. Conflicting views would bedevil the life of the commission from 1909 onward, and would contribute to its ultimate demise twelve years later.

The first clear evidence of the differing views came over the composition of the commission. The act provided that there would be twelve ex-officio members, the federal ministers of the interior, agriculture, and mines, and the member of each provincial government who had charge of natural resources. The commission itself would consist of twelve unpaid members appointed by the federal government, at least one member from each province being a member of the faculty of a university. The latter provision was intended to provide the Commission with the necessary scientific and technical expertise. Sifton had hardly heard from Fisher about his appointment as chairman when he began to make suggestions about the appointed members, particularly those from Ontario. He wanted men who would emphasize the non-partisan nature of the commission, whose presence would add weight to its recommendations, and, in the case of Ontario, a prominent provincial Conservative or two who would facilitate communication with a very touchy Tory government in Toronto. He suggested Sir Sanford Fleming, B.E. Walker, Professor Fernow of the University of Toronto Faculty of Forestry, Senator W.C. Edwards, Professor A.P. Coleman of the School of Practical Science, University of Toronto, and either Lt.-Col. John S. Hendrie of Hamilton, a minister without portfolio in the Whitney government and a leading capitalist, or George Tate Blackstock, a prominent Conservative lawyer and imperial unionist. At the same time, he strongly opposed the proposed appointment of J.F. Mackay, Liberal business manager of the *Globe*, and Charles A. McCool, a Liberal Ottawa lumber merchant. Both, he insisted, would be merely partisan appointments who would add no weight to the commission. [16]

George P. Graham, minister of railways and canals, was more than a little sensitive about Sifton's suggestions. "I find," he told him, "that all the other Provinces are willing to accept their own members, and then insist on selecting those from Ontario as well." The only person on whom he and Sifton were in complete agreement was Fleming. Sifton replied, restating his case and emphasizing that "I am leaving personal considerations entirely out of the question." He only wished to see appointments which would be widely recognized "as eminently in the public interest." [17] Inevitably the result was a compromise, in which the Ontario members were Fleming, Edwards, McCool, Mackay, Fernow, Sifton, and E.B. Osler. Although a leading Tory and businessman, Osler had been a member of Parliament since 1896 and did not fulfil Sifton's desire for a man closely linked to the Whitney government. [18] While some of the appointments tended to be more partisan and less prestigious than Sifton would have liked, neither he nor most observers of the time were critical of the relatively low proportion of scientific expertise. The idea behind the Commission, he pointed out in 1910, "was that men of affairs should be induced to act upon this commission gratuitously, and give the benefit of their judgment and experience in the public interest." [19] The commission in turn would hire the scientific experts required.

How did Sifton view the functions and purposes of the commission of conservation? First, he constantly stressed its necessarily non-partisan nature. He informed the first annual meeting of the commission in January 1910 that "I determined, when accepting the position of Chairman to dissociate myself altogether from active participation in party political affairs, believing that the work of the Commission will occupy a great share of my time and attention, and that, by such a course, I can reasonably hope to secure the complete and hearty co-operation of all the members of the Commission.''[20] Only in a limited sense can any credence be given to this statement. As previously seen, Sifton already had his own reasons for adopting a non-partisan public posture in 1909-10. More importantly, when he so desired, he was quite prepared to ignore the principle. At the very time he was addressing the commission he was heavily funding the Manitoba Liberals. A year later he would be enveloped in the reciprocity struggle, and in 1917 in the conscription election, in both cases while chairman of the commission. In fact, there can be little question that it was only his active services on the Tory side in 1911, and the strong links then formed with Robert Borden, that enabled Sifton to continue in his post under the new administration. Other politicians, such as Osler and F.D. Monk, also continued in their partisan activities while members of the commission. It is, rather, in a different sense that the commission was non-partisan: there would appear to be very little evidence that its postures on various resource issues were influenced by partisan considerations. It was that fact, rather than any alleged restraint from political activity, that gave the commission's recommendations considerable weight. Nevertheless, Sifton's constitutional inability to refrain from public comment or activity on important issues and his long list of political enemies, both Grit and Tory, meant that his chairmanship would always be the subject of controversy.

A second problem was that of the relationship of the commisssion to the government and to Parliament. Sifton informed the commission in 1910 that it was ''not a portion of the ordinary governmental administration for which the Government is politically responsible.'' Parliament had created the commission and given it certain responsibilities ''upon the performance of which it is to report from time to time.'' Except for the necessity of relying upon the government of the day to put through the required estimates each year, ''the work is totally independent of the ordinary administration of affairs.''[21] A few weeks later Sifton repeated these views to the Commons, adding that the reports of the commission would be transmitted to the House through the Governor General in Council. Fisher, however, appeared partly to contradict Sifton when he asserted that there was a department—Agriculture—which would act as an intermediary between the commission and Parliament.[22] Sifton's view inevitably caused difficulties, because as he evidently envisaged it, the commission would be nearly so independent as not to have to justify or defend its actions to the government. Although the estimates were included with those of the Department of Agriculture until 1919, successive ministers confessed that they had ''no control over it.''[23] Thus there was another reason for criticism. Ministers disliked being responsible for a body over which they had no control or even, as ex-officio members, little influence. Members of Parliament similarly were uncomfortable voting estimates for a body which they could not seriously question.

The commission would have been difficult for any minister to influence or control in any case, given Sifton's highly decentralized approach to administration. He believed that the chairman's administrative responsibilities should be minimal, probably for two reasons. First, the field was at once so vast and so specialized that no single person could master it. Second, Sifton believed that his responsibilities were best centred on the broad lines of policy, and of selling the commission and its recommendations. As a result the membership was divided into seven committees: fisheries, game and fur-bearing animals; forests; lands; minerals; public health; water and water-power; and press and co-operating organizations. A member of the commission chaired each committee, which could meet as often as it thought necessary and conduct its own business. There would be but one general annual meeting.[24] Thus the independence from Parliament and the decentralization of the structure allowed the scientists and technical experts a great deal of freedom to pursue diverse areas of interest and concern, under the protection and enthusiastic encouragement of one of the most influential and dynamic men in Canadian public life. The committees responded with a staggering number of publications, nearly two hundred by 1919. They ranged from books and periodicals to pamphlets, from popular summaries to the specialized and technical in each of the fields.[25]

A good administrator must not only devise an effective plan of operation and be prepared to delegate authority, but must be capable of selecting able personnel. As so often in the past, Sifton was very fortunate in his appointments, particularly that of James White to the post of secretary to the commission. He had come to value White's abilities when the latter was chief geographer in the Department of the Interior. In his letters to Sifton, White sometimes emerges as an unlikely success story, seemingly ready to complain at any slight or inconvenience, sometimes a bit narrow, fussy, and stiff, at best a difficult and prickly personality. But he also was an enthusiastic advocate of conservation and an efficient office administrator. He was the person responsible for seeing that the committee and annual meetings went smoothly, that the publications appeared regularly and quickly, that memoranda or speeches or briefs required by Sifton or other members of the commission were prepared as required. Few studies of the commission have given White the credit he so clearly deserves.[26]

The commission, as Sifton repeatedly pointed out, had neither executive nor administrative powers. It was empowered to investigate any subject bearing upon the conservation of natural resources, to collect and weigh information, to advise governments on related policy issues, and to publish and otherwise make available its findings for the general public. The commission's advice would have weight only insofar as its conclusions were based upon the most careful and advanced scientific investigation. Concluding his inaugural address to the Commission in 1910, Sifton declared:

> This Commission can exert a powerful influence in the right direction. It can strengthen the hands of all who are desirous of following progressive policies. It can help to render the labour of investigations in the various branches of scientific thought available for the service of the country. It can be the vehicle by which enlightened and educated men can bring an influence directly to bear on the administration of affairs. In a word, it can, if it will, be the embodiment of public spirit and advanced thought. [27]

There were two other characteristics of the commission to which the chairman frequently referred. The first was that it must reflect the federal nature of the country and the divided jurisdiction over natural resources. The provinces, he noted, might well "look with jealousy upon any Commission created by Federal legislation." He hoped that the composition of the commission would preclude such sentiment. "The Commission is," he proudly observed, "in fact, probably the most truly national in its composition of any body that has ever been constituted in Canada." [28] The second point was that the commission must not attempt "to exercise the functions of any Department of government, Provincial or Dominion." Occasionally some of the work would appear to fall under the various departmental jurisdictions, but "we should never carry this work to a greater length than is necessary to arouse interest in it, to point a way to improvement and, in some cases, to collect the information necessary to the formation of intelligent judgment." [29] The commission was quite sensitive to the problems of overlapping jurisdictions, the inefficiency and the jealousies thereby created. From time to time officials of the commission sat on interdepartmental committees investigating various problems; scientific and technical experts in some federal departments were periodically consulted; and such men were regularly asked to address the commission's annual meetings. Regrettably, these measures were unable to prevent the anticipated rivalries from emerging.

Sifton began his tasks as chairman with great enthusiasm, delivering at least sixteen public addresses on the subject between January 1910 and January 1911. [30] Conservation was urgent, he warned his audiences, or Canada's prosperity and progress would come to an abrupt halt, her remaining resources would be seized by rapacious Americans, and western civilization would be one step nearer to the fate that befell the Assyrians, Babylonians, Egyptians, Persians, Greeks, Romans, and Incas. Those civilizations had wasted their resources and allowed their agricultural base to deteriorate. England herself was in danger: "Where will she be when her iron and coal disappear, if her agricultural population is not restored? Decline must inevitably set in."[31] Many contended that the situation in Britain or the United States did not apply to Canada, where a sparse population had scarcely begun to exploit the available resources.

> I have heard the view expressed that what Canada wants is development and exploitation, not conservation. This view, however, is founded upon an erroneous conception, which it must be our work to remove. If we attempt to stand in the way of development, our efforts will assuredly be of no avail either to stop development or to promote conservation. It will not, however, be hard to show that the best and most highly economic development and exploitation in the interests of the people can only take place by having regard to the principles of conservation.[32]

Canada ought to learn from the example of the United States, which was three or four decades ahead of the Dominion in exploitation of its resources and the resultant problems. Wasteful and unscientific farming methods, the reckless destruction of the forests, the depletion of the fisheries were all well known. Formerly rich districts had become "totally unproductive." Even worse, "the vast resources yet remaining to them, through loose and unsatisfactory laws, are practically monopolized by large financial interests, so that the people cannot participate in them on moderate and reasonable terms." It was time for Canadians "to get rid of the old shibboleths and to learn that new problems have arisen. The great problem in Canada today is how to arrive at a system of government whereby laws can be framed to protect resources permanently and to prevent them falling under monopolistic control."[33]

Two issues arose early in 1910 which not only illustrated Sifton's concerns, but also permitted him to undertake the kind of vigorous advocacy role that he favoured for the commission. The first concerned a project to dam the St. Lawrence just above Cornwall at the Long Sault rapids to generate electricity for the markets of northern New York state and eastern Ontario. Behind the project was the Aluminum Company of America (Alcoa), which required substantial amounts of electricity to expand its operations.[34] In 1901 the Canadian Parliament had incorporated the St. Lawrence Power Company, empowered to construct the dam, subject to the approval of the cabinet. Its charter had subsequently been acquired by the Long Sault Development Company, chartered in New York State in

1907. Legislation to empower the company to build on the American side was introduced into the House of Representatives late in 1909, and then referred to the International Waterways Commission for a report. The proposal entailed constructing a dam 4,500 feet long and forty-five feet high, anchored by several islands in the river. It would produce 200,000 horsepower immediately, and would have an ultimate capacity of 600,000 horsepower; the projected cost was $20,000,000. It would have the effect of shifting navigation from the existing main channel to an alternative channel on the American side.[35] The referral to the IWC permitted Canadian as well as American representations to be made, and Sifton seized the opportunity to oppose construction during hearings in Toronto on 7 February 1910. He objected that the company was showing little concern for Canadian interests, that most of the power would be generated on the American side, and only one-sixth of the total available power would ever reach Canada. The plans, he insisted, "contemplate an absolute monopolization of the whole power available from the rapids." The small Canadian market, moreover, could not absorb the electricity at present; almost certainly the company would divert the excess to American customers, creating vested interests that would make it impossible in future to withdraw the power to meet developing Canadian needs. The new channel proposed for navigation was inferior to the existing channel, the approach would be "beset with dangerous currents, and ice jams and floods might well occur in winter." This would make it impossible for the Canadian government to deepen the navigation channel, if it so desired. Worse still, "an all-Canadian route from Lake Superior to the ocean would become a dream of the past." Finally, the dam would destroy a part of the river which was internationally appreciated for its scenic beauty. It was, concluded Sifton, "the plain duty of Canada to maintain her rights of ownership and jurisdiction absolutely unimpaired and untrammelled."[36]

Sifton and the conservation commission were but one of many Canadian voices raised in opposition. A strong array of Montreal and Toronto interests were joined by the Ontario government in their protests. On the other hand, representatives of the towns of Brockville, Cornwall, and Prescott all supported the project in the expectation of attracting industrial development to eastern Ontario through the availability of cheap power.[37] Subsequent to the hearings, Sifton advised Laurier of another reason to oppose the dam: the Webster-Ashburton Treaty of 1842 provided that the channels of the river which would be affected by the project "shall be equally free and open to ships, vessels and boats" of both countries. "This application has been before us for more than three years," the prime minister reassured Sifton. "I never viewed it favourably and it always seemed to me that for many reasons it would be inexpedient, if not worse, to destroy the Long Sault Rapids."[38]

The question was debated in the House of Commons on a different occasion, since Parliament had already given the Governor-General-in-Council the duty of deciding the construction of the dam. It was on a bill sponsored by F.F. Pardee, Liberal member for Lambton West, to incorporate the St. Lawrence Power Transmission Company that the parliamentarians had opportunity to express their views in an all-night debate.[39] The bill would allow the St. Lawrence Power interests to transmit the electricity to market. Sifton did not participate in the debate directly, but the Conservation Commission did offer a negative opinion on the bill. And Sifton's concerns evidently struck a sympathetic chord among the parliamentarians, for Pardee's bill emerged heavily amended to limit the Company's powers, and to require that all plans for damming the St. Lawrence must first be submitted to Parliament.[40] The effect was to halt the project for the time being.

The second issue concerned a bill sponsored by James Conmee, Liberal MP for Thunder Bay-Rainy River to incorporate the International Waterways, Canal and Construction Company. The ostensible aim of the Company was to build a canal system linking Lake Superior to Rainy River, Lake of the Woods, the Winnipeg River, and eventually to Lake Winnipeg. However, the bill also would have given the company control over the waters of Cedar Lake, Cross Lake, the Saskatchewan and Assiniboine rivers, and lakes Manitoba and Winnipeg, "with power to exact tolls on goods transported over these waterways."[41] Once again, although he did not participate in the debate in the House, Sifton did write the prime minister, speak publicly, and represent the conservation commission before the railway committee in expressing his concern. The bill was "entirely opposed to all sound principles of public policy." It was obvious that the immense capital required to build the canals could not be raised or justified on the basis of available traffic. "This being so, it becomes clear that the Bill is a cloak for some ulterior object"—in all probability, effective control over all water power in the region. "I need only suggest that if this Bill be passed and its stock subsequently acquired by, for instance, American power interests our whole situation along an important strip of international waters will be seriously prejudiced and, in fact, imperilled." [42] As a result of Sifton's vigorous stand, combined with strenuous opposition from the towns and cities affected, from Thunder Bay to Edmonton, the bill failed to emerge from the committee.

Perhaps the clearest statement of Sifton's views arose on a less publicly contentious issue, the issuance of a licence to the Ontario and Minnesota Power Company to export power developed in Canada on the Rainy River, at Fort Frances, Ontario. The company had developed 7,000 horse power in Canada, with little or no market, and applied to export 6,000 horsepower. By the time the conservation commission was apprised of the situation, the export had been approved by the railway commission, and the rate fixed. Fort Frances and other municipalities then appealed to the conservation commission to use its influence to try to prevent the export. Sifton told William Templeman, then minister of inland revenue:

> We are of the opinion that the power developed upon the Canadian side of the International boundary line belongs of right to Canada and the Canadian people and should be held intact and available for use when it is required in Canada. The time is rapidly approaching when all the power available on the Canadian side will be required for Canadian industries....We regard the idea that the power can be exported to the United States, allowed to be used there for the purpose of building up important industries and creating vested rights, and afterwards summarily withdrawn and applied to Canadian purposes entirely misleading. There is, in our judgment, not even a slight probability that any Canadian Government will feel itself justified in crippling great American industries by withdrawing the power necessary to their maintenance.

Moreover there were specific concerns about the Fort Frances situation. The same interests that controlled the power company were purchasing pulpwood in Canada and shipping it across the river to an American mill. Indeed, the power company reportedly had refused to grant power to any independent Canadian pulp company.[43] In this case, however, Sifton's pleas were of but limited use. The government did allow further hearings, but ultimately decided to grant a licence for the export of 3,500 horse-power.[44]

There is little doubt but that Sifton relished the opportunities to affect public policy in this way. As he reflected on what he termed "a perfect epidemic of water-power legislation" in 1910, he concluded that "no perpetual franchise on water-power should ever be given by a Government. Limited franchise might be granted, but the rate to be charged for power should be under public control." This was in keeping with his long-held view that public utilities, whether railways or hydro-electric companies, ought to have their rates regulated in the public interest. And the public interest, or national interest, must always prevail. Concerning the St. Lawrence dam issue, he declared, "The interests of navigation are paramount on the St. Lawrence....Let the local interest bow to the general good of the Dominion."[45] Finally, his attitude on these power questions lends an important perspective to his attitude toward the United States during the reciprocity debate in 1911.

Most of the duties of the conservation commission were neither so glamorous nor so controversial. In 1910 Sifton called for "a comprehensive and accurate inventory of our natural resources." Although the commission made some substantial strides in this direction, by 1918 it was still far from the goal because so much basic spadework had to be undertaken before any inventory could even begin.[46] The one area in which the commission was clearly successful was that of a stocktaking of national water powers, in three volumes.[47] This was scarcely surprising given Sifton's assertion that "the flowing waters of Canada are, at the moment, apart from the soil, our greatest and most valuable undeveloped natural resource." Properly utilized, Canada's hydro-electric potential was capable "of supplying our entire urban population with light, heat and power, operating our tramways and railways, and abolishing the present methods with their extravagance, waste and discomfort." What sense did it make, for example, to pollute the atmosphere by burning coal—some of which was imported from the United States—not only for these purposes, but to generate electricity, when sufficient clean, cheap power was readily at hand in Canada? Conservation meant the most efficient utilization of the available resources. In the case of water, this did not entail the right to pollute it with sewage; and Sifton cited the case of typhoid resulting from Montreal's proverbially wasteful system as illustrating what he termed "the monumental misuse" of water in Canada.[48] Similarly wasteful were agricultural techniques which failed to conserve soil moisture and allowed water to run off, not only eroding the soil, but carrying valuable fertilizers which in turn polluted the water. Also the commission was concerned about the effects of deforestation and certain agricultural techniques in lowering the water table levels in various regions. What is remarkable is the airing of many such issues as much as fifty years before they attracted widespread public concern.

It is scarcely surprising that the commission should have expended a great deal of energy on forest conservation. This was the oldest forebear of the commission itself and, as Sifton recognized in 1910, was the one area in which he and his fellow commissioners could rest assured that public opinion was aroused and largely sympathetic.[49] At first in his public speeches Sifton played on this sentiment with an almost apocalyptic portrayal of American designs on Canadian forests. He estimated that the United States had about 2,200,000,000,000 board feet of timber left, or at best a thirty-year supply at existing rates of consumption. "You can imagine the plight of about 120,000,000 people without lumber! What will they do? Why, they will come to Canada for it if proper measures are not passed to protect our forests." Canada, by contrast, had only 200,000,000,000 board feet, scarcely a seven-year supply for the Americans. "I believe there are men in this room today," he told the Empire Club in Toronto, "who will see the time when the people of Canada will be compelled to ask for the prohibition of the export of lumber. Why not now conserve our forests and ensure the supply for all time to come?'' Good management in both countries could make the North American supply both adequate and permanent.[50] Perhaps because the alleged threat was less pressing than that with respect to water and hydro-electricity, this anti-American theme soon disappeared from his public speeches and rarely appeared even in his private correspondence. Two other ideas that Sifton did hold, however, were consistent with those expressed on the water and other issues: he opposed the export of pulpwood, which in his opinion ought to have been processed in Canada; and he believed that a system of limited leases of forest lands was preferable to outright sale, or unlimited lease.[51]

Apart from attempting to inventory Canada's forest resources, the main goals of the conservation commission with respect to forestry were two: to reduce wastage of timber by forest fires and to expand national parks, forest reserves, and reforestation programmes. A related third goal was the upgrading and professionalization of the forestry services in the dominion and provincial governments.

The first concern was to persuade governments to force the railways to protect the forests from fires caused by their locomotives. Existing laws penalized individuals who inadvertently or deliberately started fires, but not the companies. ''You cannot secure the enforcement of a law,'' declared Sifton indignantly, ''which requires the camper who carelessly sets out a fire to be put in gaol, while railway companies are permitted to start fire after fire all along their lines with no one to say a word to them. That is contrary to natural law and justice and you never could get such a law enforced and it never was enforced.''[52] Public opinion needed to be roused, because ''you cannot make progress without breaking some heads, without somebody having to do something that he was not doing before.''[53] Action also was needed to force lumber companies to clear the dead trees and branches resulting from their operations; the dense detritus not only posed a fire hazard, but hampered forest renewal and even served as a breeding ground for certain pests harmful to live timber. Except in Ontario, the various governments responded reasonably quickly to the exhortations of the Commission, and even the railway companies became quite co-operative. In 1916 the province of Ontario suffered a serious outbreak of fires, causing Sifton to snort, ''Ontario is the most backward province of the dominion in respect to fire protection....I think it should be plainly stated that the Government of the province of Ontario has deliberately and persistently refused to adopt any modern ideas about fire protection, and these fires are the consequence.'' Perhaps the experience was salutary, because the following year the Ontario government adopted a Fire Protection Act which Sifton warmly greeted as the beginning of ''a new era.''[54]

Few incidents better illustrate the utilitarian approach of the commission and the federal government—as opposed to a preservationist approach—than the Rocky Mountains Forest Reserve created in 1911. All the land above 4,000 feet along the eastern slope of the Rockies in Alberta was set aside as a forest reserve, some 18,000 square miles in total, stretching from the international boundary to a point over one hundred miles northwest of Jasper. At the same time, however, within these limits the national parks at Banff and Jasper were sharply reduced in size. Within the parks exploitation of timber and mineral resources was severely limited and protection was provided for the flora and fauna. In the remaining territory, however, the act contemplated cutting and removal of timber, the working of mines, quarries and mineral deposits, removal of sand, gravel, earth and stone, pasturage of cattle, use of hay lands, creation of reservoirs, development of water power sites, and hunting of animals in much of it. Of course it was to be strictly controlled development to preserve the watershed of the eastern Rockies, to prevent forest fires, and so forth. By 1914 public opinion would force the government to enlarge the park boundaries once again, but the episode reflected the predominant "doctrine of usefulness."[55]

Sifton firmly believed that no measure would do more to put Canada's forests to efficient use, and reduce fires, than the appointment by all levels of government of a professional forest service. The forest service of the federal government was part of the "outside service," exempted from the provisions of the Civil Service Act, and therefore wholly subject to the patronage system. Sifton pleaded with the government to reclassify the foresters in the "inside service," to require proper qualifications and examination. So too did Sir George Murray, an Englishman who investigated the reorganization of the civil service in 1912.[56] "From the head of the service to the least important of its employees," insisted Sifton, "the merit system should absolutely govern, and no one should be allowed to be employed except upon the basis of qualification for the work. The success of the work will depend entirely upon the adoption of this principle. No effective forest service can be carried on when foresters are expected to combine the work of forest protection, political canvassing and general representation of the political interests of the government." He urged members of the commission to seize every opportunity to speak with cabinet ministers and inform them that their public duty required this reform. "It may be that after awhile the members of the Government may feel a little like the unjust judge, that though they fear not God, yet they will do it because we ask them."[57] While progress was made but slowly in this field, there is no question that the commission's work bore fruit in greater government regulation of Canadian forests.

On the subject of mines and minerals, Sifton had much less to say. He was wholly in favour of the rapid expansion of Canada's mineral production, but he believed that there was much to be learned concerning the efficient production and use of these minerals. The industry as it stood not only tended to be wasteful, but also careless of human life. When it came to mine accidents, observed Sifton, "my information is that Canada makes almost the worst showing in the world." The Mining Institute of Canada responded that Sifton was "not acquainted with the facts," but a sobering admitted fatality rate of twelve per 1,000 miners employed underground still left much room for improvement. "While it is most undesirable that the mining industry should be too much hampered by governmental interference," concluded Sifton, "public opinion would surely...support the Goverment in going much farther in the way of regulation and inspection."[58]

Sifton's main concern was, however, similar to when he was responsible for the Geological Survey. He wanted information concerning Canada's minerals made readily available in useful form to the interested public. The commission undertook both an inventory of resources and a compilation of all dominion and provincial laws affecting mines and mineral production. And the committee on minerals conducted studies on specific concerns: the use of phosphate lime, found in the Rockies, to fertilize western soils; the use of waste by-products from the coal and coking industries; the use of low-grade western coals; the evils of environmental pollution from mining, factory and power plant stacks, particularly in slum areas of cities. "After all," the committee noted, "the conservation of humanity is even more important than the conservation of coal." Once again, however, the commission was promoting such ideas long before the public was seized with their importance and willing to force governments to act.[59]

The Committe on Fisheries, Game and Fur-Bearing Animals made a significant contribution as well, but with much less interest being evinced by Sifton. In his inaugural address he referred to the fisheries as "one of the greatest of our national resources," but his remarks were perfunctory, and he had nothing whatever to say on the subjects of game and fur. In subsequent years he appeared to deprecate what had been accomplished by the commission in this field because of the lack of a fisheries expert.[60] Preservation was, as already noted, never a serious concern of the commission, and the preservationist movement developed mainly in the Parks Branch of the Department of the Interior and in bodies outside the government service. Ironically, two of Sifton's civil service appointees, Howard Douglas and J.B. Harkin, developed into leaders of the preservationist movement.[61] The commission eventually strongly backed the Migratory Bird Treaty of 1916 between Canada and the United States, perhaps the most important single advance toward preservation taken in the era.[62] But the commission still tended to understand preservation simply in terms of economic benefit, particularly the attraction of tourists, hunters, and fishermen. Studies undertaken by the commission in this field ranged from fur farming to the cultivation of oysters and methods to restore the west coast salmon fishery.[63]

The Committee on Lands might better have been termed the "Committee on Agriculture," for that was almost its sole concern. It was, in Sifton's opinion, central to the purposes of the commission:

> Agriculture is the foundation of all real and enduring progress on the part of Canada. It is one of the striking facts of the present social condition in the United States and in Canada that, with a few exceptions, those men who, by reason of strength of character and intellectual pre-eminence, take the lead in public affairs, in professional life and in scholarship are, as a rule, removed not more than one or, at most, two generations from ancestors who tilled the soil.
>
> The possession of a preponderating rural population having the virtues and strength of character bred only among those who follow agricultural life, is the only sure guarantee of our national future. The possession of such a population depends upon the maintenance of the fertility of the soil.[64]

There was some danger of overlapping with work already being done by the federal and provincial governments, but Sifton believed that there was plenty of room for the commission to make a significant contribution.

The most visible undertaking of the commission was a series of thirty-three illustration farms. These were different from the dominion experimental farms, which were founded for scientific agricultural research. The illustration farm, as its name implied, was intended to demonstrate to farmers in a given district the benefits to be derived from intelligent scientific agriculture. The idea had first been proposed to the government before 1900, but it had never been implemented. Now Sifton and the Commission took up the farms with enthusiasm. After consulting with the farmers of a particular district—in most provinces, but concentrated in Québec, Ontario, and the West—a farmer was selected who would be advised by the Commission about methods of cultivation and fertilization, the best strains of crop for the district, crop rotation, effective weed control, and the use of labour-saving devices and up-to-date machinery. The farms were tremendously popular, leading to demands for illustrated lectures in the winter on such topics as the production, care, and uses of manure; soil cultivation; growing of clover; and use of farm machinery. The instructors also advised on methods of making "the farm home and its surroundings more comfortable and attractive" especially encouraging the planting of flowers, vegetables and some fruits. The instructors even claimed that trying the new methods added "zest" to farming, particularly for the children of the farmers, who would be more inclined to remain on the farm if the work were interesting: "It is not all a matter of dollars and cents."[65]

The work of the Commission helped to force the various governmental departments of agriculture to increase appropriations for "improvements in agriculture," a subject they often had ignored. This and the popularity of the farms caused Sifton to conclude in 1915 that the commission's goals had been achieved. "It is not our business to conduct a department of agriculture, and obvious inconveniences will arise if, even upon a small scale, we continue the work which we have been doing." Public opinion had been roused as the value of the work became evident, and it was hoped that the federal Department of Agriculture would assume the work in future.[66]

By no means did the illustration farms reflect the full scope of the commission's activities in agriculture. It conducted an agricultural inventory across the country, research on effective use of fertilizers, investigation of new technology—even the generation of electricity by windmills, and sanitation on farms. Most such findings found their way into publication as well as practical demonstration. Beyond a certain point, however, it was difficult to make significant advances in face of the conservative individualism of the farmers themselves. "The unfortunate feature of farming in Ontario, and in Canada generally," concluded Sifton, "has been that each individual farmer has jealously regarded himself and his farm as a unit separated from the rest of the community and to be managed without any reference to the views or interests of any other person." Significant improvement in most areas of concern to the farmer could only be achieved by co-operative endeavour.[67]

If the inclusion of agriculture within the purview of the commission appeared to broaden its original purpose somewhat, the subject of public health seemed, in the minds of some critics, to be a significant departure. Sifton, as usual, had no reservations. "The physical strength of the people," he affirmed, "is the resource from which all others derive. Extreme and scrupulous regard for the lives and health of the population may be taken as the best criterion of the degree of real civilization and refinement to which a country has attained."[68] One of the first national conferences that the commission convened was the Dominion Public Health Conference held in Ottawa in October 1910. "This is a business meeting and not a scientific conference," Sifton told the delegates; the country expected some practical results. In particular he wanted solutions suggested to conflicting federal and provincial jurisdictions; a serious effort to confront tuberculosis, preferably with federal leadership; effective measures to deal with pollution of rivers and streams; and some method of dealing with the proliferation of slums. Earlier he had told a Toronto audience, "If we allow men and women to herd together a race of degenerates will grow up, which years and years of legislation will not stamp out, in fact I have never known of a race of people who have become degenerates regaining their former physique.'' A slum, he told the Ottawa conference, was ''a back yard of a town, where undesirable people live, and undesirable conditions prevail.'' Once established, slums spread faster than remedial measures could cope with. Public opinion needed to be roused on the subject, so that effective planning would be implemented to avoid slum development.[69] Thus it will be understood how readily town and city planning became a major concern of the conservation commission.

The notion that public health care and especially preventive medicine ought to be a government responsibility was a comparatively recent development. Ontario established the first provincial board of health in 1882; and over the two decades preceding the founding of the Commission of Conservation all other provinces followed suit.[70] The federal government had little interest in the subject beyond perfunctory inspection and care for immigrants and Indians and sanitation measures within various departmental jurisdictions, regarding public health as constitutionally a wholly provincial responsibility. Nevertheless, as public health care became professionalized, and as the appalling scope of the difficulties was revealed through studies and sad experience, those engaged in the public health field began to see themselves almost as crusaders engaged in a holy war. Infant mortality rates were shockingly high; an estimated one in three Canadian deaths was caused by tuberculosis; typhoid fever could slaughter Canadians in numbers comparable to highway fatalities in contemporary Canada.[71] The First World War intensified this concern, shattering ''the patriotic legend that Canada had the healthiest of all climates.'' States one authority, ''Between 1914 and 1918, the country lost almost as many people from tuberculosis as it did from the fortunes of war. The influenza epidemic had taken about as many again.''[72]

In some respects the conservation commission was frustrated as it met a massive wall of federal indifference to its recommendations. Repeated suggestions that a federal department of health be established were ignored until after the experience of the Great War.[73] So were recommendations to adopt modern methods of stream control used in Britain and Germany. Requests for federal aid for tubercular care and crown lands for sanatoria were rejected on the ground of provincial constitutional responsibility. A proposed National Public Health Laboratory was approved by the Laurier government in 1911 but rejected by the Borden administration.[74] The commission did establish a committee of medical men and scientists to try to develop a plan for combatting tuberculosis that would ''command public confidence and support.''[75] Yet little seems to have been achieved in practice.

There also were successes. The first was Sifton's selection of Dr. Charles Alfred Hodgetts, an official with the Ontario Board of Health since 1891, to head the medical work of the commission. Hodgetts was a zealot in the cause of public health and, supported strongly by Sifton, was bound to generate vigorous activity. Perhaps the first significant impact on public opinion was the commission's investigation into the causes of the typhoid epidemic which struck Ottawa during the winter of 1911, killing over two hundred people. The resulting report was published as a pamphlet; the Committee on Public Health drafted a bill to regulate disposal of sewage in navigable waters; and a broader study soon appeared, *The Prevention of the Pollution of Canadian Surface Waters*.[76] Hodgett's most lasting contribution to the commission, however, was in the connection he was forever drawing between inadequate housing and lack of town planning, and the spread of disease. "The failures of public health work in Canada have been due to the Governments not taking more direct control in administration," he declared:

> From the standpoint of hygiene it would seem the cart has gone before the horse in the eight hour day movement, for the average mechanic working in the modern, up-to-date factory spends his time in a better environment than he does the remaining hours of each twenty-four. Physically, he is better off at the factory than at home....
>
> It is somewhat farcical that a state should decline to accept any responsibility, financial or otherwise, to provide the means whereby crime and disease may be minimized, if not prevented, by bettering the housing conditions. Yet that same state will plan and devise the most approved and up-to-date sanitary home for a man after he has become a criminal. It damns him first and then attempts his reclamation after ....Certainly the criminal of to-day is better housed and fed after incarceration than he is in his own slum home.[77]

Sifton endorsed these views when he addressed the National Conference on City Planning in May 1914. "It seems a terrible indictment of modern civilization," he observed, "that the growth of insanitary, unhealthful conditions, the growth of slums and slum populations, are in direct ratio to what we call progress." In Canada, the situation had become serious in Montreal, Toronto, and Winnipeg. Nevertheless, he added optimistically, "our cities are not so large that they are out of control, and it is still possible within the next ten or twelve years to relieve any evil conditions which exist at the present time, and to lay foundations which will effectually prevent any serious growth of undesirable conditions in the future."[78]

Thus it may be seen that Sifton shared many of the beliefs of the social reformers of his era: that social problems such as crime and disease were largely products of the physical environment and that the application by experts of scientific planning and principles, backed by government regulation, could eradicate the problems. Sifton and Hodgetts had quickly identified the Conservation Commission as the most prominent national body concerned with city planning; and in 1912 a nationwide petition was raised, sponsored by groups ranging from the CMA and the IODE to the Canadian Public Health Association, asking the commission to hire as an expert adviser a British town planner, Thomas Adams. He was regarded as the leading authority on planning working class housing and suburban subdivisions, had written a book on the idea of the Garden City, and had created a sensation in North America in 1911 with a speech to a planning conference in Philadelphia.[79] After protracted negotiations, involving the intervention of Sir Robert Borden himself, Adams agreed in July 1914 to become town planning adviser to the conservation commission, a position he would occupy through the remaining life of the commission. When Hodgetts took leave from his duties in 1915 to serve with the Canadian forces overseas, the public health work gave way almost entirely to that of town planning.

If Hodgetts had been an enthusiast, Adams was nothing less than a dynamo. In the years that he was associated with the commission he published no less than 139 articles and books and almost certainly gave as many public addresses. He was called on to advise governments from coast to coast, including the reconstruction of Halifax after the explosion of 1917.[80] He stimulated the publication of the periodical *Conservation of Life* (1914-21), and the formation of the Civic Improvement League of Canada to generate public interest. He persuaded most of the provinces to adopt planning acts modelled on a British statute of 1909. He promoted the establishment of planned satellite towns near larger cities and the planning of new resource towns in Ontario and Quebec.[81] There is no question that he did more than any other single person to give the work of the Commission an international reputation.[82]

Adam's work, and the philosophy underlying it, had their shortcomings. Undoubtedly, they were too strictly utilitarian, too concerned with efficiency.[83] Adams's plans often envisioned more government intervention than Canadian governments were prepared to accept. It has been argued that "the suburban movement accentuated rather than alleviated the problem" of working-class housing by increasing the fragmentation of the city into rich and poor enclaves.[84] Yet if the planning movement was not a panacea, it was a serious effort to confront an intractable problem and led to improvements in urban life, particularly in new districts and communities.

Broadly as Sifton conceived of the scope of the commission's work, he imposed some arbitrary limits. J.S. Woodsworth wrote him on behalf of the Canadian Welfare League in September 1914, noting the recent inclusion of housing and town planning among the commission's interests. Could it not expand that into "a fully equipped 'welfare department'?" Woodsworth apparently had in mind the same kind of facilities to collect and disseminate statistics and research on various "social needs" that had been established for other areas of concern. Although he claimed some sympathy for the league's work, Sifton flatly refused, on the ground that "the conduct of our work calls for a very great discretion to avoid interfering with other recognized Government agencies, and I think for the present we have gone as far in extending the scope of our work as it is possible to do."[85] Perhaps that was true, although it is difficult to see that the problem of overlapping jurisdictions was worse in the area supported by Woodsworth than in those already covered by the commission. It is more likely that Sifton believed that town planning held greater promise for ultimately solving social problems.

He also felt free to use his position as chairman to push some of his favorite hobby-horses. For example, he enthusiastically endorsed a report to the commission on the introduction of technical education in Ontario, adding, "I do not hold with the idea of establishing grammar schools and collegiate institutes to teach boys to make critical examinations of Shakespeare's plays and Milton's poems, when they know nothing about agricultural chemistry and have not the faintest idea of mechanics or other branches of technical education."[86] At a more advanced level, he promoted the idea of a national laboratory for industrial research, and extensive federal aid to technical education.[87] More specifically, he had always believed that Canadian peat held great potential as a fuel, both for domestic use and export, promoting it through the Commission and having some sent to Britain for analysis and testing.[88] When he decided that a debate in Britain was significant for Canada, about why German agricultural productivity was allegedly superior to that of England, he ordered that scientific studies on the use of chemical fertilizers should constitute part of the next annual meeting of the commission. White was directed to "get the best man you can in America to write a paper, setting out fully the fertilizers that are used, and the results that have been attained by the use of these fertilizers, with details as to their method of manufacture and cost." In particular the papers should distinguish the uses of phosphate and nitrate fertilizers. "My purpose is that the discussion... would present a reliable and condensed epitome of information on the subject."[89] The point is, that while he did pursue his own interests very often, it was precisely that enthusiasm for the best current research in a wide range of topics that give the commission much of its vitality.

Hence the enormous loss to the commission when Sifton submitted his resignation as chairman on 22 November 1918.[90] The reasons were complex and the decision was not entirely sudden. He told one correspondent that he found himself "unable to give the necessary time to the various lines which require attention in connection with the work."[91] Possibly this was true, as the commitment of time was considerable for what was an unpaid, voluntary position. While heavy business and political commitments in previous years, especially 1911 and 1917, had not led to consideration of resignation, it is likely that with the close of the war Sifton anticipated spending more time abroad in connection with his personal affairs.

More serious was the growing hostility toward the commission on the part of certain leading members of the government, such as Arthur Meighen, George Foster, and Martin Burrell, and also among certain civil servants. The sentiment became more public after Sifton's resignation, but he must have been aware of it. At least as early as 1913 charges were raised that the commission was duplicating work done in the Department of the Interior, charges constantly reiterated in later years.[92] The response of the commission was that it tried to initiate work not being done by others, that this led to others beginning work that they should already have been doing and then complaining about the commission, and that wherever possible the commission tried to co-operate with experts in other departments. Still, rivalries were bound to arise in such a situation, and it was made worse when the government decided to establish a scientific research committee which, in Sifton's view, was deliberately designed to encroach on the work of the commission and limit its scope.[93]

Furthermore, James White was not a diplomatic secretary to the commission. He tended to react angrily toward those he thought biased against the commission, and tactlessly toward those he should have been cultivating. "All the redundants & incompetents in the Civil Service," he once wrote, "are saying that we are duplicating the work of the Departments & that we 'annex' ('steal' is, I believe the phrase they use) work done by the Depts. Of course one can not run the slanderers down." On another occasion he wrote a vigorous letter defending the commission's activities to Martin Burrell and denouncing its critics as "mediocrities and incompetents who have neither original ideas nor initiative." The letter, Burrell promptly told Borden, "apparently sets forth the Commission's view of its own powers and functions," and, as he was in disagreement with much of it, he circulated copies of the letter to the cabinet. He pointedly added "that from such information as I have the National Conservation Commission of the United States, which was established by Mr. Roosevelt, became merged a year later in the National Conservation Association, a voluntary body having no connection with the Government."[94] Evidently the government also was concerned about the anomalous position of the commission, being supported by Parliament, yet remaining independent of it. Either it should be an independent, private body as in the United States, or it should be attached to a government department. However, it appears that as long as Sifton was chairman, the government was reluctant to broach the subject directly.[95]

The government had no less an authority than Sir George Murray to back up its views. When Murray reported on the civil service in 1912, he declared that the commission lacked sufficient technical expertise, and was unwieldy in size. He recommended a small permanent commission of three to five members (rather than thirty-two), assisted by a large technical staff. He believed it should carry out its "thinking, planning and advising" functions at the federal level and also act as a training ground for technical experts in the government service. Finally, it should be under the control of, and responsible to, the prime minister.[96] Advised of the report's conclusions, Sifton responded irritably, "Sir George Murray seems to be one of those men who are somewhat set in their own opinions. I discussed the question and constitution of the Commission with him and I tried to explain to him that it was not a Commission that reported to the Government or was under Government control, but he seems to have failed to get the idea into his head." Murray failed, he told another correspondent, to grasp that the value of the Commission "consists almost entirely to the fact that it is indifferent to party affairs, [and] able to take an unbiased view of matters which come before it."[97] Sifton might have added that the apparently unwieldy composition of the commission had been necessitated by the federal nature of the country and that a small, permanent federal commission would have little influence with the provinces. Murray ignored the fact that technical experts were hired on a limited contract basis, and were not part of the permanent staff, though some, like Adams, remained many years with the commission. As to efficiency, Sifton could let the Commission's record speak for itself. Nevertheless, Murray's report constituted effective ammunition for those anxious to attack the commission.

Sifton himself, of course, was a controversial figure who was not trusted by several of the old-line Tory cabinet ministers. But he was confident that as long as he had the backing of Borden, he could maintain his conception of the commission and do useful work. In 1918 the relationship changed. First, Borden did not back Sifton's recommendations regarding salary increases for the commission staff. By the fall Sifton was annoyed and a bit touchy, as was Sir Robert, who was exhausted by the strain of four years of war. The two men had an angry exchange of correspondence over what appears in retrospect to have been a rather silly and certainly a reconcilable difference, but one which probably was the immediate precipitating factor in Sifton's resignation.

The concern which produced the conflict was an old one, the determination of Alcoa to secure the St. Lawrence dam it needed to expand its aluminum processing plant and hydro-generating capacity at Massena, N.Y. The company had not given up after its defeat in 1910; it had renewed its application in 1911 and 1912 and had been successfully opposed by the Conservation Commission and the Canadian government. In succeeding years the company stated publicly that its goal had not altered, and in 1917 the American involvement in the First World War provided the perfect occasion for it to renew its application on the ground that aluminum was a strategic metal required for the war effort. The Canadian government, using an argument originally suggested in part by Sifton, contended that the International Joint Commission, which had been asked to rule on the project, had no jurisdiction in light of the Webster-Ashburton Treaty. The IJC ignored the Canadian position and approved the project. Canada responded by declaring that the decision was not binding on the Dominion; but the project, now reduced to a weir which could be constructed wholly in American waters, went ahead.[98]

It seems ironic that the issue should have produced a conflict between Borden and Sifton. Both the government and the commission appeared to be on the same side, historically opposing the power scheme, and urging public ownership of power sites on the St. Lawrence. By 1917 both recognized that the construction was probably necessary and inevitable, but neither wanted the IJC to approve private American construction. The government's view was that the IJC had no jurisdiction, that the project infringed on long-standing treaty rights, and therefore should be covered by diplomatic negotiations that would revise the treaty and perhaps make some concessions to Canadian interests. The Commission of Conservation, meanwhile, had prepared a brief for the IJC with Sifton's approval but in his absence, which neither opposed the weir nor questioned the IJC's authority in the matter. It simply reiterated the traditional points that public ownership was preferable and that any construction should safeguard Canada's interests.[99]

When Borden upbraided White for the Commission's action, Sifton replied that the commission had had little notice to prepare its case, that its case was in line with its past position, and that in any event "the Commission had no intimation from the Government as to what its wishes were in regard to the matter."[100] Borden responded in some irritation, contending in effect that it was the responsibility of the commission to co-ordinate its case with that of the government, not vice versa: "Such a situation as this, which appears to make the Government speak with two voices, is clearly undesirable; it might easily result in confusing and weakening the Government's case before the International Joint Commission; it might even have the unfortunate result of giving an appearance that this Government was wanting in frankness and straightforwardness."[101]

If the prime minister was exaggerating the probable effect of the Commission's action on the IJC decision, Sifton was in no mood for compromise:

> With regard to the suggestion that the Government has been made to speak with two voices, I desire to say that the Commission of Conservation has never been regarded as a Department of the Government or a part of the administration for whose opinions the Government is directly responsible. It has never been recognized that the Commission was bound to harmonize its views on public questions with those of the Government.
>
> Were this not the case, the usefulness of the Commission would have been seriously curtailed.

He continued with a forceful, almost angry, defence of the policies and staff of the commission, claimed that the commission had practically fought the battle against the power interests singlehanded since 1910, and sarcastically concluded "that it is a matter of much gratification to those who have devoted time and attention to the question of St. Lawrence Power that the Government has now adopted a comprehensive national policy on this subject." [102] Although more conciliatory in tone, Borden's response of 7 November 1918 essentially offered no concession of principle. [103] Sifton must have believed that Borden's position effectively undermined his own conception of the commission's proper role. Yet in retrospect it is hard to believe that the two men could not have resolved their differences in a conference had the will to do so existed. By the end of the War, however, Sifton's limited respect for the prime minister was beginning to evaporate.

Following Sifton's resignation the commission began to limp badly. His successor, Senator W.C. Edwards, carried little weight. The commission's next annual meeting, of 7 February 1919, reflected the planning begun by Sifton; it was also the last meeting of which the proceedings were published. In 1921 the commission was not even allowed to proceed with its annual meeting because the government, headed since the summer of 1920 by Arthur Meighen, was preparing to abolish it altogether. The excuses given were readily predictable: the commission was allegedly duplicating work better done by departments, was costly, and was independent of government control. [104] Pointedly, all the commission's staff were offered positions in various departments, except James White, who was abruptly superannuated. During the entire twenty-five years since he had first gone to Ottawa, Sifton sympathetically told White, "I never heard of a public servant being treated in as venomous and contemptible a manner as the Government has treated you." [105]

It was a sad conclusion to a remarkable story. Early in the life of the commission Sifton wrote, "Sometimes it seems a little flat to be hammering away at the same things all the time but there are many subjects of great interest and occasionally we succeed in doing something that is really important."[106] That sense that they were engaged in a work of vital importance to the country had constantly fuelled the fires of enthusiasm among members of the commission. They had taken the relatively new concept of conservation, broadened its original meaning, and identified it with the spirit of progressive reform and social renewal that had so seized many Canadians of that generation. A significant debate was generated over the responsibilities of both government and the private sector with respect to conservation and the public interest; unprecedented levels of research were undertaken; and systematic publicity lent momentum to the movement. "In many ways," writes one authority, "the Conservation Commission was years, and even decades, ahead of its time."[107] The reform enthusiasm which peaked before and during the War dissipated rapidly after 1918. The loss, first of Sifton, then of Borden, and the accession to power of the enemies of the commission, all further sealed its fate, and its work was quickly almost forgotten. Yet its legacy could be found in dozens, if not hundreds, of federal and provincial statutes regulating resource exploitation, encouraging farmers and fishermen, and requiring public health standards and city planning. The commission in fact may well have been one of Sifton's greatest achievements.

12

Through the Great War
(1911-1918)

Clifford Sifton's strenuous public labours in the interest of conservation in 1910 and in opposition to reciprocity in 1911 inexorably exacted a physical toll. "The fact is," he wrote in 1912, "I have been troubled with my head and nerves for the last couple of years and....I shall have to refrain from speaking in public for some time."[1] Not only had the stress caused a recurrence of insomnia, severe headaches, and high blood pressure, but Sifton also suffered a serious worsening of his deafness and, in the fall of 1912, a dangerous bout of pneumonia. As soon as he was able to undertake it, he arranged a trip to England for treatment of his ears, followed by a holiday in Italy. Neither was very successful. Naples, in fact, "was the meanest and most disagreeable place I had ever been in." Rome, particularly the Alban hills, was somewhat better: "The atmosphere is rare and free from moisture and has a most beneficial effect upon the stomach and nerves."[2] Nevertheless, there was no improvement in his hearing and he pursued treatments in future more to prevent further worsening than with much hope of improvement or a cure. He still experimented with hearing aids of various kinds, but more and more relied on either a standard ear trumpet, or a "speaking tube" comprising a length of hose held to the ear at one end and fitted with a cone at the other end for the speaker.[3]

The death of John Wright Sifton on 19 September 1912 at the age of seventy-nine was not unexpected, but it cannot have helped Clifford Sifton's physical condition. He and his father had been quite close, and the elder Sifton had remained president of the Free Press Company despite failing health. "We all feel his loss very much now," wrote Clifford a few days later, "because although in a way his death was expected nevertheless when it came it seemed like breaking off the last link that bound us to the past."[4] Scarcely a year later his wife Arma also became seriously ill, necessitating a prolonged recuperation in the southern United States.[5] The truth was that Sifton himself remained in poor health until well into 1914. According to an acquaintance, "his face seemed to change almost each day and now instead of a firm and strong face it was getting all puffy and soft." In the opinion of another friend, his countenance was "but a reflex of his mentality which is by no means what it was. His life is a tragedy."[6] The judgment was a trifle hasty. By the summer of 1914 Sifton appeared largely recovered and, when the war began, able to call on his old reserves of energy.

He continued to expand his business interests prior to the war. "The man who is going to make good in this age," he told the Canadian Clubs of Port Arthur and Fort William, "is the man who puts his money and his confidence on the side of progress, and who believes in progress rather than stagnation."[7] As in the past, many of Sifton's investments tended to be speculations rather than direct involvement in material progress. One example was his quarter interest in the Chehalis Lumber Company, which held 6,418 acres in dominion timber berths and a provincial berth in British Columbia. Up to 1913 the Company had paid $149,200 for its holdings, and it anticipated rapid profits, particularly when the opening of the Panama Canal made British Columbia lumber economically accessible to the east coast markets. Depression and war temporarily discouraged these hopes, but the expected profits were amply realized during the boom of the 1920s.[8] Another speculation was in several hundred acres of land between Port Arthur and Fort William in the expectation that the development of the Lakehead ports would enhance their value. Although some land was disposed of before the War, the bulk of it never produced the anticipated return and remained in the Sifton family holdings for several decades.[9]

Perhaps more indicative of the speculative optimism of the inflationary spiral during 1911 and 1912 was an investment in irrigation. In the spring of 1912 Sifton was contemplating purchasing a block of land near Winnipeg and, after some improvement, selling it in small plots of ten to forty acres to market gardeners from Europe. However, on venturing further West he encountered J.D. MacGregor, his old crony from Brandon, who promptly sold him on the agricultural potential of irrigated land in southern Alberta— specifically, the holdings of the Southern Alberta Land Company, in which MacGregor was a leading shareholder. In June Sifton agreed to purchase 25,000 acres of land from the company at an average price of $33.75 per acre, together with an option to purchase a further 50,000 acres. At first he expected to be able to sell it, when irrigated, at $50.00 per acre, for a profit exceeding $400,000. By September, however, the projected sale price was up to $55.00, and by October $100.00 per acre, for a theoretical profit of over $1.6 million.[10] Such greed assumed, of course, that the inflation of western land prices in recent years would continue unabated, and undoubtedly was encouraged by the hundreds of thousands of dollars worth of profits already extracted from the land and irrigation scheme by MacGregor and his cohorts.[11] Fortunately for Sifton the company was unable to deliver the water as contracted; an option to purchase the 25,000 acres was substituted for the original sale agreement, and eventually he declined to take up the option in 1920 when the water was at last available. By then there was not the slightest prospect of the depressed land prices producing any profit whatsoever.[12] It might be argued that this was not merely a speculative proposition for Sifton, because he intended to attract settlers to a hitherto undeveloped part of the plains. However, the correspondence makes clear that his interest was far more in the immediate profits to be realized by land sales than in the long-term viability of a complex and costly enterprise.

Undoubtedly Sifton's interest in quick profits in 1912 was stimulated by heavy losses he suffered at the same time in his Colombian oil investments. The Atlantic Oil Company had been converted into the Colombian Oil and Gas Company of Canada, Limited. The two principal shareholders were Sifton, and a "Mr. Kelly";[13] Sifton paid $100,000 for $400,000 worth of stock, while Kelly paid $150,000 for $600,000 worth of shares, though Sifton had had to act as a guarantor for some $38,000 of Kelly's obligations. In addition, Sifton had loaned the company $65,835. Two holes drilled by the company in 1912 had failed to find more than traces of oil, though plenty of natural gas, and finally in October the company exhausted its funds and the discouraged owners decided to wind up its affairs. Neither Sifton nor any of the directors had made any profit from the concern. "On the contrary," noted a final statement to the shareholders, "they are all substantial losers"—in Sifton's case, probably over $200,000.[14] The sobering reverse caused him to be very cautious about oil investments even in Canada.[15]

Increasingly important in Sifton's private activities was work as an agent for British capitalists seeking profitable investment opportunities in Canada, most frequently in lands, and in the bonds issued by various levels of government. In 1912 he decided to regularize this activity by purchasing control of the British Empire Agency Company for a total of £3,000, or approximately $15,000.[16] At the time the agency served primarily as booking and shipping agents, and also published the *Empire Magazine*. Sifton's real interest appears to have been to develop a land sales department, which in the fall of 1912 published a collated list of lands for sale in Canada, including farms, orchards, timber lands, townsite lots, and so forth, from coast to coast, though emphasizing the prairies. The Company also made available mortgages at rates from 7 to 9 per cent.[17] Once again the optimism generated by the boom of the previous decade was crushed by the abrupt change in the investment climate. Early in 1913 Sifton wrote,

> The money market in Europe is as bad as it can possibly be and the worst part of it is the Canadian section. There is absolutely nothing doing in the way of new business. All the money that is coming to Canada is coming upon securities of the gilt-edge type which are being handled by houses in England only for clients of long standing. New issues, and especially real estate deals, will not command a penny during the next few months.[18]

Sifton's interest in encouraging British capital to invest in Canada had been whetted in 1911 and 1912 by his role in the formation of the Canadian Western Natural Gas, Light, Heat and Power Company Ltd., a concern formed to supply natural gas from fields near Medicine Hat to Lethbridge and Calgary, and to towns along the pipeline route. It was, he enthusiastically told Arthur Grenfell of the British Empire Trust Company in London, "about the best business proposition that has been put in shape in Canada for a good while and involving little or no risk." He hoped that Grenfell's company could handle the sale of bonds "as one proposition in London."[19] The prospects were excellent as $8,000,000 in common stock and $4,500,000 in 5 per cent first mortgage debenture stock was quickly taken up, the former probably realizing less than half its face value for the company.[20] Construction of the pipeline commenced 8 April 1912, the gas to reach Calgary by 1 September. With fourteen producing wells and a monopoly of the southern Alberta market, the optimism of the company was understandable.[21] Exactly how much Sifton invested in the concern himself is unknown, but he held 26,438 of the 80,000 common shares; he probably also held an equivalent proportion of the debenture stock.[22] His desire for quick profits was made clear to one of the company's officials who favoured reinvesting profits in expansion of the pipeline network: "We have no idea of putting our surplus profits into extensions for the next two or three years and allow the shareholders to go without Dividends. This Company is being operated for Dividends, and when it earns the Dividend there is no reason why it should not pay it."[23] The dividends were not unusually high, averaging 8.98 per cent between 1913 and 1919 on the original $4,500,000 actually invested in the company.[24] At the very least, Sifton was able to depend on an income from his common shares alone of from $52,000 to $104,000 each year. With this kind of performance the British Empire Trust Company was very happy and told Sifton, "We have always placed our confidence in having you as the presiding genius of the Company.[25]

A more curious and still somewhat murky episode in Sifton's business affairs was his relationship with the *Toronto World*. Its publisher, William Findlay Maclean, had been both an independent Liberal and an independent Conservative, a strong protectionist, and an advocate of public ownership of railways and other public utilities, policies with which Sifton had never demonstrated much sympathy. The paper was constantly in financial difficulty, despite the fact that it had the third largest circulation in Toronto, after the *Globe* and the *Mail and Empire*.[26] Sifton evidently had become friendly with Maclean, and in 1909-10 lent the paper as much as $20,000 to tide it over some financial embarrassment, causing the Conservatives to believe that he actually owned it.[27] Such a conclusion was erroneous, though understandable, given Sifton's connection with the *Manitoba Free Press*. As time went on, he seemed to be drawn more deeply into supporting his friend financially, though there is no evidence that this had any significant impact on the *World's* editorial stance. It would appear that by 1915 Sifton was a heavy investor in the Central Press Agency, which in turn controlled the *World*, and he was talking of investing $30,000, and perhaps as much as $67,000, in return for some of Maclean's private property, to bail out the paper. Shortly the connection became even more personal when, in 1916, Sifton's third son, Harry, married Maclean's daughter, Mary Lewis (Mollie). Nothing, however, could save the floundering *World* in the financial pressures of the late war and post-war years. Although Clifford Sifton was involved in attempts to reorganize its finances, the paper finally succumbed in 1921, when its assets were taken over by the *Mail and Empire*.[29]

Information concerning the financial status of Sifton's most important investment, the *Manitoba Free Press*, is particularly thin for these years. In 1911 the decision was made to sell the building constructed in 1903 and build another, which was occupied in the spring of 1913.[30] That reflected the rapid development of the paper and its readership during the Laurier boom. The only observation that Sifton offered about the new facility was an expectation "that a strict discipline system may be enforced in the new offices which discipline was lacking very woefully when last I saw the Editorial Department of the paper." With the new building should come a new order, and he suggested that the office manager "buy a couple of guns and keep everyone right up to the mark."[31] Obviously neither Dafoe's defence of his employees nor the continued high quality and success of the paper had overridden Sifton's conviction that the management was unduly lax.

The profitability of the paper was curtailed briefly during the war years owing to a price war in Winnipeg. A decline in advertising revenues and a rise in the price of newsprint and other costs led many newspapers in Canada to increase their price from one cent to two cents per copy. In Dafoe's opinion, the subscription price of the paper should at least cover newsprint and distribution costs. When the *Free Press* increased its rate to ten cents a week in 1915, the *Tribune* and *Telegram* refused to comply, seriously reducing the *Free Press* circulation. The fear of papers like the *Tribune*, and the *World* in Toronto, was that if rates were significantly increased, the large number of households that subscribed to two or more papers would cut back to one, and the leading papers, like the *Free Press* or the *Globe*, would emerge big winners. Beginning in October 1915, therefore, the *Free Press* slashed its rates and began an aggressive and successful campaign to regain its lost circulation. Operating from a position of strength, and realizing that the same cost squeeze faced the *Tribune* and the *Telegram*, Dafoe and Macklin finally forced the other papers to agree to a near doubling of subscription prices early in 1917. The effect on the smaller papers is unclear; but Dafoe was pleased to note no adverse effects on *Free Press* circulation and complacently predicted a substantial increase in profits for the year. Sifton remained determined that the paper must vigilantly oppose any attempt by the newsprint industry to raise prices further and syphon off the new profits.[32]

The defeat of Laurier in 1911 meant that the *Free Press* could enjoy "the luxury of opposition," not having to worry about embarrassing or defending the Laurier Liberals.[33] Yet Dafoe's partisanship was insufficiently relaxed for Sifton, as several times he faulted the paper for being too ready to defend the Liberal leader.[34] Dafoe's violent attacks on Sifton's old enemy R.P. Roblin, and the use of investigative journalism to uncover scandal and graft in the Manitoba government occasioned a strong cautionary statement. "Speaking generally," he told Dafoe, "it is not the business of a great newspaper to be a detective of graft in the public service." Apart from all the energy and expense consumed in such investigations, the overwhelming majority of readers, whatever their political affiliation, would not see the charges as anything more than another partisan attack. Let the opposition make the case, which the newspaper could duly publicize. A "Democracy gets the kind of a Government that it is entitled to," and a province that would turn out the "honest, economical and businesslike" Greenway government and keep re-electing the Roblin Tories would not easily be persuaded by publishing charges of corruption in the *Free Press*. "It is for this reason that I have often urged you to take a really independent stand in regard to all public questions; not looking back, and making personal references but dealing impartially with the facts and leaving the public to draw their own inferences."[35]

Such comments reflected Sifton's own political isolation after 1911. He had burned his bridges to the Liberal party during the reciprocity campaign, but could never be a very enthusiastic supporter of the new Borden government. Yet he bore at least a little responsibility for the composition of that government, as well as for its election. Borden had pledged in March 1911 to consult with Sifton, Lash, Walker, and Willison when drawing up the cabinet, and he fulfilled his promise. Sifton supported the appointment of Thomas White, the former Liberal, as minister of finance. Despite his pious words about reforming the civil service in 1908, and the idealistic words of the March agreement with Borden, Sifton also supported the appointment of unreformed party bosses from the provinces, including Frank Cochrane of Ontario, Robert Rogers of Manitoba, and W.J. Bowser or Sir Richard McBride from British Columbia; of these men, Cochrane and Rogers were appointed, although the urbane Martin Burrell became minister of agriculture and representative of the Pacific province. Finally, Sifton gave his blessing to the appointment of the mercurial and controversial Sam Hughes as minister of militia.[36] Dafoe, probably unaware of his employer's precise role, allowed that the new cabinet, despite some weaknesses, could be as good or better than that of Laurier. He nevertheless feared Rogers in the Department of the Interior, predicting that "he will set about building up a machine to capture the West, just as he has rounded up and branded Manitoba."[37] Of course Dafoe was correct; and the fact that Sifton could not only look upon the situation with equanimity but encourage it suggests the extent to which he had distanced himself from his former western supporters.

Thereafter until after the outbreak of war Sifton's contacts with the new prime minister were infrequent. Indeed, he appeared increasingly disillusioned with the government's ability to handle important issues. Of these, none was more critical than that of naval policy. The Laurier government's Naval Service Act of 1910 had provided for the establishment of a small Canadian navy, voluntarily manned, and under the control of the Canadian government. Before Laurier's defeat in 1911 two second-hand cruisers, the *Niobe* and the *Rainbow*, had been purchased to serve as training vessels. Borden and most Conservatives from English-speaking Canada had contended in 1910 that the Laurier plan did not meet the threat posed to the Royal Navy by German naval rearmament. A Canadian navy would take too long to construct, would be of limited use at a time when naval strength was measured mainly in terms of the numbers of Dreadnought-type battleships possessed by each side, and could be rendered utterly ineffective by a Canadian government trying to make up its mind whether to join the battle or not. Imperialists also believed that a Canadian-controlled navy was but another step, thinly veiled, toward separation from the Empire. As prime minister, Borden clearly would not be content to follow his predecessor's lead; but what policy would he substitute?

Among the Canadians whose views he desired while formulating his policy was Clifford Sifton. Sifton's views were both firm and consistent with his privately expressed opinion of 1909. The first consideration was Canada's own defence. No prospective Canadian naval force could hope to fight successfully at sea against the navy of a major power. Canada could, however, effectively protect its ports and seacoast with a small fleet of cruisers, destroyers, and submarines, a plan for mining the ports and sea lanes, and a co-ordinated system of coastal batteries. The small naval force would gradually provide Canada with a trained cadre of men capable of assuming larger responsibilities in the future. But defence was not the only consideration. Canada also ought to contribute to the offensive power of the Royal Navy by providing "two battleships of the first class," one to be built immediately, and the other three years hence, "so as to get the advantage of any improvements in the meantime." The ships would be Canadian government property, paid for and maintained by Canada, but completely under the direction of the Royal Navy. Canada was in a strong financial position, Sifton optimistically concluded, with "a large surplus over all ordinary requirements," so that there should be no question of her being able to afford such a scheme.[39] Thus he supported both a permanent Canadian navy and a contributory policy. No one, however, could have accused him of being an imperialist in his response. He believed his suggestions derived from a realistic assessment of Canada's capabilities and responsibilities.

Borden apparently gave Sifton's opinions little weight. His policy, announced in December 1912, was to grant $35 million to Britain to build two or three battleships or armoured cruisers, which apparently would remain British property with no Canadian support for maintenance or operating expenses, and no clear agreement that the ships would ever revert to Canada. Meanwhile Laurier's policy was scuttled, and although Borden spoke of eventually establishing a Canadian navy, there was no commitment. The prime minister's policy was to be sold in the expectation that the British would allow Canada some indeterminate voice in the foreign policy of the Empire.[40] Borden "seems to have simply fallen over himself," expostulated Sifton. "I do not wish to see Canada under the heel of the Americans but I wish just as little to see her give up her right to a complete national development. The same principles which made me resist reciprocity cause me to resist this lying down policy which has apparently been adopted by Borden."[41] Dafoe was more succinct, perhaps because he also instinctively was more hostile to Borden. The prime minister, he declared, was attempting "to reverse the whole national policy of Canada, and seek to commit us to a programme of permanent subordination....[T]he Tories are not to be trusted. In office, they are certain to revert to type." That, concurred Sifton, "summarizes the situation perfectly well."[42]

Generating somewhat less public emotion than the navy, but more complex and enduring, was the railway question. The Borden government was having to face the consequences of the high-flown extravagance of the Laurier administration in 1903-4. By the end of 1911 there were already signs that the long years of economic expansion were nearing their close. The London financial markets were flooded with Canadian securities, making it difficult, if not impossible, for the Grand Trunk Pacific and Canadian Northern to raise the funds necessary to complete their lines. Inevitably they turned to the Canadian government to bail them out. Sifton, when he heard of the GTPR application, was incensed. "I think that ample provision has been made for the financing of this enterprise," he told Dafoe. "Hopeless incompetence" had made an earlier loan necessary and had led to this further application. "I have never known so cold-blooded a raider of the treasury," he added, as C.M. Hays, the general manager of the Grand Trunk.[43]

Sifton was particularly irritated by what he deemed the Grand Trunk's refusal to fulfil the intent of the Laurier policy. That included leasing by the GTPR of the National Transcontinental line between Winnipeg and Quebec City and Moncton, and payment of 3 per cent per annum of the construction cost of the latter line. The government was anxious to lease the completed sections of the NTR, and the Grand Trunk was anxious to have access to the line which could be linked up at Cochrane and North Bay with the main line of the Grand Trunk to place a substantial volume of transcontinental traffic for the first time wholly under GTR control. However, the fixed charges on the NTR lease were so enormous because of increased construction costs that the Grand Trunk wanted to be relieved and only have to pay on that section of the NTR (Winnipeg-Cochrane) that it expected to use. Borden countered with a proposal to have the government take over the whole of the GTP-NTR system; but the Grand Trunk, on the verge of realizing its dream of over half a century of becoming a transcontinental line, rejected the offer. Angrily, Sifton pointed out to Dafoe that the original contract had been for the construction of "a Canadian National road with Canadian National ports." "The idea," he fumed, "of letting them drop ports of the National Transcontinental that they do not want and operate the Grand Trunk Pacific and part of the National Transcontinental to run their stuff down to American ports and to the Hill system is intolerable." If the Grand Trunk refused to fulfil its obligations, the Borden scheme should be imposed.[44] The government, as it turned out, was not yet ready to force the issue.

On both the naval and railway questions Sifton had refrained from public comment, although he did expect Dafoe and the *Free Press* to voice his views editorially. Once or twice Borden had sought his views on the railway question and the navy, yet there is no evidence that he became a confidant of the prime minister. At the same time, Sifton began cautiously to rebuild his relationship with Laurier, whose policies, especially on the naval issue, he still found more acceptable than those of Borden. This in turn convinced some Tories that 1911 was an aberration and that Sifton was back advising his fellow Liberals.[45] Such an impression was mistaken. Sifton valued his independence and the opportunity to have some influence on both sides. Furthermore, neither party wholly trusted him, though they both respected his judgment and political acumen.

In light of the passion with which Sifton embraced the war effort, it is salutary to recall that his sympathy with the Allied cause had not been quite immediate and instinctive. At the end of July 1914, in fact, as armed conflict became inevitable, he wired Dafoe, "Do not commit yourself on our participation in war." He hoped that Britain could remain aloof, and suspected that if she entered, she would be "pushed into it by the jingo element. In that case I would be entirely opposed to Canada taking any part"[46] Only when he was convinced that Germany had attacked Belgium and France without excuse and that the fall of Britain's European allies would be but a prelude to a further attack on the Empire and all that it stood for, did Sifton endorse wholehearted Canadian participation.

There was neither joy nor jingoism, nor even great confidence when he sombrely told Dafoe, "I realize what apparently very few people do; that this war is a dreadful business, and only imperative necessity can excuse any participation in it....The question...simply resolves itself into this, whether the British Empire is to lie down and let Germany destroy its allies preparatory to destroying the Empire. There can only be one answer to this question, and that is we must stand by the British Government to the last man and the last dollar." Contrary to the optimists, he could not believe that the Allied armies would be enjoying Christmas turkey in a defeated Berlin. Rather, in another year Canada would still be raising contingents to send overseas in a bitter war of attrition. If Canadians were to join the battle, "I do not expect more than one-half of them to come back."[47]

At the age of fifty-three Sifton was too old for active service; but like thousands of other parents he had the wrenching experience of seeing his sons—four of them by summer 1915[48]—off to war. It was, he concluded, "a time when men have to show whether they are worthy to live in a free country or not."[49] Neither of his two eldest sons, however, reached the trenches in Europe. Winfield had had militia experience in the Corps of Guides since 1909 and sailed with the first Canadian contingent in September 1914. Along with the rest of the Canadians, he spent dreary months training on the muddy Salisbury Plain, serving as ADC at divisional headquarters. Before the contingent embarked for Europe, however, he was invalided and spent the remainder of the conflict pursuing a business career in London. The eldest of Sifton's sons, John Wright (usually called "Jack"), had no more distinguished a career. He too had been with the Corps of Guides since 1909, having been promoted to major in July 1914. He did not enlist until 1915, perhaps because his wife and infant daughter were both precariously ill. He never sailed to Europe, being detailed as staff officer to the inspector general for western Canada. The closest he came to actual fighting was when he joined the Canadian Siberian Force in 1918-19.[50]

The two younger brothers, by contrast, had distinguished war records. Clifford enlisted in December 1914, although he did not reach the front until November 1915. Thereafter, in service with the Canadian Field Artillery, he saw action in all the principal battles that became synonymous with the record of the Canadian Expeditionary Force, including St. Eloi, Courcelette, Vimy Ridge, Hill 70, Passchendaele, and Amiens. Wounded three times, he retired from the CEF in 1919 with the rank of major and with a DSO.[51] Victor Sifton, the youngest, joined the Mississauga Horse in October 1914, although he did not reach the front in Europe for over a year, serving with the 4th Canadian Mounted Rifles. He was twice wounded and, like Clifford, retired as major with the DSO.[52]

The involvement of his sons made the war deeply personal for Sifton. He was determined to make his own contribution, and in August and September 1914 he was instrumental in the formation and financing of the Automobile Machine Gun Brigade No. 1, later renamed 1st Canadian Motor Machine Gun Brigade.[53] The purpose was to present to the Canadian Expeditionary Force some of the latest technological advances in mobile, armoured vehicles carrying heavy machine guns. The brigade was to have sixteen machine guns mounted on eight armoured cars, together with six trucks and four automobiles for officers, and was to be constituted of nine officers and 114 other ranks. The total cost of providing the equipment exceeded $70,000 and was borne by some fourteen men at Sifton's request, including T.A. Burrows, Donald Mann, J.R. Booth, Sir Henry Egan, Sir Thomas Shaughnessy, Herbert Holt, and Huntley Drummond, as well as Sifton himself.[54] Within three weeks of the outbreak of war orders had been placed with the Autocar Company of Avonmore, Pa., for the vehicles, and with Colt's Patent Fire Arms of Hartford, Conn., for the guns, the whole being delivered by early September, and ready to embark from Gaspé by early October.[55] It was unusually quick work and much appreciated by a force that was desperately short of such modern equipment. An indicator of the situation was the fact that the brigade's "auto ambulance" was the only such vehicle available to the Canadian contingent in England and was in constant demand.[56] The gift was a grand and sincere patriotic gesture on the part of Sifton and the others, but all would discover that it was but a small first instalment toward the ultimate demands and costs of the war.

It was indubitably a struggle to preserve liberty, "the greatest fight for liberty since the Dutch & English broke the power of Spain in the sixteenth century." The Germans, Sifton told Dafoe, were "a worse menace to liberty than even Napoleon was. Now the modern arms & munitions of war make despotic power absolutely irresistible once it gets the upper hand." [57] The liberty for which Britishers, and those of other nations such as the Dutch and the Swiss, had fought and died over the years, was "ordered and regulated by law," which prevented even the rulers of the country from "arbitrary interference with rights of person or property." Canadians must rally behind the mother country, because "cradled behind the watery rampart [of the English Channel], the British nation has developed its proud position as the home of liberty, and has carried the spirit of freedom to the ends of the earth." The lesson of history, he asserted, was that "the free man's arms must aid the free man's laws....No nation ever won its liberty except at the price of blood. No nation has ever preserved its liberty except by freely shedding its blood whenever necessary. We on this continent are not exempt from this law." The battle against the German campaign for "world dominion" was "the noblest cause in which men have ever contended." [58] Beyond that, in the course of a wholehearted commitment to the war by Canada, the Dominion might well "find the national soul which of late has seemed sometimes to be lacking." [59]

"Liberty" to Sifton meant reasonable freedom of speech, among other things. He was incensed when a barber was jailed in 1917 for making statements "calculated to discourage recruiting." "We are," he fumed, "supposed to be fighting for liberty but there could be no worse & more outrageous tyranny than this in Germany....Men who do not agree with us about the war have as good a right to their opinions as we have & *just as much* right to express them." [60]

"Liberty" did not, however, extend to the right of French Canadians outside Quebec, or any other minorities, to obtain bilingual education. On this subject Sifton's views were as fixed as they had been two decades earlier in Manitoba. When the Liberals under T.C. Norris finally defeated the Roblin Tories in Manitoba in 1915, they were pledged to dismantle the bilingual schools provided in the "Laurier-Greenway compromise" of 1896-97. Sifton wanted Dafoe to hold the new government to its promise, against any possible concessions: "The whole bilingual system so far as possible ought to be wiped out....The American principle is the only safe one; to stand firmly and make no compromise." [61] Efforts to retain, or obtain, bilingual schools in Manitoba and Ontario were simply brushed aside by Sifton as "anti-national movements." In 1916 Sir Wilfrid Laurier nearly broke the Liberal party in his efforts to persuade Parliament to pass a resolution supporting Franco-Ontarians in their fight with their provincial government for bilingual schools. His passionate plea for compromise and tolerance was rebutted by Borden's stolid stance that the courts had upheld Ontario's power to eliminate bilingual education, and it was incumbent on Parliament not to interfere. "Borden's attitude was first rate & his speech good," pronounced Sifton. "Laurier's attitude was that of a school boy & his speech twaddle." In Sifton's opinion the aging Liberal leader had lost his sense of national vision and responsibility, had caved in to a narrow faction, and "the quicker he gets out of leadership the better for the country at large."[62]

By 1916, indeed, Sifton's view of the two party leaders had altered appreciably. One reason, perhaps, was that Borden appeared more ready than Laurier ever had been to recognize Sifton's contributions to Canadian public life, particularly in wake of the organization of the Automobile Machine Gun Brigade, and in the fall of 1914 he recommended Sifton for a knighthood, duly bestowed on 1 January 1915.[63] Even more significant, however, was his growing conviction that it was Borden rather than Laurier whose priorities were correct during the war years. Party strife, he believed, should be suspended for the duration of the conflict, and all efforts bent toward victory in Europe. Prime Minister Borden, angry at what he conceived to be the Liberal party's continued partisan attacks on his government, seriously contemplated an election in the spring of 1915. By the fall, however, charges of corruption, resurfacing railway difficulties, and the certainty that Laurier would be massively supported in Quebec, all made the outcome of an election uncertain. The prime minister now hoped to avoid an election altogether by obtaining Laurier's support for an extension of Parliament until a year after the conclusion of the war. Early in October he decided that Sifton—now Sir Clifford—should be his inter-mediary in the delicate preliminary negotiations with the Leader of the Opposition. Sifton found Laurier amenable, though not to the indefinite term proposed by Borden. The Liberal leader was prepared to discuss a one-year extension of the life of Parliament (to the fall of 1917); but this arrangement was not finally concluded between the two cautious leaders when they met in November.[64] The experience certainly created doubts in Sifton's mind about Laurier's willingness to place the war effort ahead of partisan advantage.

Another factor drawing Sifton's sympathies to the government was Sam Hughes, minister of militia. Upon the outbreak of war, Hughes proceeded to ride roughshod over the established mobilization procedures of the militia, erecting the base at Valcartier almost overnight, from which the first troops would embark for overseas service. He was determined to create an efficient Canadian army out of the tradition-bound, parochial militia in which political preferment had been the traditional means of promotion. Hughes had to cast aside claims to leadership based on length of service and political influence and seek to secure men of competence as officers.

Inevitably feathers were ruffled, from the governor general on down, as a result of Hughes's impetuosity, aggressiveness, and giant ego. The minister's display of energy strongly appealed to Sifton: "He has stood off the grafters & jobbers to the best of his ability," he told Dafoe, "& is turning out an army in record time." In fact, he continued, "We never before had a minister of militia who would not be bullied by the whiskey drinking cliques of militia officers who have been playing toy soldier & trading on their alleged military knowledge."[65] Despite the bizarre excesses that finally would force Borden to dismiss Hughes in November 1916, Sifton stubbornly—perhaps obtusely—remained a staunch defender. His presence in the government represented a wholehearted commitment to the Allied cause and his impulsive decisiveness and battles with his colleagues probably struck a familiar chord in Sifton's memory of his own cabinet experience.[66]

Borden, for his part, went out of his way to consult with Sifton on many questions of public policy, particularly with respect to the thorny railway question. There is little evidence that Sifton's views had much influence on government policy, but Borden recognized the value of working with a man of Sifton's proven political astuteness. Predictably, at first he generally opposed nationalization of the railways, especially a broad proposal to take over all the lines including the CPR. Such a policy, he insisted, would be "sheer lunacy. The fact is that the war excitement has unhinged people's minds." Anyone who had ever experienced living in a town or province monopolized by a single railway would understand the folly of the proposal. In the case of Manitoba, he asserted, "It was not rates—nor service—It was the impertinent indifference of the management which drove the people wild." A government-controlled monopoly would merely be worse.[67] The continual financial troubles of the Canadian Northern, Grand Trunk, and Grand Trunk Pacific lines created a perpetual drain on the government, and Sifton, despite his coolness to the principle of government ownership, found himself in general agreement with the terms of the Drayton-Acworth commission which reported in the spring of 1917 on the railway problem.[68] The recommendation was essentially for nationalization of these lines, combining them with existing government lines into an efficient transcontinental system, and placing the whole system under a board of directors largely independent of government control and patronage. Thus the worst of the alleged defects of government ownership would be avoided, and there would be an effective competitor for the CPR.[69]

The government's policy, however, did not go quite so far. It decided to make yet another loan to the Grand Trunk interests, thus providing a stay of execution. The Canadian Northern, by contrast, would be nationalized, with compensation to Mackenzie and Mann to be determined by a board of arbitrators. Sifton was highly critical of the fact that the original announcement of the policy placed no limit on the compensation, and he believed that it was only the influence of the Liberals about to enter the Union Government in the fall of 1917 that caused Borden finally to impose a $10 million ceiling on the compensation. Privately, however, he admitted to "a good deal of satisfaction" in "the fact that the promoters of this Railway are finally eliminated from Canadian politics."[70] Clearly Sifton's sympathies for Mackenzie and Mann were not as deep-seated as many of his opponents suspected.

Sifton's potential influence on public affairs was considerably minimized by his extended absences in England. Probably for as much as half the war he remained there, first in London, then at Springhill, Rugby, while Lady Sifton lived in England for most of the last three years of the conflict and into 1919. There they kept a home for their sons and their friends when they were on leave, ill or recuperating from wounds. There too the Siftons maintained a stable of horses, rode to the hounds with many of the aristocracy, and extended their social and business contacts. Greater proximity to the theatre of war, however, did nothing but arouse Sifton's nationalism and contempt for the Allied command. Back in Canada for a few months in 1916, and freed of the censorship of trans-Atlantic mail, he unburdened himself to Dafoe. He was especially incensed that British generals, Alderson and Byng, had been put in charge of the Canadian forces. "Why in the name of heaven are these incompetents put in?" Consider the fate of the Australians and New Zealanders, also under British generals: "Sent like sheep to the slaughter without a chance of success through sheer stupidity." The Canadians had suffered nearly as badly, and in Sir Clifford's opinion, Canadian leadership would have produced "several thousand less casualties."[71] By 1917, when the constitutional relations of the Empire were under discussion by the Imperial War Conference, he concluded that the imperial connection had become a burden. Sifton was, noted Borden in his diary after an interview "out for complete independence."[72]

Proximity to the war, and to his sons and their comrades, did reinforce his convictions about the conflict, that it was being fought for freedom and not the imperial tie. He feared that an attempt might be made to sue for "an inconclusive peace" rather than outright victory. "It is quite clear to me that if it were done it would give British connection with Canada a very serious blow."[73] Plainly this also implied that Sifton wanted to see the government in Ottawa continue to support the war effort at almost any cost; that, however, was becoming more and more uncertain. Laurier had finally agreed in 1916 to a one-year extension of the life of Parliament, but by late in the year it was becoming apparent that a further extension beyond the fall of 1917 was improbable. The main reason was, in all likelihood, that Laurier

ate 18. North American con-
rence on conservation, Wash-
gton, 1909. Seated on President
heodore Roosevelt's right are the
anadian delegates: Sydney Fisher,
ifford Sifton, and Dr. Henri S.
eland.

DOT LEETLE HERO OF HAARLEM

TARIFF
DIKE

CLIFFY VON SIFTON: Hellup! Hellup!!

ate 19. Opponents of the 1911
ciprocity agreement with the
nited States believed that even a
aall breach in the dikes of pro-
ction would lead to a flood of
nerican control of the Canadian
onomy.

Plate 20. Sir Wilfrid Laurier.

Plate 21. Sir Robert Laird Borden.

Plate 24. An armoured vehicle from the First Canadian Motor Machine Gun Brigade, sponsored by Sifton in 1914.

Plate 22. William Lyon Mackenzie King.

Plate 23. Arthur Lewis Sifton.

Plate 25. A labour newspaper's view of Union government. Clipping from PAC, Sifton Papers, vol. 311.

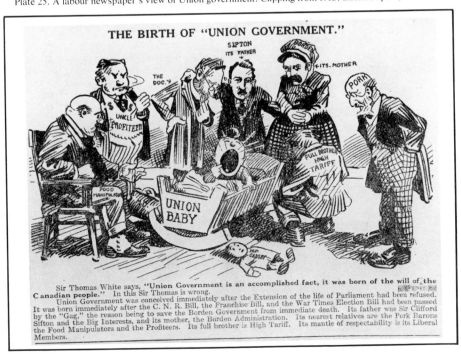

Plate 26. Sir Clifford Sifton in 1917.

and his advisers believed they could win an election. Certain that they could sweep the French-Canadian constituencies in Québec and convinced that Tory blundering and corruption would weaken the government elsewhere, the Liberals' thirst for power was asserting itself over the early pledges to suspend partisan strife. Borden, meanwhile, seemed inclined to leave his party in the control of what Sifton termed "hard shell party Conservatives," making a broadly based appeal to those not committed to the Tory party extremely difficult. Sir Clifford evinced little enthusiasm for Borden's government, yet it was the lesser evil: "I regard the return of Laurier without control of his actions & policy as fraught with possible disaster." Although he had no desire to become involved in another election, the growing possibility of a Laurier victory might leave him with little choice.[74]

The first few months of 1917 transformed the Canadian political scene, and seemingly inevitably Sifton was drawn once more into the heart of the political struggle that produced conscription, Union Government, and a climactic, bitter December election. In October 1915 the authorized strength of the Canadian Expeditionary Force had been set at 250,000 men; less than three months later Borden decided to raise the figure to 500,000, a decision "made without any clear idea whether the necessary men were available or of the means that might be needed to secure them."[75] The commitment having been made, it became a matter of national honour to uphold it. Yet by early 1917 it was clear that voluntary enlistment was falling far short of the numbers required to sustain the strength of the force in light of the high levels of casualties at the front in Europe. Conscription was being urged on the government as a means not only to raise the required manpower, but to distribute the burdens of war more "equitably" by producing a higher enlistment rate in areas such as Québec which allegedly had been delinquent in fulfilling their duty to the Allied cause. Furthermore, the prime minister's visits to the front and to military hospitals in England and France in the spring of 1917 confirmed his resolve that the government and people of Canada must not fail to uphold the troops, whatever the sacrifice. He returned to Canada, quickly obtained the approval of his cabinet, and on 18 May announced to Parliament that conscription was now the policy of the government. A week later, on 25 May, he sought out Laurier and proposed a coalition government composed equally of Liberals and Conservatives, apart from himself as prime minister.[76] Both proposals would shake Canadian politics to its foundations.

At this crucial juncture, having been out of the country for nearly a year, Sifton returned to Ottawa. The events of late May and early June constitute one of the most difficult episodes of his life to explain satisfactorily. He appeared at first to side with Borden; then to attack conscription and support Laurier, while deprecating the potential racial division in the country attendant upon conscription; and finally to reverse himself once more, supporting Borden, conscription, and coalition, and becoming a leader in exploiting the very racial divisions he had previously denounced. He had opposed a wartime election and reversed himself. He declared that there could be no moral justification for imposing conscription without either an election or a referendum on the issue and then supported a government which was committed to neither before compulsory service was implemented. All this happened within the space of a month. Small wonder that observers at the time and since have denounced his actions as duplicitous, and suspected self-serving motives.[77]

One difficulty in unravelling the events of this period, so far as Sifton is concerned, is the sparsity of documentation. None the less, it would appear that some—though by no means all—of the above concerns are susceptible of a more rational explanation than might at first appear. Several points might fairly be made on Sir Clifford's behalf. First, it is possible to argue that he was consistently committed from at least early May 1917 to the idea of a coalition government; careful study of the documents does not show conclusively that he ever actually abandoned this preference. Second, he opposed a war-time election until persuaded that it was inevitable; he preferred, and worked to secure, an extension of parliament for the duration of the war. Third, he feared that a Laurier Liberal government would fail to sustain Canada's war effort; he respected Sir Wilfrid's ability and admitted the desirability of trying to accommodate Québec's views, but he believed that a majority Laurier government would be dominated by French Canada. Fourth, he had far less personal respect for Borden and his government, but believed that they nevertheless were willing to make winning the war a priority. Finally, it is arguable that his stance on conscription was not wholly inconsistent, that his quarrel was with the Borden government's methods more than the principle. He believed that there were alternative ways of achieving the same end and that in any event it was vital for the government to seek proof of widespread support to vindicate its policy.

Beginning in January 1917, J.W. Dafoe undertook a campaign in the *Free Press* to secure a national government coalition.[78] In this, as in most of the events of 1917, the initiative lay with Dafoe, while Sifton eventually came to agree with him and follow his lead. On 5 May Sir Clifford saw Borden shortly before the latter embarked for Canada and pushed the idea of coalition, "if it can be made stable," while opposing any election. On 26 May, Sir Clifford, just returned to Canada, again interviewed Sir Robert about coalition. "He thinks Laurier will support coalition," noted Borden, "but I do not."[79] Perhaps Sifton assumed that compulsory service would be very popular, forcing Laurier to support it, possibly with some face-saving compromise. At the same time there is no statement about Sifton's own views on the subject. It would appear, none the less, that his initial reaction was fairly sympathetic to the prime minister's initiative.

As events unfolded and he began to get a grip on events in Ottawa and public opinion, Sir Clifford's views began to alter. He concluded that Borden had made a serious tactical error in announcing his commitment to conscription prior to inviting Laurier to join the government. The prior commitment would make it very difficult for any compromise, such as a referendum and a renewed recruiting campaign in the interim, to be accepted. He assumed that Borden had "bungled" the affair under pressure from hardline Tories such as Robert Rogers who wished "to play the party game with the object of isolating & destroying Laurier." Conscription, by this calculation, would ally the English-speaking provinces against Laurier and Québec and ensure the Tories of another electoral victory.[80]

If that were the case, the government had sadly miscalculated. Opposition to conscription was "intensely strong" not only in French Canada, but also in labour circles. Sifton anticipated little enthusiasm among the "population of foreign origin," nor had much warmth been found "in the villages and rural districts in Ontario." Even among its ostensible supporters the issue was potentially divisive:

> In the letters which the Members of Parliament are receiving on both sides, the people who say that they are in favor of conscription invariably elaborate the scheme which they are in favor of. Needless to say it is carefully drawn up so as to exclude themselves and their employees.

Under the circumstances, no government could be formed which would have the moral authority to implement conscription without either a referendum or an election. Otherwise it would be unenforceable. Given the state of public opinion, however, it was far from certain that conscription could be carried either way.[81]

This was roughly the state of Sifton's opinion when he interviewed Laurier, who had consulted his advisers and decided to oppose both conscription and coalition. They sensed that the government was divided on Borden's policy and knew it was unpopular with the electorate. Sir Clifford had a good deal of sympathy for their point of view and doubtless was further influenced by Sir Wilfrid's persuasiveness. Indeed, according to a witness of the meeting, he declared "that the proposed Conscription measure of the Government is the most iniquitous piece of legislation ever proposed in a free parliament; we must fight the Government and we will lick them." Pro-conscription Liberals, such as those in Toronto, he confidently predicted "could be brought into line." He also told Laurier that he "should agree to a further extension of the life of parliament if

Conscription were dropped," perhaps even for the duration of the war.[82] Thus he remained consistent: extension was the patriotic policy, and a war-time election should be avoided.

Unfortunately the vehemence of Sifton's remarks about the proposed conscription bill—and he evidently repeated their substance to other leading Liberals—left the understandable impression that he was irrevocably opposed to the Borden government and the principle of coalition and conscription and would stand by Laurier even in an election on these issues. That, insisted Dafoe, was an interpretation that went well beyond Sir Clifford's intentions: "Sifton, like all men of his nervous, sanguine temperament, was apt at times to let his speech outrun his judgment."[83] Dafoe might have been correct. Strictly speaking, not only had Sifton said nothing about holding an election, there is little evidence that he would have welcomed a Laurier government. Conscription could have been fought effectively if the Liberal opposition were united, given the divisions in, and unpopularity of, the Tory ministry. Perhaps a less divisive compromise could yet be worked out and an election avoided.

If that was Sifton's reasoning—and it is impossible to be certain— the debate on the Military Service Bill, introduced on 11 June, confirmed his fears that it would lead to racial division. He asked the prime minister to postpone the measure because of the manifest hostility in Québec; surely Laurier would see the need for compromise. Unhappily the two sides were irreconcilable: there would be no coalition with the Liberal leader, no extension of the parliamentary term, and the two sides became more concerned with manoeuvering for the advantage in the now inevitable election. Laurier believed that he had a good chance of winning such a contest, and the biggest concession he seemed willing to offer was a post-election referendum. What use would such a promise be if a new government were dominated by Québec and committed to a limited war effort? Sifton was now forced to make a choice. Inconsistent as he appeared, it could not have been difficult. Borden's measure signified a commitment to the war effort; possibly a coalition with the Liberals of English Canada would legitimize it and give the government a broad enough base to win. Laurier, whose policy Sifton had once described as "patriotic," would once more be attacked as the man who had sold out the broad interests of Canada for the narrow concerns of his home province.[84]

The shocked Liberals could scarcely believe their eyes when they read of Sir Clifford's "defection" from their cause. They could only attribute the change to the basest opportunism and personal motives: perhaps Laurier had refused a request, or possibly a Borden government would better protect his alleged interests in the Canadian Northern. Not a scintilla of evidence has been advanced to support such allegations. Though not an unbiased observer, Dafoe—who was intimately involved with the coalition negotiations of the early summer and saw Sifton constantly—declared, "I saw no signs whatever that any interest, outside of what he regarded as the interest of the country, was in his mind."[85] Probably in his own peculiar way that was true, but it is equally true that the seemingly inconsistent way he acted in that difficult month after his return can add little lustre to his reputation.

The decision made, Sir Clifford emerged as Borden's chief contact with the dissident Liberals, particularly those of the West. He moved quickly and decisively. It seemed clear that any coalition with the parliamentary Liberals was impossible; the only hope lay with support from the Liberal-dominated western provinces and from the Liberal opposition in Ontario. Accordingly, he arranged that his brother Arthur (premier of Alberta since 1910, and returned to power in a provincial election earlier in June), James Calder of Saskatchewan, and A.B. Hudson of Manitoba, along with J.W. Dafoe, should all be in the capital early in July. All apparently supported conscription, and all soon came away from interviews with Laurier aware of the aging statesman's unalterable opposition to it. But the universe did not unfold quite according to Sifton's plan. Late in June he had confidently assured Borden that a coalition could be formed; Borden enthusiastically responded by offering Sifton a senatorship and a post in the cabinet without portfolio, to which Sifton agreed. After the westerners' interview with Laurier, however, their interest in coalition began to dissipate. Even worse, N.W. Rowell, the pro-conscription Ontario Liberal leader, appeared far more anxious to avert a break with Laurier than to support conscription through a coalition. In a rage Sifton reported to Borden that the Ontario and Manitoba provincial Liberals in particular "were obdurate that they were like men under a spell, that their brains had gone to seed, that nothing could be done with them."[86]

Perhaps not all was lost, however. On 5 July, the day after Sir Clifford's emotional meeting with Borden, it was announced that the western conscriptionist MPs had met with the western provincial representatives and decided to call a convention of Liberals of the four western provinces to meet in Winnipeg on 7 and 8 August. There it was expected that pro-conscription sentiment combined with disgust at Laurier's rejection of compulsory military service would produce a party committed to coalition and enforcement of the conscription policy. Despite rumours at the time, there is no concrete evidence to indicate that Sifton had anything to do with engineering the call for the convention.[87] Two weeks later, however, the plan was dealt a serious blow. A meeting of Ontario Liberal MPs, called by conscriptionist members who had supported the Military Service Act, was held on 20 July. They anticipated not only a firm endorsement of conscription, but also of some "suitable arrangement" for coalition. This in turn would rouse the flagging spirits of conscriptionists in the rest of the country. The result, however, was a rejection of coalition, of immediate conscription, and of parliamentary extension; and an endorsation of Laurier's leadership.[88]

It was a staggering setback for the coalitionists and almost certainly propelled Sifton to public activity once more, since he realized that the outcome of the western convention would be very much in doubt. The first shot in his campaign was an open letter to Hewitt Bostock, Liberal leader of the Senate, published in newspapers across the country on 24 July. It was time, he asserted, to bring Canadians to their senses. The 80,000 or so Canadian men actually in the front lines in Europe at any one time were being decimated in action and, he argued, were nearing the point of exhaustion because of the lack of reserves to relieve them. In a war where "liberty, human rights and free modern civilization" were at stake, Canada had to make every sacrifice, including compulsory service, to sustain her share of the Allied cause. "At this supreme moment," he continued, Canadians "care nothing for Borden or Laurier, Conservatism or Liberalism." Only the cause of the war mattered. Laurier, he thought, had loyally supported the war effort until the time when conscription became an indisputable military necessity. Sir Wilfrid's refusal to recognize this fact constituted an abdication of the responsibilities of leadership, allowing himself to be controlled by the minority opposed to conscription. Under a Laurier government there would be no recruiting in Québec (a distortion of Laurier's position), making recruiting elsewhere insupportable, and finally undermining the Canadian Corps in Europe. The issue boiled down to a simple choice for Canadians: either total support for the war effort, or abandonment of the fighting men and dishonour for the dominion.

> I will go further. The decision of this issue will determine, once for all, whether Canada is a nation, dominated and held together by a national will and national sense of honor, or is a helpless aggregation of sectional communities, held together only by time-serving considerations of sectional interest....We are not fighting for sentiment, for England, for imperialism; we are fighting for the rights of ourselves and our children to live as a free community.[89]

Immediately after the publication of this letter, Sifton took the train to Winnipeg where he held a public meeting and also met with seven members of the three prairie governments. "I am informed," he told Borden optimistically, "that they are unanimous for a coalition war government." They anticipated little trouble in having a resolution to that effect passed at the convention.[90] Following a few days planning strategy for the August meetings in consultation with Dafoe and the Liberal leaders, he continued westward to speak in Regina and Moose Jaw on 31 July and 1 August and to meet with some Liberals in Calgary. Quickly he sensed that the result of the convention was unpredictable. Both in Regina and Calgary he observed that "machine liberals" (who were generally pro-Laurier or anti-conscription) dominated the meetings that were electing delegates to the convention. The government representatives who had apparently supported conscription and coalition were now "hedging considerably" in their speeches. Saskatchewan, he thought, would oppose coalition. "They do not seem to be greatly concerned about the war." Alberta too appeared to be against conscription. "Perhaps the Convention may do better than I anticipate," he told Dafoe, "but on the whole the situation looks very bad to me."[91] Recognizing that he was no longer a Liberal in good standing, nor a westerner, he had no role to play at the convention itself and left Winnipeg for Ottawa on 6 August to await the results.

Sifton's political instincts about the direction the convention would take were substantially accurate. In the first place, it was a convention representative of partisan constituency organizations, with delegates often selected by constituency executives. They were in an intensely partisan mood, having regarded the Borden government as incompetent or worse since 1911 and as having bungled the war effort. They were convinced that a Liberal party united behind Laurier could win an election. Then coalition or compulsory service might be considered—but on Liberal terms. They arrived in Winnipeg firmly believing that putting the Borden government out of office was "the immediate and chief patriotic duty to perform".[92] In the second place, Sifton himself had become a factor. Western Liberals had not forgotten his role in the defeat of reciprocity in 1911; he was widely regarded as an apostate, and any project with which he was associated, such as the convention or the coalition movement, was doubly suspect. His old enemy R.L. Richardson commented in the *Tribune* that it was widely believed that "in trying to elbow his way into public position again, [Sifton] has some selfish or sinister object in view." The newspaper approvingly quoted an editorial from the Toronto *Telegram* which suggested that seeing Canadian politics dominated again by Sifton would be only marginally preferable to being under Kaiser Wilhelm.[93] He was variously denounced by Liberals as "Judas the second," a "traitor," the "arch-manipulator." The Tories, fumed Frank Burnett of Vancouver, "made him a knight for his apostacy in 1911. No doubt if he succeeds in pulling off this nefarious scheme [of coalition] he will be created a lord. Baron Sifton of Klondike would sound well and would help to remind him of his greatest triumphs."[94] "Sifton in the West is a dead dog," another assured Laurier, probably substantially correctly.[95]

Thus it was not entirely surprising that the convention, which considered resolutions on a wide range of subjects, from the tariff to senate reform and women's suffrage, should prove stiffnecked on the two issues that mattered most to Sifton and Borden. It did call for maintaining the "unimpaired strength" of Canada's fighting forces at the front and "the taking of all steps necessary to secure the required reinforcements for this purpose." However, it expressly rejected an amendment, "by conscription if necessary," proposed by J.G. Turriff, MP for Assiniboia and known to be a friend of Sifton. It also endorsed Laurier's leadership, and called for formation of a national government after an election.[96] "Sir Clifford Sifton has found his Waterloo," wrote an enthusiastic Laurier loyalist.[97]

Yet, if on the face of it the convention was a bitter disappointment to those sympathetic to conscription and coalition, it was by no means a total disaster. Anyone bothering to read the debates on the resolutions as printed in the press would readily understand that there was in fact a great deal of sympathy for conscription, if shown to be necessary, and for the principle of a national war government. Many of those who rejected the conscription amendment, for example, claimed that the main resolution in fact already meant conscription of both wealth and manpower. Others claimed that Borden's bungling had not given voluntary enlistment a fair chance, but that if enlistment did not improve under a Liberal government, they too would support conscription. Still others claimed that the resolution endorsing Laurier was only in appreciation of his past leadership. Some were as crass as to admit to supporting him because he could win the election, after which he would be dumped if he refused to support conscription. The reasoning might have been fuzzy, but it revealed considerable divisions about the meaning of the resolutions. Furthermore, the Liberals of Winnipeg lost no time in rejecting the views of the convention, declaring their support for conscription and national government, and rejecting Laurier as leader—positions publicly endorsed by Liberals as diverse in their attitudes to Sifton as E.D. Martin, T.A. Crerar, Isaac Pitblado, and Frank Fowler. Even Premier Norris, who had waffled woefully at the convention, now supported the Winnipeg position.[98]

Moreover, the apparent failure of the convention had not noticeably weakened Sifton's position with the prime minister. Immediately upon his return to Ottawa he was summoned to a meeting with the governor general, Lord Devonshire, along with Borden, Laurier, Shaughnessy, and several other prominent Liberals and Tories. Sifton and Shaughnessy proposed postponing an election by a further extension of Parliament, formation of a national war council, and a renewed recruiting campaign to try to avoid the divisions bound to result from conscription. Borden renewed his offer of coalition. But Laurier, probably expectant of electoral victory in a straight party fight, and undoubtedly heartened by the events of the previous three weeks, refused.[99]

Thus an election by the end of the year became inevitable. But Sifton was doubtful that the Tories could win in a straight party fight, so coalition was still essential if what he deemed a "win-the-war government" was to be returned. In the West he had discovered tremendous hostility among Liberals directed at Borden, though at least in part because of the presence of Robert Rogers, a great symbol both of corruption and of Tory machine politics, in the cabinet. He proposed that the chief justice of the Supreme Court, Lyman Duff, should head a war administration, in which case western Liberals would be more readily reconciled to coalition. When Duff declined, he proposed Sir William Meredith, elderly chief justice of Ontario. Borden's cabinet colleagues opposed a change of leadership, however, and by 14 August Sifton agreed that attempting a change of leadership would create more difficulties than it could possibly solve. Two days later Rogers, who had been one of the strongest Tory opponents of coalition, was forced out of the cabinet, putting a new face on matters from a western perspective.[100]

At first it appeared that Sifton would indeed act on his June understanding with Borden and enter the government. He had not wanted to re-enter public life, but told Dafoe in mid-August, "I have finally decided to go in & fight it out to a finish. I will get the best arrangement I can but if the arrangement is not good I am not on that account going to run away." There would in any case be some advantages to working with the prime minister: "I know Borden & he knows me & we can get along & run the machine effectively." Yet a few days later he changed his mind and told Borden that he would not enter the government.[101] Not only did he appear to have no ambition to be in the government if effective alternative arrangements were possible, but Sifton must have realized that his presence would be nearly as great a stumbling block for western Liberals as that of Rogers. In particular the sensitivities of two western agrarian leaders, T.A. Crerar and Henry Wise Wood, from Manitoba and Alberta respectively, had to be considered. The restive farmers whom they represented had for some years called for reform of the old corrupt political system, of which Sifton, Rogers, and even Borden were considered symbols. Ultimately Wood declined to come in when it was clear that Borden would not go; Crerar, more flexible, was prepared to discuss the situation with the prime minister after being assured that Sifton and Rogers would not be included.[102]

Also in the capital during the negotiations were A.L. Sifton and James Calder of Saskatchewan. The Alberta premier readily indicated his willingness to serve, solving the problem of Alberta representation. Calder, whose constant wavering in face of opposition from Saskatchewan Liberals exasperated both the Tories and Sifton, would have to be the representative of the central prairie province. Crerar, Calder, and A.L. Sifton, along with A.B. Hudson, attorney general of Manitoba, told Borden after meeting in Winnipeg that they would join a coalition government, provided it was not led by Sir Robert. Instead they proposed one of George Foster, Duff, Sir

Adam Beck (of Ontario Hydro), or Sir William Mulock. Borden took the proposal to his cabinet and caucus, even offering to resign, but both unanimously rejected the condition and supported the prime minister.

At once Sifton went to Winnipeg to talk to the would-be unionists. Only Hudson, it turned out, would have difficulty accepting Borden's leadership. The others may well have demanded his resignation in order to retain the support of their own party organizations.[103] It was agreed to drop negotiations until the end of the parliamentary session.

Those remaining weeks of the session would help to tip the scales even further toward western Liberal acceptance of coalition. The government completed passage of two pieces of legislation designed to ensure its return to office: the Military Voters Act, and the Wartime Elections Act. The bills enfranchised every British subject serving with the Canadian forces, regardless of age, sex, or country of origin, and permitted the government to manipulate the enormous military vote to its advantage. The female relatives of soldiers, likely to be sympathetic to conscription, were enfranchised. At the same time, conscientious objectors, Doukhobors. Mennonites, and anyone who applied for exemption under the Military Service Act were denied the vote. Also disfranchised were all persons born in enemy countries or who were born in Europe and spoke as their mother tongue the language of an enemy country, who had become naturalized British subjects after 31 March 1902.[104] It was nothing less than "a bald, reprehensible gerrymander,"[105] where men like Borden and Sifton could justify the means only by claiming the overriding importance of the end of winning the war. Sifton was not a major player in the drafting and passage of the legislation. But he had been consulted. Apparently his only objection was to the partial enfranchisement of women, which he hoped to avoid altogether. Evidently it was also partly at his suggestion that the introduction of the legislation was postponed until after the Winnipeg convention.[106] For a man who so frequently claimed that the war was being fought for liberty and freedom of expression, for a democratic political system, the approval of this legislation certainly calls into question the depth of his devotion to those principles.

As the parliamentary session drew to a close, and in the succeeding week or so, desperate efforts were made by anti-coalition Tories and Liberals to sidetrack the union movement. On the Liberal side, Laurier tried everything from his enormous persuasive powers to floating rumours that he would resign in favour of a conscriptionist Liberal leader, Frank Carvell of New Brunswick. At the same time, hard-line Conservatives believed that the electoral legislation recently passed would guarantee the return of the government with or without the conscriptionist Liberals, so they renewed their efforts to abort the union movement. By early October, however, when Borden returned to the capital after a brief holiday, the union began to take shape. For the first time it appeared that the coquettish coalitionist Liberals were anxious to come in, rather than insisting on being wooed. Sifton slipped into the background of the negotiations as the westerners and Rowell dealt directly with Borden, and James Calder emerged as the leading negotiator of the final details and some necessary concessions by the Liberals. Finally, on 12 October the new government was announced. It included only nine Liberals (A.L. Sifton, Crerar and Calder from the West), and twelve Conservatives; and the Liberals generally occupied less prestigious portfolios. It was none the less a remarkable accomplishment and appeared to put the government in an unassailable position facing the election in December.[107]

Sir Clifford Sifton, who had been anxiously hovering behind the scenes, trying repeatedly to steady the vacillating resolve of the Liberal unionists, wrote to Dafoe, ''I suppose you are feeling somewhat the sensations of 'the day after.' It has been a prolonged strain but the victory is complete.''

Desperate efforts were made at the last moment to upset the coach. The effort from the Tory reactionists was the most dangerous & was very nearly successful. If I had not been at hand to resist firmly it would undoubtedly have been successful.

The new Govt is I think strong enough to attend to its own business, & I shall therefore be free to attend to mine....

There are a good many private heartburnings but such things must be in every famous victory.[108]

It was not, in Sifton's estimation, a perfect government. He thought several of the Conservative members were weak and that the cabinet was much too large for efficient decision-making. Yet he believed that the Union Government would "undoubtedly carry the country at the approaching election"; that it would vigorously enforce the Military Service Act; that Canada could send a fifth division to the front and anticipate sufficient reinforcements to maintain the strength of all units "no matter how long the war lasts"; and that Canada had demonstrated "its national will to stand by its allies in full strength to the end."[109]

Predictably, a man of Sifton's political interests could not merely attend to his own business, particularly when he was so emotionally committed to a Unionist victory in the election, now set for 17 December. He was disillusioned with the government very quickly. The ministers had been too concerned about cultivating their constituencies and had not undertaken important measures expected of them. The things that the government *was* doing were so inadequately presented to the press as to make no impact. The implementation of the Military Service Act was, in his opinion, turning out to be a disaster. On 13 October the government had ordered all Class I men under the act (those who were single, or childless widowers, 20-32 years of age) to report by 10 November; by that date only 21,500 had reported for service, while fully 316,000 applied for exemption, and 70,000 had failed to complete the forms. Thereupon the exemption tribunals in Montreal granted exemptions to 80 per cent of 2,600 cases heard in two days. [110] This level of exemption was totally unjustified, claimed Sifton, and the government ought to file thousands of appeals against the Québec exemptions in the courts. Otherwise hostility against the government in English Canada would be magnified. [111] When a report came in that western farmers were dissatisfied because the draft was absorbing farm labour, making it difficult even to maintain production levels, Sifton replied, "There are tens of thousands of women in the Eastern Provinces who would be perfectly willing to take on farm work....This has been done in England, and as a matter of fact...they not only do the work but they do it well and like it." A similar organization ought to be undertaken in Canada. [112]

Most disturbing, however, were the reports of rural hostility in Ontario to the government, and Sifton began to seek information about the "general attitude of the rank and file of the electors towards the Union Government." He believed that there was "a very decided reaction...amongst the poorer class of voters in favor of Laurier. It is hard to say how far it will extend, but I am very uneasy about it." He anticipated little trouble in the West, by comparison. [113] Furthermore, the Liberal and Conservative Unionists were fighting among themselves over nominations in Ontario constituencies. Finally Borden himself met with Rowell, Frank Cochrane, and Sifton in Toronto on 30 November and concluded that Sifton must be placed in charge of the Ontario organization, with special responsibility to resolve the constituency conflicts. One of the first effects of this conference was the passing at Sifton's insistence of an order in council on 2 December exempting farmers' sons from the draft. [114] It was a political necessity in the short term, despite Sifton's belief that women could fill the gap in the long term.

Operating out of his suite in the King Edward Hotel, Sifton quickly established contacts across the province and began to bring some order out of the organizational chaos. A rare memoir of Sir Clifford at this time was written by Main Johnson, private secretary to Secretary of State N.W. Rowell. At his first meeting Johnson was shown in by Sifton's slightly cross-eyed secretary, and found him "sitting in a chair in the middle of the room, alone and apparently idle....Sir Clifford picked up from the table what appeared to be a piece of garden hose: put one end to his ear, and handed the other to me. The aperture was very small, and I wasn't certain at first exactly how to use it, or how loudly it was necessary to speak." It was a difficult meeting, because Johnson had to relay a message from Rowell reminding Sifton of his great unpopularity and advising him to remain behind the scenes and independent of Cochrane, the Tory organizer. Thereafter Johnson saw Sifton daily, "and never have I been impressed more by any personality I have met."

> He is not spectacular: he talks little, but he has an air of strength, and of calm, which seems to ride above all the conflicting winds and storms.
>
> Never in Canadian politics was there greater chaos than in the Ontario situation during these critical weeks. There seemed to be no road, no way out of the difficulties pressing on every side. Public opinion seemed to be strongly against us, and getting worse all the time.
>
> To go to Sifton, however, was like going to the one power which could grapple with it. Not that he was unaware of the crisis, or minimized it. But he was dealing with it. He had his hand on the throttle, and although it was shaken hither and thither in the commotion, it never loosened its grasp, and gradually, relentlessly, it began to get control.

Johnson was struck by the resemblance of Sifton's profile to that of the Kaiser. Yet, "full face, when Sifton smiles, there is an extraordinary transformation. What in repose and in thought, is stern, becomes benignant, soft and shining—a most attractive, winning countenance."[115]

It is possible that the somewhat awe-struck Johnson, and Sifton, may have exaggerated the seriousness of the situation. Certainly from the disorganized Laurier Liberal side matters appeared even worse. Yet surviving reports from the period of late November and early December show persistent hostility to the government in rural Ontario, and those involved on both sides attributed the Unionist victory very much to Sifton. On 17 December 153 Unionist members were returned to 82 Laurier Liberals; in Ontario the majority was 74 to 8, with the Unionists taking 62.7 per cent of the popular vote.[116] "I still believe that we were in serious difficulty two weeks before polling and that your energetic handling of the situation saved the day," John M. Godfrey of Toronto told Sifton. "I never saw such a rapid change in public opinion. The Tory farmers were placated and the Liberals simply came over to us in droves."[117] Laurier, who believed the Liberals would have won on the original franchise, also attributed much to Sifton. Sir Clifford, he had been informed, had told Borden on 30 November that his government was doomed unless it assured the farmers that their sons would not be conscripted and also that it must carry out a hard-hitting religious and racial campaign. "These instructions were followed from that day to the end, and you know the result."[118]

For his part, Sifton was satisfied with the result and believed that Canada's renewed commitment to the cause would have a positive effect among all the Allies.[119] On 31 December he sailed once more from New York for England, confident at last that the new government could work from a solid foundation. Few, however, would have believed—perhaps including Sifton himself—that the 1917 election had marked his last serious involvement in politics, fully thirty-five years since his first faltering campaign speeches on behalf of his father, and nearly thirty years since his own first successful campaign.

13

The Closing Decade
(1919-1929)

The armistice of 11 November 1918 finally removed the lid from the pressure cooker of more than four years of war. The world that emerged was transformed: bitter, resentful, and disillusioned, seeing its dreams for a return to ''normalcy'' and peace shattered by the realities of wartime and post-war social, economic, and political dislocation. The stated great purposes of war, for which so many lives had been sacrificed, had produced neither a strong sense of moral victory nor a certainty of future peace. Inevitably, the relief that the war was over was tempered for many people by frustration and recrimination, sentiments certainly shared by Sir Clifford Sifton.

He had returned to Canada during the summer and autumn of 1918, but on 23 November—the day after he resigned the chairmanship of the Conservation Commission—he embarked from New York on *S.S. Megantic* to begin wrapping up his affairs in England and preparing to bring his wife back to Canada. He was accompanied on the voyage by J.W. Dafoe, who was on his way to cover the peace conference. There was little to do on the cold, foggy voyage but read and chat, so Dafoe gave Sifton the latest novel by H.G. Wells, *Joan and Peter*. Wells's caustic, cantankerous attacks on the monarchy, British politics, the church, and above all the army, appealed to Sifton's temper and judgment of the British war effort. For Peter, crippled in action during the war, the pre-war world had ''defaulted'' in its promise to the younger generation. ''This war was an outrage by the senior things in the world upon all the hope of the future.'' ''With a vast fleet,'' reflected another character, ''with enormous armies, with limitless wealth, with the loyal enthusiasm behind them of a united people and with great allies, British admirals and generals had never once achieved any great or brilliant success, British statesmen had never once grasped and held the fluctuating situation.''[1] The novelist's acerbic comments on the upper classes met with Sifton's approval. ''Wells' furious, biting indictment of all the English institutions—church & schools, social hierarchy & governing machinery, what he calls Anglicanism marched with [Sifton's] mood,'' observed Dafoe; ''and he chortled over every page.''[2]

Sifton's wartime experience, and the nature of the peace, led him to believe that Canada's interests would be best served by freeing the country from all foreign entanglements, including those within the Empire, and focusing on restoring the kind of domestic development that had charac- terized the decade and a half before the war. That meant, among other things, a resumption of the flow of agricultural immigrants, a moderate tariff fashioned in the best interests of all regions of the country, moral reform of the political system, and maintenance of at least two strong, competitive national railway systems. Yet at the very time when Canada needed a vigorous national party system, the parties were fragmenting and becoming the tools of various regional, economic, or rigidly partisan interests.

The Union Government was a major disappointment to him. Whether justly or not, the government and its leader had acquired an aura of indecision and inertia, if not incompetence. Many of its supporters hoped that it would be more than a ''win-the-war government.'' Ideally it was to have become an agency of reform, its members working together to bury the hatchet of partisan conflict and attempting to realize a new, regenerated Canada.[3] Unfortunately the members of the government remained prisoners of their partisan pasts. Sir Robert Borden, who might have done much to overcome the problems inherent in his creation of 1917, remained aloof, unwell, preoccupied first with the war, then with the peace settle- ment, and was eventually forced by ill health to retire in July 1920. An exchange between Sir John Willison and Sifton reflected the contempt with which even Borden's former allies had come to regard him. ''You have no doubt heard,'' wrote Sir John, ''why the ship that Borden was to christen at Halifax slipped into the water before the ceremony could be performed. It could not wait for Borden to make up his mind.'' Replied Sifton, ''I had not heard that joke about Borden but it is extremely good. He will go down to posterity (as far as he goes) as Robert the Unready.''[4] Cruel as the remark appears, Sifton was convinced that Borden lacked both the courage and sense of responsibility required of a good prime minister. He was angered when Borden took an extended vacation in the fall of 1919 in a futile attempt to recover his failing health, while the bill to nationalize the Grand Trunk Railway was before Parliament, the farmers' revolt was gathering momentum, and a series of by-elections was under way. The prime minister's absence under such circumstances, Sifton told Dafoe, "is a spectacle such as we have not ever had in Canada before. He has funked the whole position and run away. He is not any more sick than you or I."[5]

The truth was that Borden had lost both his health and his enthusiasm for politics. His successor in 1920, Arthur Meighen, was more dynamic and decisive, impressing Sifton at first with his ability, if not his policies. But the new prime minister had never been a warm supporter of the concept of Union Government. He made no apology for his determination to see Conservatism dominate the government; he appeared to Sifton to have an imperfect appreciation of the implications for Canada of the imperial connection and to run his government altogether too much in the interests of the corporate elite of the Dominion. When Meighen, facing a general election and declining popularity in 1921, reorganized his cabinet, Sifton depreciated it as "worse than anybody could have anticipated. [Meighen] seems unable to get anybody except Corporation Lawyers who have heretofore not manifested any capacity for public affairs. [R.B.] Bennett's appointment [as Minister of Justice] strikes me as being a joke."[6] The government stood utterly bereft of its earlier patina of reform. Two days after the cabinet shuffle, Meighen invited Sifton to consult with him about the forthcoming election. Sir Clifford's reply was curt and categorical: the new cabinet was "a Government which I could not support under any circumstances whatever."[7]

Four years earlier, when he had been supporting the formation of the Union Government, Sifton had published his views on reform in *The New Era in Canada*. The book was intended to raise funds for the Red Cross and contained essays by several prominent Canadians on how the war was shaping Canada and how the national life of the country could be regenerated to justify the great sacrifices of the war. Few, least of all Sifton, could have claimed any originality of thought. Yet his forceful exposition of ideas then current drew widespread approval. His great concern was for the cleansing of the body politic, in the conviction that all other necessary reforms would flow readily from a morally healthy polity. Accepting the inevitability of female suffrage, he advocated a universal suffrage for Canadian citizens, but with a longer naturalization period for immigrants of non-British or non-French heritage. The war, however, demonstrated that certain people were not deserving of the privilege: "Canada should bar her doors against the German, the Austrian, the Turk and the Bulgarian, and no person of any of these nationalities should be admitted to Canadian citizenship." He wanted to eliminate gerrymandered constituencies, introduce proportional representation, reduce patronage, further reform the civil service, control election expenses, place an age limit of seventy-five on senators, and broaden the base of membership of the Upper House to help strengthen it. He insisted that Canada must secure the right to a-mend her own constitution, a theme he would develop more fully in future. "The foundations of the New Era," he concluded, "should be the best electorate that we can get, the cleanest elections that we can get, the best constitution that we can get, and the freest political thought that we can get. Upon these foundations the superstructure should be reared." In the new era, the liquor traffic, slums, and poverty would be eliminated. "The ideal State is that in which all citizens, without exception, have the opportunity of living a sane, clean and civilized life, partaking of at least all the necessary comforts provided by modern science, and enjoying the opportunity of spiritual and intellectual development. To build such a state should be the ambition of the young men of Canada."[8]

Though sometimes trite and derivative, Sifton's views reflect a firm faith in the basic institutions of the society and no desire to question them. The war was a means of purification, and a justification; it was not a precursor of revolution. By implication, it was the duty of government to provide leadership to those forces desiring reform, to the liberal, progressive element in society.

The Union Government had acted decisively in only one area of concern to Sifton and like-minded reformers. Within a week of the 1917 election it prohibited interprovincial transportation and importation of liquor, rounding out a movement toward total abolition of the liquor traffic that had developed in the provinces since 1915. "I am immensely pleased at the prohibition move," Sifton told Dafoe. "I only regret that my dear old dad did not live to see the success of the cause for which he gave a lifetime of work & kept himself poor."[9] None of the other achievements of the government produced much credit, at least in the eyes of those like Sifton who longed for some evidence of a new spirit to enliven the post-war government.[10]

There were, none the less, some hopeful signs. Whatever its character would prove to be, a new era in Canadian politics was quickly and definitely taking shape. It was first marked by the death of Sir Wilfrid Laurier in February 1919 and the selection a few months later of William Lyon Mackenzie King as the new leader of the Liberal party. Scarcely seven months after the armistice T.A. Crerar resigned from the government to lead what became the Progressive party; his action simply confirmed the rapid spread of anti-government sentiment among agrarian voters, particularly of the prairie provinces and Ontario. "The present party organizations are illogical and absurd," Sifton had commented in 1916, and he claimed to look forward to "a complete upheaval in Canadian politics."[11]

He had contributed to the "upheaval" in 1917, and had high hopes that the continuing uncertainty of the post-war period would produce a reformed, genuinely progressive Liberal party. Dafoe, reflecting much western opinion, suspected that King would be controlled by a reactionary Québec caucus. Sifton did not agree:

> At the present time the Province of Québec represents the only substantial popular element in Canada that can be relied on to stand for Liberal principle. Not all the followers of King from Québec are genuine Liberals but the majority of them are, and the only hope for anything that can be called a Liberal Government or a Progressive Government in Canada comes from an alliance between King and the farmers. [12]

Hoping to realize that result, Sifton began rebuilding his bridges to the Liberal party, as well as consulting regularly with Crerar. His efforts produced a highly suspicious response from King. The Liberal leader believed (erroneously) that Sir Clifford had been the real power behind the throne of the Union Government in the first year or so after its formation and that he was seeking a position of similar influence in the Liberal party in 1920 and 1921. Even after being told frankly that Sifton's object was simply to bring the Liberals and Progressives together—a goal King himself supported—all King could conclude was that "plainly, Sifton felt aggrieved at Borden not giving him an overseas portfolio during the war, or using his services in a prominent way after he had made Borden." Then he imagined that Sifton's real purpose in proposing coalition was to prevent the defeat of Meighen's government to further some alleged railway intrigues. Supposedly Sir Clifford's plan was to use railway money to support the Progressives, "destroy Liberalism and let Tories win to Help him in Railway schemes." [13] There is absolutely no corroborating evidence to support King's bizarre scenario, but his suspicions may help partially to explain his reluctance to endorse the idea of coalition immediately prior to the 1921 federal election. Sir Clifford, by contrast, was a bit more generous to King, whose abilities he had recognized over two decades, understanding that the inexperienced Liberal leader's task of rebuilding the shattered party was formidably difficult. [14]

More congenial than the mystifying King was T.A. Crerar, whom Sifton greatly admired. Despite the fact that some of the radical, class-conscious "Alberta Progressives" struck Sifton as eccentric, if not dangerous, Crerar's brand of "Manitoba Progressivism" came very close to Sir Clifford's own idea of the philosophy a progressive Liberal party should endorse. "I think a great deal of Crerar," he remarked after a productive interview, "and would like to see him stay in public life." [15] The Progressive leader, however, was even less able than King to pursue the idea of coalition prior to an election placing Sifton in a dilemma during the 1921 campaign. He finally decided to remain aloof and make no speeches whatever. He did sit on the platform in silent support of Crerar during a triumphant Progressive election rally at Massey Hall; he gave E.C. Drury, the "Farmer Premier" of Ontario, some private advice on organization; and he attempted to minimize the number of constituencies where both a Liberal and a Progressive were running against a Meighen government candidate. [16] Yet his influence on the outcome, which produced a Liberal minority government, a Tory rout, and an astonishing sixty-five progressive seats, was minimal. [17]

The possibility of coalition came to the fore immediately. Sifton contended that the Progressives should hold out for a fifty-fifty share in the government, with a written agreement on policy. He believed that if King were sincere about forming a strong national government capable of dealing effectively with Canada's national problems, he would accept such an arrangement, which would at the same time free him from the domination of the reactionary Liberals of Montreal. With anything less, the Progressives would "share the fate of the Liberals who went into the Union Government." Given his own predilections and pressure from his Liberal supporters, King was neither willing nor able to go so far, though he did seek to attract some strong Progressives, such as Crerar, into his cabinet. Such a move, Sifton recognized, would merely result in dividing the Progressives and probably lead to their demise. [18] Throughout the negotiations, which ultimately failed on 24 December, Sifton was in touch with the leadership of the Progressive party, though once again there is no reason to suppose that he had great influence. The new prime minister, however, was infuriated at what he imagined had been a failure owing to Sifton's malign and sinister machinations:

> Sifton has been a thoroughly pernicious influence in our public life. He and Fitzpatrick are two of a kind—conspiring powers behind the throne. Fitzpatrick for love of power—Sifton for love of money. There will be no power behind my throne so long as I have a knowledge of what is going on, other than the power of the people from whom government is derived. I feel genuinely indignant at Sifton. What poor tools men are who will permit themselves to be the puppets of such a man. I am shocked at Drury, Crerar and others.

King still believed that the Progressive campaign had been financed by "the Sifton-Bank of Commerce and Canadian Northern outfit." "I will," he vowed, "bring [them] to their knees before long." [19] Fortunately King's private maunderings were usually confided to his diary; to Sifton's face he always managed a degree of civility, courtesy, and sometimes even warmth.

Sir Clifford, for his part, was very disappointed with the result of the negotiations which, he claimed, had been "done in a crude and amateurish fashion." The cabinet was weak, and "the Montreal crowd" were "definitely in the saddle." On the other hand, "it is clear that the Progressives must take the responsibility for having refused to come in." He suggested to Dafoe that the *Free Press* attitude should be "equally independent towards the Government and towards the Progressives."[20]

Meanwhile, Sifton was no fool, and well understood his isolation from the citadels of power at Ottawa. In October 1919 he and his family had moved to Toronto after twenty-three years' residence in the capital, perhaps symbolic of the change. Many of the older generation of Liberals he had alienated in 1905, 1911, or 1917; the younger generation scarcely remembered his power and contribution under Laurier, and he represented to them, if anything, the less desirable characteristics of a passing age. Friendly as Sifton was with Crerar, both men knew that he was mistrusted by most of the Progressives, so his influence could at best be slight and indirect. Yet there were several national issues which concerned him, and on which he hoped he could exercise some influence, so he turned to the one avenue left open to him. As a public speaker and writer he still could command a national audience, newspapers across the land would publish his remarks and reflect on them editorially, and in this way his views might carry some weight with those shaping public policy.

Among domestic policies, none was nearer his heart than immigration. A strong flow of settlers to the remaining unoccupied agricultural lands of the West, and to the northern clay belt of Ontario and the West, would renew the expansion of the Canadian economy. There was, in his judgment, no greater single responsibility before the government; and he considered that, given his experience, he had a singular contribution to make to the development of policy. Virtually nothing had changed in his mind, however, in the fifteen or more years since he had left office. In some measure he was a physiocrat, believing that society and the economy were only as strong as their agricultural base, which needed to be renewed and extended after the war with a larger permanent peasant population.

The first requirement was to abandon Anglo-Saxon particularism and the indiscriminate encouragement of all British settlers, irrespective of social or economic background. The floodgates had been opened by Frank Oliver, who had abandoned Sifton's selective policies, cancelled the North Atlantic Trading Company contract, and equalized the bonus to agents for all British immigrants, whether agricultural or not. "The mechanic, the artisan and the drifter....flooded Canada," maintained Sifton, "and would have precipitated a crisis in labor if it had not been for the war."[21] What was needed was a return to principles of quality rather than quantity in immigration policy.

> When I speak of quality, I have in mind, I think, something that is quite different from what is in the mind of the average writer or speaker upon the question of immigration. I think a stalwart peasant in a sheep-skin coat, born on the soil, whose forefathers have been farmers for ten generations, with a stout wife and a half-dozen children, is good quality. A Trades Union artisan who will not work more than eight hours a day and will not work that long if he can help it, will not work on a farm at all and has to be fed by the public when work is slack is, in my judgment, quantity and very bad quality. I am indifferent as to whether or not he is British born. It matters not what his nationality is; such men are not wanted in Canada, and the more of them we get the more trouble we shall have.

The peasants he had in mind were to be found in Scandinavia, Belgium, Bohemia, Hungary, and Galicia. "These men are workers. They have been bred for generations to work from daylight to dark. They have never done anything else and never expect to do anything else. We have some hundreds of thousands of them in Canada now and they are among our most useful and productive people."22

Sifton agreed that renewed efforts should be made to obtain agricultural settlers from the United States and Britain. But these people would not come in large numbers, and in any case would not be prepared to endure the marginal farming conditions likely to obtain in the clay belt. Even so, he went out of his way to minimize the difficulties of farming in the region. Conditions in the clay belt, he contended, were "a good deal easier than they were when my grandfather went with his family on a bush farm in the county of Middlesex and started to clear it." The government should get the movement started by hiring crews to clear a few acres on each quarter section and erect a rudimentary cabin and shelter for animals, making the expenses a charge on the land. In this manner, he calculated, it would not be long before 500,000 farmers and their families would have settled the region and made it productive.

There were critics of Sifton's ideas. E.J. Ashton of the Soldier Settlement Board, for example, pointed out that 500,000 farmers would require eighty million acres of land at a time when government figures showed only thirty-four million acres of unoccupied lands within a reasonable distance of railways, and much of it quite unsuited to any form of agricultural settlement. "As there are just under 50,000 individual farmers in the Province of Manitoba, the settlement of 500,000 individual farmers would mean the adding of ten Manitobas to Canada in ten years from a farming standpoint.'' Furthermore, prior to the war immigrants had been able to rely on income from railway and other construction to help get them established; in the 1920's no comparable development seemed likely, while the land itself would be much more costly. Sifton quickly dismissed such difficulties: ''People's ideas of what kind of land is fit for settlement undergo radical changes.'' Most of the ''foreign settlers'' on the prairies had occupied land thought unfit for settlement when he had taken office in 1896. ''It will be found that the land is available when required.''[23]

Sir Clifford was destined to be frustrated in his efforts to persuade the government. He had expounded his notions to James Calder under the Union Government, ''but he has never shown any capacity whatever to assimilate an idea on the subject, and has shown himself, in my judgment, entirely incapable.'' He hoped for change under King, but soon found that the responsible minister, Charles Stewart, a former Premier of Alberta, was no better. In disgust he noted that ''Stewart showed his incapacity first when he started to organize an Immigration Board. The Lord Almighty could not conduct an immigration policy with an Immigration Board. Then he went up West to find out what kind of settlers they wanted in the Western Provinces, having himself been a settler and for years in a Western Government.'' Sifton was instrumental in persuading King to replace Stewart with James A. Robb, MP for Chateauguay-Huntingdon, in 1923. He provided the new minister with a careful resumé of his ideas, adding that ''the immigration problem can no doubt be solved, but the solution of it depends upon the capacity and the driving energy of the Minister, and upon that alone....It is a tremendous task. The Minister has to work, suggest, devise, inspire, every day.'' Quick, decisive action along the lines suggested by Sifton would ''at once secure the confidence of the country.''[24]

While levels of immigration did recover somewhat by 1923 and 1924, and while some settlement of the clay belt regions did occur during the decade, the development fell far short of Sifton's expectations. Farming in most of the clay belt, despite a few pockets of marginal success, was not generally viable. With most of the good land occupied, only the Peace River region emerged as a new settlement frontier, so that, despite Sifton's assertions, there was limited opportunity for agricultural immigrants compared to the pre-war years. Finally, the government could not ignore public opinion, which remained cool or even hostile to the kind of European peasant that Sifton wanted to attract. As had been the case earlier, Sifton shared such prejudices only in a limited degree, regardless of his crude notions of ethnic distinctiveness. He did concur with one observer who favoured limiting of Poles, presumably because they were often viewed as urban slum dwellers or else a poor class of farmers. Similarly, southern Europeans should be avoided; and Orientals, particularly the Japanese, excluded altogether. ''I am unequivocally opposed to the allowing [of] Asiatics to settle in

Canada," he wrote. "They are not adapted to our country, and they will create difficulty and wholly unnecessary economic and social problems, of which we have enough on our hands at the present time."[25]

For Sifton, Canada's economic problems were susceptible of fairly straightforward solutions, provided the government would act as a tough minded regulator of a free enterprise economy, encouraging reasonable competition and protecting both individuals and regions against exploitation. This conviction underlay his ideas on railways, freight rates, tariffs, banking and taxation policy.

The Canadian Pacific Railway had deeply feared the emergence of a massive government-owned competitor, such as that which took shape between 1917 and 1923 as the Canadian National Railway system. The president of the CPR, Sir Thomas Shaughnessy, had vigorously lobbied the federal government to adopt a scheme whereby the CPR could control the whole system, a policy which Sifton strenuously opposed both during the war and when Shaughnessy resurrected it in 1921. There were, he confessed, some attractive short-term benefits that might seduce the public to support the plan. But there were also in his estimation four "insuperable objections" to it. First, it would "destroy the virility and efficiency of the C.P.R." Second, "it would certainly create a monopoly of management and service which would be intolerable." Third, "it would create a monster of patronage and financial power which would dwarf everything else in the country, the Government amongst the rest." Fourth, within a short time a single union of all railway workers would emerge, "which would make it its business to hold up the Management for whatever terms it saw fit to exact and an inevitable conflict would follow between the public and the operating staffs of the railway."[26] In fact, Sifton would have much preferred to see the government make concessions that might have enabled the Grand Trunk to survive as a strong third railway in a competitive Canadian system.

A further proposal of a senate committee in 1925 to merge the managements of the rival systems under a committee of fifteen was equally intolerable. In all probability, he told Dafoe, it would mean effective CPR monopoly:

> The fact is that we have got a lot of half-baked, half-educated busybodies in public life who simply cannot keep still and are continually propounding some Smart-Alex proposition, which they think will bring prosperity to the country. The fact is that we have at the present time the best railway service in the world without any exception whatever, and it is rapidly getting itself into a position when it will not only be self-supporting, but will pay interest on a fair reasonable capitalization; thereafter within reasonable time it will probably pay back all the

money that has been sunk in it....Our policy should be that these two railways must be kept separate at any cost whatever; [and] that the country will have to pay the deficit in the meantime until the Canadian National catches up.[27]

Sifton, Dafoe, and the *Free Press* were, however, preaching to the converted so long as Mackenzie King was in power, for he too opposed so great a concentration of power.

Even a strongly competitive system required some regulation if the interests of the consumers and producers of the country were to be safe-guarded and the national economic objectives of the government were to be realized. Inevitably the issue of freight rates arose once more as the western Progressives sought to have the Crow's Nest Pass rates of 1897 imposed once more, following a three-year suspension which was to end on 7 July 1922. It was a difficult test for the new King administration, which was naturally under heavy pressure from the railways to continue the suspension under which freight rates had risen as much as 45 per cent. At the same time, however, wheat prices had declined sharply since the war, so that the issue had become extremely sensitive in the West. Sifton was firm in his belief that the railways could still operate profitably under the "Crow rates" and that the onus ought to be on them to prove that they could not do so. In April he shrewdly told King that restoring the low freight rates and creating a wheat marketing board would solve two of the major grievances of the western farmer and undercut the need for a separate Progressive party. King was impressed with the advice and eventually a compromise was worked out which provided for reinstatement of the "Crow rates" on grain and flour, while the other rates remained suspended for one or possibly two more years. This in turn became the basis of a permanent solution in 1925.[28]

The railways responded, as might have been expected, by raising rates significantly for carrying wheat and flour east of Thunder Bay to Québec and Halifax, a matter of considerable moment to the farmers because not all their crop could be shipped from Lakehead ports during the shipping season. Much of this traffic, as a consequence, began to move in American channels. Sifton was infuriated. It struck at the very heart of Canada's historic policy of keeping Canadian trade within Canadian channels, and particularly undermined the viability of the National Transcontinental policy of 1903-4. He sought out Sir Henry Thornton, president of the CNR, and explained "very briefly what the reasons for building the Trans-continental were and why it had been so extravagantly constructed, pointing out that the main reason for the standard of construction was to enable wheat to be carried cheaply." Sir Clifford bluntly told Thornton that he would fight the railways to the bitter end on the issue. "I pointed out to him that if he succeeded in carrying the 'carry-over' wheat to Canadian ports that he would be doing more for the unity of Canada than anything that had been done since the Canadian Pacific was built.'' The railways responded by claiming to fear that the Americans would retaliate with lower rates of their own, leading to a ruinous rate war. That line of argument, Sifton told Dafoe, "leaves me entirely cold.''

> The wheat which is in question is only a small fraction of the Canadian crop which they carry over at Port Arthur and Fort William and the idea that the United States Railways are going to make war on us because we presume to carry our own wheat which is left over after the navigation season at the price which we think is a good paying price for our own Railroad, is the most impudent and preposterous proposition that I ever heard of. I don't think that the Interstate Grain Commission [*sic*] would for an instant allow the rate of the United States Railroads to be upset by any such proposition. And I am entirely in favour of going ahead and fighting it out with bare knuckles....If we are to be told by the United States Railways that we cannot carry our own wheat on our own Railways to our own ports because they will start a rate war on us if we do, then we had better start the rate war now.

Once again, despite his vigorous advocacy and that of the *Free Press*, only a limited victory was achieved.[29]

Of no less concern to the western farmer was the manipulation of rates for grain, flour, and cattle by combinations of shippers on the Great Lakes and the Atlantic Ocean. Sifton had always contended that a Canadian national transportation policy would encourage shipment of goods from Canadian ports in Canadian bottoms, but once again the transportation interests were conspiring to avoid competition, skim profits from the producers, and the ultimate result could be damaging to Canada's national interests. He was suspicious of the situation in 1920, but it was not until September 1922 that the *Free Press* unleashed a steady and detailed assault which led directly to government commissions to investigate both monopolies.[30] During the agitation, Sifton himself wrote a series of front-page articles for the *Free Press* in a racy trenchant style—in fact, the only time he became directly involved in writing for the paper.[31] His concern was not to present a detailed analysis, but to provide a stark outline of the issues in a manner that would rouse western opinion and stimulate the Progressives to pressure the government. "Your writing must have some punch in it," Dafoe reported. "At any rate it has raised a certain amount of hell around here."[32]

Sir Clifford urged Dafoe to go to Ottawa, once the commission reports had substantiated the newspaper's charges, to see that the Progressives were firmly united on the issue and to attempt to pledge King to definite action. In 1924 Sifton personally interviewed several cabinet ministers, telling them "that if they merely promised and did not perform, the Progressives would drift away from them and necessarily assume an attitude of antagonism." Besides legislation to deal with the combine on the Great Lakes, Sifton wanted the government to challenge the fixed cattle rate on the Atlantic by being prepared if necessary to "charter a fleet of ships and carry the cattle themselves" for $10 a head instead of the prevailing $25 between Montreal and British ports.[33] The government did agree to legislation to destroy the Great Lakes combine, but it was inclined at first to try subsidizing the steamship companies to carry cattle at $10 a head. Eventually, however, they decided to offer a contract to an English shipping magnate, Sir William Peterson, to compete with the Atlantic combine and force down rates; but Peterson died before the contract became effective. In the latter part of the decade a growing market in the United States for Canadian cattle took much of the pressure from the government. Sifton had been very disappointed both at the government's failure to act and at the weak support given his campaign by the Progressives and the Canadian Council of Agriculture. "These farmers' bodies," he remarked sourly, "always make fools of themselves whenever an opportunity comes to perform a real service for their constituents."[34]

Sir Clifford was no more impressed with the Progressive stance on the tariff. At first he was inclined to agree with the farmers that the Union Government was unduly wedded to protection, and he saw the development of the Progressive movement as a logical response to a legitimate grievance. Despite some Progressive rhetoric about abolishing the tariff, he thought that the majority of farmers were "reasonable and moderate in their views," The minority government of Mackenzie King proved somewhat more responsive to Progressive demands, though of course never satisfying them. None the less, in 1922 there had been a slight general reduction in duties, followed in 1924 by substantial reductions on agricultural implements and many other imports. The benefit was pronounced for the agricultural community, and the Progressives began to clamour for more as the government was preparing its 1925 budget. The agitation angered Sifton. "The plain fact is," he told Dafoe, "that speaking in general terms the tariff has been as much reduced as it is possible for any Government to carry out. I think that the West has got about as much as they can reasonably expect in that line, and there is no sense whatever in a persistent and incessant howl for what has been found by Government for thirty years to be impracticable, that is to say, we cannot have a tariff framed exclusively with regard to the ideas and desires of Western Canada. That was the stand I took when I was in office and I would take it again now if I were in office."[36]

Sifton's consistent position since 1896 had been to support a moderate protectionist tariff, flexibly adjusted to the advantage of the whole nation. The tariff must not be dominated by any single class or region or Canadian unity would suffer. The Progressives, he thought, should be grateful for what they had gained and recognize that they could procure more for their constituents in other directions. Thus the drastic reductions in the automobile tariff in 1926, made largely to satisfy the Progressives, struck Sifton as "a piece of lunacy." He perceived King as caving in to western pressure and likely to alienate the manufacturing community.[37]

One of the issues in the twenties which Sifton believed ought to have been of more interest to the Progressives was banking policy. A significant series of bank failures and amalgamations was resulting in greater dominance of the field by a relatively few large banks, a trend which seemed to Sifton to strike at the heart of a vitally competitive economy. The Bank Act in his opinion stifled the establishment of new small or local banks, leading to demands for a greater governmental role. In the fall of 1922 the Canadian Council of Agriculture, partly in response to western frustration with the major banks, called for a royal commission, a central bank of rediscount similar to the American Federal Reserve Bank, and restriction of the right to issue bank notes to the federal government. Sifton declared that a commission would be a waste of money; that a rediscount bank would have powers that could easily be abused; and that federal power to issue bank notes should be even more restricted than it was, presumably because its policies could be influenced by political pressures. The one thing that Sifton agreed with was that the Bank Act should be amended to "induce local capital to engage in banking." That is, Canada should encourage the development of small banks with capital of $100,000 to $250,000, similar to the situation in the United States, subject to reasonable regulations. "We should have comparatively free trade in banking. This is especially necessary in the Western country." Meanwhile, banking capital had been concentrated in the Dominion "to an extent that is almost criminal." All amalgamations should be prohibited; weak banks, or those not fulfilling the terms of their charters, should simply "be obliged to...wind up or liquidate or go out of business." As to western complaints about the inaccessibility and inflexibility of the major chartered banks, Sifton was categorical: it was "sheer nonsense. The whole of my observations throughout life have led me to the conclusion that borrowed money is too easy to get and more men are ruined by easy loans than by inability to get loans at all." In fact, "the trouble in the west is not that there is not enough money loaned. It is that the Banks should be to some extent local & sympathetic to & conversant with local conditions."[38]

Sir Clifford further elaborated his views in a memorandum for the Progressive MPs in March 1923 and in a speech to the Cobourg Rotary Club in January 1924."[39] He decided that a "Central Board" of three or five experienced businessmen should be appointed by the government to serve two or three major purposes. Under its auspices banks should be audited regularly in the hope that some of the discreditable activities that had led to bank failures would be prevented or uncovered. The board should act as a bank of rediscount, issuing Dominion notes, and attempting to bring stability to the banking situation, particularly for smaller banks. It would study the entire credit system systematically and be thus able to warn the banks of policies that were too strongly inflationary or deflationary. He also contended that banks should have to cover their liabilities to the extent of at least 25 per cent in paid-up capital, rather than going as low as 10 per cent, which he claimed was quite common. This, he believed, would slow the growth of the large banks.

When the Royal Bank swallowed up the Union Bank in 1925, he expressed his concern that the "Bank of Montreal crowd and [Herbert] Holt crowd" were slowly acquiring a stranglehold on the business community, making it more and more difficult for anyone out of favour with the small clique who controlled the banks to acquire substantial investment capital.[40] Sifton's purpose in all this was to develop a banking system that would reinforce a vigorous capitalist economy, not sap its vitality through monopoly. The capitalist system, he declared, was the product of hundreds of years of development, and of millions of people engaged in commerce; although it could be improved in details, the basic concept could not be altered. The duty of government lay in a different direction:

What we want, what we must constantly devote our attention to, is the correction of the admitted evils of the system which we have. The commerce of the world is a huge affair. Millions of men are engaged in carrying it on. Its powerful currents at times bear hardly on the weak and unfortunate. It is the supreme task of our modern legislators to remedy these evils, to protect the weak against those whose capacity, good fortune or circumstances, render too strong. In short, to prevent undue aggregation by the strong at the expense of the weak.[41]

Protecting the weak, however, must not lead to undue curbs on the well-to-do. Sifton was resigned to the inevitability of the income tax, but he did not like many of its features. The exemptions, he declared in 1920, were too high. "Everybody who is above the starvation line ought to pay something." He believed that only a relatively few people—mainly those worth more than $75,000—were paying the tax at all. "The income tax is as high as it can safely be made as far as rich men are concerned." Any higher taxes would lead to "a Hegira of the brains and capital of the country." He also objected to the method of collection, whereby the taxpayer had to assess himself, but could be subject to prosecution for errors in calculation. The law was not enforceable, but would place thousands of law-abiding citizens in fear of government bureaucrats. "It is my considered opinion that this is the most flagrant outrageous & utterly indefensible piece of tyranny that I have ever heard of in a supposedly free country." Far preferable as a means of raising revenue was the sales tax. It was "the most logical, sensible method...and perfectly fair. If a man spends $2000 supporting his family, he pays the tax on $2000. If he spends $50,000 he pays the tax on $50,000, If he builds an expensive house he pays the tax on all the materials." The higher income and inheritance taxes promoted by the Progressives would only stifle the brains and initiative of the country.[42]

In the years after the 1921 election Sifton grew increasingly disillusioned with the Progressives. To his mind they had a magnificent opportunity, if united and aggressive, to achieve much for their constituents and force King to come to terms with them. Instead, the indecisiveness born of internal conflict over the purposes and methods of the party drastically curtailed their effectiveness. In November 1922 T.A. Crerar resigned the leadership in frustration and was succeeded by Robert Forke, described by W.L. Morton as "a bluff, amiable Scots Canadian of transparent honesty and transcendent modesty."[43] Though regretting Crerar's loss, Sifton thought that Forke was the best possible successor. Unhappily, Forke did not have the force of character necessary to impose unity on his fractious party; on some occasions, in fact, he was embarrassingly inept. In 1925, for example, when the Liberal government presented a pre-election budget that did not offer additional concessions to the Progressives, Forke managed to produce a critical amendment that was ruled out of order, and the Progressives subsequently divided on the main motion. The whole affair, wrote Sifton in disgust, "is about the most ill-judged and injudicious political proceeding that I can think of in the last fifty years."[44] By 1925 he had concluded that the Progressive party had largely destroyed itself. "My own notion is," he informed Dafoe, "that the Progressive Party may possibly live usefully through the next election, but it has shot its bolt as far as usefulness is concerned and every purpose would be served if they could take the place of a Western, and perhaps more radical wing of the Liberal Party."[45]

Meanwhile Sifton's relations with the Liberal party had warmed somewhat. Prime Minister King went out of his way to consult with him fairly frequently, though he was usually still suspicious that Sir Clifford had devious personal motives underlying every statement—perhaps a cabinet post or other appointment or some concessions to benefit his mysterious investments. It is possible that Sifton would have accepted a cabinet post if strongly pressed by the prime minister, but there is no corroborating evidence that he desired or actively sought one. As with other contemporaries, King was struck with the force of Sifton's analysis of conditions and the options available to the government, noting in his diary that Sir Clifford was "a clear thinker." For his part, Sifton concluded that King was a weak leader, well intentioned but badly advised and altogether too much under the influence of the "Montreal crowd." By 1923 he thought the government was losing strength, adding, "in fact the leadership of Meighen is the only asset that the Government has," the Tory leader being "too extreme and vindictive" to capture widespread support. Early in 1924 he bluntly told King and several of his colleagues that "they were on the toboggan slide" and would certainly lose the next election unless they acted decisively on such policies as the lake and ocean freight rates, development of the St. Lawrence seaway and power, and promotion of immigration. The country would respond to a strong, positive lead from the government.[46]

As an election drew nearer in 1925 and it became evident that the government was in difficulty, speculation mounted that Sifton would enter the cabinet. "There are signs," Sifton noted, "that some people are very much alarmed as a result of having got the idea that I was going back into active politics. It is a bit amusing. However, they need not lose any sleep over it as I have no such intention at present." Nor did King make any offer. Nevertheless, just ten days before the election the prime minister, recognizing at last that his government was in trouble, wired Sifton urgently asking him to speak in its support.[47] Sir Clifford responded with two speeches, at Aurora on 23 October, and four days later at Brampton. He appealed to the Progressives and Liberals to join to gether to defeat Meighen and the Tories. He attacked Meighen's promise to retaliate in kind to high American protective tariffs. The existing tariff, he insisted, was about as fair to all parts of the country as could be devised. The Tory proposals would seriously affect the cost of living, and benefit only the "idle rich." "It passes the wit of man to explain how that is going to benefit the ordinary ratepayer of Canada." The main result would be the disruption of Confederation. Canadians should stop complaining and try to appreciate their advantages: "It is my deliberate and considered opinion that, man for man, the people of Canada are the best off of any people in the world."

While also alluding to his views on railway and ocean freight rates, and on bank mergers, Sifton declared that his main purpose in entering the fray was to warn Canadians of the alleged plot of Québec interests, led by E.L. Patenaude, to win a substantial part of Québec for the Conservatives. Their reward would be the control of the government by the Montreal financial community, the raising of tariffs, and the destruction and "looting" of the Canadian National Railway system for the benefit of the CPR. The proposed railway monopoly would be an unmitigated disaster for the

Dominion, as would government by "arrogant" and "conceited" businessmen. "As a matter of fact, in a great many cases, the men who are successful in making money are extremely ignorant in regard to anything outside of their own business, and my experience has been that men who are in a large way in business, and whose minds are concentrated on their business, are very unsafe guides in regard to the conduct of public business." Never, he declared, had "any more nefarious, more sordid and more contemptible conspiracy" been "hatched against the interests of the people of any country."[48]

Once again congratulations poured in on him, one supporter going so far as to claim, "Those speeches of yours were the only life in the Liberal platform." However, as he himself admitted, he had not started early enough in the campaign to have much appreciable effect. On 29 October the government appeared to have been defeated, as the Conservatives gained 116 seats, to ninety-nine for the Liberals, twenty-four Progressives and six Independents.[49] The result was not unexpected, admitted Sifton. There was widespread dissatisfaction with King and his government, particularly the "narrowness in the view which they took of large questions, which very materially impaired the confidence of the businessmen in Ontario in the ability of government."[50]

Unfortunately, the results of the election were unlikely to produce a more decisive government. Meighen was well short of a working majority, particularly since the majority of the Progressives and Independents were less likely to co-operate with the Tories than the Liberals. Yet King had undeniably suffered a major reverse. Among those whom he consulted on his future course was Sifton. Sir Clifford's advice was forthright: "There are apparently one hundred and twenty five members elected on low tariff against one hundred and seventeen elected on a high tariff leaving out the three labor members. Under these circumstances I think it is your clear duty to carry on." Not only did the advice coincide with King's own desires, but as he reflected on the election he concluded that the party organization had been woefully weak. Who better to undertake the necessary rebuilding than the legendary Sifton? Probably swallowing a good deal of pride, King sent one of his inimitably convoluted and flattering appeals to Sifton:

> I feel confident that the present is a moment in which to realize all that we most wish for in the way of a Party united from coast to coast, and prepared to put the supreme interests of the Dominion over all lesser considerations. The key to it all is effective organization. In that all important requirement no one can bring so much in the way of experience and knowledge and resource as yourself.[51]

It cannot have taken Sifton long to decline the offer. He had no more desire to resume organizational responsibility than he had had twenty years earlier for Laurier. Furthermore, he had little confidence in the ministry. His "disgust," he told one correspondent, stemmed "principally from the apparent inability of the Government to frame a comprehensive policy of a national character which would unite the different sections of the Country." He had offered his advice whenever asked, but "I cannot say that anybody has shown much comprehension of what I have suggested."[52]

As it happened, Sifton's speeches in 1925 marked his last intervention in Canadian elections. He stood aloof from the events of the spring of 1926 which led to the resignation of the King government, the short-lived Meighen ministry, and the calling of another election in the summer. Once again King made an elaborate appeal for Sifton's aid, but this time Sir Clifford's reply was curt: "I expect to go to England shortly and have no intention of taking any part in the election." The Progressives were a wasted force; Meighen's Toryism was quite insupportable; and King seemed to lack the courage, decisiveness, and vision to be an effective national leader. Best, perhaps, to stand free of them all.[53]

There was one area, nevertheless, where Sifton and King had much in common: Canada's relations to the British Empire and the League of Nations. That they shared common ground so often seemed little less than miraculous to Sifton. "King does not manifest a very keen appreciation of the details of the constitutional law," he once wrote, "but he seems to have a very unerring instinct for getting to the right spot and jumping over any artificial defects."[54] "The right spot" was essentially isolationism, a desire to ensure that Canada would be free of any entangling alliances, whether in the Empire or the League of Nations, that might draw her against her will into conflicts in which she had no interest. From that position stemmed Sifton's desire to secure a clarification of Canada's constitutional status so that the Dominion's complete independence of action would not again be in doubt.

Neither Borden nor Meighen had clearly understood the situation, in Sifton's opinion. The government's "ignorance & ineptitude," he warned in 1919, were getting Canada "committed to all kinds of things."[55] As the Imperial Conference of 1921 drew near, he feared that the British politicians were hatching a plot to "take Canada in and make her responsible for everything the British government does," a position he believed Meighen willing to accept. "Canada," he asserted, "will have to conduct her own foreign policy and let Great Britain do the same, neither having any responsibility for the other."[56] Dafoe tended to think that Meighen would protect Canada's interests at the conference, but Sifton remained sceptical. When the prime minister returned and spoke of Canada's continued support and commitment to the Empire, Sir Clifford almost sneered at Dafoe: "So your prize package statesman Meighan [*sic*] has sold the pass—gate, moat, portcullis & drawbridge. His Québec speech means a united Empire with a consultative council of premiers and the whole empire responsible, financially, militarily & navally....It means responsibility for Great Britain's foreign policy in Europe & the whole world. It means we are a part of the quarrelling & warring world of Europe instead of the peaceful world of America."[57]

Sir Clifford was no less vehement in denouncing the League of Nations and the international aggression committed by several of its leading members, including Greece, France, and Britain. The League was "a preposterous and expensive farce and amounts to nothing more than a part of a machine designed to involve us in European and Imperialistic complications." Canadian supporters of the League of Nations Society were mere "busybodies" who did not comprehend the dangers before them.[58] The proper role of the League should be as a voluntary association of nations desiring to keep the peace through arbitration and discussion. Canada ought to follow the American lead, partly because they accurately perceived the risks of League membership and partly because Canada's proper foreign policy ought to be "to avoid any trouble with the United States, and we have no business in the League when the United States is staying out." Without the Americans, the League would be nothing more than "an Agency for the European countries to use in settling up their disputes, which we have absolutely nothing to do with. Our participation is expensive, will do us no good and may possibly get us into trouble."[59]

Once Mackenzie King was installed in office, Sir Clifford lost no time in attempting to educate him with respect to Canada's international situation. The prime minister was among the dignitaries at a meeting of the Ottawa Canadian Club in April 1922 when Sifton spoke on "The Political Status of Canada." He pointed out that despite the evolution of Canada's constitutional powers since 1867, the Dominion did not have the power to amend her own constitution:

> So long as we lack full powers of government, so long as we have to go to the British parliament for amendments to our constitution relating to the relative jurisdictions of the provinces and the dominions, so long as the Privy Council holds to be ultra vires attempts of the Provinces to alter their constitutions and no power exists in Canada to validate these changes, so long as we are powerless to change the constitution of our Senate, so long as we lack the power to regulate the conduct of Canadian citizens the moment they step over the boundary line, so long

as for all these things we have to go to the British Parliament for leave and power, it is in my judgment idle to talk about equality of status, idle to talk about our sovereign power, idle to talk about having achieved national status.

There was, he insisted, no question that Canada remained legally and constitutionally subordinate to Britain, a situation affecting her international standing. Even though Canada had in practice acquired the power to negotiate her own treaties, formal ratification still lay with the British government. Even worse, "with respect to making peace or war, Canada has no legal or constitutional power whatever." Even at the Washington Disarmament Conference Canada participated, not in her own right, but because she was part of the British Empire. "We have no right to expect any foreign country to recognize us as a separate political entity until we have taken proper means to legally constitutionally and internationally define our status." Even membership in the League and the Peace Conference did not in Sifton's opinion have anything more than a psychological impact. He wanted "a constitutional instrument which shall specifically contain provisions which confer upon the Dominion of Canada complete sovereignty and national status," with no vestige of subordination.

Sir Clifford quoted Lloyd George as saying, "The Dominions since the war have been given equal rights with Great Britain in the control of foreign policy of the Empire....The advantage to us is that joint control means joint responsibility" for "the burden of Empire." That, asserted Sifton, was a distinct repudiation of Canadian policy for fifty years; instead of Parliament having the power of decision on matters of participation in war, Canada was assumed to have undertaken "responsibility for the wars of Great Britain all over the world in return for being consulted." With astonishing prescience, Sir Clifford gloomily predicted that "if [the British] get into a war over oil concessions in Mesopotamia or Persia and get an army massacred or captured...our Government is liable to get a cable calling on it to implement its responsibility and send an army to take part in the war."[60] The prime minister thought it a "splendid address" and promptly called on Sifton for further discussion of Canada's status.[61]

Five months later the telegram foreseen by Sifton arrived. Britain indeed appeared to be on the verge of serious conflict in Asia Minor and sent cables requesting support from the Dominions. Sifton was appalled at the "military enthusiasm, swashbuckling & froth" among many Canadians in response. "Is it possible," he demanded, "that the Canadian people have learned nothing and are prepared to bequeath to their children the legacy of warfare hate & bloodshed which makes Europe a shambles?" The *Manitoba Free Press*, at least, must stand firmly opposed to any involvement. Dafoe responded with editorials stating that only the Canadian

Parliament could involve Canada in war and certainly not the British government. It was the same position staked out by the King administration. But Sifton attributed much to the effectiveness of Dafoe's editorial work: "The whole press of Canada was on the verge of an hysterical shriek for war. Your first article steadied them. I think the danger is over." He certainly did not minimize his own role in Canada's response to the so-called Chanak crisis either. "In my own mind," he wrote, "I accept full responsibility for furnishing MacKenzie [*sic*] King with a ready-made policy. His declarations on the subject were almost word for word what I said in an address at Ottawa [the Canadian Club speech] where King was present." The prime minister's cable to the British government declaring that Canada would not go to war except by decision of Parliament was, in Sifton's opinion, "a definite constitutional advance."[62]

Whether the response to the crisis marked a significant step in the evolution of Canada's national status has been much debated, although there is no doubt that the affair vindicated and heightened the suspicions of men like Sifton and King about the imperialists. But Sir Clifford was not at first much impressed by the prime minister's next attempt at constitutional advance, the signing of the Halibut Treaty early in 1923. The Canadian government asked the King through the Colonial Office to appoint Ernest Lapointe, minister of marine and fisheries, as the sole British-Canadian signatory of this treaty between Canada and the United States, omitting the customary British signature. No one argued that Canada had long had the power to negotiate her own treaties; it was the formal power of being the sole signatory that Mackenzie King desired to secure. In Sifton's opinion, the fact that Lapointe had been appointed on the advice of the British ministers meant that his signature bound the whole Empire, just as the British signature on a treaty had always done. What Canada should have insisted upon was direct access of the Canadian government to the monarch through the king's secretary, in the same way that the British government approached the king. Then the treaty would have been binding on Canada alone, and the Canadian government would clearly have equal status as one of His Majesty's governments.[63] Yet, insofar as there was a constitutional advance in the proceedings (and Sifton did later term it a "turning point" in the history of Canada's foreign affairs), it may again have been partly owing to Sifton's influence. On 9 January 1923 he addressed the Canada First Club of Toronto on the constitution, in the course of which he alluded to the limitations on Canada's treaty-making powers. Two days later when the federal cabinet took up the Halibut Treaty, they "decided to have it signed only by Lapointe." Mackenzie King did not refer to Sifton's speech directly in his diary, but there is every indication that he followed Sir Clifford's pronouncements on such matters carefully, and he had secured a copy of the speech.[64]

Sifton's views naturally found full expression through J.W. Dafoe in the *Free Press*. The editor was then at the height of his powers; his views largely coincided with those of King; and the prime minister decided that he wanted Dafoe to cover the Imperial Conference in the autumn of 1923 to effectively offset the "Tory imperialist" despatches that otherwise would predominate. Sifton was happy to let Dafoe go. He believed that an effort would be made "to misrepresent Canada's position" and that at the Conference there would be an attempt "to involve Canada in commitments which neither her duty nor her interest will warrant her in undertaking." The conference probably would "result in a showdown," and he fully expected that "King will stand by the right views."[65] Dafoe was much less sanguine. "I must say I have very little confidence in King," he told Sifton. "I am afraid his conceit in his ability to take care of himself is equalled only by his ignorance and I should not be surprised if he should find himself trapped." Dafoe was especially fearful that the issue of status would be shelved, while specific policy matters would be discussed "which may qualify or destroy the present status of the Dominion." King should submit a resolution and have the status question settled first.[66]

Sifton evidently concurred, and drafted such a resolution. During the voyage to England, Dafoe showed King Sifton's "proposed definition of equality," but the prime minister "fought shy of it." He said he had to consider the effect on Canadian politics and clearly preferred not to press the issue in so definite a form. Nevertheless, Dafoe left the resolution with King, who eventually did make use of it. During the conference he steadily resisted any and all attempts at centralization of the empire or recognition of common responsibility for policy and defense. Despite everything, Lord Curzon presented the conference with a draft statement about its proceedings which to the Canadians "meant the acceptance in its most unqualified form of the Doctrine of the joint foreign policy with joint responsibility." At this King reportedly "went up in the air" and blasted the British proposals in vigorous terms. He subsequently went further and read out Sifton's draft resolution. "He said he was asked if that represented his own views and he said it did; but he was not sure, he told them, it was yet an opportune time to make this a matter of record."[67] The conference thus produced none of the ringing declarations of equality of status that Dafoe and Sifton would have liked, but King had earned their grudging respect as a defender of Canada's national interests. The conference, in Dafoe's opinion, was "a triumph for the idea of a voluntary association of autonomous nations."[68]

Still, the failure to secure a firm declaration of equality of status left Sifton uneasy. The fact that Britain retained the power to declare war or peace for the entire empire was exceedingly dangerous. "England is like the other great nations of the world—militarist and imperialist," he told the

Toronto Women's Liberal Association in 1925. "She holds large portions of the earth's surface. She means to keep them, peacefully if she can, but by force if she has to. We are a great, young, peaceful nation whose sole desire is to develop our resources in peace....Canada will never agree to be responsible for the colonial wars of Great Britain.''[69] Furthermore, there were additional constraints on Canadian sovereignty: the Dominion still could not amend her own constitution; the Judicial Committee of the Privy Council overruled a dominion statute abolishing appeals of criminal cases to the Privy Council; the British Merchant Shipping Act was held to have precedence over Canadian legislation even in Canadian waters; so did British bankruptcy laws have precedence over Canadian provincial legislation; Canada did not have extra-territorial powers over her citizens as other countries did; and during the so-called "King-Byng crisis" of 1926 the governor general had presumed to exercise powers (in denying his prime minister a dissolution) which the British monarch would never have attempted to assume. Mackenzie King had declared that "the destiny of Canada is to be found as a continuing member of the British Common-wealth of Nations.'' "I concur with his statement,'' noted Sifton, "but upon the condition that as a member of the Commonwealth we have equal powers and that our powers are precisely and exactly the same as those of Great Britain.''[70]

Thus both Sifton and Dafoe were anxious that the Imperial Conference of 1926 should produce the sort of definition of equality that had been avoided in 1923. King was unlikely, they agreed, to "give anything away,'' but they doubted that his habitual caution could produce anything definitive. They had decided to send D.B. MacRae, assistant editor of the *Free Press*, to cover the conference, and Dafoe drafted (and Sifton approved) a memorandum for MacRae setting out their concerns, along with a draft resolution:

> That the Dominion of Canada should of right be and is of equal status with Great Britain in the management of its own affairs; and the Parliament of Canada and the Legislatures of the provinces should, under the British Crown, possess the same rights in regard to the management of the affairs of Canada, domestic and foreign, as the Parliament of Great Britain possesses in regard to the affairs of Great Britain.[71]

Much to Sifton's irritation, King seemed prepared once more to temporize while South Africa and Ireland pressed the issue. Finally he told Dafoe to cable MacRae "to tell King we expect Conference definitely to settle Canada's complete and plenary competence to deal with her own affairs external and internal and will not be satisfied if he accepts anything less.''

Shortly thereafter King did move to help draft a resolution that the disputing parties at the conference could accept; his action undoubtedly derived mainly from the situation in London, but Dafoe and Sifton came to believe that their intervention was not without effect. At last there was a declaration on status which Sir Clifford could find "perfectly satisfactory." The self-governing Dominions were declared to be

> autonomous Communities within the British Empire, equal in status, in no way subordinate to one another in any aspect of their domestic or external affairs, though united by a common allegiance to the Crown, and freely associated as members of the British Commonwealth of Nations....Every self-governing member of the Empire is now the master of its destiny. In fact, if not always in form, it is subject to no compulsion whatever.

But if that statement, and those affecting the signing of treaties and the status of the governor general, were adequate, Sifton was displeased with those aspects of the declaration covering shipping and foreign policy. On the whole, however, he concluded that the declaration marked "a very distinct advance...though, as I expected, we have no particular reason to thank King, whose qualities become less and less admirable as they are more closely exposed."[72]

The affirmation of dominion status reduced the pressure for Canada to secure the power to amend the constitution, though Sifton naturally hoped to see some such measure succeed. Recognizing that the conference declaration had no legislative effect, he thought that the imperial Parliament should be asked to take the next logical step, namely to pass an act amending the BNA Act, and "divesting itself expressly of any authority over the domestic or external affairs of Canada." He was aware that the federal government could not unilaterally ask the British government to act and indeed had warned King that the provinces must be consulted on constitutional change.

> I do not take an extreme view with regard to the rights of the Provinces, but I think it goes without saying that, when put in charge of our own affairs, it is quite out of the question that the Dominion Parliament should be able to amend the constitution in such a way as to affect the jurisdiction of the Provincial Legislatures without their consent. As to whether the consent should be unanimous, which I would not advocate because that would nullify the provision, by a two-thirds majority, or by a simple majority, or by a popular vote, is a matter for consideration....
> When Canada is put in entire control of her own affairs, by the

instrument which gives her that control, a statement should be made setting forth the constitutional guarantees which at present exist with a declaration that these guarantees are assented to by every Province and that they are the basis and condition of Confederation.[73]

Any such instrument, furthermore, would have to protect "clauses respecting the French language, the Province of Quebec, and the educational rights of the minorities, Protestant and Catholic, as contained in the British North America Act, the Manitoba Act and other Constitutional legislation which should remain permanent and unamendable as part of the fundamental law."[74] This position marks a striking reversal of Sifton's attitude to the rights of the same minorities thirty or forty years earlier. It probably represents not only the mellowing of age and his removal from western politics, but a realistic assessment of what would be necessary to make an amendment formula workable. Mackenzie King and Ernest Lapointe did raise the issue at the 1927 Dominion-Provincial Conference, but did not press it in light of the hostility of Québec and Ontario.[75] If he was disappointed at the result, Sifton apparently did not record his views.

By contrast with the problems of the Empire and the League, Canada's difficulties with the United States seemed much less serious to Sifton. "The main business of Canada in foreign relations," he once told Dafoe, "is to remain friendly with the United States while preserving its own self-respect."[76] The most obvious concern was Canada's relative impotence should serious disputes arise. For this reason, "the more we get working with the U.S. by joint commissions the better for us. It builds up a body of precedents which may be of great use to Canada in times of stress in holding the U.S. steady." More broadly, a tradition of peaceful and amicable settlement of disputes would stand Canada in good stead. Sifton's views also were predicated on the perception that the United States was more peace-loving than any other major power. He was, for example immensely impressed with the Harding government's disarmament proposals at the Washington Conference in 1921, while anticipating that they would be opposed by "the armament and munitions clique in England."[77]

Of course Canadians had to be aware of the need to preserve their own independence. That was one reason that Sir Clifford so strongly opposed the bank amalgamations of the twenties. When there were only five or six banks left in the country, he feared that it would be a simple matter for the Rockefellers or Duponts to acquire control. "This," he noted, "is really the kind of annexation that we have reason to be afraid of." Similarly, he regarded American action in driving up the protective tariff during the decade as ample justification for his course in opposing reciprocity in 1911. The reality was that Canada was "not an important factor in American tariff-making, and I do not think that we should seek to be so." Had Canada been aligned with the American economy in 1911, the adjustments of the 1920s would have been immensely disruptive.[78] Curiously, given these concerns, Sifton was wholly sanguine about heavy American investment in Canada. "American capitalists who come to Canada," he told a reporter in 1925, "are as a rule shrewd and sensible men of affairs. They are good citizens and never attempt to exert any undue influence on the conduct of our affairs."[79] That was a proposition that later generations of nationalists would seriously question. Nonetheless it underscored Sifton's tremendous optimism concerning the potential vitality and strength of Canada's future internal development.

The years after 1919, wrote J.W. Dafoe, "constituted one of the happiest periods of Sir Clifford Sifton's life."[80] Free from public responsibility and financially secure, he was able not only to indulge his interest in public questions, but also to lead a more relaxed private life than he had known in over thirty years.

His sons had matured through the war and now sought to find their own niches in the business world. Jack, the eldest, joined the *Manitoba Free Press* in 1908, eventually becoming secretary-treasurer of the company. Those who knew him regarded him as a man of undistinguished talents and possibly somewhat lazy. The second son, Winfield (or "Win"), was undoubtedly the most ambitious of Sir Clifford's sons. He seems, however, to have inherited his grandfather's propensity for spreading his energies in many areas at once and ultimately failing in most things he tried. Although admitted to the Ontario bar in 1913, he quickly decided on a business rather than a legal career. He was associated with Royal Securities Corporation in Montreal before the war and with Neptune Trust and the marine insurance business in London during the war. At the end of the war he was managing director of Thynne, Nicholson and Duncan, an export trade company in which his father appeared to have an interest, and a director of at least four foreign trade companies. He also claimed to have been the "inventor and patentee" of "various chemical and mechanical processes in connection with manufacture of explosives, optical glass and scientific instruments." Then Sir Clifford brought Winfield back to Montreal where, along with his youngest son, Victor, he hoped his boys could salvage the Export Association of Canada, Limited. However the post-war collapse in international trade proved too much for the company, which went into liquidation in 1921. Sir Clifford appears to have lost as much as $202,000 in the venture.[81] By no means did he believe his sons responsible, and there is every indication that he was particularly proud of Winfield's determination in the succeeding years to establish himself independently.

The third son, Harry, had been partially crippled by, and evidently nearly died from, some hip disease as a child. Yet he was the most engaging and popular of Sir Clifford's sons and served as his father's private secretary from 1919 to 1929. In this capacity he relieved Sir Clifford of the need for routine administrative concerns about his investments and also performed many of the functions about which, because of his deafness, Sifton felt awkward—not the least of which was the problem of conversing on the telephone. The immediate post-war careers of the two younger sons, Clifford and Victor, remain somewhat obscure, though Clifford finally decided on a legal career and was admitted to the bar in 1927, following which he did practise law for some years. Victor was shy and awkward in dealing with others, often appearing brusque or tactless. Yet it was the opinion of Dafoe, who knew the family well, that Victor was "the ablest of all the Siftons." He was as brilliant as his father, but "Sir Clifford was impulsive and frequently made mistakes which had later to be recovered." Victor rarely did. [82]

It was especially fortunate that Sir Clifford's sons could take over his affairs, because Lady Sifton was very frail, apparently at least in part from goitre problems, and also a heart condition, while Sifton himself had a succession of assorted health problems as a result of which he seems to have become something of a hypochondriac. As always, he had little faith in Canadian doctors and frequently sought out physicians whom he deemed to be the leading international figures in their fields, or sometimes even mechanical cures. For example, when he was diagnosed as having high blood pressure, he concluded that "there are no Doctors who know anything about successful treatment for high blood pressure," but claimed great relief from a "High Frequency Violet Ray instrument." [83] He and his wife regularly sought relief through extended stays at various spas and resorts in New York, New Jersey, Virginia, and Florida, all the while complaining about the excessive costs. "These resorts," he told Harry with unconscious irony, "have become simply hold up places, encouraged by the newly rich or by people who do not know any better & the expense is quite out of proportion to any value received." [84]

In 1922 he went to Philadelphia for a tonsillectomy, which was promptly followed by painful gout. "This," he told a friend, "is surely unfair to one who is the third in a direct line of total abstainers. There is a tradition in our family that on the paternal side there was for several generations a line of whiskey drinking fox hunters in Ireland. I fear that I am getting the benefit of some of their excesses." [85] Despite such flashes of humour, it is clear that Sifton no longer had his great reserves of energy. In 1924 he wrote to Harry from a New York resort, "I am getting fed up with walking to and from the [golf] links. The distance does not seem much when one is chasing his golf ball but it is different after the excitement of the game is over." [86] He was periodically depressed as well by the continued worsening of his deafness.

In June 1924 he had another ear operation, hoping that "the nightmare of being practically stone deaf which has been hanging over me for the past year will...be removed." Apparently a slight improvement was achieved, but the chief benefit was that further deterioration was arrested.[87]

A few months after moving to Toronto in 1919 the Sifton's fifteen-room house at 57 Douglas Drive was seriously damaged by fire.[88] Shortly thereafter Sir Clifford decided to build a more substantial residence, as well as nearby homes for Harry and Clifford, on Lawrence Avenue, about a mile east of Yonge Street. He found the cost "appalling," but seems to have spared no expense and included a large barn for as many as seventy horses, with exercise areas.[89] "Armadale," Sir Clifford's residence, was occupied in 1924. That Christmas four of his sons, three daughters-in-law, and his several grandchildren celebrated together. "I think they all were very happy," he told T.A. Burrows, "and for myself I think the Lord has been a great deal better to me than I deserve."[90]

The warm pleasures of the family reunion were shattered less than two months later with the death of Lady Sifton, aged sixty-three, on 19 February 1925. Apparently Sir Clifford did not record his sentiments, but there can be no doubt that it was a shattering blow to him. His letters to his sons in the 1920s show constant solicitousness about how "Mama" was faring; but the loss was the greater because in the deepest darkness of the despair and isolation resulting from his deafness she was the one person with whom he could readily communicate and count on for reassurance. His purely social contacts with others had been limited for years, and he had long since dropped his memberships in the clubs—a major source of male fraternization in that era—because of his hearing impairment. Hence his dependence upon his wife was greater than was often appreciated, and he never wholly recovered from her loss.[91]

In the post-war years Sifton appeared not to be interested in significant new departures with respect to his business affairs. Unfortunately, the available records provide only scanty information, and certainly nothing reliable about many of his sources of income. The Canadian Western Natural Gas, Light, Heat and Power Company is a case in point. In the post-war years the extent of Alberta's vast reserves of natural gas was scarcely understood. The company feared that its proven reserves might soon be exhausted and wanted some of its industrial customers to convert to coal. It also sought and gained from the Public Utilities commission in 1921 permission to increase rates from 35 cents per thousand cubic feet to 48 cents in hope of increasing conservation, maintaining a reasonable return on investment, and providing capital for further exploration. The cities of Calgary and Lethbridge violently opposed the increases, a situation which caused uneasiness among the British stockholders. Eventually the provincial government permitted the increase, but the profits of the company were tightly controlled, and Sifton finally sold off his interest early in 1925.[92] What profits he might have made are unclear, but it would appear that he sold at an opportune time.[93] Apart from this concern, Sir Clifford continued to have sizeable investments in British Columbia timber lands and in property, including an interest in the Canadian Northern Prairie Lands Company. He also became a director of the British Empire Steel Corporation in 1920, because the company wanted his advice on how to handle the western Canadian press and the western MPs, "who only see in every big industrial consolidation in the East, a menace to themselves."[94]

Sifton's main business concern during the decade of the twenties was preserving the viability of the *Manitoba Free Press*. It was, of course, far more than a business proposition to him; he told one enquirer in 1920, "just at present I have not the least desire to sell [the *Free Press*] and it would have to be more than a commercial price that would tempt me."[95] Not only was the paper profitable, but it had become a source of pride to him, enhanced by his relationship with John W. Dafoe. Yet there is no question that from a business standpoint the paper was at a crossroads. The commercial situation of Winnipeg had changed, new forms of competition were emerging, and even the functions of a newspaper had altered dramatically within the previous decade or so.

Since the early 1870s Winnipeg had assumed that it was inevitably the gateway to the West and the region's natural distribution centre. The *Free Press* had always supported and benefitted from that metropolitan pre-eminence, and for a while it gained a position of leadership among western papers, successfully marketing both the daily and weekly as far west as Alberta and as far east as the Lakehead. By the early twentieth century, however, its position was being challenged, as was that of Winnipeg itself, by the rapid growth of new prairie centres—Calgary, Edmonton, Saskatoon, Regina—and commercial competition was even being felt from the port of Vancouver. The opening of the Panama Canal already had an effect on transcontinental commerce, and the prospect of a Hudson Bay Railway at last being completed would further detract from Winnipeg's position. By the early twenties the *Free Press*'s constituency had contracted to include only Manitoba and some parts of eastern Saskatchewan, and it began to fear competition from the Regina and Saskatoon dailies in western Manitoba.

Moreover within Winnipeg it faced a new kind of competition from the *Tribune*, since 1920 a Southam paper. Although the *Free Press* continued to boast a strong edge in circulation,[96] as part of a chain the *Tribune* could, at least theoretically, become a dangerous competitor. The *Tribune* at first lost money for the Southams, and they proposed a scheme to eliminate competition between the papers and maximize profits. The *Free Press* as the stronger paper responded coolly, and nothing seems to have come of the proposals.[97] The *Tribune* naturally became much more aggressive, with all the advantages of a large chain of newspapers behind it: access to national news services formerly beyond the resources of the paper, national promotions and features, syndicated columnists, and so forth. It could, and did, lure *Free Press* staff members with higher salaries. Fortunately, the *Tribune* management also wanted the paper to be profitable, so it was not inclined to reduce subscription rates. But *Free Press* management was keenly aware of how vulnerable their position had become; if the Southams were willing to run their paper at a loss for a few years in serious competition, the *Free Press*, without additional resources, could readily be destroyed.

Furthermore, the paper had discovered that its readership had little inherent loyalty to the paper. During the battle over subscription rates in the war period, the desertion of its subscribers had forced the paper to meet the *Tribune*'s rates. Later, during a six-week battle with Eaton's over advertising costs, the paper lost 8,000 subscribers. Many of those who switched told the *Free Press*, according to E.H. Macklin, "We are sorry to discontinue the old Free Press. We have taken it in our family for years, and always liked it, but the 'Missus' wants to see the Eaton advertisement and as the Eaton advertisement is only carried in the Tribune we have to take that paper and we cannot afford to subscribe for two."[98] The quality of the newspaper, faced with such questions, ultimately meant little. In addition, as Sifton told a friend, the paper had to take care not to offend any large segment of the community:

> Of course you know that the old-time custom of large newspapers taking a violent stand on every question that comes up in a community, and trying to bludgeon their views into their readers, is a thing of the past. It rarely does any good and sometimes does a great deal of harm. In questions where the community is violently divided the general attitude of the newspaper is to give the news and articles on both sides, as they are presented.[99]

A memorandum drawn up for Sifton in 1923 considered all these issues and concluded that the shareholders should either consider sale of the property or contemplate acquisition of additional newspaper properties. The Free Press Company property was valued in 1923 at $2,079,615.86, and its average annual net earnings over the previous six years were $208,054.41, or better than 10 per cent on valuation. That was a good profit margin, and far better than in any previous period, but increased competition from either the *Tribune* or the Saskatchewan dailies could significantly reduce it.[100] Under the circumstances, for Sifton there could be only one answer. The *Free Press* had entered into radio broadcasting in 1922 to maintain its communications edge.[101] Now expansion was essential to rationalize the newspaper market and give the *Free Press* a broader foundation. In March 1924 the Siftons opened negotiations to try to acquire the *Saskatoon Star* and *Regina Post*, both evening papers. Unfortunately, the owners of the papers, who also owned the *Saskatoon Phoenix* and *Regina Leader*, wanted an all-inclusive sale of the four papers for $1.5 million and the assumption by the purchaser of nearly $200,000 in additional debt. Such a price was utterly out of the question; Sifton countered with an offer to buy 51 to 53 per cent of the stock for about $600,000, but the negotiations ultimately collapsed.[102] Four years later the Siftons succeeded in purchasing the papers, which survived as the *Star-Phoenix* and *Leader-Post*. By then, however, the purchase was substantially in the hands of Sir Clifford's sons, and the details of the purchase have not been made available. There is no question about the papers' profitability, however: in 1928, profits from the *Free Press* were $574,581.02; from the *Leader-Post*, $168,451.54; and from the *Star-Phoenix*, $120,941.25.[103]

Yet it would be misleading to portray Sifton's concern with the paper as focusing wholly, or even largely, on profits. In one of his last letters to his sons, he wrote:

> Finally with respect to your newspaper properties, when great prosperity comes I adjure you not to regard it as a spending fund to spoil yourselves and ruin your families. Regard it as a sacred trust to buttress and strengthen these properties, and enable you to hand them down as a great and powerful influence for the good of Canada. In time of prosperity prepare for trouble. Follow the policy that I have followed.[104]

A burden of concern for the welfare of the country dominated Sifton's interest in newspaper ownership. From the beginning of his association with J.W. Dafoe in 1901 he had committed himself to leave the details of policy and business in the hands of the editor and the business manager. It was understood, however, that he would be fully consulted and informed; and when in the post-war years his greater freedom from public responsibility permitted it, he constantly supplied Dafoe with his opinions — occasionally in two, or even three, letters a day. Often he was simply bursting to express his views directly in the paper: "Several times lately I have composed in my mind elegant & inspiring editorials for the F.P.," he told Dafoe in 1919. "Always however when it comes to dictating them I relent. You have a very slight conception of the value of what you have been deprived of."[105] Only once—during the freight rate dispute of 1923—did he give in to the temptation. "The range of his knowledge was so great and his power of penetrating to the kernel of an intricate question so remarkable," Dafoe wrote in 1929, "that his views always threw a strong and penetrating light on the most intricate subjects. But he always played the game with the men in charge and on the spot. He gave us the best of his mind and his thought, but the decision was ours and ours was the responsibility."[106]

Generally Dafoe was correct. But he overlooked a few occasions in which Sifton issued practically direct orders about editorial policy. When he was concerned about proposals to increase the levels of income tax, which he knew to be popular among the farmers, he bluntly told Dafoe, "I positively will not allow the Free Press to lead any such movement." On another occasion, when the spectre of western separatism raised its head and Dafoe had not been sufficiently vigorous in denouncing it, Sifton wrote, "under no circumstances whatever can the Free Press have anything to do with people who advocate secession or disruption of confederation. We will stand for a united Canada under any and all circumstances and use the sledge hammer if we have to." When the paper ran a full-page article on his old enemy, Sir George Foster, Sir Clifford simmered in fury: "I very seriously object to a page of the Free Press being taken up for the purpose of advertising a useless, garrulous, crooked old humbug." Dafoe had long known of Sifton's hostility to Foster and admitted that the article normally never would have appeared but for an oversight on his part.[107] In fact, this last case was a fairly accurate reflection of the relationship between publisher and editor, because Dafoe well understood the limits of Sifton's tolerance, and certain topics were normally ignored by the paper. On other topics the editor's own proclivities were held in check or modified by the owner's views; a case in point was Dafoe's internationalism, which was largely restrained by Sir Clifford's isolationism, but enjoyed freer rein after Sifton's death.

On the other hand, Sir Clifford understood that there were limits to how far Dafoe could be pushed, and beyond a certain point he would not insist on his views. One of those limits was direct interference with the staff of the paper. He was absolutely livid when the Ottawa correspondent of the *Free Press*, E.H. Chisholm, failed to report his celebrated Canadian Club speech in 1922. When Chisholm pleaded that he had had no notice of the speech, Sifton retorted, "he is not attending to his job. The Prime Minister, the leader of the Opposition, all the leading members of the Government, the Chief Justice of the Supreme Court and all the leading citizens of Ottawa were there." For months, he declared, he had been dissatisfied with the substandard Ottawa service in the *Free Press*, and this episode had brought matters to a head. Chisholm must be replaced and the bureau reorganized:

> Now, my dear Dafoe, I hope you will not feel either irritated or hurt at what I have been saying. The whole staff of the Free Press and everybody connected with it look upon you with a sort of reverence, which prevents them from expressing any opinion about matters that are within your direction. The time has come, however, when it has become necessary for me to speak....There is no use in showing the slightest consideration to anybody. Any attempt at kindness will confer no permanent benefit on the recipient. There is only one test that can be applied and that is efficiency.

Dafoe replied very mildly, deflecting Sifton's wrath, and pointing out that it would cost substantially more to provide the kind of service that the owner appeared to desire. He naturally spoke to Chisholm about Sifton's complaints, but left him at his post. Sifton subsided, and a year and a half later Dafoe quietly informed him, "We had to let Chisholm go and he ceases to be our correspondent at the end of the year. His trouble, of course, was drink."[108] Dafoe appears never to have permitted Sifton to dictate to him concerning the staff of the paper; he was admired by his staff because he would shield them and give them every opportunity to prove themselves.

At the same time, Sifton did not hesitate to tell Dafoe when he approved of his editorial work, which was frequently; and there was no question of his enormous pride in his editor and the quality of the paper. He saw that Dafoe and Macklin were well paid and rewarded with substantial bonuses for their efforts. After receiving one such reward, Dafoe expressed their great pleasure at this recognition: "E H [Macklin] & I have never been vocal on the subject but I think you know that we understand and appreciate the generosity and consideration wh[ich] we h[a]v[e] always received from the chief proprietor."[109] The formality of this understated emotion was characteristic of the two men's correspondence. Despite all their years of friendship, they appear never to have been on a casual first-name basis, always beginning their letters, "My dear Dafoe," or "My dear Sifton," or "Dear Sir Clifford." There was always an element of reserve, if not secrecy, in Sifton; not until Dafoe was preparing his biography of Sifton after the latter's death and had access to Sifton's papers did he realize how unique and privileged his position had been as Sir Clifford's chief confidant.[110]

No chapter of Sifton's adult life would be complete without locating him at or near the centre of some major public controversy. In the 1920s the issue was the construction of the Georgian Bay canal, enormously complicated by the question of who controlled the right to hydro-power development on the Ottawa and St. Lawrence rivers.

In 1894 one Joseph Kavanagh McLeod Stewart succeeded in having Parliament incorporate the Montreal, Ottawa and Georgian Bay Canal Company. It was empowered to construct a canal for shipping from Montreal to Georgian Bay via the Ottawa and Mattawa rivers, Lake Nipissing, and the French River. The charter also included the right to develop hydro power along the route, a concession then deemed to be of little value. The idea of the canal went at least as far back as 1819 when, oddly enough, the Legislative Council and Assembly of Nova Scotia recommended that the British undertake the project as a means of creating an inland route well protected from the United States. There was no doubt that the project was feasible from an engineering standpoint, and that a system of dams, locks, and dredging could permit most ocean-going vessels to use the route. It would be 282 miles shorter and nearly three days faster than the Welland Canal route between Montreal and Port Arthur.[111]

From the beginning it was assumed that the project could only be realized by some form of marriage between private capital and federal government assistance, in much the same manner as the nation's railways had been constructed. The senate investigated and commended the plan in 1898; Israel Tarte endorsed the scheme in 1899; in 1904 Laurier publicly committed the government to it; and by 1908 he was reiterating his intent to proceed "as soon as the resources of the country permit." Also commending the scheme were such luminaries as Robert Borden, Sir William Van Horne, and J.J. Hill.[112] In 1899 a British company, the New Dominion Syndicate, headed by Sir Robert W. Perks, acquired control of the Canal Company charter, with an unquestionably serious intent to proceed as soon as the government co-operated. Perks himself had exceptionally strong qualifications as a lawyer, civil engineer, and British Liberal MP; he had constructed railways and harbour works in the United States and South America.[113]

Frustrated by the government's constant stalling, despite its verbal assurances, and having invested sizeable sums in engineering studies and some preliminary work, the Syndicate decided in June 1909 to hire Sifton as a lobbyist for its interests; in return, Sifton was to obtain one-third of "all profits derived from the promotion of the said enterprise, the construction of the said canal, the development of water powers, or other transactions incidental to or arising out of the said enterprise."[114] Sifton hoped for quick approval by Parliament and began to search for allies, ranging from the Bank of Montreal to Nova Scotia coal interests who could anticipate greatly increased sales in central Canada. Early in 1910, however, Sifton concluded that there would be a conflict of interest between his post as chairman of the Conservation Commission and his representation of

Perks's interests, because the commission would have to advise the government on navigation and power on the Ottawa. He asked that the 1909 agreement be terminated.[115]

The syndicate continued negotiations with the government, and Laurier finally promised the London officials in the summer of 1911 that he would propose taking up the project in 1912, either by supporting the Syndicate, or by government construction, in which case he would ensure that the British investors "were not unfairly treated." Following Laurier's defeat in September 1911, the syndicate lost no time in pressing the Borden government and met with the new prime minister's assurances that he wanted to push an arrangement through Parliament in 1913. Procrastination once more became the order of the day as the country slid into depression and the government found its depleted resources swallowed up in bailing out the railways. Eventually it appointed a commission to evaluate the project, and then after the outbreak of war it intimated that it would take over the charter with reasonable compensation; but once again repeated postponements dashed the syndicate's hopes.

Throughout the more than two decades since the charter was first granted, the project had repeatedly come in second on the government's list of priorities. There were always railways to be built or salvaged from disaster, and the Borden ministry also decided to deepen the Welland Canal, an action which implied a continuing commitment to the St. Lawrence-Great Lakes route. Furthermore, even before the war the issue of whether the charter should include the right to develop water power was raised. Frank Cochrane, minister of railways and canals in the Borden cabinet, told Sifton, "I feel that the Federal Government is not entitled to the use of the water of canals, other than for navigation purposes." The right to develop hydro power, and the revenues deriving therefrom, properly belonged, in his judgment, to the provinces. Thus the jurisdictional dispute also was a factor in the endless delays.[116]

The British investors found "the whole business...extremely disappointing." Sir Robert Perks told Sifton in 1919, "I have been personally busy on this affair constantly for 15 years, and on four separate occasions ...I have arranged practically for the raising of the capital on each occasion, after what we thought was a distinct and clear arrangement with the Canadian Government." In 1920 the syndicate appointed Sir Clifford their attorney and agent in an effort to consummate the sale to the government.[117] Despite his great abilities, Sifton was not a fortuitous choice, given Arthur Meighen's frigid attitude to him. To an enquiry from Sir Clifford, Meighen curtly replied, "The fact is the subject of the Georgian Bay canal dropped pretty well out of sight during the war, and has not to my knowledge been up for discussion in any form since."[118] Out of sight the matter remained until after the 1921 election.

The advent of the King ministry marked a new level of cooling toward the project. Officially the government declared that the canal was desirable, and in 1924 another of the triennial renewals of the charter which had occurred since 1894 without opposition was granted in Parliament. Yet in April 1923 Mackenzie King had told Perks that the government had before it plans to develop both the St. Lawrence and the Georgian Bay routes. Each was very costly, and "in the present state of affairs we cannot advise any action which would in any way commit Canada to any obligation concerning either of them." Furthermore, in 1924 King flatly rejected the idea that any compensation was due if the project did not materialize. [119]

Cost was a factor, but the situation was far more complex than King intimated. First, Canada was under some pressure from the United States to co-operate in deepening and widening the St. Lawrence waterway to allow full passage of ocean-going vessels. The enormous costs could well divert capital from the Georgian Bay project and kill it, though the King government was busily putting off the Americans. Second, and even more important within Canada, was a furious jurisdictional battle. The federal government would have liked to finance the St. Lawrence project from the revenues derived from hydro-electric development incidental to the seaway development. It also likely would have favoured private development. Ontario and Québec both insisted that under the constitution the federal control extended only to water required for navigation; that used for hydro-electricity fell under provincial control, as did the vast revenues. Québec, however, favoured private development, while Ontario favoured public control, as had prevailed with Ontario Hydro. On top of these disputes were bitter metropolitan rivalries and the lobbying of vested interests. Montreal opposed any project that would permit ocean vessels to proceed west of its port; the railways saw the canals as competitors for similar business; and Toronto opposed the Georgian Bay route as likely to divert business from Lake Ontario ports. At the same time, there was pressure for some settlement fairly quickly because of anticipated power shortages in Ontario.

As it happened, the Montreal, Ottawa and Georgian Bay Canal Company's right to develop hydro power along its route was also under challenge by the National Hydro-Electric Company which had acquired the right to develop power at the substantial Carillon site on the Ottawa River, with a view to exporting the power to the United States. By 1925 the latter company had been taken over by the huge Shawinigan Power Company of Québec, which was anxious to develop the Carillon site. [120]

At this juncture the Siftons entered the picture once more. The canal company's future on the old basis was bleak: government support plainly would not be forthcoming in the foreseeable future, and compensation had been rejected. Winfield Sifton appears to have been the guiding genius behind a new approach. The ever-expanding market for electricity in Ontario could provide the majority of the revenues necessary to complete the canal, with the remainder to be raised in the private market. Simply by developing all the hydro-power sites, including Carillon, as the canal was built, the project would pay for itself, the government would be under no financial obligation, and all that was necessary was to give permission to proceed. Winfield had made the acquaintance of Perks and the other British investors during the war, and they were quite willing to let him have control if he could succeed.

In March 1924 and again in January 1925, as Winfield's plans were taking shape, Sir Clifford used interviews with King to sound out the prime minister on the project. The pressure increased in the fall of 1925. A new company, Great Lakes Securities Corporation, was incorporated by Sifton's sons in October, which in turn purchased control of the canal company. In December Sir Clifford had a new holding company, Armadale Corporation, established, which took over the holdings of the Canadian Assets & Brokerage Company. Early in 1926 he sold his sons the equity stock in Armadale, then valued by the Siftons at $2,510,000, in return for the brothers' holdings in the canal company, which they claimed was worth at least $2,820,000. [121] While this transaction had a subsequent significance for the Siftons, it meant in 1926 that Sir Clifford officially controlled the canal company, though in practice most of the work on promoting the project remained in the hands of his sons.

In November 1925, as these plans were taking shape, the Siftons interviewed King three times. Winfield assured King that he had reached an agreement with Ontario Hydro to take the electricity and that no power would be exported from the canal route sites to the United States. King replied that if the government were to support the scheme, Sir Clifford should guarantee that the *Manitoba Free Press* would, in effect, be a government supporter. The Siftons would go further than that, responded Winfield. They would spend up to $2 million to acquire control of the *Globe* to ensure its support of the King government. On the one occasion that King saw Sir Clifford himself, the latter informed the prime minister, perhaps somewhat disingenuously, that he was not behind the project for the money; he had all he needed and his sons had all that was good for them. Instead, this was a project essential to Canada's development that would mean the expenditure of many millions at no charge to the government. [122] King nevertheless appeared sympathetic to the project, even considering the political shoals that he knew lay ahead.

1927 was the critical year for the project. The canal company's charter was up for renewal by 1 May, as—coincidentally—was the National Hydro-Electric Company's lease on the Carillon site. Renewal, it was understood, was tantamount on this occasion to permission to proceed.

The King government now had to make some difficult choices. The Ontario government was opposed to both projects, and Ontario Hydro was under orders not to promise to purchase electricity from either interest. The Québec government supported the Shawinigan Power interests, although co-operating with Ontario against federal pretensions. The Siftons, as King laconically recorded, "have few if any friends," a situation perhaps worsened by the fact that Sir Clifford's declining health permitted him little more than an advisory role as his sons conducted the battle. His reputation as a corrupt, self-interested Croesus underlay much of the opposition; the Siftons, in the opinion of Ontario Premier G. Howard Ferguson, were "buccaneers determined to put the power users of Ontario to ransom."[123] As the two provincial governments, Ontario Hydro, the private power and railway interests, and Toronto and Montreal combined against the Georgian Bay Canal project, it seemed that it was really the Siftons who were under attack. They were represented as having no interest in the canal itself, merely being interested in a power monopoly with which they would gouge the Ontario consumer and sell the excess to the United States, while tens of millions of dollars in profits rolled into their massive coffers.

This image of immense, ill-gotten wealth seemed to be the public's main impression of Sifton. A western correspondent chided him: "Now, Sir Clifford, surely you are tired of making money, you have more of it than you will ever know what to do with. What good is it? Remember, all that you can carry away, clenched in the cold hand of death, is the memory of the good deeds left behind." Even the prime minister was not immune to such notions. After visiting Sifton at "Armadale" in 1925, he wrote in his diary, "I noticed a huge vault etc. on the way. It is all indicative of his 'power.' He has amassed great wealth somehow and is a sort of medieval baron."[124]

It would be difficult to maintain that the Siftons were unaware of the long-term potential for profit from the venture, and it is nonsensical to argue, as Dafoe did, that Sir Clifford "put his whole fortune...in jeopardy" by becoming involved with so "highly speculative" an enterprise.[125] Nevertheless, a fair assessment of the available records would suggest that Sifton was primarily motivated by his conviction that the canal would be a major contribution to Canadian development and to a wholly Canadian-controlled water transportation system. Nowhere is there any indication that the power development intrinsically interested the Siftons, except as it would contribute to completion of the project.

Winfield drafted a lengthy brief, revised by Sir Clifford, to put forward the case to the Members of Parliament, and to rebut the main objections being made.[126] It emphasized the all-Canadian features of the route and contended that the shorter route would attract traffic from American ports and that Montreal's total business would substantially increase. It would not cost the public treasury anything, construction would further stimulate the Canadian economy, and rates for carriage of freight and electricity, as well as profits, would be subject to government control. Nova Scotia coal would be accessible to much of Ontario and the interior of the continent. The great power monopolies of Québec were fighting the project because it would undercut their control and their rates. "The insinuation that the Canal Company is trying to use its Canal project to get control of the water-power is a malicious falsehood." On the contrary, if the Carillon and other sites fell into the hands of the Québec power interests, the route could not be developed in the foreseeable future. The document undoubtedly made the strongest possible case for the project. It even contended that *all* the water on the route was required for navigation and that the only water power that would be developed would be on sites where dams were necessitated for navigation purposes. Therefore the federal government should control the power development, which was incidental to navigation. Logical or not, such an argument could not obscure the emotional federal-provincial jurisdictional dispute.

The federal cabinet was in somewhat of a quandary. Charles Dunning, minister of finance, denounced the Sifton project as a "'blackmailing' proposition." "I corrected him," noted King, "to speak of it as a 'dog in the manger attitude' which he accepted." And these were the Siftons' supposed friends! Even so, the cabinet could not ignore that they were Liberals and hence more worthy of support than Tory claimants. The private member's bill which would have extended the charter to 1 May 1936 by which time the project was to be completed had a very rough second reading. The cabinet declined to make it a government measure, a decision which they well knew would seal the bill's fate; yet for the sake of relations with the Siftons they wanted to appear sympathetic, so arranged for most of the cabinet to support the bill, get it to the committee stage, and allow it to die there. [127]

Harry and Winfield Sifton carried their case once more, to the special Commons Committee on Railways, Canals and Telegraph Lines, and sought to meet the opposition charges raised in second reading by proposing three amendments to the charter. The first would prevent the investors from deriving any profit until the entire canal was open for navigation. The second would require that a majority of directors be Canadian citizens. The third would prohibit the export of power generated along the route. It was a first-class presentation, as even King admitted. But after two hearings the bill was, inevitably, voted down. "There was," King recorded, "almost unanimity in opposition to the measure on both sides of the House." [128]

Sir Clifford received the news of defeat while convalescing in Florida from an operation. His sons had been taken in by King's professions of sympathy with their cause, and they proposed to write the prime minister hoping to find some way to keep the project alive. Sir Clifford had seen through King's attitude for some time and bluntly told Harry that such a letter would be "futile and absurd." Despite being in full possession of the facts, the government "deliberately & treacherously knifed you."

> You remember that I said before I came away that you and Win should make a stand to have the Govt get behind the bill & declare they were behind the enterprise *in toto*. Up to that time the Govt had been stalling. When you wrote me that the Govt would not take a stand I gave up any idea of the bill passing. I knew perfectly well that the Govt would knife you but they were more clever about it than I anticipated. I expected it would be defeated on the second reading but they held their hand until Committee.
>
> I don't want to "come the senior" on you too much but when you are as old as I am you will know better than to appeal to men who have just got through putting the knife into you....
>
> With regard to the Govt of course what I have written is between ourselves. No necessity to quarrel with anybody or exhibit any spleen. [129]

Upon the defeat of the bill Sir Robert Perks indicated that he wished to proceed, by court action if necessary, to secure compensation from the federal government for money invested in the project over the previous thirty years. Sifton, however, flatly refused to join in seeking compensation for his own investment and indeed was willing to transfer all of his stock to Perks at no charge. [130] It would appear that Sir Clifford was not especially disappointed at the failure of the enterprise; he was far more distressed at the methods used and the professions of sympathy from those who he believed had actually killed it. Most especially was he disgusted with Charles Dunning, whom he had formerly regarded as a friend. When the personal abuse of Sifton was at its height, he had wired Dunning a message to read to the House of Commons denying that he had ever benefitted "by any concession or favor from any government in Canada." Dunning merely suppressed the message. "I have not heretofore known of a minister of the crown making so complete a skunk of himself as Dunning has done in this case," fumed Sifton. "The quicker he is relegated to the obscurity of private life the better for everyone." [131]

Sifton himself enjoyed private life, but he could never be relegated to obscurity. Indeed, one of the problems for Mackenzie King was how to deal with so prominent a personage as Sir Clifford. The prime minister never lost his suspicion that Sifton wanted control of the government, a notion inadvertently encouraged by Winfield, who told King that although his father did not want to enter the government, he was sure that he and his brothers could persuade him to do so. King hedged; perhaps the chairmanship of the tariff commission? Privately, King made it clear that he wanted no strong rival, and added, "now is the time to get in younger and more active men—men with a future not with a past." [132] Later the prime minister suggested to Winfield that his father might be made "a Comm'r on Immigration." [133] Given Sir Clifford's poor health and the lack of any corroborating evidence in his other papers, it would seem unlikely that he would have encouraged such discussions.

The one public appointment that he received from King was to the Canadian National Advisory Committee on the St. Lawrence, in May 1924. The development of the waterway had long been one of Sifton's interests; he had supported deepening the channel to fourteen feet during the Laurier years as a means of reducing the shipping costs for western farmers. By the end of the First World War there had been several disputes between Canada and the United States over the development of hydro power and problems of navigation; there was a great American demand for the electricity that could be produced; and there were fears that without access to ocean-going vessels the region would lose industrial development to ocean ports and the Panama Canal. In Canada the market for electricity was smaller, and there was less sense of urgency. None the less, the question was referred to the International Joint Commission in 1920; at the beginning of 1922 its report recommending development reached both governments. The Canadian government threw cold water on it because of the tremendous cost. Further pressure from the Americans in November 1923 produced a Canadian decision in 1924 to appoint engineers to a board to assess the ultimate cost and an advisory committee to "enquire fully from a national standpoint into the wide questions involved." In November 1926 the Joint Board of Engineers made its report, and the following year the Americans again pressured Canada to agree to act. The advisory committee, which had met only twice, in 1924, was called on early in 1928 by the reluctant King government to produce a report. [134] And once again many of the same forces that had opposed the Georgian Bay development were united in opposing the St. Lawrence seaway.

Sifton had never wavered in his support of its development and told the government in 1924 to ignore the pressures and push ahead with deepening the channel and securing the hydro power at the same time, simply disregarding the provincial claims. No export of Canadian power should be permitted; eventually it all would be required by the domestic market. He anticipated that much or all of the cost could be defrayed from the sale of the electricity. [135] Given the Board of Engineers' estimates, Sifton concluded that the costs would be "appalling" if they were to be underwritten by the respective governments. "There is only one basis upon which it can be built and that is that the power shall pay for the canal completely and entirely." He had little confidence that the members of the advisory committee fully appreciated the complexities of the construction, financing and politics involved, and he knew that Ontario and Québec would continue fighting "to get the power free of canal costs."[136]

Mackenzie King had little confidence in the committee either, regarding most of its members as representatives of various vested interests and Sifton as "the dominating figure & mind." Nevertheless he called it together early in 1928, "pointedly reminded" the members that they had an advisory role only, and asked for a report, which was presented on 11 January.[137] The committee supported the construction of a minimum twenty-seven-foot waterway covering the entire St. Lawrence-Great Lakes system, but its method of apportioning the costs and its timetable were immediately controversial. Essentially, it suggested that Canada be credited with expenses already incurred in the Canadian sections of the waterway: dredging the St. Lawrence below Montreal and the improvements to the Welland Canal. In addition, Canada would undertake improvements on that portion of the St. Lawrence between the international boundary and Montreal. This would be constructed by private interests in return for the privilege of exploiting the waterpower. Sale of this power from Québec to Ontario Hydro would alleviate any power shortage in Ontario and ensure no export of the Canadian power.

Meanwhile, the United States would be responsible for financing and developing the international section of the St. Lawrence under the technical supervision of an international commission. But this section could not be undertaken until the Canadian sections were complete and additional power would be required by the Canadian market, at which point Canada could claim half the power produced in the American-built section. Additionally, the United States would be required to complete the channels connecting Lake Superior with Lake Huron and Lake Huron with Lake Erie. For Canada it was a marvellous scheme. The new costs to Canada would be small, and the major remaining expense would be undertaken at no cost to the federal treasury, while the Americans would provide power from their expensive sections at no charge to Canada.[138] Of course the United States would never agree to a plan so one-sided in its advantages to Canada, but the report was another tool for King to employ in his strategy of delay.

The report also shows the marks of Sifton's influence: his determination that Canada should fight for maximum advantage in dealing with the Americans, his conviction that Canada must not ever export power which she might need in future, and his belief that private enterprise could complete the project without any assistance from government. Implicit too was the assumption that the federal government had the power to act unilaterally to develop the hydro power, a position consonant with that taken on the Georgian Bay Canal project but curiously at odds with his concern for provincial rights when he spoke of amending the constitution.

Sir Clifford frequently appeared to be something of an old curmudgeon in his declining years, certainly when he contemplated what he deemed to be the sorry state of post-war society. Morosely he contemplated the rise of sloth, the disappearance of the work ethic, and the dissipation of the undisciplined younger generation—an exercise undoubtedly as old as mankind. "To a man like me," he moralized to Harry Sifton, "brought up to work long hours & take no amusements whatever the community seems to be crazy." He told the American Association for the Advancement of Science, "Everywhere we are getting away from simple methods of living." Especially deplorable was the accelerated movement of people from farm to city. Life was so much more attractive in the towns, where people could find improvements ranging from sewers and sidewalks to movie houses and "amusements of all descriptions." More effort needed to be made to regenerate the agrarian life-style, for herein lay the very moral fibre of the nation.[139]

Especially since the war, he warned the Westerners' Club of Montreal, all sorts of theories had been advanced as to how people should be governed. These theories came in the guise of religion, charities, education, social welfare, and similar matters, "but sift them out and you will always find that they are directed against the stern, orderly administration of the community. They are directed against law and order. They are subversive to the principles on which the State is built...that a man's prosperity is founded on his own integrity, his own work, honesty and virtue. That is the only foundation for the well-being of a State."[140] On another occasion he wrote, "I was taught when a boy, as all boys were taught then, that if a man did not have an occupation and work hard at it he was an idler and a loafer." Canadians needed to return to that principle, remembering that "without labor, persistent and prolonged, no good thing is accomplished, no great end is achieved and no real character built up."[141]

Sir Clifford was experiencing the difficulty of trying to reconcile the values of his youth and early manhood with the reality of post-war Canada. To some extent he recognized the problem. Canada's progress had earlier been based on sheer physical growth, the struggle to overcome obstacles of geography and environment to create a nation. The problem for the post-war generation was that with the completion of the process of western settlement and construction of the industrial and transportation infrastructure for the domestic market, Canadians needed to define new objectives. Sifton realized that, but desired somehow to retain the old and apparently simple values of a pre-industrial, pre-urban era.

None the less, nothing could long cloud Sifton's fundamental liberal optimism, his conviction that any country so blessed with human and material resources as Canada was destined to make a major contribution in human history. Like others of his era, he took great pride in the Canadian discovery of insulin and hoped it would be the forerunner of future great medical discoveries.[142] Canadians, he pointed out, led the world in certain diverse fields including aspects of hydro-electrical engineering, pest control and aerial photography. All this suggested a great future, provided that Canadians did not neglect the traditions on which "a progressive, orderly and prosperous community" had been built. He believed in the mythology of Canadians as an inherently law-abiding people who had built their nation on the basis of individualism and free enterprise. Do not be misled by the false gods of socialism, he warned: "Socialistic theories without exception always and everywhere break down completely when they are tried. Their fruit is starvation, disease, poverty and death."[143] On all these issues Sifton was consistent with his ideas of the previous thirty years.

Thus, his last years found him somewhat uncomfortable and isolated, as were so many of his generation, from the new directions of society after the war. But it was also true in his personal life. His greatest pleasures seemed to derive from the breeding and training of horses, in which he became a recognized expert; and his sizeable stable enjoyed marked successes in shows and competitions.[144] Even so, he often was not well enough to attend the meets himself. Beginning early in 1927 his health declined markedly. He underwent an operation in Philadelphia that entailed a long recuperation, and he was still not fully restored when he returned to Toronto in June.[145] Late in 1927 some further treatment was required, but this time there was little improvement. Whatever hope he had for recovery was dealt a devastating blow in June 1928 when Winfield, the son for whom he had held such high hopes, suddenly died. In January 1929 he wrote despondently, "I have been more or less an invalid for the last year." [146]

Sir Clifford had been suffering from high blood pressure and a weakened heart; it is also possible that his condition was complicated by some kind of abdominal cancer.[147] His condition seriously deteriorated in November 1928, and he went to a favourite resort at Daytona Beach, Florida, half expecting not to return to Canada. Those, like Dafoe, who visited him found him in an unusually reminiscent and reflective mood, but also quite frail and depressed. His formerly firm handwriting often became nearly undecipherable, and writing was always a strain for him; his analytical mind no longer had the same force, despite efforts to maintain his interest in public affairs. By late February he began to feel somewhat better and told Harry he hoped to be able to return home by 1 May: "I am playing a little golf, but taking great care not to over do it. Am extremely comfortable in my cottage, and have gotten over my stomach trouble entirely. For the first time since I left home I am feeling cheerful and confident & a little like a human being." Four weeks later his health was about the same, and he was looking forward to seeing Canada again. "Can't see that my brain is fading yet," he told Dafoe, "but you are a better judge of that."[148]

In early April he wired Harry to come to accompany him from Florida to the Roosevelt Hospital in New York, where he was to consult with a heart specialist. There, at 10 o'clock in the morning of 17 April, as he was sitting in a chair talking, he suddenly dropped his hand which was holding his earphone, saying, "Just a minute Harry. I feel weak." His head rested against the chair, and he quietly died.[149]

A private funeral service was held 19 April from "Armadale". He had asked that there be no "ostentation" about the service, and in accordance with his wishes not even a eulogy was offered. Sir Clifford's four living sons, with Dafoe and Macklin, were the pallbearers, with burial taking place in Mount Pleasant Cemetery in Toronto.[150]

His death evoked tributes ranging from the governor general and prime minister to a nationwide spectrum of acquaintances, friends, and old enemies. Two will be noted here. Wes Spiers, a civil servant in the Department of the Interior who had often ridden on hunts with Sifton, recalled, "He was a true sportsman....a fearless rider, nearly always in front, no fence too high, no hazard too great for him to attempt." That would summarize much about his approach to life and politics. The *Ottawa Journal*, never friendly to Sir Clifford, none the less wrote: "His policies may have been open to criticism, and were abundantly criticized; but no one ever denied that they were inspired by vision, by a restless vigor and imagination, by a deep and sustained faith in the country's future."[151] That was a tribute which Sir Clifford Sifton would have been happy to accept.

Epilogue

In death, as in life, Sir Clifford Sifton remained controversial. Prime Minister King perhaps captured the Canadian ambivalence as well as anyone: upon hearing of Sifton's death, he noted that "it was with the greatest difficulty that I got something written out in the nature of an appreciation." For King, at least, his memory was not easily exorcised, as Sifton's spectre evidently returned from time to time to haunt the prime minister's dreams and participate in his séances.[1] He has continued to haunt historical writing in Canada as a spirit both benevolent and malevolent.

It appeared for a while that Dafoe's sympathetic 1931 biography of Sifton would set many of the less flattering myths to rest. "For [Sifton's] intellectual abilities and courage I had always much admiration," noted one satisfied reader, "but the abuse by which he was assailed over so many years raised suspicions in my mind that, I am glad to say, your book has effaced. You will recall that it was Sifton's rapid acquirement of wealth that had much to do with creating these doubts, and I must confess my regret that the scope of your work did not give you an opportunity to deal with this feature of his career, as probably it was as consistent with honor as were his political activities."[2] The reader of the present work will perhaps find the comparison less reassuring than it appeared early in 1932.

The reader also may regret that even now the evidence is not available to bring the means by which Sifton acquired his wealth altogether out of the shadows. What can be said with some confidence is that Sifton was not as fabulously wealthy as many contemporaries suspected. A fairly conclusive estimate of his wealth was made public in April 1932 as a result of an action by the Ontario government to obtain a large sum in unpaid succession duties. At his death his estate was valued at $3,287,231, on which a duty of approximately $480,000 was paid.[3] That, claimed the Ontario government, was only a fraction of the total real value of the estate. In effect, the province appeared to argue that the transfer of "Armadale" stock in 1926 to Sifton's sons had been a massive tax-dodge because it had been traded for worthless stock in the Georgian Bay Canal enterprise. If the province could show that the latter stock was indeed worthless at the time of transfer, or at least did not represent a fair equivalent for the Armadale stock, then the transfer would represent a gift by Sir Clifford to his sons and be subject to taxation.

The government valued the "Armadale" shares owned by Sifton's sons at the time of his death at $5,978,415.98, alleged that the "debenture stock of the said Montreal, Ottawa and Georgian Bay Canal Company was of no value whatever" in February 1926, and claimed that Sir Clifford's heirs and successors owed an additional $1,752,669.05 in duties plus accrued interest.[4] Sifton's sons naturally contended for a lower valuation of the "Armadale" stock; and argued that the Canal Company stock indeed had a high value in 1926, that it was not until much later that the opposition formed that ultimately killed the project and rendered the stock valueless, and that indeed it was because the project had such high value that so strong an opposition to it did take shape.[5] The controversy resurrected all the old suspicions about Sifton's devious methods and considerable wealth. Yet the figures showed that by the highest estimate Sifton's fortune was less than $10 million—rich indeed in 1929, but much less than the rumours of the era surmised. Finally, it must be admitted that the suspicions about his illegitimate or corrupt acquisition of wealth remain unsubstantiated, as they did during his lifetime despite massive efforts to prove otherwise.

The suspicions nevertheless clouded contemporary judgments of his achievements; by contrast Sir John A. Macdonald, whose knowledge of devious politics and flexibility of principle was at least equal to that of Sifton, had a saving and ingratiating sense of humour and never became conspicuously wealthy while in office, with the result that much is forgiven the country's first prime minister. Even Sir Clifford's enemies willingly conceded his administrative ability, energy, and courage. But he was widely seen as a man ruthless and unprincipled. "In the full meaning of the word, he can never be described as a statesman," opined one editorialist, "for he thought first and always of Sifton. He came to Ottawa a poor man, even more than that, a man in debt. [An erroneous impression.] He left Ottawa a few years later a wealthy man, which to the ordinary man carries the inference that while he did not love Canada less, he loved himself more, and by such tests is determined a man's national greatness."[6]

While not ignoring such factors, one must go much further to provide a balanced assessment of Sifton's career and contribution to Canada. He was, like most people, complex and not always consistent. He well understood that, and was fond of quoting Emerson's dictum that "a foolish consistency is the hobgoblin of little minds." Mid-nineteenth-century liberal notions had been milk and meat to him in his formative years, many of which values he never lost. He believed throughout his life in the virtues of hard work, self-denial, self-sufficiency, and the struggle for success.[7] Moreover, to liberal-democrats such as Sifton, "the real road upward for the common man lay in the adoption of a certain kind of character. A growing economy would solve all social ills. Sloth alone prevented success." This was part of his own self-image, for he believed that everything he had achieved in the way of material or political success had resulted from precisely these virtues. Like other liberal-democrats of his age, he believed that the role of the state should be confined to providing equality of opportunity for individuals (or businesses) who adopted such virtues to make use of their talents and strive for success; beyond that, the state owed the individual nothing.

Despite his frequently stated devotion to the principle of economy in government, and of small government, he had a practical enough mind to discard the principle when circumstances seemed to require it. Far more than Laurier, for example, he accepted the proposition that the federal government in Canada needed to be dynamically involved in stimulating and shaping economic development. The Liberal party, in his view, must shed its devotion to principles both outdated and inapplicable to the realities of dominion politics and geography. Frank Underhill put his contribution to Laurier liberalism in perspective:

> It was not until Laurier took charge that the Liberal party acquired sophistication and felt really at ease with railway promoters, land companies and industrialists. Laurier put an end to the anti-clerical Rouge tradition. Fielding put an end to the stiff-necked Cobdenism of Cartwright. And in Sifton, who was apparently the main driving force of the administration, Laurier had a disciple of Alexander Hamilton who believed with all his heart in the gospel of creating prosperity by tying to the government all the private profit-seeking interests who could most effectively exploit the material resources of the country. The Laurier-Fielding-Sifton party had thus emancipated itself from its narrow English liberalism; it was now North American; it was truly national in its appeal. It had become all things to all men, and could compete on equal terms with the so-called Conservative party which Macdonald had created.[8]

Small wonder that Sifton came to view Macdonald as a great constructive statesman who had knit the country together with railway and tariff policies well adapted to the nation's circumstances. His encouragement and shaping of immigration and western settlement fitted in closely with his view of the role of government.

Similarly, his support of a regulatory role for government, his opposition to private or state monopoly in any economic sector, and his suggestions for state encouragement of competition, as in the case of banking law, were applications of liberal principles to encourage competition and equality of opportunity. There was, in his mind, a clear distinction between such a role for government and ''socialistic'' measures designed to buffer individuals or companies from the harsh economic realities. Rather than seeking state intervention, those like the farmers who considered themselves disadvantaged by the system should support co-operative buying and selling as a means of strengthening themselves.

There always was a slight radical or populist streak in Sifton's thinking. He denounced millionaires as a young politician for reaping their industrial and transportation fortunes at the expense of the hard-working farmer; when he himself became a millionaire, he never seemed to see himself as part of the establishment, was at pains to point out that he had no industrial or manufacturing investments, and often took positions on issues such as banking or transportation that had less in common with the Canadian business elite than with agrarian populism. Throughout his career he retained his suspicion of the motives of large business interests. While disagreeing with farmers on the desirability of state ownership, he agreed with the main thrust of the farmers' demands, namely, that the rapacity of the large interests must be controlled by the state in the public interest. Similarly, he believed that the political system needed to be purified and freed from the domination of selfish business interests.

Whether Sifton ever appreciated the irony of his stance on political purity is unclear. There is no evidence, however, to suggest that he at any time abandoned his somewhat elitist and severely practical (if not un-principled) approach to democratic politics. Whatever rhetoric might be mouthed concerning grass-roots democracy, Sifton clearly believed in tight control of the political machinery and had no qualms about manipulation of the electoral process. Despite his later attacks on the patronage system, he had earlier been a masterful and thorough devotee, using it to the advantage of himself and the Liberal Party. Of course his opponents used the same tactics; of course he was right in believing that the electorate was all too willing to be corrupted; but he certainly saw little purpose while in active politics in campaigning for a more ideal system.

For Sir Clifford the Liberal party ought to be a party of consensus which should try to reflect the interests of the moderately progressive elements of society, to balance the interests of farmer and businessman, of West and East. Politics had purposes greater than the mere exercise of power. The goals included maintaining a strong national unity and economy and promoting development; they excluded, in Sifton's mind, any movement toward the welfare state. He also believed that the Liberals were the party most committed to Canadian nationalism—independence of both the British Empire and the United States. Yet his notions of nationalism and unity never fully grasped the French fact in Canada; even his recognition of French-Catholic constitutional rights late in life appeared to arise more because of his desire for constitutional independence than from any deep appreciation of minority rights.

There has long been a tendency to view Sifton as always having been a westerner in his point of view. Not only did he represent a prairie constituency and act as a western representative in the Laurier cabinet, but the immigration and settlement policies for which he is best remembered focused on western development, completing the final phase of the national policy of domestic expansion. It is true that he had to battle strenuously at times for the interests of the west. Yet it is doubtful that he ever would have described himself as principally a spokesman for the region. The national policy, after all, was designed among other things to achieve an integration of Canada's regions, a philosophy with which Sifton certainly was in sympathy. His concerns were for the development of the entire country; western views could be promoted as long as they contributed to that end. It would be difficult to see his policies on the tariff or on transportation, for example, as merely regional. He removed from the region physically in 1896; after 1905 he spent little time in the west except on business; in 1911 the public finally saw, if they had not understood previously, that he was espousing views far more characteristic of central Canada than of the west. It was somewhat ironic that the man who had done so much to develop the prairie region should have been vilified by westerners in 1911 and 1917 as a turncoat and traitor, when in fact his views on the national interest had remained quite consistent for fifteen or twenty years.

Why was Sifton so prominent? As a political organizer, men like Rogers or Cochrane may well have been his equals. As an administrator, his record on immigration and settlement was exceptional by any reasonable standard, but the Yukon could hardly be termed a great achievement, let alone other lesser areas to which he could not give adequate attention. As an orator he was widely respected, but he could never move people like Laurier. As a thinker, his ideas were derivative, though he certainly expressed many current notions with force and was blessed with formidable analytical powers. While wealthy, he was never truly a member of the business elite—the industrialists, manufacturers, bankers or transportation and utility magnates. His fortune was to have gifts in many areas, to have a broad and incisive grasp of issues, a willingness to work hard and tremendously energetically, combined with an indefinable charisma. "Sifton had a faculty of fastening men to him with hooks of steel," recalled T.A.Crerar: "He was a man of action and compelling power. No one can estimate how far his physical disability influenced his action. His was the energetic, restless nature that must always be doing. Shut off from his fellows by his deafness, his mind naturally turned to other things."[9]

"Sir Clifford Sifton is of course nearest to a real statesman of any of our leaders," wrote Sir B.E. Walker in 1918, "while he has a curious reputation arousing admiration and dislike in about equal proportions in his fellow Canadians. He is, in my opinion, so able that were it not for his deafness he would probably have been Premier of this country. As it is he wields a great influence.''[10] Little has changed in some respects. The ambivalence remains. The flaws in Sifton's character certainly entailed more than his deafness. His coldly calculating, ruthless approach to politics, his failure to develop a sensitivity to French Canada, his seeming deviousness, his apparent departure from principle in politics—all arouse disapproval. On the other hand, his sheer talent cannot be denied. His grasp of so broad a range of issues, his incisive analytical mind, his executive capacity, were rare. He had a vision of how Canada ought to be developed, at least materially, and for better or for worse went a long way in seeing it realized. If he was not quite a statesman, he was an extraordinary politician of great influence, and in his own way a remarkable Canadian.[11]

Appendix 1

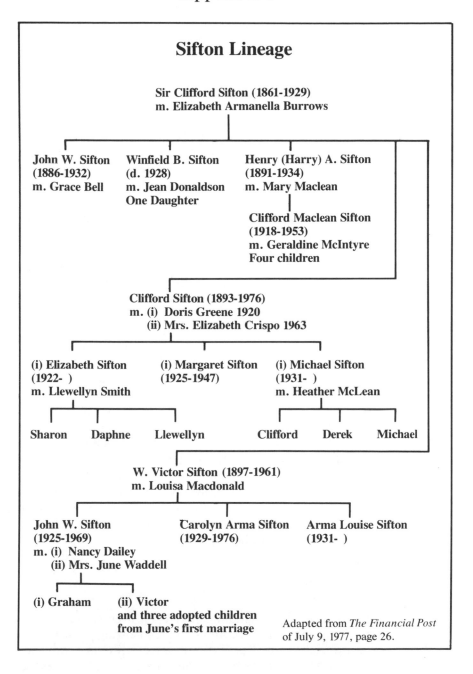

Sifton Lineage

Sir Clifford Sifton (1861-1929)
m. Elizabeth Armanella Burrows

John W. Sifton
(1886-1932)
m. Grace Bell

Winfield B. Sifton
(d. 1928)
m. Jean Donaldson
One Daughter

Henry (Harry) A. Sifton
(1891-1934)
m. Mary Maclean

Clifford Maclean Sifton
(1918-1953)
m. Geraldine McIntyre
Four children

Clifford Sifton (1893-1976)
m. (i) Doris Greene 1920
(ii) Mrs. Elizabeth Crispo 1963

(i) Elizabeth Sifton
(1922-)
m. Llewellyn Smith

(i) Margaret Sifton
(1925-1947)

(i) Michael Sifton
(1931-)
m. Heather McLean

Sharon   Daphne   Llewellyn   Clifford   Derek   Michael

W. Victor Sifton (1897-1961)
m. Louisa Macdonald

John W. Sifton
(1925-1969)
m. (i) Nancy Dailey
(ii) Mrs. June Waddell

Carolyn Arma Sifton
(1929-1976)

Arma Louise Sifton
(1931-)

(i) Graham   (ii) Victor
and three adopted children
from June's first marriage

Adapted from *The Financial Post*
of July 9, 1977, page 26.

Appendix 2

CLAUSE OF 21 FEBRUARY 1905

16. 1. The provisions of section 93 of the British North America Act, 1867, shall apply to the said provinces as if, at the date upon which this Act comes into force, the territory comprised therein were already a province, the expression "the union" in the said section being taken to mean the said date.

2. Subject to the provisions of the said section 93, and in continuance of the principles heretofore sanctioned under the Northwest Territories Act, it is enacted that the legislature of the said province shall pass all necessary laws in respect of education, and that it shall therein always be provided (a) that a majority of the ratepayers of any district or portion of the said province or of any less portion or subdivision thereof, by whatever name it is known may establish such schools therein as they think fit, and make the necessary assessments and collection of rates therefor, and (b) that the minority of the ratepayers therein whether Protestant or Roman Catholic, may establish separate schools therein, and make the necessary assessments and collection of rates therefor and (c) that in such cases the ratepayers establishing such Protestant or Roman Catholic separate schools shall be liable only to assessment of such rates as they impose upon themselves with respect thereto.

3. In the appropriation of public moneys by the legislature in aid of education, and in the distribution of any moneys paid to the government of the said province arising from the school fund established by the Dominion Lands Act, there shall be no discrimination between the public schools and the separate schools, and such moneys shall be applied to the support of public and separate schools in equitable shares or proportion.
(*Debates*, 1905, cols. 1852-53, 1 March 1905)

CLAUSE OF 3 MARCH 1905

In and for the Province the Legislature may exclusively make laws in relation to education subject and according to the following provisions—

1. Nothing in any such law shall prejudicially affect any right or privilege with respect to separate schools which any class of persons have at the date

of the passing of this act under the terms of Chapter 29 of the Ordinances of the North West Territories, passed in the year 1901, known and cited as "The School Ordinance."

2. An appeal shall lie to the Governor General in Council from any act or decision of any Provincial Authority affecting any right or privilege of the Protestant or Roman Catholic minority of the King's subjects in relation to education.

3. In case any such Provincial law, as from time to time seems to the Governor General in Council requisite for the due execution of the provisions of this section is not made, or in case any decision of the Governor General in Council or any appeal under this section is not duly executed by the proper Provincial authority in that behalf, then and in every such case, and as far only as the circumstances of each case require, the Parliament of Canada may make remedial laws for the due execution of the provisions of this section and of any decision of the Governor General in Council under this section.

(PAC, Grey of Howick Papers, vol. 27, pp. 5003-6, Laurier to Grey, 5 March 1905, and encl.)

FINAL VERSION

17. Section 93 of *The British North America Act*, 1867, shall apply to the said province, with the substitution for paragraph (1) of the said section 93, of the following paragraph: —

"(1) Nothing in any such law shall prejudicially affect any right or privilege with respect to separate schools which any class of persons have at the date of the passing of the Act, under the terms of chapters 29 and 30 of the Ordinances of the North-West Territories, passed in the year 1901, or with respect to religious instruction in any public or separate school as provided for in the said ordinances.

(2) In the appropriation by the Legislature or distribution by the Government of the province of any moneys for the support of schools organized and carried on in accordance with the said chapter 29 or any Act passed in amendment thereof, or in substitution therefor, there shall be no discrimination against schools of any class described in the said chapter 29.

(3) Where the expression "by law" is employed in paragraph 3 of the said section 93, it shall be held to mean the law as set out in the said chapters 29 and 30, and where the expression "at the Union" is employed, in the said paragraph 3, it shall be held to mean the date at which this Act comes into force.

(*Statutes of Canada*, 4-5 Edward VII, c. 3, s. 17 [1905])

Note on Sources

As with the first volume of this biography, this book is derived mainly from the Sir Clifford Sifton Papers in the Public Archives of Canada. While the bulk of the papers are concentrated on the period to 1905, there is sufficient material here and in other collections to permit some re-evaluation of his influential remaining years. Recently deposited material on Sifton's business career is useful, but it tells more about failed investments and enterprises than about how his fortune was accumulated. As was the case for his early career, the collection remains almost devoid of material about his personal or private life, apart from a scattering of letters from the 1920's.

Especially valuable for the later period of Sifton's life, particularly the last decade, are the papers of John W. Dafoe. There is a large collection of Dafoe-Sifton correspondence between 1901 and 1905 in the Sifton Papers. For the following years their correspondence survives in only a scattered fashion, mostly in the Sifton Papers, until after the First World War. Thereafter both the Dafoe and Sifton collections have between them fairly complete files of an extensive correspondence until 1925, after which the Sifton material inexplicably ends. Many of the most interesting letters have been published by the Manitoba Record Society in *The Dafoe-Sifton Correspondence 1919-1927*, ed. R. Cook; this volume, however, is based mainly on the Dafoe collection and is by no means complete, so scholars seriously interested in the period should still consult the originals.

The papers of Sir Clifford's fourth son, Clifford Sifton (1893-1976), contain not only useful biographical material, but some insights into Sir Clifford's business affairs. The papers of prime ministers Laurier, Borden, and King, and those of Sir John Willison, illuminated much of Sifton's career. Also invaluable was the *Manitoba Free Press*, which not only recorded the main events of Sir Clifford's career, but mirrored his opinions on most public issues.

John W. Dafoe's 1931 biography of Sifton becomes in many respects a personal memoir for the period after 1901, and is in this sense a primary source of great significance. It was a semi-official biography; Dafoe had enormous respect for Sifton and certainly succeeded in creating a sympathetic portrait of his subject; yet, when due allowance is made for these facts, it remains an important contribution to Canadian biography.

With a very few exceptions, the bibliography is confined to those sources mentioned in the footnotes. I hope that the bibliography not only will be useful to readers of this biography, but will serve as an acknowl-edgement of the enormous debt owed to those who have laboured to illuminate various facets of this period of history.

Bibliography

ARCHIVAL COLLECTIONS

Archives de l'Archevêché de St. Boniface
  J.S. Ewart files
  Langevin Correspondence and "Post Scriptum"
Glenbow Alberta Archives
  Canada Land and Irrigation Company Limited Papers
Public Archives of Alberta
  Premiers' Papers, file 291, Public Utilities Commission—General
Public Archives of Canada
  Manuscripts
    Sir Robert Borden Papers
    Sir Mackenzie Bowell Papers
    Acton Burrows Papers
    A.K. Cameron Papers
    Canadian Pacific Railway Records
    Charles Constantine Papers
    John Wesley Dafoe Papers
    A.R. Dickey Papers
    Sir Charles Fitzpatrick Papers
    W.L. Grant Papers
    Lord Grey of Howick Papers
    Charles M. Hays Papers
    William Lyon Mackenzie King Papers
    William Lyon Mackenzie King Diary
    Sir Wilfrid Laurier Papers
    Liberal Party of Canada Papers
    Sir John Alexander Macdonald Papers
    Arthur Meighen Papers
    Lord Minto Papers
    William Ogilvie Papers
    Sir George Parkin Papers
    Sir Joseph Pope Papers
    Sir Richard William Scott Papers
    Sir Clifford Sifton (1861-1929) Papers
    Clifford Sifton (1893-1976) Papers
    H.H. Smith Papers
    Marcus Smith Papers
    Joseph Israel Tarte Papers

Sir John Thompson Papers
Sir Charles Tupper Papers
Sir Charles Hibbert Tupper Papers
Frederick Coate Wade Papers
Sir John Stephen Willison Papers
Selwyn Wilson Papers
Zachary Taylor Wood Papers
  Public Records
    Department of Indian Affairs Records
    Department of National Defense Records
    Immigration Branch Records
    Royal Canadian Mounted Police Records
Public Archives of Manitoba
  C. Acton Burrows Papers
  James Colcleugh Papers
  W. Sanford Evans Papers
  Thomas Greenway Papers
  Letterbooks of Inspector of Public Institutions and Buildings,
      and of the Chief Clerk, Department of Public Works, 1891-1900.
  Manitoba, Railway Commissioner, Mortgages, Leases, Agreements
      between the Railway Commissioner of the Province of
      Manitoba and the Canadian Northern Railway Company
      Lines, 1896-1916.
  Sir Daniel Hunter McMillan Papers
  J.J. Moncrieff Papers
  Arthur W. Puttee Papers
  Alexander Reid Papers
  John Christian Schultz Papers
  Clifford Sifton Papers
  James Morrow Walsh Papers
Public Archives of Nova Scotia
  Sir Frederick Borden Papers
  William Stevens Fielding Papers
Public Archives of Ontario
  Historical Sketch of Canada Southern Railway Company [1946]
  Sir James P. Whitney Papers
Public Archives of Saskatchewan
  Walter Scott Papers
Queen's University Archives
  T.A. Crerar Papers
Toronto Public Library
  William Main Johnson Papers
University of Manitoba, Elizabeth Dafoe Library
  John Wesley Dafoe Papers
University of Toronto Archives
  James Mavor Papers
  B.E. Walker Papers

University of Western Ontario Library
  David Mills Papers
Winnipeg Free Press Library

PUBLISHED GOVERNMENT DOCUMENTS

Canada. Commission of Conservation. *Annual Reports*, 1910-1919
Canada Gazette (Ottawa)
Canada. Parliament. House of Commons. Special Committee on Railways, Canals
    and Telegraph Lines, *Minutes of Proceeding and Evidence*, Nos. 1, 2, 3, 5-7
    April 1927
Canada. Parliament. House of Commons. *Debates*
Canada. Parliament. House of Commons. *Journals*
Canada. Parliament. *Sessional Papers*
Census of Canada 1890-91
Census of Manitoba, 1885-86
Manitoba Gazette
Manitoba. Legislative Assembly. *Journals*
Manitoba Reports
Olmstead, R.A., ed., *Decisions of the Judicial Committee of the Privy Council
    relating to the British North America Act, 1867 and the Canadian
    Constitution 1867-1954*. Ottawa: Queen's Printer, 1954
Province of Manitoba. *Sessional Papers*
Report of the Canadian Pacific Railway Royal Commission, 3 vols. Ottawa: S.
    Stephenson & Co., 1882
Report of the Department of Education, Manitoba, for the Year 1894. Winnipeg,
    1895
Report of the Royal Commission on the Liquor Traffic. Ottawa, 1895
Statutes of Canada
Statutes of Manitoba
Supreme Court of Canada, *Reports*

NEWSPAPERS AND PERIODICALS

Acta Victoriana (Victoria University Archives)
Brandon Blade
Brandon Daily Mail
Brandon Sun
The Canadian Magazine
Collier's, The National Weekly (Canadian Edition)
Dawson Daily News
Edmonton Bulletin
Eye-Opener (Calgary)
The Gazette (Montreal)
The Globe (Toronto)
The Inter-Ocean (Selkirk, Manitoba)
Mail and Empire (Toronto)

Manitoba Free Press (Winnipeg)
The Monetary Times
Montreal Daily Star
Montreal Herald and Daily Telegraph
The Morning Albertan (Calgary)
Morning Chronicle (Halifax)
The News (Toronto)
Northwest Review
Ottawa Evening Citizen
Ottawa Journal
Saturday Night (Toronto)
The Times (London)
Toronto Daily Star
Western Law Times
Winnipeg Daily Tribune
The World (Toronto)
The Yukon Sun

PAMPHLETS

The Administration of the Yukon. Law and Order Prevail. n.p., n.d. [Liberal election pamphlet, 1900].

All Red Route: Great Britain to Australia, New Zealand and Hong Kong via Ireland and Canada. n.p., n.d. [1908].

Ames, H.B. *Our Western Heritage and How it is being Squandered by the Laurier Government*. [Conservative election pamphlet, 1908].

Dafoe, John W. *Sixty Years in Journalism*. Address to Winnipeg Press Club, 16 October 1943.

Ewart, John S. *The Manitoba School Question. A Reply to Mr. Wade*. Winnipeg: Manitoba Free Press Co., 1895.

Facts for the People: Pages from the Record of the Laurier Administration from 1906 to 1908. [Conservative election pamphlet, 1908].

Livesay, J.F.B. *The Canadian Press and Allied Organizations*. Toronto: n.p., 1924.

Ogilvie, William. *Information Respecting the Yukon District from the Reports of William Ogilvie...and from Other Sources*. Ottawa: Department of the Interior, 1897.

A Session's Diclosures, Second Series: Some Transactions of the Laurier Administration Exposed in the Session of 1907. [Conservative election pamphlet, 1908].

Sifton, Sir Clifford. *Some Historical Reflections Relating to the War*. Address to Women's Canadian Historical Society of Ottawa, 4 November 1915.

Victor Sifton of the Winnipeg Free Press. Winnipeg Free Press, [1961].

Wade, F.C. *The Manitoba School Question*. Winnipeg: Manitoba Institute for the Deaf and Dumb, 1895.

BOOKS

Armstrong, Christopher, *The Politics of Federalism: Ontario's Relations With the Federal Government, 1867-1942*. Toronto: University of Toronto Press, 1981.

Bankson, Russell, A. *The Klondike Nuggett*. Caldwell, Id.: Caxton Printers, 1935.

Beck, J.M. *Pendulum of Power: Canada's Federal Elections*. Scarborough: Prentice-Hall, 1968.

Berger, Carl, ed., *Imperialism and Nationalism 1884-1914: A Conflict in Canadian Thought*. Toronto: Copp Clark, 1969.

Berton, Pierre. *Klondike: The Life and Death of the Last Great Gold Rush*. Toronto: McClelland and Stewart, 1958.

———. *The Last Spike*. Toronto: McClelland and Stewart, 1971.

Bliss, Michael. *The Discovery of Insulin*. Toronto: McClelland and Stewart, 1982.

Borden H., ed. *Robert Laird Borden: His Memoirs*. 2 vols. Toronto: Macmillan, 1938.

Brebner, J.B. *North Atlantic Triangle*. New York: Columbia University Press, 1945.

Breen, David H. *The Canadian Prairie West and the Ranching Frontier, 1875-1922*. Toronto: University of Toronto Press, 1983.

Brown, Robert Craig. *Canada's National Policy, 1883-1900: A Study in Canadian-American Relations*. Princeton: Princeton University Press, 1964.

———. *Robert Laird Borden, A Biography*. 2 vols. Toronto: Macmillan, 1975, 1980.

———, and R. Cook. *Canada 1896-1921: A Nation Transformed*. Toronto: McClelland and Stewart, 1974.

Bruce, Charles. *News and the Southams*. Toronto: Macmillan, 1968.

Burwash, Nathanael. *The History of Victoria College*. Toronto: Victoria College Press, 1927.

Campbell, Charles S., Jr. *Anglo-American Understanding, 1898-1903*. Baltimore: Johns Hopkins Press, 1957.

Clark, Lovell, ed. *The Manitoba School Question: Majority Rule or Minority Rights?* Toronto: Copp Clark, 1968.

Clark, W. Leland. *Brandon's Politics and Politicians*. Brandon: Brandon Sun, 1981.

Colquhoun, A.H.U. *Press, Politics and People: the Life and Letters of Sir John Willison, Journalist and Correspondent of the Times*. Toronto: Macmillan, 1935.

Cook, G. Ramsay. *The Politics of John W. Dafoe and the Free Press*. Toronto: University of Toronto Press, 1963.

———, ed. *The Dafoe-Sifton Correspondence 1919-1927*. Manitoba Record Society Publications, vol. II. Altona, Man.: D.W. Friesen & Sons, 1966.

Coyle, David C. *Conservation: An American Story of Conflict and Accomplishment*. New Brunswick, N.J.: Rutgers University Press, 1957.

Craven, Paul. *"An Impartial Umpire": Industrial Relations and the Canadian State 1900-1911*. Toronto: University of Toronto Press, 1980.

Crunican, Paul. *Priests and Politicians: Manitoba Schools and the Election of*

1896. Toronto: University of Toronto Press, 1974.

Currie, A.W. *The Grand Trunk Railway of Canada*. Toronto: University of Toronto Press, 1957.

Dafoe, John W. *Clifford Sifton in Relation to His Times*. Toronto: Macmillan, 1931.

———. *Laurier: A Study in Canadian Politics*. Toronto: McClelland and Stewart, 1963.

Dawson, R.M. *The Civil Service of Canada*. London: Oxford, 1929.

———. *William Lyon Mackenzie King*, I, 1874-1923. Toronto: University of Toronto Press, 1958.

Donnelly, Murray, *Dafoe of the Free Press*. Toronto: Macmillan, 1968.

Easterbrook, W.J., and H.G.J. Aitken. *Canadian Economic History*. Toronto: Macmillan, 1956.

Eayrs, James. *The Art of the Possible: Government and Foreign Policy in Canada*. Toronto: University of Toronto Press, 1961.

Eggleston, Wilfrid. *The Queen's Choice: A Story of Canada's Capital*. Ottawa: Queen's Printer, 1961.

Elford, Jean Turnbull. *History of Lambton County*. 2d. ed. Sarnia: Lambton County Historical Society, 1969.

Ellis, L.E. *Reciprocity, 1911*. New Haven: Yale University Press, 1939.

English John. *The Decline of Politics: The Conservatives and the Party System 1901-20*. Toronto: University of Toronto Press, 1977.

Fergusson, Bruce. *Hon. W.S. Fielding*. 2 vols. Windsor, N.S.: Lancelot Press, 1970, 1971.

Foster, Janet. *Working for Wildlife: the Beginning of Preservation in Canada*. Toronto: University of Toronto Press, 1978.

Fowke, V.C. *Canadian Agricultural Policy: The Historical Pattern*. Toronto: University of Toronto Press, 1947.

———. *The National Policy and the Wheat Economy*. Toronto: University of Toronto Press, 1956.

Fumoleau, René. *As Long As This Land Shall Last: A History of Treaty 8 and Treaty 11, 1870-1939*. Toronto: McClelland and Stewart, 1975.

Gibson, Dale and Lee. *Substantial Justice: Law and Lawyers in Manitoba 1670-1970*. Winnipeg: Peguis, 1972.

Graham, Roger. *Arthur Meighen*. 3 vols. Toronto: Clarke, Irwin, 1960, 1963, 1965.

Granatstein, J.L., and J.M. Hitsman. *Broken Promises: A History of Conscription in Canada*. Toronto: Oxford, 1977.

Grant, George P. *Philosophy in the Mass Age*. Rev. ed. Toronto: Copp Clark, 1966.

Green, Lewis. *The Gold Hustlers*. Anchorage: Alaska Northwest Publishing Co., 1977.

Gruening, Ernest. *The State of Alaska*. New York: Random House, 1968.

Harkness, Ross. *J.E. Atkinson of the Star*. Toronto: University of Toronto Press, 1963.

Harris, Theodore H. *The Economic Aspects of the Crowsnest Pass Rates Agreement*. McGill University Economic Studies, no. 13. Toronto: Macmillan, 1930.

Hays, S.P. *Conservation and the Gospel of Efficiency*. Cambridge: Harvard University Press, 1959.

Hedges, J.B. *Building the Canadian West: the Land and Colonization Policies of the Canadian Pacific Railway*. New York: Macmillan, 1939.

———. *The Federal Railway Land Subsidy Policy of Canada*. Cambridge: Harvard University Press, 1934.

Higham, John. *Strangers in the Land: Patterns of American Nativism 1860-1925*. New York: Atheneum, 1963.

Innis, H.A. *Settlement and the Mining Frontier*. Toronto: Macmillan, 1936.

Johnson, George, ed. *The All Red Line: The Annals and Aims of the Pacific Cable Project*. Ottawa: James Hope & Sons, 1903.

Kavanagh, Martin. *The Assiniboine Basin*. Winnipeg: Public Press, 1946.

Kaye, Vladimir J. *Early Ukrainian Settlement in Canada 1895-1900: Dr. Josef Oleskow's Role in the Settlement of the Canadian Northwest*. Toronto: University of Toronto Press, 1964.

Kelley, Robert. *The Transatlantic Persuasion: The Liberal Democratic Mind in the Age of Gladstone*. New York: Knopf, 1969.

Kostash, Myrna. *All of Baba's Children*. Edmonton: Hurtig, 1977.

Lamb, W. Kaye. *History of the Canadian Pacific Railway*. New York: Macmillan, 1977.

Lambert, Richard S., and Paul Pross. *Renewing Nature's Wealth: A Centennial History of the Public Management of Lands, Forests & Wildlife in Ontario 1763-1967*. Toronto: Ontario Department of Lands and Forests, 1967.

Landon, F., and O. Miller. *Up the Proof Line: The Story of a Rural Community*. London, Ont.: D.B. Weldon, 1955.

Lauriston, Victor E. *Lambton's Hundred Years 1849-1949*. Sarnia: Haines Frontier Printing Co. [1949].

Lingard, C.C. *Territorial Government in Canada: The Autonomy Question in the Old North-West Territories*. Toronto: University of Toronto Press, 1946.

Lupul, Manoly R. *The Roman Catholic Church and the North-West School Question: A Study in Church-State Relations in Western Canada, 1875-1905*. Toronto: University of Toronto Press, 1974.

Macdonald, E.M. *Recollections, Political and Personal*. Toronto: Ryerson, 1938.

Macdonald, Norman. *Canada: Immigration and Colonization, 1841-1903*. Toronto: Macmillan, 1966.

MacDougall, John. *Rural Life in Canada*. Toronto: University of Toronto Press [1913], 1973.

MacEwan, Grant. *The Battle for the Bay*. Saskatoon: Western Producer Books, 1975.

Mackenzie, Norman and Jeanne. *H.G. Wells*. New York: Simon and Schuster, 1973.

Macleod, R.C. *The NWMP and Law Enforcement 1873-1905*. Toronto: University of Toronto Press, 1976.

Martin, Albro. *James J. Hill & the Opening of the Northwest*. New York: Oxford, 1976.

Martin, Chester. *"Dominion Lands" Policy*, ed. Lewis H. Thomas. Toronto: McClelland and Stewart, 1973.

Marunchak, M.H. *The Ukrainian Canadians: A History*. Winnipeg: Ukrainian Free Academy of Science, 1970.

McCluskey, Neil G., S.J. *Catholic Viewpoint on Education*. Garden City: Hanover House, 1959.

McDougall, J.L. *Canadian Pacific: A Brief History*. Montreal: McGill University Press, 1968.

McNaught, Kenneth. *A Prophet in Politics: A Biography of J.S. Woodsworth*. Toronto: University of Toronto Press, 1959.

Miller, Carman. *The Canadian Career of the Fourth Earl of Minto: The Education of a Viceroy*. Waterloo: Wilfrid Laurier University Press, 1980.

Morrison, D.R. *The Politics of the Yukon Territory, 1898-1909*. Toronto: University of Toronto Press, 1968.

Morton, A.S. *History of Prairie Settlement*. Toronto: Macmillan, 1938.

Morton, W.L. *Manitoba: A History*. Toronto: University of Toronto Press, 1957.

———. *One University: A History of the University of Manitoba*. Toronto: McClelland and Stewart, 1957.

———. *The Progressive Party in Canada*. Toronto: University of Toronto Press, 1950.

Munro, John A., ed. *The Alaska Boundary Dispute*. Toronto: Copp Clark, 1970.

Neatby, H.B. *Laurier and a Liberal Quebec*. Toronto: McClelland and Stewart, 1973.

———. *William Lyon Mackenzie King*, II, *1924-1932*. Toronto: University of Toronto Press, 1963.

Nelles, H.V. *The Politics of Development: Forests, Mines & Hydro-Electric Power in Ontario, 1849-1941*. Toronto: Macmillan, 1974.

Nelson, J.G., ed. *Canadian Parks in Perspective*. Montreal: Harvest House, 1970.

Official Report of the Liberal Convention, Held in Response to the Call of Hon Wilfrid Laurier Leader of the Liberal Party of the Dominion of Canada. Ottawa, Tuesday, June 20th, and Wednesday, June 21st, 1893. Toronto: The Budget Printing & Publishing Co., 1893.

Ogilvie, William. *Early Days in the Yukon & the Story of Its Gold Finds*. Ottawa: Thorburn & Abbott, 1913.

Oliver, E.H., ed. *The Canadian North-West: Its Early Development and Legislative Records*. 2 vols. Ottawa: Government Printing Bureau, 1915.

Oliver, Peter. *G. Howard Ferguson: Ontario Tory*. Toronto: University of Toronto Press, 1977.

Ollivier M., ed. *The Colonial and Imperial Conferences from 1887 to 1937*. 3 vols. Ottawa: Queen's Printer, 1954.

Owram, Douglas. *Building for Canadians: A History of the Department of Public Works 1840-1960*. Ottawa: Public Works Canada, 1979.

———, ed. *The Formation of Alberta: A Documentary History*. Calgary: Historical Society of Alberta, 1979.

Patton, H.S. *Grain Growers' Cooperation in Western Canada*. Cambridge: Harvard University Press, 1928.

Peers, Frank W. *The Politics of Canadian Broadcasting 1920-1951*. Toronto: University of Toronto Press, 1969.

Penlington, Norman. *The Alaska Boundary Dispute: A Critical Reappraisal*. Toronto: McGraw-Hill Ryerson, 1972.

———. *Canada and Imperialism, 1896-1899*. Toronto: University of Toronto Press, 1965.

Perkins, Bradford. *The Great Rapprochement: England and the United States, 1895-1914*. New York: Atheneum, 1968.

Pinkett, Harold T., *Gifford Pinchot: Private and Public Forester*. Urbana: University of Illinois Press, 1970.

Porritt, Edward. *The Revolt in Canada against the New Feudalism: Tariff History from the Revision of 1907 to the Uprising of the West in 1910*. London: Cassell, 1911.

———. *Sixty Years of Protection in Canada 1846-1907, Where Industry Leans on the Politician*. London: Macmillan, 1908.

Prang, Margaret. *N.W. Rowell: Ontario Nationalist*. Toronto: University of Toronto Press, 1975.

Preston, R.A. *Canada and "Imperial Defense"*. Toronto: University of Toronto Press, 1967.

Preston, W.T.R. *The Life and Times of Lord Strathcona*. London: Eveleigh Nash, 1914.

———. *My Generation of Politics and Politicians*. Toronto: D.A. Rose, 1927.

Regehr, T.D. *The Canadian Northern Railway: Pioneer Road of the Northern Prairies 1895-1918*. Toronto: Macmillan, 1976.

Robbins, Roy M. *Our Landed Heritage: the Public Domain, 1776-1936*. Lincoln: University of Nebraska Press, 1962.

Rodney, William. *Joe Boyle: King of the Klondike*. Toronto: McGraw-Hill Ryerson, 1974.

Ross, A.H.D. *Ottawa Past and Present*. Ottawa: Thorburn and Abbott, 1927.

Rutherford, Paul. *A Victorian Authority: The Daily Press in Late Nineteenth-Century Canada*. Toronto: University of Toronto Press, 1982.

Saywell, J.T., ed. *The Canadian Journal of Lady Aberdeen 1893-1898*. Toronto: Champlain Society, 1960.

Schmeiser, D.A. *Civil Liberties in Canada*. London: Oxford University Press, 1964.

Schull, Joseph. *Edward Blake*. 2 vols. Toronto: Macmillan, 1975, 1976.

———. *Laurier: the First Canadian*. Toronto: Macmillan, 1965.

Sissons, C.B. *Church & State in Canadian Education*. Toronto: Ryerson, 1959.

———. *A History of Victoria University*. Toronto: University of Toronto Press, 1952.

Skelton, O.D. *Life and Letters of Sir Wilfrid Laurier*. 2 vols. New York: Century, 1921.

Spence, Ruth Elizabeth. *Prohibition in Canada* . Toronto: Ontario Branch of the Dominion Alliance, 1919.

Stacey, C.P. *Canada and the Age of Conflict*, I, *1867-1921*. Toronto: Macmillan, 1977.

———. *Canada and the Age of Conflict*, II, *1921-1948*. Toronto: University of Toronto Press, 1981.

Stevens, Paul, ed. *The 1911 General Election: A Study in Canadian Politics*. Toronto: Copp Clark, 1970.

Stevens, Paul, and J. T. Saywell, eds., *Lord Minto's Canadian Papers*, vol. 1. Toronto: Champlain Society, 1981.

Stewart, Robert. *Sam Steele: Lion of the Frontier*. Toronto: Doubleday, 1979.

Stuart, J.A.D. *The Prairie W.A.S.P.: A History of the Rural Municipality of Oakland, Manitoba*. Winnipeg: Prairie Publishing, 1969.

Sutherland, Neil. *Children in English-Canadian Society 1880-1920: Framing the Twentieth-Century Consensus*. Toronto: University of Toronto Press, 1976.

Talbot, Edward Allen. *Five Years' Residence in the Canadas*. London: Longman, 1824.

Tansill, C.C. *Canadian-American Relations, 1875-1911*. Gloucester: Peter Smith, 1964.

Thomas, Lewis H. *The Struggle for Responsible Government in the North West Territories 1870-97*. Toronto: University of Toronto Press, 1956.

Thompson, John Herd. *The Harvests of War: The Prairie West. 1914-1918*. Toronto: McClelland and Stewart, 1978.

Thomson, Don, W. *Men and Meridians: The History of Surveying and Mapping in Canada*, vol. 2, *1867-1917*. Ottawa: Queen's Printer, 1967.

Troper, H.M. *Only Farmers Need Apply: Official Canadian Government Encouragement of Immigration from the United States 1896-1911*. Toronto: Griffin House, 1972.

Underhill, F.H. *In Search of Canadian Liberalism*. Toronto: Macmillan, 1960.

Vaughan, W. *The Life and Work of Sir William Van Horne*. New York: Century, 1920.

Walker, Franklin A. *Catholic Education and Politics in Ontario*. Toronto: Nelson, 1964.

Wells, H.G. *Joan and Peter: The Story of an Education*. New York: Macmillan, 1918.

Willison, J.S. *Sir Wilfrid Laurier*. Toronto: Oxford, 1927.

Wilson, C.F. *A Century of Canadian Grain*. Saskatoon: Western Producer Prairie Books, 1978.

Wood, L.A. *A History of Farmers' Movements in Canada*. Toronto: Ryerson, 1924.

Woodcock, G., and I. Avakumovic. *The Doukhobors*. Toronto: Oxford, 1968.

Young, Scott and Astrid. *O'Brien*. Toronto: Ryerson, 1967.

Zaslow, M. *The Opening of the Canadian North, 1870-1914*. Toronto: McClelland and Stewart, 1971.

———. *Reading the Rocks: the Story of the Geological Survey of Canada 1842-1972*. Toronto: Macmillan, 1975.

ARTICLES

Armstrong, Alan H. "Thomas Adams and the Commission of Conservation," In *Planning the Canadian Environment*, edited by L.O. Gertler, 17-35. Montreal: Harvest House, 1968.

Artibise, A.F.J., and G.A. Stelter. "Conservation Planning and Urban Planning: the Canadian Commission of Conservation in Historical Perspective." In *Planning for Conservation*, edited by Roger Kain, 17-36. New York: St. Martin's Press, 1981.

Avery, Donald. "Canadian Immigration Policy and the 'Foreign' Navvy 1896-1914." Canadian Historical Association, *Historical Papers* 1972.: 135-56.

Baker, W.M. "A Case Study of Anti-Americanism in English-Speaking Canada: the Election Campaign of 1911." *CHR*, 51, no. 4 (December 1970): 426-49.

Ball, Norman. "The Development of Permafrost Thawing Techniques in the Placer Gold Fields of the Klondike." In Department of Indian and Northern Affairs, National Historic Parks and Sites Branch, *Research Bulletin*, no. 25, (November 1975).

Betke, Carl. "The Mounted Police and the Doukhobors in Saskatchewan, 1899-1909." *Saskatchewan History*, 27, no. 1 (Winter 1974): 1-14.

Brown, Gerald H. "The Georgian Bay Canal." *Collier's* (Canadian Edition) (22 August 1908): 21.

Brown, R.C. "The Doctrine of Usefulness: Natural Resource and National Park Policy in Canada, 1887-1914." In *Canadian Parks in Perspective*, edited by J.G. Nelson, 42-62. Montreal: Harvest House, 1970.

———. "For the Purposes of the Dominion: Background Paper on the History of Federal Public Lands Policy to 1930." In *Canadian Public Land Use in Perspective*, edited by J.G. Nelson, R.C. Scace and R. Kouri, 5-15. Ottawa: Social Science Research Council, 1974.

Caldwell, J. Warren. "The Unification of Methodism in Canada, 1865-1884." The *Bulletin*, 19 (1967) (United Church of Canada, Committee on Archives): 3-61.

Cook, Ramsay. "Dafoe, Laurier, and the Formation of Union Government." In *Conscription 1917*, edited by C. Berger, 15-38. Toronto: University of Toronto Press, n.d.

Cooper, John A. "The Editors of the Leading Canadian Dailies." *The Canadian Magazine*, 12, no. 4 (February 1899): 349-50.

Creighton, D.G. "Confederation: the Use and Abuse of History," *JCS*, 1, no. 1 (1966): 3-11.

———. "John A. Macdonald, Confederation, and the Canadian West." In *Minorities, Schools, and Politics*, edited by R.C. Brown, 1-9. Toronto: University of Toronto Press, 1969.

Currie, A.W. "Freight Rates on Grain in Western Canada," *CHR*, 21 (1940): 40-55.

Dafoe, J.W. "Sir Clifford Sifton." *Dictionary of National Biography*, Twentieth Century, 1922-30, pp. 772-73.

Daniel, Richard. "The Spirit and Terms of Treaty Eight." In *The Spirit of the Alberta Indian Treaties*, edited by Richard Price, 47-100. Montreal: Institute for Research on Public Policy, 1979.

Dreisziger, N.F. "The Canadian-American Irrigation Frontier Revisited: the International Origins of Irrigation in Southern Alberta, 1885-1909." Canadian Historical Association, *Historical Papers 1975:* 211-29.

Eager, Evelyn. "Separate Schools and the Cabinet Crisis of 1905." *The Lakehead University Review*, 2, no. 2 (Fall 1969): 89-115.

Eagle, John A. "Monopoly or Competition: the Nationalization of the Grand Trunk Railway." *CHR*, 62, no. 1 (March 1981): 3-30.

Epp, A. Ernest. "The Lake of the Woods Milling Company: an Early Western Industry." In *The Canadian West*, edited by H.C. Klassen, 147-62. Calgary: University of Calgary, 1977.

Foster, Keith. "The Barr Colonists: Their Arrival and Impact on the Canadian North-West." *Saskatchewan History*, 35, no.3 (1982): 81-100.

Fowke, V.C. "Royal Commissions and Canadian Agricultural Policy." *CJEPS* 14 (1948): 163-75.

Fraser, Blair. "The Many, Mighty Siftons." *Maclean's*, (19 December 1959): 18-19, 52-54.

———. "The vast and turbulent empire of the Siftons." *Maclean's* (5 December 1959): 15-17, 83-86.

Friesen, Gerald. "Homeland to Hinterland: Political Transition in Manitoba, 1870 to 1879." Canadian Historical Association, *Historical Papers, 1979*: 33-47.

Gadsby, H.F. "Has Canada a Political Boss?" *MacLean's* (31 March 1918): 38-40, 75-76.

Hall, D.J. "Clifford Sifton and Canadian Indian Administration 1896-1905." *Prairie Forum* 2 (1977): 127-51.

———. "Clifford Sifton: Immigration and Settlement Policy, 1896-1905." In *The Settlement of the West*, edited by H. Palmer, 60-85. Calgary: University of Calgary, 1977.

———"A Divergence of Principle: Clifford Sifton, Sir Wilfrid Laurier and the North-West Autonomy Bills, 1905." *Laurentian University Review*, 7, no. 1 (November 1974): 3-24.

———. "The Half-Breed Claims Commission." *Alberta History*, 25, no. 2 (1977): 1-8.

———. "The Manitoba Grain Act: An 'Agrarian Magna Carta'?" *Prairie Forum*, 4, no. 1 (Spring 1979): 105-20.

———. "'The Spirit of Confederation': Ralph Heintzman, Professor Creighton, and the bicultural compact theory." *JCS*, 9 (November 1974): 24-43.

———. "T.O. Davis and Federal Politics in Saskatchewan, 1896." *Saskatchewan History*, 30 (1977): 56-62.

Harney, Robert F. "Men Without Women: Italian Migrants in Canada, 1885-1930." *Canadian Ethnic Studies*, 11, no. 1 (1979): 29-47.

Hawkes, Arthur. "Clifford Sifton and the Reciprocity Election of 1911." *MFP*. (21 September 1929): 33.

Heintzman, Ralph. "The Spirit of Confederation: Professor Creighton, Biculturalism and the Use of History." *CHR*, 52 (1971): 245-75.

Hulchanski, John David. "Thomas Adams: a biographical and bibliographical guide." *Papers on Planning & Design*, no. 15, Department of Urban and Regional Planning, University of Toronto, 1978.

Johnson, Gilbert. "James Moffat Douglas," *Saskatchewan History*, 7 (1954): 47-50.

Lederle, John W. "The Liberal Convention of 1893." *CJEPS*, 16 (1940): 47-50.

Leslie Genevieve. "Domestic Service in Canada 1880-1920." In *Women at Work: Ontario, 1850-1930*, 71-125. Toronto: Canadian Women's Educational Press, 1974.

Lupul, M.R. "The Campaign for a French Catholic School Inspector in the North-West Territories, 1898-1903." *CHR*, 47 (1967): 332-52.

Macleod, R.C. "The Mounted Police in Politics." In *Men in Scarlet*, edited by H.A. Dempsey, 94-114. Calgary: McClelland and Stewart West, 1975.

MacDonald, Norbert. "Seattle, Vancouver and the Klondike," *CHR*, 49 (1968): 234-46.

MacFarlane, R.O. "Manitoba Politics and Parties after Confederation," Canadian Historical Association, *Annual Report* (1940): 45-55.

McCormack, A.R. "Arthur Puttee and the Liberal Party: 1899-1904," *CHR*, 51 (1970): 141-63.

McCutcheon, Brian R. "The Patrons of Industry in Manitoba, 1890-1898." In *Historical Essays on the Prairie Provinces*, edited by Donald Swainson, 142-65. Toronto: McClelland and Sewart, 1970.

Miller, J.R. "D'Alton McCarthy, Equal Rights, and the Origins of the Manitoba School Question." *CHR*, 54 (1973): 369-92.

Morton, W.L. "Confederation, 1870-1896: The end of the Macdonaldian constitution and the return to duality." *JCS*, 1, no. 1 (1966): 11-24.

Osler, Richard, "The Siftons: a tale of two brothers." *The Financial Post* (16 July 1977): 30-31.

———. "The Siftons: to live enough is to conquer," *The Financial Post* (9 July 1977): 26-27.

Percy, M. B., K.H. Norrie and R.G. Johnston, "Reciprocity and the Canadian General Election of 1911." *Explorations in Economic History*, 19, (1982): 409-34.

Perdue, W.E. "Fusion of Law and Equity in Manitoba," *Canadian Law Times*, 2 (1882): 428-31.

Phelps, Edward. "Foundations of the Canadian Oil Industry, 1850-1866." In *Profiles of a Province: Studies in the History of Ontario*, edited by E.G. Firth, 156-65. Toronto: Ontario Historical Society, 1967.

Raby, Stewart. "Indian Land Surrenders in Southern Saskatchewan." *The Canadian Geographer*, 17 (Spring 1973): 36-52.

Renfrew, Stewart. "Commission of Conservation." *Douglas Library Notes* (Queen's University), Spring 1971, pp. 17-26.

Sifton, Clifford. "Canada's Conservation Commission," *American Conservation*, 1, no. 5 (June 1911): 171-78.

———. "The Canadian People and Their Problems." *MFP*, Diamond Jubilee Issue, 1927, p.11. Address to Canadian Daughters' League of Canada, Vancouver.

———. "The Conservation of Canada's Resources." In *Empire Club Speeches* (Toronto), *1910-1911* (20 October 1910), edited by J. Castell Hopkins, 57-63. Toronto: Saturday Night Press.

———. "The Foundations of the New Era." In *The New Era in Canada: Essays Dealing with the Upbuilding of the Canadian Commonwealth*, edited by J.O. Miller, 37-57. Toronto: J.M. Dent, 1917.

————. "Immigration." *Proceedings of the Canadian Club, Toronto, for the Years 1921-22.* vol. 19 (3 April 1922): 182-91.

————. "The Immigrants Canada Wants." *MacLean's* (1 April 1922): 16, 22-24.

————. "The Manitoba School Question." *Review of Reviews.* (12 October 1895), 452-53.

————. "The Needs of the Northwest.," *The Canadian Magazine,* 20, no. 5, (March 1903): 425-28.

————. "Reciprocity." In *Canadian National Problems,* edited by Ellery C. Stowell, 20-28 Philadelphia: American Academy of Political and Social Science, 1913.

————. "Some Canadian Constitutional problems." *CHR*, 3 (1922): 3-23.

————. "Some Matters of National Interest to Canadians." In *Addresses Delivered before the Canadian Clubs, Ottawa Club, 1903-04,* edited by G.M. Brown, pp. 71-73.

Simpson, Michael. "Thomas Adams in Canada, 1914-1930, *"Urban-History Review,* 11, 2 (October 1982): 1-16.

Smith, C. Roy, and David R. Witty. "Conservation, Resources and Environment: an Exposition and Critical Evaluation of the Commission of Conservation, Canada." *Plan Canada*, 11, no. 1 (1970): 55-71, and 11, no. 3 (1972): 199-216.

Smith, P.J. "The Principle of Utility and the Origins of Planning Legislation in Alberta, 1912-1975." In *The Usable Urban Past: Planning and Politics in the Modern Canadian City,* edited by A.F.J. Artibise and G.A. Stelter, 196-225. Toronto: Macmillan, 1979.

Sterner, W.E. "Sir Clifford as a Young Campaigner." *Toronto Saturday Night.* (27 April 1929).

Stevens, Paul. "Wilfrid Laurier: Politician," In *Les idées politiques des premiers ministres du Canada/The Political Ideas of the Prime Ministers of Canada,* edited by M. Hamelin, 69-85. Ottawa: Les Editions de l'Université d'Ottawa, 1969.

Thomas, Greg, and Ian Clarke. "The Garrison Mentality and the Canadian West." *Prairie Forum,* 4, no.1 (Spring 1979): 83-104.

Thomas, Lewis H. "From the Pampas to the Prairies: the Welsh Migration of 1902." *Saskatchewan History*, 24 (1971): 1-12.

Thorpe, F.J. "Historical Perspective on the 'Resources for Tomorrow' Conference." *Resources for Tomorrow, Conference Background Papers*, vol. 1. Ottawa: Queen's Printer, 1961.

Timlin, M.F. "Canada's Immigration Policy, 1896-1910." *CJEPS* 26 (1960): 517-32.

Wade, F.C. "The Alaska Boundary Dispute: Its Practical Side." *The Empire Review*, 4 (January 1903): 577-86.

Wessel, Thomas R. "Prologue to Shelterbelt, 1870 to 1934," *Journal of the West*, 6 (1967): 119-34.

Wickett, S.M. "Yukon Trade." *Industrial Canada,* (October 1902): 164-72.

Winearls, Joan. "Federal Electoral Maps of Canada 1867-1970." *The Canadian Cartographer*, 9, no. 1 (1972): 1-24.

THESES AND DISSERTATIONS

Allan, John. "Reciprocity and the Canadian General Election 1911: a Re-examination of Economic Self-Interest in Voting." M.A. thesis, Queen's University, 1971.

Avery, D.H. "Canadian Immigration Policy and the Alien Question, 1896-1919: The Anglo-Canadian Perspective." Ph.D. diss., University of Western Ontario, 1973.

Bocking, D.H. "Premier Walter Scott: A Study of His Rise to Political Power." M.A. thesis, University of Saskatchewan, 1959.

Bray, Robert Matthew. "The Role of Sir Clifford Sifton in the Formation of the Editorial Policy of the *Manitoba Free Press*, 1916 to 1921." M.A. thesis, University of Manitoba, 1968.

Brennan, J.W. "A Political History of Saskatchewan, 1905-1929." Ph.D. diss., University of Alberta, 1976.

Brooks, William Howard. "Methodism in the Canadian West in the Nineteenth Century." Ph.D. diss., University of Manitoba, 1972.

Bush, Edward Forbes. "The Canadian 'Fast Line' on the North Atlantic, 1886-1915." M.A. thesis, Carleton University, 1969.

Byrne, A.R. "Man and Landscape Change in the Banff National Park Area before 1911." M.A. thesis, University of Calgary, 1964.

Calnan, David M., "Businessmen, Forestry and the Gospel of Efficiency: the Canadian Conservation Commission, 1909-1921." M.A. thesis, University of Western Ontario, 1976.

Clague, R.E. "The Political Aspects of the Manitoba School Question, 1890-1896." M.A. thesis, University of Manitoba, 1939.

Clark, Lovell C. "A History of the Conservative Administrations, 1891 to 1896." Ph.D. diss., University of Toronto, 1968.

Clippingdale, Richard T.G. "J.S. Willison, Political Journalist: From Liberalism to Independence, 1881-1905." Ph.D. diss., University of Toronto, 1970.

Cooke, Ellen Gillies. "The Federal Election of 1896 in Manitoba." M.A. thesis, University of Manitoba, 1943.

Coutts, R.M. "The Railway Policy of Sir Wilfrid Laurier: Grand Trunk Pacific— National Transcontinental." M.A. thesis, University of Toronto, 1968.

Crunican, Paul E. "The Manitoba School Question and Canadian Federal Politics, 1890-1896: a Study in Church-State Relations." Ph.D. diss., University of Toronto, 1968.

Curtis, Christopher. "The Parting of the Ways: the Manufacturers, the Liberals, and the 1911 Election." M.A. thesis, Carleton University, 1977.

Dreisziger, N.A.F. "The International Joint Commission of the United States and Canada, 1895-1920." Ph.D. diss., University of Toronto, 1974.

Driessen, Martin. "William Lyon Mackenzie King and the St. Lawrence Seaway, 1921-1930." B.A. Honours thesis, Department of History, University of Alberta, 1976.

Eagle, John A. "Sir Robert Borden and the Railway Problem in Canadian Politics, 1911-1920." Ph.D. diss., University of Toronto, 1972.

Fisk, Larry John. "Controversy on the Prairies: Issues in the General Provincial Elections of Manitoba 1870-1969." Ph.D. diss., University of Alberta, 1975.

Friesen, Gerald A. "Studies in the Development of Western Canadian Regional Consciousness 1870-1925." Ph.D. diss., University of Toronto, 1974.

Gibson, Frederick W. "The Alaskan Boundary Dispute." M.A. thesis, Queen's University, 1944.

Gilbert, Angus D. "The Political Influence of Imperialist Thought in Canada." Ph.D. diss., University of Toronto, 1974.

Grayson, Linda M. "The Formation of the Bank of Canada, 1913-1938." Ph.D. diss., University of Toronto, 1974.

Guest, Henry James. "Reluctant Politician: A Biography of Sir Hugh John Macdonald." M.A. thesis, University of Manitoba, 1973.

Hall, D.J. "The Political Career of Clifford Sifton 1896-1905." Ph.D. diss., University of Toronto, 1973.

Harris, James G. "*The News* and Canadian Politics, 1903-1914: a Study of the Policies of *The News* under the Editorship of Sir John Willison." M.A. thesis, University of Toronto, 1952.

Hett, R.R. "John Charlton, Liberal Politician and Free Trade Advocate." Ph.D. diss., University of Rochester, 1969.

Hilts, Joseph A "The Political Career of Thomas Greenway." Ph.D diss., University of Manitoba 1974.

Holmes, John L. "Factors Affecting Politics in Manitoba: a Study of the Provincial Elections 1870-99." M.A. thesis, University of Manitoba, 1936.

Holmgren, Eric J. "Isaac M. Barr and the Britannia Colony." M.A. thesis, University of Alberta, 1964.

Jackson, E.V. "The Organization of the Canadian Liberal Party, 1867-1896, with Particular Reference to Ontario." M.A. thesis, University of Toronto, 1962.

Jackson, James A. "The Disallowance of Manitoba Railway Legislation in the 1880's: Railway Policy as a Factor in the Relations of Manitoba with the Dominion, 1878-1888." M.A. thesis, University of Manitoba, 1945.

Kemp, Herbert Douglas. "The Department of the Interior in the West 1873-1883: An Examination of Some Hitherto Neglected Aspects of the Work of the Outside Service." M.A. thesis, University of Manitoba, 1950.

Kirkland, Herbert Donald, III. "The American Forests, 1864-1898: A Trend toward Conservation." Ph.D. diss., Florida State University, 1971.

Koester, C.B. "The Parliamentary Career of Nicholas Flood Davin, 1887-1900." M.A. thesis, University of Saskatchewan, 1964.

LaPierre, Laurier J.L. "Politics, Race and Religion in French Canada: Joseph Israel Tarte." Ph.D. diss., University of Toronto, 1962.

MacIntosh, A.W. "The Career of Sir Charles Tupper in Canada, 1864-1900." Ph.D. diss., University of Toronto, 1960.

McCutcheon, Brian Robert. "The Economic and Social Structure of Political Agrarianism in Manitoba: 1870-1900." Ph.D. diss., University of British Columbia, 1974.

McGinnis, Janice P. Dickin. "From Health to Welfare: Federal Government Policies Regarding Standards of Public Health for Canadians, 1919-1945." Ph.D. diss., University of Alberta, 1980.

McLaughlin, K.M. "Race, Religion and Politics: The Election of 1896 in Canada." Ph.D. diss., University of Toronto, 1974.

McMurchy, D.J.A. "David Mills: Nineteenth Century Canadian Liberal." Ph.D. diss., University of Rochester, 1968.

Miller, J.R. "The Impact of the Jesuits' Estates Act on Canadian Politics, 1888-1891." Ph.D. diss., University of Toronto, 1972.

Mitchner, E. Alyn. "William Pearce and Federal Government Activity in Western Canada, 1882-1904." Ph.D. diss., University of Alberta, 1971.

———. "William Pearce: Father of Alberta Irrigation." M.A. thesis, University of Alberta, 1966.

Noble, Edward James. "D'Alton McCarthy and the Election of 1896." M.A. thesis, University of Guelph, 1969.

Pross, August Paul. "The Development of a Forest Policy: A Study of the Ontario Department of Lands and Forests." Ph.D. diss., University of Toronto, 1967.

Regehr, T.D. "Canadian Northern Railway: Agent of National Growth, 1896-1914." Ph.D. diss., University of Alberta, 1967.

———. "The National Policy and Manitoba Railway Legislation 1879-1888." M.A. thesis, Carleton University, 1963.

Richardson, George, "The Conservative Party in the Provisional District of Alberta 1887-1905." M.A. thesis, University of Alberta, 1977.

Scace, R.C. "Banff: A Cultural-Historical Study of Land Use and Management in a National Park Community to 1945." M.A. thesis, University of Calgary, 1967.

Shaw, W.T. "The Role of John S. Ewart in the Manitoba School Question." M.A. thesis, University of Manitoba, 1959.

Stevens, Paul Douglas. "Laurier and the Liberal Party In Ontario, 1887-1911." Ph.D. diss., University of Toronto, 1966.

Stotyn, Keith. "The Bow River Irrigation Project 1906-1949." M.A. thesis, University of Alberta, 1982.

Thompson, John H. "The Prohibition Question in Manitoba 1892-1928." M.A. thesis, University of Manitoba, 1969.

Van Kirk, Sylvia M. "The Development of National Park Policy in Canada's Mountain National Parks, 1885 to 1930." M.A. thesis, University of Alberta, 1969.

Wilson, Keith. "The Development of Education in Manitoba." Ph.D. diss., Michigan State University, 1967.

Wright, Norman Ernest. "An Historical Survey of Southwestern Manitoba to 1899." M.A. thesis, University of Manitoba, 1949.

REFERENCE WORKS

Calendar of the University of Victoria College, Cobourg, 1877-1881.
Canada Year Book.
Canadian Annual Review.

The Canadian Newspaper Directory. Montreal: A. McKim & Co., 1899, 1901, 1905, 1907.

Canadian Parliamentary Companion and Annual Register, 1879.

Carrigan, D.O. *Canadian Party Platforms 1867-1968*. Toronto: Copp Clark, 1968.

City of London and County of Middlesex Gazetteer and Directory 1874-75. London: Irwin & Co., 1874.

Dictionary of Canadian Biography. Toronto: University of Toronto Press, 1966-.

Directory of Members of Parliament and Federal Elections for the North-West Territories and Saskatchewan, 1887-1953. Regina: Saskatchewan Archives Board, 1956.

Electoral Atlas of the Dominion of Canada as Divided for the Revision of the Voters' List made in the Year 1894. Ottawa: Government Printing Bureau, 1895.

Electoral Atlas of the Dominion of Canada as Divided for the Tenth General Election Held in the Year 1904. Ottawa: Government Printing Bureau, 1906.

Mitchell and Company's Canada Classified Directory for 1865-66. Toronto: Mitchell & Co. [1865].

Morgan, H.J. *Canadian Men and Women of the Time*. 2d ed. Toronto: William Briggs, 1912.

Rose, George Maclean. *A Cyclopedia of Canadian Biography*. Toronto: Rose Publishing, 1888.

Sifton Family Record. n.a., n.p., 1955.

Urquhart, M.C., and K.A.H. Buckley, eds. *Historical Statistics of Canada*. Toronto: Macmillan, 1965.

Who's Who and why.

Who's Who in Canada.

INTERVIEWS:

R.S. Malone
Douglas Murray
Clifford Sifton (1893-1976)
Michael Sifton

Abbreviations

CAR	*Canadian Annual Review*
CCAR	Commission of Conservation *Annual Report*
CHR	*Canadian Historical Review*
CJEPS	*Canadian Journal of Economics and Political Science*
CSP	Canada, Parliament, *Sessional Papers*
Debates	Canada, House of Commons, *Debates*
DIA	Department of Indian Affairs
GAA	Glenbow Alberta Archives
JCS	*Journal of Canadian Studies*
Journals	Canada, House of Commons, *Journals*
MFP	*Manitoba Free Press*
PAA	Public Archives of Alberta
PAC	Public Archives of Canada
PAM	Public Archives of Manitoba
PANS	Public Archives of Nova Scotia
PAO	Public Archives of Ontario
PAS	Public Archives of Saskatchewan
RCMP	Royal Canadian Mounted Police
TPL	Toronto Public Library

Notes

1. PAC, Lord Minto Papers, vol. 24, pp. 124-29, Memo: on Yukon affairs, 31 October 1900.
2. Ibid., vol. 14, pp. 70-72, Chamberlain to Minto, 22 October 1900; letterbooks, vol. 2, pp. 122-23, Minto to Chamberlain, 7 November 1900. See also Carman Miller, *The Canadian Career of the Fourth Earl of Minto: the Education of a Viceroy* (Waterloo: Wilfrid Laurier University Press, 1980), pp. 174-75; and Paul Stevens and J.T. Saywell, eds., *Lord Minto's Canadian Papers*, 1 (Toronto: Champlain Society, 1981),especially the Introduction.
3. See D.J. Hall, "Clifford Sifton and Canadian Indian Administration, 1896-1905," *Prairie Forum*, 2, no. 2 (November 1977): 137.
4. PAC Minto Papers, vol. 25 pp. 1-12, Minto to Queen Victoria, 14 May 1899.
5. Ibid., letterbooks, vol. 2, pp. 79-81, Minto to Chamberlain, 19 August 1900; vol. 24, pp. 124-29, Memo: on Yukon affairs, 31 October 1900. For a description of Minto's tour, see ibid., "Across Canada to the Klondyke, Being the Journal of a Ten Thousand Mile Tour through the 'Great North West', July 19th to October 13th, 1900 by Col. D. Streamer [hereafter, "Klondyke Journal"].
6. Ibid., letterbooks, vol. 2, pp. 79-81, Minto to Chamberlain, 19 August 1900; vol. 24, pp. 124-29, Memo: on Yukon affairs, 31 October 1900.
7. PAC, Sir Clifford Sifton Papers, vol. 229, pp. 404-10, 554-57, Sifton to Ogilvie, 21 and 26 November 1898.
8. Ibid., vol. 61, p. 43602, Fielding to Sifton, 5 January 1899; and see vol. 230, pp. 894-931, Sifton to Ogilvie, 15 February 1899.
9. Ibid., vol. 231, pp. 596-608, Sifton to Ogilvie, 24 March 1899.
10. Ibid.
11. Ibid., vol. 230, pp. 894-931, Sifton to Ogilvie, 15 February 1899.
12. Ibid., vol. 295, file "Ogilvie, William 1899-1903," Ogilvie to Sifton, 15 July 1899; PAC, Sir Wilfrid Laurier Papers, vol. 134, pp. 40158-74, J.E. Girouard to Laurier, 23 December 1899, and reply, 23 janvier 1900, and lists and salaries of government employees in the Yukon.
13. PAC, Sifton Papers, vol. 230, pp. 894-931, Sifton to Ogilvie, 15 February 1899; vol. 231, pp. 596-608, Sifton to Ogilvie, 24 March 1899.
14. Ibid., vol. 104, pp. 81609-10, R. Lowe to Sifton, 6 January 1901; vol. 240, pp. 396-97, Sifton to Ogilvie, 28 December 1900.
15. PAC, Laurier Papers, vol. 124, pp. 37041-42, H.J. Woodside to Laurier, 1 September 1899; and see PAC, Sifton Papers, vol. 69, pp. 51290-98, A. Bowen Perry to Sifton, 7 November 1899.
16. "Fractions" were small areas between properly surveyed claims.
17. PAC, Sifton Papers, vol. 74, p. 55741, J.S. Willison to Sifton, 19 April 1899; vol. 230, pp. 894-931, Sifton to Ogilvie, 15 February 1899.
18. PAC, Laurier Papers, vol. 122, pp. 36727-30, D.A. Dugas to J.E. Girouard, 21 August 1899; vol. 116, pp. 34961-71, D.A. Dugas to L.O. David, 29 June 1899; vol. 142, 42504-8, C.A. Dugas to J.I. Tarte, le 18 fevrier [*sic*] 1900 (italics in original).
19. PAC, Sifton Papers, vol. 231, pp. 596-608, Sifton to Ogilvie, 24 March 1899; PAC, RCMP Records, vol. 268, file 247. The commission was not paid in 1899, but was introduced in 1900; the officers immediately sought retroactive payment for the previous year, which was finally granted in December 1902. See also D.R. Morrison, *The*

Politics of the Yukon Territory, 1898-1909 (Toronto: University of Toronto Press, 1968), p. 28.

20. PAC, Sifton Papers, vol. 228, pp. 471-72, Sifton to Ogilvie, 23 September 1908; pp. 703-4, 5 October 1898; vol. 229, pp. 453-56, 23 November 1898.
21. Ibid., vol. 230, p. 493, Sifton to Sir Louis Davies, 28 January 1899.
22. *CSP*, 1901, no. 25, pt. 8; 1902, no. 25, pt. 9; 1903, no. 25, pt. 7.
23. See below, chapter 6; and Morris Zaslow, *The Opening of the Canadian North 1870-1914* (Toronto: McClelland and Stewart, 1971), pp. 118-19.
24. PAC, Sifton Papers, vol. 80, pp. 60686-87, W.S. Fielding to Sifton, 15 January 1900; Minto Papers, vol. 29, pp. 5-6, Z.T. Wood to Minto, 27 September 1900; Morrison, *Politics of the Yukon Territory* p.36; Order in Council 1742, 20 July 1900; 2117, 4 September 1900; 573, 13 March 1901.
25. For example, he claimed that the government received $2 million annually in taxes from the Yukon, and spent only $50,000 on roads. In fact the government received $1.475 million during the fiscal year ending 30 June 1900, and expended some $105,609.72 on roads and trails. PAC, Minto Papers, "Klondyke Journal," pp. 132-33; *CSP*, 1901, no. 25, pt. 8.
26. PAC, Sifton Papers, vol. 230, p. 1, Sifton to Tarte, 3 January 1899; pp. 894-931, Sifton to Ogilvie, 15 February 1899; pp. 933-34, Sifton to Ogilvie, 17 February 1899; vol. 73, pp. 54295-305, Tarte to Sifton, 31 May, 2 June, 3 June, 4 June 1899; Laurier Papers, vol. 156, pp. 45775-77, Ogilvie and Dugas to Laurier, 12 May 1900.
27. See Douglas Owram, *Building for Canadians: A History of the Department of Public Works 1840-1960* (Ottawa: Public Works Canada, 1979), pp. 171-75. The evidence suggests, however, that a substantial amount of money was wasted on unnecessary projects. For example, Public Works continued to improve the Stikine-Teslin route long after it had been discredited, and many miles of roads were built in an area where they were quickly superseded by construction of the White Pass Railway. See ibid.; and PAC, Sifton Papers, vol. 295, file

"Ogilvie, 1900," Ogilvie to Sifton, 11 July 1900.
28. Ibid.
29. Ibid., vol. 238, pp. 532-33, Sifton to Ogilvie, 22 August 1900.
30. Ibid., pp. 188-89, Sifton to David Mills, 6 August 1900.
31. PAC, RCMP Records, vol. 174, file 594; and see R.C. Macleod, "The Mounted Police in Politics," in H.A. Dempsey, ed., *Men in Scarlet* (Calgary: McClelland and Stewart West, 1975), pp. 95-114; R.C. Macleod, *The NWMP and Law Enforcement 1873-1905* (Toronto: University of Toronto Press, 1976), pp. 59-60, 93-94.
32. PAC, Laurier Papers, vol. 102, pp. 30685-90, Steele to H. Harwood, MP, 22 February 1899.
33. PAC, Minto Papers, vol. 24, pp. 124-29, Memo: on Yukon affairs, 31 October 1900; Sifton Papers, vol. 66, pp. 48376-85, J.D. McGregor to Sifton, 24 May 1899.
34. Ibid., vol. 231, p. 31, Sifton to Walter Scott, 27 February 1899.
35. PAC, RCMP Records, vol. 174, file 594; vol. 74, pp. 55616-7, F. White to Steele, 12 September 1899; Sifton Papers, vol. 234, p. 278, Sifton to White, 15 September 1899; vol. 236, p. 271, Sifton to White, 1 February 1900.
36. PAC, Laurier Papers, vol. 125, p. 37353, Woodside to Sifton, 12 September 1899 (copy).
37. For an account of this episode much more sympathetic to Steele, see Robert Stewart, *Sam Steele: Lion of the Frontier* (Toronto: Doubleday, 1979), pp. 229-33. In 1900, Perry succeeded L.W. Herchmer as Commissioner of the North West Mounted Police, a post he would occupy for more than twenty years.
38. PAC, Sifton Papers, vol. 100, pp. 79265-68, Mrs. Hodgkin to Sifton [undated, 1901].
39. See ibid., vol. 69, pp. 51290-98, A.B. Perry to Sifton, 7 November 1899; vol. 77, 58219, David Mills to Sifton, August 1900; PAC, Laurier Papers, vol. 171, pp. 49295-299A, E.L. Bond to Sifton, 15 September 1900 (copy).
40. CSP, 1901, no. 25, pt. 8.
41. PAC, Sifton Papers, vol. 230, pp. 894-931, Sifton to Ogilvie, 15 February 1899; vol. 229, pp. 43-44, Sifton to Mrs.

M.M. Brownlee, 31 October 1898; RCMP Records, vol. 164, file 174, Memo, 8 February 1899.

42. PAC, Sifton Papers, vol. 59, pp. 41695-96, W.H.P. Clement to Sifton, 13 April 1899.

43. Ibid., vol. 231, pp. 922, 924, Sifton to Smart, 13 April 1899; pp. 935-36, Smart to Ogilvie, 13 April 1899; vol. 234, pp. 314-16, Sifton to Ogilvie, 16 September 1899.

44. Ibid., vol. 236, pp. 177-78, Sifton to A.B. Perry, 29 January 1900; pp. 179-80, Sifton to Z.T. Wood, 29 January 1900; p. 182, Memo: for McGregor, 29 January 1900.

45. PAC, Laurier Papers, vol. 179, pp. 51116-26, Smart to Laurier, 26 November 1900; Sifton Papers, vol. 74, p. 55358, Notice of Action, Edgar Dewdney vs. Clifford Sifton, 2 August 1899.

46. PAC, Laurier Papers, vol. 179, pp. 51116-26, Smart to Laurier, 26 November 1900; vol. 156, p. 45775-77, Ogilvie and Dugas to Laurier, 12 May 1900. PC 1870 of 26 July 1900 authorized the Minister of the Interior to issue permits. The standard kickback to the Liberal Party was $1 per gallon, in addition to an official fee of $2 per gallon.

47. PAC, Minto Papers, letterbooks, vol. 2, pp. 79-91, Minto to Chamberlain, 19 August 1900.

48. PAC, Sifton Papers, vol. 96, pp. 75332-34, "Regulations governing the importation of liquors into the Yukon Territory, as authorized by Orders in Council, dated respectively 25th February, 1901, and 18th March, 1901."

49. Ibid., vol. 238, pp. 203-5, Sifton to W. Templeman, 6 August 1900.

50. *CSP*, 1901, no. 25, pt 8.

51. PAC, Sifton Papers, vol. 69, pp. 51290-98, Perry to Sifton, 7 November 1899.

52. Ibid., vol. 238, pp. 352-53, Sifton to Ogilvie, 14 August 1900; Morrison, *Politics of the Yukon Territory*, p. 36.

53. PAC, Laurier Papers, vol. 171, pp. 49300-301, Laurier to Col. E.L. Bond, 21 September 1900.

54. PAC, Sifton Papers, vol. 93, p. 72908, A.N. Belcourt to Sifton, 8 March 1901; vol. 115, pp. 90769-72, F.C. Wade to Sifton, 3 March 1901.

55. PAC, Laurier Papers, vol. 190, pp. 54469-70, A.S. Grant to Laurier, 19 March 1901; pp. 54471-73, Sifton to Laurier, 9 April 1901.

56. Judge Dugas wrote, "Je ne crois pas que même le vote des hommes de la Police et de la Milice seront suffisants pour boulverser cette majorité." Ibid., vol. 142, 42504-8, Dugas à Tarte, le 18 fevrier 1900; and see vol. 143, pp. 42766-69, J.E. Girouard à Laurier, le 25 fevrier 1900; PAC, Sifton Papers, vol. 295, file "Ogilvie, 1900," Ogilvie to Sifton, 7 and 19 March 1900.

57. Morrison, *Politics of the Yukon Territory*, pp. 31-32. Legislation permitting such a move had been passed in 1899.

58. Ibid., p. 36.

59. PAC, Sifton Papers, vol. 241, pp. 540-41, Sifton to F.C. Wade, 5 February 1901; Minto Papers, "Klondyke Journal," p. 251. The Mintos noted that Kirchhoffer was "better known under the title of Lord Burleigh of Brandon."

60. Ibid., vol. 36, pp. 162-73, Minto to Arthur Elliot, 19 October 1900.

61. The cost of entertaining the Governor General for the three days he was in Dawson was $15,144.81. *CSP*, 1902, no. 1, pp. L163-64.

62. PAC, Minto Papers, vol. 36, pp. 175-203, Minto to Arthur Elliot, 25 November 1900.

63. PAC, Sifton Papers, vol. 231, pp. 596-608, Sifton to Ogilvie, 24 March 1899.

64. Ibid., vol. 240, pp. 991-92, Sifton to Ogilvie, 21 January 1901.

65. Ibid., vol. 242, pp. 454-57, Sifton to Ogilvie, 15 March 1901. On Ross's reasons for accepting the position, see Morrison, *Politics of the Yukon Territory*, p. 111n44.

66. PAC, Sifton Papers, vol. 96, pp.75410-12, O.H. Clark to Sifton, 29 April 1901.

NOTES TO CHAPTER TWO

1. PAC, Sifton Papers, vol. 81, pp. 61683-84, R.B. Harstone to Major J.M. Walsh, 28 July 1900.
2. On the negotiations, see T.D. Regehr *The Canadian Northern Railway: Pioneer Road of the Northern Prairies 1895-1918* (Toronto: Macmillan, 1976), pp. 86-93.
3. Ibid., p. 91; PAM, Manitoba Railway Commissioner, Indentures dated 15 January 1901 and 11 February 1901.
4. PAM, J.J. Moncrieff Papers, Moncrieff to James Fisher, 18 February 1901; Moncrieff to C.S. Mellen, 22 February 1901.
5. PAC, Sifton Papers, vol. 241, pp. 110-13, Sifton to Magurn, 23 January 1901.
6. Ibid., vol. 94, pp. 74019-23, T.A. Burrows to Sifton, 19 February 1901; vol. 98, p. 77306, p. 77311, E. Farrer to Sifton, 21, 24 February 1901.
7. Ibid., vol. 242, pp. 36-39, Sifton to Magurn, 26 February 1901; *MFP*, 26 February 1901.
8. PAC, Sifton Papers, vol. 242, pp. 36-39, Sifton to Magurn, 26 February 1901.
9. Ibid., vol. 241, p. 955, Sifton to D.H. McMillan, 20 February 1901; vol. 242, p. 333, Sifton to McMillan, 12 March 1901; vol. 95, pp. 74924-26, J.D. Cameron to Sifton, 14 March 1901.
10. Ibid., vol. 98, pp. 7713-14, E. Farrer to Sifton, 28 February 1901.
11. Ibid., vol. 242, pp. 339-40, Sifton to Magurn, 12 March 1901; p. 602, Sifton to C.J. Mickle, 21 March 1901; vol. 100, p. 78703, J.W. Greenway to W.W. Cory, 2 March 1901. Isaac Campbell suggested that the businessmen had been influenced by large supply orders from Mackenzie and Mann; ibid., vol. 95, pp. 75097-99, Campbell to Sifton, 13 March 1901.
12. Ibid., vol. 242, pp. 673-74, Sifton to J.W. Sifton, 25 March 1901.
13. PAC, Laurier Papers, vol. 196, pp. 55802-3, Sifton to Laurier, 1 May 1901.
14. PAC, Sifton Papers, vol. 103, p. 81291, Laurier to Sifton [ca. 3 May 1901]; vol. 98, pp. 77471-72, W.S. Fielding to Sifton [ca. 3 May 1901]; Canada, House of Commons, *Debates*, 1901, cols. 4372-75, 4436-534, 4688-702,

4902-16, 4940-5090, 3, 6, 8, 10, 13 May 1901. It is worth noting that the counsel for Manitoba during these proceedings was none other than Walter Barwick of Toronto, a close friend of Sifton who often conducted legal transactions for the Minister of the Interior.
15. *Debates*, 1901, cols. 4983-97, 13 May 1901.
16. Opposed were H. Bourassa, J. Charlton, A. Puttee, R.L. Richardson, and C. Wallace. Puttee and Richardson, both strong advocates of government ownership, deprecated the failure of the Conservative ministry in Manitoba to act on the plank of government ownership, part of the 1899 Tory platform. On the views of Bourassa and Charlton, see Regehr, *Canadian Northern Railway* pp. 95-99.
17. PAC, Sifton Papers, vol. 244, pp. 269-70, Sifton to McMillan, 25 June 1901; vol. 104, pp. 82295-96, Mann to Sifton, 25 June 1901; vol. 244, p. 376, Sifton to Smith, 5 July 1901; and see Regehr, *Canadian Northern Railway*, p. 93.
18. PAC, Sifton Papers, vol. 101, pp. 79795-96, H.M. Howell to Sifton, 19 July 1901.
19. Ibid., vol. 76, pp. 57587-88, Brierley to Sifton, 27 December 1900; vol. 240, p. 331, reply, 28 December 1900.
20. Ramsay Cook, *The Politics of John W. Dafoe and the Free Press* (Toronto: University of Toronto Press, 1963), pp. 4-16; Murray Donnelly, *Dafoe of the Free Press* (Toronto: Macmillan, 1968), pp. 11-35, 134; J.W. Dafoe, *Clifford Sifton in Relation to His Times* (Toronto: Macmillan, 1931), pp. 22, 23; PAC, Sifton Papers, vol. 234, pp. 403-4, Sifton to T.O. Davis, 19 September 1899; J.W. Dafoe Papers, vol. 4, Dafoe to R.L. Borden, 2 July 1929.
21. John W. Dafoe, "Sixty Years in Journalism," Address to Winnipeg Press Club, 16 October 1943, p. 9; PAC, Sifton Papers, vol. 97, p. 76245-1, Dafoe to Sifton, 3 January 1901.
22. Ibid., vol. 240, pp. 634-35, Sifton to Magurn, 7 January 1901.
23. Ibid., vol. 104, pp. 82083-85, Magurn to

Sifton, 23 January 1901.
24. Ibid., vol. 97, p. 76245-4, Dafoe to Sifton, 27 March 1901; vol. 242, p. 830, reply, 29 March 1901.
25. Ibid., vol. 104, p. 82347, Mather to Magurn, 19 June 1901 (copy); vol. 244, p. 181, Sifton to H.M. Howell, 19 June 1901; vol. 101, p. 79787, Howell to Sifton, 24 June 1901.
26. Ibid., vol. 104, pp. 82146, 82154-57, Magurn to Sifton, 28, 29 June 1901; vol. 267, p. 150, Sifton to Magurn, 2 July 1901.
27. Ibid., vol. 104, pp. 82167-74, Magurn to Sifton, 9 July 1901; vol. 245, p. 686, Sifton to J.W. Sifton, 9 October 1901.
28. Ibid., vol. 201, p. 159221, Sifton to R.M. Coulter, 14 February 1914; Winnipeg Free Press Library, obituary notice.
29. PAC, Sifton Papers, vol. 244, pp. 523-34, Sifton to J.D. Cameron, 15 July 1901.
30. Dafoe, "Sixty Years of Journalism," p. 11.
31. PAC, Sifton Papers, vol. 241, pp. 101-2, Sifton to Magurn, 22 January 1901.
32. See, for example, ibid., vol. 115, pp. 90860-62, J.M. Walsh to Sifton, 20 January 1901; vol. 241, p. 93, reply, 21 January 1901.
33. Ibid., vol. 115, pp. 91207-10, Willison to Sifton, 29 January 1901.
34. Ibid., vol. 241, pp. 547-51, Sifton to Willison, 7 February 1901.
35. Ibid., vol. 97, p. 76245-12, Dafoe to Sifton, 17 July 1901.
36. Ibid., vol. 287a, Clippings, Lethbridge *Herald*, 17 April 1929; PAC, Sir Robert Borden Papers, vol. 321, p. 190490, unidentified clipping.
37. Ibid.
38. PAC, Sifton Papers, vol. 131, pp. 104071-72, Philp to Sifton, 21 May 1902.
39. Cited in Blair Fraser, "The Many, Mighty Siftons," *Maclean's* (19 December 1959): 53.
40. PAC, Sifton Papers, vol. 296, file "Masten, C.A. 1901," Masten to Sifton, 17 January 1901.
41. Ibid., Masten to Sifton, 15, 26 December 1901; 6, 26 May 1902. The law required five shareholders, so Sifton had to transfer two more shares to other persons.
42. Ibid., vol. 178, file "Masten, C.A.,

1905," Masten to Sifton, 13 February 1905.
43. Ibid., vol. 255, pp. 518-20, Sifton to Col. J.M. Gibson, 3 February 1904; vol. 296, file "Masten, C.A. 1902," Masten to Collier, 9 December 1902.
44. Ibid., vol. 255, pp. 518-20, Sifton to Col. J.M. Gibson, 3 February 1904; *Debates*, 1902, cols. 4803-5, 13 May 1902.
45. Ibid., vols. 5056-64, 15 May 1902; *Joint Stock Companies Incorporation Act*, 2 Edw. 7, ch. 15.
46. PAC, Sifton Papers, vol. 296, file "Henderson, F.G.A. 1901"; file "Walsh, Louis, 1904," Walsh to Sifton, 18, 20 August 1904; file "Masten, C.A. 1904," passim. Despite its name, The Canadian Northern Land Company does not appear to have had any connection with the various enterprises of William Mackenzie and Donald Mann.
47. Ibid., vol. 249, p. 948, Sifton to W.H. Barnes, 2 January 1902 [*sic*; should be 1903]. Sifton was selling 210 shares of stock in the Company, and anticipated a minimum price of at least $210 per share, or some $52,500.
48. Ibid., vol. 248, pp. 883-86, A.P. Collier to Sifton, 24 July 1902.
49. Ibid., vol. 251, pp. 847-48, Sifton to Burrows, 31 March 1903. After his resignation, Sifton's activities became the object of concerted opposition attacks; see below, chapter 9.
50. Ibid., vol. 104, p. 82349, Mather to Sifton, 16 July 1901; vol. 245, pp. 587-89, Sifton to Mather, 4 October 1901.
51. Ibid., vol. 249, Sifton to Sir D.H. McMillan, 11 December 1902.
52. Ibid., vol. 238, Sifton to Walter Scott, 17 December 1900.
53. Ibid., vol. 101, 79728-29, 79731-32, 79736-40, H.M. Howell to Sifton, 7, 17, 25 January 1901; vol. 241, p. 309, Sifton to Howell, 29 January 1901; vol. 101, pp. 79769-72, Howell to Sifton, 7 June 1901; PAC, Laurier Papers, vol. 198, pp. 56534-35, J.E. Cyr to Sifton, 28 May 1901 (forwarded to Laurier).
54. PAC, Sifton Papers, vol. 101, pp. 79731-32, 79765, 79769-72, 79793, H.M. Howell to Sifton, 17 January, 4, 7 June, 13 July 1901; vol. 244, p. 685, Sifton to J.D. Cameron, 26 July 1901.
55. *Tribune*, 20 July 1901; *MFP*, 30

August 1901, 20 February 1902; PAC, Sifton Papers, vol. 113, p. 89017, circular letter of the independents, dated 8 July 1901; vol. 247, pp. 296-97, Sifton to Dafoe, 23 January 1902; PAM, Arthur W. Puttee Papers, *Constitution and By-Laws of the Political Reform Union* (1902).

56. PAC, Sifton Papers, vol. 101, 79736-40, H.M. Howell to Sifton, 25 January 1901; vol. 244, p. 521, Sifton to I. Campbell, 15 July 1901.

57. Ibid., vol. 99, pp. 77871-72, F.O. Fowler to Sifton, 25 July 1901; vol. 244, pp. 757-58, 761 Sifton to Fowler, 3, 4 August 1901; vol. 100, pp. 78794-96, Greenway to Sifton, 14 November 1901.

58. Ibid., vol. 246, pp. 151-53, 245, Sifton to J.M. Robinson, 11, 16 November 1901; vol. 134, p. 106537, Andrew Strang to Sifton, 15 January 1902; vol. 133, pp. 105988-90, 105992-93, J.W. Sifton to Sifton, 16, 18 January 1902; vol. 247, p. 54, Sifton to Strang, 14 January 1902; pp. 148-49, Sifton to J.D. Cameron, 18 January 1902; p. 161, Sifton to J.W. Sifton, 20 January 1902; vol. 121, pp. 96720-22, E. Farrer to A.P. Collier, 15 January 1902; *MFP*, 28 January 1902. Early in 1901 the Manitoba ministers had interviewed Sifton and Laurier about the school lands fund; *MFP*, 4, 8 January 1901. In December 1901 the British government rejected a petition from Manitoba to refer the school lands issue to the Judicial Committee of the Privy Council; see Sifton Papers, vol. 94, pp. 74320, 74347, 74349-54.

59. PAC, Sifton Papers, vol. 247, p. 530, Sifton to Richardson, 31 January 1902; pp. 532-33, draft address for D.A. Stewart.

60. Ibid., p. 542, A.P. Collier to J.W. Sifton, 20 February 1902. The actual vote was Stewart, 3,370; Richardson, 2,354; Toombs, 1,646 (*CSP*, 1905, no. 37).

61. See PAC, Sifton Papers, vol. 125, file "Howell, H.M. 1902" passim. This file reveals that a local prostitute could have told a great deal, but instead decided to blackmail T.O. Davis and T.A. Burrows; they in turn made the mistake of threatening her, a move which backfired and led to some frantic manoeuvering to prevent her from telling what she knew. See also vol. 120, pp. 95936-39, 95941, 95942, T.O. Davis to Sifton, 29 July, 21 August 1902.

62. Ibid., vol. 125, pp. 99109-14, Howell to Sifton, 3 November 1902.

63. Ibid., vol. 118, pp. 94060-61, J.D. Cameron to Sifton, 20 February 1902.

64. C.F. Wilson, *A Century of Canadian Grain* (Saskatoon: Western Producer Prairie Books, 1978), p. 32; J.W. Brennan, "A Political History of Saskatchewan, 1905-1929," Ph.D. thesis, University of Alberta, 1976, p. 23.

65. L.A. Wood, *A History of Farmers' Movements in Canada* (Toronto: Ryerson, 1924), pp. 171-72.

66. PAC, Sifton Papers, vol. 97, p. 76245-38, Dafoe to Sifton, 6 November 1901, with Sifton's written reply; *MFP*, 1, 7, 8, 9, 22 November 1901.

67. PAC, Sifton Papers, vol. 97, pp. 76245-40—43, Dafoe to Sifton, 7 November 1901; vol. 103, 81018, Alfred Lovatt to Sifton, 13 November 1901.

68. Ibid., vol. 97, pp. 76245-51—54, Dafoe to Sifton, 27 November 1901.

69. 44 Vict. ch. 1, *An Act Respecting the Canadian Pacific Railway* (1881), Schedule A, section 20.

70. PAC, Sifton Papers, vol. 247, pp. 233-37, Sifton to Dafoe, 21 January 1902; *Debates*, 1902, cols. 2938-40, 17 April 1902; cols. 4583-89, 10 May 1902; *MFP*, 27 January, 18, 19 April 1902; *CSP*, 1902, no. 48.

71. See below, ch. 4.

72. 2 Edw. 7, ch. 19 (1902), *An Act to Amend the Manitoba Grain Act 1900*; D.J. Hall, "The Manitoba Grain Act: an 'Agrarian Magna Charta'?", *Prairie Forum*, 4, no. 1 (Spring 1979): 116.

73. *Debates*, 1902, cols. 4354-56, 4468-515, 4578, 7, 9, 10 May 1902; *MFP*, 9, 10, 27 May 1902.

74. PAC, Sifton Papers, vol. 133, p. 105806, Shaughnessy to Sifton, 10 November 1902.

75. Ibid., vol. 249, pp. 379-80, Sifton to A.D. Chisholm, 24 November 1902.

76. Ibid., pp. 623-24, Sifton to Dafoe, 10 December 1902.

77. For a summary of the case, see Wilson,

Century of Canadian Grain, p. 35;
Wood, *History of Farmers' Movements*, pp. 179-80.
78. *MFP*, 14, 15 January 1903; PAC, Sifton
Papers, vol. 251, pp. 371-73, Sifton to
Dafœ, 19 March 1903.
79. Ibid., vol. 250, p. 595, Sifton to John
McLaren, 12 February 1903; vol. 251,
pp. 356-57, Sifton to Cartwright, 17
March 1903.
80. Wilson, *Century of Canadian Grain*,
pp. 35-6; *Debates*, 1903, cols. 7294-95,
7988-8008, 24 July, 4 August 1903;
MFP, 25 July, 5 August 1903; 3 Edw. 7,
ch. 33 (1903); PAC, Sifton Papers, vol.
256, pp. 858-59, Sifton to Cartwright,
21 March 1904
81. 4 Edw. 7, ch. 15 (1904); Wilson,
Century of Canadian Grain, pp. 35-36.
82. PAC, Sifton Papers, vol. 251, pp. 371-
73, Sifton to Dafoe, 19 March 1903.
83. H.B. Neatby, *Laurier and a Liberal
Quebec: a Study in Political Management* (Toronto: McClelland and Stewart, 1973), pp. 97-98; PAC, Laurier
Papers, vol. 164, pp. 47881-86, E.
Farrer to R. Boudreau, 29 July 1900.
84. Ibid., vol. 217, p. 60974, Langevin to
Laurier, 23 December 1901; PAC, Sifton Papers, vol. 94, pp. 74349-54,
Petition, Manitoba Government to
Federal Government, re: transfer of
school lands.

85. Ibid., vol. 133, pp. 105988-90, J.W.
Sifton to Sifton, 16 January 1902; vol.
134, p. 106537, Andrew Strang to
Sifton, 15 January 1902.
86. Ibid., vol. 247, pp. 233-37, Sifton to
Dafoe, 21 January 1902; and see p. 54,
Sifton to A. Strang 14 January 1902;
pp. 148-49, Sifton to J.D. Cameron, 18
January 1902; p. 161, Sifton to J.W.
Sifton, 20 January 1902.
87. Ibid., vol. 242, p. 484, Sifton to A.
McLeod, 18 March 1901; vol. 99, pp.
77862-64, Fowler to Sifton, 6 July 1901.
88. Ibid., vol. 103, pp. 80748-52, E.F. Lang
to Sifton, 29 August 1901.
89. *MFP*, 17 September 1901.
90. Ibid., 15 October 1901.
91. PAC, Sifton Papers, vol. 245, pp.
844-46, Sifton to Greenway, 22 October
1901.
92. *MFP*, 9 December 1901, and subsequent issues. G.O.M. refers to
Grand Old Man, popularly associated
with W.E. Gladstone in his later years.
93. Ibid., 11-14 December 1901.
94. PAC, Sifton Papers, vol. 249, pp. 512-
13, 633-64, Sifton to J.D. Cameron, 4,
11 December 1902; pp. 606-7, Sifton to
C.A. Young, 8 December 1902.
95. Ibid., vol. 247, p. 661, Sifton to J.W.
Greenway, 25 February 1902; vol. 133,
p. 105898, Sifton to Collier, 11 March
1902.

NOTES TO CHAPTER THREE

1. PAC, J.S. Willison Papers, vol. 74, pp.
27454-56, Sifton to Willison, 26 April
1902.
2. Dafoe, *Clifford Sifton*, p. xiii. -
3. *Debates*, 1901, col. 2763, 10 April
1901; and see Hall, "Clifford Sifton
and Canadian Indian Administration," pp. 127-51.
4. *Debates*, 1902, cols. 3035-37, 18 April
1902; *CSP*, 1904, no. 27, p. xvii.
5. See Hall, "Clifford Sifton and
Canadian Indian Administration,"
pp. 138, 141, 149n54, 150 n73.
6. PAC, Sifton Papers, vol. 102, pp.
80470-73, Kennedy to Sifton, 14

January 1901.
7. Ibid., vol. 265, pp. 423-24, Sifton to
Rev. John Fraser, 29 March 1901.
8. *Debates*, 1902, col. 3040, 18 April
1902; 1903, col. 6329, 9 July 1903.
9. Ibid., cols. 6326-52, 6408-9, 9 and 10
July 1903; and see 1902, cols. 3051,
3053, 18 April 1902.
10. Ibid., 1904, cols. 6960-64, 18 July
1904.
11. *CSP*, 1906, no. 27, pp. xx, 271-78;
Zaslow, *The Opening of the Canadian North*, pp. 227-29; Hall "Clifford
Sifton and Canadian Indian Administration," pp. 140-41, 150n66, 67.

12. *Debates*, 1904, cols. 6946-56, 18 July 1904; 1903, cols. 7260-61, 23 July 1903.
13. Ibid., 1904, cols. 6946-56, 18 July 1904.
14. PAC, Sifton Papers, vol. 265, pp. 403-5, Sifton to Bishop Legal, 22 March 1901.
15. *Debates*, 1902, cols. 3043-46, 18 April 1902.
16. PAC, DIA Records, vol. 3920, file 11675-A, Benson to the Deputy Superintendent General, 23 June 1903.
17. PAC, Sifton Papers, vol. 106, pp. 83483-92, J.A.J. McKenna to Sifton, 10 December 1901.
18. *Debates*, 1902, cols. 3054-56, 18 April 1902; 1903, cols. 6422-24, 10 July 1903; 1904, cols. 6942-45, 6954-57, 18 July 1904; and see DIA Records, vol. 3878, file 91839-7; vol. 1124, p. 440, Sifton to Governor General in Council, 4 February 1901.
19. PAC, Sifton Papers, vol. 201, p. 159135, Sifton to Laurier, 19 November 1914.
20. Stewart Raby, "Indian Land Surrenders in Southern Saskatchewan," *The Canadian Geographer*, 17 (Spring 1973) 37, 43.
21. PAC, Sifton Papers, vol. 106, 83569-74, J.O. McLean to Sifton, 13 August 1901.
22. *Debates*, 1904, cols. 6952-53, 18 July 1904; 1903, cols. 6410-15, 10 July 1903.
23. PAC, DIA Records, vol. 3558, file 67-18, vol. 3571, files 130-18, 130-19.
24. Ibid., vol. 4015, file 273023 vol. 1; Raby, "Indian Land Surrenders," pp. 42, 44; Regehr, *The Canadian Northern Railway,* pp. 172-74.
25. PAC, Laurier Papers, vol. 248, pp. 69214-20, Minto to Laurier, 16 January 1903.
26. Ibid., vol. 252, pp. 70325-29, Minto to Laurier, 17 February 1903.
27. For an excellent, detailed critical discussion of Sifton's period as Minister, see Morris Zaslow, *Reading the Rocks: the Story of the Geological Survey of Canada 1842-1972* (Toronto: Macmillan, 1975), chs. 10-12.
28. Ibid., pp. 199-200, 215.
29. *Debates*, 1901, col. 5318, 15 May 1901.
30. *CSP*, 1904, no. 26, pp. i, xxix-xxxii. Many still believed that the reports were too theoretical and impractical compared, for example, to those of the Ontario Bureau of Mines. See H.V. Nelles, *The Politics of Development: Forests, Mines & Hydro-Electric Power in Ontario, 1849-1941* (Toronto: Macmillan, 1974), pp. 124-25.
31. *CSP*, 1902, no. 25, p. ii; Zaslow, *Reading the Rocks*, pp. 243, 246.
32. *Debates*, 1903, cols. 13762-69, 12 October 1903; Zaslow, *Reading the Rocks,* pp. 249-50.
33. PAC, Sifton Papers, vol. 255, pp. 226-27, Sifton to R. Bickerdike, 25 January 1904; *Debates*, 1904, cols. 7056-62, 19 July 1904; *CSP*, 1905, no. 25, pt. 8; 1906, no. 25, pt. 8.
34. *CSP*, 1907-8, nos. 26-26b; Zaslow, *Reading the Rocks*, pp. 255-59.
35. The best general examination of the historical development is S.M. Van Kirk, "The Development of National Park Policy in Canada's Mountain National Parks, 1885 to 1930" (M.A. thesis, University of Alberta, 1969) See also A.R. Byrne, "Man and Landscape Change in the Banff National Park Area before 1911" (M.A. thesis, University of Calgary, 1964); R.C. Scace, "Banff: a Cultural-Historical Study of Land Use and Management in a National Park Community to 1945" (M.A. thesis, University of Calgary, 1967), J.G. Nelson, ed., *Canadian Parks in Perspective* (Montreal: Harvest House, 1970).
36. Van Kirk, "Development of National Park Policy," pp. 42-44; Byrne, "Man and Landscape Change," pp. 118-19; *CSP*, 1898, no. 12, p. 4, and pt. 1 p. 44.
37. Ibid., 1901, no. 25, pt. 4, p. 4.
38. PAC, Sifton Papers, vol. 247, p. 139, Sifton to T.G. Shaughnessy, 18 January 1902; *Debates*, 1902, col. 3305, 23 April 1902; Van Kirk, "Development of National Park Policy," pp. 19-20; Byrne, "Man and Landscape Change," pp. 119-201. The vast size of the Rocky Mountains Park proved unwieldy, and in 1911 it was reduced to 1,800 square miles.

39. See R.C. Brown, "The Doctrine of Usefulness: Natural Resource and National Park Policy in Canada, 1887-1914," in Nelson, ed *Canadian Parks in Perspective*, pp. 46-62; Janet Foster, *Working for Wildlife: the Beginning of Preservation in Canada* (Toronto: University of Toronto Press, 1978), chs. 1-2.

40. *CSP*, 1905, no. 25, pt. 5, p. 11; Byrne, "Man and Landscape Change," pp. 94-108; *MFP*, 17 May 1902.

41. *CSP*, 1902, no. 25, p. xiv; 1906, no. 25, p. xxxvi; pt. 5, p. 14; *MFP*, 3 July, 14 August 1901.

42. Herbert Donald Kirkland III, "The American Forests, 1864-1898: a Trend toward Conservation" (Ph.D. thesis, Florida State University, 1971), pp. 1-2; Roy M. Robbins, *Our Landed Heritage: the Public Domain, 1776-1936* (Lincoln: University of Nebraska Press, 1962), chs. 17-20; S.P. Hays, *Conservation and the Gospel of Efficiency* (Cambridge: Harvard University Press, 1959), ch. 3.

43. Kirkland, "The American Forests," pp. 83-84.

44. Ibid., pp. 15-16, 89.

45. On the Ontario case, see August Paul Pross, "The Development of a Forest Policy: a Study of the Ontario Department of Lands and Forests," Ph.D. thesis, University of Toronto, 1967, chs. 2 and 3; Nelles, *Politics of Development*, pp.182-214.

46. *CSP*, 1898, no. 13, pt. 1, p. 43; 1899, no. 13, p. ii; pt. 1, p. 70.

47. *MPP*, 29 November, 11, 22 December 1897; 6, 14, 26 January, 21, 26 February, 18 March, 11 May, 20 July, 4 August 1898. Stephenson's report was dated 26 November 1897, and the coincidence is remarkable between that date and the first of the series of editorials. Almost certainly Sifton inspired the editorials, even though he was still negotiating for control of the paper. Through publicizing the subject, the editorials were intended to prepare the way for government action.

48. *CSP*, 1899, no. 13, pt. 1, p. 32.

49. Ibid., p. xxi.

50. *Debates*, 1899, cols. 9006-15, 31 July 1899; *CSP*, 1900, no. 13, pp. xix-xx; pt. 9, "Report of the Chief Inspector of Timber and Forestry for Canada."

51. Ibid., 1900, no. 13, pt. 9, p. 19; 1901, pt. 5, pp. 5-7.

52. Ibid., p. 4; 1901, pp. xxxii-xxxiii. The Association took over some pages in *Rod and Gun in Canada*, a monthly journal, as an initial means of publication.

53. PAC, Sifton Papers, vol. 244, pp. 90-91, Sifton to W.T.R. Preston, 18 July 1901. In the United States the German-trained B.E. Fernow had been appointed Chief Forester in 1886; he later became first Dean of the Faculty of Forestry in the University of Toronto. Kirkland, *The American Forests*, p. 89; Pross, *The Development of a Forest Policy*, p. 62.

54. PAC, Laurier Papers, vol. 220, p. 61815-34, Report of C.A. Schenck to Sifton, 21 January 1902 (forwarded to Laurier); *CSP*, 1902, no. 25, pt. 8. p. 3; Dafoe, *Clifford Sifton*, pp. 247-48; H.T. Pinkett, *Gifford Pinchot* (Urbana: Univerity of Illinois Press, 1970), p.30.

55. PAC, Laurier Papers, vol. 220, pp. 61815-34, Report of C.A. Schenck to Sifton, 21 January 1902; A.P. Pross, *The Development of a Forest Policy*, p.62; *MFP*, 29 March 1902.

56. *CSP*, 1904, no. 25, pt, 9, p. 7; 1905, no. 25, pt. 10, pp. 4-5; PAC, Sifton Papers, vol. 301, W.W. Cory to Sifton, 11 December 1923; Dafoe, *Clifford Sifton*, pp. 247-48.

57. *Debates*, 1901, col. 2681, 9 April 1901.

58. Ibid., 1901, cols. 2668-98, 9 April 1901; 1903, cols. 6773-86, 16 July 1903; 1904, cols. 7070-74, 19 July 1904.

59. Greg Thomas and Ian Clarke, "The Garrison Mentality and the Canadian West," *Prairie Forum*, 4, no. 2, (Spring 1979): 96-99.

60. Thomas R. Wessel, "Prologue to Shelterbelt, 1870 to 1934," *Journal of the West*, VI, (1967): 127; *MFP*, 29 March 1902.

61. *CSP*, 1905, no. 25, p. xxv.

62. Ibid., pp. xx-xxi.

63. Ibid., 1902, no. 25, p. xi; and pt. 6.

64. Ibid., 1897, no. 13, p. xxix; 1902, no. 25, pp. xxii-xxiii; 1905, no. 25, pt. 1, pp. 31-32.

65. Ibid., p. 34; 1897, no. 12, p. xxx.

66. Ibid., p. xxxi; 1905, no. 25, part 1, p. 34.
67. Ibid., 1902, no. 25, pp. xxv-xxvii. The development of coal lands also was encouraged by new regulations in 1901; see p. xxviii.
68. Ibid., p. xxx; 1897, no. 13, p. xxvii; 1905, no. 25, pt. 1, p. 45. Inconsistency in departmental reports makes it difficult to be precise on the expansion of irrigation facilities. Figures given for 1900, for example, are noticeably larger than those given for 1901. This discrepancy is unexplained, although it seems highly improbable that there was a decline in the irrigated area during the year. See also ibid., pp. 7-8.
69. *Debates*, 1901, col. 82, 13 February 1901; cols. 1871-74, 12 March 1901; *CSP*, 1906, no. 25, pp. xxx, xxxii; 1897, no. 13, pp. xiv-xv. The total area surveyed fell by about one-sixth in the year 1904-5. In 1883 some 27.2 million acres, or 170,000 farms had been surveyed. By 1905 the total area surveyed for settlement in the West was some 115.5 million acres, or 722,000 farms.
70. J.B. Hedges, *The Federal Railway Land Subsidy Policy of Canada* (Cambridge: Harvard University Press, 1934), pp. 61-67; Hedges, *Building the Canadian West: the Land and Colonization Policies of the Canadian Pacific Railway* (New York: Macmillan, 1939), pp. 55-58.
71. Dafoe, *Clifford Sifton*, p. 133; Chester Martin, *"Dominion Lands" Policy*, edited by L. H. Thomas (Toronto: McClelland and Stewart, 1973), pp. 96-97.
72. *MFP*, 3, 4 April, 23 August, 13, 14 December 1901; 7 April 1902; *Debates*, 1901, cols. 325-26, 881-92, 1116-66, 2492-546, 5417-32, 25 February, 4, 7 March, 2 April, 17 May 1901; 1902, cols. 4410-11, 7 May 1902. Sifton argued that while Parliament might have had the legal power to violate a contract or override vested rights, it did not have the right to do so. See ibid., 1901, cols. 2520ff., 2 April 1901.
73. PAC, Sifton Papers, vol. 143, pp. 114452-55, 114469, H.M. Howell to Sifton, 20 February, 16 March 1903.

The judgments of the Manitoba Supreme Court are contained in *CSP*, 1903, no. 79. See also *MFP*, 7 April, 3 October 1902; 14, 19 February, 16 March, 11, 12 August 1903; Hedges, *Building the Canadian West*, pp. 8lff. The Manitoba judgments were sustained in the Supreme Court of Canada, litigation continuing until 1911.
74. PAC, Sifton Papers, vol. 252, pp. 434-36, Sifton to Turriff, 1 August 1903.
75. Martin, *"Dominion Lands" Policy*, p.172.
76. *Debates*, 1903, cols. 6771-72, 16 July 1903.
77. Martin, *"Dominion Lands" Policy*, p. 211.
78. Ibid., p. 418.
79. Norman Macdonald, *Canada: Immigration and Colonization, 1841-1903* (Toronto: Macmillan, 1966), ch. 12.
80. Ibid., pp. 253-54; Hedges, *Building the Canadian West*, pp. 143-64; Hedges, *Federal Railway Land Subsidy Policy*, pp. 123-33; A.S. Morton, *History of Prairie Settlement* (Toronto: Macmillan, 1938), p. 120; Martin, *"Dominion Lands" Policy*, pp: 91-93; Dafoe, *Clifford Sifton*, pp. 306-9; *Debates*, 1904, cols. 7034-56, 19 July 1904; 1906, cols. 4286-309, 31 May 1906; *MFP*, 14, 31 May 1902; 3 October 1904; PAC, Sifton Papers, vol. 248, pp. 220-21, Sifton to Arthur Hitchcock, 4 June 1902. According to Hedges, J. Obed Smith, Commissioner of Immigration, wrote to Sifton on 10 April 1902, commending the project in general terms; on 25 April, Colonization Agent C.W. Speers submitted the company proposals; on 30 April they were approved; and on 24 May the appropriate order in council was passed. No evidence has yet been submitted to support widespread allegations at the time that Sifton benefitted personally from the scheme.
81. *Debates*, 1901, col. 1249, 11 March 1901; *MFP*, 12 March 1901.
82. By far the best source on this subject is David H. Breen, *The Canadian Prairie West and the Ranching Fron-*

tier, 1875-1922, (Toronto: University of Toronto Press, 1983), ch.4.

83. Ibid., p. 126.

84. Hedges, *Federal Railway Land Subsidy Policy*, p.67; Hedges, *Building* the *Canadian West*, pp. 51-52.

85. *MFP*, 30 April 1901. See also D.J. Hall, "Clifford Sifton: Immigration and Settlement Policy 1896-1905," in H. Palmer, ed., *The Settlement of the West* (Calgary: University of Calgary, 1977), pp. 60-85.

86. M.C. Urquhart and K.A.H. Buckley, eds., *Historical Statistics of Canada* (Toronto: Macmillan, 1965), p. 23, series A 254; *CSP*, 1902, no. 25, pt. 1, p. 6; 1906, no. 25, p. xxiii.

87. Ibid., no. 25, pt. 2, pp. 36-45.

88. Ibid., 1902, no. 25, p. xiv; 1903, no. 25, p. xii; 1904, no. 25, p. xxiv; 1905, no. 25, pp. xxv, xxxii; 1906, no. 25, p. xxiii; pt. 2, pp. 36-45.

89. PAC, Minto Papers, letterbooks, vol. 2, p. 293, Minto to A. Cohen, 17 May 1901.

90. PAC, Sifton Papers, vol. 138, pp. 110340-41, Memorandum, Smart for Sifton, 2 July 1903; H.M. Troper, *Only Farmers Need Apply: Official Canadian Government Encouragement of Immigration from the United States, 1896-1911* (Toronto: Griffin House, 1972), pp. 57-78.

91. Ibid., p. 154; PAC, Willison Papers, vol. 51, pp. 18971-74, S. Lyon to Willison, 20 April 1902; Sifton Papers, vol. 198, pp. 157697-98, Sifton to J.M. Shortcliffe, 22 March 1911.

92. Canada, House of Commons, *Journals*, 1901, App. no. l, pp. 263-376; see also 1906, pt. 2, pp. 281-449. In 1906 Sifton supplied Laurier with a list of the companies involved; PAC, Laurier Papers, vol. 400, pp. 106546-48, Sifton to Laurier, 29 May 1906, and encl. On the reasons for secrecy, see W.T.R. Preston, *My Generation of Politics and Politicians* (Toronto: D.A. Rose, 1927), pp. 259-61.

93. PAC, Dafoe Papers, vol. 2, file 1921, Sifton to Dafoe, 8 February 1921.

94. Mabel F. Timlin, "Canada's Immigration Policy, 1896-1910," *Canadian Journal of Economics and Political Science*, 26, (November 1960): 512-22; PAC, Laurier Papers, vol. 336, pp. 89865-69, Order in Council, 20 Sep-

tember 1904.

95. In Canada, the Tories were always quick to defend Colmer and attack Preston; see *Debates*, 1901, cols. 2879-984, 4818-53, 12 April, 9 May 1901.

96. PAC, Sifton Papers, vol. 246, p. 23, Sifton to Strathcona, 2 November 1901; vol. 113, p. 89319, Strathcona to Sifton, 5 November 1901.

97. Ibid., vol. 251, pp. 979-80, Sifton to Preston, 7 May 1903; vol. 150, pp. 120087-92, Smart to Sifton, 24 February 1903; vol. 148, 118319-20, Preston to Sifton, 6 June 1903; 118333-34, Preston to A.P. Collier, 20 June 1903. See also ibid., vol. 254, pp. 526-27, Sifton to Sir R. Cartwright, 2 January 1904; vol. 170, pp. 125104-105, Cartwright to Sifton, 6 December 1904; vol. 262, pp. 52-53, Sifton to Cartwright, 7 December 1904.

98. Robert F. Harney, "Men Without Women: Italian Migrants in Canada, 1885-1930," *Canadian Ethnic Studies*, 11, no. 1 (1979): 32-33; Donald Avery, "Canadian Immigration Policy and the 'Foreign' Navvy 1896-1914," Canadian Historical Association, *Historical Papers 1972*,: 142; PAC, Sifton Papers, vol. 97, pp. 76514, 76530-32, 76534-37, F.J. Deane to Sifton, 10, 31 July 1901; pp. 76523-24, H.A. Harper to Sifton, 11 July 1901; vol. 114, pp. 90720-22, Rev. P. Wright to Sifton, 28 November 1901; vol. 108, pp. 85514-15, Alfred Parr to Sifton, 5 October 1901; vol. 97, p. 75903, Guelph Trades and Labor Council to Sifton, 9 December 1901 (example of many identical petitions); vol. 126, pp. 99743-44, D.W. Kennedy to Sifton, 25 April 1902; 1 Edw. 7, ch. 13, 1901.

99. PAC, Sifton Papers, vol. 126, pp. 99751-52, Memo: Smart for Sifton, 6 May 1902 (words in parentheses added in Sifton's hand).

100. PAC, Laurier Papers, vol. 263, pp. 72951-55, Laurier to Rev. C.W. Gordon, 18 May 1903; vol. 258, pp. 71671-73, Laurier to W.S. Calvert, MP, 1 April 1903; Sifton Papers, vol. 168, p. 135855, *The Toiler* (Toronto), 22 July 1904.

101. PAC, Laurier Papers, vol. 181, pp. 51600-602, Memo: Smart for Sifton,

10 December 1900; Memo: Sifton for Laurier, 15 April 1901. It should be noted that in this case, Smart, presumably with Sifton's concurrence, had recommended allowing some of the Jewish farmers to come. The Prime Minister however, strongly opposed the movement, and asked the Department of the Interior to recast its original memorandum, putting clearly the case that "whilst the doors of the country are open to all, we favour only agricultural immigration." The racial prejudice in this case seems to have been distinctly that of Laurier himself. See ibid., vol. 186, pp. 53204-206, Smart to Laurier, 5 February 1901, and p. 53207, reply, 7 February 1901; Minto Papers, vol. 5, p. 90, Laurier to Minto, 13 April 1901.

102. PAC, Sifton Papers, vol. 113, p. 89315, Memo: Sifton for Smart, n.p., n.d. [1901]; p. 89316, Sifton to Smart, 16 November 1901; pp. 89317-18, Smart to Strathcona, 19 November 1901.

103. Ibid , vol. 255, pp. 51, 139, Sifton to Smart, 22, 25 January 1904; p. 301, Sifton to Preston, 29 January 1904; p. 304, Sifton to Smart, 29 January 1904; vol. 256, p. 407, Sifton to Sir William Mulock, 9 March 1904.

104. Ibid., vol. 255, p. 139, Sifton to Smart, 25 January 1904; p. 156, Sifton to W.D. Scott, 25 January 1904.

105. Ibid., pp. 462-63, Sifton to Smart, 2 February 1904. See also Genevieve Leslie, "Domestic Service in Canada, 1880-1920," in Janice Acton et al., eds., *Women at Work: Ontario, 1850-1930* (Toronto: Canadian Women's Educational Press, 1974), pp. 71-125.

106. See, for example, *Debates*, 1901, cols. 2879-2920, 2927-84, 12 April 1901. Sifton's short but pointed speech is found in cols. 2970-76.

107. PAC, Sifton Papers, vol. 246, pp. 137-40, Sifton to Dafoe, 11 November 1901. The cost per immigrant was calculated on the basis of all costs— advertising, commissions, salaries, bonuses—required to attract and locate the settlers. The government normally gave a figure of less than five dollars per head for Galician immigrants, much lower than the figure for the Doukhobors.

108. *CSP*, 1904, no. 25, p. xxiv; PAC, Sifton Papers, vol. 135, pp. 107401-2, J.G. Turriff to Sifton, 11 February 1902; vol. 132, pp. 105154-60, Sifton to Ivan Ivin and Feodor Suchorukoff, 15 February 1902; vol. 248, pp. 68-69, Sifton to Alex Thom, 28 May 1902; vol. 133. pp. 106345-49, J. Obed Smith to Frank Pedley, 11 July 1902.

109. George Woodcock and Ivan Avakumovic, *The Doukhobors* (Toronto: Oxford University Press, 1968), p. 178.

110. Ibid., pp. 192-95; PAC, Sifton Papers, vol. 149, pp. 94-95, Sifton to James Mavor, 4 November 1902; vol. 135, pp. 108068-70, Robert Watson to Sifton, 1 November 1902; *MFP*, 27 October-15 November 1902, 20 December 1902; 7 May 1903.

111. PAC, Sifton Papers, vol. 118, pp. 93835-37, Smart to F. Charlton, 29 December 1902; vol. 253, pp. 863-64, Sifton to J.O. Smith, 8 December 1903; vol. 150, pp. 120421-23, C.W. Speers to J.B. Harkin, 15 December 1903. See also Carl Betke, "The Mounted Police and the Doukhobors in Saskatchewan, 1899-1909," *Saskatchewan History*, 27 no. 1 (Winter 1974): 5-9.

112. See Eric J. Holmgren, "Isaac M. Barr and the Britannia Colony" (M.A. thesis, University of Alberta, 1964); Keith Foster, "The Barr Colonists: Their Arrival and Impact upon the Canadian North-West," *Saskatchewan History*, 35, no. 3 (Autumn 1982): 81-100.

113. PAC, Sifton Papers, vol. 150 pp. 120083-84, 120087-92, Smart to Sifton, 20, 24 February 1903.

114. Ibid., vol. 142, pp. 113650-53 Griffith to A.P. Collier, 28 February 1903.

115. Ibid., vol. 251, p. 423, Sifton to A.G. Blair, 20 March 1903; vol. 150, p. 120119, Smart to Sifton, 23 March 1903.

116. *Debates*, 1903, cols. 6354-404, 10 July 1903.

117. E.J. Holmgren, "Isaac M. Barr," pp. 54-63, 71-75, 168-70.

118. PAC, Sifton Papers, vol. 255, pp. 809-10, Sifton to Col. S. Hughes, 11 February 1904; vol. 150, pp. 120610-11, Turriff to Hon. J. Sutherland, 26

May 1903. Despite these statements, Sifton did allow one exception, a small reservation for Mennonites in Manitoba. See ibid., vol. 260, pp. 69-71, Sifton to Smart, 14 July 1904.
119. Ibid., vol. 169, pp. 137000-7002, Calgary Board of Trade Resolution, 28 December 1904.
120. *MFP*, 19 September 1901.
121. Ibid., 16 October, 16 November 1901; 1 March, 21 April, 23 September, 1 October 1902. It must be noted, however, that in later years—especially after 1911—Dafoe himself led a series of vigorous attacks on "foreigners" and on the schools which failed to make them English-speaking. See M. Donnelly, *Dafoe of the Free Press* (Toronto. Macmillan, 1968), pp.70-73.
122. *MFP*, 2 November 1901.
123. Ibid., 1, 9, 14 April, 12 June 1902.
124. Ibid., 19, 23 January 1903. See also Lewis H. Thomas, "From the Pampas to the Prairies: the Welsh Migration of 1902," *Saskatchewan History*, 24 (1971): 1-12.
125. PAC, Dafoe Papers, vol. 2, Sifton to Dafoe, 3 March 1922; Sifton Papers, vol. 150, p. 120119, Smart to Sifton, 23 March 1903.
126. Ibid., vol. 252, pp. 461-63, Sifton to Jaffray, 5 August 1903.
127. *MFP*, 22 November 1902 (speech of November 21).

NOTES TO CHAPTER FOUR

1. Nelles, *The Politics of Development*, p. 41.
2. Toronto *Globe*, 18 November 1902.
3. *MFP*, 22, 24 November 1902.
4. In a later speech he went so far as to state that Sir John A. Macdonald was "unquestionably...the greatest constructive statesman of the past generation, a man who began his public life by advocating as a practical measure the building of a waggon road from Kingston to Toronto, and who saw the achievement of that greater idea, the building of a railway from sea to sea." *MFP*, 27 July 1904.
5. Ibid., 12, 14, 17, 19 January 1903; "The Needs of the Northwest," *The Canadian Magazine*, 20, 1902-3, no. 5 (March 1903): 425-28. In this article Sifton stated that in the prairies there was "abundance of room to sustain from fifteen to twenty millions of people."
6. PAC, Sifton Papers, vol. 249, pp. 748-53, Sifton to Fitzpatrick, 18 December 1902.
7. *MFP*, 27 July 1904.
8. Ibid., 24 November 1902.
9. Ibid., 12 January 1903.
10. Ibid., 21 May 1903. Sifton's real thoughts were somewhat less warm toward the British connection than these remarks might suggest. He had just written to Sir William Mulock, "I have avoided saying anything in the newspapers or making any speeches, calling to mind the fact that most visiting Ministers keep their colleagues at home explaining their utterances. I have to say a few words to-night at the Colonial Institute dinner, but I will try and make my remarks so commonplace as not to cause anyone any annoyance." PAC, Sifton Papers, vol. 251, pp. 944-46, Sifton to Mulock, 1 May 1903.
11. Ibid., vol. 253, pp. 216-17, Sifton to Hamar Greenwood, 22 October 1903. The reference to the takeover of Halifax seems extraordinary because, according to one authority, the matter then had not even been considered by the Canadian cabinet. R.A. Preston, *Canada and "Imperial Defense"* (Toronto: University of Toronto Press, 1967), p. 338.
12. PAC, Sifton Papers, vol. 253, pp. 146-47, Sifton to Sydney Fisher, 19 September 1903; and reply, vol. 141, pp. 112860-63, 5 October 1903. See also vol. 142, pp. 113696-99, W.L. Griffith to Sifton, 29 May 1903; vol. 268, p. 162, Sifton to Laurier, n.d. [September or October 1903].

13. *MFP*, 12 January 1903.
14. PAC, Sifton Papers, vol. 253, pp. 413-14, Sifton to Dafoe, 21 November 1903; reply, vol. 140, pp. 118898-83—86, 28 November 1903.
15. *MFP*, 12 January 1903.
16. Ibid., 27 July 1904.
17. Paul Stevens, "Wilfrid Laurier: Politician," in M. Hamelin, ed., *Les idées politiques des premiers ministres du Canada/The Political Ideas of the Prime Ministers of Canada* (Ottawa: Les Editions de l'Université d'Ottawa, 1969), p. 74; R.T.G. Clippingdale, "J.S. Willison, Political Journalist: from Liberalism to Independence, 1881-1905" (Ph.D. thesis, University of Toronto, 1970), p. 412; PAC, Laurier Papers, vol. 202, p. 57717, Laurier to Fielding, 12 August 1901.
18. See, for example, PAC, Sifton Papers, vol. 230, Sifton to Tarte, 10 January 1899.
19. Ibid., vol. 61, pp. 49976-79, Mulock to Sifton, 13 February 1899.
20. Ibid., vol. 126, pp. 100379-80, Laurier to Sifton, 3 December 1902.
21. Ibid., vol. 237, p. 665, Sifton to Robert Adamson, 4 July 1900; vol. 244, p. 434, Sifton to S.J. Jackson, 13 July 1901.
22. Ibid., vol. 241, pp. 600-601, Sifton to Fielding, 8 February 1901; and references in notes 19 and 20, above.
23. See D.J. McMurchy, "David Mills: Nineteenth Century Canadian Liberal" (Ph.D. thesis, University of Rochester, 1968) pp. 520-47.
24. PAC, Sifton Papers, vol. 61, p. 43829, Fitzpatrick to Sifton, 14 September 1899; McMurchy, "David Mills," pp. 535-36. Scott was the elderly Secretary of State. So far as is known the scheme did not succeed. Fitzpatrick could not seek the position himself because as Solicitor General he was not a member of the cabinet.
25. PAC, Laurier Papers, vol. 297, pp. 80490-93, Sifton to Laurier, "Saturday" [probably October 1901].
26. *MFP*, 31 January 1902.
27. PAC, Sifton Papers, vol. 126, pp. 100343-46, Laurier to Sifton, 8 February 1902. Carroll had been MP for Kamouraska since 1891; his career was without apparent distinction. See

also *MFP*, 8 February 1902.
28. PAC, Laurier Papers, vol. 223 pp. 62775-76, 15 February 1902.
29. Despite many later comments upon rivalry between Sifton and Fitzpatrick, there is little contemporary evidence that their relations were unusually strained at this time. Differences on railway policy in 1903, and on the North-West schools in 1905, were later developments. See, for example, the exaggerated dramatization in Joseph Schull, *Laurier: the First Canadian* (Toronto: Macmillan, 1965), p. 414. The earliest concrete evidence of the Sifton-Fitzpatrick rivalry that I have discovered is in a letter to the Minister of Justice in September 1903, from one of his supporters: "If you can succeed in getting Sifton to read his valedictory to Laurier, you will be Captain of the whole Brigade. The game of politics is a great one...one sometimes gets beaten with a full hand." PAC, Fitzpatrick Papers, vol. 6, M.F. Hackett to Fitzpatrick, 2 September 1903.
30. Miller, *Canadian Career of the Fourth Earl of Minto* p. 174.
31. PAC, Minto Papers, vol. 2, pp. 362-64, Minto to Kirchhoffer, 15 August 1901.
32. PAC, Sifton Papers, vol. 97, pp. 76245-16—17, Dafoe to Sifton, 24 September 1901; Miller, *Canadian Career of the Fourth Earl of Minto*, pp. 179-83; PAC, Sir G. Parkin Papers, vol. 20, pp. 5764-99, Minto to Parkin, 26 September 1904.
33. *MFP*, 14, 19, 22-25 October, 4, 7 November 1901; PAC, Sifton Papers, vol. 97, pp. 76245-24—30, Dafoe to Sifton, 18 October 1901, and encl.; Cook, *The Politics of John W. Dafoe*, pp. 20-23; Donnelly, *Dafoe of the Free Press*, p. 44.
34. PAC, Laurier Papers, vol. 210, pp. 59627-34, Minto to Laurier, 31 October 1901; Sifton Papers, vol. 97, pp. 76245-46, Dafoe to Sifton, 9 November 1901.
35. *MFP*, 2 November, 4 December 1901.
36. Ibid., 7, 10 February 1902. The phrase quoted by Sifton was not precisely correct; he probably was paraphrasing the qualifying language, "while not doing injustice to any class." See

D.O. Carrigan, *Canadian Party Platforms 1867-1968* (Toronto: Copp Clark, 1968), p. 34.

37. E.M. Macdonald, *Recollections, Political and Personal* (Toronto: Ryerson, 1938), pp. 59-60; J.S. Willison, *Sir Wilfrid Laurier* (Toronto: Oxford University Press, 1927), part 2, pp. 459-60; O.D. Skelton, *Life and Letters of Sir Wilfrid Laurier*, 2, (New York: Century, 1922), pp. 165-84; J.W. Dafoe, *Laurier: a Study in Canadian Politics* (Toronto: McClelland and Stewart, 1963) pp. 76-77; Schull, *Laurier: the first Canadian*, pp. 410-12. On Tarte's campaign, see L.L. LaPierre, "Politics, Race and Religion in French Canada: Joseph Israel Tarte" (Ph.D. thesis, University of Toronto, 1962), pp. 441ff.

38. H.B. Neatby, *Laurier and a Liberal Quebec: a Study in Political Management* (Toronto: McClelland and Stewart, 1973), p. 139.

39. Ibid.

40. PAC, Sifton Papers, vol. 97, pp. 76245-40—43, Dafoe to Sifton, 7 November 1901.

41. PAC, Sifton Papers, vol. 130, pp. 103735-36, D.A. Poe to W. Templeman, 29 July 1902 (copy); LaPierre, "Politics, Race and Religion," p. 452.

42. *MFP*, 4 September 1902; CAR, 1902, pp. 21-22.

43. MFP, 5, 11, 13, 16, 22 September, 2 October 1902.

44. PAC, Sifton Papers, vol. 119, 94347-49, Cartwright to Sifton, 6 September 1902; see also vol. 118, pp. 90499-501, J.D. Cameron to Sifton, 4 September 1902; vol. 134, 106590-91, A. Strang to Sifton, 16 September 1902; Minto Papers, letterbooks, vol. 3, pp. 257-59, Minto to Laurier, 23 September 1902; Laurier Papers, vol. 241, pp. 67273-75, Cartwright to Laurier, 15 September 1902; pp. 67284-90, Fielding to Laurier, 18 September 1902.

45. Ibid., pp. 67434-35, C.A. Gordon to Laurier, 11 October 1902.

46. PAC, Sifton Papers, vol. 120, pp. 95836-32—36, Dafoe to Sifton, 28 October 1902; vol. 118, p. 94131, Cameron to Sifton, n.d. [October 1902]; Public Archives of Saskatche-

wan, Walter Scott Papers, p. 1130, Sifton to Scott, 30 October 1902.

47. PAC, Minto Papers, letterbooks, vol. 3, pp. 261-65, Minto to Chamberlain, 23 September 1902. Minto over-simplified Tarte's position as much as that of Sifton; see LaPierre, "Politics, Race and Religion," pp. 445-46.

48. PAC, Minto Papers, vol. 4, pp. 40-41, Conversation with Tarte, 17 September 1902; pp. 49-51, same, 22 October 1902; pp. 46-47, Conversation, Lady Minto with Tarte, 22 October 1902; vol. 2, pp. 18-22, Conversation with Laurier, 20 October 1902; letterbooks, vol. 3, pp. 261-65, Minto to Chamberlain, 23 September 1902; vol. 36, pp. 246-47, Minto to Arthur Elliot, 2 November 1902. Hon. James Sutherland, a close friend of Sifton, was principal Ontario organizer in the cabinet. He was Minister without Portfolio, 1899-1902, briefly Minister of Marine and Fisheries in 1902, and then succeeded Tarte as Minister of Public Works in November, 1902.

49. Ibid.

50. *MFP*, 14, 23 January 1903.

51. Ibid.

52. Ibid.; and 16, 17 January 1903; Toronto *News*, 21 January 1903.

53. Ibid., 27 July 1904; PAC, Sifton Papers, vol. 253, pp. 469-71, Sifton to Dafoe, 23 November 1903.

54. Ibid., vol. 251, p. 884, Sifton to Fielding, 18 April 1903. He considered that the Americans "are trying to play us on the question for the purpose of their election next November."

55. Ibid., vol. 253, pp. 413-14, Sifton to Dafoe, 21 November 1903.

56. Ibid., pp. 469-71, Sifton to Dafoe, 23 November 1903.

57. Ibid., vol. 140, pp. 111898-83—86, Dafoe to Sifton, 28 November 1903; see also vol. 253, p. 669, Sifton to Dafoe, 2 December 1903, agreeing "exactly" with Dafoe's views.

58. Ibid., p. 750, Sifton to Dafoe, 5 December 1903; vol. 254, p. 765, Sifton to B.J. McDonnell, 14 January 1904; pp. 289-91, 483, Sifton to Walter Scott, 24, 30 December 1903; vol. 255, p. 24, Sifton to Scott, 21 January 1904.

59. Ibid., vol. 254, pp. 961-64, Sifton to Dafoe, 19 January 1904; p. 965, Sifton to W. Paterson, 20 January 1904; vol. 157, pp. 127183-19—23, Dafoe to Sifton, 25 January 1904; vol. 255, pp. 296-97, Sifton to Laurier, 29 January 1904; p. 326, Sifton to Dafoe, 29 January 1904; pp. 324-25, Sifton to Paterson, 29 January 1904.

60. *MFP*, 8 June 1904.

61. PAC, Laurier Papers, vol. 334, p. 89405, Senator McMullen to Laurier, 7 September 1904; reply, pp. 89407-8, 9 September 1904; vol. 337, pp. 90170-71, McMullen to Laurier, 27 September 1904.

62. *Debates*, 1901, cols. 3599-607, 23 April 1901. In 1903 he strongly supported the idea of requiring the Grand Trunk Pacific to purchase rails in Canada by imposing a duty on imported rails. Otherwise American manufacturers would undervalue their rails "for the purpose of killing off the steele [*sic*] plants in Canada, which are just now struggling into existence." PAC, Laurier Papers, vol. 276, pp. 76042-43, Sifton to Laurier, 10 August 1903.

63. *MFP*, 6, 9 December 1904; *CAR*, 1904, p. 456.

64. See J.L. McDougall, *Canadian Pacific: a Brief History* (Montreal: McGill University Press, 1968), pp. 143-45; the CPR argument is found in PAC, Laurier Papers, vol. 184, pp. 52446-53, T.G. Shaughnessy to Laurier, 14 January 1901, and encl.; the Great Northern argument in the Sir Mackenzie Bowell Papers, vol. 15, 6597-600, J.J. Hill to Bowell, 4 March 1900; the Coal Company view, in a series of articles in the Toronto *Globe* early in January 1901; and Sifton's view in Sifton Papers, vol. 240, pp. 703-6, 835-36, Sifton to Magurn, 9, 15 January 1901; p. 831, Sifton to D. McMillan, 14 January 1901; vol. 241, pp. 521-22, Sifton to H. Bostock, 5 February 1901. See also *MFP*, 4, 7 January 1901; and Clippingdale, "J.S. Willison, Political Journalist," pp. 427-30.

65. W.K. Lamb, *History of the Canadian Pacific Railway* (New York: Macmillan, 1977), pp. 236-37.

66. PAC, Laurier Papers, vol. 193, pp.

55162-63, Shaughnessy to Laurier, 6 April 1901. It had been revealed in March that Hill had purchased $500,000, or 30 per cent of the Coal Company stock; see Clippingdale, "J.S. Willison, Political Journalist," p. 428; Albro Martin, *James J. Hill & the Opening of the Northwest* (New York: Oxford University Press, 1976), p. 593.

67. PAC, Sifton Papers, vol. 95, pp. 7462-68, documents on Crow's Nest Pass Coal Company; vol. 96, pp. 75829-34, Cox to Sifton, 4 May 1901; vol. 246, pp. 961-63, Sifton to Dafoe, 13 January 1902. Opposition to the charter when brought to Parliament was so strong that it was withdrawn and a charter subsequently obtained from British Columbia. Clippingdale, "J.S. Willison, Political Journalist," pp. 428-29.

68. *MFP*, 5 January 1901.

69. PAC, Sifton Papers, vol. 241, pp. 85-86, Sifton to Magurn, 21 January 1901.

70. Ibid., pp. 612-13, Sifton to A.G. Blair, 8 February 1901; vol. 242, pp. 882-83, Sifton to Blair, 3 April 1901; vol. 246, pp. 961-63, Sifton to Dafoe, 13 January 1902.

71. *MFP*, 15 March 1901.

72. PAC, Sifton Papers, vol. 101, p. 79734, H.M. Howell to Sifton, 17 January 1901.

73. Ibid., vol. 242, p. 689, Sifton to I.R. Stratton, 22 March 1901; vol. 241, pp. 521-22, Sifton to H. Bostock, 5 February 1901; *MFP*, 11, 15 February 1901, and many subsequent editorials.

74. Ibid., 11 February, 5, 6 March 1901.

75. Ibid., 14 February 1901; this editorial in particular seems to have been inspired by Sifton.

76. PAC, Laurier Papers, vol. 230, p. 64426, Laurier to R. Holmes, MP, 19 April 1902.

77. PAC, C.M. Hays Papers, vol. 1, pp. 61-62, Hays to Rivers Wilson, 9 December 1902.

78. John A. Eagle, "Sir Robert Borden and the Railway Problem in Canadian Politics, 1911-1920," Ph.D. thesis, University of Toronto, 1972, pp. 27-28.

79. PAC, Hays Papers, vol. 1, pp. 73-74,

Hays to Rivers Wilson, 13 January 1903; Laurier Papers, vol. 248, pp. 69079-87, Hays to Laurier, 12 January 1903, and encl.

80. Regehr, *The Canadian Northern Railway* pp. 106-7.

81. Ibid., p. 113.

82. PAC, Laurier Papers, vol. 252, pp. 70245-52, Mulock to Laurier, 14 February 1903.

83. PAC, Sifton Papers, vol. 250, pp. 604-7, "Memorandum on the subject of a Commission to be appointed for the purpose of making a report on the general subject of Transportation", 12 February 1903; vol. 251, pp. 430-36, Memo: re: the Grand Trunk Pacific Railway, 20 March 1903.

84. Ibid., Memo: 12 February 1903.

85. PAC, Laurier Papers, vol. 260, pp. 72004-2009, Sifton to Laurier, 9 April 1903, particularly the "P.S."

86. PAC, Sifton Papers, Vol. 251, Memo: 20 March 1903. It is worth noting that in May of 1903 Laurier accepted Sifton's idea of a broad investigation into all aspects of transportation, appointing a Royal Commission headed by Sir William Van Horne. But the basic decisions had been made by the time it was appointed, and it did not report until the end of 1905. See R.M. Coutts, "The Railway Policy of Sir Wilfrid Laurier: Grand Trunk Pacific —National Transcontinental," (MA thesis, University of Toronto, 1968), p. 13.

87. PAC, Laurier Papers, vol. 260, pp. 72004-9, Sifton to Laurier, 9 April 1903.

88. PAC, Sifton Papers, vol. 144, pp. 115545-47, Laurier to Sifton, 28 May 1903.

89. PAC, Hays Papers, vol. 1, pp. 167-70, Hays to Rivers Wilson, 24 June 1903; pp. 175-76, Hays to Rivers Wilson, 29 June 1903; Eagle, "Sir Robert Borden and the Railway Problem," p.29.

90. PAC, Hays Papers, vol. 1, p. 176, Hays to Rivers Wilson, 29 June 1903.

91. Eagle, "Sir Robert Borden and the Railway Problem," pp. 30-32.

92. PAC, Hays Papers, vol. 1, correspondence, July 1903.

93. Eagle, "Sir Robert Borden and the Railway Problem," p. 29; *Debates*, 1903, cols. 7658-97; *MFP*, 31 July 1903.

94. PAC, Laurier Papers, vol. 272, pp. 74954-62, Blair to Laurier, 10 July 1903.

95. PAC, Sifton Papers, vol. 138, pp. 110236-40, T.A. Burrows to Sifton, 21 July 1903.

96. Ibid., vol. 213, pp. 164848-49, J.S. Willison to Sifton, 6 April 1925; and reply, 11 April 1925. See also J.S. Willison, *Sir Wilfrid Laurier* (Toronto: Oxford University Press, 1927), part 2, p. 360.

97. *MFP*, 15 July 1903; PAC, Hays Papers, vol. 1, pp. 236-37, Rivers Wilson to Hays and reply, 23 July 1903; pp. 238-39, Rivers Wilson to Hays, 24 July 1903; Laurier Papers, vol. 273, pp. 25298-99, J.A. Macdonald (editor, Toronto *Globe*) to Laurier, 21 July 1903. Macdonald had been influenced by Robert Jaffray; it should be recalled that Jaffray, perhaps correctly, blamed Sifton for his failure to obtain a coveted Senatorship two years earlier. See Sifton Papers, vol. 102, pp. 80253-56, 80258-59, Jaffray to Sifton, 28 January, 14 February 1901; vol. 241, pp. 863-64, Sifton to Jaffray, 15 February 1901; vol. 102, pp. 80441-45, L.M. Jones to Sifton [n.d.].

98. *MFP*, 16 April 1904.

99. *Debates*, 1903, cols. 8617-80, 13 August 1903. The Geological Survey Report and Map is found in *CSP*, 1903. no. 143.

100. PAC, Laurier Papers, vol. 306, pp. 82781-82, Sifton to Laurier, 21 February 1904.

101. *MFP*, 27 April 1904; PAC, Sifton Papers, vol. 172, p. 139668, W.F. McCreary to Sifton, 17 March 1904; vol. 167, pp. 134787-88, Justice McGuire to Sifton, 4 June 1904; and reply, vol. 259, p. 184, 11 June 1904; Eagle, "Sir Robert Borden and the Railway Problem," p. 30; R.C. Brown, *Robert Laird Borden, A Biography*, 1, *1854-1914* (Toronto: Macmillan, 1975), p. 69.

102. H. Borden, ed., *Robert Laird Borden: His Memoirs*, I (Toronto: Macmillan, 1938), p. 124; *Debates*, 1904, cols. 794-824, 6 April 1904.

103. Regehr, *The Canadian Northern Railway*, pp. 122-24.

NOTES TO CHAPTER FIVE

1. *MFP*, 18 November 1903.
2. PAC, Sir Joseph Pope Papers, vol. 49, Pope to Anderson, 10 July 1899.
3. See James Eayrs, *The Art of the Possible: Government and Foreign Policy in Canada* (Toronto: University of Toronto Press, 1961), pp. 124-25.
4. Norman Penlington, *The Alaska Boundary Dispute: a Critical Reappraisal* (Toronto: McGraw-Hill Ryerson, 1972), p. 45; Charles S. Campbell, Jr., *Anglo-American Understanding, 1898-1903* (Baltimore: Johns Hopkins Press, 1957), p. 145.
5. See the excellent map in Penlington, *Alaska Boundary Dispute*, p. 51; Campbell, *Anglo-American Understanding*, pp. 147-50.
6. PAC, Laurier Papers, vol. 209, pp. 59301-6, Minto to Chamberlain, 12 October 1901.
7. PAC, Minto Papers, letterbooks, vol. 3, pp. 204-5, Minto to Col. Kitson, 17 May 1902; and see pp. 203-04, Minto to Laurier, 17 May 1902.
8. Dafoe, *Clifford Sifton*, p. 217.
9. Campbell, *Anglo-American Understanding*, pp. 257-58; PAC, Minto Papers, letterbooks, vol. 3, pp. 219-21, Minto to Lansdowne, 4 June 1902; vol. 2, pp. 14-16, Conversation with Laurier, Mulock and Lansdowne, 24 June 1902; pp. 18-22, Conversation with Laurier, 20 October 1902.
10. Dafoe, *Clifford Sifton*, p. 217; for further evidence of cabinet dissatisfaction with Laurier's position, see PAC, Minto Papers, letterbooks, vol. 3, pp. 271-76, Minto to Sir Michael Herbert, 21 October 1902; vol. 2, p. 27, Conversation with Laurier, 19 January 1903; Miller, *The Canadian Career of the Fourth Earl of Minto* p. 165.
11. Penlington, *Alaska Boundary Dispute*, pp. 68-69.
12. PAC, Minto Papers, letterbooks, vol. 3, pp. 332-33, Minto to Sir Michael Herbert, 30 December 1902; vol. 2, pp. 24-25, Conversation with Laurier, 8 January 1903.
13. On the process of selecting the Agent, and the names raised, see PAC, Pope Papers, vol. 44, Diary, 19 January, 12, 17-19 February, 4-7, 9 March 1903.
14. PAC, Sifton Papers, vol. 250, pp. 410-13. Sifton to Dafoe, 4 February 1903.
15. C.C. Tansill, *Canadian-American Relations, 1875-1911* (Gloucester: Peter Smith [1943], 1964), p. 231; Campbell, *Anglo-American Understanding*, pp. 309-12.
16. PAC, Sifton Papers, vol. 250, p. 810, Sifton to Fielding, 20 February 1903; vol. 273, Minto to Colonial Office and reply, 20 February 1903; Minto Papers, vol. 2, pp. 29-31, Conversation with Laurier, 25 February 1903; letterbook, vol. 3, pp. 397-402, Minto to Chamberlain, 2 March 1903; *MFP*, 23 February, 9 March 1903.
17. PAC, Sifton Papers, vol. 150, pp. 119973-74, Sifton to W.H. Dickson, 23 March 1903; pp. 119980-83, draft of press release, corrected by Sifton; pp. 119976-79, final draft, 23 March 1903. During his stay in England, Sifton kept a close eye on treatment of the question in Canadian papers; see ibid., vol. 267, p. 991, Sifton to Dafoe, 22 May 1903; vol. 252, pp. 144-47, Sifton to Hon. J. Sutherland, 5 May 1903.
18. PAC, Laurier Papers, vol. 260, pp. 72004-9, Sifton to Laurier, 9 April 1903; Joseph Schull, *Edward Blake*, 2, *Leader and Exile (1881-1912)* (Toronto: Macmillan, 1976), pp. 222-25. The Canadian staff also included Christopher Robinson, F.C. Wade, A. Geoffrion, and (from July) L.P. Duff as counsel; and Joseph Pope, W.F. King and J.J. McArthur as civil servants expert in facets of the case. They were assisted by British counsel S.A.T. Rowatt and J.A. Simon; and by Sir Robert Finlay and Sir Edward Carson, respectively the Attorney General and the Solicitor General of England.
19. PAC, Sifton papers, vol. 268, p. 3, Sifton to Laurier, 1 May 1903.
20. PAC, Pope Papers, Memoirs, p. 194.
21. PAC, Minto Papers, vol. 27, p. 104, Anderson to Minto, 22 April 1903. Anderson also reported that Blake was proving difficult.
22. Ibid., letterbooks, vol. 4, pp. 60-61, Minto to Anderson, 1 May 1903.
23. Ibid., vol. 36, pp. 310-25, Minto to Elliot, 20 May 1903; vol. 27, pp. 13-16,

A. Bigge to Minto, 28 June 1903.

24. Penlington, *Alaska Boundary Dispute*, pp. 85-87. Penlington greatly overstates the importance of these problems, which he terms "Sifton's Political Blunders."

25. PAC, Sifton Papers, vol. 144, pp. 115545-47, Laurier to Sifton, 28 May 1903.

26. Ibid., vol. 252, pp. 144-47, Sifton to Hon. J. Sutherland, 5 May 1903; PAC, Fitzpatrick Papers, vol. 5, Christopher Robinson to Edward Blake, 23 March 1903; Robinson to Fitzpatrick, 13 April 1903.

27. PAC, Sifton Papers, vol. 251, p. 823, Sifton to Anderson, 15 June 1903; vol. 252, pp. 163-66, Sifton to Wade, 15 June 1903.

28. Ibid., p. 238, Sifton to J.D. Cameron, 21 July 1903; pp. 366-68, Sifton to L.P. Duff, 29 July 1903.

29. Campbell, *Anglo-American Understanding*, pp. 323-28.

30. Penlington, *Alaska Boundary Dispute*, pp. 91-96, argues this point of view very strongly.

31. PAC, Pope Papers, vol. 48, Special Journals, Alaska Boundary, 1903, Diary entry, Sunday, 13 September 1903. The "mountain line" would give the Americans an unbroken *lisière*, but it would be narrower than the American contention. Another version of Pope's conversation with Alverstone appears in John A. Munro, ed., *The Alaska Boundary Dispute* (Toronto: Copp Clark, 1970), pp. 74-76.

32. Penlington, *Alaska Boundary Dispute*, p. 94.

33. Ibid.

34. Ibid., p. 95.

35. PAC, Sifton Papers, vol. 253, pp. 146-47, Sifton to Sydney Fisher, 19 September 1903.

36. PAC, Laurier Papers, vol. 282, pp. 77108-10, Sifton to Laurier, 19 September 1903.

37. PAC, Pope Papers, vol. 1, Laurier to Pope, 4 October 1903, and undated note; Laurier Papers, vol. 284, p. 77602, Sifton to Laurier, 8 October 1903.

38. PAC, Sifton Papers, vol. 275, telegram, Laurier to Sifton, 8 October 1903.

39. Ibid., Laurier to Sifton, 18 October 1903; Laurier Papers, vol. 286, p.

77891, Sifton to Laurier, 17 October 1903; Penlington, *Alaska Boundary Dispute*, p. 97.

40. See ibid., pp. 96-102.

41. Sifton did cling to the notion long enough to defend it to Lord Minto; but Laurier and Cartwright confessed that there was nothing in it, and publicly Sifton hardly mentioned it. PAC, Minto Papers, vol. 4, pp. 62-73, Conversation with Sifton, 11 November 1903; vol. 2, pp. 52-53, Conversation with Laurier, 18 November 1903; vol. 4, pp. 75-82, Conversation with Cartwright, 13 November 1903.

42. PAC, Sifton Papers, vol. 252, p. 990, Sifton to A.N. McPherson, 10 November 1903.

43. Ibid., vol. 253, pp. 248-49, 799, Sifton to Campbell, 17 November, 7 December 1903.

44. PAC, Minto Papers, vol. 4, pp. 62-73, Conversation with Sifton, 11 November 1903.

45. Ibid., vol. 14, pp. 130-34, Chamberlain to Minto, 28 December 1903; Brandford Perkins, *The Great Rapprochement: England and the United States, 1895-1914* (New York: Atheneum, 1968), pp. 167-68.

46. PAC, Sifton Papers, vol. 253, pp. 91-92, Sifton to A.M. Peterson, 13 November 1903; Dafoe, *Clifford Sifton*, pp. 239-40.

47. Clifford Sifton, "Some Matters of National Interest to Canadians," in G.M. Brown, ed., *Addresses Delivered before the Canadian Clubs, Ottawa Club, 1903-04*, pp. 71-73; *MFP*, 8 December 1903; PAC, Sifton Papers, vol. 253, pp. 874-75, Sifton to Dafoe, 9 December 1903. Minto dismissed Sifton's speech as "only...pandering to a thoughtless and somewhat dangerous young Canada." PAC, Minto Papers, vol. 36, pp. 381-407, Minto to Arthur Elliot, 2 January 1904.

48. PAC, Sifton Papers, vol. 253, pp. 937-38, Sifton to Shortt, 11 December 1903. Shortt did indeed produce a frank statement in 1904; see Carl Berger, ed., *Imperialism and Nationalism 1884-1914: a Conflict in Canadian Thought* (Toronto: Copp Clark, 1969), pp. 79-81.

49. PAC, Sifton Papers, vol. 285, Confidential Opinions of Sir Allen Ayles-

worth on the Alaskan Boundary Dispute [1942] (partially reprinted in *CHR*, 52, 1971, pp. 476-77); Mr. Clifford Sifton to F.W. Gibson, 11 November 1942; J.W. Dafoe to Mr. Clifford Sifton, 15 November 1942; Mr. Clifford Sifton to Mr. Justice McLennan, 19 November 1968 (in possession of author); Dafoe, *Clifford Sifton*, pp.

50. Cited in Munro, ed., *Alaska Boundary Dispute*, p. 47.

51. PAC, RCMP Records, vol. 229, files 149, 150; vol. 232, file 195; vol. 237, file 528; Sifton Papers, vol. 117, pp. 93221-23, Sifton to F.W. Borden, 22 January 1902; vol. 135, pp. 107940-43, J.M. Walsh to Sifton, 17 March 1902, and encl.; F.C. Wade Papers, vol. 1, F. White to Wade, 11 October 1902; Laurier Papers, vol. 753, pt. 1, Minto to Chamberlain, 20 November 1901.

52. Tansill, *Canadian-American Relations*, p. 224; Penlington, *Alaska Boundary Dispute*, p. 62.

53. Ibid., p. 55; PAC, Pope Papers, vol. 49, no. 200, Memo: re: Wales and Pearse Islands at the entrance to the Portland Canal (17 December 1902). A more complete contemporary description of the problems and growing Canadian-American friction is F.C. Wade, "The Alaska Boundary Dispute: Its Practical Side," *The Empire Review*, 4, (January 1903): 577-86. This article was drafted in the early fall of 1902 and approved by Sifton, who termed it "timely and practical." PAC, Sifton Papers, vol. 249, p. 13, Sifton to Wade, 1 November 1902.

54. See Zaslow, *The Opening of the Canadian North*, ch. 10, pt. 2, esp. pp. 243-48; and ch. 11.

55. PAC, Sifton Papers, vol. 249, pp.

690-92, Sifton to Smart, 15 December 1902; RCMP Records, vol. 235, file 296.

56. PAC, Sifton Papers, vol. 251, pp. 461-62, Sifton to Smart, 21 March 1903.

57. Ibid., vol. 252, pp. 140-42, Sifton to Smart, 31 March 1903.

58. Ibid., vol. 136, p. 109067, R.L. Borden to Sifton, 3 August 1903; PAC, Constantine Papers, vol. 3, Reports, 1903; RCMP Records, vol. 235, file 296.

59. Ibid., Sifton to White, 19 November 1903; PAC, Sifton Papers, vol. 152, pp. 121817-18, 121325-26, White to Sifton, 10 November 1903, and encl.; pp. 121831-32, White to Laurier, 17 November 1903 (copy).

60. PAC, Laurier Papers vol. 290, pp. 78866-67, Ami to Laurier, 17 November 1903; Fitzpatrick Papers, vol. 6, Ami to Fitzpatrick, 22 October 1903; Zaslow, *Opening of the Canadian North*, p. 262. Ami had tutored Sifton's sons in French. His suggested declaration is found in Sifton Papers, vol. 136, pp. 108762-64, Ami to Sifton, 1 December 1903.

61. PAC, Minto Papers, vol. 2, pp. 55-59, Conversation with Laurier, 3 December 1903.

62. PAC, Sifton Papers, vol. 253, pp. 962-63, Sifton to King, 11 December 1903. King's report appeared in 1904; see Zaslow, *Opening of the Canadian North*, pp. 254-55, 264-65.

63. PAC, Sifton Papers, vol. 153, pp. 122486-92, Ami to Fitzpatrick, 15 January 1904 (sent to Sifton); vol. 255, pp. 173, 827, Sifton to Laurier, 25 January, 11 February 1904; Laurier Papers, vol. 303, p. 81846, Sifton to Laurier, 1 February 1904.

NOTES TO CHAPTER SIX

1. *MFP*, 20, 28 August 1901; 21, 23, 31, July, 6 September 1902; PAC, Sifton Papers vol. 96 p. 75658, F.T. Congdon to Sifton, 16 August 1901; vol. 248, pp. 831-32, A.P. Collier to Rev. S.J. Taylor, 21 July 1902; vol. 133. pp. 106137-41, J.A. Smart to Sifton, 18 August 1902; Morrison, *Politics of the*

Yukon Territory, p. 47. Ross was reported to have had "an attack of apoplexy, which resulted in partial hemiplegia and motor aphasia."

2. PAC, Laurier Papers, vol. 192, p. 54992, Woodside to Laurier, 2 April 1901.

3. PAC, Sifton Papers, vol. 242, pp.

392-93, Sifton to J.I. Tarte, 13 March 1901; and reply, vol. 114, p. 89837, 14 March 1901.

4. Ibid., vol. 110, p. 86976-78, Ross to Sifton, 18 July 1901.
5. Ibid., .vol. 96, pp. 75691-703, Cory to Sifton, 2 October 1901; vol. 249, pp. 725-28, Sifton to A. Pattullo, 17 December 1902. See also vol. 246, pp. 128-30, Sifton to Alexander Dawson, 11 November 1901; vol. 93, pp. 72956-58, N. A. Belcourt to Sifton, 20 June 1901; vol. 110, pp. 86959-61, Ross to Sifton, 9 July 1901.
6. Ibid., vol. 110, pp. 89971-74, Ross to Sifton, 18 July 1901.
7. Ibid., vol. 96, pp. 75691-703, 75705-10, Cory to Sifton, 2 October, 6 November 1901.
8. PAC, Minto Papers, letterbooks, vol. 2, pp. 79-91, Minto to J. Chamberlain, 19 August 1900.
9. Morrison, *Politics of the Yukon Territory*, pp. 40-42.
10. PAC, Sifton Papers, vol. 110, pp. 86980-84, Ross to Sifton, 18 July 1901; vol. 96, pp. 75705-10, Cory to Sifton, 6 November 1901; RCMP Records, vol. 268, file 247; *MFP*, 11 March, 18 April, 28 August 1901; Zaslow, *The Opening of the Canadian North*, p. 114.
11. Both Ross and James Smart supported an assay office for Dawson, commenting on the high profits made by the banks in purchasing gold in Dawson. Smart also noted the high interest rates (18 to 24 per cent) charged by the banks on loans, and concluded that "the banks are the greatest 'grafters' in the [Yukon] country." It might be added that the banks sold their gold, like the miners, in the U.S. PAC, Sifton Papers, vol. 133, pp. 106189-202, Smart to Sifton, 15 September 1902; vol. 110, pp. 86980-84, Ross to Sifton, 18 July 1901.
12. *CAR*, 1901, p. 500; PAC, Sifton Papers, vol. 90, pp. 74041-46, W. Templeman to Sifton, 20 October 1900.
13. PAC, Laurier Papers, vol. 202, p. 57562, Sifton to Laurier, 15 July 1901; Sifton Papers, vol. 96, pp. 75604-5, A.P. Collier to Sifton, 4 August 1901; vol. 110, pp. 87010-12, Ross to Sifton, 15 August 1901. Between 1898 and 31 October 1901, the Seattle assay office

treated nearly $54.9 million worth of gold, of which $45.95 million came from the Yukon and British Columbia. PAC, Sifton Papers, vol. 105, Thos. McCaffry to Sifton, 2 December 1901.

14. PAC, Laurier Papers, vol. 190, pp. 54471-73, Sifton to Laurier, 9 April 1901.
15. Morrison, *Politics of the Yukon Territory*, p. 40; Zaslow, *Opening of the Canadian North*, pp. 136-37; PAC, Minto Papers, vol. 35, pp. 36-39, Wood to Minto, 26 July 1901.
16. PAC, RCMP Records, vol. 219, file 905, Houses of prostitution at Dawson, F.C. Wade to E.L. Newcombe [1902]; Sifton Papers, 1901, correspondence of F.C. Wade, F. White and E.L. Newcombe.
17. PAC, Sifton Papers, vol. 248, pp. 631-32, Sifton to Rev. Dr. Bryce, 28 June 1902.
18. Morrison, *Politics of the Yukon Territory*, p. 42.
19. PAC, Sifton Papers, vol. 110, pp. 86980-84, Ross to Sifton, 18 July 1901.
20. Ibid., vol. 295, file "Walsh, J.M., 1897," H.J. Barton to Walsh, 20 August, 1897; Laurier Papers, vol. 368, pp. 98165-74, W.W. Cory to R. Boudreau, 3 June 1905, and encl.; Lewis Green, *The Gold Hustlers* (Anchorage: Alaska Northwest Publishing Company, 1977), p. 19. See also William Rodney, *Joe Boyle: King of the Klondike* (Toronto: McGraw-Hill Ryerson, 1974), chs. 5 and 6; Morrison, *Politics of the Yukon Territory*, ch. 6.
21. Zaslow, *The Opening of the Canadian North*, p. 114. On the technology of mining in the Yukon, see H.A. Innis, *Settlement and the Mining Frontier* (Toronto: Macmillan, 1936), ch. 2; Norman Ball, "The Development of Permafrost Thawing Techniques in the Placer Gold Fields of the Klondike," Department of Indian and Northern Affairs, National Historic Parks and Sites Branch, *Research Bulletin*, No. 25, November 1975; and Green, *The Gold Hustlers*, passim.
22. Morrison, *Politics of the Yukon Territory*, pp. 43-44; Green, *The Gold Hustlers*, pp. 20-28. Though lacking conclusive evidence, both authors imply that Sifton had a direct interest in

the Treadgold scheme, and Morrison believes that he kept the royalty in place until 1902 purposely to drive out the placer miners. No doubt some statements in Treadgold's letters can be read this way, but the case is far from certain. The delays in implementing the project, subsequent correspondence, and Sifton's attitude when the scheme failed, do not suggest any deep personal involvement. If he was involved, he certainly covered his tracks well. See also PAC, Sifton Papers, vol. 73, pp. 54568-81, letters, Treadgold to Sifton, 30 May to 27 September 1899.

23. PAC, Laurier Papers, vol. 138, pp. 41363-69, Sifton to Laurier, 22 January 1900, and encl.

24. PAC, Sifton Papers, vol. 236, pp. 797-99, Sifton to Laurier, 8 March 1900.

25. *CSP*, 1903, no. 63, p. 9.

26. PAC, Sifton Papers, vol. 151, pp. 121080-97, Treadgold and others to Sifton, 9 June 1903; *CSP*, 1902, no. 81; Green, *The Gold Hustlers*, p. 28.

27. PC 1293, 12 June 1901.

28. PAC, Sifton Papers, vol. 238, pp. 532-33, Sifton to Ogilvie, 22 August 1900. It should be noted that a number of the concessions were authorized by James Sutherland, Acting Minister of the Interior, during Sifton's absence in Europe.

29. Ibid., vol. 93, pp. 72871-79, A. Beaudette to the Assistant Gold Commissioner, 7 August 1901; vol. 110, pp. 87021-23, Ross to Sifton, 17 August 1901.

30. Ibid., vol. 96, pp. 75419-20, O.H. Clark to Sifton, 24 August 1901; vol. 102, pp. 80321-30, H.B. Jayne to Sifton, 23 August 1901; vol. 110, pp. 87032-34, Ross to Sifton, 10 October 1901; Minto Papers, vol. 24, pp. 119-22, Jos. McGillivray to David Mills, 11 November 1901 (copy).

31. PAC, Sifton Papers, vol. 267, pp. 114-15, Sifton to E.C. Senkler, 6 September 1901; Green, *The Gold Hustlers*, pp. 34-37.

32. PAC, Sifton Papers, vol. 151, pp. 121105-8, Order in Council, 7 December 1901.

33. Morrison, *Politics of the Yukon Territory*, p. 45.

34. PAC, Sifton Papers, vol. 129, p. 102985, Postmaster Hartman to W. Mulock, 15 February 1902 (copy).

35. PAC, Sifton Papers, vol. 246, pp. 827-29, Sifton to Ross, 3 January 1902 (Sifton's emphasis).

36. Morrison, *Politics of the Yukon Territory*, p. 46; Green, *The Gold Hustlers*, p. 42; PAC, Sifton Papers, vol. 128, pp. 100709-10, H.C. MacAulay, A.E. Wills, F.T. Congdon, and O.H. Clark to Sifton, 17 February 1902.

37. PAC, Sifton Papers, vol. 119, pp. 94646-51, Clark to Sifton, 26 February 1902.

38. Ibid.; vol. 127, p. 102109, Order in Council, 21 April 1902; and Green, *The Gold Hustlers*, pp. 44-45.

39. PAC, Sifton Papers, vol. 247, p. 129, Sifton to Ross, 16 January 1902; vol. 133, 106149-52, Smart to Sifton, 21 August 1902; vol. 248, pp. 636-38, Sifton to Ross, 28 June 1902.

40. Ibid., vol. 116, pp. 92321-22, 92327, 92343-45, W. Barwick to Sifton, 31 July, 5, 30 September 1902; vol. 133, pp. 106157-61, Smart to Sifton, 25 August 1902.

41. PAC, Minto Papers, vol. 4, pp. 40-41, Conversation with Tarte, 17 September 1902.

42. PAC, Sifton Papers, vol. 120, pp. 95142-50, Congdon to Sifton, 29 September 1902; Laurier Papers, vol. 244, 68192-98, Ross's election declaration and platform, 19 November 1902.

43. *CSP*, 1905, no. 37; PAC, Sifton Papers, vol. 249, pp. 695-96, Sifton to J.D. McGregor, 15 December 1902.

44. PAC, Laurier Papers, vol. 258, pp. 71626-30, Ross to Laurier, 31 March 1903.

45. PAC, Sifton Papers, vol. 151, pp. 121129-32, Turriff to Sifton, 3 April 1903; and reply, vol. 252, pp. 157-59, 15 April 1903.

46. Ibid., vol. 151, pp. 121141-42, Turriff to Sifton 28 April 1903.

47. *Debates*, 1903, cols. 2796-915, 12 May 1903; vols. 4486-548, 11 June 1903; PAC, Sifton Papers, vol. 150, pp. 120570-81, 120585-87, J. Sutherland to Sifton, 23 May, 1 June 1903; pp. 120143, 120149-53, Smart to Sifton, 27 May and 3 June 1903; and reply, vol. 267, p. 984, 3 June 1903; vol. 268, p. 5,

Sifton to Laurier, 29 May 1903; and reply, vol. 144, p. 115549, 29 May 1903; Laurier Papers, vol. 261, pp. 72318-21, Mulock to Laurier, 20 April 1903, and encl.; vol. 285, pp. 77772-77, J.S. Willison to Laurier, 12 October 1903; Green, *The Gold Hustlers*, pp. 68-71.

48. PAC, Sifton Papers, vol. 150, pp. 120585-87, Sutherland to Sifton, 1 June 1903; *CAR*, 1903, pp. 233-40.

49. PAC, Sifton Papers, vol. 252, pp. 127-28, Sifton to Sutherland, 4 June 1903; vol. 151, pp. 121080-97, Treadgold and others to Sifton, 9 June 1903; Laurier Papers, vol. 268, pp. 74020-27, Treadgold to Laurier, 9 June 1903; and reply, 3 July 1903; vol. 277, pp. 76227-29, Treadgold to Laurier, 17 August 1903.

50. PAC, Sifton Papers, vol. 259, pp. 182-83, Sifton to Orr Ewing, 11 June 1903.

51. Ibid., vol. 296, file "Ewing, H. Orr 1904," Orr Ewing to Sifton, 4 July 1904; vol. 299, file "Orr Ewing, H. 1917," passim. On Treadgold's later activities, see Innis, *Settlement and the Mining Frontier*, pp. 249, 268-69; Green, *The Gold Hustlers*, ch. 5.

52. PANS, F.W. Borden Papers, letterbook 4, pp. 870-72, Borden to Captain Norwood, 2 September 1901; letterbook 6, p. 881, same, 23 March 1903; letterbook 7, pp. 467-68, same, 23 July 1903; letterbook 10, pp. 554-55, same, 2 January 1906; letterbook 11, p. 425, same, 28 May 1906; letterbook 12, pp. 599-600, same, 11 February 1907; and see PAC, Laurier Papers, vol. 368, pp. 98165-74, W.W. Cory to R. Boudreau, 3 June 1905 (enclosing list of concessions); Sifton Papers, vol. 156, pp. 126230-38, "Memo Re Yukon Corruption," [n.a., n.d.].

53. S.M. Wickett, "Yukon Trade," *Industrial Canada*, (October 1902): 164-72; PAC, Sifton Papers, vol. 273, F.C. Wade to Sifton and Prof. Wickett, 13, 14 March 1903.

54. PAC, Sifton Papers, vol. 107, pp. 84309-54; final version, pp. 84266-307 [October 1901].

55. *CSP*, 1904. no. 142. Bell died in February 1904, so the final report was solely Britton's work. Of a large amount of evidence taken during a month of hearings and investigation in the Yukon,

the evidence of only three persons—all government officials—was published. Britton dismissed most of the evidence given as of no weight.

56. Zaslow, *The Opening of the Canadian North*, p. 115. It is worth noting that the *Manitoba Free Press* resolutely refused to take notice of the Treadgold agitation. Only in announcing the cancellation of the concession did it tersely admit that the scheme was "looked upon as a curse by all miners" in the Yukon (*MFP*, 27 June 1904; and see Dafoe, *Clifford Sifton*, pp. 187-88).

57. PAC, Sifton Papers, vol. 252, pp. 157-59, Sifton to Turriff, 15 April 1903.

58. Ibid., vol. 98, pp. 77441, 77491-92, Fielding to Sifton, 28 February, 26 September 1901; vol. 110, pp. 86967-69, Ross to Sifton, 16 July 1901; vol. 86, p. 75417, O.H. Clark to Sifton, 17 July 1901; Morrison, *Politics of the Yukon Territory*, p. 57.

59. PAC, Sifton Papers, vol. 120, pp. 95213-14, W.W. Cory to Sifton, 29 July 1902; vol. 133, pp. 106137-41, J. Smart to Sifton, 18 August 1902; vol. 135, pp. 107898-904, F.C. Wade to Sifton, 27 October 1902; vol. 132, p. 104933, Ross to Sifton, 24 December 1902; Laurier Papers, vol. 312, pp. 84348-54, A. Noel to Laurier, 9 April 1904.

60. This information is pieced together from a wide range of sources: Morrison, *The Politics of the Yukon Territory*, chs. 6 and 7; PAC, Sifton Papers, correspondence from Pringle, Pattullo, Wood, Major Woodside, O.H. Clark, Congdon, F.C. Wade, 1902-5; Laurier Papers, correspondence from Pattullo, Woodside, A. Noel, J. C. Noel, J.E. Girouard, Judge Dugas, Congdon, Pringle, Beddoe, Joe Clarke and others, 1902-5; Willison Papers, correspondence from F.C. Wade and Frederick Hamilton, 1904-6; R.C.M.P. Records, correspondence, 1904 and 1905, especially in volume 295; Minto Papers, vol. 4, pp. 40-41, conversation with Tarte, 17 September 1902; and from *Dawson Daily News* and the Yukon *Sun*; PANS, W.S. Fielding Papers, no. 1257, 1258, Congdon to Fielding 21 September, 14 October 1904; no. 1259, J. Pringle to Fielding, 3 January 1905.

61. PAC, Sifton Papers, vol. 178, pp.

144551-60, Pringle to Sifton, 3 January 1905.
62. The new Commissioner, appointed in May 1905, was W.W.B. McInnis. See Morrison, *The Politics of the Yukon*

Territory, p. 71.
63. *MFP*, 17 June 1904, 20 January, 7 February 1905 (partial list of dismissed employees).

NOTES TO CHAPTER SEVEN

1. PAC, Willison Papers, vol. 55, pp. 20422-23, C.A. Matthews to Willison, 24 February 1902.
2. See Ross Harkness, *J.E. Atkinson of the* Star *(*Toronto: University of Toronto Press, 1963), pp. 19-24.
3. PAC, Sifton Papers, vol. 112, p. 88665, Sifton to A. P. Collier, 8 July 1901. The papers were the *Free Press*, *Tribune* and *Telegram* of Winnipeg; the *Globe*; the Ottawa *Journal*; and the *Gazette* and *Herald* of Montreal.
4. *The Canadian Newspaper Directory* (Montreal: A. McKim & Co.), 1899 ed., p. 187; 1901 ed., p. 184; 1905 ed., p. 199. The *Telegram* weekly was consistently weaker than the others.
5. PAC, Sifton Papers, vol. 239, p. 839, Sifton to William Mackenzie, 16 November 1900.
6. PAM, W. Sanford Evans Papers, vol. 3, Evans to W. M. Southam, 8 January 1900 [should read 1901]; Evans to R. T. Riley, 21 November 1900; Evans to Irene Evans, 19 December 1900.
7. PAC, Sifton Papers, vol. 112, pp. 88710-12, J.W. Sifton to Sifton, 22 January 1901; vol. 155, p. 124929, J. D. Cameron to Sifton, 26 April 1904. Richardson controlled 51 per cent of the stock in the *Tribune*; the other leading shareholders were Alexander MacDonald and A.B. Bethune.
8. Sifton had offered ten cents on the dollar. PAC, Sifton Papers, vol. 101, file "Howell, H. M. 1901," passim.; vol. 241, pp. 670-71, Sifton to Howell, 9 February 1901; p. 914, same, 19 February 1901; vol. 112, 88758, J. W. Sifton to Sifton, 19 October 1901.
9. Ibid., vol. 247, p. 350, Sifton to E.H. Macklin, 25 January 1902.
10. Ibid., vol. 241, pp. 42-43, Sifton to Howell, 21 January 1901; vol. 104, p. 81871, Macklin to Sifton, 5 October

1901.
11. Ibid., vol. 246, pp. 7-8, Sifton to Howell, 2 November 1901; and reply, vol. 101, pp. 79799-800, 8 November 1901; vol. 104, pp. 8190-92, Macklin to Sifton, 9 November 1901; vol. 101, 79804-5, Howell to Sifton, 19 November 1901; pp. 79807-8, same, 23 December 1901. The mortgage was to be in the name of C. A. Masten of Toronto, in the amount of $67,837.12; Sifton also held another chattel mortgage for $22,500 at six per cent.
12. Ibid., vol. 250, pp. 262-63, Sifton to Macklin, 29 January 1903.
13. Ibid., vol. 241, p. 710, Sifton to Macklin, 13 February 1901; p. 913, Sifton to J.W. Sifton, 19 February 1901; vol. 242, p. 479, Sifton to Macklin, 18 March 1901; p. 480, Sifton to J.W. Sifton, 18 March 1901. With a delicious sense of irony, the Roblin government appointed the impecunious W.F. Luxton to J.W. Sifton's old sinecure; it was believed that he thereafter did considerable writing for the *Telegram*.
14. PAC, Sifton Papers, vol. 253, pp. 675-77, Sifton to J.W. Sifton, 2 December 1903. Macklin, Dafoe and J. W. Sifton would comprise the new company; see ibid., pp. 966-67, Sifton to Macklin, 14 December 1903.
15. Ibid., vol. 255, pp. 828-30, 908, Sifton to J.W. Sifton, 11, 15 February 1904.
16. Ibid., vol. 242, pp. 600-601, Sifton to J. W. Sifton, 21 March 1901.
17. Ibid., vol. 133, pp. 106031-32, 106042-44, J.W. Sifton to Sifton, 31 March, 29 April 1902. In one two-month period the *Free Press* distributed over 12,000 free copies of its weekly edition; ibid., pp. 105985-86, J. W. Sifton to Sifton, 15 January 1902.
18. Ibid , vol. 145, p. 116004, clipping from

Morden Chronicle (undated).

19. Ibid., vol. 97, pp. 76245-48—49, Dafoe to Sifton, 25 November 1901.

20. Ibid., vol. 120, pp. 95836-15—19, Dafoe to Sifton, 12 April 1902.

21. Ibid., vol. 140, pp. 111898-63—67, Dafoe to Sifton, 23 November 1903; vol. 254, pp. 172-74, Sifton to Dafoe, 21 December 1903.

22. See, for example, ibid., vol. 245, p. 694, Sifton to Dafoe, 11 October 1901; vol. 246, pp. 219-20, 429-30, same, 13 and 29 November 1901; vol. 253, pp. 950-51, same, 12 December 1903.

23. Ibid., vol. 254, p. 421, Sifton to Dafoe, 29 December 1903; vol. 258, p. 785, same, 25 May 1904.

24. The hard line on socialism and government ownership had been continued to the end by Magurn, without restraint from Sifton (*MFP*, 11 May, 11, 17 June 1901).

25. PAC, Laurier Papers, vol. 321, p. 86300, "Regular List of Papers."

26. PAC, Sifton Papers, vol. 255, p. 908, Sifton to J.W. Sifton, 15 February 1904; vols. 250-52, correspondence, passim; vol. 296, file "Sifton, C. 1904," W. F. McCreary to Dafoe, 19 March 1904 (copy); and reply, 26 March 1904. Sifton may also have controlled a French paper, *L'Echo de Manitoba*. The ethnic papers were controlled through a subsidiary of the Free Press Company, The Northwest Publishing Company.

27. PAC, Sifton Papers, vol. 140, pp. 111898-38—47, Dafoe to Sifton, 3 November 1903; and reply, vol. 253, pp. 67-72, 12 November 1903.

28. Ibid., vol. 256, pp. 548-50, Sifton to Dafoe, 12 March 1904.

29. When occasion demanded it, Sifton was also prepared to obtain control of important local weeklies, such as the *Neepawa Press*. See PAC, Sifton Papers, vol. 140, p. 111884, A. Dunlop to J.O. Smith, 8 September 1903; vol. 258, pp. 85-86, Sifton to J.D. Cameron, 28 April 1904.

30. *MFP*, 14 December 1901.

31. PAC, Sifton Papers, vol. 120, pp. 95836-26—28 Dafoe to Sifton, 1 October 1902; vol. 122, pp. 97361-62, A.C. Fraser to Sifton, 4 October 1902; PAS, Walter Scott Papers, p. 1130, Sifton to Scott, 30 October 1902.

32. PAS, Scott Papers, 1130, Sifton to Scott, 30 October 1902. On Borden's tour, see Brown, *Robert Laird Borden:* pp. 52-54.

33. PAC, Sifton Papers, vol. 119, pp. 94347-49, Cartwright to Sifton, 6 September 1902; vol. 150, pp. 120570-81, J. Sutherland to Sifton, 23 May 1903. The Conservative-dominated Senate had thrown out a redistribution bill in 1898, forcing Laurier to go to the country in 1900 on the basis of the old system. As soon as the Liberals controlled the Senate they began their plans for another bill.

34. Joan Winearls, "Federal Electoral Maps of Canada 1867-1970," *The Canadian Cartographer*, 9, no. 1 (1972): 3; *Electoral Atlas of the Dominion of Canada as Divided for the Tenth General Election Held in the Year 1904* (Ottawa: Government Printing Bureau, 1906); *MFP*, 2, 25 July 1903, 7 January 1904.

35. PAC, Sifton Papers, vol. 255, pp. 618-19, Sifton to A. McLeod, 5 February 1904.

36. PAC, Sifton Papers, vol. 252, pp. 716-17, Sifton to Robertson, 20 August 1903.

37. Ibid., vol. 243, pp. 114229-35, J.B. Harkin to A.P. Collier, 7 September 1903. For a later comment on election expenses, see PAC, Willison Papers, vol. 36, pp. 13418-24, F. Hamilton to Willison, 18 December 1905. The Conservatives claimed having only half what the Liberals estimated, but believed the Liberals had a war chest of $1.5 million. The accuracy of these figures is difficult to assess.

38. PAC, Laurier Papers, vol. 282, pp. 77108-10, Sifton to Laurier, 19 September 1903.

39. PAC, Sifton Papers, vol. 253, Sifton to Harkin, 19 September 1903; p. 141, Sifton to A.F. Martin, 19 September 1903; pp. 146-47, Sifton to Fisher, 19 September 1903; vol. 144, pp. 115559-77, 115567-69, Laurier to Sifton, 2 and 4 October 1903.

40. Both priests had worked in the Conservative interest in the provincial election of 1903, but were unimpressed with the Roblin government's inaction on election promises. PAC, Sifton Papers, vol. 148, pp. 118413-17,

Prud'homme to Sifton, 3 October 1903. Prud'homme had general charge of organizing the French vote in Manitoba and the Territories.

41. Ibid.

42. Ibid., vol. 253, p. 288, Sifton to Harkin, 24 November 1903; see also vol. 140, pp. 111898-38—47, Dafoe to Sifton, 3 November 1903; and reply, vol. 253, pp. 67-72, 12 November 1903; pp. 316-17, Sifton to Dafoe, 19 November 1903.

43. Ibid., vol. 152, pp. 122121-25, Young to Sifton, 24 November 1903; and reply, vol. 253, pp. 570-72, 27 November 1903; vol. 138, pp. 110168-69, Bulyea to Sifton, 3 December 1903; and reply, vol. 253, pp. 836-38, 8 December 1903; vol. 138, pp. 110173, 110189-90, Bulyea to Sifton, 9 December 1903, and details of territorial organization.

44. Ibid., vol. 253, pp. 874-75, Sifton to Dafoe, 9 December 1903.

45. Ibid., vol. 254, pp. 374-77, Sifton to Scott, 26 December 1903. Sifton believed that Ontario, New Brunswick and Québec (apart from Laurier) opposed a winter campaign; and he was not enthusiastic about such a campaign in the West.

46. PAC, Sifton Papers, vol. 255, pp. 876-79, Sifton to Bole, 13 February 1904. Part of the story was that McCreary had been offended because he had not been given the GTPR solicitorship; he threatened revolt, and hoped Bole would support him. Sifton denied to Bole that he knew anything of the solicitorship, which was an utter fabrication, because in the fall of 1903 he had arranged with Hays that J.D. Cameron should have it.

47. PAC, Sifton Papers, vol. 154, pp. 123961-63, Bole to Sifton, 22 February 1904.

48. Ibid., vol. 255, pp. 839-40, Sifton to T. A. Burrows, 12 February 1904.

49. PAC, Laurier Papers, vol. 327, pp. 87768-71, Bole to Laurier, 20 June 1904.

50. Ibid., vol. 324, pp. 86980-82, Power to Laurier, 20 June 1904.

51. Ibid., pp. 86994-96, Laurier to Dafoe, 28 June 1904.

52. PAC, Sifton Papers, vol. 157, pp. 127183-225—226, Dafoe to Sifton, 4 July 1904.

53. There is a voluminous correspondence on this subject, particularly from Finlay Young, T.A. Burrows, Bole and Dafoe in the Laurier and Sifton Papers in 1903 and 1904. See especially PAC, Sifton Papers, vol. 259, pp. 301-3, Sifton to Dafoe, 21 June 1904.

54. MFP, 1 January, 17 March 1904; PAC, Sifton Papers, vol. 261, pp. 128-29, Sifton to McMillan, 14 September 1904. Additional projects were provided for in supplementary estimates.

55. PAC, Sifton Papers, vol. 155, pp. 125086-88, Cartwright to Sifton, 12 July 1904.

56. Ibid., vol. 258, p. 240 Sifton to Frank Fowler, 3 May 1904.

57. J. M. Beck, Pendulum of Power: Canada's Federal Elections (Scarborough: Prentice-Hall, 1968), p. 106; detailed election results are in CSP, 1905, no. 37. It should be added that there is extensive correspondence in the Sifton Papers for 1903 and 1904 on the preparations for the campaign, particularly with Dafoe, Bole, Young, Fowler, Scott, Smith, Bulyea, Burrows, T.O. Davis, J.M. Douglas, Greenway, R. E. A. Leech, and others. It is especially informative on the selection of candidates.

58. MFP, 10, 20 October 1904.

59. Ibid., 13 October 1904.

60. Ibid., 29 October, 1 November 1904.

61. PAC, Sifton Papers, vol. 262, pp. 292-94, 345-46, 460-61, Sifton to J.M. Howell, 15, 17, 21 December 1904; p. 351, Sifton to J. F. Kilgour, 17 December 1904; pp. 457-59, Sifton to Dafoe, 21 December 1904.

62. Ibid., pp. 348, 349-50, Sifton to Bole, and to William Chambers, 17 December 1904.

63. Ibid., vol. 261, pp. 844-45, Sifton to W. A. Galliher, 29 November 1904.

64. PAC, Laurier Papers, vol. 344, pp. 91988-89, Stewart to Laurier, 9 November 1904 (quoting Prov. 29:2); Sifton Papers, vol. 155, pp. 125098-99, Cartwright to Sifton, 14 November 1904 (alluding to Judges 15:8).

NOTES TO CHAPTER EIGHT

1. C.C. Lingard, *Territorial Government in Canada: the Autonomy Question in the Old North-West Territories* (Toronto: University of Toronto Press, 1946), p. 16.
2. PAC, Laurier Papers, vol. 118, pp. 35558-60, G.H.V. Bulyea to Laurier, 17 July 1899; and reply, p. 35561, 24 July 1899.
3. E.H. Oliver, ed., *The Canadian North-West: Its Early Development and Legislative Records*, 2 (Ottawa: Government Printing Bureau, 1915), pp. 115-57.
4. Ibid., pp. 1158-60, Haultain to Sifton, 30 January 1901; and reply, 21 March 1901.
5. *Debates*, 1901, cols. 1368-69 (12 March 1901).
6. PAC, Sifton Papers, vol. 245, pp. 749-50, Sifton to Editor of Montreal *Witness*, 15 October 1901; Oliver, ed., *The Canadian North-West*, pp. 1163-202, Haultain to Laurier, 7 December 1901; Sifton to Haultain, 27 March 1902.
7. L.H. Thomas and L.G. Thomas, "Introduction," in D.R. Owram, ed., *The Formation of Alberta: a Documentary History* (Calgary: Historical Society of Alberta, 1979), pp. xxix-xxx.
8. *Debates*, 1902, col. 3101 (18 April 1902). A little later (col. 3112) he suggested that a population of 600,000 or 700,000 might be a prior condition to autonomy; in 1901 there were 158,940 people in the Territories (See J.W. Brennan, "A Political History of Saskatchewan, 1905-1929" [Ph.D. dissertation, University of Alberta, 1976], p. 20). See also *MFP*, 8 April 1902.
9. *Debates*, 1902, cols. 3101-102 (18 April 1902).
10. PAC, Sifton Papers, vol. 118, p. 93603, T.A. Burrows to Sifton, 26 March 1902.
11. Brown, *Robert Laird Borden*, p. 54.
12. Thomas and Thomas, "Introduction," pp. xxxiii-xxxiv.
13. PAC, Sifton Papers, vol. 150, pp. 119788-89, Scott to Sifton, 23 November 1903.
14. Debates, 1903, cols. 12844-45 (1 October 1903); Lingard, *Territorial Government*, pp. 90-91, 258.

15. Lingard, *Territorial Government*, pp. 92-93; Owram, ed., *The Formation of Alberta*, pp. 230-51, esp. documents IV-17 and IV-29.
16. PAC, Sifton Papers, vol. 252, pp. 707-9, Sifton to Fielding, 20 August 1903. L.H. Thomas and L.G. Thomas claim that the issue emerged "as the major element in the parliamentary debates of that year." (See Thomas and Thomas, "Introduction," p. xxxiv.) This is erroneous; Borden did not push the issue until 13 October, the dying days of a session preoccupied with railways. See Lingard, *Territorial Government*, pp. 84-89; Owram, ed., *The Formation of Alberta*, p. 244.
17. The episode is related in D.H. Bocking, "Premier Walter Scott: a Study of His Rise to Political Power" (M.A. thesis, University of Saskatchewan, 1959), pp. 67-72.
18. Owram, ed., *The Formation of Alberta*, pp. 237-39.
19. PAS, Walter Scott Papers, pp. 2692-96, Scott to Sifton, 23 November 1903.
20. Lingard, *Territorial Government*, p. 98. Haultain had asked Sifton for an increase of $400,000; Haultain to Sifton, 19 May 1904, in Oliver, ed., *The Canadian North-West*, pp. 1237-41.
21. Haultain to Laurier, 1 June 1904, in Owram, ed., *The Formation of Alberta*, pp. 252-54.
22. PAS, Scott Papers, p. 4632, Scott to Sifton, 1 September 1904.
23. Laurier to Haultain, 30 September 1904, in Owram, ed., *The Formation of Alberta*, pp. 256-57.
24. The Laurier Papers for 1903 in PAC contain a great deal of correspondence on this topic.
25. See PAC, Laurier Papers, vol. 302, pp. 81735-36, Laurier to Charles Russell, 16 January 1904. Sbaretti also favoured using Roblin's territorial ambitions as a lever by requiring that not only would existing minority privileges be protected in any territory annexed, but that they be extended to all Manitoba.
26. PAC, Laurier Papers, vol. 110, pp. 33148-57, Grandin à Minto [n.d.]; Minto Papers, vol. 5, pp. 68-69, Laurier to Minto, 30 November 1900;

M.R. Lupul, "The Campaign for a French Catholic School Inspector in the North-West Territories, 1898-1903," *CHR*, 47 (1967): 332-52.

27. PAC, Sir R.W. Scott Papers, vol. 2, pp. 685-91, Legal to Sbaretti, 4 October 1903. The most complete study of the evolution of the issue is M.R. Lupul, *The Roman Catholic Church and the North-West School Question: a Study in Church-State Relations in Western Canada, 1875-1905* (Toronto: University of Toronto Press, 1974).

28. PAC, Laurier Papers, vol. 307, pp. 82980-81, 82982-84, Sbaretti to Laurier, 1 March 1904; and reply, 7 March 1904.

29. Ibid., vol. 309, pp. 83411-12, Sbaretti to Laurier, 15 March 1904.

30. Ibid., vol. 340, pp. 90803-4, Laurier to Sbaretti, 24 October 1904. See also Lupul, *The Roman Catholic Church*, pp. 168-71.

31. H.B. Neatby, *Laurier and a Liberal Quebec: a Study in Political Management* (Toronto: McClelland and Stewart, 1973), p. 152. This of course was not binding on opposition papers, or independent papers such as the Toronto *News*, which endeavoured to stir up agitation on the subject.

32. Lingard, *Territorial Government*, p. 129n5; PAC, Sifton Papers, vol. 263, pp. 209-12, Sifton to Dafoe, 25 February 1905. Sifton's comments do not appear to have survived.

33. Lupul, *The Roman Catholic Church*, p. 176.

34. *MFP*, 31 December 1904; PAC, Sifton Papers, vol. 177, pp. 143868-76, Lord Grey to Sifton, 14 January 1905.

35. PAC, Laurier Papers, vol. 352, pp. 93969-73, Sifton to Laurier, 22 January 1905.

36. Ibid.

37. Lingard, *Territorial Government*, ch. 10; PAC, Sir John S. Willison Papers, vol. 36, pp. 13212-15, F. Hamilton to Willison, 19 January 1905.

38. See D.J. Hall, "A Divergence of Principle: Clifford Sifton, Sir Wilfrid Laurier and the North-West Autonomy Bills, 1905," *Laurentian University Review*, 7 no. 1 (November 1974): 3-24; Evelyn Eager, "Separate Schools and the Cabinet Crisis of 1905," *The Lakehead University*

Review, 2, no. 2, (Fall 1969): 69-115; C.B. Sissons, *Church & State in Canadian Education* (Toronto: Ryerson, 1959), pp. 253-73.

39. PAC, Laurier Papers, vol. 354, p. 94548, Laurier to Cameron, 10 February 1905.

40. Most of the various drafts of the school clause are conveniently collected in Lupul, *The Roman Catholic Church*, pp. 213-21.

41. PAC, Laurier Papers, vol. 352, pp. 93974-76, Laurier to Sifton, 26 January 1905.

42. Ibid., vol. 354, pp. 94354-61, Sifton to Laurier, 1 February 1905.

43. *MFP*, 19, 21 January, 17 February 1905.

44. PAC, Laurier Papers, vol. 356, pp. 94915-17, Laurier to Sifton, 20 February 1905.

45. PAC, Willison Papers, vol. 36, pp. 13235-40, C.F. Hamilton to Willison, 5 March 1905.

46. PAC, Laurier Papers, vol. 356, p. 94931, Sifton to Laurier, 20 February 1905.

47. Ibid., p. 94932, Laurier to Sifton, 21 February 1905.

48. The former possibility was the opinion of Walter Scott; see O.D. Skelton, *Life and Letters of Sir Wilfrid Laurier*, 2 (New York: Century, 1922), p. 234n1. The latter view is best articulated in Dafoe, *Clifford Sifton* ch. 10. Lupul, *The Roman Catholic Church* p. 179, rejects both explanations, attributing Laurier's actions to innocence and sincerity; even if this is accepted, Laurier still bungled the issue politically.

49. *MFP*, 24 February 1905; PAC, Willison Papers, vol. 36, p. 13224, C.F. Hamilton to Willison, 23 February 1905.

50. PAC, Sifton Papers, vol. 263, pp. 209-12, Sifton to Dafoe, 25 February 1905.

51. Ibid.; and pp. 213-15, Sifton to Laurier, 26 February 1905; vol. 177, pp. 144137-39, Laurier to Sifton, 28 February 1905; PAC, Laurier Papers, vol. 357, pp. 95194-95, Sifton to Laurier, 27 February 1905.

52. PAC, Sifton Papers, vol. 263, pp. 209-12, Sifton to Dafoe, 25 February 1905.

53. See Appendix 2, Clause of 21 February 1905.

54. *Debates*, 1905, cols. 1852-53 (1 March

1905).
55. Ibid., cols. 1441-59 (21 February 1905).
56. Sbaretti, R.W. Scott, Fitzpatrick, Henri Bourassa.
57. R.C. Brown and R. Cook, *Canada 1896-1921: a Nation Transformed* (Toronto: McClelland and Stewart, 1974), p. 78.
58. PAC, Laurier Papers, vol. 356, pp. 91913-14, Laurier to P.L. Potter, 25 February 1905.
59. As quoted in Toronto *Saturday Night*, 18 February 1905.
60. PAC, R.W. Scott Papers, vol. 2, pp. 735-39, Scott to Sbaretti, 30 December 1907; see also Eager, "Separate Schools and the Cabinet Crisis of 1905," p. 108.
61. Professors L.H. Thomas and L.G. Thomas reject this argument, claiming that Sifton feared that the Catholics would try to use the courts to restore the 1884 system, and that the court case and remedial legislation required would make the procedure so cumbersome that Laurier would have recognized its futility.(See Thomas and Thomas, "Introduction," p. xiv). They ignore Scott's evidence; they also miss the point of Laurier's experience with the Manitoba school issue when the courts declared that the province had taken away privileges granted in law since Confederation, and that the minority therefore had a legitimate grievance. Laurier did not try to satisfy the grievance by remedial legislation. He achieved significant gains for the minority by quiet diplomacy and pressure. It is by no means improbable that he and his advisors thought he might be able to achieve something in the same indirect manner in Alberta and Saskatchewan.
62. PAC, Sifton Papers, vol. 177, pp. 144137-39, Laurier to Sifton, 28 February 1905.
63. Ibid., vol. 263, pp. 209-12, Sifton to Dafoe, 25 February 1905.
64. Ibid., pp. 213-15, Sifton to Laurier, 26 February 1905; see also pp. 228-29, Sifton to Dafoe, 27 February 1905, for further elaboration.
65. Ibid., vol. 263, pp. 228-29, Sifton to Dafoe, 27 February 1905. Sifton doubted that Laurier's threat was serious, with good reason. A few days later Laurier confided to a friend, "The whole thing is purely bluff. I have no intention of resigning at all, and will hold on as long as my health will allow." PAC, Laurier Papers, vol. 358, p. 99596, Laurier to J.S. Brierley, 9 March 1905.
66. See Appendix 2, Clause of 3 March 1905; PAC, Sifton Papers, vol. 263, p. 400, Sifton to Laurier, 3 March 1905.
67. PAC, Grey of Howick Papers, vol. 27, pp. 5003-6, Laurier to Grey, 5 March 1905, and encl. This new draft was published in the press; see Lupul, *The Roman Catholic Church* , pp. 219-20 ("Clause No. 9"). Ordinance 31 was dropped in the final version of the clause, which spelled out certain financial provisions otherwise covered in the Ordinance. See *Debates*, 1905, col. 2926 (22 March 1905); and Appendix 2, Final Clause.
68. PAC, Sifton Papers, vol. 263, pp. 660-63, Sifton to Dafoe, 11 March 1905.
69. See Appendix 2, Final Clause.
70. *Debates*, 1905, cols. 2915-26 (22 March 1905).
71. Ibid., cols. 3092-3121 (24 March 1905).
72. Writing earlier to Dafoe, Sifton took the same line even more strongly: "The point to be made in discussing it with our friends is to show that the Church is absolutely eliminated. There is no possibility of the Church getting its finger in the schools known as 'separate schools' under the present North West Ordinances, and the result is that they are shut out forever unless they can get the people of the North West Territories to give them something more, which I apprehend is putting it upon very safe ground." PAC, Sifton Papers, vol. 263, pp. 660-63, Sifton to Dafoe, 11 March 1905.
73. PANS, W.S. Fielding Papers, vol. 509, file 29, p. 1313, Sifton to Fielding, 1 March 1905.
74. *MFP*, 24 and 27 February, 1, 2, 6, 9, 14, 15, 20, 21, 27 and 28 March 1905; Cook, *The Politics of John W. Dafoe,* pp. 32-33.
75. PAC, Sifton Papers, vol. 263, pp. 660-63, Sifton to Dafoe, 11 March 1905.
76. Ibid.
77. PAS, Walter Scott Papers, p. 6740, Scott to G. Spring-Rice, 6 March 1905.
78. See below, chapter 9.

79. PAC Willison Papers, vol. 59, pp. 22043-45, J.J. Moncrieff to Willison, 3 and 5 March 1905; vol. 36, pp. 13229-32, C.F. Hamilton to Willison, 3 March 1905; pp. 13235-40, Hamilton to Willison, 5 March 1905; W.L. Grant Papers, Hamilton to Grant, 24 October and 30 November 1905; Minto Papers, A.F. Sladen to Minto, 24 March 1905; PAS, Walter Scott Papers, pp. 6804- 6, Scott to J.S. Telfer, 16 March 1905; pp. 6754-55, Scott to D.A. Stewart, 28 March 1905; Toronto *Saturday Night*, 18 March 1905; *CAR*, 1905, p. 29; Calgary *Eye-Opener*, 25 February and 4 March 1905.

80. Dafoe, *Laurier*, p. 24.

81. PAC, Sifton Papers, vol. 263, p. 576, Sifton to A.C. Fraser, 7 March 1905.

82. Ibid., pp. 577-78, Sifton to Gordon, 7 March 1905.

83. See Dafoe, *Laurier*, pp. 77-80; Brown and Cook, *Canada 1896-1921*, pp. 78-79.

NOTES TO CHAPTER NINE

1. PAC, Laurier Papers vol 358, pp. 95540-42, Duncan to Laurier, 5 March 1905.

2. *Debates*, 1906 col. 2449, May 1906.

3. Ibid., cols. 1815-16, 20 April 1906.

4. PAC. Minto Papers. vol. 23, pp. 121-27, A.F. Sladen to Minto, 31 October 1906; Brown, *Robert Laird Borden*, 1, pp. 122-25.

5. *Debates*, 1906, cols. 2457-59 2 May 1906; cols. 4606-7, 5 June 1906; 1908, col. 13416, 17 July 1908.

6. Ibid., 1906, cols. 4267-325, 31 May 1906.

7. H.B. Ames, *Our Western Heritage and How it is being Squandered by the Laurier Government* (Conservative election pamphlet, 1908), pp. 18-19.

8. Dafoe, *Clifford Sifton*, p. 308.

9. *Debates*, 1906, cols. 4300-301, 31 May 1906; *CAR*, 1906, p. 573.

10. Dafoe, *Clifford Sifton*, p. 326.

11. PAC, Willison Papers, vol. 36, pp. 13532-36, C.F. Hamilton to Willison, 2 June 1906.

12. *Debates*, 1906, cols. 4341-43, 31 May 1906. On Sifton's lease policy, see D.H. Breen *"The Canadian Prairie West"* pp. 122-23, 126.

13. PAC, Willison Papers, vol. 36, pp. 13532-36, C.F. Hamilton to Willison, 2 June 1906; and p. 13540, Hamilton to Willison, 5 June 1906; *Debates*, 1906, cols. 4605-7, 5 June 1906.

14. PAC, Willison Papers, vol. 36, pp. 13537-39, Willison to Hamilton, 4 June 1906.

15. *Debates*, 1907-8, cols. 2595-614, 6 February 1908; 1906, cols. 4277-84, 31 May 1906; *CAR*, 1908, pp. 73-78; Ames, *Our Western Heritage*, pp. 4-6.

16. Ames, *Our Western Heritage*, p. 8; *Facts for People: Pages From the Record of the Laurier Administration from 1906 to 1908* (Conservative election pamphlet, 1908), p. 13; H.J. Morgan, *The Canadian Men and Women of the Time* (Toronto: William Briggs, 1912), p. 1023. In 1908 Sifton denied having any association with the Imperial Pulp Company. *Debates*, 1908, cols. 3578-79, 21 February 1908.

17. Ames, *Our Western Heritage*, p. 8; *Facts for the People*, p. 13.

18. Ames, *Our Western Heritage*, pp. 10-12.

19. *Facts for the People*, p. 13.

20. Dafoe, *Clifford Sifton*, p. 312. On 19 December 1907 the government ordered that notice for disposal of timber berths must be at least sixty days, and that henceforth disposal was to be by public auction. *CAR*, 1908, p. 73.

21. *Debates*, 1906, cols. 4277-84, 31 May 1906; 1907-8, cols. 2608-11, 6 February 1908.

22. PAC, Sifton Papers, vol. 296, file "Mann, Donald 1908"; McMillan to Sifton, 8 February 1908.

23. *Debates*, 1907-8, col. 2615, 6 February 1908.

24. Ibid., cols. 13,095-139, 15 July 1908;

PAC, Liberal Party of Canada Papers, vol. 988, *Records of the Laurier Government...1896-1908* (Conservative election pamphlet, 1908), p. 58; PAC, Sifton Papers, vol. 296, file "Philp, A.E. 1908," Sifton to Philp, 7 August 1908, and reply, 15 August 1908.

25. Dafoe, *Clifford Sifton*, p. 327.
26. PAC, Laurier Papers, vol. 350, pp. 93603-5, Sifton to Laurier, 11 January 1905 [*sic*; should read 1906]; and reply, 13 January 1906.
27. Brown and Cook, *Canada 1896-1921*, p. 68.
28. PAC, Laurier Papers, vol. 445, pp. 118909-10, Sifton to Laurier, 30 January 1907; Sifton Papers, vol. 179, pp. 145185-87, D.H. Cooper to Sifton, 28 September 1907, and reply, 8 October 1907; Chester Martin, *"Dominion Lands" Policy*, ed. Lewis H. Thomas (Toronto: McClelland and Stewart, 1973), pp. 162-66.
29. PAC, Hays Papers, vol. 3, p. 927, C.M. Hays to C. Rivers Wilson, 8 August 1905; PAC, Laurier Papers, vol. 581, pp. 157547-49, Sifton to Laurier, 2 July 1909, and reply, 3 July 1909.
30. PAS, Scott Papers, pp. 6699-703, Sifton to Scott, 18 August 1905; Brennan, "Political History of Saskatchewan," pp. 58-60; Regehr, *Canadian Northern Railway*, p. 178.
31. PAC, Sifton Papers, vol. 184, p. 148526, Sifton to M. Lawrie, 16 November 1908.
32. See George Johnson, ed., *The All Red Line: the Annals and Aims of the Pacific Cable Project* (Ottawa: James Hope & Sons, 1903).
33. *All Red Route: Great Britain to Australia, New Zealand and Hong-Kong via Ireland and Canada* [n.a. n.p. 1908], (pamphlet outlining Blacksod Bay scheme); *CAR*, 1907, p. 342.
34. M. Ollivier, ed., *The Colonial and Imperial Conferences from 1887 to 1937*, 1, *Colonial Conferences* (Ottawa: Queen's Printer, 1954), p. 322.
35. PAC, Laurier Papers, vol. 464, pp. 125226-32, Sifton to Laurier, 10 May 1907, and encl.
36. Edward Forbes Bush, "The Canadian 'Fast Line' on the North Atlantic,

1886-1915" (MA thesis, Carleton University, 1969), p. 131.
37. *CAR*, 1907, p. 345.
38. See Laurier-Sifton correspondence in PAC, Laurier Papers, vol. 490, pp. 132364-76, 19-27 November 1907; and vol. 694, pp. 133609-16, telegrams, 10 December 1907.
39. *The Times* (London), 4 December 1907.
40. PAC, Laurier Papers, vol. 499, pp. 134717-20, Sifton to Laurier, 4 January 1908, and encl.; Sifton Papers, vol. 186, pp. 149720-21, Sifton to Strathcona, 18 January 1908.
41. *Debates*, 1907-8, col. 5356, 20 March 1908.
42. Ibid., cols. 5353-55; *Times*, 4 December 1907; *The Monetary Times*, 3 July, 17 August 1907; Bush, "The Canadian 'Fast Line'," p. 132.
43. Bush, "The Canadian 'Fast Line'," p. 133; *Debates*, 1907-8, col. 5352, 20 March 1908.
44. *CAR*, 1908, p. 598.
45. *CAR*, 1907, p. 345.
46. *Debates*, 1907-8, cols. 12439-48, 9 July 1908.
47. See, for example, PAC, Sifton Papers, vol. 195, p. 155375, Sifton to C.C. McKechnie, 31 January 1910; vol. 200, p. 158719, Sifton to William Davies, 7 June 1913.
48. Dafoe, *Clifford Sifton*, p. 333.
49. PAS, Scott Papers, vol. 6741-42, Scott to Spring-Rice, 20 March 1905; PAC, Sifton Papers, vol. 263, p. 516, Sifton to J.W. Bettes, 6 March 1905; p. 517, Sifton to A.N. McPherson, 4 March 1905.
50. PAC, Sifton Papers, vol. 296, file "Turriff, J.G. 1906," John Crawford and J.G. Turriff to Sifton, 20 June 1906.
51. Ibid., file Colwell, C.F. 1906, Horace Chevrier to Sifton, 29 November 1906; and in the same volume, letters from John Brown, A.C. Fraser, J.W. Fleming, George Graham, C.J. Mickle and Isaac Pitblado. As noted above, Hyman did not finally resign until August 1907.
52. Ibid., vol. 181, pp. 146190-98, Metcalfe to Sifton, 4 June 1907, and encl.
53. Ibid. p. 146199, Sifton to Metcalfe, 7 June 1907.

54. PAC, Grey Papers, vol. 2, pp. 469-72, Conversation with Laurier, 25 August 1907. See also Laurier Papers, vol. 481, pp. 129948-49, Laurier to J.S. Climo, 2 October 1907; vol. 537, pp. 145483-84, John McVicar to Laurier, 1 October 1908, and reply, 8 October 1908.
55. PAC, Willison Papers, vol. 74, pp. 27483-88, Sifton to Willison, 27 August 1907.
56. Dafoe, *Clifford Sifton*, pp. 333-34.
57. Ibid.
58. Ibid., p. 335.
59. PAC, Willison Papers, vol. 37, pp. 13979-80, C.F. Hamilton to Willison, 21 June 1908; Sifton Papers, vol. 297, file "Sifton, Arthur 1908," Sifton to A.L. Sifton, 13 August 1908; *Collier's, The National Weekly*, Canadian Edition, 41, no. 22, 22 August 1908.
60. *Debates*, 1907-8, cols. 5338-57, 20 March 1908.
61. *CSP*, 1907-8, no. 29a, *Report of the Civil Service Commission, 1908*; 7-8 Edw. VII, c. 15. On the subject generally, see Robert MacGregor Dawson, *The Civil Service of Canada* (London: Oxford University Press, 1929), pp. 74-77.
62. *Debates*, 1907-8, cols. 5343-45, 20 March 1908.
63. PAC, Willison Papers, vol. 37, pp. 13893-95, 13920, Hamilton to Willison, 11 February, 21 March 1908.
64. PAC, Sifton Papers, vol. 183, pp. 147590-91, Flavelle to Sifton, 22 March 1908; vol. 185, pp. 148724-27, Prof. S.J. McLean to Sifton, 21 March 1908, and reply, 23 March 1908.
65. Ibid., vol. 185, pp. 149110-11, E.W. Nesbitt to Sifton, 17 December 1908, and reply, 18 December 1908.
66. *Tribune*, 23 September, 15 October 1908; Fraser, "The many, mighty Siftons," p. 53; *CAR*, 1908, p. 215.
67. *CAR*, 1908, pp. 200-201; PAC, Sifton Papers, vol. 186, p. 149640, F. Schultz to Sifton, 9 November 1908; vol. 278, pp. 165042-54, Reports of operative no. 138, 23-30 September 1908.
68. PAC, Sifton Papers, vol. 181, pp. 146382-83, Sifton to J.G. Rattray, 24 December 1907.
69. Ibid., vol. 296, file "Philp, A.E.

1908," Sifton to Philp, 31 January 1908; Philp to Sifton, 14 April 1908.
70. Ibid., vol. 278, file 7, "General Election 1908," passim; vol. 184, pp. 148444-49, correspondence with J.K. Kerr, 25 August-11 September 1908; vol. 296, file "Bain, J. 1908," Sifton to John Bain, 8 September 1908; Dafoe, *Clifford Sifton*, pp. 341-42.
71. *CAR*, 1908, pp. 48-56; Brown, *Robert Laird Borden*, 1, p. 135.
72. PAC, Sifton Papers, vol. 182, pp. 146885-87, Sifton to A.B. Aylesworth. 5 May 1908; vol. 183, pp. 147479-45—49, 147479-51—55, Dafoe to Sifton, 15 and 21 June 1908.
73. Ibid., 147479-50, Sifton to Dafoe, 19 June 1908.
74. *CAR*, 1908, p. 214; PAC, Sifton Papers, vol. 183, p. 147511, newspaper clipping, 21 October 1908 [probably *Winnipeg Telegram*].
75. *MFP*, 24 September 1908; PAC, Sifton Papers, vol. 278, pp. 165084-88, reports of operative no. 56, 17 and 24 October 1908.
76. *MFP*, 24 September 1908.
77. Ibid., 16 September, 3 October 1908.
78. Ibid., 22 and 23 October 1908; *Tribune*, 22 October 1908.
79. *MFP*, 22 October 1908. The Tories claimed that only 365 timber leases were in force; *CAR*, 1908, p. 74.
80. On the Act, see Paul Craven, *"An Impartial Umpire": Industrial Relations and the Canadian State 1900-1911* (Toronto: University of Toronto Press, 1980), ch. 9. To be fair, Sifton had taken the side of the labouring men and asked Laurier to press Shaughnessy into making some concessions. PAC, Laurier Papers, vol. 536, pp. 145297-301, Sifton to Laurier, 26 September 1908, and reply, 1 October 1908.
81. *CAR*, 1908, pp. 191, 196.
82. *MFP*, 14-15 October 1908; PAC, Dafoe Papers, vol. 1, Sifton to Dafoe, 14 October 1908, and clipping from the *Winnipeg Telegram*, 14 October 1908; PAC, Sifton Papers, vol. 183, p. 147479-143, Sifton to Dafoe, 31 December 1908.
83. *CSP*, 1909, no. 18, pp. 344ff.; J.M. Beck, *Pendulum of Power*, pp. 106, 119; Brown, *Robert Laird Borden*, 1, pp. 138-39; University of Manitoba,

Elizabeth Dafoe Library, Dafoe Papers, McKenzie to Dafoe, 3 February 1932.

84. *Tribune*, 27 October 1908.

85. PAC, Sifton Papers, vol. 187, p. 149928, Sifton to Wade, 3 November 1908; *MFP*, 11 February 1909; *CAR*, 1908, p. 234.

86. *MFP*, 20, 22, 23 March 1909.

87. PAC, Sifton Papers, vol. 297, file "Sifton, Arthur 1908," correspondence August-September 1908.

88. Ibid., vol. 183, pp. 148034-35, W.L. Griffith to Sifton, 4 July 1908.

89. Ibid., vol. 297, file "Nesbitt, Wallace 1909," Nesbitt to Sifton, 1 March 1909; vol. 190, p. 152551, Sifton to W.F. MacLean, 4 March 1909; vol. 297, file "Orr Ewing, H. 1910," Sifton to Orr Ewing, 17 October 1910; *Montreal Daily Star*, 18 November 1910.

90. PAC, Sifton Papers, vol. 297, file "Orr Ewing, H. 1910," Sifton to Orr Ewing, 17 October 1910.

91. *McKims: The Canadian Newspaper Directory*, 1907, p. 199. No figures on the *Tribune's* weekly circulation are given.

92. J.F.B. Livesay, *The Canadian Press and Allied Organizations* (Toronto: n.p., 1924), pp. 4, 6-9.

93. Donnelly, *Dafoe of the Free Press*, pp. 58-60; Cook, *The Politics of John W. Dafoe*, pp. 37-39.

94. Unfortunately most of the letters from this period do not survive, but those that do certainly imply a much more extensive correspondence.

95. PAC, Sifton Papers, vol. 193, pp. 154512-80—82, Sifton to Dafoe, 13 December 1910.

96. Ibid., vol. 188, pp. 151155-34—35, Sifton to Dafoe, 14 January 1909.

97. Ibid., vol. 186, pp. 149607-8, Sifton to Prof. John Squair, 23 March 1908.

98. Ibid., vol. 193, pp. 154612-67—73, Dafoe to Sifton, 16 August 1910; PAC, Dafoe Papers, vol. 1, Sifton to Dafoe, 31 August 1910; Regehr, *The Canadian Northern Railway*, pp. 175-76.

99. PAC, Sifton Papers, vol. 193, pp. 154612-4—19, Dafoe to Sifton, 4 January 1910, and reply, 7 January 1910.

100. Ibid., vol. 296, file "Cameron, D.C. 1908," Sifton to Cameron, 9 June 1908.

101. Ibid., vol. 296, file "Boland, H.J. 1907," Sifton to Boland, 26 December 1907; file "Bain, John 1907," passim; *Financial Saturday Night* (Toronto), 15 October 1910, p. 23.

102. PAC, Sifton Papers, vol. 296, file "Cameron D.C. 1908," Sifton to Cameron, 24 August 1908; "Charlton file, W.A. 1908," passim.

103. Ibid., vol. 297, file "Wade, F.C. 1909," Sifton to Wade, 19 October 1909.

104. Scott and Astrid Young, *O'Brien* (Toronto: Ryerson, 1967), pp. 106-8.

105. PAC, Sifton Papers, vol. 296, file "Fraser, J.A. 1907," Fraser to Sifton, 22 January 1907; file "Clingan, George 1908," D.A. Coste to Sifton, 28 February 1908; file "Nesbitt, Wallace 1908," Sifton to Nesbitt, 2 September 1908; file "O'Grady, G. de C. 1908," file "Colwell, C.F., 1906," Colwell to Sifton, 29 November 1906; vol. 297, file "Fraser, A.C. 1909," Sifton to Fraser, 22 April 1909; Clifford Sifton [1893-1976] Papers, vol. 1, passim.

106. PAC, Sifton Papers, vol. 296, file "Cameron, D.C. 1907," Sifton to D.C. Cameron, 18 August 1907; vol. 297, file "Cameron, D.C. 1909," Sifton to Cameron, 25 August 1909.

107. Ibid., vol. 296, file "Cameron, D.C. 1908," Sifton to Cameron, 12 December 1908.

108. University of Manitoba, Elizabeth Dafoe Library, Dafoe Papers, Philip McKenzie to Dafoe, 3 February 1932. This story is still told by the Sifton family.

109. PAC, Sifton Papers, vol. 296, file "Boland, H.J. 1907," Sifton to Boland, 26 December 1907.

110. Ibid., vol. 298, file "Scott, Robert 1911," Sifton to Walter Scott, 24 March 1911.

111. At Brandon on 30 March 1908 Sifton had described the relationship as that of "a daughter State in full co-ordinate partnership with Great Britain as a member of the Empire." *CAR*, 1908.

112. *The Globe* (Toronto), 20 November 1908.

113. PAC, Sifton Papers, vol. 183, pp. 148006-10, Grey to Sifton, 8

December 1908; Laurier Papers, vol. 532, pp. 114268-69, Sifton to Laurier, Wednesday [25 November] 1908.

114. PAC, Sifton Papers, vol. 194, p. 154914, Sifton to R.R. Hall, 24 December 1910.

115. PAC, Willison Papers, vol. 37, pp. 14174-77, C.F. Hamilton to Willison, 5 April 1910.

116. See PAC, Sifton Papers, vol. 196, p. 156573, Sifton to J.J. Foy, 21 April 1911. On 1 March 1911 the Toronto *Globe* observed, ''Mr. Sifton has not voted with the Liberal party for the last two sessions. He did not vote even on the navy question, an issue of great importance, and some time ago he informed the Liberal Whips that he would give no more party votes.''

117. See below, chapter 11

118. PAC, Sifton Papers, vol. 191, pp. 152717-20, McMillan to Sifton, 31 March 1909, and reply, 3 April 1909.

119. See *Debates*, 1909-10, cols. 856-57, 2 December 1909.

120. Ibid., cols. 6485-92, 6 April 1910; *CAR*, 1910, pp. 239-42; PAC, Sifton Papers, vol. 194, pp. 155185-89, John Lewis to Sifton, 6 April 1910, and reply, 9 April 1910.

121. On this notion, see R.C. Macleod, *The North-West Mounted Police and Law Enforcement 1873-1905* (Toronto: University of Toronto Press, 1976), pp. 114-130.

122. PAC, Sifton Papers, vol. 191, file ''Perry, H.E. 1909,'' passim.

123. Ibid., vol. 189, pp. 151493-96, F.O. Fowler to Sifton, 8 November 1909, and reply, 18 November 1909; vol. 194, p. 154752, Sifton to Fowler, 26 February 1910.

124. Ibid., vol. 194, p. 154759, Sifton to Fowler, 31 August 1910.

125. Ibid., vol. 191, pp. 152718-20, Sifton to McMillan, 3 April 1909.

NOTES TO CHAPTER TEN

1. E. Porritt, *The Revolt in Canada against the New Feudalism: Tariff History from the Revision of 1907 to the Uprising of the West in 1910* (London: Cassell, 1911) pp. 185-91; *CAR* 1910, p. 267.

2. Christopher Curtis, ''The Parting of the Ways: the Manufacturers, the Liberals, and the 1911 Election'' (MA thesis, Carleton University, 1977), pp. 36-37, 106-7.

3. A.H.U. Colquhon, *Press, Politics and People: the Life and Letters of Sir John Willison, Journalist and Correspondent of the Times* (Toronto: Macmillan, 1935), p. 187.

4. Bruce Fergusson, *Rt. Hon. W.S. Fielding*, 2, *Mr. Minister of Finance* (Windsor, N.S.: Lancelot Press, 1971), p. 88; *Globe*, 4 November 1910; and see L.E. Ellis, *Reciprocity, 1911* (New Haven: Yale University Press, 1939), p. 100.

5. James G. Harris, ''*The News* and Canadian Politics, 1903-1914: a Study of the Policies of *The News* under the

Editorship of Sir John Willison'' (MA thesis, University of Toronto, 1952), pp. 155-56.

6. Fergusson, *Mr. Minister of Finance*, p. 92.

7. *CAR*, 1910, pp. 328-34.

8. Curtis, ''The Parting of the Ways,'' pp. 116-22; *Globe*, 30 December 1910.

9. Paul Stevens, ed., *The 1911 General Election: a Study in Canadian Politics* (Toronto: Copp Clark, 1970), pp. 8-18. Some agricultural implements were reduced from 17-1/2 per cent to 15 per cent, but many remained at twenty per cent or higher. See Fergusson, *Mr. Minister of Finance*, p. 105.

10. *The News* (Toronto), 10 January 1911; *Montreal Daily Star*, 9 January 1911.

11. Skelton, *Life and Letters of Sir Wilfrid Laurier*, 2, pp. 371-72; PAC, Dafoe Papers, vol. 1, Laurier to Dafoe, 24 February 1911; Dafoe, *Clifford Sifton*, pp. 354-59.

12. PAC, Laurier Papers, vol. 664, pp. 180773-74, Sifton et al. to Laurier, 1 February 1911; *The News* (Toronto), 2

February 1911. It should be noted that there was widespread speculation that Congress would never pass the agreement. See, for example, PAO, J.P. Whitney Papers, Whitney to A. Broder, 2 February 1911.

13. See, for example, *The World* (Toronto), 27 February 1911.

14. PAC, Sifton Papers, vol. 193, pp. 154612-67—73, Dafoe to Sifton, 16 August 1910; Dafoe Papers, vol. 1, Sifton to Dafoe, 31 August 1910.

15. PAC, Dafoe Papers, vol. 1, Dafoe to Sifton, 7 April 1910; Cook, *The Politics of John W. Dafoe*, pp. 43-44.

16. Interview with Col. Clifford Sifton, 18 December 1968; Donnelly, *Dafoe of the Free Press,* pp. 62-64. Nevertheless, it must be noted that Sifton later wrote that "the arrangement under which [Dafoe and Macklin] took charge some years ago was that they should control the editorial policy of the paper. There has been no change in this respect and it would have been contrary to the agreement that had been made if I had sought in any way to interfere with their discretion." PAC, Sifton Papers, vol. 197, Sifton to J.C. Hopkins, 3 November, 1911.

17. *CAR*, 1911, pp. 37-43; *The News*, 11 and 16 February 1911.

18. PAO, Whitney Papers, Borden to Whitney, 14 February 1911.

19. Stevens, ed., *The 1911 General Election*, pp. 66-67; PAC, Sifton Papers, vol. 198, pp. 157910-12, B.E. Walker to Sifton, 18 February 1911; and reply, 20 February 1911. A good discussion of the episode is in Eagle, "Sir Robert Borden and the Railway Problem," pp. 15-20.

20. PAC, Laurier Papers, vol. 667, p. 181847, Sifton to Laurier, 20 February 1911.

21. Ibid., vol. 297, file "Philp, A.E. 1911," Philp to Sifton, 27 February 1911; and reply, 28 February 1911. For other details on the developing agitation, see Curtis, "The Parting of the Ways," pp. 141-43.

22. PAC, Sifton Papers, vol. 196, pp. 156293-94, F. Cook to Sifton, 24 February 1911; and reply, 28 February 1911.

23. *Debates*, 1910-11, cols. 4385-4409, 28 February 1911.

24. PAC, Grey Papers, vol. 5, pp. 1498-1500, Laurier to Grey, 1 March 1911; Laurier Papers, vol. 670, 182767-68, Frank Burnett to Laurier, 8 March 1911; vol. 669, pp. 182487-88, A. Fortin à Laurier, le 3 mars 1911.

25. PAC, Sifton Papers, vol. 198, pp. 157913-14, Sifton to Walker, 20 February 1911; and reply, 23 February 1911; H.J. Morgan, *Canadian Men and Women of the Time*, 1912 ed., pp. 504, 638-39, 1134-35, 1171-72.

26. PAC, Willison Papers, vol. 105, pp. 38488-92, undated memorandum (reprinted in Stevens, ed., *The 1911 General Election*, pp. 69-70); see also Brown, *Robert Laird Borden*, 1, pp. 179-80.

27. PAC, Borden Papers, p. 150602, Borden to Dafoe, 17 December 1931.

28. Even the meeting with Sifton angered many Tories; see Brown, *Robert Laird Borden*, 1, pp. 183-84.

29. Arthur Hawkes, "Clifford Sifton and the Reciprocity Election of 1911," MFP, 21 September 1929, p. 33.

30. Ibid.; Curtis, "The Parting of the Ways", pp. 152-62; Brown, *Robert Laird Borden*, 1, pp. 190-91. See also Stevens, ed., *The 1911 General Election*, pp. 78-85.

31. *The News* (Toronto), 17 and 22 March 1911; *Montreal Star*, 21 March 1911; PAC, Dafoe Papers, vol. 1, S. Fisher to Dafoe, 23 March 1911.

32. PAC, Liberal Party of Canada Papers, vol. 991, "The Fielding Reciprocity," pamphlet issued by the Ontario Liberal Association, 1911, p. 55; Sifton Papers, vol. 197, p. 156585, Sifton to Editor of *Free Press*, Ottawa, 3 March 1911.

33. A. Hawkes, "Clifford Sifton and the Reciprocity Election of 1911." According to J.W. Dafoe (*Clifford Sifton*, p. 372), "In his book of reminiscences *My Generation of Politics and Politicians*, [W.T.R.] Preston says that Laurier permitted him to convey the intimation to Sifton [while in London] that he was considering dissolution, and that Sifton returned the courtesy by advising him not to submit himself and his cause at that time to the electors. This must have been an act of private friendliness, for Sifton's public position was that it was the duty of the government to submit the pact to the

electors." I was unable to confirm Dafoe's reference in Preston's memoirs; certainly the anecdote does not appear in chapter 41, which concerns the 1911 election.

34. PAC, Sifton Papers, vol. 297, file "Philp, A.E. 1911," Sifton to Philp, 2 March 1911; vol. 196, p. 156299, S.A. Coxe to Sifton, 6 March 1911.

35. PAC, Dafoe Papers, vol. 1, Sifton to Liberal Association of Brandon, 28 July 1911; *MFP*, 1 and 3 August 1911.

36. PAC, Sifton Papers, vol. 297, file "Philp, A.E. 1911," Philp to Sifton, 14 August 1911, and reply, 18 August 1911; vol. 196, p. 156348, Sifton to F. Cochrane, 18 August 1911. One of the ironies of the campaign was 'that the federal authorities decided to prepare their own voters' lists for Winnipeg and Brandon, after Laurier had consistently refused to do so in previous elections. Ibid., p. 156226, D.C. Cameron to Sifton, 9 August 1911.

37. Arthur Hawkes, "Clifford Sifton and the Reciprocity Election of 1911; *The News*, (Toronto), 23 August 1911.

38. *The News*, 24 August 1911.

39. Ibid., 26 August 1911.

40. Ibid., 23, 24, 26 August 1911.

41. Beck, *Pendulum of Power*, pp. 119, 135; Sifton Papers, vol. 196, p. 156285, Sifton to G.B. Coleman, 28 September 1911. On the Campaign in Brandon, see W. Leland Clark, *Brandon's Politics and Politicians* (Brandon Sun, 1981), pp. 55-59.

42. PAC, Borden Papers, p. 150602, Borden to Dafoe, 17 December 1931; Sifton Papers, vol. 251, p. 141137, Borden to Sifton, 22 September 1911;

vol. 193, pp. 156350-51; Cochrane to Sifton, 22 September 1911; vol. 196, p. 156258, J.B. Chambers to Sifton, 22 September 1911. See also Donnelly, *Dafoe of the Free Press*, pp. 65-66.

43. PAC, Sifton Papers, vol. 197, p. 156640, Sifton to James Gillespie, 7 October 1911; Clifford Sifton, "Reciprocity," in Ellery C. Stowell, ed., *Canadian National Problems* (Philadephia: American Academy of Political and Social Science, 1913), pp. 22-23, 25-26.

44. John Allan, "Reciprocity and the Canadian General Election of 1911: a Re-examination of Economic Self-Interest in Voting," (MA thesis, Queen's University, 1971). Allan concludes that "the Liberals had not appreciated the extent of the structural change in the economy from 1854....It appears that a decisive Liberal defeat at the polls in 1911 was not without economic justification, and did not represent irrationality on behalf of the Canadian voter." See also M.B. Percy, K.H. Norrie, and R.G. Johnstone, "Reciprocity and the Canadian General Election of 1911," *Explorations in Economic History*, 19 (1982): 409-34.

45. Clifford Sifton, "Reciprocity," pp. 24-25, 27-28.

46. Ibid., pp. 26-28. On this theme, see W.M. Baker, "A Case Study of Anti-Americanism in English-Speaking Canada: the Election Campaign of 1911," *CHR*, 51, no. 4 (December 1970): 426-49, esp. 435-36.

47. Clifford Sifton, "Reciprocity," p. 26.

NOTES TO CHAPTER ELEVEN

1. The best general survey of the history of the Commission is C. Roy Smith and David R. Witty, "Conservation, Resources and Environment: an Exposition and Critical Evaluation of the Commission of Conservation, Canada," *Plan Canada*. vol. 11, no. 1 (1970): 55-71, and vol. 11, no. 3 (1972): 199-216. See also Stewart Renfrew,

"Commission of Conservation," *Douglas Library Notes* (Queen's University) (Spring 1971): 17-26; "The Driving Power of Conservation: a Sketch of the Work Performed by the Commission of Conservation in Canada," *Saturday Night* (1 January 1921): 8; Alan F.J. Artibise and G.A. Stelter, "Conservation Planning and

Urban Planning: the Canadian Commission of Conservation in Historical Perspective," in *Planning for Conservation*, ed. Roger Kain (New York: St. Martin's Press, 1981), pp. 17-36; David M. Calnan, "Businessmen, Forestry and the Gospel of Efficiency: the Canadian Conservation Commission, 1909-1921" (MA thesis, Univerty of Western Ontario), 1976.

2. *CAR*, 1906, pp. 81-83, 528; F.J. Thorpe, "Historical Perspective on the 'Resources for Tomorrow' Conference," *Resources for Tommorrow*, *Conference Background Papers*, vol. 1 (Ottawa: Queen's Printer, 1961), pp. 2-3; Janet Foster, *Working for Wildlife: the Beginning of Preservation in Canada* (Toronto: University of Toronto Press, 1978), pp. 34-35.

3. Smith and Witty, "Conservation, Resources and Environment," pt, 1, p. 58; Thorpe, "Historical Perspective," p. 2.

4. Foster, *Working for Wildlife*, p. 35.

5. On this notion, see P.J. Smith, "The Principle of Utility and the Origins of Planning Legislation in Alberta, 1912-1975," in *The Usable Urban Past: Planning and Politics in the Modern Canadian City*, ed. A.F.J. Artibise and G.A. Stelter (Toronto: Macmillan, 1979), pp. 198-202; Samuel P. Hays, *Conservation and the Gospel of Efficiency: the Progressive Conservation Movement 1890-1920* (Cambridge, Mass.: Harvard University Press, 1959); Brown, "The Doctrine of Usefulness."

6. David C. Coyle, *Conservation: an American Story of Conflict and Accomplishment* (New Brunswick, N.J.: Rutgers University Press, 1957), pp. 64-66.

7. Ibid., p. 67.

8. Fisher was a member of the Canadian Forestry Association, and the Canadian Association for the Prevention of Tuberculosis, was active in both fruit and dairy farming in Québec, and had long been interested in the application of scientific and conservationist principles to farming.

9. Béland was a physician and Liberal MP for Beauce, and was interested in both the pulpwood and dairy industries, and in creation of a federal department of health.

10. PAC, Grey Papers, vol. 9, pp. 2286A-88A, Grey to Bryce, 3 February 1909.

11. CSP, 1909, no. 90, North American Conservation Conference, Declaration of Principles. Roosevelt's successor, W.H. Taft, was much less enthusiastic about conservation, and the idea of a world-wide conference was dropped.

12. *Debates*, 1909, cols. 355-69, 1 February 1909; col. 688, 8 February 1909; col. 1556, 25 February 1909. See also Foster, *Working for Wildlife*, pp. 37-38.

13. 8-9 Edw. VII, Ch. 27; *CCAR*, 1919 p. 12; Alan H Armstrong "Thomas Adams and the Commission of Conservation," in *Planning the Canadian Environment* ed., L.O. Gertler (Montreal: Harvest House, 1968), p. 18.

14. *Debates*, 1909, col. 5249, 30 April 1909; 6362-83, 12 May 1909.

15. PAC, Sifton Papers, vol. 189, 151436-39, Fisher to Sifton, 28 May 1909.

16. PAC, Laurier Papers, vol. 576, pp. 156367-68, Sifton to Laurier, 31 May 1909; Sifton Papers vol. 189, pp. 151440-42, Sifton to S. Fisher, 31 May 1909, and reply, 1 June 1909; pp. 151596-98, Sifton to G.P. Graham, 31 May 1909.

17. Ibid., pp. 151599-602, Graham to Sifton, 1 June 1909, and reply, 3 June 1909.

18. PC 1831, 3 September 1909. This order-in-council names the entire Commission. See also Thorpe, "Historical Perspective," pp. 3-4.

19. *Debates*, 1909-10, col. 6333, 5 April, 1910.

20. *CCAR*, 1910, p. 5. See also *Debates*, 1909-10, col. 6334, 5 April 1910; Clifford Sifton, "Canada's Conservation Commission," *American Conservation*, 1, no. 5, June 1911, p. 171.

21. *CCAR*, 1910, p. 2.

22. *Debates*, col. 6337, 5 April 1910.

23. Foster, *Working for Wildlife*, p. 40, quoting Martin Burrell, 1913.

24. *Debates*, 1910, col. 6363, 5 April 1910; *CCAR*, 1910, pp. 6, 170.

25. *Canada Year Book*, 1919, pp. 635-36; 1920, p. 705.
26. On White's appointment, see PAC, Sifton Papers, vol. 188, pp. 151450, 151460, Sifton to S. Fisher, 21 October, 1 November 1909; vol. 192. pp. 153943-47, White to Sifton, 22 October 1909; Calnan, "Businessmen, Forestry and the Gospel of Efficiency," pp.37-38.
27. *CCAR*, 1910, p. 27; see also pp. 3, 5, 172; 1914, p. 17; 1915, p. 232; 1917, p. 21; Sifton, "Canada's Conservation Commission," p. 178.
28. *CCAR*, 1910, p. 5; *Morning Chronicle* (Halifax), 22 February 1910 (reporting Sifton speech to Halifax Canadian Club, 21 February 1910); Clifford Sifton, "Canada's Conservation Commission," pp. 171-72.
29. *CCAR*, 1914, p. 17.
30. *CCAR*, 1911, p. 112, lists fourteen in 1910; in addition, Sifton spoke at London and Montreal early in January 1911.
31. Clifford Sifton, "The Conservation of Canada's Resources," *Empire Club Speeches* (Toronto), *1910-1911* (20 October 1910), ed. J. Castell Hopkins (Toronto: Saturday Night Press, 1911), p. 59; *CCAR*, 1910, pp. 24-25.
32. *CCAR*, 1910, p. 6.
33. Sifton, "The Conservation of Canada's Resources," pp. 57-59.
34. N.A.F. Dreisziger, "The International Joint Commission of the United States and Canada, 1895-1920," (Ph.D. diss., University of Toronto, 1974), pp. 337-39.
35. *CAR*, 1910, p. 246; *CCAR*, 1911, pp. 113-14; Dafoe, *Clifford Sifton*, pp. 349-50.
36. *MFP*, 9 February 1910; *CAR*, 1910, p. 247; *CCAR*, 1911, p. 114.
37. *CAR*, 1910, pp. 246-47.
38. PAC, Laurier Papers, vol. 615, pp. 167027-29, Sifton to Laurier, 15 February 1910, and reply, 17 February 1910. Sifton seems in later years to have forgotten this letter and to have exaggerated his own role at the time. "It is now nearly twenty years," he told Dafoe in 1925, "since I locked horns with Laurier and Graham when they intended to grant legislation to enable the Aluminium Company of America to get away

with the power at the Long Saulte. It was all but done when I discovered it. I declared war on it and ultimately defeated it. I have been against this large export of power ever since." PAC, Sifton Papers, vol. 212, pp. 164667-103—106, Sifton to Dafoe, 23 May 1925.
39. *Debates*, 1909-10, cols. 5317-5491, 14 March 1910; 5557-60, 16 March 1910.
40. Dafoe, *Clifford Sifton*, p. 350; *CAR*, 1910, pp. 247-49; *CCAR*, 1911, pp. 114-15.
41. *Debates*, 1909-10, col. 2672, 28 January 1910; *CAR*, 1910, pp. 249-50.
42. PAC, Laurier Papers, vol. 618, pp. 167906-8, Sifton to Laurier, 7 March 1910; *MFP*, 19 March 1910; *CAR*, 1910, p. 250; *CCAR*, 1911, p. 115.
43. PAC, Laurier Papers, vol. 613, pp. 166630-33, vol. 614, p. 166877, Sifton to Templeman, 5 and 11 February 1910.
44. *CCAR*, 1911, pp. 116-17.
45. Clifford Sifton, "Conservation of Canada's Resources," pp. 60-61; *Montreal Daily Star*, 9 January 1911; *CCAR*, 1910, p. 15.
46. *CCAR*, 1910, p. 7; 1918, p. 28.
47. *The Water Powers of Canada* (1911); *The Water Powers of Manitoba, Saskatchewan and Alberta* (1916); *The Water Powers of British Columbia* (1918).
48. *CCAR*, 1910, pp. 13-14. The Commission did produce a volume entitled *Waterworks and Sewage Systems*.
49. *CCAR*, 1910, p. 18.
50. Clifford Sifton, "The Conservation of Canada's Resources," pp. 61-62; *CAR*, 1910, pp. 368-73; *Morning Chronicle* (Halifax), 22 February 1910.
51. *Gazette* (Montreal), 24 February 1910 (reporting speech at Fredericton, 23 February 1910, to Canadian Forestry Association).
52. *CCAR*, 1912, pp. 54-55.
53. *Montreal Daily Star*, 9 January 1911.
54. PAC, Sifton Papers, vol. 205, pp. 161227-28, Sifton to J. White, 25 August 1916; *CCAR*, 1918, p. 6; Richard S. Lambert and Paul Pross, *Renewing Nature's Wealth: a Centennial History of the Public Management of Lands, Forests & Wildlife in Ontario 1763-1967* (Toronto: On-

tario Department of Lands and Forests, 1967), pp. 194, 213.
55. *CCAR*, 1911, p. 5; 1912, pp. 54, 64-75 (includes map); Clifford Sifton, "Canada's Conservation Commission," pp. 173-74; and see Van Kirk, "Canada's National Park Policy, 1885-1930," ch. 1.
56. *CSP*, 1913, no. 57a.
57. *CCAR*, 1915, pp. 20, 194; 1918, pp. 6-7; PAC, Borden Papers, vol. 175, pp. 95142-43. Sifton to Borden, 29 November 1912.
58. *CCAR*, 1910, pp. 8-11; *The News* (Toronto), 2 March 1910.
59. See Smith and Witty, "Conservation, Resources and Environment," pt. 2, pp. 199-201.
60. *CCAR*, 1910, p. 11; 1912, pp. 84-85; 1915, pp. 178-79.
61. Foster, *Working for Wildlife*, pp. 62, 72-73, 77-82.
62. Ibid., ch. 6, esp. pp. 133-34.
63. PAC, Borden Papers, vol. 157, pp. 84071-76, M. Burrell to Borden, 2 January 1917, and encl. (J. White to Burrell, 12 December 1916); Smith and Witty, "Conservation, Resources and Environment," pt. 2. pp. 205-8.
64. *CCAR*, 1910, p. 24.
65. *CCAR*, 1913, pp. 142-50; 1914, pp. 8, 134-38; 1915, pp. 5-6, 210-22.
66. *CCAR*, 1915, pp. 5-6.
67. *CCAR*, 1918, p. 14; Smith and Witty, "Conservation, Resources and Environment," pt.2, pp. 208-10.
68. *CCAR*, 1910, p. 12.
69. *CCAR*, 1911, pp. 118-219 esp. pp. 119-23; Clifford Sifton, "The Conservation of Canada's Resources," p. 60.
70. Neil Sutherland, *Children in English-Canadian Society 1880-1920: Framing the Twentieth-Century Consensus* (Toronto: University of Toronto Press, 1976), p. 40.
71. *CCAR*, 1915, p. 178; Armstrong, "Thomas Adams and the Commission of Conservation," p. 22; Sutherland, *Children in English-Canadian Society*, pp. 56-57, 69-70.
72. Janice P. Dickin McGinnis, "From Health to Welfare: Federal Government Policies Regarding Standards of Public Health for Canadians, 1919-1945" (Ph.D. diss., University of Alberta, 1980), pp. 1, 8-13; *CCAR*,

1919, p. 208; Sutherland, *Children in English-Canadian Society*, ch. 6.
73. *CCAR*, 1912, pp. 7-9; 1914, p. 87; on the establishment of the Department of Health in 1919, see McGinnis, "From Health to Welfare," ch. 1.
74. *CCAR*, 1912, pp. 2-5; 1914, pp. 24-25; 1919, pp. 206-8; Armstrong, "Thomas Adams and the Commission of Conservation," p. 21.
75. PAC, Sifton Papers, vol. 196, pp. 156250-54, undated memorandum [1911].
76. Smith and Witty, "Conservation, Resources and Environment," pt. I, p. 69; *CCAR*, 1912, p. 10.
77. *CCAR*, 1911, pp. 66-67.
78. *CCAR*, 1915, pp. 238-39.
79. John David Hulchanski, "Thomas Adams: a biographical and bibliographical guide," *Papers on Planning & Design*, no. 15 (Department of Urban and Regional Planning, University of Toronto, 1978), pp. 9-10; Artibise and Stelter, "Conservation Planning and Urban Planning," pp. 23-24; *CCAR*, 1913, p. 8; Michael Simpson, "Thomas Adams in Canada, 1914-1930," *Urban History Review*, 11, 2 (October 1982): 1-16.
80. Hulchanski, "Thomas Adams," pp. 14-24; PAC, Sifton Papers, vol. 206, p. 161794, Sifton to J.D. Reid, 29 December 1917; *CCAR*, 1919, pp. 95-96, 106-9.
81. Artibise and Stelter, "Conservation Planning and Urban Planning," pp. 24-25.
82. See, for example, PAC, Sifton Papers, vol. 201, pp. 159207-9, C.H. Cheney to Sifton, 19 December 1914, and reply, 31 December 1914.
83. See Smith, "The Principle of Utility."
84. Artibise and Stelter, "Conservation Planning and Urban Planning," pp. 25-27.
85. PAC, Sifton Papers, vol. 202, pp. 159830-32, Woodsworth to Sifton, 9 September 1914, and reply, 19 September 1914. On the League, see Kenneth McNaught, *A Prophet in Politics: a Biography of J.S. Woodsworth* (Toronto: University of Toronto Press, 1959), pp. 60-78.
86. *CCAR*, 1915, p. 33.
87. PAC, Sifton Papers, vol. 201, pp. 159280-81, A.P. Drummond to Sifton,

29 December 1914, and reply, 2 January 1915; Borden Papers, vol. 209 pt. 2, pp. 117945-46, Sifton to Borden, 16 May 1916; *CCAR*, 1912, pp. 13-15; Dafoe, *Clifford Sifton*, pp. 455-59. On the subject generally, see Brown and Cook, *Canada 1896-1921*, pp. 95-96.

88. *CCAR*, 1912, pp. 31-34, 82-83; 1918, pp. 29-42; PAC, Sifton Papers, vol. 205, pp. 161233-35, Sifton to J. White, 25 August 1916, and reply, 12 September 1916.

89. PAC, Sifton Papers, vol. 205, pp. 161229-30, Sifton to White, 9 August 1915; *CCAR*, 1917, pp. 40-74.

90. PAC, Borden Papers, vol. 233, p. 130048, Sifton to Sir Thomas White (Acting Prime Minister), 22 November 1918.

91. PAC. Sifton Papers, vol. 207, p. 162316, Sifton to Laura B. Durand, 29 August 1919.

92. See, for example, PAC, Borden Papers, vol. 175, pp. 95206-8, J. White to Borden, 27 March 1913; Sifton Papers, vol. 205, pp. 161216-17, White to Sifton, 1 August 1916.

93. PAC, Sifton Papers, vol. 205, pp. 161216-17, White to Sifton, 1 August 1916; PAC, Borden Papers, vol. 233, p. 130049, Sir Thomas White to Borden, 26 November 1918.

94. PAC, Sifton Papers, vol. 205, pp. 161216-17, White to Sifton, 1 August 1916; PAC, Borden Papers, vol. 157, pp. 84071-76, Burrell to Borden, 2 January 1917, and encl. (White to Burrell, 12 December 1916).

95. Even as he informed Borden of Sifton's resignation, Sir Thomas White noted that the cabinet wanted to accept it and to seize the opportunity to place the Commission under a department. PAC, Borden Papers, vol. 233, p. 130049, White to Borden, 26 November 1918.

96. *CSP*, 1913, no. 57a, p. 25.

97. PAC, Sifton Papers, vol. 201, pp. 159032-41, J. White to Sifton, 15 January 1913, and reply, 6 February 1913; vol. 200, Sifton to C.A. Magrath, 6 October 1913.

98. *CCAR*, 1917, p. 30; 1918, pp. 23-24; N.A.F. Dreisziger, "The International Joint Commission," pp. 337-45.

99. N.A.F. Dreisziger, "The International Joint Commission," pp. 345-47; PAC, Borden Papers, vol. 244, pp. 136497-98, Sifton to Borden, 21 September 1918, and encl. ("Statement of the Commission of Conservation in Response to the Application of the St. Lawrence River Power Company....Ottawa, 1918").

100. PAC, Borden Papers, vol. 244, pp. 136477-78, Sifton to Borden, 18 September 1918.

101. Ibid., pp. 136518-19, Borden to Sifton, 22 October 1918.

102. Ibid., p. 136575-79, Sifton to Borden, 1 November 1918.

103. Ibid., pp. 136586-88, Borden to Sifton, 7 November 1918.

104. On the abolition of the Commission, the best discussion is in Foster, *Working for Wildlife*, pp. 210-16. See also Smith and Witty, "Conservation, Resources and Environment," pt.2, pp. 212-14. A defence of the Commission's record, possibly by Sifton, is in PAC, Sifton Papers, vol. 278, 164890-902.

105. PAC, Sifton Papers, vol. 209, p. 163064, Sifton to White, 29 October 1921. See also Foster, *Working for Wildlife*, p. 215.

106. PAC, Sifton Papers, vol. 193, p. 154220, Sifton to B.E. Chaffey, 12 December 1910.

107. Foster, *Working for Wildlife*, p. 215.

NOTES TO CHAPTER TWELVE

1. PAC, Sifton Papers, vol. 199, p. 158060, Sifton to J.H. Burnham, 21 June 1912.

2. Ibid., vol. 298, file "Coste, Eugene 1912," J. Bain to Coste, 24 October 1912; vol. 199, pp. 158133-16—18,

Sifton to Dafoe, 21 November 1912; vol. 298, file "Edwards, W.C. 1912," Sifton to Edwards, 27 November 1912; vol. 201, pp. 159261-62, Sifton to Sir Louis Davies, 23 February 1914.

3. Ibid., vol. 201, p. 159285-11, Sifton to Dafoe, 2 January 1915; vol. 299, file "Parrish to Phippen 1915," W.L. Parrish to Sifton, 19 November 1915; and reply, 22 November 1915.

4. Ibid., vol. 298, file "Sifton, Arthur 1912," A.L. Sifton to Clifford Sifton, 20 September 1912; file "Webster, John 1912," Sifton to Webster [1912]; *MFP*, 20 September 1912.

5. PAC, Sifton Papers, vol. 200, p. 158873, Sifton to W.F. Maclean, 6 October 1913; vol. 299, file "Sifton, Arthur 1914," Sifton to A.L. Sifton, 27 October 1914.

6. PAC, Laurier Papers, vol. 694, p. 190566, Alex. Smith to Laurier, 17 December 1913; and see Borden Papers, vol. 450, Diary, 27 October 1912, 6 April 1913.

7. *MFP*, 23 May 1912.

8. PAC, Sifton Papers, vol. 298, file "Cameron, D.C., 1912," Sifton to Cameron, 29 January 1912, and reply, 5 February 1912; file "Phippen to Piper 1913," Chehalis Lumber Company Balance Sheet, 31 January 1913; vol. 299, file "Lacey, James 1914;" file "Boyle to Burrows 1917;" file "Phippen to Preston, 1917;" Interview with Col. Clifford Sifton, 18 December 1968. Also involved in the Chehalis Company were the Rat Portage Lumber Company owned by D.C. Cameron (one quarter interest), and the Brooks Timber Company of Minneapolis (half interest).

9. PAC, Sifton Papers, vol. 298, file "Philp, A.E. 1913"; Interview with Michael Sifton, 1 July 1981.

10. GAA, Canada Land and Irrigation Company Ltd. Papers, file 627, J.D. MacGregor to W.J. Challis, 7 June 1912; Challis to Southern Alberta Land Company, 7 June 1912; MacGregor to Sifton, 11 June 1912; Sifton to MacGregor, 4 July, 3 September 1912; MacGregor to Sifton, 9 October 1912.

11. For an excellent treatment, see Keith Stotyn, "The Bow River Irrigation Project 1906-1949" (M.A. thesis, University of Alberta, 1982), ch. 2.

12. GAA, Canada Land and Irrigation Company Papers, file 627, W.J. Challis Southern Alberta Land Company, 11 March 1913; file 83, J.W. Sifton to A.C. Newton, 28 November 1913, and reply, 30 December 1913; file 311, W.J. Challis to D.W. Hays, 7 September 1920.

13. Kelly's identity is uncertain; he might have been Andrew Kelly of Brandon, a prominent grain merchant. See Morgan, *Canadian Men and Women of the Time*, 1912, p. 602. Sifton and Kelly had tried and failed to persuade Sir William Mackenzie to become a majority shareholder; see PAC, Sifton Papers, vol. 297, file "Mackenzie, Sir William, 1911," Sifton to Mackenzie [1911].

14. PAC, Sifton Papers, vol. 310, file "Columbia Oil and Gas Company of Canada Ltd 1912," statement to shareholders.

15. Ibid., vol. 298, file "Coste, Eugene 1912," Sifton to Coste, 23 September 1918.

16. Ibid., vol. 310, file "British Empire Agency Limited 1912," Memorandum. Sifton's shares were held in trust by a Mr. Devereux, otherwise unidentified.

17. Ibid.

18. Ibid., vol. 298, file "Philp, A.E. 1913," Sifton to Philp, 19 March 1913.

19. Ibid., vol. 297, file "Grenfell, Arthur 1910," Sifton to Grenfell, 13 December 1910.

20. *Monetary Times*, 28 August 1914, p. 17; PAC, Sifton Papers, vol. 298, file "McLeod, Alexander 1913," statement of assets and liabilities; vol. 300, file "Coste, E., 1920," statement of earnings and expenditures; PAA, Premiers' Papers, File 291, Public Utilities Commission—General, N.B. Gash to J.E. Brownlee, 24 February 1927.

21. *The Morning Albertan* (Calgary), 8 April 1912; PAC, Sifton Papers, vol. 298, file "Bain, John 1912," Bain to Sifton, 8 April 1912; file "Coste, to Sifton," 9 July 1912.

22. PAC, Sifton Papers, vol. 298, file "McLeod, Alexander 1913," state-

ment of assets and liabilities; vol. 299, file "Coste, Eugene 1917," Sifton to Coste, 17 November 1917.

23. Ibid., vol. 298, file "McLeod, Alexander 1913," Sifton to McLeod, 14 November 1913.

24. Ibid., vol. 300, file "Coste, E. 1920," statement of earnings and expenditures.

25. Ibid., vol. 299, file "Coste, Eugene 1917," Coste to Sifton, 20 November 1917, file "Horne-Payne to Housser 1916," R.M. Horne-Payne to Sifton, 8 September 1916. Sifton's "presiding genius" as usual was not involved in the day-to-day running of the company; that was handled by Eugene M.A. Coste, a mining engineer and authority on natural gas. Coste was president of the Company, and held 11,765 common shares in it. Sifton had also used Coste as a consulting engineer in his Colombian oil ventures.

26. Paul Rutherford, *A Victorian Authority: the Daily Press in Late Nineteenth Century Canada* (Toronto: University of Toronto Press, 1982), p. 239; Morgan, *Canadian Men and Women of the Time*, 1912, pp. 709-10.

27. PAC, Sifton Papers, vol. 190, pp. 152551, 152553, Sifton to Maclean, 4 March, 22 April 1909; vol. 194, pp. 154894-97, Sifton to W.H. Greenwood, 8, 9, 15 April 1910, and Greenwood to Sifton, 8 April 1910; vol. 195, pp. 155450-54, Maclean to Sifton, 27 March [1910]; Willison Papers, vol. 37, pp. 14086-87, C.F. Hamilton to Willison, 19 February 1909.

28. PAC, Sifton Papers, vol. 203, file "Maclean, W.F. 1915," passim; *Who's Who in Canada*, 1930-31, p. 46. The marriage produced a son in 1918, Clifford Maclean Sifton.

29. PAC, Sifton Papers, vol. 206, files "Maclean, W.F. 1917" and "Maclean, W.F. 1918," passim.

30. Ibid., vol. 297, file "Finnie, D.M. 1911," Sifton to Finnie, 11 May 1911; vol. 200, pp. 158727-1—3, Dafoe to Sifton, 1 March 1913.

31. Ibid., vol. 298, file "Payne, J.L. 1913," Sifton to W.F. Payne, 11 April 1913.

32. Ibid., vol. 204, pp. 160906-7—15,

Dafoe to Sifton, 17 October 1916; vol. 205, pp. 161401-13—19, Dafoe to Sifton, 12 February 1917; pp. 161401-56—57, Sifton to Dafoe, 4 October 1917; PAC, Dafoe Papers, vol. 1, Dafoe to Sifton, 27 February 1917.

33. Cook, *The Politics of John W. Dafoe* ch. 4.

34. See, for example, PAC, Dafoe Papers, vol. 1, Sifton to Dafoe, 12 May 1916.

35. PAC, Sifton Papers, vol. 200, pp. 158727-6—10, Sifton to Dafoe, 17 November 1913.

36. PAC, Borden Papers, vol. 16, p. 4197, Sifton to Borden, 30 September 1911, and encl.; Brown, *Robert Laird Borden*, 1, pp. 198-200, 204.

37. PAC, Sifton Papers, vol. 196, pp. 156494-10—15, Dafoe to Sifton, 11 October 1911.

38. See Brown, *Robert Laird Borden*, 1, pp. 148-63, 235-36.

39. PAC, Borden Papers, vol. 125 pt. 1, pp. 67191-94, Sifton to T.W. White, 11 July 1912; see also PAC, Dafoe Papers, vol. 1, Sifton to Dafoe, 4 January 1913.

40. Brown, *Robert Laird Borden*, 1, pp. 239-40; PAC, Dafoe Papers, vol. 1, Sifton to Dafoe, 4 January 1913.

41. PAC, Dafoe Papers, vol. 1, Sifton to Dafoe, 4 January 1913.

42. PAC, Sifton Papers, vol. 200, pp. 158727-1—3, 158727-5, Dafoe to Sifton, 1 March 1913, and reply, 19 March 1913.

43. PAC, Sifton Papers, vol. 199, pp. 158133-1—3, Sifton to Dafoe, 9 January 1912; Brown, *Robert Laird Borden*, 1, pp. 223-24; A.W. Currie, *The Grand Trunk Railway of Canada* (Toronto: University of Toronto Press, 1957), p. 410.

44. Brown, *Robert Laird Borden*, 1, pp. 224-25; Currie, *Grand Trunk Railway*, pp. 412-13; PAC, Sifton Papers, vol. 199, pp. 158133-16—18, Sifton to Dafoe, 21 November 1912.

45. Dafoe, *Clifford Sifton*, pp. 384-85; PAC, Borden Papers, vol. 450, Diary, 7 June 1913.

46. PAC, Dafoe Papers, vol. 1, Sifton to Dafoe, 31 July 1914; Dafoe, *Clifford Sifton*, pp. 385-86.

47. Dafoe, *Clifford Sifton*, p. 386.

48. The only one not in uniform was

Harry, who was ineligible because of a physical disability.

49. PAC, Sifton Papers, vol. 299, file "Sifton, Arthur 1914," Sifton to A.L. Sifton, 30 September 1914.

50. PAC, RG 9, II, B4, vol. 30; *Who's Who and Why*, 1921, p. 1280.

51. PAC, RG, 9, II, B 4, vol. 11; Clifford Sifton (junior) Papers, vol. 13, file "Sifton, Clifford, Biographical Material 1965, 1971, n.d.;" Selwyn Wilson Papers, Diary of the 13th Battery, Canadian Field Artillery 1914 to 1919.

52. PAC, RG 9, II, B 4, vol. 12; Winnipeg Free Press, *Victor Sifton of the Winnipeg Free Press* [Winnipeg, 1961]. I also am indebted to Barbara Wilson of the Public Archives of Canada, and to W.A. MacIntosh of the Directorate of History, Department of National Defense, for providing information on the war records of Clifford Sifton's sons.

53. Its history is outlined in PAC, RG 9, III, D 1, vol. 4687, Folder 38 file 1; see also *London Chronicle*, 2 April 1918.

54. PAC, Sifton Papers, vol. 202, p. 159797, Sifton for Sir Robert Borden, 3 October 1914. Others were W.A. Downey and C.W. McLean of Brockville, R. Brutinel, H. Paton and Mortimer B. Davis of Montreal, and Ahearn & Soper Ltd. of Ottawa. Sifton and J.R. Booth shared the largest contributions, $6220.28 each; Sifton Papers, vol. 202, p. 159905, Sifton to Booth, 27 January 1915.

55. PAC, Sifton Papers, vol. 202, p. 159662-63, F. Nichol to R. Brutinel, 11 August 1914; vol. 201, pp. 159493-96, D.S. Ludlum to R. Brutinel, 19 August 1941; RG 9, III, D 1, vol. 4681, folder 38, file 1.

56. PAC, Sifton Papers, vol. 201, pp. 159199-202, R. Brutinel to Sifton, 12 November 1914.

57. PAC, Dafoe Papers, vol. 1, Sifton to Dafoe, 21 September 1914.

58. Sir Clifford Sifton, "Some Historical Reflections Relating to the War," Address to Women's Canadian Historical Society of Ottawa, 4 November 1915, pp. 7, 9, 16-17, 19-20. See also *Montreal Herald and Daily Telegraph*, 25 January 1915.

59. PAC, Dafoe Papers, vol.1, Sifton to Dafoe, 21 September 1914.

60. Ibid., Sifton to Dafoe, "Saturday 1917."

61. Ibid., Sifton to Dafoe, 18 May 1915; W.L. Morton, *Manitoba: a History* (Toronto: University of Toronto Press, 1957), pp. 351-53.

62. PAC, Dafoe Papers, vol. 1, Sifton to Dafoe, 30 July 1915, 11 and 12 May 1916; Brown and Cook, *Canada 1896-1921*, pp. 252-62; Brown, *Robert Laird Borden*, 2, pp. 53-54.

63. PAC, Borden Papers, vol. 450, Diary, 8 October 1914.

64. Ibid.; and Diary, 30 September-19 November 1915; Brown, *Robert Laird Borden*, 2, pp. 19, 45-46.

65. PAC, Dafoe Papers, vol. 1, Sifton to Dafoe, 21 September 1914; Sifton Papers, vol. 202, pp. 159596-97, Sifton to W.F. Maclean, 9 September 1914.

66. PAC, Borden Papers, vol. 36, p. 14906, Sifton to Borden, 27 March 1916; Sifton Papers, vol. 204, p. 160985, Sifton to Agnes C. Laut, 8 May 1916.

67. PAC, Dafoe Papers, vol. 1, Sifton to Dafoe, 11 May 1916; "Saturday 1917"; Borden Papers, vol. 450, Diary, 28 April 1916.

68. PAC, Borden Papers, vol. 450, Diary, 2 May 1917.

69. Regehr, *Canadian Northern Railway*, pp. 414-29; J.A. Eagle, "Sir Robert Borden, Union Government and railway nationalization," *JCS*, 10, no. 4, (Nov. 1975): 59-66.

70. PAC, Sifton Papers, vol. 205, pp. 161401-62, Sifton to Dafoe, undated [October 1917?]; Brown, *Robert Laird Borden*, 2, p. 97; Regehr, *Canadian Northern Railway*, pp. 443-44.

71. PAC, Dafoe Papers, vol. 1, Sifton to Dafoe, 12 May 1916 (two letters).

72. PAC, Borden Papers, vol. 450, Diary, 1 May 1917.

73. PAC, Sifton Papers, vol. 204, pp. 160906-5—6, Sifton to Dafoe, 1 August 1916.

74. PAC, Dafoe Papers, vol. 1, Sifton to Dafoe, 11 November 1916, 14 January 1917; Dafoe, *Clifford Sifton*, pp. 392-93, 398-99.

75. J.L. Granatstein and J.M. Hitsman, *Broken Promises: A History of Conscription in Canada* (Toronto: Ox-

ford University Press, 1977), p. 36; Brown, *Robert Laird Borden*, 2, pp. 33-34.

76. Brown, *Robert Laird Borden*, 2, pp. 76, 83-86.

77. See English, *The Decline of Politics*, pp. 137-38.

78. Dafoe, *Clifford Sifton*, p, 399; Cook, *Politics of J.W. Dafoe* , pp. 73-74; PAC, Sifton Papers, vol. 205, pp. 161401-13—19, Dafoe to Sifton, 12 February 1917; Dafoe Papers, vol. 1, Dafoe to Sifton, 27 February 1917.

79. PAC, Borden Papers, vol. 450, Diary, 5, 26 May 1917.

80. PAC, Dafoe Papers, vol. 1, Sifton to Dafoe, 28 May, 5 June 1917; Sifton Papers, vol. 206, p. 162049, Sifton to G.M. Wrong, 5 June 1917. Contemporary evidence does not support Sifton's analysis of the motives underlying Borden's actions; indeed it has been argued that no one was more distressed at the Prime Minister's course than Rogers. See English, *The Decline of Politics*, p. 132; Brown, *Robert Laird Borden*, 2, pp. 84-90.

81. PAC, Dafoe Papers, vol. 1, Sifton to Dafoe, 5 June 1917; Dafoe, *Clifford Sifton*, pp. 403-4.

82. Queen's University Archives, T.A. Crerar Papers, Box 98, Ser. 3, A.K. Cameron to J.W. Dafoe, 21 December 1931 (copy).

83. PAC, A.K. Cameron Papers, vol. 16, Dafoe to Cameron, 2 January 1932.

84. PAC, Borden Papers, vol. 450, Diary, 26, 27 June 1917; Dafoe, *Clifford Sifton*, p. 405.

85. PAC, A.K. Cameron Papers, vol. 16, Dafoe to Cameron, 2 January 1932; Queen's University Archives, Crerar Papers, Box 98, Ser. 3, A.K. Cameron to J.W. Dafoe, 21 December 1931.

86. PAC, Borden Papers, vol. 450, Diary, 28, 29 June, 3, 4 July 1917; Margaret Prang, *N.W. Rowell: Ontario Nationalist* (Toronto: University of Toronto Press, 1975), pp. 191-97; Ramsay Cook, "Dafoe, Laurier, and the Formation of Union Government," in C. Berger, ed., *Conscription 1917* (Toronto: University of Toronto Press, n.d.), pp. 28-29.

87. Dafoe, *Clifford Sifton*, p. 418, asserts that Sifton did not call the convention;

see also *MFP*, 6 July 1917; and *Tribune*, 6 July 1917.

88. English, *The Decline of Politics*, pp. 144-46; Prang, *N.W. Rowell*, pp. 198-99.

89. *MFP*, 24 July 1917. See also Dafoe, *Clifford Sifton*, pp. 412-13, 415.

90. PAC, Borden Papers, vol. 78, pp. 40337-39, Sifton to Borden, 25 July 1917; Borden Diary, 30 July 1917.

91. PAC, Dafoe Papers, vol. 1, Sifton to Dafoe, "Wednesday 1917," [1 August 1917?]; and "Saturday 1917" [4 August 1917?]; undated [1917].

92. Dafoe, *Clifford Sifton*, p. 418; John Herd Thompson, *The Harvests of War: the Prairie West, 1914-1918* (Toronto: McClelland and Stewart, 1978), p. 125; TPL, William Main Johnson Papers, Diaries, vol. 8, Johnson to N.W. Rowell, 7 August 1917.

93. *Tribune*, 1 and 9 August 1917.

94. PAC, Laurier Papers, vol. 712, pp. 196781-84, Burnett to Laurier, 22 August 1917; vol. 711, pp. 196484-87, Sir Allen Aylesworth to Laurier, 2 August 1917; pp. 196574-76, J.K. Barrett to Laurier, 9 August 1917.

95. Ibid., vol. 713, pp. 197012-14, J.K. Barrett to Laurier, 15 September 1917, In the same vein, T.A. Crerar had earlier commented that "Sifton in the West is...as dead as a doornail." Cited in English, *The Decline of Politics*, p. 143.

96. *MFP*, 9, 10 August 1917; *Tribune*, 9, 10 August 1917.

97. PAC, Laurier Papers, vol. 711, pp. 196574-76, J.K. Barrett to Laurier, 9 August 1917. See also TPL, Main Johnson Papers, Johnson to N.W. Rowell, 7 and 9 August 1917; Johnson commented that Sifton's "unpopularity among the rank and file of Western Liberals seems to be unanimous."

98. *MFP*, 10-22 August 1917.

99. PAC, Borden Papers, vol. 450, Diary, 9 August 1917; Brown, *Robert Laird Borden*, 2, p. 104.

100. PAC, Borden Papers, vol. 450, Diary, 6, 8, 10, 13, 14, 15 August 1917; Brown, *Robert Laird Borden*, 2, p. 105; English, *The Decline of Politics*, p. 150.

101. PAC, Dafoe Papers, vol. 1, Sifton to

Dafoe, 14 August 1917; Borden Papers, vol. 450, Diary, 19 August 1917.

102. PAC, Borden Papers, vol. 450, Diary, 13, 16, 20 August 1917; Dafoe Papers, vol. 1, Dafoe to Sifton [12 August 1917?]; PAC, Sifton Papers, vol. 206, p. 162056, Sifton to G.M. Wrong, 24 August 1917.

103. PAC, Borden Papers, vol. 450, Diary, 29 August, 7 September 1917; Dafoe, *Clifford Sifton*, p. 427; English, *The Decline of Politics*, pp. 152-53; Brown, *Robert Laird Borden*, 2, 105-7.

104. 7-8 Geo. V, ch. 34 (Military Voters Act); 7-8 Geo. V, ch. 39 (Wartime Elections Act).

105. Brown, *Robert Laird Borden*, 2, p. 100.

106. PAC, Borden Papers, vol. 450, Diary, 27 June, 22 July 1917.

107. English, *The Decline of Politics*, pp. 154-57; Brown, *Robert Laird Borden*, 2, pp. 107-10; PAC, Dafoe Papers, vol. 1, Sifton to Dafoe, 15, 21, 27 September, 4, 9 October 1917.

108. PAC, Dafoe Papers, vol. 1, Sifton to Dafoe, 15 October 1917.

109. PAC, Sifton Papers, vol. 206, pp. 162010-12, 162013, Sifton to Sir John Willison, 12 and 16 October 1917.

110. Granatstein and Hitsman, *Broken Promises*, p. 85; English, *The Decline of Politics*, p. 191; PAC, Sifton Papers, vol. 299, Sifton to J.G. Rutherford [November 1917].

111. PAC, Sifton Papers, vol. 299, Sifton to John Bain, 23 November 1917.

112. Ibid., A.E. Philp to Sifton, 30 November 1917; and reply, 8 December 1917.

113. Ibid., vol, 205, pp. 161455-58, Sifton to J.M. Godfrey, 8 November 1917, and reply, 9 November 1917; Sifton to F.O. Fowler, 12 November 1917.

114. PAC, Borden Papers, vol. 450, Diary, 30 November 1917; Brown, *Robert Laird Borden*, 2, pp. 120-21; TPL, Main Johnson Papers, Diary, vol. 9, "Sir Clifford Sifton."

115. TPL, Main Johnson Papers, Diary, vol. 9, "Sir Clifford Sifton."

116. Beck, *Pendulum of Power*, p. 148. A week before the election Sifton had told Dafoe that in Ontario "Laurier might get 35 seats and he might get only five." He thought a pro-government trend was developing and Laurier might get ten or twelve. With strong leadership, he believed the Liberals could have secured 25-35 seats. PAC, Sifton Papers, vol. 205, p. 161401-71, Sifton to Dafoe, 10 December 1917.

117. PAC, Sifton Papers, vol. 205, p. 161459, Godfrey to Sifton, 19 December 1917. Evidence supporting this from the Liberal side may be found in PAC, A.K. Cameron Papers, vol 2, W.H. Cameron to A.K. Cameron, 21, 24 November, 8 December 1917; A.K. Cameron to W.W. Wilkinson, 12, 22, 24 November, 7 December 1917.

118. PAC, Laurier Papers, vol. 718, 198988 Laurier to W.T.R. Preston, 3 January 1917. Of course no direct evidence substantiating Sifton's involvement in a "religious and racial campaign" appears to have survived.

119. PAC, Dafoe Papers, vol. 1, Sifton to George W. Allen, 6 February 1918, Sifton also praised Dafoe for his role in the Union government movement and its results; he "grasped the whole situation very clearly from the beginning, never lost his courage, and from his editorial chair directly dominated the situation." On Dafoe's role, see Cook, "Dafoe, Laurier, and the Formation of Union Government."

NOTES TO CHAPTER THIRTEEN

1. University of Manitoba, Elizabeth Dafoe Library, Dafoe Papers, Diary of Peace Conference, 1919; H.G. Wells *Joan and Peter: the story of an*

Education (New York: Macmillan, 1918), pp. 549-51; Norman and Jeanne Mackenzie, *H.G. Wells* (New York: Simon and Schuster, 1973), pp. 317-18.

2. University of Manitoba, Elizabeth Dafoe Library, Dafoe Papers, Diary of Peace Conference, 1919.

3. Brown and Cook, *Canada 1896-1921*, pp. 294-95; Thompson, *The Harvests of War*, pp. 145-46, 153ff.

4. PAC, Sifton Papers, vol. 208, Willison to Sifton, 28 December 1920; Willison Papers, vol. 74, Sifton to Willison, 29 December 1920.

5. PAC, Sifton Papers, vol. 207, pp. 162316-18, Sifton to Dafoe, 20 November 1919. See also John A. Eagle, "Monopoly or Competition: the Nationalization of the Grand Trunk Railway," *CHR*, 62 no. 1, (March 1981): 3-30.

6. Brown, *Robert Laird Borden*, 2, pp. 176-78; PAC, Sifton Papers, vol. 207, p. 162563-28, Sifton to Dafoe, 16 October 1920; p. 162563-53, Sifton to Dafoe, 22 December 1920; vol. 208, p. 162823-46, Sifton to Dafoe, 22 September 1921; Roger Graham, *Arthur Meighen*, 2, *And Fortune Fled* (Toronto: Clarke, Irwin, 1963), p. 115.

7. PAC, Sifton Papers, vol. 209, p. 162937, Meighen to Sifton, 23 September 1921; Meighen Papers, vol. 22, p. 12207, Sifton to Meighen, 26 September 1921; Sifton Papers, vol. 208, p. 162823-50, Sifton to Dafoe, 26 September 1921.

8. Clifford Sifton, "The Foundations of the New Era," in J.O. Miller, ed., *The New Era in Canada: Essays Dealing with the Upbuilding of the Canadian Commonwealth* (Toronto: J.M. Dent, 1917), pp. 37-57.

9. PAC, Dafoe Papers, vol. 1, Sifton to Dafoe [December 1917?]; Thompson, *The Harvests of War*, p. 153; Brown and Cook, *Canada 1896-1921*, pp. 300-301.

10. The record of the Union Government was by no means negligible; see English, *Decline of Politics*, p. 220; and Brown and Cook, *Canada 1896-1921*, pp. 321-26.

11. PAC, Dafoe Papers, vol. 1, Sifton to Dafoe, 11 May 1916.

12. PAC, Sifton Papers, vol. 207, p.
162563-28, Sifton to Dafoe, 16 October 1920; and see pp. 162563-40—41, Sifton to Dafoe, 19 November 1920.

13. W.L. Mackenzie King Diary, 18 September 1917; 7 December 1920; 18 January, 25 February, 3, 17 March, 18, 24, 29, 31 October 1921.

14. Dafoe tended to be harsher in his judgment, regarding King as weak and ineffective. See, for example, PAC, Sifton Papers, vol. 207, pp. 162316-11—12, 162316-15—16, Dafoe to Sifton, 26 August, 5 September 1919, and many subsequent references. See also W.L. Morton, *The Progressive Party in Canada* (Toronto: University of Toronto Press, 1950), p. 126.

15. PAC, Dafoe Papers, vol. 2, Sifton to Dafoe, 19 November 1920.

16. PAC, Sifton Papers, vol. 208, pp. 162823-56, 162823-77—78, Sifton to Dafoe, 4, 31 October 1921; vol. 209, p. 162965, Sifton to W.T.R. Preston, 11 November 1921; *Toronto Daily Star*, 12 November 1921.

17. The elections results on 6 December 1921 were: Liberal, 116; Conservative, 50; Progressive, 65; Labour, 2; Independent, 2. Beck, *Pendulum of Power*, p. 160.

18. PAC, Sifton Papers, vol. 208, pp. 162823-105—106, 162823-115—116, 162823-124, Sifton to Dafoe, 8, 12, 16 December 1921; Dafoe Papers, vol. 2, Sifton to Dafoe, 14, 18, 30 December 1921; R. MacGregor Dawson, *William Lyon Mackenzie King, a Political Biography*, 1, *1874-1923* (Toronto: University of Toronto Press, 1958), pp. 357-73; Morton, *The Progressive Party*, pp. 130-44.

19. Mackenzie King Diary, 28 December 1921.

20. PAC, Dafoe Papers, vol. 2, Sifton to Dafoe, 30 December 1921; Sifton Papers, vol. 209. p. 163251-56, Sifton to Dafoe, 7 February 1922.

21. PAC, Sifton Papers, vol. 207, p. 162563-38, Sifton to Dafoe, 18 November 1920; vol. 208, p. 162823-25, Sifton to Dafoe, 8 February 1921; Sir Clifford Sifton, "The Immigrants Canada Wants" *Maclean's Magazine*, (1 April 1921): 16, 22-24; Sifton, "Immigration," *Proceedings of the Canadian Club, Toronto, for the*

Years 1921-22, vol. 19, (3 April 1922): 182-91.

22. Sifton, "The Immigrants Canada Wants."

23. PAC, Sifton Papers, vol. 209, pp. 163075-77, E.J. Ashton to Sifton, 13 March 1922; and reply, 14 March 1922.

24. Ibid., vol. 208, p. 162823-25, Sifton to Dafoe, 8 February 1921; vol. 209, p. 163251-106, Sifton to Dafoe, 1 December 1922; vol. 210, p. 163766-40, Sifton to Dafoe, 15 March 1923; vol. 211, pp. 164039-43, Sifton to J.A. Robb, 25 October 1923; Mackenzie King Diary, 10 March 1923.

25. PAC, Sifton Papers, vol. 207, p. 162563-38, Sifton to Dafoe, 18 November 1920; vol. 210, pp. 163766-11—12, Sifton to Dafoe, 16 January 1923; vol. 209, p. 163310, Sifton to W.T.R. Flemington, 13 March 1922; p. 163186, Sifton to Bryce Coleman, 5 April 1922; vol. 210, p. 163654, Sifton to T.A. Burrows, 19 November 1923. See also Dafoe, *Clifford Sifton*, pp. 491-96.

26. PAC, Sifton Papers, vol. 208, pp. 162823-15—19, Sifton to Dafoe, 25 and 27 April 1921. On Shaughnessy's scheme, see Lamb, *History of the Canadian Pacific Railway*, pp. 290-99.

27. PAC, Sifton Papers, vol. 212, pp. 164667-92—94, Dafoe to Sifton, 29 April 1925; PAC, Dafoe Papers, vol. 3, Sifton to Dafoe, 24 April 1925; and see Dafoe, *Clifford Sifton*, pp. 496-98.

28. Lamb, *History of the Canadian Pacific Railway*, pp. 302-4; Dawson, *William Lyon Mackenzie King*, 1, pp. 394-96; H. Blair Neatby, *William Lyon Mackenzie King, 2, 1924-1932* (Toronto: University of Toronto Press, 1963), pp. 24-30, 46-48.

29. PAC, Dafoe Papers, vol. 3, Sifton to Dafoe, 3, 11, and 23 January 1926; Dafoe, *Clifford Sifton*, pp. 500-502.

30. PAC, Dafoe Papers, vol. 2, Sifton to Dafoe, 4 December 1920; *MFP*, 7, 10, 12 April 1923; Dafoe, *Clifford Sifton*, p. 503.

31. *MFP*, 16-21 April, 23-27 April 1923; two of these articles are reproduced in Dafoe, *Clifford Sifton*, pp. 504-6.

32. PAC, Sifton Papers, vol. 210, pp. 163766-52—53, Dafoe to Sifton, 21 April 1923.

33. Ibid., pp. 163766-60, 163766-83, 163766-88—89, Sifton to Dafoe, 3 May, 4, 5, 7 June 1923; PAC, Dafoe Papers, vol. 3, Sifton to Dafoe 16 February, 1 March 1924; Sifton Papers, vol. 211, pp. 164244-70—71, Sifton to Dafoe, 21 April, 1924.

34. PAC, Dafoe Papers, vol. 3, Sifton to Dafoe, 7 May 1924; 12 March 1925; Sifton Papers, vol. 212, pp. 164667-43—44, 164667-59, Sifton to Dafoe, 10 and 27 March 1925; vol. 213, pp. 164715, 164719-20, Sifton to W.L.M. King, 10 March 1925, and reply, 13 March 1925; vol. 212, pp. 164622-23, Sifton to T.A. Burrows, 25 August 1925; Cook, *Politics of John W. Dafoe*, pp. 125-27, 151.

35. PAC, Sifton Papers, vol. 207, p. 162316-6, Sifton to Dafoe, 12 May 1919; pp. 162563-36—37, Sifton to Dafoe, 13 November 1920.

36. Ibid., vol. 212, pp. 164667-16—18, Sifton to Dafoe, 27 January 1925; Morton, *Progressive Party in Canada*, pp. 155, 190; Dawson, *William Lyon Mackenzie King*, 1, pp. 391-92; Neatby, *William Lyon Mackenzie King, 2*, p. 18. Indeed, Sifton generally was coming to have less sympathy for the western farmers who, he claimed, had made sizeable profits in the war years and "squandered" them. "I do not recognize the idea that it is the duty of the Government and Parliament to make farms pay for the people who are on them, and the sooner we get over this nonsense, the better." PAC, Sifton Papers, vol. 301, Sifton to T.A. Burrows, 15 January 1923.

37. PAC, Dafoe Papers, vol. 3, Sifton to Dafoe, 23 April 1926. Sifton considerably exaggerated the impact of what was a very skilful budget. See Neatby, *William Lyon Mackenzie King, 2*, pp. 122-24; Morton, *Progressive Party*, p. 252.

38. PAC, Sifton Papers, vol. 209, pp. 163251-108—13, Dafoe to Sifton, 10 December 1922; Dafoe Papers, vol. 2, Sifton to Dafoe, 14 December 1922. See also Sifton Papers, vol. 209, pp. 163094-95, Sifton to W.L. Baker, 14 October, 1922; vol. 210, p. 163609, Sifton to G.W. Allan, 5 March 1923.

For criticisms of the Canadian banking system in the 1920's, focussing on the question of establishing a central bank, see Linda M. Grayson, "The Formation of the Bank of Canada, 1913-1938" (Ph.D. diss., University of Toronto, 1974), ch. 3.

39. PAC, Sifton Papers, vol. 211, pp. 164109-14, Sifton to Thomas Wayling, 14 March 1923; *Globe*, 12 January 1924; Dafoe, *Clifford Sifton*, pp. 508-10.

40. PAC, Sifton Papers, vol. 212, pp. 164667-103—106, 164667-120, Sifton to Dafoe, 23 May, 1 June 1925. He expressed similar concern when the Bank of Commerce took over the Standard Bank in 1928; see Dafoe Papers, vol. 4, Sifton to Dafoe, 14 and 19 July 1928; and Dafoe to Sifton, 17 July 1928.

41. Dafoe, *Clifford Sifton*, pp. 510-11.

42. PAC, Dafoe Papers, vol. 2, Sifton to Dafoe, 10 February 1920, 16 January 1921; Sifton Papers, vol. 209, pp. 163251-67—68, Sifton to Dafoe, 25 May 1922. See also Dafoe Papers, vol. 3, Sifton to Dafoe, 1 June 1926.

43. Morton, *Progressive Party*, p. 164.

44. Ibid. pp. 205-6; PAC, Sifton Papers, vol. 209, p. 163251-101, Sifton to Dafoe, 13 November 1922; vol. 210, p. 163766-89, Sifton to Dafoe, 7 June 1923; vol. 212, p. 164667-59, Sifton to Dafoe, 27 March 1925.

45. PAC, Sifton Papers, vol. 212, pp. 164667-16—18 , Sifton to Dafoe, 28 January 1925.

46. Mackenzie King Diary, 22 April 1922, 10, 11 March 1923, 16 January 1924, 5 January 1925; PAC, Sifton Papers, vol. 210, pp. 163766-25, 163766-30—31, Sifton to Dafoe, 27 February, 8 March 1923; Dafoe Papers, vol. 3 Sifton to Dafoe, 16 February 1924.

47. PAC, Sifton Papers, vol. 212, pp. 164667-60—61, Sifton to Dafoe, 30 March 1925; vol. 213, pp. 164723-24, King to Sifton, 19 October 1925, and reply, 20 October 1925.

48. *Toronto Daily Star*, 25, 28 October 1925.

49. PAC, Sifton Papers, vol. 212, p. 164664, R.J. Cromie to Sifton, 14 November 1925; vol. 213, p. 164683, Sifton to W.L. Griffith, 17 November 1925; Beck, *Pendulum of Power*, p. 174.

50. PAC, Sifton Papers, vol. 212, p. 164650, Sifton to D.H. Cooper, 30 October 1925; vol. 213, p. 164681, Sifton to W.D. Gregory, 31 October 1925.

51. Ibid., vol. 213, pp. 164722, 164728-29, King to Sifton and reply [undated]; PAC, W.L.M. King Papers, Correspondence, Primary Series, vol. 125, p. 106219, King to Sifton, 16 November 1925. An indicator of how blurred Sifton's political identity had become was a request that he seek to replace Forke as leader of the Progressive Party; see Sifton Papers, vol. 213, pp. 164752-57, G.A. Maybee to Sifton, 5 December 1925, and reply, 15 December 1925.

52. PAC, Sifton Papers, vol. 302, Sifton to R.J. Cromie, 24 November 1925. Sifton's most recent suggestions to King had included a coalition or fusion of Progressives and Liberals; a Hudson Bay railway; guaranteed freight rates for the West; a tariff advisory board; and tariff increases only on glass, woollens, boots and shoes. The idea, he told King, was to develop a sort of "omnibus" programme "to unite East and West." Mackenzie King Diary, 13 November 1925.

53. PAC, King Papers, Correspondence, Primary Series, vol. 139, pp. 118075-77, King to Sifton, 6 July 1926, and reply, 6 July 1926. Note too that Sir Clifford's son Harry was running (unsuccessfully) as a Liberal candidate in North York in 1926, and possibly he wished to avoid influencing the outcome.

54. PAC, Sifton Papers, vol. 211, p. 164244-64—65, Sifton to Dafoe, 16 April 1924.

55. PAC, Dafoe Papers, vol. 2, Sifton to Dafoe, 19 August 1919.

56. PAC, Sifton Papers, vol. 208, pp. 162823-21, 162823-40, Sifton to Dafoe, 30 April, 4 July 1921.

57. PAC, Dafoe Papers, vol. 2, Sifton to Dafoe, 8 August 1921; and see Graham, *Arthur Meighen, And Fortune Fled* pp. 107-8

58. PAC, Dafoe Papers, vol. 2, Sifton to Dafoe, 19 November 1920, 30 May 1921.

59. PAC, Sifton Papers, vol. 208, pp. 162823-15—17, 162823-30, Sifton to Dafoe, 25 April, 30 May 1921; and see

vol. 209, p. 163010, Sifton to J.S. Willison, 30 June 1921.

60. PAC, Meighen Papers, vol. 68, pp. 38102-20, copy of "The Political Status of Canada," 8 April 1922. Much the same concern is expressed in Clifford Sifton, "Some Canadian Constitutional Problems," *CHR*, 3 (1922): 3-23. Evidently Ernest Lapointe, Minister of Marine and Fisheries and King's Québec lieutenant, undertook to translate and circulate Sifton's article in his province. PAC, Sifton Papers, vol. 209, p. 163251-6, Sifton to Dafoe, 7 February 1922.

61. Mackenzie King Diary, 8 April 1922; and see C.P. Stacey, *Canada and the Age of Conflict*, 2,, *1921-1948* (Toronto: University of Toronto Press, 1981), pp. 14, 17-18.

62. PAC, Dafoe Papers, vol. 2, Sifton to Dafoe, 17, 26, 28 September, 4 October, 14 December 1922; Sifton Papers, vol. 210, pp. 163766-19—20, Sifton to Dafoe, 15 February 1923; C.P. Stacey, *Canada and the Age of Conflict*, 2, pp. 17-31. That Sifton's remarks had had a significant impact on King was confirmed by the Prime Minister himself; PAC, King Papers, Correspondence, Primary Series, vol. 82, p. 68976, King to Sifton, 29 May 1922.

63. PAC, Dafoe Papers, vol. 2, Sifton to Dafoe, 26, 31 March 1923; Dafoe to Sifton, 30 March 1923. According to Dafoe, King deprecated the role of the Colonial Office, regarding it as purely mechanical.

64. *Toronto Daily Star*, 9 January 1925; PAC, King Papers, vol. 87, pp. 73669-85, Address, Sir Clifford Sifton, King Edward Hotel, Toronto, 9 January 1923; Stacey, *Canada and the Age of Conflict*, 2, pp. 49-55. On the notion that the policies of King did not mark any constitutional advance, see Angus D. Gilbert, "The Political Influence of Imperialist Thought in Canada" (Ph.D. diss., University of Toronto, 1974). p. 353.

65. PAC, King Papers, Correspondence, Primary Series, vol. 95, pp. 80291-94, King to Sifton, 17 August 1923, and reply [undated]; Dafoe Papers, vol. 2, Sifton to Dafoe, August 1923 [*sic*].

66. PAC, Dafoe Papers, vol. 2, Dafoe to Sifton, 12 September 1923.

67. PAC, Sifton Papers, vol. 311, file "Imperial Conference 1923," Transcript from Dafoe's Diary, esp. 29 September, 6 and 8 November 1923; King Papers, Correspondence, Primary Series, vol. 125, pp. 106201-4 King to Sifton, 22 January 1925.

68. Cook, *The Politics of J.W. Dafoe*, p. 144.

69. *Toronto Daily Star*, 9 January 1925.

70. PAC, Sifton Papers, vol. 311, file "Constitution 1922-23," undated memorandum [1926]. The term "commonwealth" was one with which Canadian nationalists were not entirely happy, but nevertheless found useful. "There is not, and of course there cannot be a commonwealth of nations," J.S. Ewart told Sifton. "A commonwealth is a single state of democratic character. It is not a word to be used as indicative of a union of states....Dafoe and I discussed fully this subject, and agreed that, however inapplicable the word *commonwealth* is, it might be useful as a sort of bridge over which imperialists might pass from British connection to Canadian independence." With this Sifton quite concurred. Ibid., vol. 210, pp. 163782-83, Ewart to Sifton, 2 March 1923; and reply 5 March 1923.

71. PAC, Dafoe Papers, vol. 3, Sifton to Dafoe, 28 October 1926; and reply, 1 November 1926; Sifton Papers, vol. 311, "Outline of Memorandum for D.B. MacRae... [re: Imperial Conference, 1926]", vol. 285, Dafoe to Clifford Sifton [son], 15 November 1942.

72. PAC, Dafoe Papers, vol. 3, Sifton to Dafoe, 4, 9, 23 November, 15, 21 December 1926; Dafoe to Sifton, 20, 29 November 1926; Cook, *The Politics of John W. Dafoe*, pp. 180-82; Neatby, *William Lyon Mackenzie King*, 2, pp. 180-90. The points alluded to by Sifton, including the passage on status, are covered in the "Report of Inter-Imperial Relations Committee," in Ollivier, ed., *The Colonial and Imperial Conferences from 1887 to 1937*, 3, pp. 145-57. Taken by themselves, the well-known lines on status may not constitute an advance over the

position of 1917, but there is little doubt that the entire extended declaration does mark an advance in a number of significant areas.

73. PAC, Sifton Papers, vol. 212, pp. 164667-41—42, Sifton to Dafoe, 16 February 1925; Dafoe Papers, vol. 3, Sifton to Dafoe, 21 December 1926.

74. PAC, Sifton Papers, vol. 210, pp. 163724-26, Sifton to T.A. Crerar, 14 February 1923.

75. See Neatby, *William Lyon Mackenzie King*, 2, pp. 232-43.

76. PAC, Sifton Papers, vol. 208, pp. 162823-74—75, Sifton to Dafoe, 29 October 1921; vol. 301, Sifton to R.J. Cromie, 11 March 1924.

77. PAC, Dafoe Papers, vol. 2, Sifton to Dafoe, 25 February 1922; Sifton Papers, vol. 208, pp. 162823-93—94, Sifton to Dafoe, 14 November 1921.

78. PAC, Dafoe Papers, vol. 4, Sifton to Dafoe, 14 July 1928; Sifton Papers, vol. 207, p. 162563-53, Sifton to Dafoe, 22 December 1920; vol. 311, file "American Investment in Canada 1925," transcript of interview, 28 February 1925.

79. PAC, Sifton Papers, vol. 311, file "American Investment in Canada 1925," transcript of interview, 28 February 1925.

80. Dafoe, *Clifford Sifton*, p. 491.

81. *Who's Who and Why*, 1921, p. 1280; *Who's Who in Canada*, 1930-31, p. 1544; PAC, Sifton Papers, vol. 300, file "Nicholson, F.W. 1919;" vol. 311, file "Export Association of Canada Ltd. 1920-21"; Clifford Sifton (jr.) Papers, vol. 1, J.W. Killam to W.B. Sifton, 7 February 1919.

82. *Who's Who in Canada*, 1930-31, pp. 46, 62; PAC, Clifford Sifton (jr.) Papers, vol. 13, file "Sifton, Clifford, Biographical Material, 1965, 1971, n.d."; Winnipeg Free Press, *Victor Sifton of the Winnipeg Free Press* [Winnipeg, 1961?], p. 14; PAC, Sifton Papers, vol. 302, file "Sifton, Harold [*sic*] 1924," Sifton to Harry Sifton, 5 June 1924; vol. 210, pp. 163630-31, Sifton to Sir Allen Aylesworth, 4 June 1923.

83. PAC, Sifton Papers, vol. 299, file "Denison 1918," Sifton to Senator W.C. Edwards, 20 November 1918; vol. 301, file "Burrows, T.A. 1921,"

Burrows to Sifton 12 May 1921.

84. Ibid., vol. 300, file "Sifton 1921," Sifton to Harry Sifton, 29 March, 7 April 1921.

85. Ibid. vol. 301, file "Sifton, Harold [*sic*] 1922," Sifton to Harry Sifton, 4 October 1922, and reply, 1 November 1922; vol. 210, p. 163370, Sifton to W.L. Griffith, 14 October 1922; PAC, Dafoe Papers, vol. 2, Sifton to Dafoe, 1, 4 October 1922.

86. PAC, Sifton Papers, vol. 302, file "Sifton, Harold [*sic*] 1924," Sifton to Harry Sifton, "Friday" [probably April 1924].

87. PAC, Sifton Papers, vol. 302, file "Sifton, Harold [*sic*] 1924," Sifton to Harry Sifton, 5 June, 30 November 1924; Harry Sifton to Sifton, 6 June 1924; vol. 301, file "Macklin, E.H. 1924," Macklin to Harry Sifton, 3 July 1924.

88. *Toronto Daily Star*, 20 January 1920, pp. 4, 8.

89. The final costs were: Sir Clifford's house ("Armadale"), $421,188.38; Harry's house, $118,604.10; Clifford's house, $130,464.74. PAC, Sifton Papers, vol. 302, file "Sifton, Harold [*sic*] 1924," Harry Sifton to Sifton, 15 November 1924, and reply, 18 November 1924.

90. Ibid., vol. 301, file "Burrows, T.A. 1924," Sifton to Burrows, 26 December 1924; vol. 212, p. 164548, Sifton to J.G. Turriff, 26 December 1924.

91. *Toronto Daily Star*, 19 February 1925, pp. 1, 13; 20 February 1925, p. 29; Dafoe, *Clifford Sifton*, pp. 534-35. Lady Sifton died of heart failure; she had required an unspecified operation for some time, but her weak heart prevented the doctors from acting.

92. PAC, Sifton Papers, vol. 207, pp. 162446-47, William Pearce to Chairman of Conservation Commission, 11 November 1919, and Sifton to A.L. Sifton, 18 November 1919; vol. 300, file "Sifton 1921," Sifton to Harry Sifton, 4 September 1921; vol. 299, file "Davidson 1916," J. Davidson to H.B. Pearson, 10 May 1922; vol. 302, file "Sifton, Harold [*sic*] 1924," Sifton to Harry Sifton, 24 June 1924; file "Cardin to Cross, 1925," Harry Sifton to A.E. Cross, 29 January 1925: PAA, Premiers' Papers, file 291,

Public Utilities Commission—
General, J.E. Brownlee to H.H.
Greenfield, 21 February 1922, and
encl.

93. PAA, Premiers' Papers, file 291,
Public Utilities Commission—
General, N.B. Gash to J.C. Brownlee, 24 February 1927; this letter in-
dicates that in 1926 the government
again reduced the rates to 35 cents/
mcf or lower, and also reduced the
valuation of the company's property
on which profit could be earned.

94. *CAR*, 1920, p. 197; PAC, Sifton
Papers, vol. 298, file "Morden 1913,"
correspondence between Col. W.
Grant Morden and Sifton, 1920-21;
vol. 302, file "Sifton, Harold [*sic*]
1924," Harry Sifton to Sifton, 24 June
1924; vol. 212, pp. 164622-23, Sifton
to T.A. Burrows, 25 August 1925.

95. Ibid., vol. 207, p. 162685, Sifton to
J.M. Robinson, 6 February 1920.

96. Daily circulation of the morning and
evening *Free Press* as of 31 October
1921 was 66,898; for the *Tribune*,
37,644. PAC, Sifton Papers, vol. 300,
file "Macklin, E. 1921," W. McCrae
[?] to Sifton, 10 November 1921;
Charles Bruce, *News and the
Southams* (Toronto: Macmillan,
1968), pp. 148, 153-54.

97. PAC, Sifton Papers, vol. 300, file
"Southam, William 1921," Sifton to
Southam, 8 November 1921. The
savings could have been substantial;
reducing the quality and size of the
paper alone would produce nearly
$13,000 per month, with thousands
more saved in other areas of the
paper's production and promotional
costs. See ibid., file "Macklin, E.
1921," passim.

98. Ibid., vol. 301, file "Macklin, E.H.
1924," Macklin to Sifton, 21 August
1924.

99. Ibid., vol. 211, p. 163864, Sifton to
T.C. Keenleyside, 12 May 1923.

100. Winnipeg Free Press Library files,
statement dated 1923, n.a.

101. PAC, Sifton Papers, vol. 201, file
"Sifton, J.W. 1922," Victor Sifton to
Harry Sifton, 22 June 1922. The
station was CJCG, begun with a
1/2-kw transmitter; a new 2-kw
transmitter would make it the most
powerful station in western Canada.

The *Tribune* broadcast on CJNC. See
Frank W. Peers, *The Politics of
Canadian Broadcasting 1920-1951*
(Toronto: University of Toronto
Press, 1969), p. 6.

102. PAC, Sifton Papers, vol. 301, file
"Macklin, E.H. 1924," passim.; vol.
302, file "Sifton, Harold [*sic*] 1924,"
passim.

103. According to an Armadale Corporation statement of 1930 (Manitoba Free
Press Library files), the Leader-Post
Publishing Company and Star
Phoenix Company became sub-
sidiaries of the Manitoba Free Press
Company: the sale included the
Saskatchewan Farmer, a wholly-
owned subsidiary of the Leader-Post
Company. However, Armadale Corporation also held a significant
portion of the shares directly. Aspects
of the early stages of negotiations are
mentioned in PAC, Dafoe Papers, vol.
4, E.H. Macklin to Dafoe, 29 October
1927; Memo, 9 November 1927 [n.a.];
Sifton to Dafoe, 4 June 1928.

104. Cited in Dafoe, *Clifford Sifton*, p.
xxiv.

105. PAC, Dafoe Papers, vol. 2, Sifton to
Dafoe, 2 October 1919.

106. Cited in Dafoe, *Clifford Sifton*, p.
xxvi. On this topic generally, see
Robert Matthew Bray, "The Role of
Sir Clifford Sifton in the Formation of
the Editorial Policy of the *Manitoba
Free Press*, 1916 to 1921" (MA thesis,
University of Manitoba, 1968).

107. PAC, Dafoe Papers, vol. 2, Sifton to
Dafoe, 10 February 1920; Sifton
Papers, vol. 208, pp. 162823-76,
162823-79—82, Sifton to Dafoe, 29
October 1921, and reply, 4 November
1921; vol. 212, pp. 164667-16—18,
Sifton to Dafoe, 28 January 1925.

108. PAC, Sifton Papers, vol. 209, pp.
163251-38—44, 163251-54—56,
173251-67—68, Sifton to Dafoe, 22
April, 1, 15, 25 May 1922; Dafoe to
Sifton, 12 May 1922, vol. 210, pp.
163766-115—118, Dafoe to Sifton, 27
December 1923; Donnelly, *Dafoe of
the Free Press*, pp. 122-24.

109. PAC, Sifton Papers, vol. 211, Dafoe to
Sifton, 10 December 1924.

110. Dafoe, *Clifford Sifton*, p. xxvii.

111. PAC, Sifton Papers, vol. 296, file
"Stewart, McLeod 1900," passim.;

Clifford Sifton (jr.) Papers, vol. 11, file "Georgian Bay Canal, 1927, 1932;" PAM, Dafoe Papers, "From the Great Lakes to the Atlantic: the Montreal Ottawa and Georgian Bay Canal Company," [1927]; *CSP*, 1909, no. 19a. Among the most useful discussions of this issue are Dafoe, *Clifford Sifton*, pp. 515-21; Neatby, *William Lyon Mackenzie King*, 2, pp. 224-28; Peter Oliver, *G. Howard Ferguson: Ontario Tory* (Toronto: University of Toronto Press, 1977), pp. 174-78, 185-87, 293-99; and Christopher Armstrong, *The Politics of Federalism: Ontario's Relations with the Federal Government, 1867-1942* (Toronto: University of Toronto Press, 1981), pp. 160-70.

112. Gerald H. Brown, "The Georgian Bay Canal," *Collier's* (Canadian Edition) (22 August 1908): 21; *MFP*, 26 September 1908; PAC, Liberal Party of Canada Papers, vol. 990, *Weekly Letters Issued by the Liberal Party Prior to the General Election of 1908* (Central Liberal Information Office, Ottawa, n.d.); LaPierre, "Politics, Race, and Religion in French Canada," p. 429.

113. PAC, Sifton Papers, vol. 296, file "Stewart, McLeod 1900," Extracts from Minutes of Directors' Meetings, The New Dominion Syndicate Ltd.; W.L.M. King Papers, vol. 577, p. C58633, biographical sketch of Perks.

114. PAC, Sifton Papers, vol. 297, file "Perks, R.W. 1909," Memorandum of Agreement between Sir Robert Perks of London, England, Arthur Frederic MacArthur of New York City and Clifford Sifton of Ottawa, Canada, 17 June 1909.

115. PAC, Sifton Papers, vol. 297, file "Perks, R.W. 1909," passim; file "Perks, R.W. 1910," passim; file "Macdonald, E.M. 1909," passim: Laurier Papers, vol. 618, p. 167904, Sifton to Perks, 18 February 1910 (copy).

116. PAC, Sifton Papers, vol. 306, file "Georgian Bay Canal Chronology of the Company 1928"; vol. 199, p. 158072, F. Cochrane to Sifton, February 1912.

117. Ibid., vol. 300, file "Perks, R. 1919," Perks to Sifton, 1 July 1919; file "Peck, Samuel 1920"; file "Sifton, A. 1920," W.B. Sifton to Sifton, 19 November 1920.

118. PAC, Meighen Papers, vol. 3, p. 1246, Sifton to Meighen, 2 June 1920; Sifton Papers, vol. 208, p. 162641, Meighen to Sifton, 4 June 1920.

119. PAC, Sifton Papers, vol. 306, file "Georgian Bay Canal Chronology of the Company 1929," King to Perks, 5 April 1923; King Papers, Series J4, vol. 77, file 567, pp. C58863-64, King to Perks, 20 February 1924.

120. Neatby, *William Lyon Mackenzie King*, 2, pp. 224-25; Oliver, *G. Howard Ferguson*, pp. 177-78, 186.

121. PAC, Sifton Papers, vol. 306, file "Georgian Bay Canal Chronology of the Company 1928"; Clifford Sifton (jr.) Papers, vol. 11, file "Georgian Bay Canal Co."; Mackenzie King Diary, 30 March 1924, 5 January 1925.

122. Mackenzie King Diary, 7, 13, 27 November 1925. Subsequently the Siftons spoke of consolidating the *Globe* and the *Mail and Empire* for the Liberals; Mackenzie King Diary, 6 January 1927.

123. Ibid., 28 March 1927; Oliver, *G. Howard Ferguson*, pp. 184-86; Neatby, *William Lyon Mackenzie King* 2, pp. 226-27.

124. PAC, Sifton Papers, vol. 213 pp. 164752-55, G.A. Maybee to Sifton, 5 December 1925; Mackenzie King Diary, 13 November 1925.

125. Dafoe, *Clifford Sifton*, p. 517.

126. PAC, Sifton Papers, vol. 303, file "Sifton, Harold [*sic*] 1927," Sifton to Harry Sifton, 28 January 1927; PAM, Dafoe Papers, "From the Great Lakes to the Atlantic: the Montreal Ottawa and Georgian Bay Canal Company."

127. Mackenzie King Diary, 19 February, 4, 14, 22, 28 March 1927.

128. Canada, Parliament, House of Commons, Special Committee [on] Railways, Canals and Telegraph Lines, *Minutes of Proceeding and Evidence* nos. 1, 2, 3, 5-7 April 1927; Mackenzie King Diary, 7 April 1927; PAC, King Papers, vol. 77, file 567, pp. C58922-31, Statement by Harry Sifton; PAC, Dafoe Papers, vol. 4, Dafoe to Sifton, 13 April 1927.

129. PAC, Sifton Papers, vol. 303, file

"Sifton, Harold [*sic*] 1927," Sifton to Harry Sifton, 16 April 1927.

130. Ibid., vol. 303, file "Malcolm-Perks 1927," Harry Sifton to Perks, 12 May 1927; PAC, Clifford Sifton (jr.) Papers, vol. 1, Clifford Sifton to Winfield B. Sifton, 5 December 1927.

131. PAC, Dafoe Papers, vol. 4, Sifton to Dafoe, 17 June 1927; Dafoe *Clifford Sifton*, pp. 520-21.

132. Mackenzie King Diary, 7 November 1925. King must have bemused and astonished Winfield nevertheless. He showed young Sifton a letter from his friend Joan Patteson concerning a dream she had had. "I then read over to him this dream—which was Mother's desire to help me, of her bringing to her assistance a certain man—who seemed to be 'Sir Clifford Sifton'. It was all there. I had intended sending off the dream to Mrs. Bleaney [a medium] to interpret....Winfield and I talked of nothing else till I took him to the hotel." There is no record of whether Winfield imparted this intelligence to his father.

133. Ibid. 27 November 1925.

134. Neatby, *William Lyon Mackenzie King*, 2, pp. 255-57; Martin Driessen, "William Lyon Mackenzie King and the St. Lawrence Seaway, 1921-1930" (BA Honours Essay, Department of History, University of Alberta, 1976), chs. 1-3; PAC, Sifton Papers, vol. 306, file "St. Lawrence Waterway Chronology of Negotiations 1927."

135. Dafoe, *Clifford Sifton*, pp. 522-23; PAC, Dafoe Papers, vol. 3, Sifton to Dafoe, 1 June 1925; PAM, Dafoe Papers, "The St. Lawrence," Sifton address, 14 February 1925.

136. PAC, Dafoe Papers, vol. 4, Sifton to Dafoe, 10 August 1927.

137. Neatby, *William Lyon Mackenzie King*, 2, p. 258.

138. Ibid., pp. 258-59; Driessen, "King and the St. Lawrence Seaway," pp. 75-79.

139. *MFP*, 5 January 1922; PAC, Sifton Papers, vol. 300, file "Sifton 1921," Sifton to Harry Sifton, 4 September 1921. Much of Sifton's thought on this topic paralleled that of John Mac-Dougall in his *Rural Life in Canada* (1913; reprinted University of Toronto Press, 1973).

140. *Montreal Gazette*, 26 February 1923.

141. PAM, Clifford Sifton Papers, draft of speech intended for Canadian Club, Regina, 1927, pp. 7-8. This speech is an excellent summary of Sifton's political and social philosophy.

142. Ibid., pp. 2, 16. In 1925 he contributed $10,000 to the Banting Research Foundation for medical research at the University of Toronto; PAC, Sifton Papers, vol. 302, file "Sifton 1925." See also Michael Bliss, *The Discovery of Insulin* (Toronto: McClelland and Stewart, 1982), p. 241.

143. PAM, Sifton Papers, draft of speech intended for Canadian Club, Regina, 1927.

144. There is little in the Sifton Papers that would add substantially to the account in Dafoe, *Clifford Sifton*, pp. 541-45.

145. PAC, Dafoe Papers, vol. 4, Sifton to Dafoe, 28 January, 13 June 1927.

146. Ibid. Sifton to Dafoe, 21 December 1927, 14 July 1928, 18 January 1929. At the time of his death, Winfield was living in Brockville, and was employed as a lawyer for Beauharnois Light, Heat and Power Co.

147. According to Douglas Murray, Sir Clifford's valet, the latter was found after his death to have a large abdominal tumor; interview with author, May 1975.

148. PAC, Dafoe Papers, vol. 4, Sifton to Dafoe, 25 February, 2, 18, 28 March 1929; Sifton Papers, vol. 303, file "Sifton, Harold [*sic*] 1929," Sifton to Harry Sifton, 1 March 1929.

149. *Toronto Daily Star*, 17, 18 April 1929; *Ottawa Evening Citizen*, 17 April 1929; *MFP*, 17, 18 April 1929.

150. *Toronto Daily Star*, 19, 20 April 1929.

151. *Ottawa Evening Citizen*, 18 April 1929; *Ottawa Journal*, 18 April 1929.

NOTES TO EPILOGUE

1. Mackenzie King Diary, 17 April 1929; *Toronto Star*, 3 January 1975.
2. University of Manitoba, Elizabeth Dafoe Library, Dafoe Papers, James Brierley to Dafoe, 3 January 1932; C.G. Gregory to Dafoe, 6 February 1932.
3. *MFP*, 29 November 1929; *Mail and Empire*, 17 March 1932.
4. PAC, Clifford Sifton (jr.) Papers, vol. 11, file "Attorney-General for Ontario vs. Siftons 1932," case filed 18 April 1932. The government placed the total value of all property passing to Sifton's sons at $9,721,374.62. As of December 1927 the Manitoba Free Press Company shares were valued by the Ontario government at $3.5 million, and the Armadale Corporation's interest was $3.2 million. Estimated values in December 1925 were, respectively, $3.19 million and $2.79 million.
5. Ibid., file "Armadale Corporation: Resale of Shares 1932"; file "Georgian Bay Canal Co." They argued that the Georgian Bay Canal enterprise shares should have been valued at from $5 million to $14 million, or, depending on potential value based on other comparable enterprises, as much as $27.7 million.
6. PAC, Sifton Papers, vol. 287a, clipping, Huntington *Gleaner*, 25 April 1929.
7. Robert Kelley, *The Transatlantic Persuasion: the Liberal-Democratic Mind in the Age of Gladstone* (New York: Knopf, 1969), pp. 263-64.
8. F.H. Underhill, *In Search of Canadian Liberalism* (Toronto: Macmillan, 1960), p. 166.
9. PAC, A.K. Cameron Papers, vol. 34, T.A. Crerar to Cameron, 18 January 1932.
10. University of Toronto Archives, Walker Papers, Walker to Cambie, 29 January 1918 (reference courtesy of Prof. J.A. Eagle).
11. A more extended assessment may be found in Hall, "Political Career of Clifford Sifton," pp. 898-916.

Index